The

Non-Commercial Food Service

Manager's Handbook

A COMPLETE GUIDE FOR HOSPITALS, NURSING HOMES, MILITARY, PRISONS, SCHOOLS, AND CHURCHES: WITH COMPANION CD-ROM

By Douglas Robert Brown & Shri Henkel

THE NON-COMMERCIAL FOOD SERVICE MANAGER'S HANDBOOK:

A COMPLETE GUIDE FOR HOSPITALS, NURSING HOMES, MILITARY, PRISONS, SCHOOLS, AND CHURCHES: WITH COMPANION CD-ROM

By Douglas Robert Brown & Shri Henkel

Copyright © 2007 by Atlantic Publishing Group, Inc.

1210 SW 23rd Place • Ocala, Florida 34474 • 800-814-1132 • 352-622-5836–Fax

Web site: www.atlantic-pub.com • E-mail: sales@atlantic-pub.com

SAN Number: 268-1250 • Member American Library Association

ISBN-13: 978-0-910627-81-8 • ISBN-10: 0-910627-81-9

Library of Congress Cataloging-in-Publication Data

Brown, Douglas Robert, 1960-
  Non-commercial food service managers handbook : a complete guide for hospitals, nursing homes, military, prisons, schools, and churches, with companion CD-ROM / Douglas R. Brown & Shri L. Henkel.
      p. cm.
  Includes bibliographical references and index.
  ISBN-13: 978-0-910627-81-8 (alk. paper)
  ISBN-10: 0-910627-81-9 (alk. paper)
  1. Food service--Handbooks, manuals, etc. 2. Food service management--Handbooks, manuals, etc. I. Henkel, Shri L., 1965- II. Title.

  TX943.B76 2007
  647.95068--dc22

                              2006030282
Printed in the United States

EDITOR: Marie Lujanac • MLujanac817@yahoo.com
ART DIRECTION & INTERIOR DESIGN: Meg Buchner • megadesn@mchsi.com
PROOFREADER: Angela C. Adams • angela.c.adams@hotmail.com
BOOK PRODUCTION DESIGN: Caroline D'Agostino • caroline05@cox.net

Table of Contents

CHAPTER 3   Using a Computer System   59

CHAPTER 4   Effective Menu Planning and Pricing   69

CHAPTER 5   Quality in Dietary and Nutritional Guidelines   109

CHAPTER 6   Purchasing and Receiving Practices   171

CHAPTER 7   Receiving, Storage, and Inventory Practices   199

CHAPTER 8   Techniques to Purchase Large Quantities of Food   231

CHAPTER 9   Choose the Proper Equipment   255

CHAPTER 10   Customer Service   275

CHAPTER 11   Food Handling and Sanitation Procedures   285

CHAPTER 12   Safety and Risk Management   359

CHAPTER 13   Interviewing and Hiring Employees   381

CHAPTER 14   Train and Manage Employees   429

CHAPTER 15   Operational Management   473

CHAPTER 16   Operate an Effective Dining Area   489

CHAPTER 17   Control Facility Costs   503

CHAPTER 18   Marketing and Promotion   529

CHAPTER 19   Catering and Special Events   563

Thank you to DayMark Safety Systems for their generous contribution of commercial food service photos used throughout this book. DayMark specializes in products that assist restaurants and other food services establishments in complying with FDA and other compliance codes. For more information visit **www.daymarksafety.com** or call 800-847-0101.

Foreword

How many times have you heard someone say, "This food is terrible!"? It's a common exclamation in hospitals, schools, military mess halls, and even in prisons. In my 25-plus years in the military, I cannot begin to tally all the reasons people have made the above comment, but I can clearly see the lack of several fundamental tasks and procedures that management did not follow. In this handbook, the author has broken down to the nth degree all the tasks and procedures an effective manager needs to know to be successful.

During my career in the military, I held a multitude of positions, such as Mess Officer for three mess halls feeding about 10,000 Marines in boot camp and DOD/Defense Logistics Agency Assistant Inspector General reviewing the acquisition procedures at buying markets around the country, inspecting many cold storage locations and perishables storage sites, inspecting meat processing plants, and reviewing procedures manuals used by military forces world-wide.

While on a training exercise in Korea, I was responsible for ensuring that 20,000 troops received three nourishing meals a day   quite a task since the temperature went as low as 50 degrees below zero! As a military joint clubs Officer in Charge, one of my prime duties was to ensure customers had an enjoyable experience at the clubs. We successfully catered organizational functions, weddings, and military formal dinners. If you want a stressful "gray-hair" experience, try satisfying hundreds of Marines at a "Mess Night"!

The detail in Douglas Brown and Shri Henkel's *Non-Commercial Food Service Manager's Handbook* can benefit any manager in improving day-to-day procedures to manage a total food service operation effectively. They have put into simple words the "how to" in managing all the tasks and procedures the most successful managers have used to produce a cost-effective, well-planned, and "taste-bud" satisfying meal experience!

Mel Trimble

United States Marine Corps Lt. Colonel (Ret.)

Supply Officer

Introduction

Are you considering food service as a career? Do feel that your only option is a commercial restaurant? There is another option that has many jobs available every year. These jobs are in the non-commercial food-service industry in hospitals, nursing homes, large companies, the military, prisons, schools, colleges, and churches.

Just as in the commercial food industry you may be required to maintain costs in the business. Increasingly, the non-commercial food industry requires managers and staff to break even or even show a profit. In many cases part or all of their funding comes from the business or the entity hosting the non-commercial food facility. This means the manager must answer for the money spent and must maintain a businesslike atmosphere.

Do you conjure images of dull, tasteless food when you think cafeteria? This mistaken impression can be one reason that many people reject this field as a career, but today non-commercial food service includes all types of food and all types of service.

Topics We Will Discuss

This book will deal with managing money, planning menus, and following dietary and nutritional guidelines, especially critical in health care and school facilities. To be an effective manager, you need to know how to purchase, receive, store, and inventory all products. We will discuss various techniques of purchasing large quantities of food effectively. Any food service manual is not complete without details about food handling and sanitation procedures along with safety and risk management.

In any business, hiring and training your staff is critical to a smooth operation.

In some non-commercial situations you may be required to cater meetings or other special events, and we'll discuss how to prepare a plan and have a successful event.

Throughout the book I also share personal case studies from experts in the non-commercial field. They have professional food experience from the military, prisons, hospitals, nursing homes, schools, and from the growing opportunities in churches.

The CD accompanying this book contains checklists, forms, and additional information that you'll find helpful and informative. It makes it easy to print copies of these forms for your use. Let's begin.

CHAPTER ONE

What Is Non-Commercial Food Service?

We are all familiar with commercial food service such as restaurants. Non-commercial food service is a separate area in a larger business and food service may be an after-thought as in the employee cafeteria, or it may be a necessary part of the overall venture: for example, health care and nursing home facilities where patients and residents must have a food service option.

In many non-commercial food-service facilities, the customers are served at predetermined times requiring large quantities to be prepared and served at regular intervals. An unusual characteristic of non-commercial food service is that the food needs to be maintained at hot or cold temperatures for extended periods of time, involving safe handling along with maintaining an appealing appearance.

To give you an idea of the large quantities we're talking about, you might prepare beef stew or potatoes for 500 or 5,000 people who must be served in a set period of time. Once the food is prepared it may be held or served to the individuals in a cafeteria line. This requires a different mentality and procedure than serving dinner to 50 to 100 people.

Customized orders are becoming popular—offering eggs cooked to order or sandwiches made to order, for example—and more appreciated than serving up all orders exactly alike.

When you look for a job in food service, remember the non-commercial industry is much more stable than commercial food service. If you are looking for a long-term career, this is a great place to go.

History of the Non-Commercial Food Service Industry

Non-commercial food service has been around for centuries in one form or another. Examples are the Egyptian Pharaohs who imported meat and grain to feed 20,000 workers building the pyramids and William the Conqueror who fed his 30,000 followers. History is replete with examples of food service developments.

Chuck Wagons

In the mid-to-late 1800s, chuck wagons fed cowboys while they were on cattle drives. Charles Goodnight is credited with developing the first chuck wagon. In 1866, he and his partner, Oliver Loving, prepared to move a herd of 2,000 longhorns from northern Texas to Denver. He purchased a government wagon, and it was rebuilt to his specifications. A special slanted box with a hinged lid was built on the side of the wagon for the cook's work table. It ran the full length of the wagon and contained shelves and drawers for storage. There was a waterproof sheet across the top and a cowhide across the bottom to carry wood and cow chips. Cowboys called food "chuck" and they called the cook, "Cookie". This first chuck wagon was copied and stayed the same over the years.

The chuck wagon was the source of food for the cowboys while they were on the range. Since this was essentially their "home away from home," the cook was expected to keep order: his authority was not to be questioned.

Working conditions for the cook were not the best. He worked from early in the morning until late at night. No matter what the weather or the time or supplies available, Cookie had to have food ready.

Cowboys were a rough bunch, but no one took any food without Cookie's permission. Each man sat on the ground and held his plate in his lap. When a man finished serving himself, he had to replace the lid on the pot to keep out dirt. No man would finish the last bit of food without being sure everyone had eaten. When the meal was done, each one was responsible for scraping his plate and putting it on the "wreck pile".

Meals on a chuck wagon usually consisted of sourdough biscuits, coffee, beans, frijoles, apple butter, grits 'n' gravy, and beef. Good chuck wagon cooks knew many ways to prepare beef on the trail—fried steak, pot roasts, short ribs, or stew. On a good day, Cookie would prepare a dessert, but the men knew this was a treat that shouldn't be taken for granted. The food wasn't elegant or fancy, but even the gruffest cowboys appreciated the work Cookie did for them.

Railroad Workers

From the mid-to-late 1800s, it was discovered that the six-month wagon train trip to San Francisco could be cut to a week by train. The appeal to the government was obvious and eventually contracts were signed. One problem was that there weren't many workers. Gold mining and homesteading were preferred to railroad building. So Chinese laborers flocked into the country and, along with Irish immigrants, built the railroad. Conditions were so bad that the workers were expected to supply their own food and housing. So they had a dedicated cook responsible for obtaining staples and preparing their meals. Chinese workers drank boiled tea instead of unsanitary water and avoided many illnesses including dysentery that plagued others on the trails.

Irish workers ate beef and potatoes day after day, but the Chinese ate seafood and vegetables. They also had live pigs and chickens that were prepared on weekends. Chinese meals were flavorful and afforded a variety compared to the Irish fare.

Industry Food Service

Around 1890 the New York and Chicago telephone companies provided food services for their employees. Sears, Roebuck and Co. followed, providing a restaurant for their employees in Chicago in 1906. They prepared meals for 12,500 employees each day. At one time, they regularly fed 8,400 people in 80 minutes, a difficult feat even today.

During World War I, many industries discovered the need to provide food service for their employees. With the push to produce supplies a shorter lunch hour evolved, which meant providing food service in the business. Manufacturers continued to learn about the benefits of providing food service and made great strides in this area during World War II. They realized a nutritious, well-balanced meal helped their employees stay healthy, efficient, and more productive on the job. With many factories located away from cities, in-house food service appealed to potential employees.

Hospitals

Hospital food service has experienced many changes through the centuries. In the Middle Ages the only foods they served were bread, broth, and beer. Patients with limited funds needed friends and relatives to bring them food. Some enterprising individuals brought food into the wards for the people who could afford it and as a result, contamination and diseases were made worse.

During the Crimean War from 1853 to 1856, Florence Nightingale worked with Alex Soyer to develop ways to provide food to patients. Soyer knew soldiers had little chance of recovering with inadequate food and possible contamination. So he went to Crimea to evaluate the situation for himself. The news he heard didn't prepare him for the situations he found. He set about to find a number of ways use to improve the conditions:

- He changed the way food was prepared.
- He created a filter to brew tea.
- He developed the idea of pouring hot soup over meat to create a hot meal.
- He created a biscuit recipe that tasted good and could be stored better.
- He designed a system to compress dried vegetables into smaller servings that could be prepared in boiling water to be eaten.
- He developed training programs for cooks.
- He found ways to help cooks prepare nourishing food.
- His Soyer Stove used less fuel and was safer than open fires.

Unfortunately providing food in the United States was no better during the Civil War in the following decade. These conditions persisted until 1890 when hospitals in the eastern United States began employing people to handle food service. Doctors at some U.S. hospitals hired women to develop diets for their patients because they believed good nutrition was therapeutic.

The hospital food-service industry changed slowly until World War II when new hospital developments came about including centralized tray service, experimenting with chilling and freezing systems, experimenting with a separate kitchen for special diets, and systems to control operations.

Today hospital food service has expanded to include nursing homes, retirement homes, and long-term care facilities with special needs to feed their residents. As with many other businesses they have developed ways to cut costs, although many times quality has suffered. Some of their problems have included poor quality food, inadequate and unclean preparation areas, poor storage and handling of food, and untrained personnel.

As our health-care options increased, so did the need for quality food service. This is especially true with the elderly. They want a homelike environment with good tasting food. As the quality of health care improves, the quality of food service has followed. These facilities may even offer carry-out service and catering options.

School Lunch Programs

In 1920 Chicago claimed to be serving lunch in all its high schools and in many elementary schools. Many other large cities claimed to have lunch programs throughout the early 1900s run by volunteers. The need for better nutrition was brought to light by the number of young people being rejected for military service because of bad nutrition.

In 1932 the Franklin D. Roosevelt administration launched a program to provide money to serve lunches in the school systems while providing work during the Great Depression of the 1930s. In 1942 this program served lunch to more than 5,000,000 students daily in more than 78,000 schools.

After World War II, the national school lunch program was established, enabling many schools to provide one nutritious meal for students at a minimal cost. This program was enhanced under the Lyndon Johnson administration in 1966 with the Child Welfare Act that reduced the price of lunches or accorded free lunches to children who qualified. An addition, the school breakfast program began in 1968.

College Food Service

During the 13th and 14th centuries in Europe, students managed hostels to provide a sort of food service facility. These regional hostels were funded by wealthy individuals to provide food and lodging for students who couldn't afford them. Eventually these facilities were taken over by universities.

Harvard University, established in 1638, provided residence and food service for students. At that time, clergymen managed the colleges and saved money by providing poor quality food. Things changed in the early 1900s when universities realized they were legally responsible for the physical well-being of the students.

College food service has become diversified over the years. Many residence halls have dining rooms for students while others have cafeterias. They may also have snack bars, vending machines, fast-food service on campus, convenience stores, dining rooms open to public, and catering services for banquets and special events.

Prison Food Service

Have you seen western movies where the sheriff's wife or girlfriend brings a tray of food to the prisoner? This is how prisoners were fed until recent times. Sheriffs were responsible for providing meals with limited funds, so no one worried about the kind of food being served, how it was prepared, or when it was served. Hiring the prisoners out to work was a way to raise money and cut feeding expenses.

We all know that when a supervisor is forced to show a profit, cuts are made. In many cases it has been the selection or quality of the prisoners' food. Minimal costs led to providing only bread, water, stew, and porridge for many prisoners. Some sheriffs and deputies felt that limiting prison food was a good way to punish inmates.

In the 1970s, things began to change. Local governments rather than private individuals were managing the prisons, and conditions were regulated bringing about changes in food service. A prison dietician got a court order in 1979 to set sanitation, quality, and nutritional standards in prisons. The cycle repeated itself when contract companies took over some segments of prison food service in the 1980s. Food quality and servings are a common reason for prisoner unrest, so these contractors walk a fine line when providing correctional system food service.

Military Food Service History

When Union soldiers were on the march, their rations contained three-fourths pound of salt pork, one pound of hard bread (hardtack), coffee, and sugar. The Army wouldn't train cooks for another 50 years. Soldiers weren't given cooking utensils beyond camp kettles and mess pans used by the entire company. These men had few tools and almost no culinary skills. The common food was a chunk of pickled pork and ten hard crackers made of flour and water. Most of the salt pork was fried, boiled, added to a stew, or it could be placed between two pieces of hardtack to create a sandwich. Over time soldiers acquired utensils such as cutlery, a tin plate, and a cup; they created boilers from an empty tin can or rigged a frying pan from discarded canteen halves, attaching a green stick for a handle.

At some point they got organized and about five soldiers would work together to prepare their meals. The soldier with the best cooking skills would cook for that group. His was the favorite job, since cooking was the only responsibility he would have in the camp. After much trial and error, soldiers determined ways to prepare the food to cut down on digestive complaints.

Salt beef, called "salt horse," was barely fit for human consumption. There was so much salt in it that it had to be soaked overnight in a running stream to be edible. Packing methods were not sufficient so it had an incredible stench. It was so bad that soldiers would throw it at the commissary's tent. The occasional fresh beef was a real treat. Cattle would be herded behind the troops and slaughtered when they stopped for the night. Beef would then be cooked for the next day's march. Most soldiers broiled their fresh beef on sticks over campfires.

Over the years and during various wars food logistics has evolved into delivering a tasty product faster. The subsistence program that the military uses now is far more refined and organized than troops in the Civil War could have imagined.

CHAPTER TWO

Account Management

All restaurants need an efficient bookkeeping system to monitor revenue that comes in, track where the money is spent, and assist in future sales projections and budgeting. Don't underestimate the importance of a good bookkeeping system, involving a good manager.

Even if the business you manage is part of a larger organization that isn't overly concerned with making a profit, you still need to account for expenses. Being able to explain them to your superiors will show initiative. If the business has a bookkeeper, learn from this person. The knowledge will help you in many aspects of your job as a non-commercial food service manager. We'll discuss ways to use a computer system in food service in Chapter 3.

Accounts Payable

First, we need to discuss accounts payable, which is critical because you need to pay your suppliers. Accounts payable is the money that the facility owes for any supplies, including food, paper products, tables, linens, or any other item that must be replenished.

Invoices

The first things you need to figure your accounts payable are the invoices for recent purchases. These should always be brought to the manager's office at the end of the day. They need to be handled carefully, not lost and certainly not thrown in the trash. An effective bookkeeping system depends on having all invoices in the hands of the manager and the bookkeeper.

It's advisable to process the invoices at the end of the day, so the information is fresh in everyone's mind. These are the steps on how to handle invoices:

1. **Verify the address on the invoice is correct.** There are times when the wrong invoice is left with a customer.

2. **Verify the invoice was signed by one of your employees.** This is the best way to be sure you actually received the merchandise.

3. **Check the delivery date.**

4. **Check the price and quantity for accuracy.** Were these numbers verified by an employee and do they correspond with your order?

5. **After you have determined that the invoice is correct, initial it or stamp it "approved".** This is an easy way for the bookkeeper to verify it needs to be entered in the ledger or computer. The bookkeeper will also know the invoice needs to be paid when the bill arrives.

6. **Check it at that time while everyone remembers what was received** and you can double check your inventory if needed in case there are questions about anything on the invoice.

CASE STUDY: CHURCH BOOKKEEPING

All purchasing receipts and invoices need to be forwarded to the church bookkeeper. It is best to determine if they will be delivered daily or weekly. The invoices need to be checked, verified, and signed and then taken to the bookkeeper. Doing so will enable the church bookkeeper to pay bills without unnecessary confusion.

Gary Douylliez, • St Francis Inn
Casa de Solana Inn • **www.stfrancisinn.com**

Code Your Invoices

Each expense can be assigned a code number, allowing the bookkeeper to enter it in the right code or category, making it easier for you to create your budget, prepare your taxes, and produce a profit and loss statement. We'll discuss budget creation later in this chapter.

The following pages has a list of codes that includes the normal expenses, provided by the National Restaurant Association (NRA). You may not need all of these codes.

Mark each invoice with the code that you want the bookkeeper to use for the expense. You can also have a rubber stamp made at any office supply store or online. A possible format would include:

Sample Stamp

Date _____	
Code # _____	
Amount Due _____	
Initials	

CHART OF ACCOUNTS		
GENERAL OPERATING COSTS	101	Cost of food
	103	Cost of wine
CONTROLLABLE OPERATIONAL COSTS	151	Cost of china and utensils
	152	Cost of glassware
	153	Cost of kitchen supplies
	154	Cost of bar supplies
	155	Cost of dining-room supplies
	156	Cost of cleaning supplies
	157	Cost of office supplies
	158	Cost of uniforms
	159	Cost of laundry and linen
SERVICES	201	Trash pickup
	202	Laundry cleaning
	203	Protection/Security
	205	Legal
	206	Accounting
	207	Maintenance
	208	Payroll
	401	Payroll-Social Security Tax
	403	Repairs: maintenance equipment
	404	Repairs: building maintenance
	405	Entertainment: music

	406	Advertising
	407	Promotion
	408	Equipment rent/lease
	409	Postage
	410	Contributions
	411	Trade dues: subscriptions
	412	Licenses
	413	Credit-card expenses
	414	Travel
	415	Bad debt/robbery
FIXED OPERATING COSTS	501	Rent
UTILITIES	301	Phones
	302	Water
	303	Gas
	304	Electricity
	305	Heat
	306	Garbage pick-up

Each line needs to be filled in with the correct information. If you expect an invoice with different coded items, ask the supplier to list the different items on separate invoices. Another solution is to enter the code number beside individual line items.

After you make the appropriate notations on each invoice, copy and file them according to the code numbers and biller's name. If an invoice has more than one code, make one copy for each code number and file in the correct folder. File the original invoices by code number and month and store in a fireproof cabinet.

Many businesses send a monthly statement with a list of all your buys for the month. These could include the invoice number and the amount due, or some companies send copies of each separate invoice. This summary allows your bookkeeper to double check your invoices to be sure your bill is correct. The individual invoices should be stapled to the statement and filed. A monthly summary gives you the benefit of only writing one check at the end of each month, leaving your cash flow available throughout the month. Be sure to save enough of your revenue to cover your monthly bills.

Most businesses close out their accounts on the last day of the month, and you should receive your bill during the first week of the following month. Your bookkeeper should log in the expense for the month of the purchase, not the month of the payment.

Purchase a separate ledger or begin a separate computer file to record your purchases. A sample of a purchase ledger is at the end of this chapter.

Use a separate page for each category:

1 – Food

2 – Wine (if applicable)

3 – Liquor (if applicable)

4 – Miscellaneous Operational Expenses such as utilities, services.

5 – Other Expenses

Enter these items on your purchase ledger with the date of delivery. Even if you won't use the items right away, still enter on the date when you received it. An example would be a utility bill—enter it for the month when the service was used and the charges created.

You will use these lists for a variety of calculations and will make any necessary adjustments at that time. At this time and for this purpose, record each expense on the date that you received the service or product. The procedure to enter an expense is to determine the expense code, enter the invoice on the correct ledger page with the date, invoice number, and the amount. These lists also need to include items that you paid for with cash. Enter these in the "Paid Out" column.

Monthly Total Purchases

At the end of the month, you need to figure the total expenditures. When the ledger has been compiled throughout the month, computing the totals is easy. You can simply add the numbers in each column and then total each page on the purchase ledger. Subtract any credits and returns on the statement. Each month should be closed out on the last day of the month. Here are some tips to compile your purchase ledger:

1. Always use a pencil for all amounts.

2. Enclose credit amounts in parentheses.

3. Have your suppliers send separate invoices for items with different codes.

Reconcile Your Accounts

Revenues for your business are generated from the sales of your products—generally food and drinks. This section will discuss how to check each transaction. This is important since it will help you track your revenue and ensure you aren't losing money.

Your Sales Report

The amount of money handled will depend on how your specific facility handles payment for meals or whether they are supplied free of charge. If you handle payments, you must reconcile the transactions for each day, much easier than trying to find mistakes a day or two later. One important part of the reconciliation is to make sure the cash drawers are correct. If you do handle cash, charges, and checks, these are the common steps to reconcile the money:

1. **Take cash drawer, sales receipts, charge slips, and all reports from the cashier's**

drawer in separate piles. Be sure to work in a locked office when you take money out of the safe.

2. **Count out new cash drawers for the day. Put the correct amount and sufficient change in the drawer before the day or the shift begins.** I like to have a small form where I list the money in the drawer when I create new cash drawers. This makes it easier when a cashier starts the day to be sure the right amount of money is in the drawer. I initial the slip and place it under the larger bills or my reserve change pile. Return the drawers to the safe and place the money in a bag in the safe. You will need the money, checks, and charge slips when you make the deposit. Some businesses create the cash drawer at the end of the shift while others do it in the morning. Either is acceptable in most instances. Check with your supervisor to see which method is used.

3. **Verify that the cashier charged the correct amount for each item.** The type of cash register you use can make this much easier. When you find errors, let the person know about the problem and be sure they know the correct way to conduct the transaction in the future. If it becomes an ongoing problem, you will need to take action. We'll discuss that in Chapter 14.

4. **Use the Food Itemization Form at the end of the chapter and place an "X" in the correct item for each menu item that was sold.** You can list how many of each item was sold. Also include any complimentary items that were given away, but these need to be listed separately.

5. **Stack all credit card receipts in one pile. Be sure each slip is signed.** If you use an imprint machine, be sure all numbers are legible, the expiration date is valid, the slip is dated, and the amount is correct. Many businesses use new credit card machines that are easier and have less chance for error.

6. **Separate the cash and checks that were received.** Verify the appropriate information is on each check, including date, amount, driver's license number, and telephone number. Total all checks and record the amount on your report. (Some possibilities are the Cashier's Report, Cash Turn in Form, Closing Bank Account Form, Change Form, and the Check Log.) There are a couple of examples at the end of the chapter. When you total your checks, paperclip the adding machine tape to the checks. List each check individually on the Check Log and fill out each column. It's also good to make a copy of the checks. You don't need to make copies if your banking service provides a copy of the front and back of the check online. Check with your bank to see what they offer and whether there is a charge.

7. **There must be receipts in the cash drawer for any money that was used for supplies.** Train your cashiers to keep these receipts in the drawer otherwise the cashier's drawer will be wrong at the end of the day. These cash expenditures should be approved by the manager or a supervisor.

8. **Your cook can also complete the Cook's Form.** This enables you to verify that each meal is paid for. If there are discrepancies, double check the cooks' numbers and your totals to find the problem.

9. **Total the food sales on the Food Itemization Form and verify that the total matches the cashier's report.** An example is at the end of the chapter.

10. **The total amount of sales multiplied by the sales tax rate must equal the amount**

of sales tax collected. These checks and double checks ensure the totals are correct and that money cannot be stolen without being detected.

11. **Compile the deposit for the day.** Use permanent ink and make two copies of your deposit slip. All checks need to be stamped "Deposit Only." When new cashiers are trained, they need to learn to initial all checks they accept enabling you to go back to them if there is a problem with any checks. All bills should be sorted and coins wrapped. If your bank requires that you submit charge slips, they should be included with your deposit, or close out your terminal for the evening and file the receipt with your sales report.

Step-by-step procedures to reconcile cash each day can save you time and money. Use a consistent method for reconciling money each time. These tips can help you maintain control over the cash handling.

1. **Count the money in the cash drawer before starting the shift and place it in the drawer.** At the end of the shift, enter each dollar bill and change denomination separately and total the amount.

2. **Total all credit card sales and enter that amount on the form.**

3. **Total all checks and enter the total on the form.**

4. **Enter all cash that was paid out during the shift for purchases in a separate column.** The cashier needs to produce a receipt for any money that was spent from the cash register.

5. **Total cash, credit cards, checks, miscellaneous sales, and cash "pay outs".**

6. **Count out money to create the till for the next shift.** Total the bills and change on an adding machine and include the adding machine tape in the drawer.

7. **Deduct the amount of the till from your drawer tally to find the "accountable funds" for that shift.** This net total needs to be entered on the "cash turn in report".

8. **Enter the gross sales total from the register "Z" report.** If the total is a positive number, the drawer is over and if the total is negative, the drawer is short for the shift. Enter that number on the reconciliation form.

The manager should take the deposit to the bank each day and should get change at the same time. Never leave two days of deposits in the safe. Night deposits are another option to get the money to the bank in a timely manner. When you get receipts from your deposits, they need to be filed with the daily paperwork. Double check the deposit ticket to verify that the amount is right. After you verify the amounts, they should be entered on the Daily Sales Report shown at the end of this chapter.

After you complete these activities, your records are reconciled, and you have identified any mistakes, be sure to include any complimentary amounts when you itemize the menu items. You need to retain these records for at least five years in a fireproof file. Keep all forms in a loose-leaf binder in the manager's or bookkeeper's office. This information must be filed away and kept confidential.

Manager's Responsibility to Maintain Costs

Many food service facilities are in business to serve a particular group of people, and even if these facilities are not striving to earn a profit, they must still break even. As a non-commercial food service manager, you must account for the money spent and can work to earn a profit. To organize and manage the facility finances, you need a long-term plan for how much it will cost you to earn the amount you need. This plan will be the basis for your budget. Many people feel that "budget" is a bad word, but a realistic budget will make all the difference in the operation and in your bottom line.

We will discuss how to project your operating costs and how to notice and resolve financial problems. A budget can also be used to gauge how effectively you are managing the business. Part of effective management is controlling costs. We will discuss that in more detail in Chapter 17, but it will be mentioned throughout this book.

When you find financial problems, you are responsible to evaluate them and find solutions. A monthly or quarterly budget is best for food service since the costs can fluctuate with the seasons. Samples of reports are provided in this book to help you figure out your budget and to make the necessary changes. You can use these monthly reports to compile your annual budget along with your profit and loss statement. Keeping up with these things each month makes your year-end reports and projections much easier.

It is time consuming in the beginning, but by the second or third month, it should only take a few hours to figure the budget for the next month. Your budget is a strong tool to control the business. It's never too early to start figuring your budget. A more experienced non-commercial food service manager can be valuable to you when you are first learning the ropes.

Don't expect to get a budget right on the first try. Some costs will be high or low. You will need to do everything possible to control costs and then figure out whether your plan should be reworked. A realistic budget is valuable. The longer you are in the job, the more information you can use to create accurate projections and budgets. It does get easier with practice.

Many times, managers are the only employees who understand the importance of maintaining operational expenses. Using a monthly budget can be a good way to help other employees understand that costs must be contained. When your staff members understand how important it is, they can be helpful in finding ways to cut costs and save money. Everyone wins when costs are controlled.

The most effective budgets are broken down by categories allowing you to find the problem areas faster and easier. If you are overusing or overspending in a certain area, it will stand out in your expenses and in your budget, helping you to see areas where you are losing control before they get bad. All these things will help you become a better and more valuable manager.

Sales Projections and Your Operational Budget

There are particular categories of expenses that you will need in your budget and sales projections.

Sales — The first things to figure are your projected sales. The amount you need to spend will be dictated by your sales. All expenses will be based on a percentage of these sales.

Total Sales — Business fluctuates from day to day, and this makes budgeting and projections complicated. The first thing is to figure which costs are variable, semi-variable, and set. Your variable and semi-variable costs will vary based on your sales. Projecting these costs will depend on accurately projecting your sales, which is a difficult thing to learn and will take time to do with any degree of accuracy. With practice, you can be on target with your projections.

You shouldn't expect to meet your budget in your first months, especially if you are managing a new business. Operational costs of a new business are higher than normal, and it's impossible to stay in an ideal budget. However, after a couple of months, operations can be streamlined as the facility becomes more efficient. This trial period should be worked out in four to twelve weeks.

After the initial trial-and-error period, you need to settle into normal operations and begin working on your sales projects. Here are the steps needed to project your sales:

- **Review customer count and facility sales for the previous year.** You can find this information in last year's Daily Sales Report. An example of this form is included at the end of the chapter. A little trick I learned was to pull out the calendar and see if there was anything unusual going on the previous year or the current year that would alter your projections. Was there a holiday, bad weather, or anything else that affected business? It's helpful to note special circumstances on your Daily Sales Report. This allows you or another manager to know why sales were unusually high or low for a specific week or day. At the end of the week, transfer the amounts to your Weekly Sales History report. An example of this form is included at the end of the chapter.

- **You can use a calendar and the Sales Projection Form to calculate the number of days in the month.** An example of this form is included at the end of the chapter. Enter the number of days in the month in the first column. Use the details in #1 to figure the average number of meals to be served per day and enter in the second column. Adjust these numbers for any holidays in the month and include any special events, meetings, and catering contracts.

- **Take the average number of meals, multiply by the number of days per month, and enter in the "subtotal" column.** Add each "subtotal" column to get the grand total.

- **When you have been there for some time, analyze the numbers and consider the business growth for the last year.** Based upon past customer counts, determine the percentage of growth or decline anticipated in the coming month, computed by subtracting the most recent period of customer counts from the past period of customer counts. The difference is then divided by the actual number of dinners served during the past period of time. A negative percentage figure shows a drop in customer counts. A positive figure indicates the percentage of increase.

Keep in mind that you need to compare like time periods using the same number of days and the same days of the week, since almost any food service facility has different types of business on different days of the week. When you compare sales numbers, use the previous week, the previous month, or the same week in the previous year. Sometimes you will need to compare the week before or after the same week in the previous year. Other things to factor into your figures are price increases that may alter your projections.

- **Multiply the percentage of growth or loss by the grand total.** Add the result to the grand total to compute the projected volume or number of dinners. Subtract this figure instead if you are multiplying by a negative percentage figure that indicates a loss in customer counts.

- **Multiply the projected volume by the average check of the past month.** The average check amount may be located on the Daily Sales Report. Adjust this figure if a price increase will be occurring during the month. Breakfast, lunch, and dinner sales may be projected together unless the percentage of growth or loss is suspected in one area and not in the other two. A separate chart should then be used to project each sales amount; simply add all three figures together for the grand total.

- **Compute food sales by simply dividing total sales by the average percentage of sales on last month's Daily Sales Report Form.**

- **The final step is to enter the budgeted amount for each day on the Daily Sales Report Form** which is computed by dividing total projected sales by the number of days in the month. Each day, enter the sales amount over or under budget in sales in the appropriate column. (Use parentheses or a red pencil to enter sales under budget.)

These amounts can be transferred to your Weekly Sales History to give you the weekly sales numbers at a glance. This is especially useful in future years. You can also use the Sales Projection Form for your projected sales. Examples of these forms are found at the end of this chapter.

Food and Beverage Costs

The amount of money you spend on food, supplies, and labor will be directly influenced by your sales volume. In turn, the more you buy, the higher your material costs. A simpler way to figure your budget costs is to use a percentage of your projected sales. The simplest way to calculate the percentage of sales is to divide the actual cost of the category by the total sales. The answer is the percentage for each category.

When we discuss maintaining your operational expenses, we will recommend having an ideal percentage amount for labor, food, and other expenses. You must keep your expenses below 100 percent to show a profit and the lower the percentage, the greater the profit. We'll discuss more about that in Chapter 17.

You can figure your food cost to be around 40 percent, so in the beginning you can use 40 percent of the projected sales. In a few months, you can use the actual amount. As your sales increase or decrease, you need to adjust your budget to reflect these changes.

Take the amount spent for supplies and subtract it from the gross sales to get the gross profit amount. You can then divide the gross profit by total sales to calculate the gross profit percentage.

Labor Cost

A number of amounts are included in your overall labor costs. They include:

- **Manager's Salary** — The manager's salary should be a fixed cost. Total the salary amount for the year and divide by the number of days in the year to determine the salary cost per day. Take the amount per day and multiply by the number of days in the month. This will give you the salary expense for that month.

- **Employee Pay** — Employee pay amounts should fluctuate with your sales amount. This is especially true when you become more experienced and learn to schedule effectively. There is a break-even point with your labor costs. When you learn to run the business and spend less on labor, the profit margin will increase. However, do not sacrifice service to save labor dollars. Your efficiency as a manager and the competence of your staff will be a determining factor in your labor costs. To find the percentage of your labor costs, divide the labor amount by your total sales amount. This percentage will fluctuate based on lower than expected sales and employee training.

- **Overtime** — You should not have overtime expenses. If there is an unusual situation that requires overtime, do everything possible to keep these amounts to a minimum. Many times the amount spent on overtime is due to poor management or an inefficient staff. A good bookkeeper will keep an eye on employees who are nearing 40 hours per week and will notify the manager. Another simple way to prevent overtime is to schedule all employees for less than 40 hours per week. There will be times when employees must exchange shifts, but these adjustments should always be approved by the manager or a supervisor to ensure employees do not work overtime.

Consistent Operational Costs

- **Dinnerware, glassware, and utensils** — Should be a consistent amount after the facility opens.

- **Dining room supplies** — Should be consistent after opening.

- **Kitchen supplies** — Should be consistent after opening.

- **Office supplies** — Should be a consistent amount each month.

- **Uniforms** — Will fluctuate depending on whether employees pay for their uniforms or the facility supplies them.

- **Laundry Expenses** — The amount can be entered as equal amounts each month, and the purchases are usually made once or twice a year. Include your laundry cleaning expenses under "services".

CASE STUDY: PRISON ACCOUNTING

The Department of Corrections has a multi million dollar budget. One Virginia prison has a population of 650-675 people inmates. It is important to stay near the daily budget of $1.70 per inmate for all three meals. If the cost exceeds $2.10 per day per inmate, the Food Service Manager can be held responsible.

The budget is approved and dispersed directly from the state government, which is Tim Kaine's office in the Commonwealth of Virginia.

Some of the smaller facilities in Virginia have a budget which slightly exceeds $2.10 per inmate, per day for a variety of reasons. Each facility has their own accountant, and receipts for food are sent or faxed to headquarters in Richmond, VA.

Lawrence Shearer, Chef

Services

- **Laundry Cleaning** — Sales will determine this cost. Figure the percentage of sales and make adjustments to allow for increases or decreases in the amount of sales.

- **Accounting Costs** — This can be a fairly consistent amount. The amount will vary during the initial set up and at tax time each year.

- **Maintenance** — You can keep this expense consistent by using a service contract with a maintenance company.

- **Telephone** — This should be consistent each month. Train all staff members to list all long distance calls in a log book. When the monthly bill arrives, compare the list with the bill for accuracy.

- **Water** — This should be a fairly consistent amount.

- **Gas and Electricity** — The sort of heat, stoves, and water heater you use will determine the consistency of your gas and electric bills. Local weather will affect your expenses at different times of the year.

Fixed Expenses

These are costs that should be consistent month after month and should not change more than once a year, and you should get advance notice if the price will change. One example is rent. If your lease or rent agreement also includes a percentage of the sales or profit amount, you can figure this amount after you complete the sales projections. Include this amount and the rent or lease amount for the year in the budgeted amount.

General Costs

- **Payroll Taxes** — Payroll taxes are the amounts deducted from each employee's paycheck. They include the matching Social Security and Medicare costs for each employee paid by the employer. These taxes also include the federal and state payroll taxes deducted from each paycheck.

- **Miscellaneous Taxes** — This includes local taxes and sales tax paid on purchases. However, it doesn't include sales tax collected by the business.

- **Equipment Repair** — These are regularly scheduled and emergency repairs or maintenance for all facility equipment. Your budget needs to include a base amount for repairs each month. Include all major expenses that you expect.

- **Building Repairs** — These include scheduled and emergency repairs. Major repairs should be minimal in a non-commercial food service facility. Include a consistent base amount in your budget and any major expense you expect.

- **Marketing and Promotional Expenses** — These are usually minimal for a non-commercial food service facility. They would include any print or media costs and any promotional items you might use to promote your facility.

- **Postage** — This is postage for business mail only.

- **Licenses** — This includes business licenses and health permits, for example. Take the amount for the entire year and divide by 12 to find the monthly cost.

- **Credit Card Costs** — This includes the monthly service charge and the average percentage for monthly charges.

- **Total Expenditures** — Total all budgeted expenditures and enter the total.

- **Net Profit** — Deduct the "Total Budgeted Expenditures" from your "Total Sales". The result is the net profit or loss. Divide the net projected profit by the projected total sales to find the projected pre-tax net-profit percentage.

Payroll Accounting

Your bookkeeper needs to compile the daily payroll numbers. You can then have the bookkeeper figure payroll deductions or hire a payroll service.

Whether time clocks compute the employees' hours worked will probably be decided before you are hired, but be sure you understand who is involved in the payroll process for the facility. This is especially important for you when the bookkeeper is sick or on vacation. These are the basic procedures involved in the manual payroll system.

Each day the bookkeeper should:

1. **Gather all time cards.**

2. **Double check time cards against the posted schedule.** Any adjustments to the schedule should be noted and initialed on the posted schedule.

3. **Figure the hours worked each day by each employee, including fractions of hours.**

4. **All employee hours need to be listed on the Daily Payroll Form.** An example of this form is included at the end of the chapter. Make a notation of any overtime hours in red on a different line. The bookkeeper also needs to notify you when any employees are close to reaching overtime. There may be ways to adjust the schedule to avoid overtime.

5. **Include the employee's hourly rate and if they are paid different amounts for various jobs, be sure the right amounts are used.** Then extend the gross amount they have earned.

6. **Divide employees' pay by the number of days in each month and include that amount each day for budgeting purposes.** List the manager's and owners' salaries at the bottom of the page.

7. **Add all payroll amounts for each employee on a specific day** and write the total at the bottom of the form. At the end of the week, total each day and enter the total gross pay. You can double check the numbers on the form to verify all numbers and totals are correct. You can also use the Payroll Cost Form to summarize the week's payroll amounts for each employee. An example of this form is included at the end of the chapter.

8. **Your daily sales and labor costs should be entered on the Labor Analysis Form.** An example of this form is included at the end of the chapter. Keep manager and owner salaries separate from employee payroll totals. The Labor Analysis Form divides the information into daily and month-to-date payroll amounts. Add each amount to the previous balance to get the month-to-date totals.

To figure the month-to-date payroll percentage, divide the month to date sales by the month-to-date payroll amount.

After you figure these amounts, you can enter them on the Operational Budget Form. A sample is included at the end of the chapter. This gives you one form to list your budget amount and percentage along with the actual costs and makes it easy to see where your cost overruns exist. You might not need every line on the form. If a line item doesn't pertain to you, leave the line blank.

Compile Your Monthly Projections and Actual Numbers

There are a number of things that need to be done each month to close out your accounts. As mentioned earlier, it's critical to enter all expenses that were incurred in the month. On the last day of the month, gather all inventory forms. Use the current invoices and check against the prices on your inventory form. When there are any discrepancies in prices, you need to check with the suppliers. It is also good to assign an employee or to organize all food and supply storage areas to make it easier to put your supplies away. Any employees who take the physical inventory should be scheduled to work early, and the cooks should arrive after the inventory is complete. We will discuss inventory in more detail in Chapter 7.

On the first day of each month, the bookkeeper needs to arrive early to complete his or her work before inventory is finished. All records for the previous date need to be reconciled and recorded just as the bookkeeper does any other day.

When you are ready to start projecting costs, you need the completed Daily Sales Report, Purchase Ledgers, Beginning Inventory Amounts, and Operational Supplies Cost Projection form. The Operational Supplies form is at the end of this chapter.

Revenue Available for Schools

Public schools have a harder time making ends meet financially. They are accountable to federal and state requirements that make it more difficult to maintain costs. This makes it advisable to put the school food service funds in a separate bank account.

Schools need to file monthly forms with the state to receive their reimbursement. The amount is based on the number of breakfast and lunch students served. Each meal needs to be broken down to indicate how many free, reduced, and full price meals were served. The state also requires the following information each month:

- Beginning cash balance

- All cash received during the month

- Total expenditures

- Ending balance for the month

There are additional information requirements in some states such as the actual cost of preparing each meal. It's best to verify the details with the state where you work.

Federal Resources

Federal law dictates how much the reimbursement will be for each meal served. Like most federal programs, if you file your paperwork late, you are running the risk of being denied.

Lunch program reimbursement is:

* A subsidy for each lunch served.

* An additional reimbursement for each free lunch.

* An additional reimbursement for each reduced price lunch.

Breakfast meals work the same way with an additional reimbursement for schools classified as "Severe Need".

State and Local Resources

Some states offer reimbursement for all lunches, while others only offer money for free or reduced lunches. You may receive these funds each month or it may be all at one time. Local support can be money, fringe benefits for employees, or some other funding. It's good to check with state and local government to be sure how the program works in your state.

Account management for any food service facility is complicated, but with some research and practice you can take advantage of any programs that may benefit your service. It's good to network with other non-commercial managers who have more experience. Ask questions and listen to their answers. If you are in a facility that is funded by the government, you need to check the federal, state, and local requirements that pertain to your facility.

Control Daily Cash Handling

A simple principle that you need to understand is that better control over the daily cash will lower costs and increase profits. It is important to keep track of how cash is handled at every stage of the daily operations. Any step in the procedure can cause major problems. Here are some procedures that are consistent in most non-commercial food service facilities.

* **Assign cash register drawers to each shift.** Keep money separate and limit accessibility to the cash. This is a quick way to identify honest or dishonest employees. When the till is compiled before the shift, add the contents on the adding machine and include that tape in the drawer. It sounds crazy, but I've discovered cash-handling errors by looking at that original calculation tape.

* **Count the cash.** Do this every day. This includes the opening till amount and any cash on hand. If this is done each day, you will spot any discrepancies in 24 hours. You can also recount the cash on hand after the bank deposit is made. It may seem redundant, but no manager wants to be called into a superior's office because of a cash shortage. When you count the cash drawer at the end of a shift, do this in a safe location. Usually a locked office is a good place, but look at your work space and find the safest place to reconcile the accounts.

- **Remove all large bills throughout the shift.** This would usually be $20 and higher, but decide what policy makes sense for your facility. If you routinely get batches of $50 bills, you need $20 bills to make change. The idea is to keep small amounts of money in the drawer. This helps with cash control and also creates a safer environment for the cashier and the facility as a whole. When this money is taken from the drawer, put it in a deposit bag or an envelope labeled to identify where it came from and lock it in the safe.

- **Routine.** This may seem boring and monotonous, but setting up a procedure and sticking to it can ensure that the money is handled properly each day and for each shift.

- **"Z" Readings.** Does your cash register have a "Z" reading feature? If so take a "Z" reading at the end of each shift. This will give you a summary of the transactions for that shift. You can compare it to the records from the cashier and the money in the drawer.

Managers need to keep track of many details in their daily operation. Many useful forms are included on the accompanying CD. If you need another log book or journal to record these specifics, take a look at **www.commlog.com**. Some of the logs they offer include: manager's, request shift, switch shift, kitchen, bar, and guest relations. Contact them 24 hours a day at 800-962-6564 (outside the United States, contact them at 602-232-2956).

Understanding Gross Profits

Your gross profit is the best indicator of the business's success. Gross profit is the difference between the item's cost and the sale price. When you reduce costs, focus on the gross profit amount. Here are some terms to help you handle and understand gross profits.

- **Cost Multiplier** — This will help you figure the selling price based on the portion cost. Divide the cost by 100 and then multiply the result by the portion cost for each product.

- **Gross Profit** — Subtract the portion cost from the sale price.

- **Gross Profit Margin** — This is the percentage of profit on each sale. Divide the amount of profit by the sales price and multiply by 100 to determine the gross profit margin.

- **Sales Percentage Profit** — Selling price is determined by dividing the portion cost by the gross profit margin percentage "reciprocal" (the figure you get by subtracting the gross margin from 100).

Troubleshoot Cash Control Issues

There may be times when your costs are escalating and you cannot find the problem. Here are some possibilities:

- **Food Cost Increase** — Have your food costs increased? If so, you need to increase food prices to compensate for price increases. Be careful not to raise your prices too much as doing so will hurt sales. Even non-commercial facility customers expect reasonable prices.

- **Include Tax in Prices** — The simplest way I've found is to include the tax in the price and make it a round number. This is especially helpful for your "impulse buys".

- **Decrease in Sales** — In some cases the competitor's prices can decrease your sales. However, in a non-commercial environment, keep in mind that your services are a convenience for staff members. They do have other options. You do not have free reign to raise your prices without considering the reasonable cost for your customers. Are more people rushing out for lunch or bringing their own lunch? These could be indicators that your prices are too high. Have you changed your staff members lately? New hires can cause some issues with your established clients. Are the menu items substandard? Has service fallen below your established standards? If this is the problem, you need to work with the new hires immediately to resolve the issues.

- **Are Sales Down and Purchasing Up?** — This could be food control problems, or items are being stolen. Some employees feel it is acceptable to give items or drinks to friends. This needs to be stopped right away.

CASE STUDY: AIRLINE CATERING

In the airline catering industry, customer service begins with accurate revenue and cost projections because contracts for both airline catering and food service facilities in airports are awarded by bid. Airline catering consists of two divisions, one serving the airlines, the other providing food and drink to travelers inside airports. A food service company, using projected traffic figures which in turn are based on economic factors, must prepare a detailed analysis of expected passenger flow and projected revenue per passenger together with food, labor, and capital expenditure costs to prepare a reasonable and mutually profitable bid on these facilities.

Sometimes a major overhaul of airport restaurant facilities is entailed, or a flight kitchen may need to be constructed, adding depreciation to the cost structure. Some airport commissions focus on the percentage of food and beverage sales that interested caterers bid; others regard the quality of proposed facilities to be equally or more important. Liquor provides the highest return on investment. (This explains why in some airports it is easier to find alcoholic drinks than milk.)

RM Zurkan - Airline Business Analyst

COMPANY _____ MONTH _____

DATE	INV #	AMT $	INV #	AMT $	INV #	AMT $	PAID OUTS
GRAND TOTAL							
						PAGE TOTAL	

DATE: _____ DAY: _____ SHIFT: _____

CASHIER: _____ PREPARED BY: _____

Total Cash/Check Guest Checks _____

Total Charged Guest Checks _____

TOTAL RECEIPTS _____

Total Cash Guest Checks _____

Total Cash Turned In _____

DIFFERENCE (note + or -) _____

REASON FOR DIFFERENCE : _____

_____

_____

_____

REGISTER READING (Taken by Manager Only)

End Reading _____

Beginning Reading _____

DIFFERENCE (note + or -) _____

REGISTER READING _____

TOTAL RECEIPTS _____

DIFFERENCE (note + or -) _____

REASON FOR DIFFERENCE : _____

_____

_____

_____

DATE: _____ PREPARED BY: _____

BILLS

Large Bills	$	_____
$20.00 Bills	$	_____
$10.00 Bills	$	_____
$5.00 Bills	$	_____
$1.00 Bills	$	_____
TOTAL BILLS	$	_____

CHANGE

Half-Dollars	$	_____
Quarters	$	_____
Dimes	$	_____
Nickels	$	_____
Pennies	$	_____
TOTAL CHANGE	$	_____

OTHER

Register Banks	$	_____
_____	$	_____
_____	$	_____
_____	$	_____
TOTAL OTHER	$	_____

CHECKS (list by name)

_____	$	_____
_____	$	_____
_____	$	_____
_____	$	_____
_____	$	_____
_____	$	_____
_____	$	_____
_____	$	_____
_____	$	_____
_____	$	_____
_____	$	_____
_____	$	_____
_____	$	_____
_____	$	_____
_____	$	_____
_____	$	_____
_____	$	_____
_____	$	_____
_____	$	_____
_____	$	_____
_____	$	_____
_____	$	_____
_____	$	_____
TOTAL CHECKS	$	_____

TOTAL CASH ON HAND:

_____
Signature of Manager

CASH REPORT

DATE: _____ DAY: _____ SHIFT: _____

CASHIER: _____ PREPARED BY: _____

ITEM	NUMBER	$ AMOUNT
BEGINNING BANK		
CURRENCY		
$100.00		
$50.00		
$20.00		
$10.00		
$5.00		
$1.00		
COINS		
$0.50		
$0.25		
$0.10		
$0.05		
$0.01		
TOTAL CURRENCY & COINS		
Checks		
Subtotal		
Less Bank		
TOTAL TURN-IN		
Notes:		

| CASHIER NAME: _____ |
| SHIFT: _____ |
| DATE: _____ |

BILLS:	$100		
	$50		
	$20		
	$10		
	$5		
	$1		
COINS:	$.50		
	$.25		
	$.10		
	$.05		
	$.01		
CHECKS & VOUCHERS:			
Total Amount Enclosed:			
- Due Back			
= Deport			
- Deposit (from cash sheet)			
DIFFERENCE (over/short)			

CASHIER NAME: _____

SHIFT: _____

DATE: _____

BILLS:	$100		
	$50		
	$20		
	$10		
	$5		
	$1		
COINS:	$.50		
	$.25		
	$.10		
	$.05		
	$.01		
	SUBTOTAL:		
	+ DUE BACK:		
	= TOTAL BANK:		

Check #	Amount	Date	Written To	Invoice #	Deposit	Acct. Balance

ITEM	USE A ✔ MARK TO DESIGNATE ONE SOLD	TOTALS
	TOTAL	

FOOD SALES RECAP

WEEK OF: _____ DATE PREPARED: _____

PREPARED BY: _____

MENU ITEM	MON	TUES	WED	THURS	FRI	SAT	SUN	TOTAL

DATE: _____ DAY: _____ APPROVED BY: _____

PREPARED BY: _____

REGISTER READINGS

DEPARTMENT	SHIFT	END READING	BEGINNING READING	DIFFERENCE

TOTAL RECEIPTS

DEPARTMENT	SHIFT	CASH	CHARGE	TOTAL	OVER/SHORT

SALES BREAKDOWN

DEPARTMENT	SHIFT	FOOD SALES	BAR SALES	TOTAL SALES

PREPARED BY: _____ DATE PREPARED: _____

WEEK OF:

	DATE	SALES	SALES TO DATE
Monday			
Tuesday			
Wednesday			
Thursday			
Friday			
Saturday			
Sunday			
TOTAL FOR WEEK			

WEEK OF:

	DATE	SALES	SALES TO DATE
Monday			
Tuesday			
Wednesday			
Thursday			
Friday			
Saturday			
Sunday			
TOTAL FOR WEEK			

DATE	# OF EACH	AVG # DINNERS	SUB-TOTAL
MONDAY			
TUESDAY			
WEDNESDAY			
THURSDAY			
FRIDAY			
SATURDAY			
SUNDAY			
HOLIDAYS			

BREAKFAST TOTAL _____

LUNCH TOTAL _____

DINNER TOTAL _____

GRAND TOTAL _____

Grand Total x % Growth/Loss = Projected Volume x Check Avg. = Projected Sales

DIVISION OF SALES

	TOTAL PROJECTED SALES x	% SALES DIVISION	= SALES DIVISION
FOOD			
LIQUOR			
WINE			

HOLIDAYS THAT MUST BE CONSIDERED:

- Washington's Birthday
- Easter
- Mother's Day
- Memorial Day
- Fourth of July

- Labor Day
- Thanksgiving
- Christmas Eve
- Christmas
- New Year's Eve

- New Year's Day
- Halloween
- Valentine's Day
- Graduation Day

DAILY PAYROLL FORM

DATE _____ MONTH _____ YEAR _____

H = HOURS   G = GROSS

EMPLOYEE	RATE	H	G	H	G	H	G	H	G	H	G	H	G	H	G	H	G	TOTAL

TOTAL   [   ]

DATE PREPARED: _____ WEEK OF: _____

PREPARED BY: _____

TOTAL PAYROLL COST

Total Gross Wages	$ _____
(+) Total Employee Meals	$ _____
(=) **Total Payroll Cost**	$ _____

PAYROLL COST PERCENTAGE

Total Payroll Cost	$ _____
(÷) Total Gross Sales	$ _____
(_____ x 100 =) **Payroll Cost**	% _____

SALES PER PERSON PER HOUR

Total Gross Sales	$ _____
(÷) Total Hours Worked	$ _____
(=) **Sales per Person per Hour**	$ _____

	DAY	DATE	DAILY SALES	DAILY PAYROLL			%	MONTH TO DATE	MONTH-TO-DATE PAYROLL			
				BUDGET	ACT	OV/UND			BUDGET	ACT	OV/UND	%
1												
2												
3												
4												
5												
6												
7												
7-DAY TOTAL												
8												
9												
10												
11												
12												
13												
14												
14-DAY TOTAL												
15												
16												
17												
18												
19												
20												
21												
21-DAY TOTAL												
22												
23												
24												
25												
26												
27												
28												
28-DAY TOTAL												
29												
30												
31												
TOTAL												

ITEM	BUDGETED	%	ACTUAL	%
SALES				
Food				
Liquor				
Wine				
TOTAL SALES				
MATERIALS				
Food Costs				
Liquor Costs				
Wine Costs				
TOTAL COSTS				
GROSS PROFIT				
LABOR				
Manager Salary				
Employee				
Overtime				
TOTAL LABOR COSTS				
Controller Oper. Costs				
China & Utensils				
Glassware				
Kitchen Supplies				
Bar Supplies				
Dining Room Supplies				
Uniforms				
Laundry/Linen				
Services				
Trash Pick-Up				
Laundry Cleaning				
Protection				
Freight				
Accounting				
Maintenance				
Payroll				
TOTAL THIS PAGE				

PAGE _____ **MONTH** _____

CATEGORY _____ # _____

    Beginning Inventory _____

    Purchases _____

    Ending Inventory _____

    Cost _____

    Sales _____

    TOTAL COST PERCENTAGE _____

CATEGORY _____ # _____

    Beginning Inventory _____

    Purchases _____

    Ending Inventory _____

    Cost _____

    Sales _____

    TOTAL COST PERCENTAGE _____

CATEGORY _____ # _____

    Beginning Inventory _____

    Purchases _____

    Ending Inventory _____

    Cost _____

    Sales _____

    TOTAL COST PERCENTAGE _____

CATEGORY _____ # _____

    Beginning Inventory _____

    Purchases _____

    Ending Inventory _____

    Cost _____

    Sales _____

    TOTAL COST PERCENTAGE _____

Depreciation Worksheet (keep for your records.)

Description of Property	Date Placed in Service	Cost or Other Basis	Business/ Investment Use %	Section 179 Deduction and Special Allowance	Depreciation Prior Years	Basis for Depreciation	Method/ Convention	Recovery Period	Rate or Table %	Depreciation Deduction

CHAPTER THREE

Using a Computer System

Computers are valuable in any business situation, and non-commercial food service is no different. Once you find the right program and learn how to use it, the software will save you time, effort, and money. There are plenty of duties to keep you busy, so find ways to use a computer to make you more efficient.

A good computer program can provide a food service manager with a wealth of information about his or her facility. Will you take the time to review these reports? Many managers don't review the reports and even fewer take the time to analyze information contained in them. The reports are critical in helping you get a grasp of the actual profitability identifying areas that need to be changed.

There are many non-commercial food-service duties which can be made easier with the right computer system. This chapter will explain ways to use a computer to make your job as manager easier.

How Do I Choose a Computer?

There are many things to consider when choosing a computer. Some are:

- What kind of computer do I need?

- How much RAM do I need?

- Do I need a Pentium or Athlon?

- What brand and size monitor do I need?

- What type of video card should I get?

- What sort of Internet connection do I need?

- What programs should I use?

Keep in mind that the computer industry is always changing. So these answers change on a regular basis. You do not need the biggest, most expensive computer for most businesses. It's better to find the most powerful system that fits in your budget. Here are some more details to consider:

- **CPU speed** — The CPU powers your computer. So the faster the CPU, the more powerful your computer will be. It's best to buy your computer with the future in mind. Again find the fastest system in your budget.

- **RAM** — RAM stores the information on your computer. You shouldn't buy any less than 128 MB of RAM, and 250 MB are preferred.

- **Operating system** — Microsoft Windows XP or Windows 2000 are stable operating systems with the ability to network multiple computers.

- **Monitor** — Monitors come in all sizes but 17" or larger is preferred. You can also choose a flat screen or an LCD monitor.

- **Graphics card** — A graphics accelerator card with at least 32 MB of RAM is sufficient. A favorite for business performance is any card based on each the GeForce Chipset.

- **Athlon or Pentium** — Either processor is a great choice.

- **Internet connection** — Dial-up is a less expensive, slower connection, sufficient for many Internet users. However, the amount of work you do may require a high-speed connection. If you need a high speed connection, check to see if DSL or cable is available in your area. Depending on your situation you may also need a router and firewall protection.

- **Computer platform** — Your choices are Windows and Macintosh. If you're uncertain, it would be good to talk to a Windows or Macintosh technician for additional information. Keep in mind that there are more software packages and long-term industry support for Windows-based operating systems.

- **Networking** — The need for networking is determined by the number of computers your facility uses. When they are networked together you can share programs, files, printers, and Internet connections. There are several networking choices, including standard wiring, phone line networks, and wireless networks.

Each has specific benefits:

1. **Standard wiring is the fastest choice**, but it requires cable installation.

2. **A phone line network is a low-cost option** that uses your existing phone lines and still allows you to talk on the phone.

3. **Wireless networks are expensive but versatile.** Most laptop owners are familiar with wireless networking and the freedom it provides.

Point-of-Sale Systems

At this time 90 percent of food-service facilities use these systems. They are simple to use and they can provide a wealth of information for managers. Here are a few benefits of the point-of-sale system:

- Customized tracking

- Inventory tracking

- Menu item performance tracking

- Employee time card tracking

- Sales breakdown

- Employee scheduling

- Purchasing and receiving

- Money management

- A wealth of useful reports

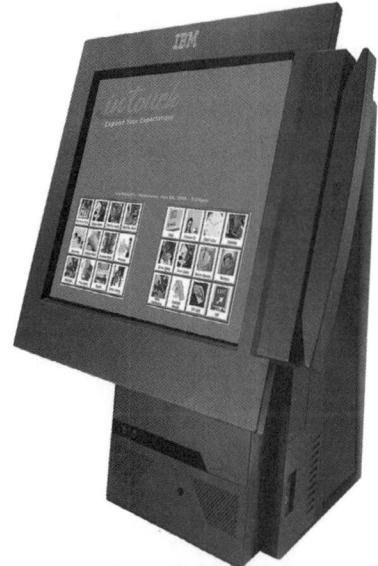

The InTouchPOS system was developed by food service operators, so it is customized to fit your needs. This system includes performance, flexibility, security, and reliability. The system can include employee information, payroll details, all discounts, promotions, and special offers. It can include various meals, ingredients, and programmed portions before it arrives at your location. It is a "turn-key" system that might be just what your non-commercial facility needs to control food and labor costs. For more information, you can visit **www.intouchpos.com/product.htm** or call 800-777-8202.

Vital Link POS helps you to track orders, modify any items, and verify the productivity of your servers and food preparation staff. You can evaluate individual menu items. It will manage your orders based on different variables including customer, table, or server. You can oversee your inventory and scheduling for better cost control. The customer history stored in the system will give you the opportunity to target your marketing efforts to your customer base. Visit **www.vitallinkpos.com/products.htm** or e-mail them at loconnor@vitallinkpos.com.

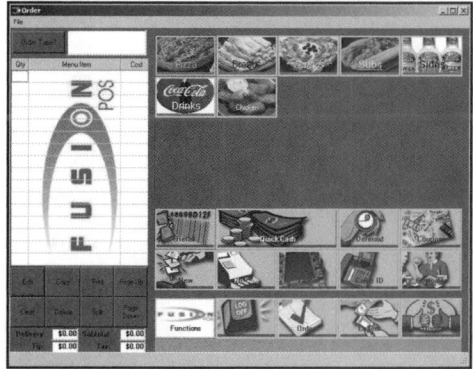

Casio offers a state-of-the-art register for your food service facility. The system uses graphics to make check-out faster for your patrons. Floating customer charge file with discount levels and credit limits can be programmed into the unit. Bar codes can be used to identify an item, to recall a customer guest check, and to reprint a transaction, all designed to eliminate input errors and decrease transaction time. An optional magnetic stripe reader (QT-6046MCR) can be used for the purpose of credit/debit operations, assigning a name to a table/check, server sign-on, and customer charge identification. Visit **www.casio.com/products/ Cash_Registers_ percent 26_POS/** for more information or call 800-638-9228.

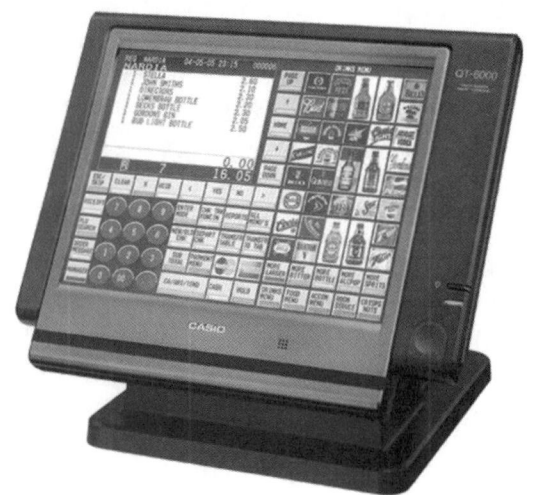

Customer Software Options

Some of the most popular software possibilities are mentioned below to give you insight into what is available and which programs would be the most advantageous for your facility.

ChefTec

ChefTec contains recipes, menu costing, inventory controls, and nutritional evaluation. Here are some additional details for each element of the program.

- **Recipe and Menu Costing**: Store, scale, and re-size unlimited recipes. Write recipe procedures with culinary spell-checker. Analyze recipe and menu costs by portion or yield amounts. Update prices and change ingredients in every recipe with the touch of a button. Create bids for catering functions. Attach photos, diagrams, and videos for bids or add pictures of plate presentation to your recipes for consistency.

- **Nutritional Analysis**: Pre-loaded with USDA information with add-on items. Calculate nutritional value for recipes and menus. Provide legally accurate information on "low-fat" and "low salt," for example. Add your specialty items for analysis. Calculate nutritional values for your recipes and menu items. See at a glance which menu items are low-calorie. Print a "Nutrition Facts" label, valuable for patients with special nutritional concerns.

- **Inventory Control**: Pre-loaded inventory list of 1,900 commonly used ingredients with unlimited capacity to add ingredients. Track fluctuating food costs and compare vendor pricing. Evaluate the impact of price increases on your recipes. Automate ordering with par values for items. This is discussed in Chapter 7. Use handheld device for inventory. Generate custom reports. Inventory control feature lets you track rising food costs automatically. Compare vendor pricing at the touch of a button from purchases or bids. Enter invoices quickly with the "Auto-Populate" feature. Generate customized reports on purchases, price changes and bids. Lists ingredients in various languages (Spanish, French, German) for Menu-Spell.

ChefTec PDA is also available. ChefTec is available from Atlantic Publishing Company (**www.atlantic-pub.com** or call 800-814-1132; Item CTC-CS).

MenuPro

MenuPro gives you the ability to create professional menus for much less than custom printing design. It can be used for simple daily special flyers, elaborate menus, or menus for catering events. It gives you the tools to create top quality designs. MenuPro is also available from Atlantic Publishing Company (**www.atlantic-pub.com** or call 800-814-1132, Item MNP-CS).

Menu-Spell

Menu-Spell was compiled and written by Arno Schmidt, a famed chef, author, and hospitality consultant. It contains more than 25,000 culinary terms in English, French, German, Spanish, and Italian. The program works with your word processor. Menu-Spell is available from Atlantic Publishing Company (**www.atlantic-pub.com** or call 800-814-1132, Item MSM-CS).

Employee Schedule Partner

This program offers a total package to create schedules for your employees by pointing and clicking. Click a button and the program fills in the schedule automatically. Click a button to replace absent employees from a list of available employees and their phone numbers. There is an online coach to help you learn the program. You can enter unlimited employees and jobs. It is simple to override any schedule suggestions to accommodate availability restrictions. Track payroll and totals for budgeting purposes. Use any day to start your work week. You have the ability to specify the maximum number of hours per day, days per week, and shifts per day per employee. Lock employees into specific shifts so the program cannot alter their schedule. The program saves old schedules for reference.

The software is password-protected to prevent unauthorized access. Employee Schedule Partner is available from Atlantic Publishing Company (**www.atlantic-pub.com** or call 800-814-1132, Item ESP-CS).

Employee Time Clock Partner

This is a preferred time-clock software. One reason is because it's powerful and simple. Employees clock in and out by entering their employee number. They can view their time card to verify their hours. It is password protected so that only a manager, owner, or bookkeeper can make changes. The program figures daily and weekly hours and overtime. Employee Time Clock Partner is available from Atlantic Publishing Company (**www.atlantic-pub.com** or call 800-814-1132, Item ETC-CS).

QuickBooks

This is my favorite accounting program. There are many built-in valuable features, and I've used it for payroll compilation and tax reports for years. QuickBooks is available at **www.quickbooks.com**.

Another popular accounting package is Peachtree, available at **www.peachtree.com**.

Purchasing and Inventory Management Software

Many large companies use software to control their inventory, saving significant time and money. Software offers numerous reports to help the manager maintain more control over the facility. All food service managers have stood in the walk-in and counted various food items to compile inventory numbers. Inventory control software allows managers to use a laser scanner to scan bar codes. Your distributors can be linked to your software that will allow you to place your orders electronically.

Here are some vendors:

- ChefTec from Atlantic Publishing was mentioned earlier.

- The National Restaurant Association's Web site, **www.restaurant.org**, offers information about software vendors. Their yearly exhibit in Chicago gives you a chance to see the latest programs available in the industry.

- You may also be interested in the information at **www.foodprofile.com**. It is used to collect and distribute information for the food industry and is part of the Efficient Foodservice Response (EFR) initiative. EFR works to improve the efficiency of the purchasing process. Distributors can list their products on this site for a fee. More than 65,000 items are listed on the site with up-to-date information, including serving suggestions, nutritional, preparation, and ingredient information. You can visit their Web site at **www.efr-central.com**.

- Another way to improve your efficiency is through placing orders online. Most distributors offer this option for their customers. The advantages are fewer errors, more convenience, discounts, simpler reordering.

Here is a partial list of vendor Web sites:

- **www.seafax.com**

- **www.tampamaid.com**

- **www.foodservicecentral.com**

- **www.foodservice.com**

- **www.fbix.com**

- **www.buyproduce.com**

- **www.gfs.com**

- **www.nugget.com**

- **www.pocahontasfoods.com**

- **www.whitetoque.com**

- **www.syscono.com**

- **www.usfoodservice.com**

- **www.sysco.com**

- **You can use purchase orders (POs) to give written authorization to your vendors to supply products at a set price on a regular schedule.** When they accept your PO, it is a legally binding contract. Vendors give you written proof of the items you ordered, the amount, and the price. A program records the invoice, adjusts your inventory amounts, and reflects any price changes.

- **Purchase orders can be printed from software programs**, and you can fax them to the vendor saving you time and money.

- **Avoid expensive, name brand products when possible.** They usually cost more because of advertising costs. Keep in mind that you can find good quality products that are not widely advertised. It is unlikely that your customers will notice a difference between "name brands" and "industrial brands".

- **Many food service facilities have found local growers who can supply their fresh produce needs.** It is possible they will be fresher, cheaper, and of higher quality. It's worth your time to check out the possibility.

- **A group of food service businesses may decide to form a cooperative to get better discounts for larger purchases.** Franchise organizations do this and even purchase trucks to deliver the supplies.

- **Keep in mind that when you buy from a vendor who is far away, the shipping costs will be more**, especially with the recent increases in gas prices.

Desktop Publishing

There are many reasons to use a computer in your job as a non-commercial food service manager. It can save you a huge amount of time and money. Here are a few of the possibilities.

- Develop and print newsletters for employees and/or patrons.

- Design and print menus or flyers.

- Design and print custom gift certificates.

- Design and print employee training manual.

- Design and print posters to promote special events.

- Design and print catering menus.

- Design your own letterhead.

Do Computers Have a Future in Food Service?

Food service operations are finding more ways to use computers and the various software programs. They can make operations more efficient and productive and even make the business more profitable. Point-of-sale systems make it easier for managers to monitor their inventory and costs.

Correct Use of E-mail

E-mail is short for electronic mail, which enables people to send messages through computers to communicate with one another through a network. You need a computer connected to the Internet and you need to establish an e-mail account to communicate with others. Your Internet service provider will usually give you at least one free e-mail account, and there are many free e-mail accounts. Think carefully about your e-mail username, especially when it's for business.

E-mail has big advantages over using the post office and the telephone: convenience and cost. It is there when it's convenient for you and for the recipient. There is no charge to send e-mails, no need to play phone tag, and you can send unlimited e-mails at once—for free.

There are distinct differences between e-mail and postal mail. E-mail is faster, free, simple to use, password protected, permanent, and useful to communicate with many people simultaneously. It may seem funny, but there are etiquette rules for e-mail. It's good to keep these things in mind when compiling and sending messages.

1. **Avoid flaming** — Flames are personal attacks for things they did or said.

2. **Avoid ambiguity** — Only forward the appropriate portions of the original message and answer their questions. It's good to include a subject line relevant to the message as it is helpful for locating the message later.

3. **Proofread your message** — Re-read your message and do spell check before you send. One problem with e-mail is that it can be misunderstood. Read your words to make sure they convey the message your have in mind. Never use all capital letters since this is tantamount to screaming.

Common Mistakes

You want to avoid these mistakes:

- Entering the message in the subject line.

- Having ambiguity in your wording.

- Not logging out of your account when you are finished.

- Not checking your e-mail regularly.

- Forgetting your username or password.

- Sending messages to the wrong address.

Should You Have a Web Presence?

If the facility is part of a large company, hospital, college, church, or another business that would attract outside interest, you should have a Web page. There are several hospitals in my area that have such good cafeterias that they attract people from the community. Colleges can always promote their cafeteria on their campus Web site. In an online search, I also discovered that many churches list their cafeterias and special food services on their Web site.

If the organization has a Web site, ask the Web master to add a page or two for your facility, and use it to announce your hours of operation. You could include weekly or monthly menus and notes about special services you offer. Take the opportunity to let people in the organization and in the community know that your non-commercial food service facility is open for business. Even if you aren't pushed to make a profit, your supervisor will appreciate the additional revenue that your efforts can produce. We'll discuss this more in Chapter 18. The Internet is a powerful promotional tool. Here are some of the benefits for the facility you manage:

1. Gather demographic information.

2. Evaluate promotional information.

3. Generate sales.

4. Lower your phone budget.

5. Improve communication with staff and potential customers.

6. Establish frequent, meaningful communications.

7. Reduce fax costs.

8. Provide additional staff training with online bulletins.

9. Submit invoices and expenses more quickly.

The Internet is the greatest medium for communication in the world. It provides exposure to more than 285 million people, 24 hours a day. About 48 percent of these people are online, one to four times a day, while 39 percent of them are online more often; 20 percent of the 285 million users are online more than 35 hours a week.

One great thing about Web sites is that you offer the information and the visitor has control over what they see and when they see it. You have a variety of ways you can present information to visitors. Downloads can be included; audio and video can present details to your visitors.

Elements of Your Web Page

Most people are familiar with various Web sites. When you look at a Web page, what catches your attention? Is there anything that makes you leave the site? If you will have pages on a larger company Web site, talk with the Web master about your ideas and get feedback. Here are some elements to consider:

1. **Pictures**: Use pictures to showcase your food, buffet line, or dining room.

2. **Bulletin Board**: Do you offer specials, events, or other noteworthy things?

3. **Menu**: If your menus are planned far in advance, why not include them on your Web page?

4. **Location**: Is it complicated to find the food service department? Include a location map and possibly parking suggestions—especially useful for special events that your department may host or oversee.

5. **Background**: Is there any special info about staff members, awards that the facility won, or any other noteworthy history? You can share this information to give the facility a more personal appeal to customers.

Keep in mind that Web site promotion has unlimited possibilities. Honestly, you are only limited by your imagination, your budget, and the ability of your Web designer.

Beware! There are some things to bear in mind when you create your Web pages. These include:

- **Don't overlook the specifics.**

- **Work with a professional for the best possible Web pages.**

- **Get a written quote for the work to be done** and include full details about all costs. Some people find ways to include hidden costs.

- **You need to get the word out about your pages.** Include the address on the bottom of menus that you circulate, letterhead, e-mail signature block, employee memos, and anywhere else to generate interest.

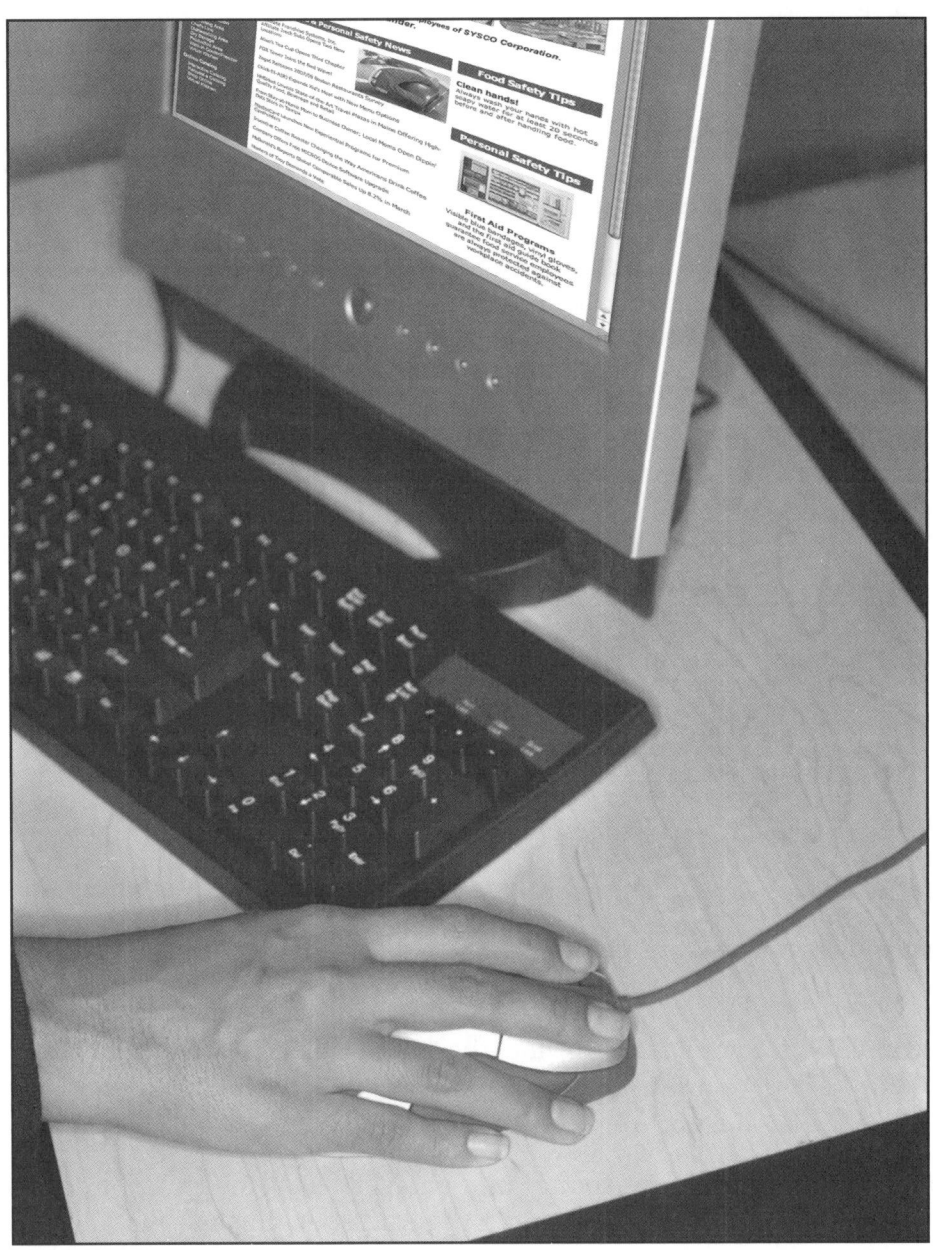

CHAPTER FOUR

Effective Menu Planning and Pricing

Y ou need to offer good food even in a non-commercial food service situation because your diners can pack a lunch or go elsewhere. If you are in a prison atmosphere, the inmates don't have other alternatives, but most other non-commercial clients have options. Hospitals have limited food service options, but you still need to make an effort to consider the needs of your clientele—their nutrition, finances, and time constraints—when meals are being planned.

This chapter will help you learn to plan a successful and profitable menu to appeal to your customers. Keep in mind that your specific recipes should come from cookbooks, but we will discuss ways to present your menu items and develop various menus for the particular situations you will face as a non-commercial food service manager.

Menu Style

How much variety will you offer in your meals? You may think that only full-service restaurants can offer variety to their customers, but you can do this. There are many types of menu items that you can offer. This is especially true in a cafeteria style non-commercial food service facility. Even if you only offer two main entrée options, you can add various vegetables, fruits, desserts, breads, and salads to appeal to a wider base of customers.

When you plan your menu items, remember that your labor and food control is critical to your success. Too many options can drastically increase your costs. There is a fine line between offering sufficient choices and giving so many options that you lose money. Over time you will learn which items are well received and which items to leave off your menu saving wasted labor and food costs. Work to find the balance to appeal to your customers without stretching your costs too far. Limited menus allow you to keep a handle on costs and will keep your kitchen work easier to manage. One of the first things to consider is how many meals you need to prepare each day. Here are some examples:

- **Health Care Facilities** — Three meals per day and maybe snacks.

- **Schools** — Lunch and maybe a light breakfast.

- **Colleges** — Three meals per day and off hour food choices.

- **Prisons** — Two or three meals per day; limited options to maintain your budget.

- **Military Facilities** — Two or three meals per day.

- **Churches** — Usually on specific days of the week such as Wednesday evening and Sunday lunch. You might offer Sunday breakfast or snack for children during Sunday school.

There are other choices, but these are some pretty common possibilities. Facilities offering two or three meals may offer fewer options than facilities serving only one meal a day.

One option is to order certain items and prepare them many different ways, saving you inventory hassles and offering various menu choices. A great example is potatoes. There are unlimited ways to prepare potatoes with limited additional work and ingredients.

Here are some advantages to each type of menu. Which menu choices work better for your facility?

Limited Menu

- Less equipment and space is needed.

- Fewer and less skilled employees are required.

- Food preparation is simpler and faster.

- Overall operating costs are lower.

- Your turnover numbers are higher

- Inventory storage space is limited.

- Purchasing is simpler and faster.

- It's easier for you to control cost and quality.

Extensive Menu

- New staff members and potential customers are intrigued.

- Your facility appeal to a more varied customer base.

- Your menu appeals to more people.

- Your menu has more flexibility.

- You can charge higher prices for special items.

- Regular customers and residents are more satisfied.

How many items should you offer? You need a variety, but not at the cost of inventory and labor control. Would you be happy to learn that research proves that only eight to twelve items make up 60 percent to 75 percent of the items sold? This is true no matter how many items are being offered. So you might want to offer 18 and 24 items.

You need to decide which items will be on the menu. There are three steps to help you make these decisions.

1. **Which courses will you offer** — appetizers, soups, entrees, desserts?

2. **What categories will you offer in these courses?** Your entrees could include beef, poultry, seafood, and vegetables. How many dishes will you offer in each category? You may want two or three entrees per day, giving you the chance to rotate the categories from day to day. The same holds true with vegetables, salads, and desserts.

3. **You will decide how each category of food will be served** — ground, chopped, marinated, broiled, baked, fried—the options are endless.

After these decisions are made, you may choose how to combine these dishes on your menu. For instance, you might offer hamburger, grilled chicken, and baked fish. This may sound like an insurmountable task, but keep the three steps in mind to assist you to make the necessary decisions.

Keep the food preparation and recipe in mind when you get ready to write the menu. This will help you maintain truthfulness in your menu listings. Any inaccuracies, whether intentional or accidental, are a problem. Your wording must give an accurate representation of the food item.

There has been a crackdown by regulatory agencies to verify the "truth in menu." Every word in your descriptions must be accurate. If you say:

- **Fresh** — it cannot be frozen.
- **Fat free** — it must be totally fat free.
- **Imported** — it must be imported.
- **Homemade** — it must be homemade.

These are just a few examples and it may sound overly simplified, but be sure to use the true and accurate words to describe your menu items. It will become routine to make an appetizing and honest menu. With a little creativity, you can write an enticing menu to meet all legal requirements.

We have provided an "Accuracy-in-Menu Checklist" to give you some common items that people word improperly on their menus. It is located at the end of this chapter and on the accompanying CD so you can print it out for your use.

Determine the accuracy of your own menu by using the checklist and answering the sample questions.

Design Your Menu for Your Customers

The basic objectives in menu planning are to provide nutritious, appetizing, and attractive foods. But these food choices need to stay within your budget limitations. The person who is the menu planner must be familiar with:

- **The people to be served**: their eating habits and preferences.

- **Their nutritional needs**: especially true in health care and school situations.

- **Food combinations, preparation, and service.**

CASE STUDY: CHURCH MENUS

Some menu choices are determined by the season. A couple of examples include: ham in April and turkey in November. Summer is a great time for outdoor barbecue for the churches who have the facilities. But one key thing is to keep the menu simple and easy because most church kitchens have only one person who is trained in food service methods and regulations. Most church food service menus have one meat or entrée, two or three vegetables, rolls or another bread, one or two cold salads and one or two dessert options.

Gary Douylliez • St Francis Inn
Casa de Solana Inn • **www.stfrancisinn.com**

Your patrons have certain eating habits and expectations. It is your job to be sensitive and realistic when you plan the menus. These are some of the things you should take into consideration, but all may not apply to your facility:

- **Ethnic or cultural foods are more important to some people than for others.** (Use your judgment about the people who patronize your facility.)

- **Many people are emphatic about maintaining a vegetarian lifestyle.**

- **It is possible the person would end up in the emergency room** or worse from eating foods that cause an allergic reaction.

- **Adequate nutritional value and recommended dietary allowances are especially important for health care and school food service facilities.**

- **American Heart Association requirements are particularly critical** in health care and nursing home environments.

It can also be helpful to define the people you will serve. This will help you develop menus to appeal to your patrons.

Each of these particular requirements is important to meet the needs and desires of your patrons. Evaluate how important each criterion is for the facility where you work. Various diets and menus will determine the equipment, purchasing, preparation, staff, and inventory you need. Various facilities will need different meal patterns. Some Hospitals offer these meal plans for patients.

- **Three meals** per day and night nourishment

- **Five meals**, two full meals, and three small meals

More than 14 hours should not pass between patients' evening meal and morning meal. There are particular nutritional challenges with five meals a day. The approach would be determined for each patient on an individual basis. Those above are simply some of the variables possible.

Choosing Menu Items

There are unlimited choices when you decide which menu items to use. Here are a few items that might fit into the plans for your facility.

Jones Soda offers unique beverage possibilities. The main categories are soda, naturals, energy, and organics. Each category offers a wide variety of flavors. Complete details are available at **www.jonessoda.com** or by calling 800-656-6050. The company has an interesting background which can be found at **www.jonessoda.com/files_new/about.html**.

Dr. Smoothie offers healthy alternatives that would fit into all non-commercial facilities, especially since smoothies are growing in popularity. They offer a cool and refreshing treat for your patrons. Dr. Smoothie's mission is to provide delicious, high quality beverage and food products that are good for your health, mind, and body. Special blends are available in Original or 100 percent crushed fruit varieties. Dr. Smoothie offers the equipment and mixes needed to serve smoothies for your customers. Visit **www.drsmoothie.com** or contact them at 888-466-9941.

Develop Appealing and Nutritional Menus

Different menu items require various types of equipment and possibly specialized training. It's advisable to make decisions about your menu items before you choose any special equipment or hire staff members. If you need special equipment, take that into consideration when deciding the kitchen layout. All of these decisions will save or cost the facility money.

Menu planning is more than just picking a selection of food items to prepare and serve each day. The items need to attract and satisfy your clientele. You may have a non-competitive situation in non-commercial food service, but diners can pack their lunch or they can have their meals delivered.

Your staff requirements depend on the food and service you offer. Cafeteria-style serving is less labor-intensive than serving patrons at their tables. Consider what level of service is needed for your menu items and for the type of facility.

You can divide your team members into groups to include food preparation, cooking, serving, clean up, cashier, and hostess. Figure how many people are needed for each activity. There can be categories in these groups. Here are some examples.

FOOD PREPARATION	COOKING
• Baking	• Frying
• Meat cutting	• Broiling
• Cold food preparation	• Carving

The amount of division will depend on the work load. You do not need a different person for each type of work if your team members are cross-trained. An employee who can perform only one job is less valuable than a flexible person who can work in many areas. We'll discuss this more in Chapter 13 about Interviewing and Hiring Employees. Here are some ways to divide the responsibilities.

FACILITY SIZE			
SMALLEST	SMALL	MEDIUM	LARGER
May have several employees who split all of the work.	Could have a few employees on each staff that split the work.	May have more team members in each group.	May have more people on the demanding and labor intensive teams.

Separate staffs for preparation and cooking make the team more efficient when you are serving large amounts of consistent products. Non-commercial facilities can benefit from training their staff to have specific duties, but I recommend that they be cross-trained.

When you choose supervisors for each area of food preparation, you need people who can communicate with others as this is critical to your success. Each phase of the work must be coordinated among team members. Your cooks need the food to be prepared and the servers need the cooks to complete their job. Each job leads to the next, and everyone must do their part in a timely manner to serve the patrons efficiently.

Some of the benefits from efficient communication include:

- Consistent food products
- Lower labor costs
- Lower food costs
- Better organization
- More efficient kitchen

Key Points to consider when choosing menu items are:

1. Superior quality.

2. Ingredients available year-round at stable prices.

3. Affordable items.

4. Consistent results when these items are prepared.

5. Ingredients that can be measured accurately with ease.

6. Items that fit into your kitchen plan and systems.

7. A long shelf-life for your food items.

8. Entrees need similar cooking times.

9. Unique dishes are a nice touch if possible in your situation.

10. Adequate and appropriate storage for the needed ingredients.

Start by collecting recipes and ideas that fit into the steps outlined above. Are these items appropriate for your facility? After you are using these suggestions as guidelines for the recipes you have chosen, other decisions should be simple. At this point, don't add recipes that require personnel or equipment that you don't have. If you are considering recipes that are questionable, you can use them as an occasional special and then see whether the patrons like them. Always remember to keep some variety in your menus.

The "Menu Planning Ideas" list found at the end of this chapter can inspire all sorts of ideas and even provide suggestions on ways to extend leftovers. The list includes lists of menu options in a wide variety of categories. These categories include meat and meat extenders, poultry, fish, meatless dishes, vegetables, salads, garnishes, desserts, and leftovers.

When choosing ways to describe items on your menu, the wording makes a big difference. Do the descriptions conjure up mental pictures for you? The appealing descriptions can make additional sales because they sound more appetizing. These examples will show what I mean:

Simple Description	Appealing Description
Beef Stew	Savory Beef Stew with Vegetables
Roast Beef	Succulent Roast Beef with Au Jus
Fried Chicken	Southern Fried Chicken with Country Gravy
Cantaloupe	Fresh Melon Balls
Prunes	Sun Ripened Prunes
Pea Soup	Zesty Split Pea Soup
Carrots	Tangy Glazed Carrots
Potatoes	Boiled New Potatoes
Cranberry Mold	Jellied Cranberry Salad
Baked Alaska	Flaming Baked Alaska
Brownies	Chewy Fudge Brownies
Peaches	Yellow Cling Peach Slices

It isn't necessary to add many menu items just to round out the menu or to include items that everyone else offers. Doing so will increase your food and labor costs. It's better to have a specialized menu. This works for a non-commercial food service facility, just as it works for commercial restaurants.

Have a "theme" for your facility to appeal to your patrons. It might be home style cooking, simple foods that can be eaten on the run, or any other theme that works for your customers. This is another area where you are only limited by your imagination.

When you strategically limit your menu, you create a number of benefits for the facility. Your team members will become experienced and skilled in the preparation of each menu item and be able to create them with consistency. They will also begin to make effective recommendations. Managing the facility is easier when there are fewer items to track and less inventory to manage. When you order larger quantities of food, you can negotiate better prices. The criteria for choosing your menu items apply to all types of food, not just entrees. After you choose the items to be served, it is time to become familiar with each dish. Through experimentation, you can tweak and adjust the recipes for the best quality items and the best labor and food costs. Evaluate each menu item to determine these factors:

- Where will you get the raw ingredients for each item?

- Which brand of these ingredients will you buy?

- What procedure should be used to prepare, handle, and store them?

Portion sizes must be determined. You want to offer the largest portion possible at a reasonable price that still allows you to make a profit. Each menu item needs a specific size and weight, and each staff member needs to maintain portion sizes. To do this, a specific size or weight must be established. Cost control isn't the only reason for portion sizes. It also helps you to maintain a consistent product for your patrons. Each of these things helps to guarantee that the dish will taste the same each time it is prepared, no matter who prepares it.

When you establish the portion sizes, keep in mind that your variation should be in half an ounce. Therefore, a 12½-ounce chicken breast can be 12 to 13 ounces. If the weight is over 13 ounces, it must be trimmed. Any chicken breast under 12 ounces must be used for something else. Many restaurants require only a ⅛ ounce variation.

You may have noticed that portion control and ingredient weights are important, so you need the best scales available. A good quality digital scale will cost more than $200, easily recouped by controlling food usage and costs. Kitchens should have at least two ounce-graduated scales. It can be good to have a backup for times when you are especially busy or if one is broken. You can also use a 150-pound floor type scale to verify the weight of ingredients when they are delivered.

Each scale has maintenance requirements that you should meet for the best possible performance. If the scale is dropped or harmed in any way, you should have it inspected and recalibrated. It is also important to clean the scales on a regular basis to ensure the best performance. You can do a simple test to verify the accuracy by weighing certain items when you know the weight of the item. When you shop for a scale, verify that it comes with a calibration kit.

What about liquid items? Do you need to measure each portion? Test the weight when using specific spoons or ladles. Soups and condiments can be placed in proper serving size containers.

You expect team members to use the portions that have been determined so you need to post portion charts throughout the kitchen. Make these charts easy to see and use. It's also important to provide measuring cups and spoons for the ingredients. Each team member is responsible to adhere to these portion controls.

You might want to list some menu items as "heart-healthy," "fat free," "low fat," "reduced fat," "cholesterol-free," and "fresh." It was mentioned earlier that you need to be sure the items meet these requirements. If you use these terms, you need to have the nutrition information available.

Since 1997, all restaurants have been included in the FDA's nutritional labeling laws. If you place health or nutrient content claims on your menu, you must comply with these regulations. The FDA defines a "restaurant" as "a place that serves food ready for consumption, including typical sit down and carryout venues as well as institutional food service, delicatessens, and catering operations." (*Restaurants U.S.A., October 1996*). Whether you use the words or a heart symbol on your menu, you still need to comply with these regulations.

These regulations indicate that when these health or nutritional claims are made on your menu, you must be able to support these claims with documentation meaning that the restaurant must be able to show their customers and any officials that their claims meet the guidelines under the Nutritional Labeling and Education Act.

Some facilities list the ingredients and "nutritional facts" on their menus for their customers. The information on the label usually includes calories, total fat, cholesterol, sodium, carbohydrates, and protein. In some states, food service businesses are required to place these labels on their take-out food items. These labels are especially important for any food products manufactured and bought for off-site consumption.

Several software programs compute these facts for you and print the labels. Labeling creation is just one of the features in these programs which were mentioned in Chapter 3. Here are the programs that print labels:

ChefTec

ChefTec is an integrated software program with recipe and menu costing, inventory control, and nutritional analysis. The nutritional analysis gives you a quick and accurate analysis of more than 5,000 common ingredients. You can add specialty items and calculate the nutritional value of your recipes. It will identify items that are low-fat or low in calories and so on. After these details are printed, you can print labels to stick on your menu or on carried-out items. ChefTech is available from Atlantic Publishing Company (**www.atlantic-pub.com** or by calling 800-814-1132).

Consider these facts about how to include nutritional information on your menu.

- **Make the information accurate and informative.**

- **You aren't required to include all the information on your menu**, but you need to have it available. You may use brochures or posters that include the nutritional information. If there are certain items that people ask about on a regular basis, it might be better to include those on the menu. These decisions will be based on the habits of your patrons.

Menu Format

Your menu should display all five food groups with more than one food in each group. The number of individual items you need is determined by whether you have a simple menu or an elaborate menu. You can also have a non-selective or selective menu.

Some points to consider about non-selective menus are:

1. The menus are less costly.

2. Fewer staff members are required to implement a non-selective menu.

3. These menus are easier to manage and help control labor and food costs.

4. The choices you offer are limited.

5. There is limited nutritional flexibility with the non-selective menu.

6. Purchasing is simpler for the simplified menu.

However, this menu styles does not offer the best patient service and is more for employee convenience rather than patient or customer satisfaction. Here are some details about a selective menu.

1. Selective menus can be inexpensive since you can add less expensive menu items.

2. People may be more satisfied since they can make their own choices.

3. People can be trained to make healthy and nutritious choices when they have selective menus.

4. Less food is wasted since the patron or patient chooses what they want.

5. You don't prepare a large quantity of food; you just offer more variety.

6. If you use a selective menu for patients and residents of a nursing home, a qualified person must monitor their choices to ensure they make adequate nutritional choices.

Determine Appropriate Menu Cycles

Be prepared for menu planning to take time. The individual who compiles the menus needs experience in food production and customer service and needs knowledge of the people whom you serve. You can make menu planning easier by establishing a format for your menus and having a menu cycle. We'll discuss both processes in this section. Here is a suggested procedure for writing a menu.

1. Choose lunch and dinner entrees for the entire week.

2. Pick vegetables and potatoes to accompany the entrees, varying the color texture, and flavor.

3. Pick several types of salads for each meal, using foods not already on the menu.

4. Provide at least one hot bread and preferably two.

5. When you provide soup and appetizer, use different ingredients.

6. Choose a dessert to complement the meal.

7. Pick breakfast entrees and use eggs at least four days a week.

8. Breakfast needs a juice.

9. Pick a hot or cold cereal, or one of each.

10. Pick one or more types of breakfast bread.

11. Breakfast beverages can include: coffee, tea, or milk.

12. Health care facilities should offer some nighttime nourishment for patients.

Menu Cycles

Many facilities use a menu cycle. You should avoid having the same menu items every third Tuesday, and this plan will let you use a menu cycle without being predictable.

Here's how it works. After you create the menus, repeat them on a cycle of every three to six weeks, sprinkling special menus on various days during the cycle. Holidays and Fridays are good days to offer something unusual. It's your chance to try out new food items in the regular menu cycle. Using a calendar, label the individual days. This works better with a number not divisible by seven. Your normal menu days are numbered. Special menu days are labeled as S-1, S-2, and so on. Holidays are labeled as H-1, H-2, and so on. Or you can find a similar system that works for you. Here's an example.

Sunday		Monday		Tuesday		Wednesday		Thursday		Friday		Saturday	
												1.	#1
2.	#2	3.	#3	4.	#4	5.	#5	6.	#6	7.	S-1	8.	#7
9.	#8	10.	#9	11.	#10	12.	#11	13.	#12	14.	S-2	15.	#13
16.	#14	17.	H-1	18.	#15	19.	#16	20.	#17	21.	S-3	22.	#18
23.	#19	24.	#20	25.	#21	26.	#22	27.	#1	28.	S-4	29.	#2
30.	#3												

In a health care facility, the number of weeks in your cycle is determined by the length of patient stays.

- **Long term facility** = four week cycle.

- **Acute care** = Shorter cycle, usually a 10-day stay.

When it's time to start the cycle over, review the previous sales to determine if changes are needed. This is the time to delete some items and add others.

Menu Review Committees

Some facilities have a menu review committee to review the menus. Each of these elements needs to be considered before an existing menu is repeated. These are some of the criteria for the committee to review.

- Food preferences
- Personnel needed
- Foods popular and unpopular
- Food acceptance
- Is there sufficient variety?
- Are there soft and crisp foods?
- Quality and quantity concerns

- Patient census
- Nutritional value of existing menus
- Flavor combinations
- Is some equipment being overused?
- Plate food waste
- Is the budget being maintained?
- Are the menu item colors appealing?

CASE STUDY: ASSISTED LIVING MENU PLANNING

We use a selective menu format for all Assisted Living and Nursing Care Residents. We offer a restaurant style menu for independent-living residents. Usually several members of my management team work together on menu planning. I use input from residents, families, and nursing staff, in addition to our professional experience. We have either a three- or five- week menu rotation. Odd numbered cycles work best, as they keep menus from falling on the same day each month.

Menus incorporate old traditional/regional favorites, ethnic recipes, salads, sandwiches, soups, casseroles, and finger foods. Finger foods are important for several reasons: 1.) They provide a convenient way for residents with dexterity or cognitive problems to eat. 2.) Many finger foods are similar to fast food offerings; lots of our folks do not go out anymore, but we can offer chicken nuggets and spiral-cut fries. Feel free to try new menu items, but be prepared to change off quickly if a new idea does not work. Simple foods work best, but there needs to be a variety for those who desire something else. This will be even truer as more baby boomers enter retirement centers.

Kathy L. Hilbert, Director of Dining Services • Bridgewater Retirement Community

Each criterion is important and needs to be evaluated honestly and thoroughly for the answers to help the committee make changes to control costs and avoid unnecessary waste. If certain items need to be removed from the menu, you can add some new menus that were well received on the special menu days. A couple of forms that could help you and the review committee determine the changes needed are listed below. They include:

Menu Tally Form: Figure the actual number of each item being sold.

Menu Item Sales Percentage: Determine if you are selling an acceptable number of each item.

Menu Sales Forecast: Using the information from past sales, determine how much you will sell in the future menu cycles.

Menu Analysis Form: Evaluates the number sold, percentage sold, cost, profit, and profit percentage to give you a complete picture of the performance of each item.

Menu Item Weekly Sales History: This can also help you determine if you are offering specific items on the wrong day.

Recipe and Procedure Manual

Every food service facility needs a recipe and procedure manual to hold all recipes, preparation procedures, handling instructions, and ordering information. Using a manual will ensure consistency each time the menu items are prepared.

Each of your recipes should be transferred to the basic format and placed in the manual. We'll share several examples of recipe formats that you can use. They are located at the end of this chapter and on the accompanying CD. You don't need to use all of these, but there is a variety for you to see which form works better for you. We offer these forms so that you will have a consistent recipe format to help you evaluate recipe costs:

- Standardized Recipe
- Standardized Recipe II
- Standardized Recipe III
- Standardized Recipe Cost Sheet
- Recipe Costing Form
- Recipe Cost Chart

The manual should be available to all kitchen personnel. No one should ever prepare your menus from memory. It is too easy to forget the recipe specifics. When you walk through the kitchen, the manual should be in front of the cook. If it isn't, it's your responsibility to have the staff member get the book out to use. Since the book will be used near food ingredients, it's best to use sheet protectors for the individual recipes pages.

The manual should have a separate page for each menu item. You can decide whether to include the "current cost" information on the page. It is usually better to delete that information from the book used in the kitchen. Using it or omitting it has different benefits so that you need to decide what to do based on your team members. The "additional comments" can include any specific information including what to serve with the items or suggestions for patrons. The following page has an example of a recipe format along with a cost breakdown.

Accurately figuring the price that you charge for a menu item means you must know the exact food cost of that item. Projecting menu costs is simply a matter of mathematics. To figure these prices, you need current price lists from your suppliers, and their sales representatives should be able to supply you with the average yearly prices for the items you order.

You can use current price lists and price projections to figure the cost of each recipe and place it in the amount column, making it easier for you to figure all costs to the nearest cent. There may be times when you need to estimate a cost, and it is always better to go over it to be sure that you have allowed enough. If you offer a meal with a salad bar or some other item, figure that cost into your projections. It is good to allow 25 cents per person to ensure you have covered the expenses.

MENU ITEM: BAKED HADDOCK		
Ingredient	**Portion / Amount**	**Cost**
Haddock	12.5 oz.	5.25
Lemon Juice	¼ tsp.	0.05
Bread Crumbs	½ tsp.	0.10
Butter	½ tsp.	0.14
Garlic Salt	¼ tsp.	0.02
Salt & Pepper	¼ tsp.	0.01
Tartar Sauce	0.5 oz.	0.05
Garnishes:	——	0.10
Parsley	——	——
Tomato Wedge	——	——
Lemon Slices	——	0.06
Salad Bar	——	1.85
Misc. Expense	——	0.55
Total Cost		$8.18

Ordering Information: Use only fresh North Atlantic Haddock.

Preparation Procedures: Remove skin and bones. Cut into 12.5 oz. portion. Place on aluminum foil. Sprinkle with lemon juice and cover with slices. Lightly cover with bread crumbs. Fold aluminum foil tightly around the fish and tighten the seams. Open the foil several minutes before the fish is finished cooking.

Cooking Procedures: Bake in oven at 350° for 10–13 minutes. Fish is done when flaked with fork.

Presentation: Remove aluminum foil. Place on #10 dinner plate. Arrange tartar sauce and garnishes: tomato wedge and parsley.

Additional Comments: Fish must be served hot. Fast service required.

Use the "miscellaneous" column to cover all condiments and any garnishes needed. If the meal includes side orders or dessert, you need to increase the price to reflect these specifics. Also figure in a slight percentage for trim and waste as part of the cost. The number of usable portions that you can get from a recipe is your yield.

To compute the yield percentage

1. Compute gross starting weight in ounces.

2. Compute net ending weight in ounces.

3. Divide the net yield in ounces by the gross starting weight. The result is your yield percentage.

To compute the actual portion of the product

1. Divide price per pound by the average yield percentage. (Actual price per pound after waste.)

2. Divide the actual price per pound by 16 to get the price per ounce.

3. Multiply the actual price per ounce by the average portion size to get the actual cost.

After these amounts are figured, compute the costs for each item, giving you the estimated total portion cost. There are variables in these computations, but it is an educated estimate to help you set your menu prices. These are your food costs only and do not include labor supplies, utilities, or rent.

Atlantic Publishing offers a computer program to help you reduce errors and lower food costs. This program allows you to enter recipe unit data into any food costing system quickly and accurately. Contact them at **www.atlantic-pub.com**, Item YLD-CS.

Menu Prices

Prices you use are important because high-priced items drive customers away while low prices will drive you out of business. There is more involved than figuring the actual cost and adding a percentage.

The market you are working in and the demand will determine the prices you can charge. In non-commercial food service facilities you have an advantage because your facility is a convenience for your patrons, but if your prices are too high and the selection is limited, remember that they can go to other places or bring a lunch to work. Here are a couple of possibilities to use when determining the prices to charge: charge as much as possible or charge as little as possible.

There are negative and positive aspects to each approach. When you charge the most, profits are higher, but you may have fewer customers and less business. The customers you have will demand a product worth a higher price. If you charge the lowest price, your customers will be satisfied with the value for their money, but your profit margin will shrink. Here are four pricing strategies to consider.

- **Be Competitive** — This may have limited benefit for you since customers have limited possibilities, but they are aware of reasonable prices.

- **Be Intuitive** — This is the practice of charging what you think customers will pay. This is not usually overly successful.

- **Be Psychological** — Low income patrons respond to this maneuver: some people consider your items to be good if you charge high prices. This could be a short-term pricing option.

- **Trial and Error** — These prices would be based on reactions from your customers. You may be able to use this tactic for some items, but it isn't a good strategy for pricing all of your items.

Managers and owners who push for the top dollar must convince their customers the items are worth the additional price. Does your non-commercial facility offer any special items? Are there feature items that are area favorites? For those you may be able to charge a higher price.

When you charge higher prices, patrons also expect superior customer service. The more patrons do for themselves, the less you can successfully charge. If you find service is lacking, either retrain the staff members to do a better job, or you will need to lower prices to keep your patrons satisfied.

Projecting Menu Prices

Projecting your menu prices is complex because many factors are involved. A business needs to maintain food cost of 35 percent to 40 percent to be profitable. The food cost percentage is figured by the total food cost divided by the total sales. However, figuring how much to charge for the menu items is reasonably easy. You figured your food cost above for the recipes. The total portion cost divided by the menu price must equal 35 to 40 percent.

Portions Costs divided by Menu Price X 100 = 35-40 percent

You can enter different menu prices into the formula until you find the food cost percentage you desire, but it's not quite that easy. To maintain 35 to 40 percent on all items, you would have to charge too much for some items. So what should you do? Seafood, poultry, appetizers, desserts, and drinks usually have lower food cost percentages. So you should promote these harder to offset the more expensive foods.

You might only be able to push certain entrees so hard, but your appetizers, side orders, beverages, and desserts can make up a large percentage of your sales. It is also good to teach your team members to up-sell these items. You can even hold competitions for employees to sell specific items to drive your food percentage down, but discourage a "hard sell." The food cost percentage doesn't tell the whole story. Here is an example:

- A $5 item with 35 percent food cost = $3.25 profit

- A $10 item with 50 percent food cost = $5 profit

This shows why higher cost foods will bring a higher gross profit. These things are all important when you are pricing your menu items.

When you find that you aren't reaching your food cost goals or that your average ticket price is too low, it can be because of your menu. You can't have all low-cost and high-profit items. There needs to be a mix to your menu. When you sell too many high-cost items, your food costs can soar. In turn, if you sell all low cost items, your ticket average and profits suffer. Keep this in mind when you are developing your sales mix.

Control Food Costs

Use these tips to effectively control your food costs.

1. **Do projections** to determine which items you will sell and how many of each item will be sold.

2. **Create an accurate food order** for the food and supplies that you need to prepare these items.

3. **Each item served needs to be the proper size portion.**

4. **Waste and theft** must be controlled to control costs.

We discussed establishing the standards to be used that all staff members must follow. Here are some standardized items which must be established and used.

Standardized Recipes help you determine the cost of all menu items and enable you to maintain consistent quality and cost for your meals. The recipe outlines the ingredients, steps to prepare, recipe yield, which equipment to use, and how the item is to be presented. These details allow you to determine the price to charge for the item.

Standardized Purchasing includes detailed descriptions of the ingredients needed for the menu items you plan to prepare with that food order, allowing you to maintain consistent quality and cost for your menu items. These are some of the advantages of using standardized recipes:

1. Consistency of your menu items.

2. Cost control through portion control.

3. Actual item cost will help you determine menu price.

4. Ordering is easier.

5. Reusing recipes makes it easier to train employees.

Keep these key points in mind when developing recipes:

1. **List ingredients** in the order they are used in the recipe.

2. **Make each dish in your kitchen with your equipment.** Different equipment may need different times and temperatures to cook. Make the needed adjustments.

3. **Verify the recipe ingredient amounts when you prepare the items.**

4. **Ensure that you have the correct pieces of equipment to prepare the recipes you plan to use.**

5. **Dry ingredients are listed by weight and liquid by volume.** Is there a scale available in the food preparation area to weigh the ingredients?

6. **Choose one responsible person** to make any needed changes to your recipes.

7. **Enforce the policy** that all staff members need to use the standardized recipes for all items prepared in the facility.

The recipes can be on index cards or in a three ring binder and stored in plastic sheet protectors or plastic envelopes to protect against any spills. The recipes also need to be organized alphabetically or by category and then alphabetically? All standardized recipes need the following details:

- **Name of the menu items.**

- **Recipe or identification number.**

- **Yield** — how many servings does the recipe make?

- **Portion Size** — includes the cooked weight, number of pieces and the utensil needed to serve the item.

- **Garnish** — list any garnishes to be used and a description of its use. You can include a picture or diagram.

- **Ingredients** — These need to be listed in the order to be used. Only the approved abbreviations should be used. List how each ingredient is prepared (chopped, sifted, packed, whole).

- **Instructions** — These details include preheating time and temperature, correct terminology, special instructions or warnings, pan-size to be used, temperature, cooking time, testing to determine if the item is done, and how to portion the finished item.

- **Finishing** — How is the item to be finished? This can include brushing with oil, topping with melted cheese, drizzling chocolate on top. At what specific temperature should the item be stored? Can it be kept at room temperature, or should it be refrigerated?

- **Cost** — The manager or owner should decide whether to include the actual cost of the recipe to be used by the staff members. The cost can be determined by getting the ingredient costs from invoices. Divide the total cost by the number of servings to find the portion cost.

Sales Mix

When you decide what to serve, determine which equipment and supplies are needed. These details can influence the kitchen size and how it will be arranged. Keep in mind that large equipment changes can be costly, so carefully consider equipment purchases and placements.

After you learn to control food costs, analyze each menu item to make it as profitable as possible. Occasionally, take some time to determine which items sell and which items don't, enabling you to make informed decisions about which items to keep on the menu and which to change. Some items may need to be promoted more, especially if they are high profit items.

It is impossible to have all high profit items on your menus. So you need to create an appetizing and profitable mix of items. It is possible to pair a less profitable item with a more profitable item to balance the expenses and increase your profit margin.

The following questions will help you analyze the sales mix on your menu:

- How many of each item is being sold?

- What price do you charge for each item?

- Are the items profitable?

Cash registers or computer systems can track the number of items that were sold. You can get a daily, weekly, or monthly report, or you can compile these reports manually based on the checks for individual customers. The cashier or hostess should compile this information accurately each day on tracking sheets.

Here is a series of classifications that you can use to classify all your menu items, providing related information to help you make appropriate decisions.

PRIME ITEMS	STANDARD ITEMS	SLEEPER ITEMS	PROBLEM ITEMS
These are popular, low-cost, high-profit items. These items need to be prominently placed on printed menus, menu boards, or daily special boards.	Higher cost items with high-profit margins. You can make these feature items and raise the prices slightly. These items can include: appetizers, desserts, entrees, salads, and soups.	These are low-cost and low-profit items. They rarely sell. It is possible for you to make these items more visible by making them specials or including them in promotions.	Some items are high-cost and low-profit items. Try raising the prices or making them more visible and if they still don't sell, get rid of them.

School Menus

Menu planning plays an important part in setting schools' budgets. Menus for a school are regulated by the government, and how the menu is developed will make a difference in financing by state and federal agencies. Two important sources are The Menu Planning Guide and Food Buying Guide from the USDA. These offer valuable information. Planning a menu includes much more than just listing foods on a sheet of paper. Here are some tips:

- Use a specially designed form to create the menus.
- Create a file with your recipes and assign a number to each one.
- Determine the portion sizes for each menu item.
- Figure the number of lunches you will need.
- Determine how much food you need to prepare the items on the menu.
- Examine each menu item for quality and quantity.
- Determine the price of the planned lunches.
- Compile your food order.
- Create the work schedule for the food to be prepared.

There are several specific things that you should consider when you create school lunch menus to ensure the nutritional value.

- Offer a variety of choices.
- Limit the amount of fat, salt, and sugar in each menu.
- Vitamin A vegetables or fruits should be served at least twice a week.
- Vitamin C fruits and vegetables should be served several times a week.

- Serve iron-rich foods several times a week.

It is advisable to research local and state requirements for school lunches. Check the Department of Education Web site for your state and see what they offer. The USDA Web site also offers a wealth of information for school food service managers at **www.usda.gov**. There is an entire section of food and nutrition. For more information about school lunch programs, please visit **www.fns.usda.gov/cnd/**.

Determine the accuracy of your own menu by using this checklist
and answering the sample questions.

Quantity Representation

YES   NO

——   ——   1. When merchandising steaks by weight, do I use the generally accepted practice of referring to the steak's weight prior to cooking?

——   ——   2. Are my double martinis really twice the size of a single drink?

——   ——   3. Are my breaded shrimp at least 50% shrimp, as government regulations require?

——   ——   4. Is my "3-egg omelette" really made with three eggs?

——   ——   5. Are my "jumbo" eggs really "jumbo," the nationally recognized egg size, or are they actually "large?"

——   ——   6. When I say "choice sirloin of beef" do I really refer to "USDA Choice Grade Sirloin of Beef," as I've implied?

——   ——   7. Do I realize that it's OK to use the words "prime rib" to describe a cut of beef (i.e., the "primal" ribs: 6th to 12th ribs), but when I combine this term with "USDA" (USDA Prime Ribs), I'm implying a *grade* of beef, not a *cut* of beef?

——   ——   8. Do I realize that "ground beef" is just what the name implies—ground beef with no extra fat (the fat limit is 30%), water, extenders or binders?

——   ——   9. Do I understand that terms like "Prime," "Grade A," "Good," "No. I," "Choice," "Fancy," "Grade AA" and "Extra Standard" are all descriptions of grades as set by federal and state standards?

Price Representation

——   ——   10. If my pricing structure includes a cover charge, service charge or gratuity, have I brought these items to my customers' attention?

——   ——   11. Do I clearly define any restrictions regarding the use of coupons or premium promotions?

——   ——   12. If extra charges are made for special requests like "all white meat" or "no-ice drinks," are these charges clearly stated at time of ordering?

——   ——   13. Are my house brands really manufactured to my own specifications, even if they are prepared off premises?

——   ——   14. Am I careful when advertising brand names that the brand advertised is always the brand sold?

YES   NO

—— —— 15. When substitutions are necessary for whatever reason (non-delivery, availability, price, etc.), do I realize these substitutions must be reflected on my menu?
Some such substitutions:

- Maple syrup and maple-flavored syrup
- Baked ham and boiled ham
- Chopped veal cutlets and shaped veal patties
- Ice milk and ice cream
- Fresh eggs and powdered eggs
- Picnic-style pork shoulder and ham
- Milk and skim milk
- Pure jams and pectin jams
- Whipped cream and whipped topping
- Turkey and chicken
- Hereford beef and Black Angus beef
- Peanut oil and corn oil
- Beef liver and calf's liver
- Cream and half-and-half
- Cream and nondairy creamer
- Butter and margarine
- Ground beef and ground sirloin of beef
- Capon and chicken
- Standard ice cream and French-style ice cream
- Cod and haddock
- Noodles and egg noodles
- White-meat tuna and light-meat tuna
- Haddock and pollack
- Flounder and sole
- Cheese food and processed cheese
- Cream sauce and nondairy cream sauce
- Bonita and tuna fish
- Roquefort cheese and blue cheese
- Tenderloin tips and diced beef
- Mayonnaise and salad dressing

Points of Origin

—— —— 16. Can I back up the following descriptions with package labels, invoices or other supplier-produced documentation to prove point of origin?

- Lake Superior Whitefish
- Maine Lobster
- Puget Sound Sockeye Salmon
- Gulf Shrimp
- Smithfield Ham
- Idaho Potatoes
- Imported Swiss Cheese
- Bay Scallops
- Florida Orange Juice
- Wisconsin Cheese

YES   NO

_____ _____   17. Do I realize that it is all right to use the following terminology in the generic sense to describe a method of preparation or service?

- New England Clam Chowder
- Irish Stew
- French Fries
- Russian Service
- Swiss Cheese
- Country Fried Steak
- French Dip
- German Potato Salad
- Manhattan Clam Chowder
- Russian Dressing
- Country Ham
- Danish Pastries
- English Muffins
- French Toast
- Denver Sandwich
- Swiss Steak
- French Service
- Florida Fresh Juice

_____ _____   18. Do I use the term "fresh juice" only for a juice without additives and prepared from the original fruit within 12 hours of sale?

_____ _____   19. Instead of using the term "homemade," do I use more accurate terminology, like "home-style," "homemade-style," "made on the premises" or "our own?"

_____ _____   20. If I use any of the following terms, am I sure I can substantiate them?

- Fresh Daily
- Flown In Daily
- Center-Cut Ham
- Aged Steaks
- Slept in Chesapeake Bay
- Corn-Fed Porkers
- Finest Quality
- Black Angus Beef
- Low Calorie
- Fresh-Roasted
- Kosher Meat
- Own Special Sauce
- Milk-Fed Chicken

Means of Preservation

_____ _____   21. Am I careful not to misrepresent canned orange juice as frozen or canned applesauce as homemade?

_____ _____   22. Do I use food preserved by the commonly accepted means: canned, chilled, bottled, frozen and dehydrated?

Verbal and Visual Representation

_____ _____   23. Am I always absolutely accurate in the terminology used to describe the method by which the food is prepared?

Some preparation methods:

- Charcoal-Broiled
- Barbecued
- Broiled
- Fried in Butter
- Deep Fried
- Baked
- Roasted
- Prepared from Scratch
- Sauteed
- Smoked
- Poached

YES   NO

—— ——   24. Do my menus, wall placard or other advertising materials containing pictorial representations always portray the actual product with true accuracy?

—— ——   25. For instance, am I careful not to:

A.   Use mushroom pieces in a sauce when the picture depicts mushroom caps?

B.   Use sliced strawberries on a shortcake when the picture depicts whole strawberries?

C.   Use four shrimps when the picture shows five?

D.   Use a plain bun when the photo depicts a sesame-topped bun?

E.   Let my waiter/waitress offer "butter or sour cream" when, in actuality, I'm using imitation sour cream or margarine?

F.   Let my waiter/waitress tell a customer, "The pies are baked in our own kitchen," when in fact they purchased prebaked, institutional pies?

Dietary or Nutritional Claims

—— ——   26. Am I sure I never risk the public's health by misrepresenting the dietary or nutritional content of a food?

—— ——   27. Do "salt-free" and "sugar-free" mean just that?

—— ——   28. Can I substantiate with specific data any special nutrition claims or claims of "low calories?"

NOTE: If you cannot answer "yes" to all these questions, it is time to revise your menu to avoid misrepresentations and potential customer misconceptions about your food.

Meats

Beef:	*Veal:*	*Pork (fresh):*
Roast beef	Veal chops	Baked ham
Pot roast	Veal cutlets	Roast pork loin
Swiss steak	Veal fricassee	Roast pork shoulder
Round steak	Veal stew	Pork chops
Steak stroganoff	Veal a la king	Barbecued pork chops
Cubed steak	Veal patties	Pork cutlets
Kabobs	Veal paprika	Spare ribs
Short ribs	Roast leg of veal	*Cured Pork:*
Beef pot pie	Roast veal shoulder	Baked ham
Beef stew	Curried veal	Ham slices
Beef ragout	*Lamb:*	Baked Canadian bacon
Hamburger	Roast leg of lamb	Ham loaf
Goulash	Roast lamb shoulder	Ham patties
Chop suey	Broiled lamb chops	*Variety Meats:*
Meat loaf	Lamb stew	Liver
Steak (broiled)	Braised lamb riblets	Sweetbread cutlets
T-Bone	Barbecued lamb	*Miscellaneous:*
Sirloin	Curried lamb with rice	Cheese stuffed weiners
Filet Mignon	Lamb fricassee with noodles	Egg rolls
Club steak		Frankfurters with kraut
Norwegian meatballs		
Meatballs with spaghetti		
Tacos		
Enchiladas		

Meat Extenders

Corned beef hash	Baked ham sandwiches	Boiled lima beans with ham
Stuffed peppers	Ham salad sandwiches	Chili con carne
Beef roll	Bacon and tomato sandwiches	Ranch-style beans
Spaghetti with meat sauce	Ham biscuit roll	Baked eggs and bacon rings
Spanish rice	Ham turnover with sauce	Pizza
Creamed beef	Sausage and dressing	Wieners with meat sauce on bun
Creamed chipped beef with peas	Sausage and apple dressing	Hot luncheon sandwich
Chipped beef with noodles	Sausage rolls	Hot roast beef sandwich
Ham and cheese sandwiches	Bacon and potato omelette	Hot roast pork sandwich
Veal croquettes	Pork and noodle casserole	Barbecued ham, pork, or beef
Veal soufflé	Ham à la king	sandwiches
Creamed ham and celery	Ham croquettes	Toasted chip beef and cheese
Cold baked ham with potato salad	Ham soufflé	sandwich
Chef's salad bowl	Ham timbales	
	Ham and egg scallop	

MENU-PLANNING IDEAS

Poultry

Turkey:	Chicken soufflé	Chicken croquettes
Roast turkey	Chicken turnovers	Chicken cutlets
Baked turkey roll	Chicken and rice casserole	Chicken timbales
Hot turkey sandwich	Chicken à la king	Chicken chow mein
Turkey loaf	Chicken with dumplings	Chicken salad
Chicken:	Chicken pot pie	Chicken salad sandwich
Baked chicken	Chicken chimichangas	Chicken loaf
Fried chicken	Creamed chicken	Chicken enchiladas
Barbecued chicken		

Fish

Fresh and Frozen Fish:	*Canned Fish:*	Tuna-cashew casserole
Salmon steaks	Salmon loaf	Tuna and noodles
Baked halibut steak	Salmon croquettes	Crab salad
Fried or baked fillets:	Creamed salmon on biscuit	Lobster salad
haddock, perch, sole	Casserole of rice and tuna	Shrimp salad
catfish,whitefish	Tuna croquettes	Tuna salad
Fried whole fish	Creamed tuna on toast	Salmon salad
Creole shrimp with rice	Tuna soufflé	Hot tuna on bun
Scallops	Scalloped tuna	
Fried clams		
Scalloped oysters		
Crab casserole		
Broiled lobster		

Meatless Dishes

Angel Hair Pasta with Basil & Tomatoes	Egg cutlets	Cheese puff
Angel Hair Pasta with Lemon and Garlic	Noodle casserole	Spoon bread
Angel Hair Pasta with Portobellas	Hot stuffed eggs	Scalloped corn
Angel Hair with Tomato Cream Sauce Cheese balls on pineapple slice	Scalloped eggs and cheese	Fruit fritters
Asparagus Pasta	Omelet	Grilled cheese sandwich
Cheese croquettes	Spanish omelet	Egg salad sandwich
Cheese soufflé	Cauliflower casserole	Fruit plates
Cheese fondue	Vegetable timbales	Cottage cheese salad
Macaroni and cheese	Spinach timbales with poached egg	Deviled eggs
Baked rice and cheese	Bow Tie Pasta & Beans	Brown bean salad
Baked Spaghetti Florentine	Bow Tie Prima Vera	Stuffed tomato salad
Rice croquettes with cheese sauce	Bow Ties and Broccoli Mushroom Alfredo	Cornbread & Bean Skillet
Chinese omelet	Baked Ziti with Three Cheeses	Country Pasta with American Cheese
Rice with mushrooms and almond sauce	Bulgar with Cabbage & Green Beans	Country Pasta with Mozzarella
Curried eggs	Buttery Veggie Couscous	Country Vegetable Lasagna
Creamed eggs	Cheese Ravioli with Pumpkin Sage Sauce	Cracked Pepper Macaroni and Cheese
Egg and noodle casserole	Cheese Tortellini in Savory Broth	Deviled Eggs Florentine
	Cheese Tortellini with Garden Vegetables	Egg Noodles with Cremini Mushrooms
	Stuffed Shells in Marinara Sauce	Farfalle with Spinach and Garbanzo Beans
		Vegetable Risotto
		Spinach Pasta Pie

Green Vegetables

Artichokes	*Types of Vegetable Preparation:*	With cheese or hollandaise sauce
Asparagus	Streamed	Au gratin
Beans	Baked	Creole
Broccoli	Grilled	Hot slaw
Brussels Sprouts	Boiled	Raw
Cabbage	Broiled	Sauteed
Celery	Buttered or creamed	
Spinach	With butter or mayonnaise	
	With mushrooms or almonds	

Other Vegetables

Beets	*Types of Vegetable Preparation:*	Creole
Cucumbers	Buttered	Creamed
Eggplant	Harvard	Mashed
Rutabagas	Julienne	With almond butter
Squash, summer	In sour cream	With cheese sauce
Carrots	With orange sauce	With peas
Cauliflower	Hot spiced	Scalloped
Mushrooms	Pickled	French fried
Tomatoes	Candied or Glazed	Mint glazed
Turnips	Lyonnaise	Baked
		Sauteed

Fruits Served as Vegetables

Apples	*Types of Preparation:*	Cooked and buttered
Grapefruit	Baked	Fried
Peaches	French fried	
Pineapple ring:	Broiled	

Other Starchy Vegetables

Corn	*Types of Vegetable Preparation:*	Baked
Lima Beans	Buttered or creamed	Scalloped
Parsnips	On cob (corn)	Glazed
Squash, winter:	Pudding	Steamed
	O'Brien	

Potatoes, Pasta, and Rice

Potatoes:	Potato cakes	*Macaroni and spaghetti:*
Boiled	Potato pancakes	Macaroni and cheese
Au Gratin	Potato salad, hot or cold	Macaroni salad
Baked	Scalloped	Scalloped macaroni
Buttered new	*Potatoes, sweet:*	*Rice:*
Creamed	Baked	Buttered
Croquettes	Candied or glazed	Curried
Fried	Croquettes	Fried rice with almonds
French fried	Mashed	Croquettes
Mashed	Scalloped	

MENU-PLANNING IDEAS

SALADS AND RELISHES

Fruit Salads

Ambrosia	Cranberry	Mixed fruit
Apple	Frozen fruit	Waldorf
Cranberry relish		

Gelatin Salads

Apple sauce mold	Frosted lime	Raspberry ring mold
Bing cherry	Jellied Waldorf	Apricot
Cranberry	Molded pear	Tomato aspic
Frosted cherry	Molded pineapple-cheese	Jellied citrus
		Grapefruit

Vegetable Salads

Acar	Cabbage	Salad greens with grapefruit
Beet pickles	Cabbage-carrot	Somen salad
Beet relish	Cabbage-marshmallow	Shopska salad
Bean salad	Cabbage-pineapple	Stuffed tomato
Caesar salad	Carrot raisin Celery cabbage	Tomato
Chef salad	Creamy coleslaw	Tomato-cucumber
Chicken salad	Cucumber-onion in sour cream	Vegetable-nut
Chinese chicken salad	Garden salad	Taco salad
Choban salad	Hawaiian tossed	
Cobb salad	Potato	
Coleslaw		

Relishes

Carrot curls	Cherry tomatoes	Radish roses
Carrot sticks	Cucumber slices	Spiced crabapples
Califlowerets	Green pepper rings	Spiced pears
Celery curls	Olives: green, ripe, stuffed	Tomato slices
	Onion rings	Tomato wedges

GARNISHES

Orange/Yellow/White

Cheese: Balls, grated, strips	Lemon sections, slices	Peach slices
Carrots: rings, shredded, strips	Orange sections, slices	Spiced peaches
Hard-cooked or sections eggs	Apricot halves, sections	Persimmons
Deviled egss	Cantaloupe balls	Tangerines
Pear balls	White raisins	Honeydew melon

Brown-Tan

Croutons	Cinnamon	Nutmeats
Cheese straws	Dates	Nut-covered cheese balls
Toasted coconut	French-fried onions	Toast: cubes, points, strips, rings
Noodle rings	Mushrooms	

Black

Caviar	Currants	Raisins
Chocolate-covered mints	Prunes	Olives
Chocolate	Walnuts	Truffles

MENU-PLANNING IDEAS

GARNISHES

Red

Fruits:	Red raspberries	*Vegetables:*
Cherries	Maraschino cherries	Beets
Apples	Strawberries	Red cabbage
Cranberries	Watermelon	Red peppers: rings, strips, shredded
Plums		Pimento: chopped, strips
		Radishes

Green

Vegetables:	Cauliflowerets	Mint
Endive	Celery cabbage	Olives
Green pepper: strips, chopped, rings	Celery: curls, hearts, strips	Parsley: sprig, chopped
Green onions	Cucumber: rings, strips, wedges, cups	Pickes: Burr gherkins, strips, fans, rings
Lettuce		Spinach leaves

DESSERTS

Cakes and Cookies

Cakes:	Coconut	Poppy seed
Angel food:	Fudge	Spice
Apple sauce	Jelly Rolls	White
Boston cream	German sweet chocolate	Yellow
Chiffon	Gingerbread	Upside-down
Chocolate	Marble	

Cookies

Brownies	Date bars	Marshmallow squares
Butter tea	Oatmeal	Peanut butter
Butterscotch	Fudge balls	Sandies
Chocolate chip	Gingercrisp	Sugar
Macaroon		

Pies and Pastries

Apple	Pecan	Mincemeat
Apricot	Pineapple	Peach
Blackberry	Pumpkin	Pineapple
Blueberry	Rhubarb custard	Plum
Banana cream	Boysenberry	Prune
Butterscotch	Cherry	Raisin
Coconut custard	Gooseberry	Rhubarb
Dutch apple		Strawberry

Puddings

Apple dumplings	Coconut cream	Peach crisp
Baked custards	Cream puffs	Pineapple cream
Banana cream	Date pudding	Shortcake
Bavarian cream	Date roll	Steamed pudding
Bread pudding	English toffee dessert	Tapioca cream
Butterscotch pudding	Fruit gelatin	Vanilla cream
Chocolate cream	Fudge pudding	

MENU ITEM TALLY FORM

| Prepared By: _____ | Week Of: _____ |

MENU ITEM	SUN	MON	TUE	WED	THUR	FRI	SAT
TOTAL CUSTOMER COUNT							

To determine the Total Sold of each menu item, use the Menu Item Tally Form on the proceeding page.

Prepared By: _____ **Week Of:** _____

MENU ITEM	Total Sold	x	Menu Price	=	Item Sales Total	÷	Total Net Sales	=	% Contribution to Sales
		X		=		÷		=	
		X		=		÷		=	
		X		=		÷		=	
		X		=				=	
		X							
		X							
		X							
		X							
		X							
		X							
		X							
		X							
		X							
		X							
		X							
		X							
		X							
		X							
		X							
		X							
		X							
		X							

DATE PREPARED:	PREPARED BY:	WEEK OF:

MENU ITEM	Sales Estimate	% of Sales	Menu Price	Plate Cost	Contribution	Sales	Food Cost
TOTAL							

DATE PREPARED:			PREPARED BY:			WEEK OF:

MENU ITEM	# Sold	% Sold	Menu Price	Plate Cost	Gross Profit ($)	Total Gross Profit	Profit Percent
TOTAL							

Prepared By: _____   **Date:** _____

MENU ITEM	SUN	MON	TUE	WED	THUR	FRI	SAT	TOTAL	AVG.
TOTAL									

Menu Item:

INGREDIENTS:

RECIPE YIELD: _____

PORTION SIZE: _____

PORTION COST: _____

PREPARATION:

NOTES:

MENU ITEM:

INGREDIENT	PORTION	UNIT COST

RECIPE PROCEDURE:

_____

_____

_____

_____

Total Recipe Cost	$ _____
Per Serving Cost	$ _____
Menu Price	$ _____
Food Cost %	_____
Gross Profit	$ _____

STANDARDIZED RECIPE III

Menu Item: ______________________________

TOOLS NEEDED:

- ❑ ______________________
- ❑ ______________________
- ❑ ______________________
- ❑ ______________________
- ❑ ______________________
- ❑ ______________________
- ❑ ______________________
- ❑ ______________________
- ❑ ______________________

photo of finished dish

INGREDIENTS	QUANTITY	PROCEDURE

MENU ITEM:

RECIPE YIELD: _____

PORTION SIZE: _____

PORTION COST: _____

INGREDIENTS		INGREDIENTS COST	
Item	Amount	Unit Cost	Total Cost

Total Recipe Cost: _____   Total Portions: _____

Portion Cost: _____   Date Costed: _____

Previous Portion Cost: _____   Previous Date Costed: _____

Menu Item: _____ **Date:** _____

Total Yield: _____ **Portion Size:** _____

| Ingredient | Quantity | COST | | | Recipe Cost |
		A.P. $	Yield %	E.P. $	

TOTAL RECIPE COST $ _____
# of Portions $ _____
Cost Per Portion $ _____

RECIPE COST CHART

Recipe: _____ Number: _____

Date Priced: _____ Total Yield: _____ Number of Servings: _____

Usage: _____ Portion Size: _____

Amount/Unit	Ingredients	Unit Price		Extension	

Total Cost $

Portion Cost $

CHAPTER FIVE

Quality in Dietary and Nutritional Guidelines

Each non-commercial food service facility needs to determine its standards of operation. In many cases, the federal, state, and local government will dictate how high the standard should be. School systems are closely monitored to ensure proper nutritional value for the students and adults. Any health care facility has similar requirements that they must meet. However, all food service facilities have an obligation to provide nutritious meals for their patrons.

One way to illustrate the quality expected is to include a color picture of each menu item on the recipe card. It's also a good policy to inform employees of the quality procedures for each food item. A few simple steps can help the quality process:

- Always provide quality products and ingredients.

- The items must be processed in a timely manner to enhance the quality of the final product.

- Test the final product for flavor and temperature.

- Continue working with employees to improve the quality.

- Consider feedback you receive from patrons.

When reviewing feedback from employees or customers always consider the negatives and positives. Did it take too long to receive the item? Was the item the correct temperature when it was served? Was the item cooked sufficiently but not overcooked? Was there too much or too little seasoning? The answers to these questions can be an equipment problem, a recipe issue, or an employee mistake. Whatever factor caused the problem, it is your responsibility to find an acceptable solution.

Test Panel

Sometimes product and service evaluation can be done in-house. At other times, it's better to bring people in from outside your department to make the critical evaluations. However, you need to pick the panel members carefully. Do they have food-service experience? Are they able to distinguish individual flavors and qualities?

For taste-testing, non-smokers are preferred. A judge could stop smoking two or three hours before your taste test and be able to regain the ability to distinguish differences to give you useful in-put. When you schedule a taste test, the best time of day is an hour before lunch or an hour before dinner.

This is the critical information you need from the panel: appearance, color, flavor, smell, taste, and texture. You want feedback regarding the four tastes: bitter, salty, sour, and sweet.

Taste and smell determine the flavor. In nursing home facilities, keep in mind taste sensitivity decreases with age. This requires that you cook with more seasoning for elderly clients.

Let's use a banana as an example of the color of your food items. Before a banana is ripe, it's green; when it's ready to eat, it is yellow; and when it is too ripe, it's black. Many foods have a different appearance pending on the stage of the food. Keep this in mind when you serve menu items. Does the color of the food entice the patron or discourage them.

Texture of your food items is important: foods may be stringy, smooth, tender, tough, crisp, mushy, or hard. Appearance includes more than just how the food looks. It can include the presentation of the food. Is the serving skimpy looking? Ask yourself whether the portion fits the container or should you find a different way to serve the item? A qualified taste test panel can provide this information and much more.

CASE STUDY: MILITARY INSPECTIONS

Military food service facilities can be inspected at any time by the Officer in Charge (OIC). For unscheduled or scheduled inspections, the food service manager is expected to make changes while the inspector is at the facility. If needed, the inspectors will work with the manager. All facilities must operate the same. When problems are found in one facility, an announcement is sent everywhere. This announcement will the problem and the procedure to fix the situation.

Mel Trimble, Retired Marine

The N

Internal Quality Control

Here are ten steps to set up a self evaluation process:

1. Assign a staff member to monitor and evaluate procedures.

2. Determine the scope of service in the facility.

3. Identify the most important parts of your service.

4. Determine indicators used to monitor your service.

5. Set up a series of plateaus to evaluate service. What will be the "trigger points" that more evaluation and possible changes are needed?

6. Collect important data as it relates to each plateau to identify problems in a reasonable time.

7. When you reach each plateau, are there new ways to improve?

8. Take all necessary action to provide better service.

9. Is your existing plan effective? If not, how can it be improved?

10. All relevant staff members need to be notified of these findings and the steps being taken to improve service.

Your employees need to be trained to implement quality control standards. An easy way to do this is to test the first tray of food that you serve each day. Some things to check include:

- Are hot and cold foods served at the correct temperature?

- Does the food look fresh and appealing?

- Is each item presented properly?

- Are there various colors, flavors, and textures in the items being served?

If you answered **yes** to each question, you are doing a good job. If not, the appropriate corrections should be made. This little test can be done before each meal or periodically if you get good results. Include your staff members in the evaluation process and help them learn to develop a better product. Each time you get positive or negative feedback from customers or upper management, share this information with your staff. This is especially important when your facility is being praised.

It is also possible changes should be made based on the feedback you receive. These changes can include types of food, staff scheduling, and the equipment you use. Some simple changes that can make a difference are steaming items instead of boiling, preparing smaller quantities to maintain, or change the temperature where specific items will be served.

Using different equipment will change your recipe requirements and the final product. Changing the preparation method and the equipment used can make a big difference in your menu items. Another possibility is scheduling your food preparation. Something that can fix this problem is to prepare items with similar preparation and cooking time. Your standardized recipes should include this information, and it needs to be considered when planning your menu items. This consideration is especially important when food is being served at improper temperature, and you need to find a solution. Consider these questions:

- Does your staff use warmed dinnerware for hot foods and chilled dinnerware for cold foods?

- When food is placed in the steam table, is it the proper temperature?

- Is there a draft near your steam table? If so, consider moving it.

- How long does it take your staff to serve the customers?

- In the health-care field, consider when the covers are removed from their trays. If they are removed too soon, the temperature of the meal is affected.

Your patrons can help you monitor the quality of the food you serve. Some non-commercial facilities ask their patrons to complete questionnaires periodically, a wonderful way to encourage feedback on the items you serve and the quality of your service. There are several ways to approach this evaluation such as individual cards placed on the dining room tables or you can use a printed questionnaire handed to your customers. Keep in mind that your customers are taking their time to give you valuable insights, and you should only pursue this if you plan to review their feedback and act on it.

At the end of this chapter is a flow chart that shows how you can gain feedback and how to implement it in the facility.

Tools to Gain Feedback

Here are some details on each feedback tool that you can use. Which seems appropriate for your facility?

Focus groups can be helpful when you are developing new products or procedures. Some funding is available for in-depth studies. Make a list of the particular information you would like to find during the focus group discussion. The best focus groups include a variety of people who are in your target market. It's good to have someone take notes to review later, or you can record the group on video or audio tape. The person who moderates the group needs to remain unbiased and should know how to draw information out of people in a helpful manner.

Individual interviews or discussions will give you honest feedback without your subjects' being influenced by their peers. However, the person asking the questions must not influence the answers. There is an art to asking the right questions, and this will be discussed in the next section. The questions need to be prepared in advance, and the interviewer needs to be familiar with them before an interview starts. This is another situation where you can tape the session to review at a later time.

Professional or mystery shopper gets a list of questions about their visit. It includes:

- Interior appearance
- Cleanliness
- Promptness
- Quality of the food

- Exterior appearance
- Quality of the service
- Cost

These are only some of the things they ask, but it gives the facility a good overview of how they are doing. When people are chosen to do mystery shopping, they need good communication skills and they need to be detail-oriented to give you the amount of information you need. All mystery shopping organizations that I'm familiar with reimburse the shopper for their meal, although they set a maximum cost. Some also pay a commission, but this is less common when the full cost of the meal is repaid.

Surveys use carefully planned questions and carefully selected participants. In any survey, choose a large enough sample of people to get accurate information.

Unsolicited feedback is given voluntarily and is usually the first source of feedback you get. Whenever someone approaches you with positive or negative feedback, take the time to consider their comments. If the comments are written, keep a copy on file, or you can make your own notes from the thoughts they shared. These comments could be divided into separate files for easier reference in the future.

The forms found at the end of this chapter are a good way to get feedback from customers about your facility. The forms ask a series of questions and have an area for people to offer comments or for you to note what was done in response to the comments you receive.

Tips to Ask the Right Questions

There is an art to asking the right questions. Here are some tips to help:

- **Ask about one specific thing with each question.** Asking about multiple things in one question distorts the answer.

- **If you use clear, easy, simple words you are much more likely to get a useful and accurate answer.**

- **Do not ask a question that can be answered with a "yes" or "no".** When you ask this sort of question the only answer you will get is either "yes" or "no" which is of limited benefit. In-depth answers are much more useful and are volunteered when the question begins with "how" or "when" or "where" rather than "Did you...?" or "Do you...?" or "Will you...?".

- **Give the person unbiased choices.** This is illustrated with a scale of one to five. If you gave these choices: extremely good, good, fair, and bad, you have balanced the scales unfairly in your favor. Rather, if you include extremely good and very good, then you need to include extremely bad and very bad.

If you decide to use interviews, you need to choose who will talk to these people. You could speak with your patrons personally or have a trusted staff member who communicates well do this for you. Some people will simply check good or excellent on your surveys. However, others will give solid feedback which can be valuable at your facility. The individuals who gave honest information will be watching to see when these changes will be implemented.

At the end of this chapter you will find food standard examples for you. They provide all information about the good qualities and bad qualities for several foods.

Another interesting way to see whether your customers like the items you prepare is to conduct a plate-waste study. This can be done by your bus staff or dishwashing staff. It will tell you whether customers are finishing their meals and which items are not being eaten. A plate-waste study should include at least 20 plates. The more plates you evaluate, the more detailed information you will gather. If your study shows certain items are not eaten, it might be good to consider deleting them from your menu. The study could also provide additional information which includes:

- Are you serving the correct food items?

- Should you change the preparation methods?

- Is the food served at the proper temperatures?

- Is your menu item selection adequate?

- Are you preparing the right quantity of food?

These are a few of the details a good study can provide.

Quality improvement and quality assurance are two different approaches that offer some differences. This chart will show how they vary in different situations.

Category	Quality Improvement	Quality Assurance
Commitment	Stress the importance of quality to staff members at all levels.	Not stressed as a major component.
Focus	Gather input about process and products to find areas to improve. Must organize your approach.	Structure your approach along with being appropriate, minimize risk, and ensure clinical performance.
Mass Inspection	Eliminate mass inspections.	Encourage broad-based inspections.
Measure and Improve Orientation	Use a cycle to improve the processes that you use. Understand the need to improve. Be proactive about improvement. Always keep customer in mind.	Identify opportunities to improve your service and care. Monitor and measure to find areas that need improvement. Be reactive when you find problems.
Problem solving	Measure quality in the unit. Cross-functioning teams.	Use multi-disciplinary committees to ensure quality throughout units.
Quality Cost	Emphasize with improvement.	Not emphasized with assurance.
Requirements	Defined by customers.	Defined by provider.
Responsibility	Everyone is responsible.	Management determines responsibility.
Standards	Standards are the starting point. Develop standards internally.	The standards are your goals. Use standards developed by others.
Statistical Method	Sophisticated method.	Rudimentary method.
Structure	Use existing structure.	Use separate assurance structure.

Each element focuses on a different segment of your facility. The quality improvement or assurance details show what is most important and how the program could be implemented in the facility. The approach you would use should be based on the specific requirements of your facility.

Operating Procedures

A thorough evaluation of operating procedures is necessary to develop a strategic long-term plan to provide quality for your customers. This is true in non-commercial food service atmospheres, and the importance should not be underestimated. Here are a few key steps to help you get started with the evaluation:

- Set goals for your department.

- Keep these goals in accord with the purpose of the facility.

- Develop a plan to attain these goals.

- Develop operating procedures to help you attain these goals.

- Create a plan to implement these procedures.

- Finally, evaluate your effectiveness and make any necessary changes.

Some key points to consider when you develop your plan are:

- Do you have adequate resources to implement your program?

- Will your plan cause other problems in the facility?

- Can you find ways to improve the quality of your food production and delivery systems?

- What quality is a major factor in all department operations including: purchasing, receiving, storage, and processing?

- Do you recruit the best personnel to maintain quality?

Sometimes more information is needed to make an effective plan. One example is the difference between knowing the department budget and being told to minimize expenses. The additional information will make a difference in how people do their job. It helps them to know where and when to minimize expenses to stay in the budget allotment. Either way, to maintain expenses certain criteria must be met, such as:

- Are your meal plans nutritious?

- Are personal and professional goals being met?

- Does the facility follow sanitary practices?

Thorough investigations and evaluations are necessary to find the answers to these questions. Keep in mind that dietary needs and nutritional requirements are priorities in any non-commercial food service facility but especially in schools and health-care markets. If dietary managers choose to ignore these facts, they're violating the trust of their patrons and cannot use their resources fully.

Conduct a Self Review

When I was in food service, we prepared for any inspections or evaluations by reviewing our procedures and policies to be sure we met the criteria and that we were doing the best possible job for our clients. So what are some ways to check and evaluate your operation to make adequate improvements?

One simple way to start is by making a checklist of each thing that should be done in the department on a daily, weekly, or monthly basis. The list will help you to identify areas that need some additional focus. You may wonder how you would develop such a checklist. This would be a great topic for a departmental meeting. All staff members can offer suggestions on areas that need improvement. You could assign several people to make concise lists of their responsibilities and then have a second or third person review the list to make sure it's complete. Once the lists are complete the manager should check them and add any additional points that were missed.

Many reference books include checklists, and I will add several to give you ideas. If the checklists at the end of this chapter are not exactly what you need, feel free to make changes as necessary for your specific facility. The procedure manual for your facility should offer additional information for creating your checklists.

After your checklist is finished, what should you do with it? The list should be used weekly or monthly to verify that acceptable standards are being met in the facility. If there are substantial problems, you may wish to use the lists more often. In a short time you should be able to implement substantial changes by improving your procedures. You may need more than one checklist. Remember to make multiple copies that can be used when training new employees or to retrain employees. It could be included with the annual employee evaluation that we will discuss in a later chapter.

Major changes will take time, but you don't want to drag your feet in starting the necessary changes in a non-commercial food service facility. After problems are identified, you can have two or three members find ways to revise your procedures. It's a good idea for the manager to try these new procedures before they are implemented throughout the facility.

Staff members will need time to become familiar with the new procedures. When you feel comfortable that your staff members are implementing the changes properly, it would be good to re-evaluate. This would help you verify that the changes are successful. If you feel the changes are not working, you should evaluate more quickly to find any new problems. This can require some trial-and-error, especially in the beginning.

After all procedure changes are made, document them in your training manual. Any time you change these documents, they need to be updated, signed, and issued to all employees to eliminate potential confusion among staff members. If any job descriptions need to be revised, that should be done at the same time and added to the procedure manual.

External Quality Control

Government agencies and private associations may evaluate dietary services in various facilities. Any dietary manager who has implemented the reviews and suggestions mentioned earlier shouldn't have a problem meeting the requirements in these evaluations.

Accompany. Offer to go with the inspector. This is a requirement for some major food corporations. Health inspectors should welcome the chance to interact with you and discuss your processes and procedures. Be sure to bring your note pad and pencil. You will get an official report documenting the day's inspection, but sometimes more minor items are pointed out for correction that never make it to the final report. Notes will also help you to remember "talk points" for your next management meeting.

Knowledge. There is an expectation that food service operators "know what they are doing" for food safety and sanitation. Managers do many things, such as make personnel decisions, assess equipment needs, adjust menus and manage money. But foremost in mind should be food safety and sanitation. Have you read your locality's regulations? Do you keep a copy in the establishment? Do you and key management staff have current certification in food safety? After all, it only takes one outbreak of illness to ruin a businesses reputation and close an establishment forever. Current knowledge and a trained staff are the best preparation you can give yourself for a health inspection.

Attitude. Be positive and think of your inspection as a learning opportunity. Most food inspection regulators enjoy helping operators be successful. While they are responsible for seeing that food safety laws are complied with, there is generally a more education-based approach to inspections. So be ready and eager to learn.

Honesty. Be forthright and honest with your regulatory representative. The inspection is your opportunity to get a consultation on how your operation is doing. Don't blow it by whispering to staff to "run and correct" this or that. If deficiencies are noted, vow to do better next time.

React. The purpose of the routine inspection is to identify deficiencies in your operation where serious health consequences to the public could occur. Be ready and prepared to make corrections as soon as they are identified. This is particularly important for those "critical" violations that are more likely to contribute to food contamination, illness, or environmental damage. Violations requiring more time to correct should be done as soon as possible. Be sure to call the health department to let them know the correction has been made.

Record keeping. Record retention is becoming more important in the inspection process. The inspector may need to see your shellfish shipping tags, or your daily HACCP logs, or your food receipts to determine that your food sources are legal. Be organized! Keep reports and logs neat, orderly, and up-to-date. It will help you to be efficient and reflect favorably on your operation.

Train for your absence. Most health inspections are unannounced. Does your staff know what to do if you are not working on the day of your inspection? Sometimes employees panic at the thought of the inspector on the premises. They keep the inspector waiting while the kitchen is being cleaned. In attempting to try to make the kitchen look better they often make mistakes in their haste, mistakes a good inspector will catch. Make sure all staff know to greet the inspector in a timely manner and keep to the normal routine.

J. Michael McMahan • District Environmental Health Supervisor
Virginia Department of Health • Central Shenandoah Health District • Staunton, VA

JCAHO focus is on imaging patient information effectively, meaning not only the quality of information but how accessible it is to staff members who need it. For more information, visit their Web site at **www.jointcommission.org**. The JCAHO standards of review include:

1. The organization must have a well-defined plan for nutritional therapy, and the plan must be implemented.

2. When patients are at nutritional risk, their plan must include goals to be measured along with a plan to achieve these goals.

3. All staff members who prescribed orders in the nutritional project must be authorized to do so.

4. Nutritional therapies must be properly prepared and stored at the proper temperature to ensure sanitation, rotation, and safety.

5. The programs must be distributed in a safe, accurate, and timely manner to the proper patients.

6. The organization must perform an ongoing evaluation and review to determine how effective the recommended nutrition is for each patient.

7. The standard must also satisfy patient's dietary needs along with meeting their religious or cultural beliefs.

8. After these practices are established, they need to become policies and procedures in the facility.

Any facility participating in Medicare and Medicaid programs must meet minimum health and safety standards, mandated by the National Social Security Act, since Medicare is a federal program and Medicaid is a state program. They apply to hospitals, nursing facilities, and providers and suppliers of health services. Each state has an agency to ensure the requirements of the National Social Security Act are followed, and member of the agency visit individual facilities to enforce the requirements. These are a few of the responsibilities they handle:

• Review surveys and certification records submitted by state agencies.

• Evaluate fiscal, administrative, and procedural aspects as related to state agreements.

• Review and evaluate Medicare and Medicaid facilities.

• Review and approve state budget expenses as they pertain to survey and certification activities.

Each of these duties ensures that the facility remains certified. Any food-service managers in charge of health care facilities need to guarantee they are in compliance with any updated requirements. This information can be found in the Journal of the American Dietetic Association, Journal of Clinical Nutrition, publications from JCAHO, and other professional journals that provide current information and requirements. Each manager is required to remain knowledgeable on these facts.

The food service departments in many hospitals need orientation, on-the-job training, and continued education coordinated with other departments in the facility. When state agencies do inspections about the things they're responsible to verify, they check to find if the facility is complying with the established requirements. They also file certification, re-certification, and

JCAHO

In the health-care industry JCAHO is a private not-for-profit organization. Their goal is to improve quality in health care facilities. Some accomplish this through setting standards, conducting survey evaluations, awarding accreditation, and educating health care staff members. Health care facilities seek accreditation with JCAHO because it boosts confidence in the level of quality and service.

JCAHO's task force has determined the important aspects of nutritional care and deals with ordering diets, communicating the orders, preparing food, and distributing items during the duration of care. Each facility is responsible to provide the most effective nutritional care and to use their resources to do this effectively. To do this, several processes must be followed including:

- Screening patients.

- Assessing and, if necessary, reassessing needs.

- Developing a solid nutritional care plan.

- Determining the need for and ordering nutritional therapy.

- Communicating these orders to the nutritional or pharmaceutical departments.

- Preparing the items as needed and as ordered.

- Monitoring the process to determine its effectiveness.

- Improving the process needed to handle the orders.

CASE STUDY: JOINT COMMISSION

Founded in 1951, the Joint Commission on Accreditation of Healthcare Organizations seeks to improve the safety and quality of care provided to the public through the provision of health care accreditation and related services that support performance improvement in health care organizations.

The Joint Commission evaluates and accredits more than 15,000 health care organizations and programs in the United States.

It includes more than 8,200 hospitals and home care organizations, and more than 6,800 other health care organizations that provide long term care, assisted living, behavioral health care, and laboratory and ambulatory care services. The Joint Commission also accredits health plans, integrated delivery networks, and other managed care entities. In addition, the Joint Commission provides certification of disease-specific care programs, primary stroke centers, and health care staffing services. An independent, not-for-profit organization, the Joint Commission is the nation's oldest and largest standards-setting and accrediting body in health care. Learn more about the Joint Commission at **www.jointcommission.org**.

One Renaissance Blvd. • Oakbrook Terrace, IL 60181
Phone: 630-792-5000

periodic reports pertaining to the facility's qualification to participate in existing programs. These agencies also send their recommendations to the federal government for facilities in the Medicare program.

The dietary manager of any facility must be familiar with rules and regulations established by the state which apply. The state requires that the dietary manager provide nutritionally adequate diets for all patients in the facility, based on the age of each patient being served.

When doctors issue nutritional orders, they cannot be changed without the doctor's permission. The dietary manager is free to offer suggestions but cannot make changes. In some cases there will be notes by the doctor stating the minimum time between the patient's last nourishment in the evening and first nourishment in the morning. This can determine whether any food item should be served to the patient in the late evening.

There are many different certification processes which health care facilities submit to, including state license requirements and professional accreditation and medical assistance standards. To coordinate each of these standards for the programs requires an exchange of information. Any manager who is familiar with the standards and guidelines will have an advantage when complying with guidelines for departmental review. The Health Care Financing Administration in 1992 issued guidelines for state survey procedures.

When reviewing this information, ask yourself the following questions.

- Does your facility meet these standards?

- Which staff member is responsible to train employees on these standards?

- Who supervises the staff to ensure the standards are met?

- Do you know how compliance will be determined?

- Are there standards included on these forms that should be typical procedures but are not?

- Do you have documentation to confirm that your facility is in compliance?

This information can be valuable when making sure you're in compliance with the established standards. Even if your facility isn't bound by these requirements, there is good information to review.

If you discover standards are not being used by your facility, you may want to check with upper management about the possibility of implementing these new practices.

Improve Dietary Services

All effective managers conduct in-house reviews periodically. The frequency depends on how often reviews are required. They can also be done whenever you see problems.

After the problems are identified your first priority is to resolve them. We all know people who are comfortable in their job and like to do things a certain way, but that may not be best for the facility when the routine needs to be changed. Many times we hear people say all they do is put out fires all day. Your job as a manager is to be prepared for problems, review the situations, and find ways to improve them. With proper planning most "fires" can be eliminated.

In the beginning, there may be a number of problems that need be addressed. In that case, you can delegate some projects to others in the department. When this is not possible, the manager needs to determine the worst problems and list them by priority. The worst problem should be handled first. In some cases, one solution can fix more than one problem. A common pitfall is to throw out the existing procedures instead of finding ways to improve on current practices. It is much easier for staff members to adjust the way they do things instead of starting over from scratch. Help your employees make changes easier by involving them in the planning stages. How a manager handles these problems reveals their management abilities.

After the changes have been determined, they must be evaluated. Any staff members who will be involved in proposed changes should be notified as early as possible. The manager needs to explain the changes, why they are needed, and may even need to defend the changes. Remember the staff that performs these jobs each day can offer valuable insights and suggestions about proposals.

CASE STUDY: MILITARY DIETARY REQUIREMENTS

In military food service the individual dietary and nutritional requirements are of concern but are not as important as in the health care organizations. Military personnel are generally given 6,000-8,000 calories a day to ensure they have the energy to maintain the rigors of their work. They are given sufficient food and calories to exist in battle conditions even when they are stateside.

In boot camp, there are programs to help people lose the weight or to bulk up and increase their weight if needed. These programs will get each person to the condition where they need to be. While individuals are in boot camp, they are given three hearty meals each day.

Mel Trimble, Retired Marine

Special Dietary and Nourishment Needs (Prescribed by Doctors)

In a health care environment, many physicians will prescribe nourishment or supplement the programs for their patients. The dietary manager should collect all information about the patient to discern their extra nourishment needs. It may be necessary for the manager to consult with the physician to ensure these are handled properly. Some facilities have a choice about how the change is communicated, while others must follow the licensing regulations and policies for that specific facility.

Chapter 4 gave you a five-meal-a-day menu option. Some facilities handle this prescribed nourishment as a between-meal feeding. The best times for these feedings would be mid-morning, mid-afternoon, early evening, or late evening nourishment which would be just before the patient goes to sleep.

There is a variety of nourishment programs that can be used. They might include high-calorie milk shakes for patients who need to gain weight or they might try to meet the specific needs, likes, or dislikes of individuals. The best plan is useless if the patient doesn't eat or drink the nourishment.

When the dietary manager compiles this information, they also need to determine the amount of time required to distribute the nourishment. This will help guarantee the temperature of any juices or other liquids, the appearance and quality of many fruits or puddings which may be offered to the patient.

CASE STUDY: ASSISTED LIVING DIETARY AND NUTRITIONAL GUIDELINES

Assisted Living Dietary and Nutritional Guidelines are met by educational knowledge of such inspection and certification requirements, physicians' orders, and diagnoses. Finalization of therapeutic menus is done by our consulting dietician. BRC uses a liberalized geriatric diet manual (approved by our Medical Staff) for the majority of our residents. Our average age is 87 years, so reversal of dietary problems is not going to happen

We believe that food and mealtime is extremely important to our residents and should be enjoyed with few restrictions. BRC has incorporated carb counting into each week of menus, so diabetics may enjoy pies or cakes about twice a week. Low Sodium diets are still very restrictive.

Kathy L. Hilbert, Director of Dining Services • Bridgewater Retirement Community

School Cafeteria Requirements

In the 1980s, more than 90 percent of public schools participated in the Child Nutrition and National School Lunch Program, which served nutritional meals to 23.9 million children per school day. With government funding comes regulations which must be met.

The Department of Agriculture through the Food and Nutrition Service administers the Child Nutrition Program, and the state agencies oversee these programs. This is a list of the programs created by this law:

- National School Lunch

- School Breakfast

- Special Milk

- USDA Donated Commodities/Food Distribution

- Nutritional Education and Training

- Child Care Food

- Summer Food Service for Children

- Emergency Food Assistance

National School Lunch Program is available for non-profit schools and requires that a specific regimen must be used. The children of low income families must receive their meals at reduced rates or free, based on the family income. Part of this program is the "offer versus serve" option. This gives high school students a choice of items they may eat. The individual school systems decide whether elementary and middle school students will be given an option. Free and Reduced Price Meals must be served at schools in the National School Lunch and Child Nutrition Program. Regulations determine the maximum amount to be charged for reduced price meals. A form letter is provided to parents to offer the option of reduced or free meals for their children. This letter is distributed to all children along with the current income scale.

School Breakfast Program is available to all public schools and reimburses the school a certain amount of money for each breakfast served based on the families' incomes. Some schools are designated as being in severe need, and they receive additional funding. There could also be an increase in schools that have a large number of reduced and free lunches or many working mothers. A nutritious breakfast could boost a student's academic performance. These are the minimum items that need to be offered:

- **One fruit or vegetable item** — Fruit or vegetable juices, not fruit drinks.

- **Milk** — This would be one half pint of milk for cereal or drink.

- **One bread or bread alternative item** — This can include bread, muffins, bagels, English muffins, biscuits, rolls, pancakes, or cereal.

The Special Milk Program encourages milk consumption.

USDA Distribution Program was funded by Congress and is distributed to schools in the Child Nutrition Program. They purchase "commodity-donated foods" to supplement the food each locality can afford to purchase. The nature of this food acquisition lends itself to fluctuating quality. However, after the food arrives at the school, the manager is responsible to store and prepare it in the best way. Schools must receive permission to serve additional or "a la carte" items. Schools choose to offer these items because they are.

- Energy sources for students who need them.

- Supplemental items for students who pack their lunch.

- An alternative to students who can't afford lunch.

There are many foods that cannot be offered on the school premises during the school day. These items include:

- Carbonated beverages
- Chewing gum
- Jellies and gums
- Many types of candy
- Marshmallow candy
- Water Ices – unless they contain fruit juices

There are various special circumstances that school food service staff members need to satisfy. The Education for all Handicapped Children Act mandates that public schools must allow an education with the least restrictions possible for all handicapped children from ages 3 to 21. It has meant that some changes are necessary in the cafeteria setup, and it may limit the variety of foods served.

Food allergies have a great impact on food service. Substitutions can be made for children with special dietary or medical needs, but the student must provide documentation from a doctor to support the need. One simple solution is to substitute juice for milk. Other food allergies need a "special exception."

The Head Start Program offers a hot lunch, a snack, and possibly breakfast for low-income children. These meals would be determined for the specific age group being served. For proper reimbursement, a decision must be made whether to file these meals under normal lunches or the Head Start Program.

Consider Food Allergies

Food intolerances are becoming more common, and the most common is "lactose intolerance." Medications are available to alleviate the symptoms.

As a food service worker, you should know the signs of food allergies or intolerances. For instance, if you see people taking antacids or other medicine for indigestion without getting relief, it could be food allergies and intolerances. There can also be other problems in children because of food allergies and intolerances. The following chart illustrates some food allergies or intolerances symptoms:

Symptom	Definition
Abdominal Cramps	Pain in the belly.
Belching:	Air which passes through your digestive tract and out of your mouth.
Bloating:	Tight abdomen caused by gas.
Diarrhea:	Loose, watery, frequent stools; chronic if it lasts more than a month.
Weight Loss:	Eating less because of illness brought on by certain foods.
Slow Growth:	Poor or unusually slow weight or height increase in children.
Floating Stools:	If the body doesn't digest and absorb fats, some of the fat leaves the body through the stools.
Foul Smelling Stools:	Stools' odor is worse than usual and is caused by diet.
Rumbling Stomach:	This can happen 30 minutes to two hours after eating. The severity depends on how much of the offending foods were eaten and how much is left in the intestinal tract.

Food allergies can be serious and life-threatening. Many foods contain lactose, not just milk and cream. People who are lactose intolerant need to read the labels for all foods before they eat including bread, cereal, instant potatoes, most baked goods, soup, margarine, lunch meats, salad dressing, biscuits, cookies, pancakes, and even candy.

Eight food groups cause allergic reactions including peanuts and other nuts, fish, shellfish, wheat, milk, soy, and eggs. A couple of unusual ingredients are aspartame, food colorings, and additives, and these are only the tip of the allergy and intolerance iceberg.

It is advisable to ensure that the ingredient information is available to your customers. You can list these ingredients specifically on your menu or have your server communicate these details to customers.

Allergies are more prevalent than most people realize. Even a small amount of an offending food can cause a person to become nauseous, vomit, develop hives, have trouble breathing, and suffer anaphylaxis. It is critical that special order requests be taken seriously and that allergens are mentioned in person or on your menu.

You can obtain more information about food allergies from the International Food Information Council at 202-296-6540 or **www.ific.org**.

PRODUCT SCORE SHEET

Name of person on taste panel:

Date:

Product name:

	Extremely Poor	Very Poor	Poor	Poor/Fair	Fair	Fair/Good	Good	Very Good	Extremely Good
Taste									
Sweet									
Salty									
Bitter									
Sour									
Odor									
Flavor									
Color									
Texture									
Appearance									

TASTE PANEL GUIDELINES

Guidelines and Number of Participants	Assign at least 10 people (and no more than 25) to be responsible for all taste test panels. The tasting should take place in a well-lighted, quiet room, separate from the food production. Participants must meet requirements as set forth below.
Test Timing	Tests should be conducted in the mid-morning (between 10:00 a.m. and 11:00 a.m.) or mid-afternoon (between 2:00 p.m. and 3:00 p.m.).
Qualifications of Participants	• Test panel participants must be trained food professionals. • Test panel participants should represent as many age ranges as possible. • Test panel participants must be nonsmokers. • Test panel participants should not have a cold or any illness that may impair their ability to taste food.
Materials Needed	Each test panel participants should have: • A writing utensil and rating cards for each sample. The cards should have the general product name only and be stacked in the order of testing. • New utensils and a napkin should be provided for each taste sample. • Glass of water. A sip of water should be taken between samples to rinse the mouth. • Sufficient food for the test panel participant enable the tester to consume 3 normal bites. • Liquids should be presented in clear glasses sufficient for 3 sips.
Comparison Samples	There should be no more than 3 different items for paired comparisons. Paired products should be at/near identical temperatures.
Acceptability Rating Test	There should be no more than 5 different items for an acceptability rating test,.
Food Temperature	All temperatures should be at or near serving temperature.
Tasting Guidelines	Test panel participants should note: • Appearance. Overall appearance as well as color, form on the plate and on the utensil. • Taste. Food should have contact with each oral taste center. • Texture. Compare texture to recognized standards.
Recording Results	Test panel participants should note feedback on each individual rating card. Additional comments should be written based on the tasting guidelines. It is preferred that the test panel participants not discuss the food offerings during the testing process.
Tabulation	A separate individual will be responsible for tallying and ranking the results of the test panel. Feedback will be given to each panel participant.

PATIENT QUESTIONNAIRE FOR FOOD AND NUTRITION SERVICE

What is your diet order?	**Regular**	**Modified**	**Don't know**	
What is your favorite meal?	**Breakfast**	**Lunch**	**Dinner**	
Did you receive the meal items you requested?	**Always**	**Sometimes**	**Rarely**	
Have your meals been served at a consistent time each day?	**Yes**	**No**		

Rating of personnel service	**Always**	**Sometimes**	**Rarely**	**Never**
Knocked on door before entering:				
Greeted you when entering:				

Rating	**Excellent**	**Good**	**Fair**	**Poor**
Food quality:				
Hot foods hot?				
Cold foods cold?				
Tray appearance				
Food variety				
Correct foods				

Comments/Suggestions:

Name: (optional)

Date: **Room number:**

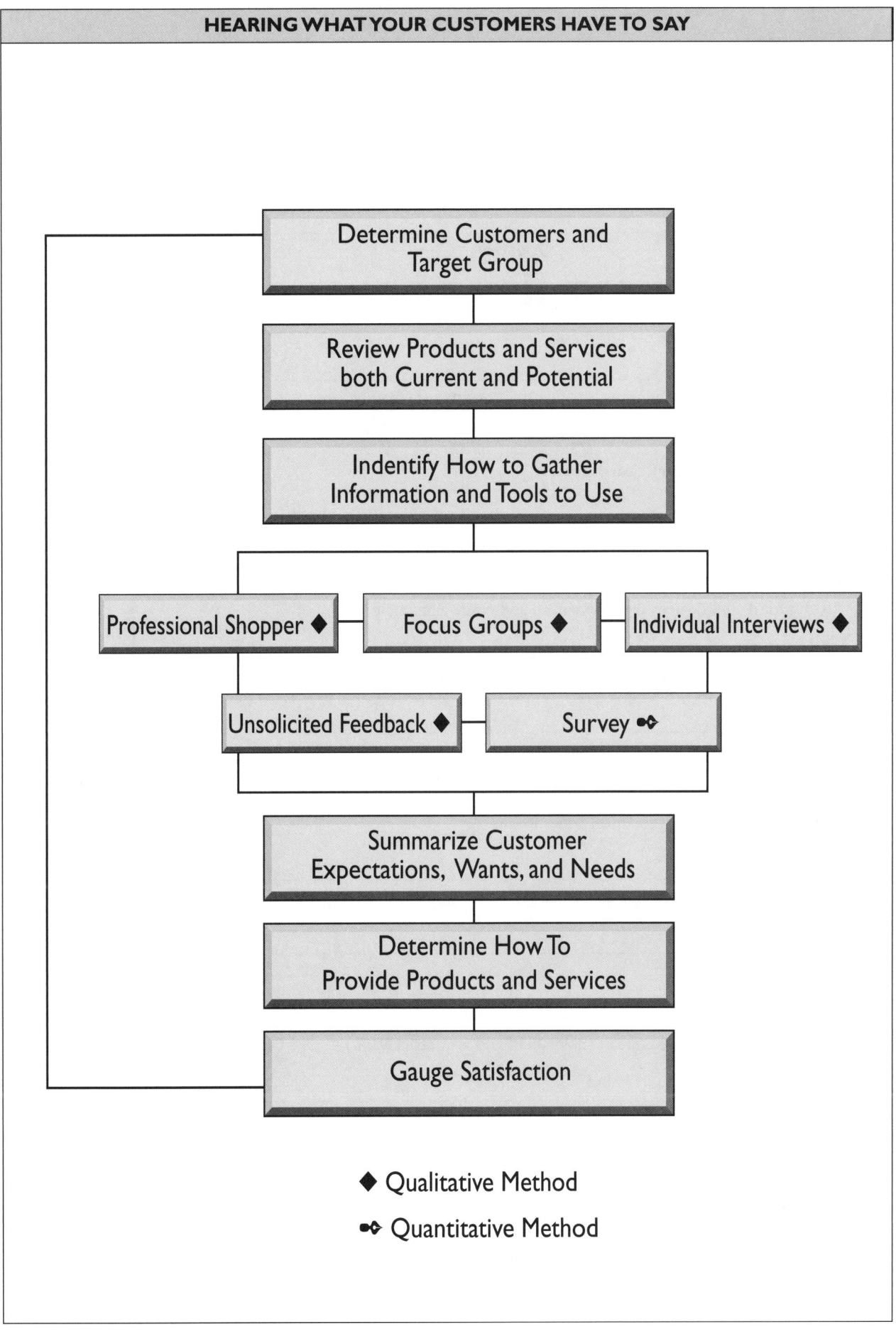

EVALUATING CAFETERIA IMPRESSIONS

Food is not the only consideration important to customers. Service, staff, variety, sanitation and convenience are also important factors. This evaluation checklist for cafeteria operations covers basic principles essential to customer service. The focus is not productivity or efficiency, but the impressions our customers get.

You may want to have numerous people complete this checklist to get a random sampling of answers including supervisors, employees and customers. Tabulate the results and provide feedback to employees. The results will help create opportunities for meaningful in-services and retraining.

Question	Yes	No
1. Are there limitations or specific times on who can dine in the establishment (visitors, staff, general employees)? COMMENTS:		
2. Do customers frequently wait outside the entrance for you to open? COMMENTS:		
3. Are the cafeteria hours clearly posted? COMMENTS:		
4. Is the first impression positive conveying a neat, clean, and organized environment? COMMENTS:		
5. Is the food service area clearly marked and easily accessible? COMMENTS:		
6. Is the lighting in the food service area sufficiently bright? COMMENTS:		
7. Are daily specials clearly posted and prices listed? COMMENTS:		
8. Are prices clearly posted for all other items? COMMENTS:		
9. Are portions consistent for all items? COMMENTS:		
10. Is the decor pleasing? COMMENTS:		
11. Are all self-service areas clean, maintained and well stocked? COMMENTS:		
12. Are spills in any area immediately cleaned up? COMMENTS:		
13. Are all self-service areas arranged in order of use to decrease cross-traffic? COMMENTS:		
14. Is the overall traffic flow of the food service efficient? COMMENTS:		

EVALUATING CAFETERIA IMPRESSIONS		
Question	**Yes**	**No**
15. Is the hot food attractively served and portioned? COMMENTS:		
16. Is the temperature of the hot food pleasing (not too hot or cold)? COMMENTS:		
17. Is the hot service area food visible to customers (not obscured by steam or other obstacles)? COMMENTS:		
18. Are employees serving food pleasant and helpful? COMMENTS:		
19. Are there enough employees serving food that customers do not have to wait to long? COMMENTS:		
20. Are there enough cashiers that customers do not have to wait to long? COMMENTS:		
21. Is the food priced competitively with other local operations? COMMENTS:		
22. Are service utensils clean, not bent and presented in an attractive manner? COMMENTS:		
23. Do the dishes match and are in good condition (no chips and fully glazed)? COMMENTS:		
24. Is the silverware accessible, stored properly, and clean? COMMENTS:		
25. Are the trays clean and dry? COMMENTS:		
26. Is an employee available to assist children or disabled customers? COMMENTS:		
27. Does the dining area appear clean overall? COMMENTS:		
28. Are tables bussed and cleaned in a timely manner? COMMENTS:		
29. Are the tables, chairs and other furnishings in good condition? COMMENTS:		
30. Are the floors clean? COMMENTS:		
31. Are all signs up-to-date, neat, clean, and relevant? COMMENTS:		

MEAL SURVEY

Our Management and Staff are proud and pleased to serve you. We welcome your comments and suggestions so we may finds ways to improve our service. Please let us know how we rate.

	Excellent	Good	Fair	Poor
Overall acceptance of food				
Value for dollar spent				
Service				
Cleanliness				

Please list what you liked most about our food service:

1.

2.

3.

4.

Please list what you liked least about our food service:

1.

2.

3.

4.

If you would like the opportunity to discuss suggestions with the Manager, please fill in the information below:

Name:	Department:	Extension:

CAFETERIA SURVEY				

Date:

Are you::	An Employee ❏		A Visitor ❏	
Meal cafeteria services were used for:	Breakfast ❏	Lunch ❏	Dinner ❏	Break ❏

Time you arrived in the cafeteria? *(choose one time only)*

1. Before 8:00 a.m. ❏		8. 12:16 p.m. - 12:30 p.m. ❏	
2. 8:00 a.m. - 9:00 a.m. ❏		9. 12:31 p.m. - 1:00 p.m. ❏	
3. 9:01 a.m. - 10:00 a.m. ❏		10. 1:01 p.m. - 2:00 p.m. ❏	
4. 10:01 a.m. - 11:00 a.m. ❏		11. 2:01 p.m. - 4:00 p.m. ❏	
5. 11:01 a.m. - 11:30 a.m. ❏		12. 4:01 p.m. - 5:00 p.m. ❏	
6. 11:31 a.m. - Noon ❏		**13.** 5:01 p.m. - 6:00 p.m. ❏	
7. 12:01 p.m. - 12:15 p.m. ❏		14. 6:01 p.m. - 7:00 p.m. ❏	

FOOD	Excellent	Good	Less than Satisfactory	Don't Know N/A
1. Food quality				
Beverages	❏	❏	❏	❏
Hot entrees	❏	❏	❏	❏
Grill items	❏	❏	❏	❏
Salad bar	❏	❏	❏	❏
Sandwich bar	❏	❏	❏	❏
Desserts	❏	❏	❏	❏
2. Variety of food available	❏	❏	❏	❏
3. Temperature of food *(hot/cold)*	❏	❏	❏	❏
4. Size of portion served	❏	❏	❏	❏

5. Food items you would like to be added to the cafeteria selection:
_____

6. Would you like to see cafeteria specials or theme days   ❏ Yes   ❏ No
    If yes, what specials or themes?_____

7. Food items you feel should not be offered in the selection:_____
_____

CAFETERIA SURVEY

SERVICES AND FACILITIES	Excellent	Good	Less than Satisfactory	Don't Know N/A
1. Speed of food service	❏	❏	❏	❏
2. Speed of cashier check-out	❏	❏	❏	❏
3. Facility cleanliness	❏	❏	❏	❏
4. Atmosphere of dining area *(appearance/decor/furniture)*	❏	❏	❏	❏
5. Courtesy of staff	❏	❏	❏	❏

If I had purchased the same items at a local eating place, I would have paid:
❏ Less ❏ Same ❏ More

Are the prices of the items posted in a convenient place for you?
❏ Yes
❏ No,
❏ Not posted at all

Generally, how responsive do you feel we are to suggestions or recommendations for changes made by employees? Would you say the our staff is:
❏ Very responsive ❏ Somewhat responsive
❏ Not responsive at all ❏ Not Sure

Overall, what is your opinion of the service you just received? Would you say:
❏ Excellent ❏ Good
❏ Less than satisfactory ❏ Don't know

Comments:
_____
_____
_____

Optional:

Name_____Dept:_____

BASIC COMMENT CARD	
Please rate your meal on a scale from 1 to 5 with 5 being excellent. Overall Quality of Meal ❏ 1 ❏ 2 ❏ 3 ❏ 4 ❏ 5 Appetizer Quality ❏ 1 ❏ 2 ❏ 3 ❏ 4 ❏ 5 Salad Quality ❏ 1 ❏ 2 ❏ 3 ❏ 4 ❏ 5 Entree Quality ❏ 1 ❏ 2 ❏ 3 ❏ 4 ❏ 5 Vegetable Quality ❏ 1 ❏ 2 ❏ 3 ❏ 4 ❏ 5 Dessert Quality ❏ 1 ❏ 2 ❏ 3 ❏ 4 ❏ 5	Additional Comments:
Name (optional):	*Date:*

PRODUCT: COOKIES

Desirable Characteristics

- Standard shape and size
- Exterior slightly brown
- Interior tender

Quality Problems and Causes

- **Crumbly Dough**
  Dough too cold (although some dough types are crumby by nature)

- **Cookies are too Hard**
  Excess flour in dough
  Overbaking

- **Cookies are not Firm**
  Excess liquid, sugar, or fat in dough

- **Cookies Spread and Flatten**
  The sugar has not been dissolved completely. There was too much fat on cookie sheet surface Dough contained too much baking powder or baking soda.

PRODUCT: MUFFINS

Desirable Characteristics

- Exterior top slightly browned
- Interior soft, even and tender
- Small uniform gas holes with no large pockets
- Slightly rounded top, that is not split or peaked

Quality Problems and Causes

Peaked	Too much mixing or oven too hot
Off-flavor	Too much leavening or poor-quality ingredients
Poor volume	Improper mixing, too much flour, not enough leavening
Tunnels and holes	Too much mixing, uneven distribution of leavening, oven too hot, or muffin cups too shallow
Tough	Not enough shortening or leavening or too much mixing
Soggy	Too much shortening, not cooked long enough, or too much mixing
Cracks in top	Oven too hot or batter too stiff
Crumbly, greasy	Too much fat

PRODUCT: BREAD
(Yeast-Leavened)

Desirable Characteristics

- Standard shape and size
- Exterior golden-brown crust
- Interior tender
- Fairly small gas holes that are uniform in size and evenly distributed throughout the bread

Quality Problems and Causes

- **Tough to Chew**
  Under-risen dough

- **Heavy**
  Did not rise long enough or rose too long
  Low-grade flour

- **Flavor too Sour**
  Oven not hot enough
  Insufficient baking time
  Dough rose too long

- **Flavor too Flat**
  Insufficient salt

- **Course or Poor Texture**
  Poor quality yeast
  Low grade of flour
  Oven not hot enough
  Too much sugar or yeast
  Too little shortening
  Dough rose too long
  Temperature of liquid too high

- **Over Crumbly**
  Flour did not have enough gluten strength
  Dough rose too long

PRODUCT: CAKE (Yellow)

Desirable Characteristics

- Even on all sides, slightly rounded top
- Pale, golden color (depending on type of cake)
- Soft, tender smooth in texture
- Moist, slightly firm interior
- Fairly small gas holes that are uniform in size and evenly distributed
- Not crumbly with sweet, delicate flavor

Quality Problems and Causes

- **Top Cracked**
  Batter too stiff
  Oven too hot at beginning

- **Tunnels**
  Over-mixed
  Air in batter at baking
  Uneven leavening agent in batter

- **Cake Falls**
  Too much butter of sugar
  Oven temperature not hot enough
  Did not bake long enough

- **Uneven Color**
  Not enough leavening agent
  Uneven oven temperature

- **Crumbly**
  Too much sugar
  Too much shortening

- **Dry**
  Not enough sugar
  Not enough shortening
  Baked too long

PRODUCT: PIES AND PASTRIES

Desirable Characteristics

- Exterior or crust light, tender, and crisp
- Golden in color
- Flaky to semi-flaky
- Blistered surface
- Crust adheres evenly to edge or rim of pan

Pie Fillings Quality Problems and Causes

- **Flat taste**
  Not enough salt
  Not enough acidity in filling (fruit pies)

- **Breaks Down**
  Not mixed well enough
  Cooled too slowly
  Too much acidity (fruit pies)

- **Cracks**
  Too much flour or cornstarch or thickening agent
  Too many eggs
  Cooked too long
  Not enough fat (cream pies)

Pastry Problems and Causes

- **Off Color**
  Too much flour or cornstarch or thickening agent

- **Large Blisters**
  Crust not vented enough
  Oven temperature not hot enough
  Pastry fitted into pan too tightly

- **Crust Shrinks**
  Too much water
  Not enough shortening
  Dough mixed too much

PRODUCT: MERINGUE

Desirable Characteristics

- Light fluffy appearance
- Smooth texture, not overly sticky
- Slightly browned on top

Quality Problems and Causes

- **Breaks down, not enough height**
  Egg whites not beaten long enough
  Insufficient sugar
  Moisture or yolk in egg whites
  Pie filling too thin
  Not baked long enough
  Improperly stored in a closed container after baking

- **Shrinks**
  Sugar added at wrong time (too soon or too late)
  Meringue fails to touch crust on all sides
  Oven temperature not hot enough

Desirable Characteristics

- Bright in color
- Firm, not mushy
- Not bruised or discolored
- Uniform in shape
- Good, crisp texture that is tender and firm
- Pleasant, typical flavor, not bitter
- Nutrients are maintained

Methods to Achieve Good Quality in Cooked Vegetables

- Wash vegetables carefully.
- Cut carefully
- Do not soak.
- Cook close to serving time.
- Cook in small batches.
- Follow recipe instructions carefully.
- Use the smallest amount of water possible.
- Do not add water to canned vegetables.
- Bring water or the liquid from canned vegetables to a boil before adding vegetables.
- Steam rather than boil whenever possible.
- Avoid overcooking.
- Cook strong-flavored and fresh green vegetables uncovered, especially at the beginning of the simmer.
- Never add baking soda to vegetables

SUPERVISOR'S DAILY REPORT OF PATIENT MEAL SERVICE

Supervisor: **Date:**

Did all scheduled employees arrive on time and work a full shift?   ❏ Yes   ❏ No

List any tardy or absent employees with reasons for missing work.

_____

_____

_____

_____

Was all food preparation material received correctly?   ❏ Yes   ❏ No

If no, list items or problems.

_____

_____

_____

Was the meal(s) served on time?   ❏ Yes   ❏ No

If no, list reasons.

_____

_____

_____

Did all equipment and dish room function and properly?   ❏ Yes   ❏ No

If no, list equipment and repairs needs (if known).

_____

_____

_____

Were all carts received and delivered on time?   ❏ Yes   ❏ No

Was meal service satisfactory?   ❏ Yes   ❏ No

List any problems.

_____

_____

_____

List any work orders sent/returned.

_____

_____

Were leftovers returned to kitchen?   ❏ Yes   ❏ No

If no, please explain:_____

_____

FOOD WASTE INFORMATION

Indicate with a slash in the first column, the number of people who did not touch their food; use the second column to show how many people left half their food on their plate, and the third column for empty plates.

Menu Cycle Week 1, Day 1, Meal 3	Plate returned full of food	Plate returned with half the food	Plate returned empty
Soup			
Juice			
Salad			
Entree			
Vegetable			
Dessert			

CLEANING CHECKLIST		
ITEM TO BE CLEANED	**CLEANING INSTRUCTIONS**	**EMPLOYEE RESPONSIBLE**
Food Preparation Areas	Remove crumbs or food debris, wipe clean	
Freezer	Clean, straighten interior, wipe exterior	
Refrigerator	Make sure food is covered and placed properly,	
Storeroom	Clean, straighten, make sure all items are labeled properly using the FIFO system	
Stove	Remove crumbs or food debris, wipe clean	
Grill	Remove crumbs or food debris, wipe clean	
Mixer, Blender	Remove crumbs or food debris, wipe clean	
Sinks	Clean and disinfect	
Paper Towels	Restocked	
Soap Dispenser	Refilled, wipe exterior	
Pots, Pans	Clean, store	
Dishes	Clean, store	
Can Opener	Wipe exterior	
Coffee Urn	Clean, wipe exterior, turn off	
Drawers	Clean, straighten	
Dining Area	Clean, straighten	
Towels	Washed	
Garbage Cans	Empty, clean, wipe exterior,	
Dishwasher	Clean, wipe exterior,	
Utensils	Clean, store	
Silverware	Clean, store	
Food Carts	Clean, store	

Food Service Supervisor Signature: *Date:*

FOOD PRODUCTION AREA

☐ Equipment, appliances, walls and screens are clean in food service area.

☐ Food preparation equipment is cleaned and sanitized after every use. This would include choppers, mixers and can openers.

☐ Frozen food is thawed using the proper thawing procedures.

☐ Cutting boards are sanitized properly after each use and when alternating between raw and cooked foods.

☐ Prior to preparation, fruits and vegetables are thoroughly washed.

☐ Foods are cooked properly and internal temperatures checked.

☐ Foods that are potentially hazardous are held at the correct temperature. Hot foods at 140°F or above; cold foods at 41°F or below. Frozen food must be at or below 0°F at all times.

☐ Steam tables or food warmers are used properly and not used to reheat or prepare food.

☐ Food service employees do not touch cooked food with bare hands.

☐ The food preparation area is not used by employees for smoking or eating. All beverage containers and cups are covered and contain some type of drinking straw.

☐ Employees who are ill are sent home or restricted to activities where he or she does not come into contact with food.

☐ Employees are wearing hair restraints.

☐ Employees wash their hands thoroughly after using the bathroom, after coughing or sneezing, after handling garbage, or after any activity that could cause food contamination.

☐ The kitchen has an easily accessible, clean sink specifically for handwashing with soap and disposable towels. A sign with proper handwashing procedures is posted near the sink.

☐ Lighting has covers or bulbs that will not shatter.

☐ In holding areas, food temperatures are checked regularly with a clean, sanitized thermometer.

☐ Uncovered glassware and dishes of food items are not stacked.

DISHWASHING AREA

☐ A high-temperature dishwashing machine is used, with wash-cycle water temperatures over 140°F, and rinse-cycle water temperatures over 160°F.

☐ A low-temperature dishwashing machine is used with a chemical agent. Manufacturer's specifications are adhered to for proper temperature and chemical concentration.

☐ For manual washing, a three-compartment sink is used. The sink has a bleach sanitizing solution or iodine, and chemical strips are used to verify the sanitizing solution's strength.

☐ Glassware and dishes are not stacked while wet.

☐ Glassware or dishes that are cracked or chipped are immediately discarded.

☐ Clean dishes, glassware, utensils, and pots and pans do not have any food residue.

CHEMICAL & NON-FOOD STORAGE

- ☐ Dirty water is discarded after use. All mops, brooms, and cleaning equipment are cleaned and put away.

- ☐ The storage area is easily accessible, and clean with no refuse or food residue.

- ☐ Toxic materials are in the proper container and clearly labeled.

REFRIGERATORS & FREEZERS

- ☐ Shallow containers are used for cooked foods in the refrigerator.

- ☐ Air can circulate freely throughout the freezer or refrigerator. Food should not be stored too closely.

- ☐ Freezers and refrigerators are clean and free from debris.

- ☐ Freezers are at a temperature of 0°F or lower. Refrigerators are at a temperature of 41°F or lower.

- ☐ Any frozen food with freezer burn or spoilage is immediately discarded.

- ☐ Frozen foods are stored in their original container, or are properly packaged, labeled and dated, using the "first in, first out" method.

- ☐ Proper storage order is observed with prepared foods on the top shelves.

- ☐ Raw items, meat and eggs are stored below thawed or cooked foods.

- ☐ Refrigerated foods are well-wrapped, labeled and dated, using the "first in, first out" method.

- ☐ Seven days is the maximum holding time for refrigerated leftovers. At 45°F, food can only be held for four days.

TRASH & REFUSE AREA

- ☐ Trash receptacles do not leak and are clean and in good condition.

- ☐ Exterior dumpsters and all trash receptacles are securely covered.

FOOD TRANSPORTATION

- ☐ Service trays are used once and then thoroughly washed and sanitized.

- ☐ Carts used to transport food are clean and well-maintained.

- ☐ Dairy items or eggs are transported in a cart at 41°F or lower. If coolers are used, they are packed with ice.

DRY FOOD STORAGE

- ☐ Storage and food handling areas are clean with no insects or rodent droppings.

- ☐ Food packages are tightly sealed.

- ☐ Labeled, clean containers are used for dry bulk food items.

- ☐ Unprotected or exposed water or sewer lines are not in or near food storage areas.

- ☐ Food is stored on shelves at least 4 inches from the floor for proper cleaning.

- ☐ The food storage shelves are clean and well-organized without debris or empty boxes.

- ☐ Foods are properly dated and shelved, using the "first in, first out" method.

- ☐ Dented cans are discarded.

- ☐ All shelving units are at least 4 inches from walls, so rodents, bugs and other pests cannot nest between walls and shelves.

- ☐ Food items have a separate storage area from cleaning agents, pesticides and other toxic substances.

Check each item when completed.

EMPLOYEES

◯ Employees have a designated area for storing all personal items, which is separate from food preparation areas.

◯ An area is designated for non-food items such as for recipes and non-food tools.

◯ Employees practice proper hand-washing between tasks, at a designated handwashing sink, with soap and single-use paper towels.

◯ Employees preparing food wear clean uniforms or aprons.

◯ Hair restraints are worn and no jewelry is allowed (except a wedding band). No false nails or nail polish is allowed.

◯ Employees do not eat, drink, smoke or chew gum in the food preparation areas.

◯ Employees with any illness are sent home. Any cuts, wounds or abrasions are bandaged and gloves are worn over the bandage.

RECEIVING FOOD

◯ Receiving trucks meet standards of cleanliness and food safety storage.

◯ Food is received by designated employee and checked for acceptable condition, date and temperature.

◯ Once food is received, it is noted on invoice and put away immediately.

◯ Any damaged or open item will not be accepted including dented or rusted cans.

◯ Food is covered, labeled and stored, using the "first in, first out" system.

◯ Cross-contamination is avoided by storing raw meats and un-rinsed vegetables away from ready-to-eat food.

FOOD

◯ Food is thawed properly in the refrigerator or under running water.

◯ Bulk food receptacles are clean and clearly labeled. Scoops with handles are used and stored separately.

◯ Ice scoops are not stored in ice.

◯ Cross-contamination is not possible between foods and food contact surfaces or staff and chemicals.

◯ If possible, pasteurized eggs are used rather than raw eggs.

◯ Food is cooked or reheated to the proper temperature (above 165°F).

◯ Food is cooled in quick-chill manner such as in a shallow pan in ice or on the top shelf of the walk-in freezer.

◯ Potentially hazardous foods are prepared according to safety standards.

EQUIPMENT

◯ Freezer and refrigerators: Record area/temperature readings

Freezer 1 _____ / _____

Freezer 2 _____ / _____

Refer 1 _____ / _____

Refer 2 _____ / _____

Refer 3 _____ / _____

◯ Equipment is cleaned and maintained according to a set schedule per manufacturer's specifications.

◯ Hand sinks are easily accessible, clean and in good condition.

◯ Towels that are in use for wiping are replaced every 4 hours. They are stored in sanitizer solution (200ppm) in labeled buckets.

◯ Refrigerators are stocked to allow adequate air circulation. Water should not be pooled on bottom shelf, and condensers should be clear and visible.

◯ Thermometers are available for all cold-holding equipment. Every thermometer is accessible, in good repair and calibrated regularly (ice water 32°F; boiling water 212°F).

◯ The gaskets are clean and in excellent condition.

◯ Preparation equipment is clean and well-maintained including range, deep fat fryer, oven, grill and broiler. Equipment with small parts are in good condition without cracks or leaks.

◯ The ice machine is sanitized, clean and free from rust, mildew, scale and deposits. The water filters are properly tagged.

◯ Beverage machines are cleaned and sanitized daily, including soda gun and holster, and soft drink nozzles are cleaned inside.

◯ Glass mats are cleaned/sanitized daily.

◯ Equipment not in use and spare parts are stored in separate area and cannot contaminate food or harbor pests.

DISHWASHING

◯ Employees wash their hands at hand-wash sinks, regularly using proper handwashing techniques.

◯ A three-compartment sink is used with separate compartments for pre-scrape, wash and rinse.

◯ The three-compartment sink uses the correct temperature water and sanitizer @ _____ (200ppm).

◯ Clean utensils are stored properly (upside down) and away from contamination and dirty utensils.

FACILITY

❍ The plumbing is in good condition with no leaking pipes, slow drains or leaking faucets. Pipes are 2 inches above drains.

❍ All fixtures, walls, ceilings and ventilation are clean and in good repair.

❍ Floors are clean and in good condition, and floor mats are pressure-cleaned regularly.

❍ Lighting is adequate and shatterproof.

❍ Break areas and wash stations are clean and free from clutter.

❍ Maintenance is done regularly and repairs made in a timely manner.

RESTROOMS

❍ Sinks are clean and stocked with soap and single-use paper towels. Hot water is at or above 110°F.

❍ Handwashing signs are posted.

❍ The facilities have adequate supplies and are disinfected, clean and in good repair.

CHEMICAL STORAGE

❍ Chemicals are labeled, stored in designated areas (away from food), with material safety data sheets (MSDS).

FIRE & SAFETY

❍ Fire extinguishers are available, charged, tagged and mounted, and employees have been instructed how to use them properly.

❍ Extension cords are not used.

❍ CO_2 tanks are stored upright and secured.

❍ Bulletin boards with tacks or pins are not used in food preparation, washing or storage areas.

PEST CONTROL

❍ There is no evidence of insects, rodents or birds (such as droppings).

❍ The building is pest-proof, with sealed doors, working fly fans and no exterior holes or cracks.

❍ Traps are tamper-proof and secured.

❍ The pest-control operator manual has pesticide lists, map of traps and emergency contacts list.

GARBAGE & REFUSE

❍ The dumpsters are clean and the lids are closed.

❍ The outside premises are clean, free from trash and debris.

❍ The grease bin and surrounding area is maintained and clean.

❍ The recycle bins and surrounding area is maintained and clean.

❍ When washing or degreasing trash cans, food bins or other equipment, wastewater does not run into storm drains.

❍ Garbage and waste food cans have plastic liners, and are pressure-cleaned and disinfected.

GENERAL

❍ Employees have been properly trained in food protection and Hazcom procedures. All training is documented.

❍ Health permits are current and prominently posted.

❍ A food-safety-certified manager is on the premises at all times.

❍ Water quality is checked annually and reports are on file.

❍ Cleaning tools such as mops and brooms are stored separately from food, dishes and utensils.

❍ The mop sink is easily accessible and clean, with hot and cold water. Mop heads are air-dried upside down and clean.

DATE: SUPERVISOR:

NOTES/COMMENTS:

Circle Yes or No for every applicable item.

RECEIVING

Y N 1. Food is received only from previously approved vendors.

Y N 2. Food deliveries are inspected immediately for proper condition and temperature, with potentially hazardous foods delivered at a temperature of 41°F.

Y N 3. Frozen foods delivered in frozen state with no evidence of thawing or refreezing.

Y N 4. Raw or frozen clams, mussels, scallops and oysters have a temperature below 45°F and are properly labeled, with labels maintained on site for at least 90 days.

Y N 5. Deliveries are rejected if the food is not at the proper temperature or in unacceptable condition.

Y N 6. Food is promptly placed in proper storage locations, with refrigerated and frozen foods stored immediately.

STORAGE

Y N 1 All food is stored away from chemicals, vermin, insects, etc., and cannot be contaminated.

Y N 2. All food is properly labeled using the "first in, first out" system, including prepackaged and bulk foods.

Y N 3. Shelving for food storage is at least 6 inches from floor and walls.

Y N 4. Items to be returned and damaged goods are stored separately.

Y N 5. Proper layering is used in refrigerated storage, with raw meat and fish stored below and away from ready-to-eat foods (produce, vegetables, beverages).

Y N 6. All food in storage is properly covered and sealed.

Y N 7. Contaminated food is promptly discarded.

PREPARATION

Y N 1. Frozen foods thawed properly using an acceptable method:

In a refrigerator.

In a microwave.

Under cold, running water.

As part of the cooking process.

PREPARATION

Y   N   2. Hot foods (which can be potentially hazardous) are cooled quickly by the following methods before placement in a refrigerator or freezer:

With a rapid, cool stirring device.

Stirring while in an ice bath.

In a blast chiller.

Adding ice to the food.

In shallow, iced pans.

Separating food into smaller portions.

Y   N   3. Separate sinks are available and used only for food preparation activities—not hand-washing or janitorial use.

Y   N   4. Potentially hazardous foods do not have sulfite added.

Y   N   5. Potentially hazardous foods are cooked thoroughly with proper internal temperatures:

Poultry–165°F (comminuted poultry, game birds, stuffed meats, stuffed pasta and reheated foods).

Beef–155°F (ground beef, other comminuted meats and foods containing comminuted meat).

Pork–155°F.

Eggs–145°F (food containing raw eggs and other cooked, potentially hazardous food).

SERVING

Y   N   1. All prepackaged foods are labeled properly with name, list of ingredients, net weight and name and address of manufacturer.

Y   N   2. Any food returned from customers uneaten is discarded (not reused or reserved).

Y   N   3. Food and utensils in self-service areas, such as salad bars, buffets, snack counters and beverage dispensers, are protected from contamination by customers (e.g., sneezing, coughing and handling).

Y   N   4. Bare hands are not used for food service and serving utensils, such as spoons, tongs and ladles, are provided.

 **TEMPERATURES**

Y   N   1. Hot, potentially hazardous foods kept at or above 140°F.

Y   N   2. Cold, potentially hazardous foods kept at or below 41°F.

Y   N   3. The danger zone for potentially hazardous foods is 42°–140°F. When cooling or reheating foods, the time spent in this temperature range is kept to a minimum.

Y   N   4. Properly calibrated thermometers are visible in the warmest part of each refrigeration and freezer unit.

Y   N   5. If serving potentially hazardous food, a metal probe-type thermometer is used to check temperature prior to service.

Y   N   6. Thermometers are sanitized before and after each use.

Y   N   7. Thermometers are calibrated regularly.

Y   N   8. While in use, tongs, scoops, spoons, ladles or other serving utensils for potentially hazardous foods are kept at or below 41°F or above 140°F, or in a dipper well that has clean water continually provided.

 **DISHWASHING**

Y   N   1. Plates, glasses and silverware are sanitized by mechanical dishwasher according to manufacturer specifications. If manually washed, they are sanitized by one of the following methods: 100ppm chlorine for 30 seconds; 25ppm iodine for 60 seconds; 200ppm quaternary ammonium for 60 seconds; or 180°F water for 30 seconds.

Y   N   2. All mechanical dishwashers are provided with dual integral drain boards.

Y   N   3. During operation of dish machines, the correct temperature is maintained as well as proper amounts of sanitizer and chemicals.

Y   N   4. When sanitizing utensils, a test strip or thermometer is used to check effectiveness.

Y   N   5. A three-compartment (preferred) or two-compartment sink is available for utensil washing.

Y   N   6. All compartments can fully submerge the largest utensil in use.

Y   N   7. Utensils are maintained and clean.

Y   N   8. Utensils used in the kitchen or for serving are regularly cleaned and sanitized.

Y   N   9. Only commercial-grade utensils that are certified by an American National Standards Institute (ANSI)-accredited program are used.

Y   N   10. Utensils are stored away from any possible contamination including dirt, rodents, insects and chemicals.

Y   N   11. Single-use customer utensils are used only once and disposed.

 **RESTROOMS**

Y N 1   Restroom facilities are provided for employees.

Y N 2. Restroom facilities are provided for customers.

Y N 3. Toilet stalls have self-closing, locking doors.

Y N 4. Restroom facilities are not used for storage of food, utensils, equipment or supplies.

Y N 5. Restroom facilities have adequate supplies such as toilet paper, single-use sanitary towels (or air dryer) and sanitizing hand cleanser.

Y N 6. A handwashing sink has pressurized hot and cold water.

Y N 7. Restroom facilities have adequate ventilation.

 **HANDWASHING**

Y N 1. A separate handwashing sink is located in, or adjacent to, restrooms and kitchens.

Y N 2. The handwashing sink has adequate supplies including single-service sanitary towels (or air dryers) and sanitizing hand cleanser.

Y N 3. The handwashing sink has pressurized hot and cold water.

Y N 4. The handwashing sink is easily accessible at all times.

Y N 5. A separate handwashing sink is used exclusively for handwashing in food prep areas and is conveniently located.

 **CHEMICALS & CLEANING**

Y N 1. Chemicals are labeled properly.

Y N 2. Chemicals are not stored in food preparation area.

Y N 3. The only pesticides used have been specifically approved for food facility usage.

Y N 4. All chemicals, pesticides and hazardous materials are used properly. Employees have access to MSDS information on all chemicals.

Y N 5. Cleaning supplies and equipment are stored in a separate area away from food preparation, food storage, dishwashing and utensil storage areas.

Y N 6. A separate janitorial sink has hot and cold water with a back-flow prevention device.

Y N 7. All mops, buckets, brooms and other cleaning equipment is kept away from food and utensils.

 **LIGHTING**

Y   N   1. In food preparation and utensil cleaning areas, lighting has a minimum intensity of 20 footcandles (fc).

Y   N   2. In dining and other areas, lighting has a minimum intensity of 10 fc, but intensity of at least 20 fc available during cleaning operations.

Y   N   3. Food preparation, food storage and utensil cleaning areas have shatterproof light covers installed and are in good repair.

 **PEST INFESTATION**

Y   N   1. Rodents, insects and other vermin are not in the building.

Y   N   2. Building does not have cracks or openings where rodents and insects can enter, and any droppings and dead insects are cleaned up.

Y   N   3. All building entrances have air curtains or tight-fitting, self-closing doors. All windows are protected by screens.

Y   N   4. Any fumigation or pest control is done by a licensed pest control operator.

 **GARBAGE**

Y   N   1. Garbage is removed frequently and proper facilities are provided for disposal and storage.

Y   N   2. Garbage containers have tight-fitting lids, do not leak and are rodent-proof.

Y   N   3. Before being placed in the dumpster, all garbage is in securely fastened plastic bags.

 **EMPLOYEES**

Y   N   1. Employees wear clean uniforms or approved clothing.

Y   N   2. Employees only use tobacco products in designated areas, away from food preparation, storage and service.

Y   N   3. Employees wash hands thoroughly and frequently. Hands are washed after engaging in any activity that may cause contamination including working between raw food and ready-to-eat foods, after coughing or sneezing, after touching soiled equipment or utensils and after using restrooms.

EMPLOYEES, CONT.

Y N 4. Ill employees are sent home or do not come to work.

Y N 5. Employees practice safe food-handling procedures and have been trained in food safety.

Y N 6. Employees check temperatures of potentially hazardous foods during storage, preparation and serving. Employees also check utensil-cleaning chemical levels, water temperatures and water pressures.

Y N 7. A separate employee changing area is provided, apart from toilets, food storage, food preparation, utensil cleaning and utensil storage areas.

PLUMBING

Y N 1. Water supply has been tested and comes from an approved source.

Y N 2. Adequate amounts of hot and cold water are available.

Y N 3. Sewage and wastewater is disposed properly into a sewer or septic system.

Y N 4. All equipment that discharges waste, such as prep sinks, steam tables, salad bars, ice machines, ice storage bins, beverage machines, display cases or refrigeration/freezer units, have a floor sink or funnel drain provided for indirect waste drainage.

Y N 5. Receptacles for indirect waste are accessible and cleaned regularly.

Y N 6. Plumbing is clean, in good repair and operating properly.

Y N 7. A licensed company cleans out grease interceptors and septic tanks regularly.

SIGNAGE

Y N 1. Restrooms have handwashing signs posted and clearly visible.

Y N 2. Handwashing sinks have signage with proper handwashing procedures posted and clearly visible.

Y N 3. "No smoking" signs are clearly visible throughout the facility, especially in food preparation, food storage, utensil cleaning and utensil storage areas.

Y N 4. A Choking First Aid poster is visible and readily accessible to employees (in facilities with sit-down dining).

FACILITY

Y　N　　1. Facility is fully enclosed, clean and well-maintained.

Y　N　　2. The building meets all applicable building and fire codes.

Y　N　　3. Exterior premises is clean and well-maintained.

Y　N　　4. All equipment is clean, well-maintained and meets applicable ANSI-accredited certification program standards.

Y　N　　5. No unused, out-dated or broken equipment is on the premises.

Y　N　　6. Cooking equipment and high-temperature dish machines have ventilation and exhaust systems installed over areas of operation.

Y　N　　7. In food preparation and storage areas, flooring is level, non-skid, durable, non-absorbent and easily cleaned.

Y　N　　8. In janitorial facilities, restrooms and employee changing areas flooring is smooth, non-skid, durable, non-absorbent and easily cleaned.

Y　N　　9. In food preparation, food storage areas, janitorial facilities, restrooms and employee changing areas, walls and ceilings are smooth, durable, non-absorbent and easily cleaned.

Y　N　　10. The health department has approved all construction, remodeling and new equipment installation prior to work.

Y　N　　11. All soiled linens are held in a clean container, and a linen storage area is provided.

Y　N　　12. Tobacco permit is valid, up to date and posted in a prominent location (if applicable).

Y　N　　13. Health permit is valid, up to date and posted in a prominent location.

DATE: _____ TIME: _____ EMPLOYEE(S): _____

JANITORIAL ROOM

Is it clean and neat?	Yes No
Are buckets empty and stored upside down?	Yes No
Are there rodent or insect droppings visible?	Yes No
Are all toxic materials (including pesticides) in their original containers and clearly labeled?	Yes No

DISHWASHING AREA

	MAIN KITCHEN	AUX KITCHEN
Wash cycle temperature	_____ °F	_____ °F
Rinse cycle temperature	_____ °F	_____ °F
Are there any obstructions or contaminants in the jets and nozzles (such as food particles)?	Yes No	Yes No
Is the dishwashing equipment cleaned daily to remove food particles, chemicals and debris?	Yes No	Yes No
Is the proper amount or level of detergent and/or sanitizer being used consistently in the wash cycle?	Yes No	Yes No
Do separate employees remove and store clean tableware?	Yes No	Yes No
Do dishwashing employees practice proper handwashing between handling soiled tableware and sanitized ware?	Yes No	Yes No
Do employees pre-scrape and flush dishes and utensils prior to washing?	Yes No	Yes No
Once dishes and utensils are cleaned and sanitized, are they stored in a clean, dry location (off the floor)?	Yes No	Yes No
Are utensils and tableware toweled properly?	Yes No	Yes No

Notes or Concerns:

| DATE: _____ | TIME: _____ | EMPLOYEE(S): _____ |

SERVICES AREA	**MAIN KITCHEN**	**AUX KITCHEN**
Are floors, tables and chairs clean and dry in the dining area?	Yes No	Yes No
Is the floor being swept or cleaned while food is being served or when customers are eating?	Yes No	Yes No
Is the temperature correct in the dining area for customer comfort?	Yes No	Yes No
Does the dining area have any unpleasant odors?	Yes No	Yes No
Are the dishes and silverware clean, sanitized and stored correctly to prevent contamination?	Yes No	Yes No
Are condiment containers clean and in good repair?	Yes No	Yes No
Are menus clean and in good repair, without food marks or stains?	Yes No	Yes No
Are food warmers or steam tables used to re-heat prepared foods?	Yes No	Yes No
Is food being held in the hot-holding equipment at or above 140°F?	Yes No	Yes No
Is cold food being held at 41°F or lower?	Yes No	Yes No
Are cold- and hot-holding cabinets equipped with thermometers?	Yes No	Yes No
Are tongs or other serving utensils available and used to pick up rolls, bread, butter pats, ice or other food to be served?	Yes No	Yes No
Are tableware towels clean, dry and only used for wiping food spills?	Yes No	Yes No
Are servers wearing proper uniforms that are clean and in good condition?	Yes No	Yes No
Do servers show any signs of illness, such as coughing or wiping their noses?	Yes No	Yes No
Do servers handle drinking glasses and silverware properly, without touching glass tops or silverware blades?	Yes No	Yes No

DATE: _____ TIME: _____ EMPLOYEE(S): _____

PERSONAL SANITATION	MAIN KITCHEN	AUX KITCHEN
Are all employees involved with food handling properly dressed in clean uniforms or attire?	Yes No	Yes No
Are employees wearing jewelry other than a wedding band?	Yes No	Yes No
Are employees wearing hair restraints?	Yes No	Yes No
Do employees have a noticeable odor (such as strong perfume or body odor)?	Yes No	Yes No
Do employees have properly groomed hands, without fingernail polish and with short, clean fingernails?	Yes No	Yes No
If employees have any wounds, are they properly covered and free of infection?	Yes No	Yes No
Do employees show any signs of illness, such as sneezing or coughing?	Yes No	Yes No
Do employees scratch their head, face or body?	Yes No	Yes No
Are employees seen eating in food preparation or serving areas?	Yes No	Yes No

GENERAL SANITATION		
Are cleaning supplies and chemicals stored separately from the food preparation and service areas?	Yes No	Yes No
Is prepared food held correctly (at the correct temperature and in the proper containers?	Yes No	Yes No
Are clean, sanitary towels available?	Yes No	Yes No
Are frozen foods thawed correctly, either in the refrigerator, under cold, running water or thawed during the cooking process?	Yes No	Yes No
Is a separate sink available for food preparation that is not used for handwashing or cleaning?	Yes No	Yes No

DATE: _____   TIME: _____   EMPLOYEE(S): _____

GENERAL SANITATION (continued)

	MAIN KITCHEN	AUX KITCHEN
Is preparation equipment cleaned and sanitized between and after each use, or at the end of the day?	Yes No	Yes No
Are equipment and utensils not in use clean?	Yes No	Yes No
Are all dishes, pots, pans and other utensils stored correctly to prevent contamination?	Yes No	Yes No
Is food stored in coolers and freezers covered and spaced correctly to allow air circulation?	Yes No	Yes No
Are cutting boards in good condition and used only for specific types of food preparation to avoid cross-contamination?	Yes No	Yes No
Are cutting boards cleaned and sanitized after each use?	Yes No	Yes No

DRY STORAGE

	MAIN KITCHEN	AUX KITCHEN
Is the food storage area enclosed, dry and free from dampness?	Yes No	Yes No
Are food supplies labeled, dated and stored to ensure "first in, first out" use?	Yes No	Yes No
Is food stored separately from non-food supplies?	Yes No	Yes No
Is there any evidence of insects or rodent droppings in the storage areas?	Yes No	Yes No
Is the food storage area clean and free of dust, empty food cartons and other debris (including shelves and floor)?	Yes No	Yes No
Are shelves at least 4 inches away from walls and floors?	Yes No	Yes No
Is the area underneath the shelves easily accessible for cleaning?	Yes No	Yes No

DATE: _____   TIME: _____   EMPLOYEE(S): _____

WALK-IN FREEZERS

	MAIN KITCHEN	AUX KITCHEN
Temperature	_____ °F	_____ °F
Are shelves and floor clean and free of empty cartons or debris?	Yes No	Yes No
Are all foods properly stored and covered?	Yes No	Yes No
Are food supplies labeled, dated and stored to ensure "first in, first out" use?	Yes No	Yes No
Can air circulate freely around stored food?	Yes No	Yes No
Does freezer need defrosting?	Yes No	Yes No

WALK-IN REFRIGERATORS

	MEAT	DAIRY	VEGE	AUX KITCHEN
Temperature	_____ °F	_____ °F	_____ °F	_____ °F
Are refrigerators clean, with no mold or offensive odors?	Yes No	Yes No	Yes No	Yes No
Can air circulate freely around stored food?	Yes No	Yes No	Yes No	Yes No
Is food stored on the the floor of the refrigerators?	Yes No	Yes No	Yes No	Yes No
Are foods labeled, dated and stored to ensure "first in, first out" use?	Yes No	Yes No	Yes No	Yes No
Are large-quantity containers used for storing cooked foods (ground meat, dressing or gravy)?	Yes No	Yes No	Yes No	Yes No
Are all containers clearly labeled with date and food item?	Yes No	Yes No	Yes No	Yes No
Is spoiled or outdated food promptly discarded?	Yes No	Yes No	Yes No	Yes No
Are proper storage techniques used, with cooked food on the top and raw meats or poultry on the bottom shelves?	Yes No	Yes No	Yes No	Yes No
Are shelves at least 6 inches from the floor to allow cleaning underneath?	Yes No	Yes No	Yes No	Yes No
Are cooked foods stored in clean, sanitized, covered containers (not their original cartons)?	Yes No	Yes No	Yes No	Yes No

Cold Food Production

Date:	Employee:

☐ YES ☐ NO 1. Before food preparation, are all equipment and utensils cleaned and sanitized (including work surfaces)?

☐ YES ☐ NO 2. Are all utensils and containers cleaned and sanitized prior to use?

☐ YES ☐ NO 3. Are potentially hazardous ingredients (including tuna fish and mayonnaise) refrigerated at least 24 hours before use?

☐ YES ☐ NO 4. Are all fruits and vegetables properly washed prior to use?

☐ YES ☐ NO 5. Before handling food, do employees wash hands properly with soap and water?

☐ YES ☐ NO 6. Is prepared food properly covered, labeled and refrigerated, and taken directly to the serving line?

☐ YES ☐ NO 7. Do all workstations have ready access to sanitizer solution?

☐ YES ☐ NO 8. After each use, are work areas cleaned and sanitized?

☐ YES ☐ NO 9. While preparing food, are employees wearing disposable gloves?

☐ YES ☐ NO 10. Are all sinks in the food preparation area sanitized after each use?

☐ YES ☐ NO 11. Are handwashing sinks easily accessible and stocked with hand soap from a proper dispenser and single-use paper towels?

☐ YES ☐ NO 12. At the end of each day, is all food production equipment cleaned and sanitized?

Action Plan:	Completed By:	Comments:
	Supervisor:	

Vending Locations

Date: **Employee:**

❑ YES   ❑ NO   1. Is the vending area cleaned and uncluttered, with no trash or other debris?

❑ YES   ❑ NO   2. Is the vending machine area clean, in good condition and protected from overhead water, waste or sewer piping leakage and condensation?

❑ YES   ❑ NO   3. Does the vending area have adequate lighting and proper ventilation?

❑ YES   ❑ NO   4. Is the vending area free of insects and rodents?

❑ YES   ❑ NO   5. Are cold, potentially hazardous foods held at the proper temperatures (41°F or less) at all times?

❑ YES   ❑ NO   6. Are hot, potentially hazardous foods held at the proper temperatures (140°F or higher) at all times?

❑ YES   ❑ NO   7. Do the vending machines have thermometers that are checked daily to ensure machines are maintaining safe, accurate temperatures?

❑ YES   ❑ NO   8. Is food sold in the vending machines properly packaged and protected from contamination?

❑ YES   ❑ NO   9. Are all vending machines cleaned on a regular basis?

❑ YES   ❑ NO   10. Is a trash receptacle located near vending machines to properly dispose of food cartons and other debris?

Action Plan: **Completed By:**   **Comments:**

Supervisor:

Vending/Catering Food Transport Vehicles

Date:	Employee:

❑ YES ❑ NO 1. During transport, are cold, potentially hazardous foods held at the proper temperatures (41°F or less) at all times?

❑ YES ❑ NO 2. During transport, are hot, potentially hazardous foods held at the proper temperatures (140°F or higher) at all times?

❑ YES ❑ NO 3. Are insulated containers used for food transport?

❑ YES ❑ NO 4. If warming cabinets are used, is the temperature 140°F or higher when handling or transporting hot foods?

❑ YES ❑ NO 5. Are foods and beverages protected from contaminations such as dirt, dust and insects?

❑ YES ❑ NO 6. Are vehicles cleaned and sanitized after each use?

Action Plan:	Completed By:	Comments:
	Supervisor:	

Hot Food Production

Date:	Employee:

❑ YES ❑ NO 1. Before and after food preparation, are all equipment and utensils cleaned and sanitized (including work surfaces)?

❑ YES ❑ NO 2. Are frozen foods thawed correctly, either in the refrigerator, under cold, running water or thawed during the cooking process?

❑ YES ❑ NO 3. Are potentially hazardous foods cooked thoroughly with proper internal temperatures: poultry, 165°F; beef, 155°F; pork, 155°F; and eggs, 145°F?

❑ YES ❑ NO 4. Are hot, potentially hazardous foods cooled quickly by one of the following methods: with a rapid, cool stirring device, stirring while in an ice bath, in a blast chiller, by adding ice to the food, in shallow, iced pans or by separating food into smaller portions?

❑ YES ❑ NO 5. Are leftovers heated to 165°F?

❑ YES ❑ NO 6. Are sinks used for food preparation cleaned and sanitized between each use?

❑ YES ❑ NO 7. Are handwashing sinks accessible and properly stocked with single-use towels and soap dispensers so employees can wash hands before food preparation?

❑ YES ❑ NO 8. Are spills wiped up immediately?

❑ YES ❑ NO 9. Are floors kept clean with regular sweeping and mopping?

❑ YES ❑ NO 10. Does every workstation have easy access to sanitizing solution?

Action Plan:	Completed By:	Comments:
	Supervisor:	

Line Serving Areas

Date: **Employee:**

❑ YES   ❑ NO   1. Do all refrigerators have properly calibrated thermometers and maintain a temperature of 41°F or below?

❑ YES   ❑ NO   2. Are all deli or line items items refrigerated until placement on the deli bar?

❑ YES   ❑ NO   3. Are all items held at 45°F while on the deli bar?

❑ YES   ❑ NO   4. Are properly calibrated thermometers used regularly to check product temperatures?

❑ YES   ❑ NO   5. Are floors kept clean with regular sweeping and mopping?

❑ YES   ❑ NO   6. At the end of each day, is all the deli bar equipment cleaned and sanitized?

❑ YES   ❑ NO   7. Does every workstation have easy access to sanitizing solution?

Action Plan: **Completed By:**   **Comments:**

Supervisor:

Line Service/Hot Foods

Date: _____ **Employee:** _____

❑ YES ❑ NO	1.	Do all refrigerators have properly calibrated thermometers and maintain a temperature of 41°F or below?
❑ YES ❑ NO	2.	Are refrigerated items stored properly, with cooked or ready-to-eat items above raw products?
❑ YES ❑ NO	3.	Are all refrigerated products stored in properly covered containers and labeled?
❑ YES ❑ NO	4.	Is raw meat refrigerated prior to cooking?
❑ YES ❑ NO	5.	Is the grill clean, in good working order and properly maintained?
❑ YES ❑ NO	6.	Is the steam table clean and in good working condition?
❑ YES ❑ NO	7.	Are all hot, cooked foods held at 140°F or higher?
❑ YES ❑ NO	8.	Do soup kettles have a temperature of 140°F or higher?
❑ YES ❑ NO	9.	Are properly calibrated thermometers used to take frequent temperature checks?
❑ YES ❑ NO	10.	Are spills wiped up immediately?
❑ YES ❑ NO	11.	Are floors mopped and swept on a regular basis?

Action Plan: **Completed By:** **Comments:**

Supervisor:

Restrooms

Date:			Employee:

❏ YES ❏ NO 1. Are restrooms clean and odor-free?

❏ YES ❏ NO 2. Are restrooms well-ventilated?

❏ YES ❏ NO 3. Do toilet stalls have self-closing, locking doors?

❏ YES ❏ NO 4. Are soap and towel dispensers well-stocked and working properly?

❏ YES ❏ NO 5. Does the sink(s) and have faucets with pressurized hot and cold water?

❏ YES ❏ NO 6. Are the trash containers cleaned and emptied on a regular basis?

❏ YES ❏ NO 7. Is the restroom used for storage of food, utensils, equipment or supplies?

Action Plan:	Completed By:	Comments:
	Supervisor:	

Dry Storage

Date: **Employee:**

❏ YES   ❏ NO   1.   Are all food goods stacked neatly, labeled and in proper containers?

❏ YES   ❏ NO   2.   Are all storage shelves or racks at least 6 inches off the floor?

❏ YES   ❏ NO   3.   Are shelves and storage area clean, free of dust, empty cartons and other debris?

❏ YES   ❏ NO   4.   Is storage area swept daily?

❏ YES   ❏ NO   5.   Are food items rotated properly using the "first in, first out" system?

❏ YES   ❏ NO   6.   Is temperature of the the dry storage area regulated (between 60°F and 70°F) and ventilated to avoid dampness?

❏ YES   ❏ NO   7.   Is the storage area large enough for ease of use?

❏ YES   ❏ NO   8.   Is the storage area inspected for evidence of rodents and insects on a regular basis?

❏ YES   ❏ NO   9.   Are food supplies stored separately from chemicals, cleaners and pesticides?

❏ YES   ❏ NO   10. Are water or sewer lines located in a separate area away from food storage?

❏ YES   ❏ NO   11. Is contaminated or spoiled food promptly discarded?

❏ YES   ❏ NO   12. Is the storage area well-lit?

Action Plan:	Completed By:	Comments:
	Supervisor:	

Dish Room/Pot & Pan Areas

Date: **Employee:**

❑ YES ❑ NO 1. Are the dish room floors cleaned and sanitized on a regular basis?

❑ YES ❑ NO 2. Are sinks cleaned and sanitized before use?

❑ YES ❑ NO 3. Are sanitizing chemicals used according to specifications and at the proper strength?

❑ YES ❑ NO 4. Is a three-compartment sink utilized for dishwashing?

❑ YES ❑ NO 5. Before washing, all are dishware, utensils, pots and pans scraped and flushed?

❑ YES ❑ NO 6. Are dishes and utensils immersed for at least 30 seconds in hot water that is at or above 170°F?

❑ YES ❑ NO 7. Are sanitizer concentrations checked using test strips?

❑ YES ❑ NO 8. Is a sanitation log book kept of test results?

❑ YES ❑ NO 9. Are all dishware, pots and pans air-dried?

❑ YES ❑ NO 10. Are all dishware, pots and pans stored in the proper manner, free from splashes and contamination?

❑ YES ❑ NO 11. If used, is the dish machine in good working order?

❑ YES ❑ NO 12. Is the final rinse temperature of the dish machine at or greater than 180°F?

❑ YES ❑ NO 13. Is the dish machine cleaned daily at the end of its use?

❑ YES ❑ NO 14. Are the detergent levels of the dish machine checked regularly?

Action Plan: **Completed By:** **Comments:**

Supervisor:

Refrigerator & Freezer Storage

Date: **Employee:**

❑ YES   ❑ NO   1.   Is the interior temperature of the refrigerators 41°F or lower?

❑ YES   ❑ NO   2.   Are all refrigerators and freezers equipped with interior and exterior thermometers?

❑ YES   ❑ NO   3.   Are the interior and exterior thermometers of the refrigerators and freezers calibrated regularly?

❑ YES   ❑ NO   4.   Are refrigerators cleaned on a regular basis (including coils, grills and compressor area) and free of mold and odors?

❑ YES   ❑ NO   5.   Isshelving at least 6 inches from the floor and free from dust or other debris?

❑ YES   ❑ NO   6.   Arefoods and products covered, dated and properly spaced to provide adequate air circulation?

❑ YES   ❑ NO   7.   Arefoods stored to allow "first in, first out" usage?

❑ YES   ❑ NO   8.   Are raw meats stored on the bottom shelves, away from cooked or prepared food?

❑ YES   ❑ NO   9.   Are all spills cleaned up immediately?

❑ YES   ❑ NO   10.   Are cooked foods labeled and stored in clean, sanitized, covered containers?

❑ YES   ❑ NO   11.   Is the temperature of freezer units 0°F or lower?

❑ YES   ❑ NO   12.   Are products in the freezer stored above floor level?

❑ YES   ❑ NO   13.   Are all frozen foods wrapped and covered to avoid freezer burn?

❑ YES   ❑ NO   14.   Are freezers clean, in good working condition and defrosted on a regular basis?

Action Plan: **Completed By:**   **Comments:**

Supervisor:

Garbage/Refuse Storage & Disposal Areas

Date: **Employee:**

❑ YES   ❑ NO   1. Is the garbage area clean and well-maintained with no spilled liquids, food materials or debris?

❑ YES   ❑ NO   2. Are garbage and refuse containers durable and easily cleaned?

❑ YES   ❑ NO   3. Is garbage area cleaned regularly and are containers washed?

❑ YES   ❑ NO   4. Are garbage and refuse containers insect- and rodent-proof with tight-fitting lids?

❑ YES   ❑ NO   5. Are garbage and refuse materials disposed of on a regular basis, so there is no overflow or odors?

❑ YES   ❑ NO   6. Are there any visible rodents or rodent droppings?

❑ YES   ❑ NO   7. Is there any evidence of insect infestation?

❑ YES   ❑ NO   8. Are dumpsters maintained and in good working condition?

❑ YES   ❑ NO   9. Are hot water and detergents available to properly wash garbage containers?

❑ YES   ❑ NO   10. Are refrigerated garbage rooms or boxes clean and in proper condition?

Action Plan: **Completed By:**   **Comments:**

Supervisor:

Cold Beverage Areas

Date: **Employee:**

❑ YES   ❑ NO   1.   Are reach-in refrigerators used for storing cold beverages at a temperature of 41°F or lower?

❑ YES   ❑ NO   2.   Are all beverage hoses and nozzles maintained in a sanitary manner and cleaned regularly?

❑ YES   ❑ NO   3.   Are beverage dispensers maintained in a sanitary manner and cleaned regularly?

❑ YES   ❑ NO   4.   Are drinking cups, lids and straws easily accessible and stored in an orderly and sanitary manner?

❑ YES   ❑ NO   5.   Are ice machines cleaned and sanitized regularly?

❑ YES   ❑ NO   6.   Is the top of the ice machine free of obstructions and not being used as a storage area?

❑ YES   ❑ NO   7.   Are ice scoops being used in a sanitary manner and placed on a clean surface when not in use?

❑ YES   ❑ NO   8.   Are the storage cabinets under cold beverage dispensers clean, organized and inspected regularly?

Action Plan: **Completed By:**   **Comments:**

Supervisor:

CHAPTER SIX

Purchasing and Receiving Practices

Principles and procedures for receiving at all non-commercial food service facilities are similar. If you work with a government agency to run the organization be sure to learn the specific details which apply to your facility.

Food Service Procurement Process Overview

What are the steps in the food service procurement process? We will discuss each element in more detail, but the chart on the next page list will provide an overview.

FOOD SERVICE PROCUREMENT PROCESS OVERVIEW

STEP 1: Assessing Your Needs

Determine menu items to be served.	Use input from evaluation team.
Use standardized recipes to guarantee consistent items.	Gather input and feedback from your staff.

STEP 2: Project Sales Figures

What are the purchasing methods to be used?	Where are your potential vendors located?
What is the size of the facility?	How much storage space is available?
What is your purchasing volume?	How many staff members do you have and what are their skills?
How often do you need deliveries?	

STEP 3: Vendor List

Who is your primary vendor?	Establish your perpetual inventory.
Who will supply other items your primary vendor doesn't offer?	Monitor your physical inventory.
Determine and maintain your inventory system	What is the dollar value of your inventory?
Which items can be "just in time" items?	How often will items be delivered?

STEP 4: Order Quantities

Project menu items and quantities.	Which supplies will be needed?
Determine standardized portions.	What food items do you have in stock?

STEP 5: Bids and Prices

Establish food item specifications.	Find best prices, quality, and service for each item.

STEP 6: Placing Orders

Price.	Method to pay.
Quantity.	Submit orders to appropriate people and places.

STEP 7: Receive Food and Supplies

Receive the minimum number of orders.	Handle any returns or problems.
Verify delivery is accurate..	

STEP 8: Store Orders

Store food using appropriate methods for each type of food.

STEP 9: Issue Items

Let's start with purchasing and receiving. Other procedures will be discussed in Chapters 7 and 8.

Purchasing is how food service managers obtain wholesome, safe ingredients for their menu items and the additional supplies needed for the operation of the facility. To satisfy your customers and offer a quality product, the items need to be available when needed. Quality depends on the standards in place. To maintain costs, these items need to be purchased at the lowest possible prices while still maintaining acceptable quality. Here are some considerations:

- **Vendors are responsible for the safety of their food.** This is the reason you must choose vendors carefully.

- **Federal and state governments monitor your suppliers to see that they use the HAACP system** and need to train all employees in safe sanitation practices. HAACP will be discussed in full detail in Chapter 11.

- **Delivery Trucks:** Trucks used by vendors should have sufficient refrigeration and freezer capabilities. Food items should be packaged in leak proof, durable packaging. Even though vendors should do these things, it is good to explain your expectations in the beginning. These quality standards should be stated in your purchase agreement with the vendor. You can also ask to see their most recent health and sanitation reports. Let the vendor know that you will inspect the cleanliness of their trucks periodically. It is much easier to make your position clear in the beginning instead of waiting until there are problems.

- **Delivery Schedule:** Quality vendors will work with you concerning inspections and are usually willing to adjust their schedule around your busy times. It can be a real nuisance to have a delivery in the middle of a lunch rush or other busy time.

- **Inventory System:** You must have a good inventory system in place. We will discuss inventory procedures in Chapter 7 along with storage practices. It is impossible to place an accurate and effective order before you inventory items you have on hand. Have your menus in place before you place your order. A delivery "cushion" is important so that you don't run out of food and supplies before your next delivery. Over time and after reviewing the sales histories, you can determine a reasonable "cushion" without causing food to expire before it can be used. Any surplus will also tie up cash flow unnecessarily. After your purchasing is established, you can simply print a copy of your order list and fill in the blanks. The amount of food you need is based on sales history, sales projections, and your proposed menus. Your order forms can include such items as supplier names, prices, and unit sizes for each item.

Purchasing or Ordering?

Is there a difference between purchasing and ordering? Purchasing includes establishing policies to cover any possible measure or description of items being bought. After these parameters are determined, your individual orders will be simplified. The facility management negotiates terms and prices with the proposed distributors. Remember there are many vendors, so you should be able to get what you want as long as your specifications are reasonable. Here are the basics of your purchasing program that need to be established.

- **Purchasing Program:** Your purchasing program includes what you will buy and which vendor you will use to provide the best quality for the best prices.

- **To create an efficient purchasing program, you need standard purchase specifications based on your standardized recipes, standardized recipe yields, and portion controls.** Each of these considerations will enable you to have accurate costs based on the portions served in the facility. The amounts you purchase need to be accurate. When you order too much, portioning suffers and you have excess spoilage, waste, and theft. Purchasing too little will raise your food costs as you may need to make costly substitutions.

- **Procedures**: Your procedures should include written specifications for each product that you buy from reliable and honest vendors.

Each of these elements is necessary to ensure a certain level of quality and standardization for your customers. A good purchasing program does these three things:

1. Allows you to acquire the items you need at the agreed upon prices.

2. Exercises control over your inventory and costs.

3. Determines procedures to guarantee the quality at the best prices.

You need to decide whether you will do the purchasing yourself or if the duty will be assigned to another team member. Whether you do the work yourself or have someone else handle purchasing, the prices must be kept up-to-date. Prices can change frequently and you need the most current prices to project and maintain food costs accurately.

It is good to check prices with various vendors periodically. Some vendors will offer lower prices for a short time, but over time they are more expensive. This is one reason why you or your purchaser needs to stay current about prices from your local vendors. If you find another vendor with lower prices, you can offer the current vendor a chance to give you an updated price quote. This will alert them that you are watching the prices, and they are accountable for the prices they charge.

Ordering Tips

It's impossible to place orders effectively until you understand the items in your inventory list. You need to be familiar with each item, and inventory counts need to be established. Par levels and projected sales amounts need to be determined. This makes it much easier to compile an accurate order. You can use a pen and paper or a computer to determine your orders, but this is what you need to accomplish:

- Create a list of which specific items are needed.

- Create a vendor contact list.

- Add prices of items on your inventory list.

- Determine a simpler way to place your orders.

After you determine par levels, the Par Order Sheet or Par Amount Requisition may be helpful. This will enable you to identify quickly where your inventory is short and help you create an accurate food order. It is shown at the end of this chapter.

Or if you prefer to keep track of items more closely, the Daily Inventory Order Sheet and Miscellaneous Order Sheet may be more helpful. (Samples of these forms are located at the end of this chapter.)

Several things need to be kept in mind when you place orders. Consider each of these factors before you complete your order and inventory.

- **Inventory Amount** — Over-stocking means you have additional items to count and less control of the items in your inventory.

- **Perishables** — Meat, produce, and seafood have a shelf life of two or three days. Keep your orders tight when the shelf life is that short.

- **Tie Up Cash** — When you order too much, money is tied up. We used to joke with a manager because he ordered too many boxes on a regular basis. No matter how many we had in stock, he always ordered more. The large piles collected dust and tied up working capital. Even though they wouldn't expire, there was no reason to tie up so much money for something that wasn't needed at that time. Do you have similar items in your inventory?

- **Food Usage Controls** — It is human nature to serve greater portions when there is too much food available. It seems easier to control usage when you have less food available.

- **Turnover** — Your inventory should be turned over every five to eight days. There may be some unusual items that won't be used that quickly, but that time frame should work.

- **Vendors** — All managers need to meet with their vendor sales reps from time to time. Schedule these meetings for a time that suits you. Remember, you're the customer and they need to work with your schedule.

- **Standing Orders** — Many times you can place a "standing order". This is especially true when your sales are consistent. There were times when I had a standing order and made slight adjustments to accommodate special events.

- **Primary Vendor** — You will save additional work if you can use one primary vendor for most of the items you purchase. You will have fewer interruptions, deliveries, orders to place, possibilities of mistakes, invoices to handle, and no sales representatives to bother you. Being a larger customer will help you receive better service.

- **Trade Magazines and Web sites** — You may find rebates from specific manufacturers. You can also check **www.foodbuy.com** for more information.

- **Food Buying Groups** — One of these groups can be found at **www.foodservice.com**. They offer you pre-negotiated prices on over 10,000 food and food-related items from over 125 suppliers. Some of the familiar companies involved include: Ecolab, General Mills, Sara Lee, and Sweetheart.

- **Buying Clubs** — There are many warehouse buying clubs. Some of the most common include Sam's Club, **www.samsclub.com**; Costco, **www.costco.com;** and Restaurant Depot, **www.restaurantdepot.com**.

- **Cash** — Many vendors offer a small discount for early payments usually made within 10 days or by the 10th of the month. Two percent may not seem like much, but if you purchase $500,000 a year, you will save $10,000.

- **Fresh versus Canned** — Take a close look at your recipes and see whether you can use canned fruits and vegetables instead of fresh. If you can make the substitution, you will save money. Remember to remove the word "fresh" from your menu if you used canned items.

These forms shown at the end of this chapter are beneficial if you prepare your order manually. There are several choices to allow you to find the one that works best for your facility.

Establish Specifications

Creating purchasing specifications enables you to control the number and quality of items you purchase and to maintain consistency in the products you order. Consistency makes it easier when more than one person places orders. This is some of the information you need:

- **Purchasing Specifications** — These indicate the amount and quality of the items you purchase. They include:

  o Product name.

  o Quantity to be ordered; establish unit size.

  o "Brand" or "grade" of the item if applicable.

  o Find what unit was used to establish prices.

- **Meats** must be inspected by the USDA or another agency. The federal or state inspection stamp should be on the packaging.

- **Eggs** are assigned a grade by the USDA. If you use frozen or dried eggs, they should be pasteurized.

- The Food and Drug Administration has a list of **Certified Shellfish Shippers** for all your shellfish orders. The supplier must have control tags available for live shellfish.

- **Record Everything** – Your record sheet needs to be available for your employees to enable them to be sure they are ordering the correct items. You can also maintain the correct costs by using a record sheet.

Some people refer to specifications as the "heart of purchasing." When they are written, keep them short and simple. Anyone who reads them needs to be able to understand them. There are three main types of specifications: internal, external, and general.

Internal

Internal menu specifications name the item, provide portion sizes, cooking instructions, a serving image or photo, handling information, and possibly cost information. These specs give employees all the information they need to prepare, cook, and serve a satisfactory menu item.

Most important, they aid in maintaining control over the product.

External

External pertains to the menu items but includes vendor specifics, details that enable the vendor to give accurate quotes on the right products for your facility. It is a good idea to make a permanent record of these item specifications for your vendors. You should not need to repeat these details every time you place an order, because they should be in the vendor's file for your facility. Should any of your specifications change, give the vendor verbal or written notification.

General

General includes delivery and food specifications included in purchasing for your facility such as delivery times, delivery practices and procedures, billing and payment, price quotes, and food specifications—brand, quality, grade, and similar details. Here are just some of the ways that specifications are beneficial:

- Costs are lower.

- Quality is better.

- You have a written record of your orders.

- You save time.

- Verification of orders is simplified.

- You have more control.

- You have more consistent customer satisfaction.

- There should be fewer stock-outs (running out of items between deliveries).

- Trained employees can make decisions about delivery problems.

- You can negotiate for competitive prices and services.

- Misunderstandings between you and your vendors are fewer.

- Purchasing is organized.

Usually managers write these specifications, but it doesn't hurt to get input from others in the facility. The specifications will have an impact on everyone in the department, so ask for their feedback. You never know where a valuable idea will originate.

Other non-commercial food service managers could offer some great insights into which specifications to use. It would be helpful to see their lists, but these should only be used as a guide. Don't just copy them. No two facilities have the same needs, and you need to customize your list to provide the best specifications for your facility.

As you work on the specifications, write down any ideas that come to mind and go back later to fine tune them. Some businesses choose to have an outsider write their specifications, but if you do this, be sure the person has sufficient knowledge of your operation to make the specifications as beneficial as possible. When an outside person or company writes your specifications, they should be reviewed by you or someone else in the facility before they are finalized.

Evaluate and Choose Your Vendors

Your suppliers can make or break you. When you have trustworthy, timely suppliers, you can run a smooth operation and satisfy your customers. The opposite is true with expensive and undependable suppliers. During your research, you may find that some suppliers charge substantially more than others. To select a vendor, consider cost, delivery, problem handling, promptness, quality, selection of products, and other services particular to your facility. There are four basic types of suppliers:

1. Full line suppliers

2. Local specialty wholesaler

3. National jobber

4. Supermarkets

Let's look at the advantages of these types of suppliers to help you determine what kind of suppliers you need.

Full Line Suppliers

Full Line Suppliers are also called one-stop or diversified suppliers. They handle large inventories and can usually supply everything you need. If you can find one supplier for most of your needs, ordering and receiving will be simplified. They may offer fresh vegetables and fruits, frozen food, meat, fish, poultry, paper supplies, equipment, and chemicals, for example. Such a wide selection can save you time, paperwork, and money because one large delivery instead of several smaller orders costs less for delivery.

Local Specialty Wholesalers

Local Specialty Wholesalers are suppliers who carry a limited selection, but their prices are often lower. They may carry only limited selections, but if they carry what you need at a better price, you should consider them a potential supplier.

National Jobbers

National Jobbers would be especially useful for large operations, such as the military, school districts, and other similar operations. Some of these only sell full lot amounts while others sell only broken lots. This is an important thing to know, because you probably won't need full lots.

Supermarkets

Supermarkets are better suited for small operations or the occasions when you run out of food. A small operation might not be able to attract the attention of larger suppliers. In this case the non-commercial food service facility may have to work with local grocery stores. If you have this problem, offer to pick up your orders from a supplier if you have suitable transportation.

When you evaluate suppliers, look for these characteristics: quality service and products and the best price. Each of these elements is important and you should consider each one individually and then make a decision based on all three plus the fact that suppliers offer many services for their customers beyond their products.

When you talk to potential suppliers, one of their most important qualities is dependability including the time they deliver your supplies and the kind of supplies they offer. When your supplier does not have a set delivery time or schedule you will have untold problems and potential dissatisfaction for your customers. Some delivery methods are easier for you to process.

One consideration is the delay between the time you place your order and the time it is delivered to your door. What is their policy on billing and returns? Do they have the ability to provide the supplies you need? Do they have friendly, knowledgeable sales representatives who can answer your questions and make helpful suggestions? Consider which supplier will form a positive long-term relationship with you.

Credit

Not all vendors are willing to extend credit to their accounts, especially new ones. Paying for merchandise later can be risky business for them; therefore, they will require the facility to complete a credit application before they decide whether to extend credit.

This is only one reason that facilities need to create and maintain a good credit rating. A better rating will help you obtain favorable credit terms and have a better overall relationship with your suppliers. When you have a good credit record with the supplier, they are more likely to work with you when money is short and you need to make payment arrangements. Be friendly with the credit managers and keep them informed of any problems or situations that develop. At the end of this chapter is a copy of a sample credit application.

Product Quality

It is important to offer a quality product to increase customer satisfaction—even the best chef cannot make a superior meal using substandard ingredients. When determining the quality and items needed, start by listing the choices of menu items to be prepared such as fresh tomato sauce versus fresh sliced tomatoes. Quality could vary between these two items. In short, you need the right ingredients to make the right menu product.

The rule of thumb is that you don't always go with the lowest price. Instead, consider the quality of the product, the menu item to be prepared, as well as the price. These three factors determine what to purchase.

Price

First-time decision makers may emphasize price and end up spending more money but not getting the best results. When considering price, also consider how many hands these items pass through. When you buy from a retailer, they purchase from a wholesaler, and they purchase from another supplier. By the time it gets to you, several separate businesses have been paid. Can you work with companies that cut out the middle man?

Some facilities have few vendors to choose from because of their location or they must get supplies from a central commissary. In these situations, look at the overall picture and not just the price.

There are some managers who like to visit the supplier's facility to see how they are set up and to inspect cleanliness and sanitation practices. It is good to check whether their trucks are refrigerated and in good working condition. Some may offer service, quality, and good prices, but an unsanitary facility might eliminate them from consideration. After you have made a list of vendors, you can use a Vendor Evaluation Form to determine which would be the best for your facility.

Dealing with Suppliers

The way you deal with suppliers can make a big difference in your job. You want to establish and maintain a good relationship with vendors and sales representatives. Here are some tips:

- **Take the time to get to know the delivery driver and the person who takes your order.** Don't take this person for granted as they play an important role in your success. It's also good to ask for the same person each time to help you establish a good working relationship.

- **Sometimes the vendor may have an overstocked item.** You can help them liquidate the inventory and negotiate a good price for your facility.

- **If you use the same items each week, the vendor might give you a small discount,** but It's not advisable to do this if you will have too much of some things.

- **Does your vendor have a Web site?** It can save you time, and some of these sites even provide industry information that might be helpful. An example would be: **www.sysco.com**.

- **Keep an eye on prices.** Do you take time each month to check on prices with other vendors? When you find someone offering your items at a lower price, you can try to negotiate lower prices with your vendor to save money and show your vendor that you are aware of their competitors' rates.

Purchasing for Health Care

Government agencies have tried for years to regulate food quality. Today food goes through many hands before it reaches us. Some are growers, processors, wholesalers, and distributors. Each of the stops offers the opportunity for mishandling and misrepresentation.

Attempting to control the quality of food in society has been done throughout history. In the 21st century great strides have been made in this area. Urbanization has worked toward better control of food safety and quality since most people don't raise their own food. However, since food goes through so many hands, there's an increased possibility of mishandling, fraud, and misrepresentation.

Science has tried to stay abreast of the use of specific chemicals that increase crop yields, shelf life, and product quality as well as development of various food items. Growers became dependent on the use of chemicals that cause major problems so the government implemented controls to prevent their overuse or misuse to protect consumers and the food industry. The public is aware that basic agricultural food is safe and nutritious. In turn, responsible growers and processors are protected against irresponsible growers who would cut corners and undermine responsible business people. There are number of purposes for the food laws in the United States:

- To monitor nutritional food used.

- To maintain and design proper procedures.

- To protect quality and quantity of basic foods.

- To keep producers, processors, and distributors honest.

- To offer informative and accurate labeling for consumers.

The Changing Face of Distributors

Distributors are expanding the products and services they offer to food service facilities. At one time they offered only food products, but they now offer supplies and equipment, including recycled packaging for the good of the environment. Their additional services may include:

- Computerized services for clients.

- Information about new products, such as nutrition and food costs.

- Instruction, development, merchandising, and marketing services.

- Consultation services regarding design, layout, and equipment.

- Coordinating recycling efforts.

- Discounts for early invoice payment.

- Quantity purchasing discounts.

- Coupons and rebates for their customers.

These are some of the ways today's food service distributors strive to earn your business. Does your sales representative offer these services to you? Today the sales representative must be a consultant, a problem solver—not just an order taker. They must offer additional information about products, packaging, economics, marketing suggestions, inventory control, product, and supply availability along with promotional and recipe ideas for your facility. Efficient sales representatives need thorough and accurate knowledge of your needs and the product lines they represent. These company representatives can be valuable to a food service manager.

Buyer Responsibilities

A buyer's responsibilities in non-commercial food service depend on the size of the facility. While large facilities may have a person dedicated to handling all buying, smaller facilities generally delegate this responsibility to the manager. The food buyer's responsibilities include:

- Evaluating and determining product equipment and service needs.

- Developing or selecting purchasing methods to be used.

- Evaluating and choosing vendors.

- Participating in awarding bids for contracts to vendors.

- Placing orders and following up with vendors or sales representatives.

- Fully training and supervising any staff members involved in receiving, storing, and issuing food and supplies.

- Establishing and maintaining proper, effective inventory control.

- Researching and evaluating new products.

- Establishing and maintaining effective relations with food vendors.

- Weighing cost-benefits of additional services offered by distributors.

- Researching and providing product information including cost and nutritional data in the department.

- Offering ways to track changes in the food market and economic conditions, attending trade and food shows, and staying abreast of trends by reading trade and professional magazines and publications.

- Learning to use technical advances to facilitate food procurement.

- Encouraging and demonstrating ways to keep communication lines open in the department and with others in the institution or facility.

Buyers who submit items for bids should find these forms shown at the end of this chapter helpful. They include the Bid Order Sheet and Bid Sheet to help you keep the specifics for each vendor organized to make an accurate decision.

The Bidding Process

1. **New Products** — Identify any new products needed. All new product sales visits should be handled by the person or department who handles purchasing. Depending on the size of the facility, this person could be the food service manager or someone who handles food service purchasing. For example, a sales representative couldn't expect to walk into a military dining room and find someone behind the counter to make a decision on a new food item.

2. **Specifications** — Be specific about the amount, size, quantity, and quality that you need. Include all of the necessary information in your specifications.

3. **Usage Levels** — How much of each item will you need? This is critical when negotiating prices. Don't inflate your numbers, but give all details.

4. **Vendor List** — The food service manager and purchasing person need to compile a list of the vendors who will be asked to place a bid.

5. **Bid Documentation and Distribution** — This documentation needs to be distributed in packets to all vendors who will bid. Include instructions, the deadline, and criteria to be used to award the bid and how questions will be handled. Include instructions about whom to contact and how questions should be submitted (in writing, by fax, or e-mail).

6. **Receiving Completed Bids** — Only the purchasing person or department should receive bids. Make that clear on the bid instructions.

7. **Analysis of Bids** — First, determine which bidders followed instructions. Eliminate any that did not. All suggested substitutions must be evaluated to determine if they are appropriate or if they should be approved. If items are not acceptable, the bidder must be eliminated.

8. **Awarding the Bids** — Purchasing recommends the winning bidder, but food service must review the recommendations. Objections and concerns need to be reviewed and handled. The actual decision to award the bid is handled by the administrators who sign contracts.

9. **Notify Vendors** — Purchasing is responsible for notifying winners and losers. Food service staff members are not to answer questions about the decisions that were made. Purchasing handles all inquiries.

10. **Verify Pricing** — Food service verifies that the items being delivered are in compliance with the bid details and needs to notify purchasing when there are discrepancies. Purchasing will take action on this information.

11. **Contract Dissolution** — If the vendor is unable or unwilling to provide items in compliance with the winning bid, the contract may be dissolved. The final decision is made by administration based on recommendations from the purchasing, food service, and legal departments.

Buyer Qualifications

Buyer qualifications include the following: food quality, background, product specifications, computer skills, marketing and distribution experience, accounting, business management, purchasing experience, soliciting and awarding bids, and contracts. A good buyer will also have personal attributes that serve them well in the non-commercial food service industry. An organized mind that pays attention to detail and accuracy is a must. New buyers and leaders who have a team mind-set along with initiatives and good communication skills can be valuable in food service.

Good buyers keep an eye open at all times for ways to improve the department. This requires initiative and creativity along with the ability to develop and execute responsibilities. An effective manager must control costs while maintaining other food service responsibilities.

Each of these abilities enables the manager and buyer to control costs and eliminate waste. Keep in mind that you should always be on the watch for better products, equipment, and ways to provide better services for your customers while working within the financial constraints of the facility.

Alternative Purchasing Systems

If no one in the food service facility has the experience to handle purchasing, you may want to use an "indirect purchasing program." There are three main types of indirect purchasing programs:

1. **Programs that guarantee pricing, specific products, brands, and grades.** Delivery, payment arrangements, and problems are handled by the institution. Some purchasing

departments handle negotiations and most purchasing for every department in the institution.

2. **Program with guaranteed pricing and some management service** to include educational services, additional product knowledge, workshops and training for managers, marketing ideas, and assistance.

3. **Some other programs offer services for the manager**, but no guaranteed prices.

Would one of these services work for your facility? Determining which program would be most beneficial depends on the qualifications your staff members have and what additional services are needed. Each of these programs will cost the institution so you must decide whether the savings outweigh the costs incurred. If not, you can obtain additional training for personnel or hire someone with the proper skills.

Purchasing Kickbacks and Gifts

Some areas of the food service industry are well known for kickbacks. One of the downsides is that people who are not involved end up paying for these kickbacks with higher prices. Below are a few tips to keep kickbacks out of your facility.

- **Purchasing and receiving should be handled by two different people to keep both people honest.** One person places the order and another verifies that correct supplies were received.

- **Have a standard policy in your employee handbook stating that no employee can receive a kickback from a vendor or a potential vendor.** Also state the action to be taken if someone does receive a kickback.

- **You may need to have employees change jobs from time to time.** If you notice problems, this can be a simple way to make people less complacent.

- **Verify prices for expensive items yourself.** Anything out of the ordinary can be checked for your peace of mind. It doesn't hurt to let your team members know that you double check invoices and their work. They are accountable to do their jobs, and you are responsible for the facility.

School Food Purchasing

All school food service managers should be familiar with five documents related to school system food service purchasing. These are available free or for a minimal charge from the State Child Nutrition Supervisor. They are: *Food Buying Guide for School Food Service, Purchasing, Volume One, Catalog to Specifications, Purchasing, Volume Two, Contract Purchasing,* and *Storage and Care.* The last two can be obtained from the USDA, Food Distribution Service, Food Safety and Quality Service (FSQS), USDA, Washington, D.C., 20250.

Procurement standards for purchasing any supplies necessary for the child nutrition program were established by the Office of Management and Budget in 1979. Guidelines were established for every School Food Authority. This pertains to any officers, employees, or agents who are involved with contracts in the food service program. This simply means none of these individuals can accept gratuities, favors, or anything of value from vendors or potential bidders. The code of conduct includes penalties, sanctions, and disciplinary action for people who violate the code.

Food service authorities developed procedures based on the standards to guarantee vendors' compliance. Open and free competition between vendors is encouraged in this program, and unnecessary or duplicate items should not be ordered by the school food service authorities.

Any invitations to bid must be based on accurate descriptions of material, product, or service to be provided. It is the responsibility of the school food authority to work with small businesses and minority businesses whenever possible.

School Food Dollar Allocation

This is a sample from one large school district to give you an idea of the percentage of each food purchased.

Buying Through Bids

If your school facility is cooling to the end-of-the-year bidding process, you may want to bid a few items at a time. If getting these items is successful, more could be added.

It's helpful to use specifications developed by the federal government when you work on the specifications. Here are a couple of reasons that this is helpful: they are widely used and well known, and they provide adequate description of products to avoid confusion.

Earlier, we discussed the idea behind cooperative buying, which can also work for school systems. In Michigan, Montana, and Colorado some school districts have saved as much as 40 percent by using cooperative buying. The school district where you work could begin this program by buying a few items and increasing purchases if the system saves money.

Brands and Quality

Various well-known brands have first, second, and third quality products identified on their labels.

A few additional notes to accompany the charts above:

- **First quality** — Grade A for canned and frozen vegetables and frozen fruits; Grade B for canned fruits except when Grade B fruits are packaged with a conditional quality label.

- **Frosty Acres French Fries** — package color indicates length of potato. Red = extra long, Brown = long, Blue = various lengths.

- **North American Buying Group** — Their "house" brand uses different colors and codes although they use the same quality standards.

- **Sysco** — the labeling system has been changed. Supreme Gold = rare items; Imperial Blue = fancy vegetables and choice fruits from prime growing areas; Classic Green = fancy vegetables and choice fruits from non-prime growing areas.

- **NIFDA** — Prime Pak = fancy vegetables and choice fruits from prime growing regions; Royal Pak = fancy vegetables and choice fruits from any region; Dandy Pak = fancy vegetables and choice fruits that meet the USDA standards.

Purchasing is a critical element in any food service organization, but effective, thorough receiving is also important.

CASE STUDY: ASSISTED LIVING INVENTORY, PURCHASING, AND RECEIVING

Assisted Living Inventory, Purchasing, and Receiving are handled with the newest computer software available to health care, university, and institutional food service: CBORD located in Ithaca, NY. Inventory is (physically) taken every Monday. Entries are coded into a handheld computer and then downloaded into the entire system. Pricing info is done online from our prime vendor.

Ordering templates were developed for each menu week and entered into the program. Based on inventory, par levels, usage, and need, orders automatically generate and go electronically to the vendor. We have the ability to check, add, and override all orders. Goods received are checked in by office staff and put away by a stockroom employee. We use computer generated requisition and issues sheets to transfer stock to other kitchens and to nursing pantries.

Kathy L. Hilbert, Director of Dining Services • Bridgewater Retirement Community

| FOOD CATEGORY: | | PURVEYOR: | | | |

ITEM & DESCRIPTION	LOW-LEVEL PAR	DELIVERY DATES				

PAR AMOUNT REQUISITION

Date: _____   Req. #: _____

Time: _____   Department: _____

Prepared By: _____   Priced By: _____

Delivered By: _____   Received By: _____

Approved By: _____

Item Description	Par	On Hand	Order	Price		Extension	

Total $

WEEK OF:

PREPARED BY:

VENDOR	ITEM	UNIT	Sunday			Monday			Tuesday			Wednesday			Thursday			Friday			Saturday		
			PAR	INV	BUY	PAR	INV	BUY	PAR	INV	BUY	PAR	INV	BUY	PAR	INV	BUY	PAR	INV	BUY	PAR	INV	BUY

MISCELLANEOUS ORDER SHEET

DELIVERY DATE:	PURVEYOR:	PHONE #

PRODUCT #	ORDER	ITEM & DESCRIPTION

COMPANY INFORMATION

PURCHASE ORDER NUMBER

Company Name: _____

Address: _____

_____

_____

Phone: _____

Fax:_____

Date Issued: _____

Issued By: _____

SUPPLIER INFORMATION

Company Name: _____

Contact/Representative: _____

Address: _____

_____

_____

Phone: _____

Fax:_____

Required Delivery Date: _____

Terms: _____

_____

Freight Charges: ❏ Collect $_____   ❏ FOB   ❏ Pre-paid

ITEMS

ITEM DESCRIPTION	QUANTITY	UNIT	UNIT COST	EXTENSION

TOTAL $

SIGNATURE OF AUTHORIZATION:

Company A: _____

Company B: _____

Company C: _____

PURCHASE ORDER #

Order Date: _____

Delivery Date: _____

ITEM	QTY	COMPARE QUOTES			ITEM COST	ITEM TOTAL
		VENDOR A	VENDOR B	VENDOR C		

SPECIAL INSTRUCTIONS:

SUBTOTAL: _____

SHIPPING: _____

TAX: _____

TOTAL: _____

NAME: SIGNATURE OF AUTHORIZATION:

Vendor name: _____

Contact/Representative: _____

Address: _____

_____

_____

Phone: _____

Fax:_____

Required delivery date: _____

Ordered by: _____

Order date: _____

Ship to: _____

_____

_____

Delivery instructions: _____

_____

_____

	ITEM PURCHASED	SPEC #	QTY ORDERED	QUOTED PRICE	EXT PRICE
1					
2					
3					
4					
5					
6					
7					
8					
9					
10					
11					
12					
13					
14					
15					

COMMENTS:

TOTAL $

VENDOR EVALUATION FORM

Vendor:_____ Date:_____

Rate Scale: Excellent = 2, Satisfactory = 1, Poor = 0

Criterion		Rate Score
Product	Quality	
	Consistency	
	Price	
	Availability	
Service	Timely delivery	
	Delivery frequency	
	Condition of product upon delivery	
	Delivery accuracy	
	Complaint handling	
	Delivery personnel courtesy	
	Emergency deliveries	
Company	Size	
	Product selection	
	Financial stability	
	Location	
	Service orientation	
	Management policies	
	Invoicing accuracy	
	Credits/invoice adjustments handled in timely manner	
Sales Personnel	Knowledge of company policies and procedures	
	Product line knowledge	
	Interest in needs of operation	
	Willingness to provide information about products	
	Price quotes provided in an accurate and timely manner	
	Makes sales calls as frequently as needed by operation	
	Schedules sales calls	
	Complaints handled promptly	
	Total	

Name of Dietary Operation

Product Name	
Product Use	Indicate product use clearly (such as pickle for garnish, chicken breast for deep-frying for fried chicken sandwich, etc.)
Product General Description	Provide general quality information about desired product. For example, pickle spears; to be juicy, firm, fresh, and crisp, not broken or spoiled. No more than 20 per jar; packed 10 jars per case.
Detailed Description	Purchaser should state additional factors that clearly identify the desired product. Examples of specific factors, which will vary, include: • Geographic origin • Grade • Size • Type • Density • Medium of pack • Style • Specific gravity • Brand Name • Variety • Container Size • Edible yield, trim • Portion size
Product Test Procedures	Test procedures occur when the product is received and as or after the product is prepared and used. For example, products to be at a specific temperature when delivered can be tested with a thermometer. Portion-cut chicken patties can be weighed. Pickles packed 10 jars per case can be counted.
Special Instructions and Requirements	Any other information needed to better indicate quality expectations can be added here. Examples include bidding procedures, if applicable, labeling and/or packaging requirements, and delivery and service requirements.
	Specification factors can include:
Meats	• Inspection (mandatory) • Fat limitations • Grading (if desired) • State of refrigeration • IMPS/MBG descriptions • Miscellaneous (tying, • Weight/thickness limitations boning, packaging, etc.)

Seafoods	• Type (fin fish or shellfish) • Quality requirements
	• Market form (whole, describe flesh, eyes, skin
	  eviscerated, etc.—fin fish; gills, etc.)
	  alive, whole, shucked, etc.— • Grade (if desired)
	  shellfish) • Inspection (voluntary)
	  • Processing requirements

Poultry	• Kind (chicken, turkey, • Style (whole, breasts, duck, goose) breasts w/ribs, etc.) • Class (typed by age) • Size (weight limitations) • Grading • State of refrigeration • Inspection (mandatory) • Grade (if desired)
Fresh Fruits and Vegetables	• Grade (if desired) • Type of pack • Variety • Count per container • Size • Growing area
Processed Fruits and Vegetables	• Grade (if desired) • Packing medium • Drained weight • Can (container) size

SAMPLE—CREDIT APPLICATION

Account No._____ Sales Representative _____ Terms Requested_____

Tax Certificate No._____

Ship To._____ Bill To._____

Corporate Name _____ Corporate Name _____

(dba) Trade Name _____ (dba) Trade Name _____

Address _____ Address _____

City, State, Zip   Phone   City, State, Zip   Phone

❏ Proprietorship   Length of time at present location_____years.

❏ Corporation   Contact:

❏ Partnership   _____ _____
                        Name   Title

Does operator own premises? ❏ Yes   ❏ No   List any existing accounts under another name:
Name, Address and Phone No.
  of Mortgagor: _____

_____   Name _____

_____   Account No. _____

_____

If Leasing: Name and Address
  of Lessor: Is your Company responsible for purchases?_____
                                               Or is food service consigned to another?_____
_____   Name of food service consignees:
_____
_____   _____

Bank Information

Bank Name _____

Address _____

City, State, Zip _____

Account No _____

List all corporate officers, partners, or an individual proprietor.

Name and Title _____ Name and Title _____

Home Address _____ Home Address _____

City, State, Zip   Phone   City, State, Zip   Phone

Social Security No. _____ Social Security No. _____

Name and Title _____ Name and Title _____

Home Address _____ Home Address _____

City, State, Zip   Phone   City, State, Zip   Phone

Social Security No. _____ Social Security No. _____

BID SHEET

Ordered By: _____ Date: _____

ITEM	Quantity	VENDORS (fill in names below)		

BID ORDER SHEET

Ordered By: _____

Date Ordered: _____ Delivery Date: _____

Vendors A: _____

Vendors B: _____

Vendors C: _____

ITEM	Quantity	VENDOR A		VENDOR B		VENDOR C	
		Unit	Total	Unit	Total	Unit	Total
Individual Invoice Total:							

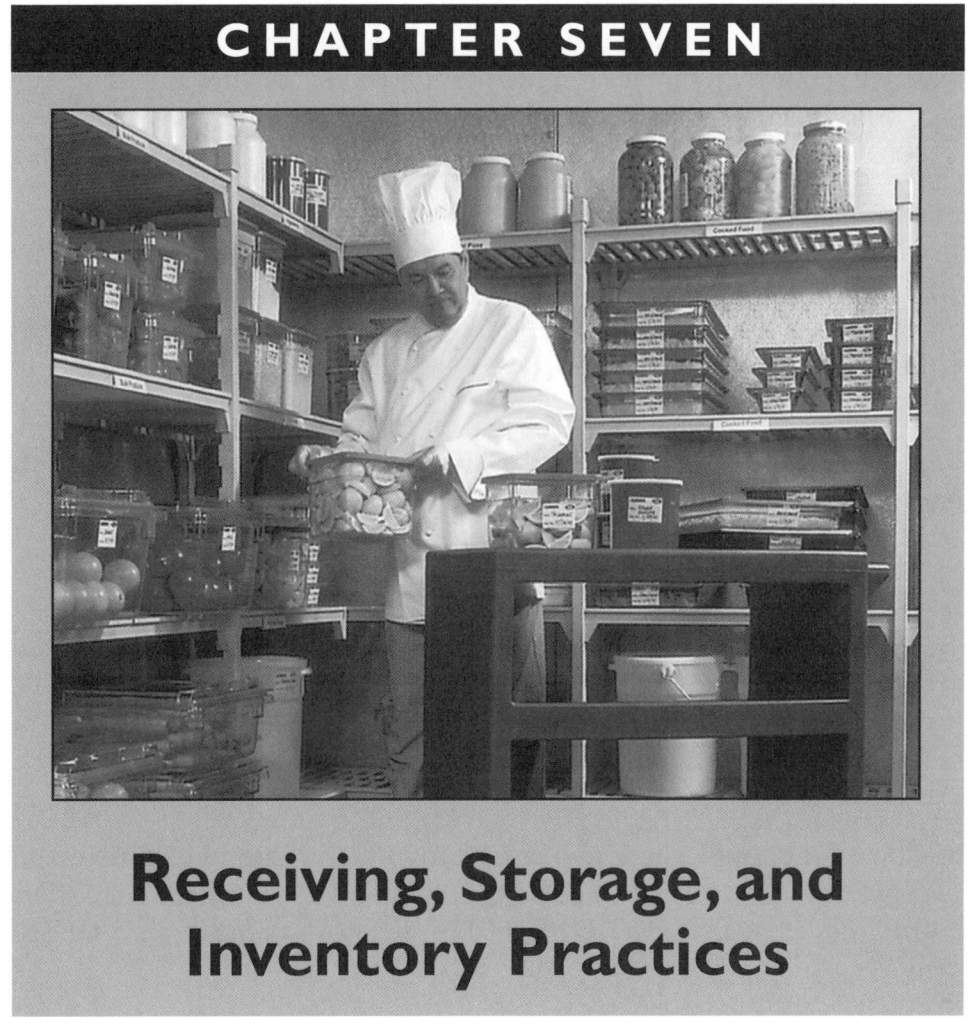

CHAPTER SEVEN

Receiving, Storage, and Inventory Practices

Receiving

Receiving means checking your purchases to ensure the correct items have been sent. The task of receiving orders can be delegated by the manager to a staff member. Even if you have a competent and well-trained staff member to receive your items, a supervisor needs to oversee the task because of quality and financial control issues. Also be aware that fewer deliveries help to control labor costs.

At the end of this chapter is a simple flow chart showing how the receiving process works.

Specific information must be checked when items are noted as received into your inventory. Receipt practices should be kept simple while still maintaining complete records and account-ability for your vendors. Keep in mind that after your delivery is received into your inventory, you become responsible for these items.

We will discuss employee scheduling in a later chapter, but remember that it is important to schedule all receiving personnel during deliveries. Basic equipment needs to be close at hand when deliveries are received, including scales, thermometers, dollies, conveyor belts, lift trucks or pallet jacks, and a laser gun scanner if you scan your PC labels.

Do you have a designated receiving clerk for your facility? This person could work part-time, or the duties could be taken on by another employee. When designating your receiving person, it is better to have another person serve as the storage and receiving clerk. It is helpful to have double checks in these areas and to involve different people in various stages of the process. For optimum benefit, your receiving person should not even move items to storage but should verify the items, quantities, quality, and that the proper items were ordered and received.

Your receiving person should be intelligent, alert, and capable of checking the quantity and quality by doing necessary calculations and compiling reports. The person must understand the importance of doing the job properly. If you determine your assigned person cannot handle the job properly, it needs to be assigned to another person right away. The receiver also needs to handle deliveries quickly while maintaining control over each step of the process. The delivery driver is on a tight schedule, and delays in receiving can cause problems for the driver and your vendor.

There is a wide variety of receiving checklists and reports which would be helpful for your receiving person. Some of these are shown at the end of this chapter.

Effective Receiving

As soon as the items are received, they need to be transferred to the proper storage facilities. There are three important elements of receiving: preparing to receive your order, inspecting the food when it arrives, then verifying that you received everything you ordered. Your receiving person needs to be sure you are not being overcharged and that you are getting consistent quality. Here are some tips:

- **Your bookkeeper should never pay for an invoice not signed by an employee.** If no one feels confident signing for the delivery, you should not pay the bill. The bookkeeper should watch for unsigned invoices each day, giving you a chance to question on-duty staff members while the details are still fresh in their minds.

- **All employees need to understand they are responsible for any items on that invoice once they sign the paperwork.** If you discover a shortage in any of the delivered items, the employee who signed the invoice must explain the discrepancy.

- **Put the items away at once.** The longer the items are left out, the more chance of losing something or having it spoil. Try to schedule deliveries at a time when employees are available to receive the order and move it into storage.

- **The delivery person must sign for any missing or damaged items before he or she leaves your facility.** You will find it much harder to get credit if you contact someone later. Handle these problems immediately.

Receiving and Storing Supplies

Usually your deliveries will arrive during the work day at times that you have designated, usually after lunch and before dinner. The manager or an assistant manager should be responsible to receive and store your orders. When another person places the order, they should verify the right items were delivered.

Proper receiving and storage are critical. Anyone involved with these practices must be thoroughly trained because any mistakes can be costly. These are the steps to process your orders:

1. **Double check** the delivery against the original order sheet.

2. **Verify** the quantity that was received.

3. **Check** the invoice to be sure the order you placed matches the items you received.

4. **Verify** the prices, totals, date, company name, and signatures on the invoice.

5. **Weigh** any items to confirm your order is correct.

6. **When food items are received,** date the containers, put the new items in back of older items, and store in the correct place right away.

7. **Mark any discrepancies on the invoice.** Call or fax to inform the vendor immediately of any overage or shortage. If the order was COD (cash on delivery), you need to take into account mistakes in your order before paying.

Many facilities have a box in the kitchen where all invoices and packing slips are placed during the day. At the end of the shift these are taken to the manager's office and filed in the designated place. Remember that any missing or incomplete invoices will make the bookkeeper's job difficult.

You can implement a receiving policy. It is easy to misplace products in the facility if no one is assigned to check in the orders. This sometimes occurs when someone moves things aside, and then the items cannot be located when someone has time to check the order. In the meantime, refrigerated or frozen food may be going bad. If they are not put into cold storage in a prompt manner, they could be unsafe, a waste of money, not to mention running short on these items before the next delivery.

Receiving Tips

Here are important guidelines to follow as you prepare to receive your order.

- Calibrate your scales and thermometers and store them in the right places. Large scales should be near your delivery entrance. Smaller scales are placed in the work areas. Each cold or heated storage area should have thermometers. A large walk-in freezer should have more than one thermometer to ensure consistent temperatures.

- Any carts you use to move food items should be sanitary.

- Clear sufficient storage area in the refrigerator and freezer before the order arrives.

- All items need to be dated when they are received.

- The receiving and delivery area should be clean and well lighted.

- As the order is moved to storage facilities, clear all empty containers and dispose of trash as soon as possible.

- The floor needs to be cleared of food particles and debris.

- Make it clear to the delivery personnel that you will verify your order before he or she leaves your facility.

- Do a quick inspection of the delivery truck when it arrives. If you see conditions that concern you, take time to look closer.

- Check the food immediately.

- Verify expiration dates for all perishable items. It is advisable to be sure they haven't expired.

- All frozen foods must be airtight, moisture-proof containers, and if they are not, check them immediately and make a note for the vendor.

- Any thawed or refrozen foods must be rejected. Signs to look for are large crystals, solid areas of ice, or excessive ice on or in containers.

- Any swollen cans or cans that have flawed seals and seams, dents, or rust should be rejected right away.

- Verify the temperature of any refrigerated or frozen foods—especially critical with eggs, dairy products, fresh meat, fish, and poultry.

- Keep your eyes open for damage or pest infestations.

- All dairy products delivered in dirty flats or crates need to be rejected.

- Meat, fish, and items shipped by the pound need to be weighed and marked. Ensure all items are counted, weighed, and date stamped. This is not a suggestion; it's a necessity. **Do not skip this step.**

- Double check your invoice for accuracy, including price, damage, brands, grades, quality, and quantity. When items are incorrect, you need to make a notation and return these items to the driver. It is important that the driver sign the invoice to reflect any returns or corrections.

- Delivery people should not enter storage areas.

- Remove any frozen items from ice before weighing them.

- Check fish and poultry for ice.

- Items can be placed on the shelves in the order they are inventoried, making inventory easier.

- Not all employees need access to your storage areas, especially critical with new employees.

- Clear trash bags can be used as a way to discourage theft.

- The delivery entrance should be locked and well lighted. It is also good to have an alarm on that door. A small peep hole is advisable to allow the employee who is receiving your delivery verify who is outside before opening the door.

- Keep storage specifications in a handy place for your employees.

- Note correct storage temperatures in convenient places.

- Are your staff members trained in your stock rotation policies?

- Any items that have questionable expiration dates should be refused or sent back on the truck. (I didn't do this on an order of pizza dough which was only a couple of days from expiration and it cost me a gold inspection award and a bonus. I learned that lesson the hard way.)

- Calibrate your scales regularly to make sure they are accurate. This should be done once a week and more often if needed.

- Are your scales adequate to weigh the items being shipped? If not, you should consider buying bigger scales. You can visit Scale World at **www.scaleworld.com** or Scale man at **www.scaleman.com.**

In Chapter 2 we discussed how important invoices are in accounting procedures for the facility. Invoices are also an important part of the receiving process. The invoice will include company name and address, quantity to be delivered, quality of product to be delivered, price of each item, total price of each item shipped, and total for each invoice.

Your invoice is a written confirmation of what you ordered and what was shipped. The person who receives the order is responsible to confirm that your facility actually received all items listed on your invoice. The documentation should also show any back order, out of stock, or cancelled items. These items should be noted on the invoice, and any discrepancies in your order should be mentioned to the driver immediately. The receiving person and driver should both sign and acknowledge any problems with the order. You can also use a discrepancy report or slip that may also be called the credit memo or a credit slip. Include all information identifying the problems in your deliveries. Examples are shown at the end of this chapter. Your facility may also use a variety of general receiving reports.

When you discover shortages on your order, complete a credit memo. Two examples are shown at the end of this chapter.

Receiving Procedures

All your orders may not be received the same way. Here are some examples of different ways to receive products. The method that is right for someone else might not be right for your facility. You can gather thoughts from other non-commercial food service managers, but make your decision based on the needs of your facility and staff.

Certified or Accepted Buying

Government agencies, large companies, or public schools may use certified or accepted buying. With this method, items are certified by an outside agent to guarantee quality and quantity. With accepted buying, federal inspectors have copies of your buying specifications and verify these requirements are met. After items are inspected, packages will be sealed and stamped to indicate approval. Keep in mind there is a cost involved for these inspections to be paid by either the buyer or the seller. You need to know these details before deciding to use this method.

Blind Receiving

Some invoices are printed with the prices and quantity on black areas so they cannot be read by the receiver. When this happens each item must be checked for count, weight, or other measuring unit. These amounts are recorded on the invoice and receiving sheet. Prices are blanked out to keep them confidential.

No Inspection

In some situations the buyer and seller may agree not to inspect the quality or quantity when items are delivered. With this method the items are delivered, the invoices are signed, and the driver leaves. This is normally used only when there is strong trust between the buyer and seller. It is advantageous to the seller and expedites faster delivery service. It could also be beneficial to the buyer since the items can be inspected later in a more accurate manner. However, when this method is used the seller agrees to accept any problems the buyer finds without question.

Night Drop Deliveries

Some vendors find it necessary to have their delivery trucks arrive during hours when your facility is not open. Night deliveries can be done quickly with less traffic on the roads, reducing labor costs. In this instance the delivery person may have a key to get into your facility and will leave the items. Obviously, this method requires strong trust between the vendor and the facility. When deliveries are made overnight or after hours, they are received and verified the following morning. Night deliveries require that refrigerated or frozen items be left in your freezer. Whenever this is done, it's a good idea to arrive early to verify the delivery before starting the day's task.

Back Orders

Your invoice may indicate that an item is no longer available or is back ordered. These discrepancies need to be noted on the invoice which is attached to discrepancy reports to ensure proper credit for missing items.

After reports are properly received, the delivery area needs to be cleaned. In some instances the receiving area may need to be hosed down or swept. All delivery debris and trash should be disposed of. Each invoice should be placed in the assigned area of the kitchen or taken to the accounting office after all notations are complete. The bookkeeper's responsibilities pertaining to delivery, invoices, and additional documentation were discussed in Chapter 2.

Food Storage

There are several goals when storing food. These include maintaining safety and responsibility for quality of the product. Any food or supply items in storage should be removed by authorized personnel. Securely organizing storage can discourage employee theft. When you enact controls over items, an effective manager can quickly detect theft.

We've already discussed how purchasing is affected by your inventory. The methods used to store your products have a bearing on your inventory practices and effectiveness. A disorganized storage area can make an accurate inventory nearly impossible. The other factor is maintaining the quality of your products while they are in storage.

Types of Storage

There are four ways to store food safely. Dry storage is used for holding less perishable items liked canned goods. Refrigeration is short-term storage for perishable items like eggs, cheese, and milk. Deep chilling is for short-term storage. Freezers are used for long-term storage of perishable foods. There are specific safety and sanitation requirements for each type of storage.

Dry Storage

Many items can be stored in a sanitary storeroom. Dry storage areas must be kept clean and pest-free to avoid sanitary and safety concerns. Some of the items you can store there include baking supplies (salt, sugar, flour), canned goods, and grain items (rice or cereal).

Some fruits should be ripened at room temperature such as bananas, pears, and avocados. Vegetables such as onions, potatoes, and tomatoes should be stored in a dry place that is kept clean and organized. Ventilation, temperature, and humidity control are important in limiting mold and bacteria. Here are some tips to remember:

- **Chemical Contamination** — Cleaning supplies and chemicals should be stored in a separate room from food to avoid accidental contamination. Store all chemicals in a safe container that is labeled to avoid confusion.

- **Common storage** — This area is set aside for flour, sugar, canned items, shortening, and oils.

- **First In, First Out** — A simple way to ensure the freshness of your products is to use the first in, first out method. In the last chapter we discussed dating each product when it is received. When you store your food items, new items need to be placed behind older ones, making it easy to use the older items first and minimizing the chances of rotten food.

- **High Temperatures** — If the temperature in your storage area reaches 100°F, storage life of these items is cut in half.

- **Pest Control** — When you clean up all messes promptly, you can avoid pest infestations and contamination. Trash cans and other garbage should never be stored in food storage areas of the facility. There needs to be a separate area, preferably outside.

- **Raised Storage** — Supplies should never be stored on the floor including paper products. Your bottom shelf needs to be at least six inches off the floor.

- **Temperature** — Maximum shelf life requires 50°F, but 60°F to 70°F is sufficient for most items.

- **Thermometers** — A wall thermometer will help you check the temperature to ensure the safest conditions. Atlantic Publishing at **www.atlantic-pub.com** offers a ThermaTwin Thermometer (Item TTT-03) and the Hanging Thermometer for your refrigerator or freezer (Item HTM-04).

Refrigerated Storage

Commercial refrigerators and walk-in units are usually equipped with mounted or built-in thermometers to let you see the interior temperature from outside the unit. Never trust just one thermometer. Keep at least one free standing thermometer inside the unit and two in a larger unit. If you have more than one, they need to be placed in different areas of the refrigerator to assure you that the unit is working properly and that the food is kept at the right temperature. Record the temperature each day on a chart kept on the outside of the unit. Keep these facts in mind:

- **Circulation** — Keep a reasonable space between items in your refrigeration unit to allow air to circulate and keep foods uniformly cool.

- **Colder the better** — Cooler temperatures will slow bacterial growth.

- **Containers** — All containers need to be clean, non-absorbent, and covered.

- **Cross contamination** — Raw foods need to be separated from cooked and prepared foods.

- **Dates** — All items need to be dated and sealed properly.

- **Dairy products** — These foods must be stored away from food with strong odors such as onions, cabbage, and seafood.

- **Fresh items** — Fresh meat, poultry, dairy products, seafood, fruits and vegetables, and hot leftovers need to be stored below 40°F.

- **Fresh fruits and vegetables** — Fresh vegetables should not be packed when they are put in storage. They need oxygen or they will turn dark and rot. Humidity around 75 percent to 85 percent is recommended to prevent dehydration. Some facilities moisten the items with a hose to keep them cool and moist. Be careful with this practice because some vegetables get too wet and rot. There is also the concern about a wet, slippery floor. It is a good practice to keep a close eye on fresh fruits and especially berries since they last only a few days.

- **Perishable items** — Perishable items must be kept below 40°F to prevent food-borne illnesses. It's also important to remember that opening and closing the refrigerator door often can change your temperature so these items should be stored inside away from the door.

- **Raw Meats** — Fluids from raw meat, fish, and poultry must not touch other foods.

- **Ready to Eat** — Store these items above raw foods—never below.

- **Root Cellar Storage** — Some root vegetables can be stored in humidity below 60 percent to 70 percent. Items like potatoes need to be kept below 60°F. Circulation is important for these items also but sacks of potatoes can be stacked.

- **Shelves** — Refrigeration units need open slotted shelves to allow cool circulation around the food. Shelves should not be lined with foil or paper.

- **Stock Tags** — Fresh shellfish will arrive with a stocking tag. Keep this information on file for at least 90 days.

U.S. Cooler manufactures premium walk-in coolers, freezers, and combination units are available at competitive prices. They are used for all types of cold storage. They also offer separate shelving, great for your walk-in freezer or storage room. Many accessories are available. For more information visit **www.uscooler.com** or call 800-521-2665.

Required Refrigerator Space — Your refrigerator space can be loosely determined by the number of meals you serve each day not counting beverages or frozen food.

Meals Served Daily	Recommended Capacity
75-150	20 Cubic Feet
150-250	45 Cubic Feet
250-350	60 Cubic Feet
350-500	90 Cubic Feet

If you will be serving more than 350 meals a day, it would be best to have a walk-in cooler. It is also advisable to have a reach-in refrigerator for small, frequently used items. Note that these capacity suggestions are minimums.

Deep Chilling

Temperatures between 26°F and 32°F are considered to be deep chilling. These temperatures have been found to decrease bacterial growth and extend shelf life of some fresh foods, such as meat, poultry, seafood, and other protein products. Lower temperatures will not compromise their quality. You can use a special unit or lower your refrigerator temperature for this storage.

Frozen Storage

Frozen meat, poultry, seafood, fruits, vegetables, and certain dairy items (ice cream) should be stored at 0°F. The lower temperature will keep items fresher and maintain flavor and texture for a longer period. It is best to store foods to be frozen as soon as they arrive. Freezing perishable foods that have been refrigerated can diminish their quality.

Frozen foods should be put in the freezer immediately upon arrival at your facility. They can only be stored in a freezer for a limited time. When left in the freezer for too long, the chance of contamination and spoilage increases. When you store food in a freezer, you need to allow room for air to circulate around it. Follow these tips:

- **Cold Loss** — Freezer doors should be opened only when necessary; otherwise, the temperature will drop. A "cold curtain" seems like a nuisance, but it will help keep the temperature colder.

- **Moisture-Proof Containers** — Frozen foods need to be stored in moisture-proof containers to keep food from losing flavor and color and to avoid their drying out and absorbing odors from nearby foods.

- **Monitor Temperature** — Earlier we discussed checking on the temperature in your refrigerator. This also applies to freezers. Record the temperature each day and use more than one thermometer for a large freezer. Keep in mind that moving warm foods to the freezer will temporarily raise the temperature in the freezer unit.

- **Frozen Food Storage Periods** — Here are some criteria for the length of time that some items can be frozen.

Sausage, ground meat, and fish	1 – 3 months
Fresh pork (not ground)	3 – 6 months

Lamb and veal	6 – 9 months
Beef, poultry, and eggs	6 – 12 months
Fruits and vegetables	One growing season to the next.

If you store items for too long, quality, flavor, and texture are lost.

Cleaning Products

Government requirements state that cleaning items and any hazardous materials must be stored separately from food items. Hazardous materials include poisons, pesticides, bleach, and strong chemicals. You may choose to store these items in a locked cabinet or in a separate section of your storeroom.

All chemicals need to be labeled properly. When a chemical is removed from its original container it must have a label and be stored in an appropriate container. Glass is usually your best option as many chemicals will eat through plastic. The label should include the chemical name and any mixing instructions, along with safety and emergency information. You may choose a storage area with hot and cold running water to mix the chemicals or for easy clean up.

Organize Your Storage Areas

Each storage area needs to be organized with a place for each item. All items used often that move quickly should be placed near the door. If it is feasible, the door should be locked. You may consider having a separate unit to store more expensive items like cooking wine or exotic mushrooms, for example. Here are some organizational tips:

- **Aisles** — Each aisle in your storage areas needs to allow easy access and to the items.

- **Five Gallon Bucket** — Dry goods like flour and sugar might be shipped in five-gallon buckets—wonderful storage containers that can be reused as they are designed for the best possible food protection. When they are empty, clean and re-label them, avoiding scraping the inside as bacteria will collect in the nicks.

- **Ice** — Some containers are specially designed for ice to avoid the risk of cross contamination if you aren't careful. Saf-T-Ice Totes are a great way to handle this safety concern. They a offer a stainless steel bucket which makes carrying and emptying easy, they meet Health Department standards, and they can be cleaned in the dishwasher. Saf-T-Ice Totes (Item # SI-6000, $79.95 for two) are available from Atlantic Publishing at **www.atlantic-pub.com** or by calling 800-814-1132.

- **Labels** — Each shelf should be labeled, making identification easier as well as leaving an obvious empty space for used-up or missing items.

- **Shelving** — It seems natural to stack items, but doing so makes it more difficult to clean and find things. The best shelving units give you the option of adjusting the shelf height to save wasted space and make it simpler to find items you need.

- **Space** — Leave enough space for the quantity of the item that you plan to stock. This should be keyed to the maximum amount you will order.

- **Stacking** – If you stack containers on top of each other, spills, breakage, and accidents are more likely. When you must stack containers, stack them in a way to make them easier to handle.

Storage Spoilage Prevention

Thorough records of all food spoilage are a must and include date of spoilage, item description, and the reason for disposing of it. Make a note about whether too much was ordered, there were equipment, cooling, or other storage problems. The information makes inventory adjustments easier.

At the correct temperatures, spices and sauces, for example, can be stored for a long time. Keep in mind the ingredients are in these sauces. If there is an ingredient that spoils easily, you can divide the sauces into small containers and freeze. When you need to use the items, defrost and serve. This saves you time and money and each batch will taste the same.

Color codes, labels, and dates need to be on all food items. The first in, first out practice will ensure you use the older food before the newer food. This practice alone will help minimize waste from spoilage. Noting the arrival date will help employees know how long the item has been in storage. Water-dissolvable labels are the best option. DayMark Food Safety Systems offers a variety of biodegradable labels that dissolve in less than 30 seconds with no residue. They are FDA approved and are available at **www.daymarksafety.com** or by calling 800-847-0101. Here are some more tips:

- **Eggs** — If they are to be used in a few hours, they should sit at room temperature to prevent yoke breakage and cracking to cut down on waste. It's best to check with the local health department for their regulations about eggs, keeping in mind that eggs are perishable.

- **Electricity Emergency** — In the event that the electricity is not restored in a couple of days, take the following steps: 1) Keep the cooler door closed. 2) Use dry ice to keep the temperature below freezing. 3) Find a dry ice supplier before there is a problem. You may call other restaurants or cold storage vendors in case you experience further problems.

- **Generator** — None of us likes to think about wide-spread emergencies, but we need to plan for the possibility. What would happen to your refrigerated and frozen items if the electricity were off for a day? It could be a problem in several ways. Not only would you lose food and money, but you also run the risk of having dissatisfied customers. You can avoid these problems by having a backup generator that you can get from any home supply or larger discount store.

- **Refreezing** — If foods thaw, do not refreeze because doing so affects the taste of food. It is better to keep refrigerated and use as soon as possible.

- **Spoilage Rate** — There are many variables in spoilage. Different qualities and brands of food spoil at different rates. Keep this in mind when you change suppliers or brands and watch the items for any variation in the spoilage rate. If there is a noticeable difference in spoilage rate, make a note on your inventory list for future reference.

- **Too Cold** — Freezer burn is a major cause of spoilage. Conducting regular checks on the cooler temperatures can help you avoid freezer burn and the resulting food spoilage. Specialty thermometers are available from Atlantic Publishing at **www.atlantic-pub.com** to enable you to look for temperature fluctuations or "cold points" in the cooler where the temperature varies in one area.

- **Walk-Ins** — Keep an eye on the temperature of your refrigerated walk-in unit. You can also talk to your alarm company about a program that monitors your freezer and walk-in temperatures. One possibility is Food Watch at **www.foodwatch.com/foodwatch.htm**. These units accurately monitor the temperature and efficiency of your food cases, refrigerators, and walk-ins. They also offer a patent pending Compressor Watch sensor which attaches to the outside of the compressor motor and tracks how long it runs. Another interesting feature is that it monitors how long the walk-in door is open, an important feature to help save on electricity and maintain the quality of your food.

Safe Storage

Food items need to be moved to storage immediately to maintain quality. Keep in mind that you need a different person for receiving and another for storage. However, if you're in a small operation, the same person may receive the items, move them to storage, take them from storage, and use the products. Sometimes there's no choice but to use one person for all these duties. It is critical that storage areas be kept clean and orderly, making it easier to find items. It's good to create a periodic cleaning schedule for simple cleaning and for sanitizing to remove mold, bacteria, and any other microorganisms.

CASE STUDY: PRISON FOOD STORAGE

At Bland Correctional Center several refrigerated trailers are behind the kitchen. Tons of produce are received from spot sales and donations. Many fruits and vegetables are grown at the facility and on many prison farms. These items include strawberries, watermelons, cantaloupes, onions, potatoes, corn, green beans, and peppers. All milk is made at the State Farm for Virginia and shipped to all facilities. Inventory is done weekly depending on what is on the upcoming menus.

Only 25 percent of the food purchased is kept in the kitchen. Most of the food is stored in warehouses and refrigerated freezers outside the facility until they are needed.

Lawrence Shearer, Chef

Inventory

There are various types of inventory providing varying degrees of protection and accountability. The types of inventory are periodic physical inventory and perpetual inventory. This is a simple formula to use to determine your inventory amounts.

Beginning Inventory + Deliveries = Food on Hand

Food on Hand – Final Inventory = Food Used

No matter how well your employees portion food and how well you keep records, there will be discrepancies in your inventory records resulting from food spoilage or theft, for example; therefore, physical inventories must be done from time to time. The frequency is determined by the number of problems the facility has. Do not allow the fact that you have few employees available prevent physical inventories from being done. The more organized your facility is, the easier a physical inventory is, and it also becomes easier with practice.

Periodic Inventory Count

A periodic physical inventory is the oldest form of inventory. At one time, people did a physical inventory at the end of the month or the quarter when they did all the other paperwork. However, many facilities want inventory details on a more regular basis. If there is a problem with inventory or usage, it's hard to identify the cause of these problems weeks or months later.

There are several different rules of thumb about how often inventory should be done—weekly, monthly, or at the close of business each day. At one time, I had an assistant manager who was drastically overusing certain items. We walked through an abbreviated inventory at the end of his shifts. This is rarely done, but I needed to prove when the shortages were happening. The proof was indisputable after we did this for several days.

In some instances you may be the person to schedule inventory, but if not and you find the current frequency is a problem, you mention it to your supervisors.

Perpetual Inventory

Perpetual inventory means checking your daily food and supply usage. It is especially important to track expensive items. An accurate perpetual inventory can guarantee that items aren't being overused or stolen. Records can be tracked manually or on a computer system and are based on an accurate count on the items served during the day.

Perpetual Order Form

All food items are listed on the Sign Out Sheet and Yield Form. The "Size" column includes the unit size used. The cook signs out food from the freezer or walk-in, noting the unit size and number of items. Each day of the month is listed across the top of the page. At the end of the day, enter the number of items remaining. This number must be subtracted from the "Amount Ordered". It is possible for an employee to hide a theft by removing items from a box and then re-sealing it, delaying discovery of the loss and making it difficult to determine the date of the theft.

We've covered this before, but be sure to note all items in your perpetual inventory as they are delivered. When you find an inventory problem, check with the employee who received the order. Don't jump to the immediate conclusion that there is a thief before investigating further. I've had well-meaning employees who wanted to help but they inadvertently moved items to the wrong storage place so that I couldn't find them when I did my inventory. It is much better to take a little time to check all possibilities before making an accusation.

How should you handle the situation if you discover theft? When you suspect theft, your first priority is to make a list of all employees who worked during the time items went missing. If you have additional theft, check to see which employees worked each of these shifts. It would be helpful to adjust the time for doing your perpetual inventory to narrow down the time the theft occurred. Placing a note on the bulletin board that you are investigating suspected theft might be all you need. Include a statement that any employee who is caught stealing will be terminated.

Inventory Forms

There are many types of inventory forms shown at the end of this chapter. Some of these will be included for you. One of these forms is perfect for the times when you need to determine the value of the items you have on hand.

Determine Inventory Levels

When you prepare a food order, you must know the amount of food and supplies on hand. You can do this manually with an inventory sheet, or use a computer program.

Take the printed sheet and work your way through the storage area marking how much of each item is "on hand" in that column. Remember to use the same unit of measure as your standard for inventory. Some items will be counted individually, others will be by the pound, and some will be by the box and other units. The unit of measure should be on the inventory sheet to avoid confusion.

You need to find the "Build to Amount" or "Order Amount" (different worksheets will use different terms). To find the amount to be ordered, you need the time for scheduled deliveries and amounts needed between deliveries. It's good to add 15 percent to the amount you figure in case a delivery is late, you need more than usual, or an item is back-ordered. Try not to cut your order short. If the facility runs out of supplies before the next delivery you risk dissatisfying your customers and causing unnecessary headaches for yourself and the staff. We've already discussed the reasons not to over-order. Precise food ordering takes practice, but you can become proficient over time.

It's good for your staff to know the following information. Place the buying schedule details on a bulletin board with easy access for staff members.

- When each order must be placed.

- When deliveries are scheduled to arrive.

- Which vendors deliver which items.

- Each sales representative's phone number and the company they represent.

- The quoted price for all items. You may prefer to keep the pricing information in your desk or a notebook in your office.

When deliveries do not arrive on time, the buyer needs to call the sales representative or the company right away. If you wait until the end of the work day, they may be closed.

You can place a "Want Sheet" on a clipboard for staff members to list any items they need, including equipment, food, and supply items that are running low or used up. This sheet works well with items used infrequently. Simply train your staff to make a note on the "Want Sheet" when they use the last item or open the last box.

Weekly or Monthly Inventory

It's good to assign teams of two people to work on inventory counts. This can include one person to count the items while the other records the amounts. It works best when the recorder listens and records the numbers. No conversation is needed. Each team needs a list of the items in their area. It is best to list these items in the order they are assigned in the storeroom.

Inventory sheets should include a slot to write any items received or issued. Inventories should be conducted at a time of limited activity and no deliveries. I worked in the purchasing department for a local hospital and we did a complete inventory first thing Friday morning. Each staff member was assigned an area to count, and we also maintained the labels, kept the area clean, and kept the items straight. It is important to recognize items when they are in different packaging.

Issuing

Usage of any food or supply items is a critical part of the inventory and cost control process. Removing food from storage to use is called issuing. Below are some suggestions for issuing and using a sign out sheet.

- **Raw Food Items** — Issue these items on a daily basis. They include meat, fish, and poultry.

- **Signing Out** — This is when you remove bulk items from the walk-in or freezer.

- **Issuing** — Managers or kitchen managers should be the only ones to remove food from storage although in some facilities other people may be involved. It depends on the facility policies and the control that the manager has over the staff members.

The Sign Out Sheet shows when each item was taken from storage to be used in the facility. Your daily usage for each menu item is determined using this information. It is also simple to verify whether food items are being over used and to determine which items are not being controlled properly. An effective sign-out procedure can help eliminate theft. Listed at the end of this chapter are two requisition forms.

Food and food related supplies can be issued just like any other supply. In a hospital a supervisor can requisition supplies to include anything needed to do their job. The food service department works the same way. Some nurses' stations may keep a supply of nourishment on their ward. They will issue these items as needed by patients.

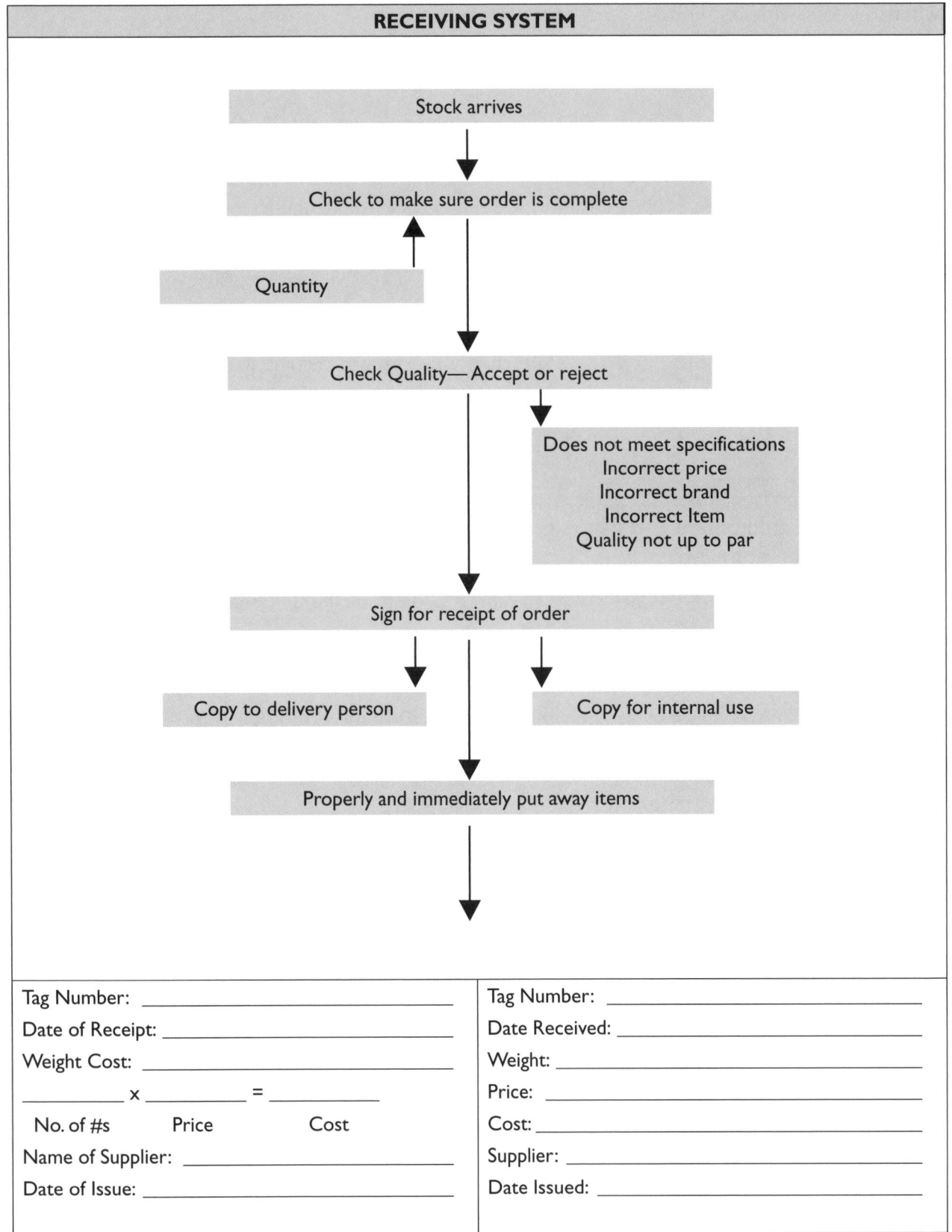

Tag Number: _____

Date of Receipt: _____

Weight Cost: _____

_____ x _____ = _____
No. of #s   Price   Cost

Name of Supplier: _____

Date of Issue: _____

Tag Number: _____

Date Received: _____

Weight: _____

Price: _____

Cost: _____

Supplier: _____

Date Issued: _____

Received By: _____ Date: _____

ITEM _____
Actual Temp. _____ °F   Packaging Intact ❏ Yes ❏ No
Valid Use-By Date ❏ Yes ❏ No
❏ **ACCEPTED**   ❏ **STORED**   ❏ **REJECTED**

ITEM _____
Actual Temp. _____ °F   Packaging Intact ❏ Yes ❏ No
Valid Use-By Date ❏ Yes ❏ No
❏ **ACCEPTED**   ❏ **STORED**   ❏ **REJECTED**

ITEM _____
Actual Temp. _____ °F   Packaging Intact ❏ Yes ❏ No
Valid Use-By Date ❏ Yes ❏ No
❏ **ACCEPTED**   ❏ **STORED**   ❏ **REJECTED**

ITEM _____
Actual Temp. _____ °F   Packaging Intact ❏ Yes ❏ No
Valid Use-By Date ❏ Yes ❏ No
❏ **ACCEPTED**   ❏ **STORED**   ❏ **REJECTED**

ITEM _____
Actual Temp. _____ °F   Packaging Intact ❏ Yes ❏ No
Valid Use-By Date ❏ Yes ❏ No
❏ **ACCEPTED**   ❏ **STORED**   ❏ **REJECTED**

ITEM _____
Actual Temp. _____ °F   Packaging Intact ❏ Yes ❏ No
Valid Use-By Date ❏ Yes ❏ No
❏ **ACCEPTED**   ❏ **STORED**   ❏ **REJECTED**

ITEM _____
Actual Temp. _____ °F   Packaging Intact ❏ Yes ❏ No
Valid Use-By Date ❏ Yes ❏ No
❏ **ACCEPTED**   ❏ **STORED**   ❏ **REJECTED**

ITEM _____
Actual Temp. _____ °F   Packaging Intact ❏ Yes ❏ No
Valid Use-By Date ❏ Yes ❏ No
❏ **ACCEPTED**   ❏ **STORED**   ❏ **REJECTED**

ITEM _____
Actual Temp. _____ °F   Packaging Intact ❏ Yes ❏ No
Valid Use-By Date ❏ Yes ❏ No
❏ **ACCEPTED**   ❏ **STORED**   ❏ **REJECTED**

ITEM _____
Actual Temp. _____ °F   Packaging Intact ❏ Yes ❏ No
Valid Use-By Date ❏ Yes ❏ No
❏ **ACCEPTED**   ❏ **STORED**   ❏ **REJECTED**

ITEM _____
Actual Temp. _____ °F   Packaging Intact ❏ Yes ❏ No
Valid Use-By Date ❏ Yes ❏ No
❏ **ACCEPTED**   ❏ **STORED**   ❏ **REJECTED**

ITEM _____
Actual Temp. _____ °F   Packaging Intact ❏ Yes ❏ No
Valid Use-By Date ❏ Yes ❏ No
❏ **ACCEPTED**   ❏ **STORED**   ❏ **REJECTED**

ITEM _____
Actual Temp. _____ °F   Packaging Intact ❏ Yes ❏ No
Valid Use-By Date ❏ Yes ❏ No
❏ **ACCEPTED**   ❏ **STORED**   ❏ **REJECTED**

RECEIVING REPORT

Supplier: _____ Date: _____

Representative: _____ Delivery Date: _____

Item Description	Quantity	Notes	Unit Price	

RECEIVING REPORT II

Received By: _____ **Date:** _____

Distribution Key: 1. _____ 2. _____

   3. _____ 4. _____

Invoice #	Supplier	Item	Unit Price	# of Units	Total Cost	Distribution			
						1	2	3	4

RECEIVING STAMPS

Date_____ Company and Invoice # _____

Received by_____ Driver _____

Approved by _____ Rejected by _____

Date _____

Weight/Count _____ O.K. ☐

Temperature _____ O.K. ☐

Prices _____ O.K. ☐

Quality _____ O.K. ☐

Received by _____ O.K. ☐

Date_____ Time_____ Invoice #_____

Shipper _____

Ordered by:

☐ PO # _____ ☐ Phone Order (date) _____

☐ Call Sheet (date) _____ ☐ Other (type and date) _____

Discrepancies if any:

_____

_____

_____

_____

_____

Received by_____

Driver _____

EXAMPLE OF A RECEIVING REPORT

General Receiving Report
Month of _____ 20_____

RECV. BY	DATE	P.O. #	COMPANY	INVOICE #	INVOICE IN	ITEM	TOTAL	DEPT.	CATEGORY	ACCURUAL $ AMOUNT	INV. ACT.

CREDIT MEMO

Credit Memo #: _____ Date Issued: _____

Vendors: _____ Vendor Invoice Number: _____

Vendor Representative: _____

Explanation: _____

_____

| ITEM | Quantity | Correction | | Price | Credit Amount |
		Short	Refused		

| Sold To: _____ Date: _____ |
| Customer Number: _____ |
| Invoice Number: _____ Invoice Date: _____ |

Instructions:
- ❏ Pickup Order Only
- ❏ Pickup and Credit Order
- ❏ Credit Only

ITEM	PRODUCT CODE	QUANTITY	PACKAGE	PRICE	AMOUNT

| SIGNATURE OF AUTHORIZATION: | DATE: |

ITEM	SIZE	QUANTITY				TOTAL	COST	EXTENSION

Location: _____

Item: _____ **Unit:** _____

Date	Beginning	Additions	Deletions	Ending	Unit Price	Extension	Initials

Date Inventoried: _____ Month Of: _____

Item Description	Unit	Counts	Total	Cost	Total Value
PAGE TOTAL $					

EQUIPMENT INVENTORY

Inventory Date: _____ **Department:** _____

Counted By: _____ **Approved By:** _____

Item Description (Name & Serial #)	Unit Count	Office Count	Difference	Explanation

Notes: _____

_____

_____

_____

CHINA AND FLATWARE INVENTORY

Inventory Date: _____ Extended By: _____

Counted By: _____ Approved By: _____

ITEM	Par	Inventory					Total	+ or - Balance
		A	B	C	D	E		

FOOD REQUISITION FORM

Date: _____ Date Needed: _____ Requested By: _____

Qty Ordered	Ingred. #	Item Description	Qty Issued	Unit Cost		Unit Total	

INVENTORY VALUATION SHEET

Inventory Date: _____ Extended By: _____

Counted By: _____

ITEM	ITEM AMOUNT	ITEM VALUE	INVENTORY VALUE
PAGE TOTAL			

Date: _____   Department: _____

Time: _____   Location: _____

Inventoried By: _____   Priced By: _____

Approved By: _____   Extended By: _____

Item Description	Unit	Quantity	Price	Extension

Notes:

Total $ _____

GENERAL REQUISITION

Date: _____   Req. #: _____

Time: _____   Department: _____

Prepared By: _____   Priced By: _____

Delivered By: _____   Received By: _____

Approved By: _____

Item Description	Unit	Quantity	Price		Extension	

Total $

CHAPTER EIGHT

Techniques to Purchase Large Quantities of Food

This information will be valuable for the people who place large orders. The first step is to determine whether large food orders are advantageous for you. Smaller orders have the advantages of offering:

- Lower storage cost for less risk, less inventory, less paperwork to maintain.

- Greater freshness for less risk of spoilage.

- Easier financial handling.

- Opportunity to take advantage of lower prices when they drop.

- Reduction in storage space.

- Greater flexibility in working with vendors.

- Less chance of theft due to having less inventory.

To make an educated decision, consider the advantages of placing large orders:

- Products can be purchased at a lower price when bought in quantity.

- There is less chance of running out of items.

- More stable prices mean more effective menu pricing.

- Buyer has more time to focus on other responsibilities.

- Lower labor cost to place, receive, and store orders.

Here we present various items to be purchased, tips to find the best quality, and negotiating the best price for your facility.

Meats, Poultry, and Fish

Meat may be the most important food item for your facility. Usually one-third to one-half the food budget is spent on meat products because they are costly and most entrees contain meat. People who have lived for years on meat, fish, or poultry are eliminating beef from their diet. Red meats are more expensive because each cow produces only one offspring a year. In turn, a sow may produce several dozen pigs, and a hen produces several hundred chicks. Another difference is the length of time it takes the animal to mature enough to go to market. Here are some of the differences:

Cattle	18 months
Chickens	12 weeks
Fish or Other Low Cost Seafood	Several weeks
Hogs	6 months
Veal or Lamb	3 months

These numbers show a drastic difference in the length of time from farm to market for beef compared to other meats.

Transporting animals to market is another costly factor. Most cattle are raised in grasslands far removed from large cities. The amount of food required to fatten cattle is significantly higher than for fish and poultry. It takes seven pounds of feed for cattle to gain one pound. Other ratios are: fish, 1:1; chickens, 2:1; and hogs, 4:1. Each of these factors pushes the price for the consumer and the non-commercial food service manager.

Meat usually sets the tone for a meal. So the buyer needs to understand properties of meat, how to pick the best quality, and meat preparation that affects what cuts or parts should be purchased. If there are any questions, speak with the cook before making the final purchase or else the menus could fail.

Properties of Meat

Raw, unprocessed meat is made up of 45 percent to 72 percent moisture and the remainder is protein, bone, fat. The muscle in meat is made up of long fibers bundled together with a threadlike appearance.

Fibers that make up the muscle contain fats, flavor minerals, moisture, proteins, vitamins, and other compounds. Younger animals have fine fibers that become coarse with age. These fibers are moist without being sticky, and they have a good color with a soft sheen indicating a good quality and tenderness, an important characteristic directly related to the amount of connective tissue. Younger muscles are tenderer, but the care and feed an animal is given also makes a difference. Animals confined and fed well are apt to be tender.

Meat that has slightly more collagen than elastin can be cooked to become tenderer, but meat with high elastin will remain tough. The length of time meat is cooked makes a difference in the tenderness. Here are some specifics:

Raw	Most tender
Rare	Less tender
Medium	Begins to toughen
Well Done	Tough

If you plan to cook something until it is well done, you need to choose a tender meat to begin. As meat is heated, it begins to coagulate and shrink because juices are cooked out. You can control the amount of shrinkage by using lower heat.

Low shrinkage allows the meat to retain more flavor and you get more servings from it; 15 percent to 20 percent shrinkage is low.

Bones increase weight and cost of meat although there is some added flavor to the meat near the bones. It is good to crack the bones and add some water to reach the marrow for added flavor. By adding a little acid to stock made with the bones, you can produce a soup richer in calcium than a glass of milk.

The trend to eat less saturated animal fat is expected to continue, so cattle is being raised to produce less fat, and more fat is being trimmed from meats. Age and feed determine the amount of fat in meat. Younger cattle have less fat and well-fed cattle have a higher amount of fat. Higher grade contains more fat.

There are three types of fat:

- **Body Cavity Fat:** located inside the body, it starts on the kidneys and heart and spreads over time.

- **Finish Fat:** located away from organs, it starts on the shoulders and rump, and moves downward and forward with time.

- **Marbling:** located in the muscles, fat appears as tiny flecks.

Fatty tissue contains 15 to 50 percent moisture and keeps the meat moist during dry cooking. Roasts are cooked upside down so the fatty juices can roll down over the meat. Turkeys are cooked backside up since that is where the fat is located. Another cooking tip is to cook lean meat in moist heat. When you try to sauté or broil lean meat, you often need to add some fat. Keep in mind that fat adds flavor and richness, but it also adds calories and cholesterol.

Myoglobin and hemoglobin make meat look red. When heat touches meat, they change to hematin, a gray pigment–the color of well-done meat. When oxygen combines with myoglobin, it creates oxymyoglobin which gives ground meat a bright red appearance on the outside but a darker color in the center. If you expose the center of ground meat to the air, it will become bright red too.

When meats are cured with nitrogen, it turns a pink color that we see in ham or corned beef brisket. Beware of brown meats: this means that the meat has deteriorated. When it is wet and slick, it has begun to spoil.

- Rare meat is red at 115 – 140°F

- Medium meat is pink at 140 – 160°F

- Well done meat is gray at 160 – 175°F

Heat builds on the outer surface of meat, so it's good to remove from the heat before it reaches the desired core temperature.

The Meat Market

Meats have changed dramatically in the last 50 years because of improved breeding and production methods to produce tenderer animals with higher meat yield. Research is being done to reduce the amount of fat animals develop. Meat is also being brought to the market younger. New scientific feeding practices promote faster growth on less feed to produce leaner animals. The practice of shipping animal carcasses has changed so that most meats are broken down and bones removed before shipping to cut shipping weight, size, and costs. All of these improvements provide a more valuable product.

Prices at all sorts of markets fluctuate, meaning that buyers need to adjust to trends and conditions. The USDA provides free daily information about market conditions, slaughter amounts, and current prices. Some of the publications you might want to check include:

- Urner Barry Publications, Inc., PO Box 399, Toms River, NJ 08754

- *The National Provisioner Daily Market Service* ("yellow sheet")

- *The Hotel, Restaurant, Institutional Meat Price Report* ("green sheet")

- USDA Publications — www.usda.gov

- *Market News Service Report*

- *Meat Sheet for Boxed Meat Items*

- Price Analysis Systems, Inc., P O Box 9626, Minneapolis, MN 55408

- *Meat Price Relationships* — published every two years. The historic prices of 74 meat and poultry items are listed along with the seasonal charts. They also predict future prices that are useful for planning, budgeting, and projecting sales and promotions.

The federal government has prevailed over the meat market for almost 100 years. *The Jungle* by Sinclair Lewis, published in 1906, caused widespread concern, prompting President Theodore Roosevelt to create a panel inquiry into actual conditions. Congress passed the Meat Act in 1906 to control operating standards that meat processing plants must follow, allowing for a series of inspections to guarantee meat is "fit for human consumption." Federal inspectors stamp the meat when it has met requirements. When the meat does not pass inspection, they are stamped "condemned," "retained" for further inspection, or "suspect."

The stamp indicates the official establishment number to help you determine where your meat actually originated. Check the number on the stamp against the federal list and you will know. See samples at right.

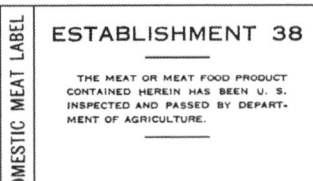 

Inspections are required by law, but grading is voluntary. When a packager puts its own "brand" on the meat, they do not have to give it a grade. The grading process was established in 1927 and the company or buyers who request grading paid an additional cost which is passed along to the consumer. Grades have been established for beef, lamb, pork, and veal. Beef has a variety of grades since there are so many different cuts and types of animals. Grading was amended in 1967 by the Wholesome Food Act which tightened the standards and gave control to state and federal governments. Some states have more stringent rules than the federal government in which case they can inspect and stamp the meat.

Frozen Meat

Large ice crystals can form on frozen meat so fast freezing is recommended so that only small crystals form. Slow freezing also causes a loss of moisture, flavor, minerals, and vitamins. If you cook meat from a frozen state, you can prevent some of these losses, but doing so increases the cooking time. Freezer burn is caused when the surface of the meat becomes dehydrated. It can be minimized by enclosing items tightly with moisture-proof wrap to eliminate air. Dry-paper cover toughens the meat and does not prevent freezer burn and flavor loss.

You might consider the cost to store frozen meat compared to making smaller purchases of fresh meat. This chart shows how long meat can be frozen under good quality conditions.

Beef	Lasts the best
Cured or Smoked Meats	1-3 months
Ground Meat	3 months
Lamb	Lasts the best
Pork	Not as well, fat becomes rancid
Veal	Lasts well

To be an effective meat buyer, you need to understand the classification and grading system used. Kinds of animals include beef, pork, sheep, and veal. There are additional classifications that include: cured meats, edible by-products, and sausage. Be aware of the prepared, canned, and substitute meat items available.

Two grading systems are used. One determines quality while the other is based on yield; age, maturity, and quality are all factors that determine the grade of beef.

Earlier we discussed marbling, tiny flecks of fat in meat. There are seven classifications which go from devoid (none) or slight to moderately abundant (heavy marbling).

The chart shown at the end of this chapter shows how grades are determined based on the variables.

Bones are graded based on their size, shape, ossification, amount of cartilage, and interior (marrow) color. These factors are indicators of the age of the animal. Younger animals have less ossification and more cartilage. The bones change shape as the animal matures. Interior bones have more red in younger animals than in older animals.

Flesh color is pink in young animals, but the color does redden with age. When you touch the flesh, it should be moist without being wet or slimy. Fibers in the meat should be silky with a soft sheen. These fibers are coarser in older animals.

Veal and calf grading are similar to beef grades although muscle structure is a factor. High grade veal and calves must have wide, thick carcasses with plump-muscled legs, shoulders, and breasts. Thin animals are graded lower.

In pork grading, age is the main factor based on body size, flesh color, and bone characteristics. Breaks in the bone indicate the animal's age. Younger animals have sharp and ragged breaks while older animals' breaks are smoother.

Identifying Portions of Meat

You must know the differences between the cuts of meat and between the muscle and bone formations to recognize various cuts of meat. When you look at a porterhouse steak and a T-bone, the biggest difference is the size of the tenderloin muscle. In a T-bone, the muscle is smaller. I've always found the shape of the bone makes it easy to recognize a T-Bone. Remember that it takes practice to identify the various cuts.

For information on meat identification see **www.ffaunlimited.org/meevandte.html** or see **www.ams.usda.gov/LSG/stand/imps.htm** for a wealth of information on specifications. Some of the publications you can download include:

IMPS FILES FOR DOWNLOAD		
Series No.	**Name**	**File Size**
--	General Requirements – pdf file	62 Kb
--	Quality Assurance Provisions – pdf file	356 Kb
100	Fresh Beef – pdf file	582 Kb
100	Fresh Beef with Pictures – pdf file	2 Mb
200	Fresh Lamb and Mutton – pdf file	668 Kb
300	Fresh Veal and Calf – pdf file	218 Kb
400	Fresh Pork – pdf file	324 Kb
500	Cured, Cured and Smoked, Cooked Pork Products – pdf file	168 Kb
600	Cured, Dried and Smoked Beef Products – pdf file	982 Kb
700	Variety Meats and Edible By-Products – pdf file	45Kb
800	Sausage Products – pdf file	119 Kb
11	Fresh Goat – pdf file	970Kb

For copies and other information concerning the IMPS write:

USDA, AMS, LS, SB
1400 Independence Ave., SW, Stop 0254
Washington, D.C. 20250-0254

To contact them call 202-720-4486 or e-mail **Thavann.Un@usda.gov.**

Wholesale and **retail** cut charts can be helpful in identifying portions of beef, lamb, veal, and pork. See charts from the USDA at **www.usda.gov**.

Processed Meat

Processed meat can be restructured, smoked, or cooked to preserve the meat, give it more flavor, or reduce labor costs, processes that are monitored by the federal government.

Nitrites or nitrates can be added to bacon, ham, and sausage as a preservative. After 1979, meats cured without nitrites or nitrates have a label that reads, "not preserved; keep refrigerated below 40°F at all times." Large canned meats can contain the same label because of their size. They may be considered fresh meats.

Cooked processed meats come in many varieties, including canned, frozen, and chilled. Some are refrigerated or frozen items which can be offered in bulk or portion packages. There is a greater chance of bacterial concerns with these products, so it is advisable to enforce bacterial standards. The federal government requires a minimum amount of meat in each of these products.

Cured Meats are salted or smoked. Salting means soaked in brine or pumped with brine for preservation. Curing offers a better flavor, improved appearance, and a tenderer product. These are some terms for cured meats and an explanation about what each term means.

- **"Country Cured"** — Meat is given a dry cure (see below) with a combination of sugar, spices, and honey. (Beef cured like this is called "cured beef brisket."

- **"Cured"** — The finished weight is the same or less before curing.

- **"Cured, Water Added"** — Finished product is 110 percent of weight before curing.

- **"Dry Cure"** — 8 percent to 9 percent salt or preservatives are added to bring out the meat's juices, making brine that soaks into the meat, preserving it.

- **"Imitation"** — More than 110 percent added weight after curing.

- **"Wet Brine Cure"** — Meat is immersed in 55 percent to 70 percent salt and soaked enough to preserve the meat.

Bacon is the most popular cured meat. It looks pink and dry, but not greasy. It usually comes in 8 to 10 pound slabs. Ham is usually 12 to 14 pounds.

Edible meat by-products are less well known but are still offered for consumption. Various types are classified as delicacies. These are some of the possibilities.

- **Brain** — Veal brains are common.

- **Heart**

- **Kidneys** — Beef and lamb are commonly used.

- **Liver**

    o Calf and veal liver are the best.

    o Lamb and pork liver are good.

    o Beef liver is tough unless it is cooked quickly.

- **Oxtails**

- **Stomachs** — First and second stomachs from cattle.

- **Honeycomb tripe** from the second stomach of cattle.

- **Sweetbreads**

- **Tongue** — Beef tongue is the most common.

- **Sausage** — Ground meat combined with spices that vary depending on which type is being made. Nitrite is added to reduce bacterial risk. Most sausages must be refrigerated. See note below for ones that do not have to be refrigerated.

A number of ground meats are classified as sausage. These include:

- **Cured Sausage** — good for 30 days, but fresh is good for one week.

- **Frankfurters** — refrigerated.

- **Pepperoni** — not refrigerated.

- **Salami** — not refrigerated.

Canned meat can be a good alternative if fresh meats are not available. They are also a good choice when refrigerated or frozen storage is an issue. However, some canned meats need to be refrigerated at 40°F to 70°F. Canned meat should not be kept for more than a year.

Some of the canned meat varieties include boned chicken or turkey, corned beef, luncheon meats, pork sausage, links, Vienna sausage, frankfurters, chili con carne, and canned ham.

Poultry

Poultry and eggs are a huge industry that changed little until the last quarter of the 20th century when it changed dramatically because science enables growers to raise heavier chickens in about half the time it used to require.

Today thousands of chickens lay eggs in large henneries. A bit of chicken trivia—the average hen lays more than 260 eggs a year. Eggs are a wonderfully versatile and inexpensive food, but demand has decreased because they are high in cholesterol.

Turkey and chicken are high in protein and cost little so the demand grows. Both are incredibly versatile and low in cholesterol and unsaturated fats.

In 1956 the government began to require that all poultry products be inspected. After an item passes inspection, it is stamped "Inspected and Passed." When poultry is processed, these are the steps needed: it is killed, bled, scalded, plucked, eviscerated, and inspected. Following are some details about the inspections performed to evaluate poultry products. Poultry items can be purchased cooked or raw.

Specifications

The specifications used to evaluate poultry include the following:

- **Kind–Poultry or Game Birds** — Poultry includes chickens, turkeys, ducks, geese, and pigeons. Game birds include pea fowl, swans, quail, wild ducks, geese, and pheasants. Rabbits are also classified as poultry.

- **Class** — Based on age and sex of poultry.

- **Grade or Quality** — Standard poultry grades are A, B, and C. Grade is based on a list of characteristics and qualities. These include conformation, fleshing, fat coverage, and lack of feathers, tears, cuts and bruises, freezer burn, and disjointed and broken bones.

- **Packaging** — Frozen poultry is wrapped in polyethylene to eliminate or limit freezer burn. The number of items in each container is determined by the type of poultry item being packaged. Some specifics are given below.

  Chicken — 12 to 24 per container

  Turkey, duck, or geese — 2, 4, or 6 per container

  Parts — 25, 30, or 50 pounds per container

- **Style** — Includes: whole, halved, quarters, and parts. Parts are drumsticks, legs, thighs, legs with pelvic meat, wings, and breasts.

- **Size, Weight, and Portion** — Vary depending on the kind of poultry.

- **Transportation and Delivery Temperature** — Frozen core temperature of poultry items is 0°F and the refrigerated temperature is 36°F to 40°F.

Eggs

Every non-commercial food service facility needs to find a reliable egg supplier. Be sure that your facility and your supplier refrigerate eggs right away. Eggs that are graded wrong can drive your price up unnecessarily. The longer they are exposed to room temperature, the lower the quality. Eggs can be purchased in these forms: in shells, as liquid, frozen, and dried. The type you need will depend on what you plan to prepare. We'll discuss that in more detail shortly. Another interesting bit of egg trivia—the weight distribution of an egg is: white = 58 percent, yolk = 31 percent, and shell = 11 percent.

Shells are a factor in the grading process and are graded on soundness, cleanliness, shape, and texture. Scanners are used to see the interior of the egg for grading and they allow the inspector to see the centering of the yolk, the aqueous nature of the white, size of the air cell, blood spots, and any deficiencies. Remember that eggs will last for several weeks if they are refrigerated properly. Egg Standards are Grade AA, A, B, and C.

This following table shows how the grading process works.

U.S. STANDARDS FOR QUALITY OF SHELLED EGGS TO MEET QUALITY FACTORS			
Factor	**AA Quality**	**A Quality**	**B Quality**
Shell	Clean, unbroken, almost normal	Clean, unbroken, almost normal	Clean or slightly stained, slightly abnormal, may be bubbly
Air Cell	1/8" or less deep, almost regular	3/16" or less deep, almost regular	3/8" or less deep, free or bubbly
White	Clear and firm	Clear and reasonably firm	Clear, may be weak
Yolk	Outline is refined slightly, mostly free from defects	Outline fairly defined, mostly free from defects	Outline may be defined, slightly enlarged, flat, and may show defects although not serious

Processed Eggs are frozen or dried and must be pasteurized. When you consider what type of eggs to use in your facility, evaluate what will be made with them. If they will only be used for cooking and baking, various cheaper options are available. The chart at the end of this chapter will show you the egg equivalents to aid in your choice.

Frozen eggs are high quality eggs used for French toast, omelets, and scrambled eggs. Lower quality eggs can and are used for cooking and baking. Frozen eggs also tend to produce a tougher finished product.

Dried eggs whites are used for meringue. "Egg Beaters" are a common product used to eliminate the yolks and lower cholesterol.

To prevent salmonella from fowl, keep eggs and poultry refrigerated below 45°F and use safe, sanitary handling and cooking methods at all times.

The Market

The poultry and egg market is volatile because of the quick turnaround time for producing poultry and eggs. Market reports are published daily. They help you to follow the poultry market when planning menus and to ensure your supplier's prices are in line. Market reports can be valuable if your facility uses a large quantity of eggs.

Selecting Fresh Produce

The fresh produce market is complex and it becomes more important as people want healthier foods. This chapter will walk you through the processes needed to buy fresh produce in the best way. An interesting tidbit is that the consumption of processed fruits and vegetables has decreased while fresh fruits and vegetable consumption has increased.

Regulations

You should know the regulations that guide the produce market. Here are a few of the most important. The Agricultural Commodities Act of 1938 required that people in the produce business be licensed and use fair business practices. Market quality and procedures improved because of this act. The Agricultural Marketing Act of 1953 and 1957 created agencies that established standards and grades for foods. The Fresh Fruit and Vegetable Division established the 160 grading standards that we have today. The Food and Drug Act also provided standards that affect the plant operations, identification, labeling, and other processes affecting fresh produce. Since 1990 prepackaged items have been required to list nutrition information.

Nutrition

People are demanding more fresh produce as they learn how healthy they are. They offer a high vitamin content—one serving of can give a daily supply of Vitamin A and C. They provide calcium, iron, phosphorous, and potassium—and no cholesterol.

Complex carbohydrates, the healthiest kind, can be found in corn, legumes, potatoes, and squash. Some produce items also offer protein and fiber. It is recommended that people eat at least four servings of fruits and vegetables each day.

The Produce Market

The produce market can be affected overnight by a storm in California or a frost or hurricane in Florida, for example. There are times when the market has too much of some items and not enough of others.

Science has had a profound effect on the produce market as advances help produce stay fresh longer. Flavor and freshness are much better with improved packaging and atmospheric control. We can create a better appearance and make produce tastier and more nutritious.

When produce is picked, it contains "field heat." The temperature needs to be raised to maintain freshness. The old way was to refrigerate produce, a slow process. Another process, hydrocooling, uses ice and water, but it is expensive. Vacucooling, a dry system, is the preferred method of cooling. A large amount of the item is pulled into a tightly sealed chamber which uses the heat in the items for evaporation. It is low cost and handles large quantities of produce quickly.

Improved shipping methods are changing the market. Items get to their destination much quicker. Harvesting, cleaning, trimming, packaging, and weighing are done in the field. Produce is then cooled and transported to market on refrigerated trucks.

Packaging options have changed the produce market. Stronger packaging is being used to protect produce en route. Special wraps are used during shipment to ensure better appearance and a fresher flavor, and bacteria static wraps are used to combat bacteria growth in items while they are being stored or shipped. Two terms for new wraps are CAP and MAP packaging, which stand for "controlled atmosphere packaging" and "modified atmosphere packaging."

Another factor that affects the market is the introduction of new varieties of produce including the number of tropical fruits that have been brought into the U.S. market, and U.S. growers are raising these items as well. Kiwi is an example of a fruit that was once scarce. It was shipped from New Zealand in containerized compartments that were loaded directly onto trucks. Now kiwis are produced in California.

Prepared fruit is another option to consider. Some facilities have eliminated fresh raw fruits and vegetables and are using prepared produce to eliminate waste and reduce equipment, space, refrigerator space, and labor needed to prepare the items. As labor costs increase, prepared produce could become even more popular with food service managers.

The season of the year can make a difference in availability and price. Most fresh produce grown in the United States is available from spring through fall. Imported produce is ungraded and varies more than items grown in the United States. It is critical that the manager and buyer know what areas produce the best products.

Perishable Items

Fresh produce needs to be handled properly. If it is stored in elevated temperatures, quality is compromised. Every 18°F elevation in temperature doubles deterioration. Produce needs to "breathe," requiring cool temperatures and good ventilation. Here are items that should be stored separately because they emit high amounts of ethylene which accelerates deterioration of nearby produce.

- Apples
- Apricots
- Berries (not cranberries)
- Cherries
- Figs (not with apples)
- Grapes
- Peaches
- Pears
- Persimmons
- Plums and Prunes
- Pomegranates
- Quinces

Not being familiar with the times for deterioration can cause waste and soaring food costs. It is also important not to buy items that are already ripe unless you plan to use them right away.

Purchasing Produce

What if your supplier insists that you must order a specific amount of produce? An example would be if you want to order three and a half crates, but they require you to buy four crates. This is quite common. When this situation arises, check your menu and see where you can make adjustments to use the additional items.

When produce is delivered, there are specific things you or your receiving person needs to confirm: amount, condition, damage, grade, net weight, packaging, rot, size, and pest infestation.

Standard grades for produce are U.S. No. 1, No. 2, No. 3, Combination Grade, and Field Grade. U.S. No. 1 is the most desirable grade. Combination Grade is a combination of items which fall in each grade. Field Grade is the items as picked.

When you figure quantity, include item count, packaging, and net weight. With produce, a variety of packaging may be used. This is a reason you need to be specific about net weight in your specifications. Many times, the quantity will be whatever amount fits in a certain size container. Several packaging terms include.

- **"Loose pack"** — Items are haphazardly placed in a package.

- **"Struck Full"** — Items are packed just below the top and scraped off if needed to level the contents.

- **"Fill Equal to Facing"** — The quality of the items on the top are equal to the quality of the products below the top and throughout the package.

It is important that you be familiar with the quantity of fresh produce to order so that you have enough to prepare food on your menus. A wonderful resource is the *Quantity to Order of Fresh Vegetables* in the *USDA Agricultural Handbook*. There is also extensive information in the book,

Quantity Food Purchasing by Lendal H. Kotschevar and Richard Donnelly by Prentice Hall in Upper Saddle River, New Jersey 07458.

Processed Foods

The processed food market is complicated partly because many government regulations are in place to oversee it. Producers and manufacturers are a small indication of the numbers of people who are involved in the industry. Foods are produced in bulk and then passed on to consumers or food service facilities.

Regulations

There are many regulations that affect processed foods, but there are several especially important to food service managers and buyers. One is the Pure Food, Drug, and Cosmetic Act which regulates what can and cannot be added to foods and sets acceptable labeling standards. The Agricultural Act gives the USDA authority to set quality standards for processed foods and should be taken seriously.

Grading

In Chapter 6 we discussed the need to establish the grade, brand, and quality desired when you establish your order list with each vendor. At times a seller may buy a product and later determine the brand after evaluating the quality. It is good for a non-commercial manager or buyer to be familiar with the usual quality of different brands to know which brands to avoid.

Surprisingly, sellers are not required to list product quality on their labels, another reason it is good to know which brands consistently offer a better quality product. The following table shows how an educated manager or buyer can identify the quality of the products from the label.

FEDERALLY APPROVED GRADES FOR FRUITS AND VEGETABLES					
	Word Terms		**Letter Terms**		
	Fruits	Vegetables	Fruits	Vegetables	Score
Top Grade	Fancy	Fancy	A	A	90-100
Second Grade	Choice	Extra Standard	B	B	80-89
Third Grade	Standard	Standard	C	C	70-79

The government doesn't recognize the word terms to indicate the produce quality, but the market hasn't caught up with the regulations. By including both techniques, you will be able to understand either designation.

Some items are rated "below standard," but they are not unusable. "Below standard" will be rated below 70. One example is canned peaches in small pieces. While they don't work as peach slices, they would be great for peach pie or peach cobbler.

Labels

The Pure Food and Drug Division dictates the elements that must be included on produce labels. When items fall below standards, the label must explain discrepancies. The label must list the style pack, variety, any artificial colors, net contents, number of pieces in the package, package size, number of servings, and serving size. The picture on the label must be a real likeness to its contents.

Standards of Identity

When the name is listed on the label it must be the proper name of the actual product in the package. An example would be sweet corn, sweet white corn, kernel corn, or cream corn.

Syrup Density

The label must list the syrup density in the container. Designations include light, medium, heavy, and extra heavy. Variations include lightly sweetened, water packed, or juice packed. Usually the higher grades contain heavier syrups although this is not guaranteed.

Standards of Fill

There are various standards of fill. A couple of these standards are

- **Contents must fill 90 percent of the water capacity.**

- **"Filled as full as practical"** — without breakage or crushing.

- **"Below Standard Fill" or "Slack Fill"** — the standard has not been met.

- **"Solid Pack"** — no water has been added.

- **"Heavy Pack"** — water has been added.

Methods to Preserve Products

There are many methods to preserve produce.

Canning

Before items are canned, they must be washed, sized, graded, peeled, trimmed, and then loaded into the cans. People have found that it's more convenient to have canneries near the production locations. Some canneries are moved into the field to speed up the process. It is recommended that the produce be blanched to hold its color, improve flavor, destroy bacteria, and remove dirt, and make rigid items easier to pack. Liquid is added to the cans; they are then closed, exhausted, and sealed. The filled, sealed containers are cooked in steam at a high pressure, then rapidly cooled. In some cases the inside of the can is finished so the can won't react to the food.

Freezing

The best way to maintain high quality is by freezing items soon after they are harvested. They can also be blanched to maintain color and destroy enzymes before freezing. When you review your product specifications with any supplier, indicate that you insist on "condition upon delivery should be the quality specified." The temperature in the transport trucks needs to be around -10°F. If the temperature fluctuates, quality can suffer. If you suspect an item wasn't stored at the correct temperatures, check for refreezing and large patches of ice on the packages.

Drying

Drying is the process of removing moisture from items. Once the moisture is removed, micro-organisms cannot grow. These are common drying methods:

- **Air Dried** — This is natural drying and it is slow.

- **Sun Dried** — This is just what it says, drying in the sun, and it is somewhat quicker. You can introduce heated, dry air to speed up the process.

- **Vacu-Drying** — Reduce air pressure and introduce heat.

- **Tunnel Drying** — Fast moving warm air or dry inert gases flow through a tunnel holding the produce.

- **Spray Drying** — Concentrated liquid is sprayed in a chamber and the moisture is extracted.

- **Drum Drying** — A drum rotates the item, lifts it, and dries it. The item is then scraped from the drum.

- **Freeze Drying** — Food is frozen and the moisture is pulled from the item with a vacuum.

Convenience Foods

We will discuss convenience foods in detail in Chapter 15. They are classified as foods prepared for longer preservation at lower labor costs. There are many convenience foods, and the list grows more every day. Some of them are high quality and can compete with products made fresh on site.

There is a variety of reasons to consider convenience foods. One would be a limit of skilled labor in your area. Another would be a way to reduce labor costs in a facility. Many facilities find that a combination of convenience foods and fresh foods works best for them. Here are some advantages to preparing items fresh on the premises:

- Overall operating expenses may be less.

- Patrons often place a higher value on homemade foods.

- Your food items can be unique.

- Nutritional value can be higher.

- Ability to limit the amount of additives used.

- More control over the food prepared.

- Less worry about downsizing.

- Convenience food instructions can be confusing or incomplete.

These are some advantages of convenience foods.

- They may be less expensive when you consider all relevant costs.

- It is simpler to track food usage.

- You can eliminate leftovers.

- You staff requires fewer skills.

- Inventory, purchasing, receiving, and clean up are easier.

- Equipment usage could be less, but a thorough evaluation is needed.

- Menu options can easily be expanded.

- Foods are easy to fix in a short time.

- Product consistency should be guaranteed.

- It is easy to keep items on hand.

A thorough evaluation is needed before making a final decision on whether to buy or make items. Positives and negatives need to be considered based on the situation in each non-commercial facility. Review all details before making a decision for your facility.

Dairy Products

We've all heard the recommendation to drink two- to eight-ounce glasses of milk every day because it is a great source of calcium, protein, and vitamins A and D. You can avoid milk fat by offering low fat and skim milk. Besides milk, dairy products include cheeses, sour cream, yogurt, ice cream, and butter.

Regulation

The dairy industry is carefully overseen and regulated by the government because it is easy to contaminate milk products. It is produced every day, and there is no effective way to shut off the market temporarily. Milk has a short shelf life, so it needs to be processed and moved to markets quickly.

Pricing

The Federal Milk Marketing Order Program establishes the pricing scale directly affecting more than 70 percent of the milk market and indirectly affecting the remainder. There are three price classifications for milk products:

1. **Class 1** — Liquid Milk Products (milk, skim, buttermilk).

2. **Class 2** — Soft Milk Products (cottage cheese, creams, ice cream, and yogurt).

3. **Class 3** — Hard Milk Products (cheese, butter, and powered milk).

Federal price setting has led to a stable market so that the supply is consistent. There is no "market destroying competition," and dairy prices are reasonable.

For information about cheese visit **www.realcaliforniacheese.com**, which provides recipes to use cheese and information about which wines to serve with cheese. You can find all these answers and much more by clicking on "World of Cheese." This site is a great resource for any non-commercial food service facilities that serve cheeses. The information will be helpful when you experiment with recipes. You can e-mail them at ed@successfoods.com.

Sanitation

Your state and local government set sanitation standards, and it is mandatory that they implement standards such as these.

- **Herds must be healthy** — USDA and public health officials inspect them.

- **Milk is obtained under sanitary conditions.**

- **Milk must be transported in modern, refrigerated, sanitized trucks.**

- **Milk is tested when it arrives to ensure it meets all relevant standards** — including: milk fat content, odor, sanitation, and taste.

- **When milk doesn't meet these criteria, it can be rejected.**

When the milk arrives at the dairy plant, it goes through an amazingly fast process. It is pasteurized, cooled, homogenized, and packaged in a few minutes. Pasteurizing can be done at various temperatures, but the highest temperature produces a cooked taste, although they are recommended for heavy milk products. The method of homogenizing milk forces it under pressures of 2,500 pounds per square inch or higher amounts, through tiny orifices which divide fat globules finely so that they are permanently suspended. The milk is packaged in non-returnable containers usually wax-coated or plasticized cardboard. The cardboard blocks any light that destroys the riboflavin in milk.

Quality Standards

There are various state and federal standards which govern milk processing and production. Milk must be "fresh, clean cow's milk free from objectionable odors and flavors." Vitamins A and D are added to milk. Normal amounts are vitamin D – 400 units and vitamin A – 2,000 units per quart of extra dry milk solids. If you want detailed information, contact your local authorities for details in your location.

Types of Milk — Quality of milk is based on flavor, odor, quantity of milk fat, and milk solids. Bacterial content can also be used in the grading process.

- **Grade A whole milk plate count** must be less than 20,000 ml and less than 10 coli form. (Some states dictate no coli form)

- **Certified Milk** — raw milk with plate count over 10,000 ml with no coli form.

- **Cultured Milk** — used for dietary purposes.

- **Filled Milk** — non-milk fat is added (must be labeled "filled").

- **Flavored Milk** — sweetener or flavoring is added.

- **Fortified Milk** — has increased nutritional content, like vitamins A and C.

- **Low Sodium Milk** — sodium is replaced with potassium.

- **Low-fat Milk** — 8.25 percent nonfat milk solids and 2 percent maximum milk fat.

- **Milk Drink** — Milk fat or milk solids have been altered.

- **Skim and Nonfat Milk** — 8.25 percent nonfat milk solids and 0 to ½ percent milk fat.

- **Soft Curd Milk** — treated to be more digestible; used in baby formulas.

- **Soured Milk** — Buttermilk is the fluid left when butter is made. Today butter is made from whole, low fat, or skim milk and is soured with bacterial cultures. Some buttermilk products contain small bits of butter. It has 8 percent to 8.5 percent milk fat content and the same milk solids as the milk used to produce it.

- **Yogurt** — is a cultured product with a spoonable consistency. It has 2 percent to 3½ percent milk fat and 8 percent to 9 percent milk solids.

- **Low-fat and Nonfat Yogurt** — self-explanatory. Yogurts can also be flavored with fruits or some other products.

Concentrated Milks

- **Evaporated Milk** — 7.9 percent milk fat and 18 percent nonfat milk solids. It can be homogenized and fortified with vitamin D. It is produced by boiling milk at 130°F to 140°F and using a vacuum to extract the moisture.

- **Nonfat Evaporated Milk** — generally purchased by the case. You can add 2.2 times the water to evaporated milk to produce whole milk. A 14½ ounce can makes one quart of milk.

- **Condensed Whole Milk** — Contains no less than 19.5 percent nonfat milk solids, 8.5 percent milk fat, and enough sugar is added to prevent spoilage—about 45 percent

- **Nonfat Condensed Milk —** may be available in bulk but doesn't have to be sterilized in the cans

- **Concentrated Whole Fresh Milk** — can be sold as a liquid or frozen product. There is a 10.5 percent milk fat content. The ratio used to create whole milk is three to one. When it is sterilized it has a three-month shelf life at room temperature or six months when refrigerated.

Dietary Milks

- **Dry and liquid diet foods produced with milk are available for sale.** They usually are high in milk solids and have been fortified with vitamins, minerals, and proteins. These can be used for dieting and are offered in various flavors. Baby formula is also offered as dry or liquid products. It is best to check the label to be sure what you are purchasing.

- **Dried Milks** — are milk solids with only 2 percent to 5 percent moisture. They must be stored in airtight containers to avoid quick deterioration.

- **Whole Dried Milk** — does not contain less than 26 percent milk fat or less than 5 percent moisture.

- **Nonfat Dried Milk** — does not contain more than 11 percent milk fat or less than 5 percent moisture. Some precautions: watch for stale taste, a cooked flavor oxidation, tallowness, caramelization, and any other unusual flavors. Dry milk should be produced from pasteurized milk.

- **Spray Dried Milk** — the highest quality dried milk. Roller dried milk under a vacuum is also high quality.

- **Malted Milk** — This is a dried milk product with about 3½ percent moisture, 7½ percent milk fat, a mixture of 40-45 percent nonfat milk, and 55 percent to 60 percent malt extract.

The federal government's grades for dried milk are: U.S. Premium, U.S. Extra, and U.S. Standard. You should use only the first two. U.S. Premium has a sweet flavor and is good for bakery production. U.S. Extra has a good flavor and aroma.

Creams

Bacterial count of cream should not be over 60,000 per ml and not more than 20 coli form per ml.

- **Half and half** — equal parts of whole milk (3¼ percent milk fat) and cream (18 percent). It is about 10½ percent milk fat.

- **Cultured half and half** — in addition to standard half and half, it has 2 percent acidity.

- **Table Cream** — has 18 percent to 20 percent milk fat.

- **Sour Cream** — is similar to table cream but has 2 percent acidity.

- **Whipping Cream** — light (30 percent to 34 percent milk fat) or heavy (34 percent to 36 percent milk fat). It is not homogenized and is ripened three days before it is marketed.

- **Filled Dairy Topping** — (18 percent fat) contains milk solids, but the fat is not milk fat.

- **Sour Cream Dressings** — 16 percent to 18 percent milk fat with 2 percent to 5 percent acidity.

Frozen Desserts

These frozen treats are pasteurized before they are frozen. The volume increase from whipping and freezing are: ice cream = 80 to 100 percent, sherbets = 40 percent, and ices = 25 percent. There are some states which forbid adding artificial flavors to frozen desserts.

Cheese

There is a wide variety of cheeses on the market. It is important for a non-commercial food service manager and buyer to know the quality factors of cheese. Various types depend on the type of milk used, bacterial cultures, milk fat content, processing method, aging process, and more. Quality depends on the ingredients being used, the age, and storage method. The grades are AA, U.S. Extra Grade, and Quality Approved.

Various types of milk can be used to produce cheese including, whole, partially de-fatted, or nonfat milk. Annatto, a yellow or orange color, can be used in cheese without being noted on the label. The milk must be pasteurized or cured for 60 days; either technique is acceptable. Interestingly, about 100 pounds of milk make 10 pounds of cheese.

Clabbered milk curd is used to produce cheese. When milk is pasteurized and cooled, a starter is added to the milk to create lactic acid and to sour the milk creating a firm curd. The curd is cut into cubes and cooked. The temperature influences the cheese product. A higher temperature creates a firmer and harder cheese. For example, cheddar is cooked below 100°F., and Swiss is cooked below 110°F.

The curd is stirred to release whey and remove it from the mix, leaving a rubbery substance. The mix is poured into each side of the trough in which it's made, and it can be cut after it solidifies. This process is called cheddaring. Other types of cheese besides cheddar are made this way. The strips are ground, salted, and piled into hoops. Specific mold or bacteria can be added at this point. When cheese is cured or aged, it undergoes a change of texture from rubbery to a softer, waxy mixture. The flavor becomes sharper and smoother. Various types of cheese are handled in different manners to create the individual tastes and textures that we love.

Hard Cheeses

There are many types of hard cheeses, but the most common are Cheddar, American, Swiss, and Monterrey Jack.

- **Cheddar and American** cheeses are the most common. Fine cheddars come from Oregon, Wisconsin, and New York. It is a hard cheese, cream to orange in color with a mild to sharp taste. The milk fat content must be below 50 percent and the moisture level below 39 percent. Grades are based on body, texture, aroma, taste, color, finish, and appearance. The grades for cheddar, curd cheddar, and Colby are AA (Extra), A (Standard) and B (Commercial). Aging is categorized with "current" (up to 60 days), "medium" (60 to 180 days) and "aged" (more than 180 days).

- **Swiss or emmental** has a creamy, yellow, firm, smooth, sweet, nutty taste and large holes. Baby Swiss is the same but has smaller holes. This cheese is cooked at 125°F to 130°F to make it hard with a glossy appearance. The curing process for Swiss is tricky because the wrong humidity can cause mold or rinds. Federal grades for Swiss are AA, A, and B. The holes should be spaced and round or oval. Keep an eye out for sticky, dry cheese that is crumbly because this is poor quality. Swiss cheese becomes whiter as it ages. Aging is rated as "current" (60-90 days), "medium" (90 to 180 months) and "aged" (over 180 days).

- **Monterey Jack** is creamy white, smooth, slightly firm, and mild flavored. It has 50 percent milk fat and is normally aged two to five weeks. Federal grades are AA, A, and

B. It has small holes and the surface is not shiny. Poor grades have large holes and a bitter taste.

Soft Cheeses

Cottage, ricotta, and feta are the most common.

- **Cottage or farm cheese is made by setting milk into a curd and cooking at 90°F.** The curd is cut, the whey removed, and 1 percent salt is added. The curd size is determined by the size of the knife used. If the moisture is below 70 percent it can become dry.

- **Ricotta cheese is a soft cottage cheese** which originated in Italy.

- **Greek feta is a soft curd cheese used in Greek, Balkan, and Arabic dishes.** It has a sharp and delicate flavor and is crumbly. The curd can be served with butter and seasonings.

Here are the specifications for hard and soft cheeses.

- **Aging** — The time needed to create a specific kind of cheese.

- **Bacteria content** — This information is not required for all cheeses.

- **Fat Content** — There are some designations that address the amount of fat: "nonfat" and "low-fat."

- **Flavor** — Each kind of cheese has a distinctive flavor, but in some cases, spices, seasonings, or wines are added for a different flavor.

- **Grade, Brand, and Quality** — Only some cheeses have grades, but it is best to indicate the quality that you want.

- **Kind** — Use the common name for each item.

- **Kind of Milk** — Goat's milk cheese would be an example of this standard.

- **Moisture Content** — There are maximum moisture contents for each cheese to classify the type of cheese; for example, hard, soft, moderately hard, and very hard.

- **Origin** — Sometimes this includes the area where it originated, and other times it could be the manufacturer.

- **Size, shape, or packaging** — Some may be distributed in normal shapes and sizes. An example would be cheddar which can come in large or small rounds, bricks, and other shapes.

Butter

The federal government says that butter should not contain more than 80 percent milk fat. It might contain salt and food coloring, but unsalted butter is on the market. It takes about 100 pounds of milk fat to produce 120 to 125 pounds of butter. After the milk is pasteurized, its acidity can be increased or decreased, and Annatto can be added for coloring. After butter and buttermilk are created, the buttermilk is drained. Then the remaining butter is washed, salted, and worked. Working is necessary to get the right consistency. If it is overworked, the butter will become sticky and greasy. Butter is graded AA, A, B, and C. Scores are based on body, color, flavor, packaging, and salt. Aroma is considered flavor. The federal government's standard for butter reads, "U.S. Grade of butter is determined on the basis of classifying first the flavor characteristics and then body, color, and salt. Flavor is the basic quality factor and is determined organoleptically by taste and smell."

Margarine

The federal government states that margarine is made from one or more various approved vegetable or animal fats combined with cream. It may also contain vitamins A and D, butter, salt, artificial flavoring, colors, and preservatives. However, labels must list any of these additional items. Beef fat used to be a favorite, but now soy oils are used more often than others. Some other oils include cottonseed, corn, other vegetable oils, or a blend of animal and vegetable oils.

Margarine is evaluated with the same standards as butter. The color, body, and texture should be consistent throughout the product. Flavors are clean, sweet, and free of unpleasant or unusual odors. You notice inconsistent colors and tastes when margarine is warm.

Food Purchasing Techniques

This chapter contains a wealth of information to help the non-commercial food service manager and buyer to make educated and informed decisions about which foods to purchase. It is helpful to know what you are talking about when negotiating a purchase. There is a great deal of information available to you, and your vendors can supply many of the details that you want to make informed decisions

CASE STUDY: ASSISTED LIVING

Promotional opportunities that work well are manufacturers' rebates. They are usually tied into contract or group purchasing programs. These programs are available to institutional operations and are based on a consistent, large volume of purchasing. This type of purchasing and rebates is not normally available to the average restaurateur. If a facility receives any type of government funding, it must be very careful about what it takes as promotional items or monies, as doing so is considered as accepting an enticement to buy and is not permitted by federal law.

Kathy L. Hilbert, Director of Dining Services
Bridgewater Retirement Community

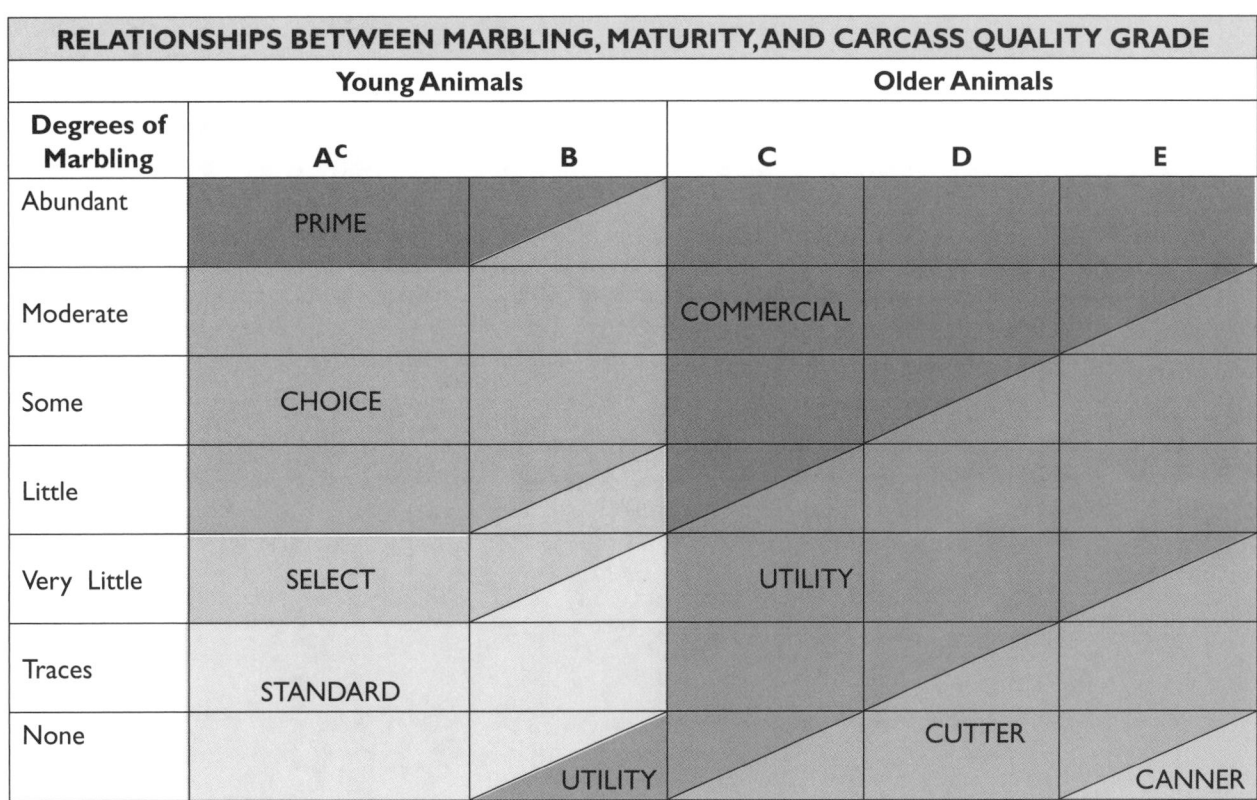

RELATIONSHIPS BETWEEN MARBLING, MATURITY, AND CARCASS QUALITY GRADE					
	Young Animals		Older Animals		
Degrees of Marbling	A^c	B	C	D	E
Abundant	PRIME		COMMERCIAL		
Moderate	CHOICE				
Some					
Little					
Very Little	SELECT		UTILITY		
Traces	STANDARD				
None		UTILITY		CUTTER	CANNER

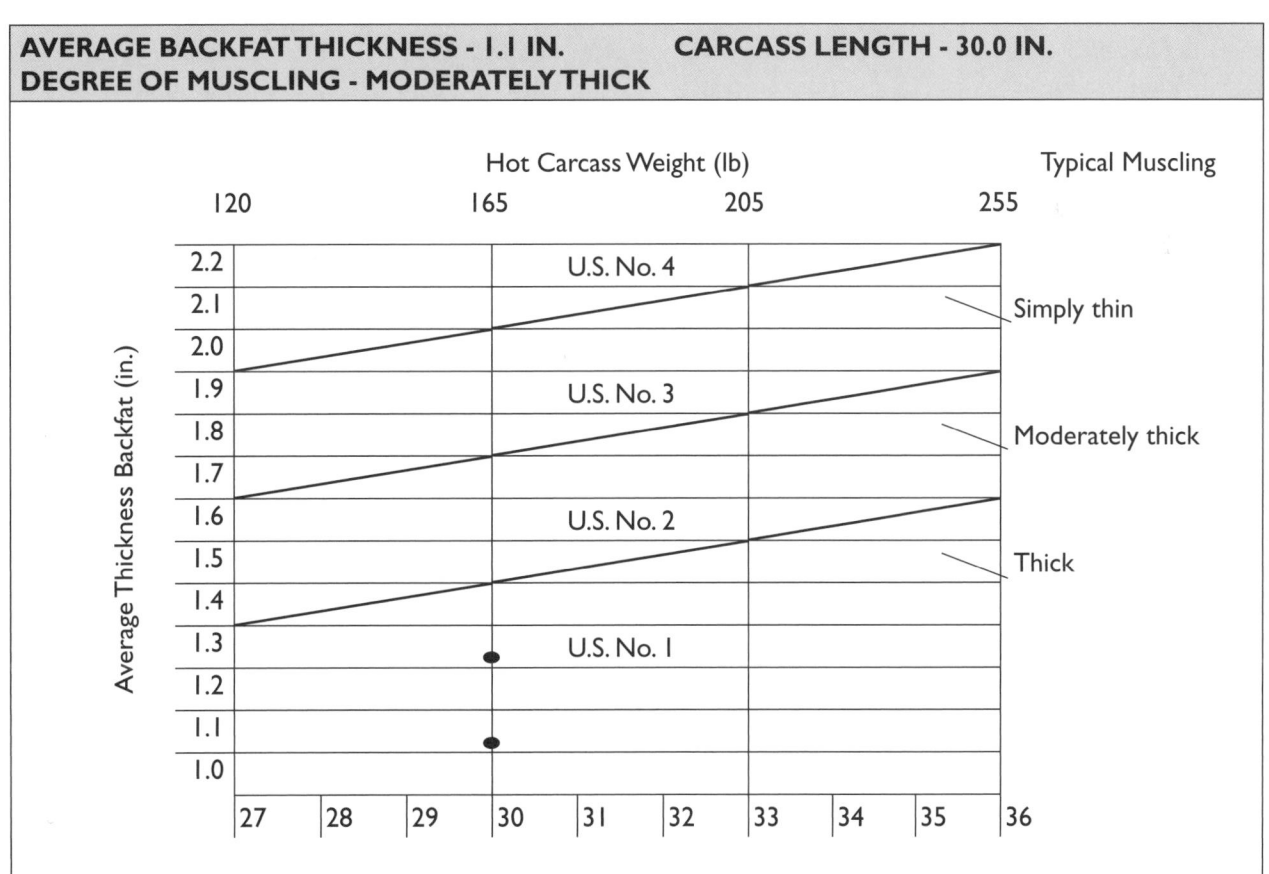

AVERAGE BACKFAT THICKNESS - 1.1 IN.   CARCASS LENGTH - 30.0 IN.
DEGREE OF MUSCLING - MODERATELY THICK

Average depth of backfat, carcass length, and degree of muscling indicate the grade of a hot packer-syle hog carcass. Thus, a carcass 30 in. long weighing 165 lb with very thick or thick muscles and an agerage fat depth or 1.1 would grade where the square is placed in the chart, but when it trades 2 fat tenths of an inch for 2 degrees of muscling, it moves up to where the dot is shown. A carcass weighing about 150 lb, 29 in. in length, which has an average backfat thickness of 1.5 with thick muscling would grade U.S. No. 2. Courtesy USDA.

All egg products should be specified USDA graded.

SHELL EGGS

Storage:
- Kept at 45°F until withdrawn for use.

Use Procedures:
- Take out only amount needed.

- Refrigerate unused eggs immediately.

- Keep raw eggs away from other foods

- Immediately clean utensils raw eggs were used with before using for other products.

FROZEN EGGS

Storage:
- Upon delivery place in frozen storage at 0°F or below.

Use Procedures:
- Keep below 45°F to prevent curdling and flavor problems.

- Defrost in refrigerator or under cold running water in closed containers. Do not defrost at room temperature.

- Mix well, since egg solids are not evenly distributed when thawing.

- Use any thawed, unused eggs in three days. Store at below 45°F until use.

LIQUID EGGS

Storage:
- Keep 45°F at all times.

Use Procedures:
- Use eggs within 7 days of receipt.

- While not in use, keep all containers in storage below 45°F and tightly closed.

DRIED EGGS

Storage:
- Keep in tightly closed containers under 70°F away from light.

Use Procedures:
- After opening store in closed containers at under 50°F or below.

- Hold products containing dry eggs at 32°F to 50°F.

CHAPTER NINE

Choose the Proper Equipment

Equipment and tools are an investment in the facility. It is impossible to turn out a quality product without the right tools and equipment. Keep in mind that equipment will pay for itself if you choose these items knowledgeably. It is best to find items you can pay off quickly. Later in this chapter we will discuss purchasing options and details about buying used or reconditioned equipment.

Here are some ways to determine the return on your investment.

- **The right equipment** makes it easier to make more money with fewer people.

- **Better equipment will help your staff members** produce better products more effectively, saving time and money.

- **Good quality equipment and tools** allow you to produce consistent items, a great way to keep your patrons happy.

- **Equipment in good condition** can reduce the number of injuries and lessen the stress of everyone in the facility.

Equipment Budget

Even if you aren't the purchaser, you should be involved in the process of selecting new or used pieces of equipment as a way to increase your knowledge and prove your worth to your supervisors. As a non-commercial food service manager, you are in touch with suppliers and other managers who could offer valuable input when making these decisions.

Equipment purchases are a major expense and there are many things to consider such as:

- How much can I spend?

- How much money is there in my budget for this equipment?

- Is there a more reasonable way to find reliable equipment?

- Should I buy or lease the equipment needed?

There are many levels of quality and pricing when you shop for equipment, but by determining your menu items before purchasing any specialty equipment, you will know which special tools or equipment are necessary. You can buy light duty or high duty equipment depending on your volume of business. When purchasing new items, review sales history to find what items are sold. Remember that you don't necessarily need the most expensive equipment. Often less expensive items are highly serviceable and serve your needs.

How can I stay in a budget? Next, develop your equipment/tool and fixture wish list and designate a priority for each item as to whether is it a "must have," "would be nice," "I'm dreaming."

The budget needs to be adhered to for the "must have" category. They are the items that make money for the business. Is there a chance the items in the "Would Be Nice" category can save you time and money? These items could become "Must Have" items. If you can find a great price, they could become a "Must Have" even quicker. The "I'm Dreaming" category includes things that you don't need at the time. If your menu items change, some of these items could become more important. This is another case where a great price could make a difference in whether they could be purchased sooner. As you review the "Would Be Nice" and "I'm Dreaming" lists, there are a couple of things to consider. How long would it take to recoup the cost of the item and can I say that it will really make more money for the facility?

When it is time to consider any equipment purchase, do your own research. Remember that a slick salesman can talk people into almost anything. Review comparison charts and evaluate whether the equipment would really fit your needs. Another important consideration is the maintenance that will be required.

After it is determined that the equipment is needed, the price can usually be negotiated. It is good to start at 50 percent of the list price.

Another alternative is restaurant supply stores who offer factory discounts that smaller suppliers can't offer. Consider buying last year's model or checking equipment dealers online. You could try an Internet search for "restaurant equipment" or use the specific name of the equipment you need. If you find something that you are interested in, verify that the company is legitimate. It would be best to have the items shipped COD to check it before paying.

Used Equipment

Buying used equipment is like buying a used car. Everything depreciates over time. A good option is to find a restaurant going out of business. The equipment isn't why they are closing. Unfortunately, in many cases the equipment may not be "like new."

It's best to shop for new items first. This will help to educate you about the options and specifics that you want. It also helps you to learn the prices before you shop for used equipment. Start your search for brands that have a great reputation and know the product details. It is also possible to research the repair history for the make and model you are considering. A good dealer or sales representative will have experience with the equipment and should share the important information with prospective buyers.

Used equipment may be available immediately instead of the wait you may have for new items. Before you shop for used equipment, be sure that you understand the difference between "reconditioned" and "rebuilt."

RECONDITIONED AND REBUILT EQUIPMENT COMPARISON	
Reconditioned	**Rebuilt**
• Clean • Worn or broken part are replaced • Usually has a short warranty • 40 percent to 50 percent of the "new" price	• Taken apart and rebuilt • Longer warranty • Usually works according to manufacturer's specification • 50 percent to 75 percent of "new" price

Before purchasing any rebuilt or reconditioned equipment, find documentation of the product's age and history. Repair history is critical. The serial number and service records reveal all this information. It is better to find out the details for yourself and do not believe the previous owner or a salesman.

Does the company have a trade-in policy? Some companies offer above average values on trade-ins when you want to trade up for newer equipment. Used equipment is available through:

- Auctions
- Bankruptcy auctions
- Food equipment groups
- Scratch and dent dealers
- Showroom and test kitchen equipment
- Direct purchase
- New equipment dealers
- Demonstration models
- Trade show items

These are all possible ways to find deals on equipment. As I mentioned above, verify the dealer is legitimate and have the equipment delivered COD, if possible, to have a chance to check the product before you pay for it. When you shop for your equipment, look for these potential problems:

- Items with rust, besides restorable cast iron
- Foreign made equipment not made for the United States
- Equipment with cosmetic problems that customers will see

- Equipment with repair parts from various items

Leasing is another alternative to consider, but you should speak with your accountant before making a final decision. Here are some specifics about leasing to consider.

- **Do they offer a service contract for a reasonable price?** If so, it might be good to verify the details.

- **Get the actual buyout in writing** and the fair market value information.

- **Interest is included in the lease,** and the price is not reduced for an early payoff.

- **Leases can provide** 100 percent financing.

- **It isn't an easy money solution.** The final cost could be substantially higher than the original price.

- **Leases are not recommended for items with a short life expectancy** or that could be deducted in the year when the purchase is made.

- **Leasing can be an effective way** to purchase costly equipment.

- **Read the agreement before signing.** It might be good to have your attorney look at the lease.

- **Talk to your accountant about the cost versus depreciation benefits,** which could vary depending on the length of the lease.

- **There could be tax benefits** to leasing equipment.

- **Verify** that your insurance covers all leased equipment.

- **Verify who is responsible for maintenance and service.** Will the manufacturer pay for these expenses, or are you required to pay for them?

CASE STUDY: CHURCH KITCHEN EQUIPMENT

Many church kitchens will not have commercial grade equipment. If the facility can locate used or refurbished commercial equipment, it would be a great idea to purchase these items. One reason is that they are heavy duty and will last longer. The commercial equipment is more convenient to repair when needed.

Gary Douylliez • St Francis Inn
Casa de Solana Inn • **www.stfrancisinn.com**

Make Wise Purchases

When you have a budget in place and you have evaluated the equipment available, decide which pieces of equipment would be the best value for your money. Here are some tips to get the performance, quality, and service you need.

Ask others in the business for their suggestions and recommendations. These people can include non-commercial food service owners and managers, used equipment dealers, and other specialists who can offer advice. Use this information to determine which features you need, how long the pieces should last and ways to extend their life. Another critical thing to ask is what brands or equipment to avoid.

Custom-built equipment may be the best option for your facility. This is especially true for facilities with limited space or unusual needs These items can be included on your list of the first, second, or third choices. Substitution is a possibility. There are times when the equipment you want simply is not available for a variety of reasons.

CASE STUDY: PRISON EQUIPMENT

The brand-name equipment the state purchases for the prison systems include Hobart, Vari mixer, and other manufacturers who service and repair their own equipment.

Lawrence Shearer, Chef

Choose a Quality Level

When considering quality, it is important to decide what level of quality you actually need. It isn't always feasible to have the best quality. Top brands are often expensive. Consider "generic" possibilities that offer the same quality for a lower price. An honest evaluation of the facility's needs will aid in making the best choice for the specific equipment. Here are some questions to consider:

- Will it fit in the budget?

- Can smaller equipment be used which may save money and space?

- Will one piece of equipment produce a better quality product?

- What is the projected return on investment?

- Will enough items be sold to justify the added expense of specialty equipment? If not, seriously consider deleting unusual items from the menu.

- Will the new equipment save labor or utility costs?

- What are the routine maintenance needs for the equipment?

- Does any local business offer affordable repair options?

- Are there added costs to operate the equipment?

- Can you purchase a reasonably priced service or maintenance agreement?

- Does the maintenance agreement last beyond the lease term?

- Does the manufacturer or wholesaler offer a chance to trade in or trade up?

- Can the seller give you a projected resale value if you want to trade up?

- Are all sanitary, plumbing, and code requirements met on the equipment?

- Would you need to make any customizations to make the equipment legal for your area?

Equipment Records

When you purchase used or reconditioned equipment, make the effort to acquire the service and maintenance records. Your details can be added to these files or you can start your own loose-leaf binder for recording equipment information, service, and maintenance schedules. Include parts lists, order forms, all necessary contact phone numbers, fax numbers, e-mail addresses, and mailing addresses.

It is also advisable to include a chart that shows the circuit breaker information. Know which circuit breaker operates each piece of equipment. This information needs to be displayed prominently in case of an emergency.

All staff members must be trained in the proper ways to use the equipment. Proper training and timely service and maintenance are necessary to have your equipment work at the highest quality level and to make the equipment last for many years.

Specific Equipment, Tools, and Supplies

Many types of equipment, kitchen tools, and supplies are needed to keep a non-commercial food service facility operating at peak performance. Some of those items will be discussed in this section. One of the most important is a good quality oven. Some facilities need multiple ovens, depending on what will be cooked and the volume of food to be prepared.

CASE STUDY: MILITARY EQUIPMENT

Most of the equipment in military food service facilities is like equipment you would find in any commercial or non-commercial facility. However, the equipment needed for a "field mess" is different. The reason for this is because the entire facility must be transportable. Equipment and supplies are sent to the site and must be set up in the field and they need to be ready to feed a large number of troops in a short period of time.

Several of the unique situations with a field mess is that you need electricity and running water to operate in the middle of nowhere. Generators are needed along with fuel to operate them. A water buffalo is used to provide troops with water while in the field. A water buffalo by military standards is a 400-gallon steel tank which sits on a trailer. The tank holds water that is purified by the (ROWPU) Reverse Osmosis Water Purification Unit, and they can turn salt water into drinkable water.

Mel Trimble, Retired Marine

Ovens

There are almost unlimited choices for ovens. The first criterion is whether to cook with electric, gas, or wood. There are computerized and manually operated ovens. The amount of space you have available is an important factor when making your decision. Two of the most important considerations are capacity of the oven—rack size and adjustability and temperature control—the stability and accuracy of the temperature. Here are some basic variables that figure into your decision:

- **Convection Ovens** — Hot air is circulated throughout the oven to speed baking and to maintain a consistent temperature in the oven.

- **Deck Ovens** — Flat steel or stone baking surface with single or multiple decks set at various heights.

- **Rack Ovens** — These contain multiple sliding racks for volume baking for items cooked at the same temperature and time requirements. This can be the best use of the floor space you have available.

- **Revolving Tray Ovens** — Sheet pans and trays are revolved in the oven for even baking throughout the item.

Below are details and contact information about different oven manufacturers.

Amana's Commercial Division offers an oven that cooks 12 times faster than a conventional oven. Visit **www.amanacommercial.com**. This page explains the benefits of the Amana Veloci compared to a conventional oven. The infrared radiant element works with the direct air flow to enhance browning, toasting, and crisping. Contact Amana at 866-426-2621 or fax 319-622-8589.

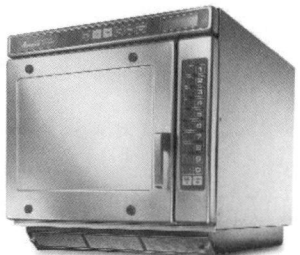

Deck Ovens

Gas deck ovens come in single or double deck configurations. These are ideal for baking and roasting many items. We will discuss conveyor ovens shortly, but items seem to taste different from conveyor ovens. Remember that deck ovens require more training and more work.

The "deck" is made from ceramic tiles, large bricks, or sections of stone. Tiles do not maintain heat as well as other decking surfaces. Items are usually placed in the oven with a paddle also used to turn the items to ensure thorough cooking. Items that need to be browned will show a marked difference when they are turned during the baking process. Another benefit of turning and rotating items is that the deck needs to reheat after an item is removed. If you use the same area over and over without a break, items will not bake thoroughly. Items must be rotated, but be careful not to open the door more than is necessary because each time the door is opened, the oven loses heat, increasing cooking time.

Deck ovens are easier to clean by closing the doors and turning the heat on high. Then you simply scrape the oven and sweep the residue out.

Deck ovens also require more time to preheat and to cool down. They have smaller capacities than conveyor ovens. These are my favorite ovens because the cook has more control over the finished product. A "well-trained" oven tender can turn out an almost perfect product every time with deck ovens. One of my former managers also proved that you can also burn an entire oven full of food if you don't pay attention.

Today, Baker's Pride is world-renowned for high quality commercial and non-commercial baking and cooking equipment. They provide a wide selection of quality deck ovens, countertop ovens, conveyor ovens, and under-fired char broilers to meet any need of the food service industries.

Baker's Pride's mission is to be the leading supplier of quality bake ovens, char broilers, conveyor ovens, and convection ovens for the food service industry. They are committed to providing leadership and innovation by delivering value-added benefits to customers through excellence in communication, problem solving, on-time delivery, and world-class, worldwide after-sales service. Visit their Web site at **www.bakerspride.com**, call 914- 576-0200, fax 914-576-0605 or 800-431-2745 U.S. and Canada, or e-mail **sales@ bakerspride.com.**

In 1848, gold was discovered in California, and Gardner S. Blodgett built his first oven. This was a turning point for California and the food service industry. Today, the Blodgett Oven Company is the leading manufacturer of commercial ovens in the world. Restaurants, fast-food chains, hotels, hospitals, institutions, small businesses, and large corporations alike rely on the Blodgett name. In fact, our ovens have been in demand overseas since the late 1800s, long before global markets and international trade became the focus of our modern world.

Many businesses rely on Blodgett ovens which have been in demand overseas since the late 1800s—before international trade became a focus for our modern world. Blodgett offers various deck ovens for your use. They come in a different sizes and configurations. Your choice depends on the volume of business you do. To see that choices are available, visit their Web site at **www.blodgett. com/deck_roasting.htm** or you can contact them at 800-331-5842 or 802-860-3700 or fax 802-864-0183.

The right oven needs the best bakeware. Genpak oven-ready baking trays are more economical than bulky permanent trays. Fill, freeze, bake, and display in the same package. The attractive design and clear lids help you market items at the counter. Genpak oven-ready meal trays work with all automated equipment. They are available with clear lids or may be film-sealed equally as well. See the full line of products at **www.genpak.com** or contact them at **www.genpak.com/cfm/inforequest.cfm.**

Conveyor Oven

Oven choices are critical for any food service operation. Consider the space available, utility considerations, and oven capacity as it relates to the volume of business you plan to do. Business volume will also dictate whether to consider single or multiple conveyors.

Typical conveyor ovens need only 15 to 20 minutes to preheat; they hold their temperature and cool down quickly. However, there are negatives to consider. When a conveyor oven malfunctions, it will not cook anything until it is shut down, taken apart, and repaired. Conveyor ovens also have noisy fans. Cleaning and repair can be time-consuming, during which time you cannot bake anything. Finally, conveyor ovens are generally more expensive than other options.

Global Cooking Systems™ offers reliable stainless steel conveyor ovens and gives the maximum cooking potential with minimal effort and investment. These ovens are built to provide easy cleaning access. Constant, even heat offers thorough baking and a consistent product every time. The design of all ovens makes them excellent for cooking many products including pizza, seafood, bagels, and ethnic foods. Contact their customer service department at 316-721-1355 or fax 316-721-0158 or check out their Web site at **www.globalcookingsystems.com/products.php**.

Cookware Options

The right choice in cookware can make a huge difference in food preparation. Some cookware is inconvenient and awkward to use. For a busy non-commercial food service facility, you need high quality and durable cookware to serve you well and last for years to come. Below is information about a couple of possibilities.

Regal Ware Food Service, a division of Regal Ware Worldwide™, offers a selection of top quality beverage and food preparation products for the non-commercial food service industry. Regal Ware Food Service offers a full range of products that were designed with the food service professional's needs in mind. Visit their Web site for more information at **www.regalwarefood-service.com** or e-mail **rfsinfo@regalwarefoodservice. com**, call 262-626-2121, or fax 262-626-8532.

Regal Ware Food Service cookware

Sitram has manufactured high quality cookware in Europe for more than 40 years. For the past 20 years they have offered their products in the United States to food service professionals. They have eight product lines to fit each user's needs. Visit **www.sitramcook-ware.com/products_foodsrv.htm** for more information. To obtain the most up-to-date information regarding pricing, availability, dealer locations, or to order directly contact Frieling U.S.A. at 800-827-2582.

Sitram cookware ▶

Beverage Equipment for Preparation and Serving

General Espresso Equipment Corporation has been in business for nine years but has already established itself as a strong player in the distribution, marketing, and promotion of Astoria espresso coffee machines in North America. They have captured a significant share of the market and continue to attract the interest of single operators, main accounts, specialty coffee roasters, specialty equipment dealers, and service companies. Designer coffees in the form of cappuccino and espresso have become extremely popular in recent years. Should your facility offer

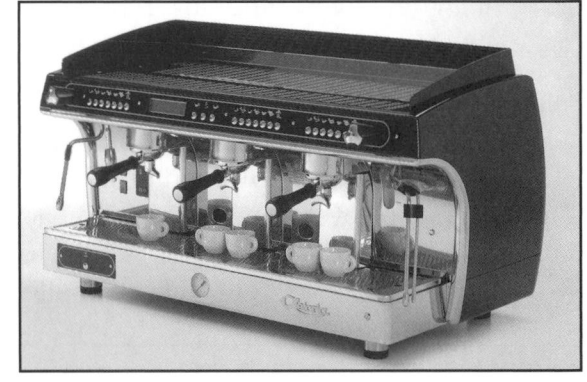

these items? If so, General Espresso probably has the equipment you need. Their full line of equipment can be seen at **www.geec.com** or you can call 336-393-0224.

Sunkist is a recognized name in fruit juices, but they also offer a quality juicer for food service facilities. This commercial grade juicer endures extended daily usage. The unit features a metal oscillating strainer to separate the juice from the pulp so you get more juice from each piece of citrus. An operator can easily extract between 10 and 12 gallons of juice per hour using pre-cut citrus. It comes with three extracting bulbs (one each for lemon/lime, orange, and grapefruit). For much more information, call 800 383-7141 or visit their Web site at **www.sunkistresearch.com/index.php?mod=category&id_ctg=67**.

Heated Tables

Non-commercial food service and cafeteria or buffet lines need heated serving tables and areas. A hot food-carving shelf is heated from the shelf base and can be placed on any surface. One

option includes two adjustable heat lamps, sneeze guard, and cutting board with gravy lane. Another item contains hot food drop-in wells and is available in one to five full-pan sizes. These items are available from Alto Shaam. For more information about their products, visit **www.alto-shaam.com/product_detail. asp?productnumber=100-HSLB**, call 800-558-8744, or fax 800-329-8744.

Refrigerated Prep Tables

Refrigerated food preparation tables are ideal for a business that produces a large quantity of pizzas, and they can be used for sub sandwich preparation as well. These tables have tubs to hold various pizza and sub ingredients and toppings. The individual bins can have lids to maintain freshness and limit contamination of toppings. In some units the bottom is enclosed and refrigerated. This is the ideal place to store additional stock on the more popular toppings for easy access during rush periods. Determining whether you need these items depends on the amount of pizza and sub production that you plan.

Instaware Restaurant Supply offers additional information about the prep tables. Visit their Web site at **www.instawares.com**. Enter "food prep tables" in the search block for a wide selection of products to fit your needs or call them at 800-892-3622.

Scales

Scales are an integral part of any non-commercial food service facility to maintain consistency in your recipes and to control food costs, both critical factors for consistency in the menu items needed to satisfy your patrons. Food cost control is also needed to keep the facility profitable and to guarantee that you don't run out of food from over-portioning. Scale usage is the easiest way to do this.

6" Portion-Control Scale from Browne-Halco.

One floor scale should be located near the delivery door to weigh incoming items. Other smaller scales should be placed at strategic places around the kitchen and food preparation areas. It is hard to expect staff members to follow portioning guidelines when they do not have scales to use.

There are various types of small, digital scales. It is good to purchase scales appropriate for the various areas in your kitchen because the wrong type of scale could be useless. Even the best quality scales must be calibrated from time to time. It's advisable to ask the sales representative about maintenance and calibration services when you shop for scales.

Good quality accurate scales are critical to maintain food costs. Scales are not a place to cut your costs. Instaware Restaurant Supply offers a variety of scales for your non-commercial facility. Visit their Web site at **www.instawares.com**. Search by "scales." Some of those choices include digital scales and platform scales. The digital scales can be used to measure individual portions and platform scales will measure the accuracy of deli orders. Contact them at 800-892-3622.

Fryer Equipment

General-purpose commercial fryers can be used for many items including: appetizers, fried chicken, eggplant parmesan, and french fries. The type and size of the fryer you choose will depend on what and how much you plan to make.

Check these distributors and manufacturers:

- Anetsberger Brothers — **www.anetsberger.com**

- Cecilware Corporation — **www.cecilware.com**

- Henny Penny Corporations — **www.hennypenny.com**

- Autofry — **www.autofry.com**

- Keating of Chicago — **www.keatingofchicago.com**

- Vulcan Hart — **www.vulcanhart.com**

Frontline International offers several systems to pump waste from your fryer into a containment tank. There is one system sufficient and appropriate for your facility. The illustrations below show two of the possibilities. For more information, contact them at **www.frontlineii.com**, call 330-861-1100, fax 330-861-1105, or e-mail **sales@frontlineii.com**.

Henny Penny is the expert in commercial and non-commercial fryers. They offer a complete line of energy efficient fryers that are durable. Pay attention to details. Their main features include: rectangular fry pots, precision controls and built in filtering systems. Visit their Web site at **www.hennypenny.com**, call 800-417-8417, or fax 800-417-8402.

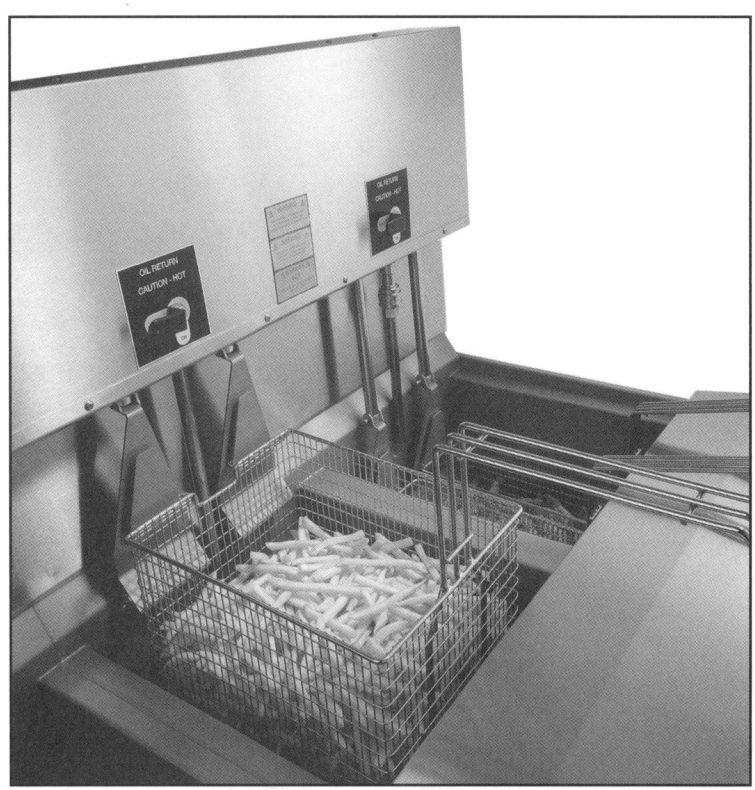

Henny Penny Open Fryer

Refrigerators and Freezers

The U.S. Department of Energy's pamphlet at is a wonderful resource. It can be founds at **www.eere.energy.gov/femp/technologies/eeproducts.cfm**. Also check the Consortium for Energy Efficiency's Web site at **www.cee1.org**.

Your menu and ingredient items dictate the amount of refrigeration needed.

U.S. Cooler manufactures walk-in coolers, freezers, and combination units. These are used for all types of cold storage. They can be constructed to suit your needs and will arrive at your non-commercial food service facility pre-assembled to ensure a quality product. Check the Web site for the configurations available. All the necessary accessories can be purchased from U.S. Cooler. These include outside ramp, rain roofs, strip curtains, shelving, glass doors, and many other items. U.S. Cooler uses the latest technology to manufacture walk-in coolers and freezers and can be purchased from a dealer or an online dealer. For more information, visit **www.uscooler.com** or call 800-521-2665.

Henny Penny—Blasters and Chillers—Proper chilling reduces the risk of contamination, and these blasters and chillers are a great way to store prepared food safely for use during peak times. For more information, see **http://www.hennypenny.com/products/index.html?pc=2** or call 800-417-8417 or fax 800-417-8402.

Axiom Equipment offers a wide range of refrigerators and freezers for your facility. These units come in many sizes and capacities. In the good ol' days, an icebox only needed to keep things cold so remember that fancy bells and whistles don't refrigerate food. Refrigerators do. Axiom offers professional-grade refrigeration at a surprisingly low price. Visit **www.axiomequipment.com** or call 888-599-5962, or fax 817-740-6758.

Smaller Equipment

There are many types of small equipment that you need for a typical non-commercial food service facility. What types of small equipment items will be needed to create the items on your menu? Is there equipment that would be needed for only one or two items? If so, should the items be deleted from the menu? Is there another way to prepare the menu item to avoid having to buy specialized equipment for one item? We will discuss some of these items below along with manufacturers who offer these products. Each of the items in this section is available from Hobart Corporation.

Mixers

The industry leader for commercial mixers is Hobart. See their Web site at **www.hobartcorp.com**. The site has calculators to help you determine the capacity needed and shows you potential savings and useful advice. Hobart produces counter and floor model mixers. Your local restaurant supply house can also help you find the right mixer. After you decide the purpose of the mixer, you can determine whether you need a heavy-use mixer. North America's dough mixer in Albany, New York offers mixers. Precision North America has distributors throughout the United States to help you find the mixer you need at a price you can afford. You can contact them toll free at 877-7-MIXERS (877-764-9377) or fax 518-462-3389 or visit **www.precision-mixers.com**.

Hobart Mixer

Food Cutters

Expand your menu using food cutters that offer the option to go from salads to dessert and will help with every course in between, many even containing attachments to handle slicing, shredding, and chopping. They can be hard-working pieces of equipment.

Coffee Makers

Coffee makers are a staple in any food service establishment. Even if you offer espresso and cappuccino, you still need real coffee. Zojirushi offers a unique coffee maker that doesn't turn the taste of coffee bitter. The Fresh Brew Stainless Steel Thermal Carafe Coffee Maker comes with a stainless steel thermal carafe that keeps the coffee hot for hours without altering the taste. It also features an electric timer clock module to set the coffee to complete brewing by the desired time. Visit **www.zojirushi.com** or call 800-733-6270 for more information.

Bread Makers

Depending on the amount of bread your facility uses, you may be interested in a bread maker. Zojirushi offers the Home Bakery Supreme® Breadmaker which bakes a large traditional shaped two-pound loaf of bread. The unit has the exclusive Home Made Menu function allowing adjustments to the knead, rise, and bake times. It also prepares dough, cake, jam, sourdough starter, and even meatloaf. The programmable timer can be used to have fresh bread when you need it. For more information visit **www.zojirushi.com/ourproducts/breadmakers/breadmakers.html** or call 800-733-6270.

Food Processors

A well-built food processor can shorten food preparation time. This product lets operators slice, dice, and chop faster, while getting consistent results. It's built for both safety of operation and enhanced productivity. You want a food processor that is easy to clean. An angles unit can also make the work easier for your staff members.

Griddles

Griddles are good for more pancakes. Fast preheating and recovery gives uniform heat distribution for the best, most consistent results. Griddles can be used for hot sandwiches, burgers, strips of chicken or steak for fajitas, or eggs and pancakes. Remember that griddles aren't just for breakfast anymore.

Serving Pans

Steam tables use pans for individual food items. There are many types of pans available from Polar Ware, offering various depths and sizes with covers. For the full line of pans and accessories, visit **www.polarware.com/view.php?catid=31** or call 800-237-3655.

Polar Ware also offers a complete line of serving pans. They can be seen at **www.polarware.com/view.php?catid=32&prodid=79** or call 800-237-3655 for more information.

Packages

Packaging you need will depend on what food items you offer. In a non-commercial food service facility there shouldn't be many carryout items, but there are employees who would like to pick up lunch at the cafeteria so you need to have carryout containers for patrons who wish to take their food with them.

Containers come in all shapes, sizes, colors, and materials including paper, plastic, and Styrofoam. It is important to have a container that closes securely for soups or gravies. Cost, environmental friendliness, and a stable package are important to you and your patrons. Ordering and receiving will be easier if you purchase all of these packaging supplies at one place, and your usual vendor may offer containers.

Here is an option in case you cannot get these items from your vendor or for price comparison.

Genpak is the perfect place to buy bakery display packaging, oven-ready baking trays, and oven-ready meal trays. The display packaging is made from crystal clear APET which extends shelf life while displaying your product at its best. Display packaging won't crack and may be opened and closed multiple times. They are available with clear lids or may be film-sealed as well. Genpak also offers a selection of disposable dinnerware and carry out containers. These items are great for your patrons who need to take the meal or leftover with them. See the full line of products at **www.genpak.com.**

Genpak disposable products

If you offer a chance for people to take leftovers with them or to carry out items, these are some containers that could fill your need. WNA is a supplier of a wide selection of quality plastic plates, cutlery, cups, and serving ware and you can choose custom packaging. View their products at **www. wna-inc.com/products/selectCategory.php.** To find the customer service information for your area, check **www.wna-inc.com/company/contactus/.**

Biocorp excels in concern for the environment. They offer environmentally friendly products for your non-commercial facility and provide quality products at reasonable prices. They also supply a line of heat-resistant cutlery that doesn't have an after taste or allergy concerns. Their full product line can be seen at **www.biocorpaavc.com/index.asp.** Contact BioCorp at 866-348-8348 Monday thru Friday from 8 a.m. to 5 p.m.

Wes Pak's food service carriers are an affordable alternative to transport food. They are easy-to-use,

WNA Pack 'n Serv Products

one-time-use packages. They are lightweight and can be used to cool drinks or store ice and hot foods. After the food is delivered, the packages can be thrown away. The selection can be seen at **www.wespakinc.com/section.asp?secID=5** or call 800-493-7725 between 8 a.m. and 5 p.m. CST.

Your Bag Lady can supply you with a large assortment of bags. When patrons take items from the facility, it offers a better way to carry food containers. Visit **www.upowerit.com/ yourbaglady.com/insulated_bags/index.php**, call toll-free 888-569-9903, fax 718-788-4218, or e-mail **marjorie@yourbaglady.com**.

Berry Plastics offers a varied selection of disposable plastic cups that are great for self-serve beverage area or for patrons who want a drink to go. These cups offer high clarity and crack resistance. The Web site is **www.berryplastics.com**.

Additional References

Hobart works with many non-commercial facilities and could be a great choice for you. Here are some instances of the type of businesses they have helped.

- Launching the Room Service Concept for Health care
  http://www.hobartcorp.com/HobartG6/sa/sage.nsf/0/8E222DC1E5CBFFC685257 09300731F2B?OpenDocument

- On-Site Foodservice for Businesses and Organizations
  http://www.hobartcorp.com/hobartg6/sa/sage.nsf/0/E5A09093E3A3AC61852570 96005400D6?OpenDocument

- The State of Collegiate Dining
  http://www.hobartcorp.com/HobartG5/sa/sage.nsf/0/1A0CEF67C65204F285257 0960061E012?OpenDocument

- Managing Costs in Foodservice has Operators Looking to Hobart – Connections
  http://www.hobartcorp.com/hobartg6/sa/sage.nsf/0/6F020ADF775BDE0685257 076001E415B?opendocument

- Grand Forks, N.D. Nursing Facility Lowers Energy and Water Consumption with New Hobart C-Line with Opti-Rinse™
  http://www.hobartcorp.com/HobartG6/sa/sage.nsf/4E995AFF2481821D8525706 E00496303/82D90A23868F70DF852570A0004A5B34?OpenDocument

- Hobart, Traulsen Target Top Foodservice Issue: Food Safety-Government Food Service
  http://www.hobartcorp.com/HobartG6/sa/sage.nsf/0/6C1FA31C3E0757158 5256 F6A0005B5D4?OpenDocument

- Managing Costs in Foodservice has Operators Looking to Hobart –
  Elementary and High Schools
  http://www.hobartcorp.com/hobartg6/sa/sage.nsf/0/6F020ADF775BDE06852570 76001E415B?opendocument

Miscellaneous Kitchen Tools

Polar Ware offers many utensils for your non-commercial food service facility. Products are steam table pans and covers, chafers, stock pots, mixing bowls, kitchen utensils, and sinks. Most of these stainless steel products are NSF listed or certified with other professional organizations. They also offer tongs, ladles, scoops, food-balers, measuring cups and spoons, kitchen spoons, whips, strainers, colanders, cutting boards, meat tenderizers, funnels, shakers, cylinders, tumblers, utility pails, and menu holders. Visit their Web site at **www.polarware.com**, call 800-237-3655 or 920-458-3561, or fax 920-458-2205.

Sabert offers the style and durability of expensive permanent-ware, with the convenience and money-saving benefits of disposable items. They are attractive and designed for precise food handling. For the full line of utensils, visit **www.sabert.com/utensils.shtml** or call 800-SABERT1 (800-722-3781).

Serving Supplies

There are occasions when platters are needed to serve items or to display food. For those times, Sabert offers a full line of platters and lids to keep the items fresh. They have a platter style for every occasion combined with superior crack and crush resistant tight-seal lids to provide the ultimate catering and food service solution. Visit **www.sabert.com/platters.shtml** or call 800-SABERT1 (800-722-3781).

Sabert's Freshpack® Bowl Collection offers a full range of bowls from 8-oz. to 320-oz., in classic and shallow bowl styles and popular clear, black, and cobalt blue colors. These attractive bowls are suitable for use on a serving table and for merchandising. All bowls come with pop-tight for leak resistant lids. They are stackable for easy handling. To view the full collection, visit **www.sabert.com/bowls.shtml** or call 800-SABERT1 (800-722-3781).

Pizza Pans

Many business people order out for pizza, so why not offer pizza to your patrons? If you plan to offer thin crust, hand tossed, and/or deep pizzas, you will need the right pans and screens. Thin crust and hand-tossed pizzas can be made on trays or screens. But deep-dish pans should be made in a pan. I really like the final product with some earthenware baking pans, but you would have to decide if it's feasible for your facility.

If you use the wrong pan, you will lose time and will not have a consistent product. It's also a problem when you buy cheap pans. They do not hold up and will need to be replaced soon. As with every other piece of cookware and bakeware, it's important to research to get the best pans for your menu items.

Most pizza pans are aluminum, but today many of these pans have a hard-anodized coating which increases the heat transfer to reduce your baking time by 6 percent to 12 percent. It also improves consistency and reduces waste since your pizzas won't stick.

A great pizza starts with a great pizza pan. A deep dish pizza, chewy on the inside and crispy on the outside, needs the right pan. Royal Industries offers basic aluminum pans and trays in various widths and depths. These pans are designed for pizza preparation, but there could be other items in your recipe file that would benefit from these quality pans. The choices are available at **www.royalindustriesinc.com/source/pizza.php**, by calling 800-782-1200, or faxing 800-321-3295.

The cleaning technique used to clean your pans will also make a difference in how long they last. Some must be pre-seasoned or you may need to "oil and bake" the new pans. All cook and prep staff should be trained that pizza pans should never be tossed into water because it harms the finish. Check out these pizza pan suppliers:

- **Lloyd Pans** — www.lloydpans.com

- **American MetalCraft** — www.amnow.com

- **Allied Metal Spinning** — www.alliedmetalusa.com

Brown Halco offers a wide selection of pizza trays and screens in a wide variety of sizes. These items heat evenly and can cook your pizzas to perfection. Brown Halco also offers pizza peels, cutters, pizza pan grippers, and other items you need to prepare irresistible pizza products. A number of their product are pictured below. Visit **www.halco.com** or call 888-289-1005.

Wash Up Afterwards

Don't forget about washing dishes, pots, and pans. Purchase a washing system to protect your customers that will be efficient and cost-effective. Some facilities can use a multi-sink system but others need a conveyor system. When you make the decision about the type of dishwashing system to use, also factor in the price of the equipment and the labor hours needed for either option.

We will discuss sanitation in more detail in Chapter 11, but it is simply combining water, chemicals, and heat properly. The purpose of washing dishes is to sanitize the dish, rinse, and dry it. It's advisable to become familiar with the local health department codes.

Water pressure needs to be sufficient to operate an automatic dishwasher. When you have low water pressure, it will slow the cycles, inhibit the automatic settings, and will not meet the sanitation standards you are responsible to meet. The temperature must be 150°F or higher depending on the machine's capabilities. You may need a water booster. Further, you need to calculate your water's hardness because rinse aids are not effective without a water softener.

Installing a low flow (1.6 gpm) pre-rinse nozzle on your dishwashing station can save up to $100 a month in energy, water, and sewer costs.

You may need a separate washer for glasses. There could be a need for a large storage area to hold dishes that must wait to be cleaned. Will your dishwasher need to soak many pans? All of these particulars make a difference in the equipment you need.

It's good to research equipment rental and chemical purchase programs, under which you are responsible for a rental fee and must buy chemicals from the supplier who will maintain the equipment. Auto-Chlor System is a well known national supplier. Their Web site is **www.autochlorsystem.com**.

Washing by Hand

A multi-sink configuration compliant with local regulations is a good option to clean oversized pots and equipment components. Be certain to:

- **Have ample counters and racks around your work area.** Local codes specify the size and amount needed.

- **Keep dirty and clean dishware separate** to avoid contamination.

- **Install a detergent dispenser over the sink area.**

- **It is easier to maintain a consistent hot water temperature** by installing sinks near a dedicated water heater.

In addition to having the proper equipment, you should make sure employees know the correct steps to wash dishes by hand. Atlantic Publishing offers a dishwashing poster which can be a great reminder. It is pictured on the next page. The full color poster measures 11" x 27" and is laminated with sealed edges. Visit **www.atlantic-pub.com** or call 800-814-1132 to order (Item # FSP8-PS, $8.95).

DISHWASHING

The correct procedure for manual dishwashing. Use a 3-compartment sink:

1 **Sort** and **Scrape** dishes.

2 **Wash** with detergent in hot water at least 110° F.

3 **Rinse** in clean water to remove detergent.

4 **Sanitize** in hot water 171° F for at least 30 seconds or chemical sanitizer 75° F.

5 **Air Dry.** Do not towel dry.

LAVAR de PLATOS

CHAPTER TEN

Customer Service

Customer service is critical in any situation. Some people may believe that non-commercial food service is different and that you don't need to worry about customer service. That is a mistake. Food service facilities on college campuses, in hospitals, or in other health care facilities are the most convenient but in many instances customers have other options. Remember that they talk to friends and co-workers. Will they say good things about your facility?

In schools, on military bases, in hospitals, and in prisons, there usually isn't another option. But that doesn't mean that you shouldn't strive to give great service anyway. Cafeteria conditions and limited food availability are the top reasons for unrest at prisons. Even when employees have few options for dining, the cafeteria staff can still provide nutritious, tasty meals.

In the instance of health care facilities, food service personnel are also helping the public to broaden its view of the hospital, retirement home, or nursing home. Friends and family members who enter these facilities are concerned with the sort of service, care, and food their loved ones receive. Why not share information about the food service portion of the facility they are considering. In small towns there are limited health care options, but the number is growing every day. Each facility needs to set itself apart from other options.

Build Customer Loyalty and Word of Mouth

All people want to know they are appreciated and your customers are no different. It's nice to have the person behind the counter remember their name or what they like. It's a simple gesture and shows you took the time to notice. Here are some other ideas to help them feel appreciated:

- **If you have a newsletter, share news about your customers.** You can even encourage them to share weddings, anniversaries, births, promotions, and any other good news,

- **Create a Wall of Fame to celebrate your best patrons.** Invite your customers to choose the criteria that constitute your best patrons and pick someone each week or month. The person's picture could be posted on the Wall of Fame, and you might even give him or her a free lunch or dessert.

- **Recognize people who contribute.** Are there patrons who make a difference in the facility where you are located or in the community? You could recognize them in the same way as your Wall of Fame.

- **Are there specific people who suggest new menu items or have a favorite item that they order frequently?** People love it when you name an item after them. This works in commercial restaurants, and it could work it the non-commercial facilities as well.

- **In the hospital where I worked, it seemed that most people had a specific table where they always sat for lunch or dinner.** You could personalize their seat or table with a simple name plate.

Know Your Customers

The easiest identifiers to learn about your customers are who they are and what they like. Let them know that you remember them and their preferences. It sounds difficult, but it can become second nature over time. This is part of showing customers that you appreciate them and that they matter.

Your existing employees probably know the people who come through your cafeteria each day. Do you have a way to help new employees learn about your regular customers? Imagine how your patrons would feel if a new employee knew them by name. You could also have a person on the front line who introduces new employees to your customers. It's a little thing that only takes a minute but will make your customers feel special. Most important, be sure the correct names are used.

Members Only

Do you have particular customers who come in every morning for breakfast? Maybe they come in each weekday for lunch. You could have a special offer for these people. It could be something like a customized mug for their coffee or a cup for them to get a refill on their drink before returning to work. Maybe they get a free dessert on Fridays. Any of these things could be a great bonus for your regular customers. Pick something that you can afford to give and that they will appreciate.

If you choose a nice mug for this promotion, others will come in and ask how they can get one. Your special customers can promote a new item for you. Personalized mugs and similar items are a good way to promote your facility and can add to the bottom line. There should be a deal that goes with the mug—a discount on drinks if they bring the mug or free refills. It can be almost anything, but figure out what works for you and for the customers.

Another way to use the "members only" idea is to give points for buying certain products. Each time customers buy a particular product, they could earn a point or ticket. When they accumulate a certain number, they would earn a prize. A local business might want to offer prizes for your customers. It could boost your sales and get valuable exposure for the business.

Lifetime Customers

The least costly way to increase the volume of business is to work with your existing customer base. Encouraging them to return more often has a dramatic impact on the amount of business you do.

Returnees are people that you know and who like your product and the service. When you make the effort to "knock their socks off," the facility will benefit. You can also feel confident that they will bring new hires to your facility. In a hospital situation there is the possibility of drawing in patient visitors and doctors who may have the flexibility to leave. Good word of mouth throughout the hospital can be a great way to increase business. Hospital visitors want to stay close to their loved ones, and the facility cafeteria can be convenient. It also helps them feel more confident about the food their loved ones are receiving.

Keep your customers coming back because of the wonderful food, interesting menus, and fantastic customer service. They will return and tell their friends about your facility; it is the most effective way to increase sales in the long term. Your goals should be to:

- Give them a wonderful meal.
- Encourage customers to return more often.
- Delight them.
- Put them first.
- Offer variety and value pricing.
- Welcome their friends and referrals.
- Win their loyalty.

CASE STUDY: SCHOOL FOOD SERVICE

I did customer satisfaction surveys with high school students several months ago. Other than a few requests for steaks, seafood, and sushi for lunch, they had some good ideas. We added more variety of fruits (kiwi and strawberries), veggies (cut up celery sticks), and more entrée choices at breakfast. We added triple-decker peanut butter sandwiches and a blatantly stolen idea from McDonalds—the yogurt and fruit parfait.

Sandy Neff • Augusta County School Board
School Nutrition Program

Communicate the Value of Loyalty

First impressions are critical in any business If there are long lines, long waits, or a dirty appearance when people come into your facility, they will get a bad first impression. It is much better to take this opportunity to make them feel welcome. Do your employees relate well to your customers? This is important and is another way to build loyalty among your patrons.

Repeat business is important and costs much less than attracting new customers. A key to creating customer loyalty is tied to the commitment you and your staff member show your repeat customers. Here are some key things to keep in mind:

- **Listen to your repeat customers.**

- **Find out what they think and how they feel about your facility.**

- **When they go to your competition, ask them why. This is especially critical when they return to the competition.** A one-time visit can be curiosity, but two times can mean problems for you.

Offer discounts or promotional items as an incentive for people to fill out comment cards. A critical question on these forms would be: "Would you eat with us again?" Each "no" requires some immediate action on your part. If customers indicate they wouldn't return, you need to find out their reasons and fix the problems.

There are an unlimited number of ways to make a visit to your facility enjoyable and to show appreciation for your customers. Later we will discuss ways to set your facility apart from competitors. In non-commercial food service this can also include reasons that they shouldn't order out or pack a lunch. Most hospital break rooms have a microwave, which makes hot lunch easy. Why should people spend their hard earned money with you? Here are some ways to show appreciation for your customers:

- Create a database and send special offers to your customers.

- Use the database to send new and updated menus to customers.

- Track which items sell and which don't and make the needed changes.

- Be on the watch for ways to improve the facility for the customers.

- Find ways to make birthdays and anniversaries special events.

- Offer specials or discounts on holidays or special events.

- Be open about saying "Thank you" to customers.

- Ask for and act on customer suggestions whenever possible.

- When you make positive changes, let your customers know.

- Explain any temporary problems or inconveniences and apologize.

- Any time a customer communicates with you, answer them promptly.

- Give employees reasonable power to solve problems that arise.

- Be available to customers and employees. In some non-commercial situations you may also need to be available to the relatives of your customers.

Show How You Are Better

Create a difference in your facility. How can you be different? Here are some possibilities:

- **The food you offer.**

- **The menu combinations that you offer.**

- **Do you use any special ingredients?**

- **Serve local spring water or bottled water.** You can also filter your tap water for a better taste.

- **Soft drinks can be offered in bottles** to allow you to have a more extensive selection.

- **Offer unique salad combinations.** Even fast food chains are jumping on the salad bandwagon. Unique bowls can make a difference. Try chilled plates, bowls, and forks. These little touches can make a big difference.

Educating Guests on the Differences

When you are planning changes, let your customers know there are new things on the horizon. If you have a newsletter, mention it there or offer a few hints each week and let people guess. The winner could receive promotional items or a coupon.

Educate your staff on the special things that you offer and encourage them to tell customers, an idea that is appropriate in a cafeteria line. Staff should never be pushy about this but teach them to mention things in a normal conversation. If you received some fresh new item, let customers know. When you try a new product, mention it in a positive way and ask for comments. If you start to offer new services, post them on your information board or place promotional pieces on the table. This will help you show customers why you are different from their other options.

Delight Your Guests

Customer satisfaction is important, but is that good enough? It is much better to exceed their expectations every time they visit your facility. Keep in mind that you serve one person at a time. Make sure that person is thrilled with your food, selection, and service.

Here are the basic things that your customers expect. I'll also include some tips on how to meet these expectations and how to exceed them.

1. **Hot food should be hot and cold food should be cold.**

2. **Serve cold food on chilled plates and hot food on warm plates.**

3. **Heat lamps are not the answer to keeping food hot and may give your staff members an excuse to dawdle.** Set the example by keeping a steady pace and not delaying when something needs to be done.

4. **Acknowledge your customers as soon as they arrive and fill the order quickly.** If something needs to be taken to their table, make sure it is served as soon as it is available.

5. **All employees should be familiar with the menu items you serve.** When a customer

asks how something is served or cooked, all employees should know the answer and be able to explain the details.

6. **Make sure your staff members show the proper concern when there are problems.**

Are there other ways that you and your staff can exceed their expectations? Any ideas should be shared with everyone who works in the facility. Show your customers that you care about them and set yourself apart from any of their alternatives. The secret is that you must actually care about the customers. Don't be phony with them but show you care because you really do. These are some things that you might do for your customers.

- **Free stuff** — If customers have to wait, do you offer them something free to compensate for the inconvenience. Many non-commercial facilities are located in businesses that provide a short lunch or dinner break. This means that a delay can be a big problem and may cause a patron to miss a meal.

- **Manager on the floor** — It is good to see the manager on the floor and especially during busy times. He or she should take a couple of minutes to greet patrons.

- **Free samples** — You can promote new menu items by offering free samples before they are offered for sale. This is a nice treat and could whet their appetite to buy the item when it is added to the menu.

- **Reading material for individual diners** — Many food service facilities offer something to draw on at the table. Offer a rack with magazines and newspapers for your patrons.

- **Armchairs for elderly or infirm** — This would be a nice touch especially at hospitals, nursing homes, and retirement homes. The arms make it easier to get in and out of the chairs and offer added support during the meal. You could escort some of your elderly patrons to the arm chairs and mention that you are providing these for them.

- **Guest book** — This may seem out of place at a non-commercial food service facility. But think about this for a minute. It gives your patrons a chance to offer a few comments. You can collect e-mail addresses, birthdays, anniversaries, and other information.

CASE STUDY: ASSISTED LIVING

Customer Service involves knowing basic waitstaff skills, being sensitive to the special needs of elderly patrons, and having a great deal of patience! We work in these persons' homes. We also must be prepared to make last-minute changes in menu choices based on physicians' orders, related to health changes.

Kathy L. Hilbert, Director of Dining Services
Bridgewater Retirement Community

Word of Mouth

Most marketing professionals understand that positive word of mouth is the best promotion there is for any business. Do you just happen to get good word of mouth? No. Great word of mouth takes effort. Do you have a plan to create great word of mouth that involves your staff? If your customers are going to talk about you, give them something positive to say.

Your effective word of mouth plan needs to meet these five goals:

1. Educate your customers.

2. Find ways to be unique and provide a personal touch.

3. Create salespeople in your customers.

4. Provide a reason to come back.

5. Set your facility apart from the other options.

The facility you manage is a part of the business or organization where it is located. How can that work for the facility? Working with and for the business will help the facility and the business grow and become stronger. This is a way to build bridges between the facility and the community which can make each work better. The goal is to make the community a better place. These are some ideas to work with the community or the business:

- **Is there something the community needs?** Can you provide it or start a project to earn the money to get what is needed?

- **Is there something that causes problems?** Find a way to eliminate this.

- **Include the less fortunate in your plans.**

- **Can you and your staff members share your space, equipment, and expertise to help students, business people, or others in the community?**

You are doing this to benefit the community, but it's also good to be sure people understand the value of the work that was done. Here are some things you can do to get the word out about these projects.

- **What does your facility bring to the community?** Jobs, tax revenue?

- **What does your facility get from the community?** Staff members, utilities, fire, police and emergency protection, trash and snow removal?

- **What are your complaints about the community?** High taxes, water and air quality, road problems, high unemployment?

Take a close look at this list. It is possible that other businesses have similar complaints. What can be done to make the community a better place? What can you do? Who can you get involved to make a difference?

These changes can make a real difference in the community. They will also help people in that community look to your business as a force for change. Something like this could bring potential employees, potential suppliers, and new patrons. This kind of program is a win-win situation for everyone involved. It is a way to improve the quality of life and opportunities for the facility and community.

Pleasing Customers

Food service is actually about the people. Without the people, there is no reason to create the food. This means that you must establish a connection with your patrons. The connection enables them to see your facility as a great place to visit and eat, more than just another meal. Treat them as important individuals and they will return. Are you mentally "there" with your patrons? They will know if you are faking it with them.

Many people are wonderful at "multi tasking," but should one person handle the phone, ordering, receiving, posting specials and giving direction?

Are employees getting the attention that they need? Most people can only focus on one thing at a time. So when you are talking to a customer or a staff member, don't do anything else. Listen and respond to what is being said. Doing so will help you to block out distractions. Keep in mind that you give partial answers when you are distracted and meaning that your staff members will have to ask the same question again, a waste or your time and theirs. If you are distracted with your customers, they may not come back.

CASE STUDY: CHURCH FOOD PREPARATION

Many food items can be prepared a day or two early. Some can be prepared ahead, frozen, and then thawed and prepared at the designated time. A key reason that you will want to prepare some items ahead of time is because with volunteer workers, anything can happen. Most church food service workers are volunteers, and they are sometimes late or absent. Having menu items prepared ahead will take some of the stress off you when some volunteers do not arrive.

Entrees, vegetables, and desserts can usually be prepared ahead. Play with your menu preparation to see how you can make the food preparation easier while still maintaining the quality that your patrons expect. Pricing is not usually an issue in church kitchens because many facilities accept donations for the meals. Sometimes tickets are sold beforehand and money is not handled at the time the meals are served.

Gary Douylliez • St Francis Inn
Casa de Solana Inn • **www.stfrancisinn.com**

Internal Relations

Speaking of your staff members, are they trained to offer the best possible service with a positive and helpful attitude? Never underestimate the importance of your staff's dealing with customers. After all, they deal with patrons more than the manager does, and they need to offer impeccable service. They need to delight your customers. These are some of the things your staff does.

- Handle most of the sales and promotional programs.

- Educate your customers and show them why your facility is better.

- Give information that can be shared with friends and co-workers.

It is a fact that your staff will treat your customers the way you treat them. Managers must lead by example. Be thoughtful, helpful, available, and gracious. Your staff will do the same. If you have staff members who do not behave like this, they need to be dealt with, and we will talk about that in Chapter 14. Here are some things your servers and other staff members can do to make a personal connection with your customers.

- **Greet guests within one minute** — Never leave a patron waiting to start their visit off on a bad note.

- **Look them in the eyes** — They will notice if you are staring at the floor or past their head. This will also help you focus on what they are saying. Don't say hello as you rush past them.

- **Make menu item suggestions** — All staff members should be familiar with menu items and be able to offer suggestions to customers. Sometimes people find it hard to make decisions. The staff can help them and this is especially true when they get to know the customers better.

- **Share good news** — When a customer compliments a staff member or a cook, share this information with the person mentioned. It is your responsibility to share the problems and complaints, but take the time to share the good news, too.

- **Ask about refills** — If your facility has servers walking around the dining room to refill glasses, ask before you refill cups or glasses. Some people feel compelled to finish everything in front of them and refilling their glass could make them uncomfortable. With tea and coffee, it takes time to get the taste just right and you can ruin a drink by refilling the cup or glass.

- **Invite customers to special events** — Some facilities may offer special events or different menu items on certain days, a nice touch on holidays for the employees who have to work. When something special is planned, have your staff members post notices and inform your patrons. There is no reason to do something special if people don't know about it.

- **Show appreciation for their business** — Most people are under stress so they appreciate gracious treatment.

- **Make recommendations** — Sometimes it is helpful to share your preferences with customers to help them make decisions and take the pressure off them. It's especially helpful when it is done with sincerity. Staff members need to be familiar with the menu items and be willing to share that information.

Do you make it easy for your staff members to do these things? If not, what changes could be made. Have they been given the opportunity to try all of your menu items? Are the standardized recipe files located in a convenient spot so that staff members can learn how items are prepared? It is good to let new employees work in the kitchen for a day or two to help them become familiar with preparation methods and specifics about your ingredients. All of these things will help them make honest and sincere recommendations. A confident server who knows about the food can be a great sales aid. You shouldn't create a script for this information. When your staff members use their own words, it is much more compelling. This enthusiasm will be a great asset to the facility.

CHAPTER ELEVEN

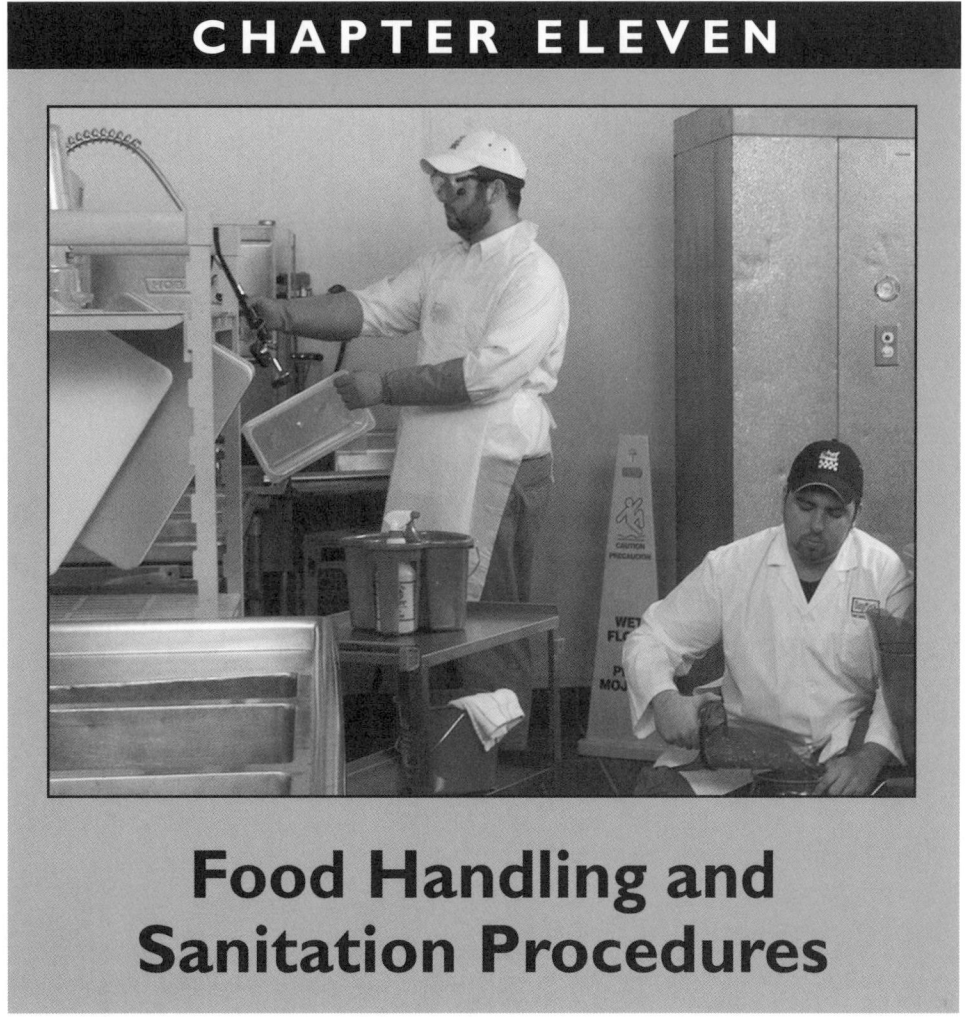

Food Handling and Sanitation Procedures

Every food service establishment has an obligation to serve quality food products in a safe environment which means that each employee must understand the basics of controlling food contamination. The actual definition of food contamination is "the spread of infectious diseases." This chapter will deal with ways to control contamination in your food storage and preparation. It also offers details about the spread of bacteria. It will help you provide an informative how to guide for your staff members. These are a few of the things you need to provide:

- **Hands on training, reminders, and an easy to understand manual.**

- **Employees need hair nets, gloves, hand and nail brushes, and germicidal hand soap.**

- **They need complete and accessible first aid kits.** We'll discuss these kits in more detail in Chapter 12.

- **Hand sinks need to be conveniently located throughout the facility** and stocked with proper hand cleaning supplies.

- **Employee bathrooms should contain scrub brushes, gloves, and disposable towels.**

- **Provide color-coded supplies and utensils.** We will discuss those in more detail later in this chapter, along with pictures of these items.

- **Approved test kits** should be supplied along with the appropriate training to use these kits effectively.

- **Provide a complete set of quality control standards.** Staff members need to be trained to use these standards. Each person on the staff is responsible to enforce them in every aspect of their work.

Many bugs, pests, and bacteria can find a home in your non-commercial food service facility, looking for food, water, and warmth, so you need to make conditions unfavorable for them.

Employees need to be trained in proper food handling and sanitary practices. The forms at the end of this chapter will be helpful in many areas of training.

There is a sample schedule at the end of this chapter which shows how your facility training program could be scheduled. It offers a wide variety of training topics that could be beneficial for your staff members.

HAACP Requirements

HACCP is the abbreviation for Hazard Analysis of Critical Control Points. This is a system to reduce food-borne illnesses by using specific procedures in food preparation. Each of your staff members needs to understand the problems that can arise when these rules are not followed.

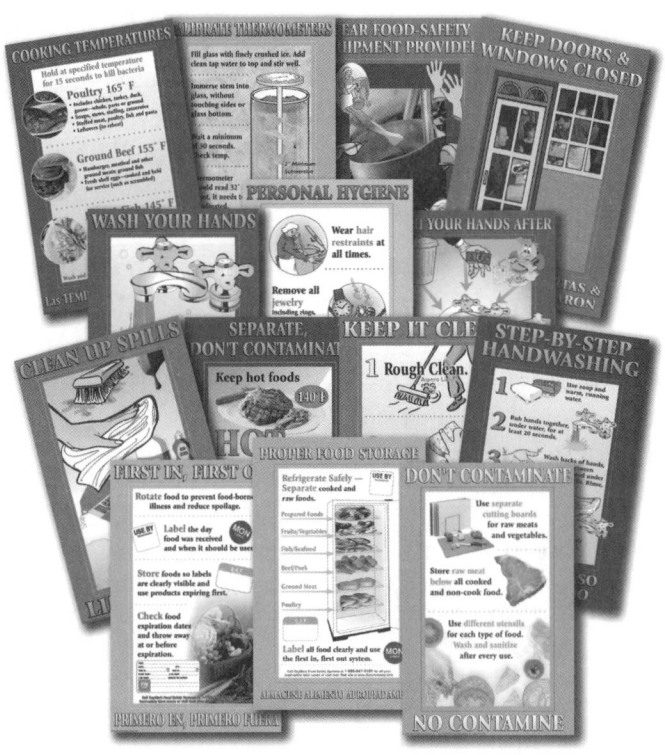

There are many critical control points where bacteria can reach the food. It is important to learn how to handle each of these potential problem areas in a way to prevent food contamination. Atlantic Publishing **www.atlantic-pub.com** offers various products to provide the in-depth information that you need. These include a training kit for your facility and labels and posters for your staff members to use. These are available at **www.atlantic-pub.com/HACCP_Main.htm**. You have the option of buying select items or the special sanitation package with includes: *HACCP & Sanitation in Restaurants and Food Service Operations: A Practical Guide Based on the FDA Food Code, With Companion CD-ROM*, 20 Safety & Sanitation Labels (five of the four different labels), 16 sanitation and safety posters, 10 workplace safety posters and a ThermaTwin thermometer.

Atlantic Publishing also offers 16 high quality posters in a series (pictured above) to help you to ensure FDA/USDA regulations and food safety practices are followed. Contact them at **www.atlantic-pub.com** (Item FSP-PS).

The HACCP Checklists shown at the end of this chapter can also be useful to your facility.

Why Should You Use HACCP?

Every non-commercial food service manager has an obligation to serve safe food. Along with this obligation is the responsibility to educate your staff members to use food safety procedures. These procedures are critical:

- **Identify all potential hazards.**

- **Implement recommended safety procedures.**

- **Keep an eye on the success of the safety system.** This is an ongoing requirement for you and the facility.

This is how it works: if the raw ingredients are safe and the process used to prepare the food is safe, the finished items are safe. HACCP gives you the ability and tools to identify foods and stages in the preparation process that are potentially hazardous, revealing each time bacterial contamination, survival, and growth are possible and likely to occur. Being aware of preventive measures will help you minimize potential problems. These are the established steps to implement HACCP and assess the hazards:

- **Put a system in place to track food items** from purchasing, receiving, storage, preparation, serving, and reheating.

- **Study your menu items with an eye for potentially hazardous foods.**

- **Can you remove these items from the menu** and reduce the chance of contamination with little effort?

- **Study the procedures you use to store, prepare, cook, and serve these items** to enable you to discover stages where contamination can occur.

- **Create a list of each potential hazard** and determine whether they are severe or probable.

"Critical Control Points" — What points in your procedures can be controlled or prevented? It is helpful to write a step-by-step list in the preparation of hazardous foods to make it easier to find the potentially critical points and find ways to prevent, reduce, and eliminate contamination. Non-commercial staff members need to:

- **Practice good personal hygiene.**

- **Avoid cross contamination** between different food items.

- **Store, cook, and cool food properly** to prevent contamination.

- **Find ways to use fewer steps when food is prepared.** Fewer steps reduce chances for possible contamination.

It is also important to study how your vendors handle the food you purchase. Is their facility clean? Do they transport items at the proper temperatures? By mishandling a product, your vendor can cause many problems for your facility. The vendor checklist at the end of this chapter will enable you to keep track of the sanitation processes of your vendors. It will also help you to know when a change may be needed.

Observe "Critical Limits" — Your limits must be visible and measurable. It could include time and temperature rules.

- **Make your descriptions precise;** include definite cooking times and temperatures to be used and to be reached during cooking.

- **It is critical to calibrate thermometers on a regular basis.**

- **Standard recipe files need to include cooking, reheating, and holding temperatures.** Include thawing time, cooking time, and cooling time.

- **Schedule enough staff members to verify food is prepared and served in a safe manner.** Minimal staff will save labor costs, but can make you run the risk of contamination.

The form shown at the end of this chapter is made to help you monitor and track critical limits in your facility.

Observe "Critical Control Points" — Step-by-step charts can help you find potentially hazardous points in your food handling processes. Review steps and when you find problem, make the needed changes immediately. Here are two possible changes. Rewash or discard any food contaminated through touch. When food temperatures are too low, food should be cooked until the required temperature is reached.

Keep Precise and Complete Records — Create a system to keep complete records of the HACCP process to enable you to monitor the results. Each employee should list compliance with these standards because doing so will keep them fresh in their minds. Records can be important in proving food-borne illnesses didn't originate in your shop. Can you prove your systems work? Here are some ways to do that:

- **Any time you need to correct your procedures, make notes of these changes.** Frequent changes indicate problems in the system. It may be necessary to rework your system or retrain your staff.

- **Review your records to be sure employees are logging the actual information about the strength of your sanitizing solution.**

- **Verify your sanitizing and dishwashing equipment works properly.** Implement a regular schedule for calibration and maintenance.

- **You may need the Board of Health to give you an unbiased assessment on the processes you are using.** If they find problems, you must change these practices right away.

HACCP Procedures

Purchasing

Here are the two main goals when you purchase food for the non-commercial facility:

1. Obtain safe and wholesome ingredients to be used in your food preparation.

2. Food is to be prepared according to your established production and menu standards.

As mentioned above, your choice of vendors is important in maintaining quality and safety. Does your vendor meet all federal and state health standards? Their employees should be using HACCP procedures. Any delivery trucks with refrigeration and freezer units need to maintain the correct temperatures. Be sure your food is in protective, leak-proof, and durable packaging.

It is important to notify your vendors from the beginning that you expect superior service, quality, and food safety procedures from them. You have the right to see their most recent Board of Health sanitation reports. It is also good to inspect their trucks quarterly and more often if you find problems. They are handling and delivering the food you will serve. You need to be happy with their procedures.

Receiving

You have two goals when receiving your food:

- Fresh, safe food needs to be delivered to your facility.

- Food items need to be moved to the proper storage area as quickly as possible.

- Be prepared to receive food.

- Food must be inspected by a qualified employee when it arrives.

Ask yourself these questions to ensure you are effectively receiving your items.

- **Do you have sanitary carts in the receiving area** to move the food to the proper storage area?

- **Is enough room prepared in the refrigerator or freezer?** Cold items need to be placed in the proper storage area right away. Preparing those areas before the food arrives makes it easier to move the items quickly.

- **Are all items labeled** with the arrival date and the use-by date?

- **Is your receiving area clean and well lighted?**

- **Is all delivery trash moved to the proper containers and area** as soon as the order is received and all items are confirmed?

- **Do your staff members keep all food and trash off the floor?**

These are important steps in the food receiving process, and any employee involved in receiving items should be thoroughly trained to observe them.

Have you noticed how the delivery truck looks? Is it clean? What do you think goes through a customer's mind when they see a dirty delivery truck bringing food to your facility? Also verify that the refrigeration units are working.

The next thing to check is the food.

- **Are the expiration dates on perishable items acceptable?**

- **Has the shelf life of the items expired** before they reach you?

- **Are all frozen items in airtight and moisture proof containers?**

- **Do you see any indication that items were thawed and refrozen?** If so, refuse to accept the items. Large crystal, solid areas of ice, and excessive ice in containers are signs of refreezing.

- **Are the cans swollen?** Are there flaws in their seams? Do you see any rust or dents on the cans? Cans with foamy or foul-smelling items should be rejected.

- **Check refrigerated and frozen items** for correct temperatures.

- **Check for bugs or signs of infestations.**

- **Are the boxes, crates, or flats dirty?** If so reject them.

Use the checklists at the end of this chapter to keep your receiving procedures in check.

Manage Food Temperatures and Storage Requirements

Use the forms at the end of this chapter to log food temperatures and as a good way to keep track of correct temperatures for food.

Storage Options and Requirements

Here are some tips for safe food storage:

- Use dry storage for holding items a long time and for less perishable items.

- Refrigeration is ideal for short-term and perishable food.

- Deep chilling units are only for short-term storage.

- Freezing is best for long-term storage for perishable items.

- It is important that everyone on your staff knows all safety and sanitation standards for each type of storage to store all types of food safely.

Dry Storage

A sanitary storeroom may hold baking supplies, canned goods, flour, grain, and dry items. Potatoes, onions, and tomatoes can be stored in a dry storage area with good ventilation and temperature control to discourage bacteria and mold. Keep these tips in mind:

- **Dry goods should be stored at 50°F**, but 60°F to 70°F is adequate.

- **Your wall thermometer must be calibrated on a regular basis.**

- **Any cans, boxes, or sacks in this area should be closed or tightly covered.** Use the "first in, first out" principal with these items. Writing or stamping the date on these packages will help ensure you use the items in the right order.

- **Any spills in this area need to be cleaned right away.** Trash and debris should never be left or stored in this area.

- **Do not place items on the floor.** They need to be raised at least 6 inches off the ground. Paper items can be placed on pallets.

- **Cleaning items or other chemicals should not be stored in the areas where food is**

stored. Label all chemicals and store them in a different container. Chemicals should be stored in their original containers. If not, use glass containers and label them.

The checklist specifically developed for tracking dry storage sanitation can be found at the end of this chapter.

Refrigerated Storage

Fresh meat, poultry, seafood, dairy products, most fresh fruits and vegetables, and hot leftovers should be stored in the refrigerator at temperatures below 40°F. Refrigeration does extend the shelf life as the cold keeps food safe from bacteria, but food can't be stored indefinitely, even in a refrigerator.

All refrigerator storage shelves need slotted shelves which allow air to circulate around the food. Do not line any shelves with paper or foil because it will hamper the air flow. It is also important that the shelves not be overloaded. Keep space on the shelves and in the refrigerator for air to circulate. Refrigerated food also needs to be dated and sealed.

Tips for effective and safe refrigerator usage:

- **Use clean, nonabsorbent, tightly covered containers.**

- **Store dairy products away from onions, cabbage, and seafood.**

- **Always store all raw and uncooked foods below prepared and ready to eat food.** This will prevent cross contamination.

- **Fish, meat, and poultry fluids must be kept away from other foods.**

- **The proper temperature for perishable items is critical to prevent food-borne illnesses.** Check regularly to be sure the temperature stays below 40°F. The inside temperature is lowered with each opening of the door.

Tucel Industries offers color coordinated brushes. Each color is used for a specific type of food as a way to prevent cross contamination. Additional details can be found at **www.tucel.com/html/haccp.htm** or contact them for more information at 800-558-8235, by fax 802-247-6826, or via e-mail at **info@tucel.com**.

In refrigerators with built-in thermometers, you still need a backup thermometer to monitor the temperature. Several thermometers should be spaced throughout the refrigerator to monitor temperatures in different areas so that it is consistent.

Use the checklist at the end of this chapter to monitor refrigerator and freezer storage.

Deep Chilling

Deep chilling foods between 26°F and 32°F decreases the growth of bacteria and extends the life of poultry, meat, and seafood without compromising their quality through freezing. You can attain this temperature by using specially designed units or by lowering the refrigerator temperature.

Frozen Storage

Frozen meats, poultry, seafood, fruits and vegetables, and some dairy products should be stored in a freezer at 0°F to keep them fresh and safe for an extended period. Make it a practice to freeze only items that you receive frozen. If you freeze perishable items, you lose some of their quality. Long-term freezer storage can cause spoilage and contamination. The freezer is another area where you must have air circulation around the shelves and the food. Use these suggestions to get maximum efficiency from your freezer:

- **Store frozen foods in moisture-proof containers** to minimize loss of flavor, discoloration, dehydration, and odor absorption.

- **Monitor temperature by using various thermometers to ensure consistent temperatures.** Keep a written record of the temperatures of each freezer.

- **Open freezer doors only when necessary.** Take multiple items each time you open the door. A "cold curtain" can guard against cold air loss.

- **Maintain temperature** by lowering the temperature of warm foods before storing.

- **Use the first-in, first-out (FIFO) method** to keep your inventory fresh.

- **Label and date all items.** Throw away anything that has been in the freezer over the suggested time limits. To make labeling easier, DayMark Food Safety Systems offers CoolMark™ freezable labels which stick to all frozen surfaces. For more information call 800-847-0101 or visit **www.daymarksafety.com.**

Issues with Food Temperatures

Cooling

You can cause food-borne illnesses by preparing foods in advance using leftovers. Two key precautions to prevent these problems are rapid cooling and protection from contamination.

Chilling It Quickly

Quick chill leftovers larger than a half gallon or two pounds to an internal temperature below 40°F, using these tips to quick chill your items:

- **Reduce food mass** — Smaller amounts of food chill quicker than large amounts so it is to your advantage to cut items into smaller pieces or divide them into several containers.

- **Shallow, pre-chilled pans** — (no more than 4 inches deep). Use stainless-steel containers because stainless steel transfers heat and cools faster than plastic.

- **Chill** — Place food in an ice-water bath or quick-chill unit (26°F to 32°F) instead of a refrigerator.

    o **Water conducts temperatures better than air** so that food cools quicker in an ice bath than in a refrigerator.

    o **Refrigeration units keep cold foods cold, but do not chill**

hot foods. It takes too long to cool foods to safe temperatures in a refrigerator.

- **Pre-chill foods in a freezer** for about 30 minutes and then refrigerate.

- **Separate items to allow air to flow around them.** Don't stack shallow pans because air cannot circulate around them. Never cool at room temperature.

- **Stir frequently** — Stirring accelerates cooling and circulates cold air to all parts of the food.

- **Check temperature periodically** — Food should reach 70°F in two hours and 40°F in 4 hours. Anything slower will put the food in the "temperature danger zone" during preparation and serving.

- **Tightly cover and label cooled foods** — List preparation date and time.

- **Store food on the upper shelves of the cooler** and cover them when they reach 45°F.

    o **Uncovered foods cool faster**, but they have an increased risk for cross-contamination.

    o **Never store prepared foods beneath raw foods.**

Reheating

Leftovers are not safe. You need to be careful when reheating and serving leftovers to avoid contamination. Here are some tips for leftovers:

- Boil sauces, soups, and gravies, heating other foods to at least 165°F. This must be done within two hours of taking the food from the refrigerator.

- Do not reheat using hot-holding equipment.

- Do not combine leftovers and fresh food.

- Food should only be reheated once.

Heated Holding Cabinets — In non-commercial food service, there are many times when you need to keep items warm. To help you keep the food free from contamination, heated holding cabinets from Henny Penny can make the difference. They offer floor or counter top units. They are energy efficient and built to last. Visit **www.hennypenny.com** or contact Henny Penny at 800-417-8417 or by fax at 800-417-8402.

Handle and Prepare Food in Safe Manner

Prepping

You need to wash fruits and vegetables with soap and water to remove any dirt, twigs, insects, and pesticides. Use food-safe disinfectant for any high risk customers. These tips will help you avoid contamination when preparing raw ingredients:

- Hands and work surfaces must be sanitized before handling food.

- Sanitize knives, choppers, and peelers between uses.

- Scrub produce before it's peeled and sliced to avoid any transfer of germs and chemicals.

When you prepare raw foods, do everything possible to avoid contamination. Colored cutting boards are an ingenious way to do this. Each board is for a specific food item. Available from DayMark Safety Systems, the durable construction provides superior heat, chemical and warp resistance in commercial dishwashers. Tough surface won't dull knives and prevents unsafe cut-grooving where dirt and bacteria can hide The color coded cutting boards help protect against cross contamination in the work place. For more information call 800-847-0101 or visit **www.daymarksafety.com**.

The appropriate brushes are also needed to scrub foods before preparation. Some are used to clean food items, and others are used to clean your work area. Available at **www.tucel.com/cgi-bin/store/agora.cgi.** Click on #1, Food Prep and Clean. Call 800-558-8235 or fax 802-247-6826.

Thawing and Marinating

Freezing will stop bacteria from multiplying, but it won't kill them. When food is taken out of the freezer, it multiplies rapidly by thawing at the wrong temperature, so these foods must be kept below the danger-zone temperatures. Never thaw foods on the counter or any other non-refrigerated area. These are the best ways to thaw food:

- Place the food item in a pan on the lowest refrigerator shelf with a temperature below 40°F.

- Place the food under drinkable running water at a temperature of about 70°F for no more than two hours or until it is thawed.

These are some tips for safe marinating:

> **Do** — Marinate meat, fish, and poultry in the refrigerator.
>
> **Do Not** — Reuse the marinade.
>
> **Do Not** — Marinate at room temperature.

While using these methods, **do not** cross contaminate the food.

Cold Food Precautions

You must be careful when preparing cold ingredients since they are at a hazardous point. It is dangerous to prepare cold foods at room temperature because contamination and cross contamination are possible. This is especially true with cold, raw foods. Items must be cleaned and prepared properly. You can chill various ingredients and then combine them while they are chilled. Keep these warnings in mind when working with cold foods:

- **Food should not be prepared too far in advance.**

- **Store cold foods below 40°F.**

- **Scrub thick-skinned produce thoroughly** with a brush.

- **Produce must be scrubbed before it is cut** to prevent contamination at the time of cutting.

- **Prepare small batches** and put into the refrigerator at once.

- **Fresh fruits and vegetables should be cleaned in plain water** to remove dirt, impurities, and pesticides.

You must avoid cross contamination. Here are some helpful tips:

- **Raw foods must be kept away from prepared foods.**

- **Cutting boards, knives, and work surfaces must be sanitized** after each different food items is prepared.

- **Hands must be sanitized** before and after handling any food item.

- **Use color-coded preparation equipment.** Each color identifies the type of food it should be used with and helps to prevent cross contamination.

- **All leftover batter, breading and marinade must be discarded after use.**

The cold food precautions are outlined on the form at the end of this chapter.

CASE STUDY: CHURCH FOOD HANDLING CONCERNS

Most of the people who work in the church kitchen are volunteers. They will not be officially trained in food handling and sanitation procedures. My volunteers review the State of Florida Restaurant Association guidelines to help them understand the basic procedures. This training program enables volunteers to understand how to prepare food safely and avoid common pitfalls in preparation. A basically "untrained" volunteer also needs quality oversight by an experienced and knowledgeable chef.

Gary Douylliez • St Francis Inn
Casa de Solana Inn • www.stfrancisinn.com

Cooking

Even when you handle food properly, there is a chance it will be contaminated, but when the internal temperature reaches the correct degree, it will kill the bacteria. It is always important to remember that conventional cooking procedures do not destroy bacteria. These are some safe cooking tips:

- **Never interrupt the cooking process** as doing so creates a dangerous environment where bacteria can grow.

- **Always stir foods that are in deep pots.** This ensures that the food is thoroughly combined and cooked.

- **Always make serving-consistent sizes** because doing so makes your cooking time uniform. All items should be finished at the same time.

- **Always calibrate heating and cooking thermometers.** Have your ovens checked regularly to be sure the food reaches proper temperatures when cooking.

- **Always use metal-stemmed, numerically scaled, or digital thermometers** to ensure the internal temperature is sufficient.

- **Always cook to an internal temperature of 165°F.**

- **When you check the internal temperature, check several different areas on the food.** This must include the thickest part that takes the longest time to cook. If you touch the thermometer against the pan, it will give you a false reading.

When you assign a person to clean your equipment, use the form at the end of this chapter to ensure sanitation practices are used.

Serving and Holding

Just cooking food doesn't guarantee that it is safe. Low holding temperatures can allow food to become contaminated. To avoid this problem, hot foods need to be held above 140°F in holding equipment and cold foods need to be kept below 40°F in a refrigeration unit or surrounded by ice.

There are specific considerations when handling hot food production. The chart at the end of this chapter will help you track your safety procedures.

Serving and Holding—the Safe Way

- **Steam tables and hot food carts** should be used during service.

- **Do not use steam tables and hot food carts to reheat foods.**

- **Cover hot holding equipment** to maintain temperatures and to prevent contamination.

- **Check the food temperature every 30 minutes** with calibrated thermometers.

- **Stir food on a regular basis** to be sure all the food is being heated.

- **Discard any food held in the "danger zone"** for more than four hours.

- **Never add fresh food to a serving pan which contains food that has already been served.**

Use the checklist at the end of this chapter for hot food-holding and serving-line monitoring.

Some important points to remember:

- **Employees need to wash their hands** with soap and warm water for at least 20 seconds before serving or preparing food.

- **When you touch food, it is best to use sanitized spoons or ladles.**

- **Staff members should never touch portions of glasses, cups, plates, and tableware** that come into contact with food or beverages.

- **Staff members should wear gloves when serving food by hand.**

- **Cuts and infections must be covered with bandages or gloves.**

- **Once gloves touch an unsanitary surface, they should be discarded.**

- **Servers need to wear gloves or use tongs to serve bread and rolls.**

- **All equipment and utensils must be cleaned and sanitized** thoroughly after each use and when you use a new food item.

- **Lids and sneeze guards must be used to protect food** for contamination.

- **Staff members should never touch cash and food without washing their hands.** If possible, have different people handle cash and food.

- **After touching raw meat or poultry, any employee must wash their hands, utensils, and working surfaces,** and before touching cooked meat and poultry.

DayMark Safety Systems is an excellent resource for personal safety items for your employees. They offer disposable aprons, hair nets, safety goggles, beard guards and a complete line of disposable gloves. For more information call 800-847-0101 or visit **www.daymarksafety.com**.

CASE STUDY: PRISON FOOD HANDLING

All guidelines are set by Food Services and Regional Sanitation Inspectors. All facilities are inspected bi-monthly and the inspections are much more meticulous than restaurant/fast food facilities. A good policy that is enforced within the prison environment is "Clean as you go."

After each meal, the linemen and floormen are responsible to sweep and mop the floor, put the trash out and to sanitize the tables, cooking, and preparation areas. The dishwasher will wash and sanitize all dishes. The milk room, freezer, walk in freezer, and fruit room are cleaned daily.

All employees handle the supervision of serving meals. Sometimes the supervisors monitor preparation depending on what the main item is, like fried chicken or pizza. They answer phones, communicate with security when there is a problem, and sign paperwork.

Food temperatures are monitored by supervisors and recorded once a day. Non-commercial food service in these conditions is a battle to stay aware of temperatures and avoiding major foodborne illnesses caused by bacteria.

Lawrence Shearer, Chef

Clean Versus Sanitary

Two common ways to bring bacteria to acceptable levels are the use of heat and chemicals which combat and destroy microorganisms. To sanitize by heat, equipment must be exposed to high heat for a sufficient period of time. The minimal time would be at least 30 seconds at 170°F to 195°F. You can also use a dishwasher that washes at 150°F and rinses at 180°F. The temperatures must be checked on a regular basis to ensure proper heat for satisfactory sanitization.

Some equipment can be sanitized by dipping or wiping with bleach or a sanitizing solution. Mix half an ounce or one tablespoon of 5 percent bleach per gallon of water. If you choose to use a commercial cleaning agent, use the manufacturer's instructions. These chemicals are regulated by the EPA. Follow these instructions carefully. You can use chemical test strips to test the sanitizing solution strength. When the solution is exposed to air, the strength of the solution is reduced, so be sure to test it often.

The Quik-Wash Hand Wash Faucet Control – The Centers for Disease Control and Prevention say "Handwashing is the single most effective means of preventing the spread of disease." This faucet control is an economical choice, better than costly electronic faucets. It offers automatic closing and hands-free positions. Visit **www.fmponline.com/featuredproduct.html** for more information. You can contact FMP at 800-257-7737, by fax at 800-255-9866, or via e-mail at **sales@fmponline.com**.

Cleaning Products and MSDS — Henny Penny offers a full line of quality cleaning products to sanitize equipment and clean your food preparation and serving areas. Visit **http://www.hennypenny.com/products/index.html?pc=6** or contact Henny Penny at 800-417-8417 or fax 800-417-8402.

Sanitize Portable Equipment

A three-compartment sink is needed to clean and sanitize portable equipment: one sink to clean, a second to rinse, and a third to sanitize.

Set aside a separate area to scrape and rinse any food and other debris into the trash before the items are washed. There needs to be another area for a drain board for clean items and an area for dirty items.

Follow this procedure to sanitize a piece of equipment:

- **Clean and sanitize** all sinks and work surfaces.

- **Scrape and rinse** all food and debris into the garbage.

- **Presoak silverware** and items that are very dirty.

- **In the first sink** have water about 120°F and clean detergent solution to dip equipment into. A brush or cloth should be used to loosen or remove any other visible soil.

- **In the second sink** — Have clean, clear water about 120°F to 140°F to remove food, debris, and detergent from the first sink.

- **In the third sink** — Have hot water about 170°F to sanitize items for 30 seconds or in a chemical sanitizing solution for one minute. All sides and surfaces of the equipment need to be covered with the hot water or sanitizing solution for the correct amount of time.

- **Watch for these warning signs.** If any of them occur, change the water.

  o If soapsuds disappear in the first sink

  o If soapsuds remain in the second sink

  o If water temperature cools

  o If any water becomes dirty and cloudy

- **Air-dry the items.** Towel drying can contaminate the equipment and remove the solution before it is finished working.

- **Do not put the equipment back together until it is dry.**

- **Any moisture can promote bacterial growth.**

Sanitizing In-Place Equipment

Some equipment must be cleaned in place. It must still be washed, rinsed, and sanitized. Use these steps to clean in-place equipment.

1. **Unplug electrical cords.**

2. **Carefully remove food scraps** and other debris.

3. **Wash, rinse, and sanitize** any removal parts using the immersion method described above.

4. **Wash all surfaces** which come into contact with food and rinse with clean water. Wipe with sanitizing solution, according to manufacturer's directions.

5. **Wipe all surfaces** which do not come in contact with food with a sanitized cloth and air dry. Once it is totally air dried, reassemble the pieces. The cloth should be sanitized before and during sanitizing. This is done by rinsing it in the sanitizing solution.

6. **After the equipment is reassembled, wipe all external surfaces** that were touched with a sanitizing cloth.

7. **Wooden surfaces should be scrubbed with a detergent solution** and a stiff bristle nylon brush. After brushing, rinse in clear, clean water and wipe with sanitizing solution after each use.

Floors, Walls, and Ceilings

Your facility must be clean and in good repair to be safe and sanitary. This is a consideration when the facility is initially laid out or if it is reorganized. Any hard-to-clean areas should be changed. Staff members will need to clean all the time. Are there ways to make it easier for them? Remember that additional labor dollars will be spent to clean a facility laid out in an awkward way.

Work Spaces

It is important to have easy-to-clean work areas that will withstand chemicals and steams.

Non-porous materials are the best choice. Limited joints are better since dirt gets trapped in the seams. Some worktables are made on wheels and can be moved to the area where they are needed.

- **Dirt and water should be kept away** from the ceilings, floors, and walls.

- **Walls should be wiped with a cleaning solution.** Floors can be swept and then cleaned with a spray cleaner and mop.

- **Ceilings can also be swabbed**, but be careful to keep water and cleaners away from lights and ceiling fans.

- **It is common to skip hard-to-reach areas**, but they need to be cleaned too.

Sanifloor is a flooring system which allows the food to go into the floor as a way to limit potential slips and falls. It controls liquids, crumbs, and other items dropped on the floor. Staff members do not need to clean the floor during the work shift. Anything collected can simply be flushed. Visit **sanifloor.com**. For prices or installation details, contact 760-345-7987 or e-mail **info@sanifloor.com**.

Various cleaning supplies are needed to maintain a clean floor. These items can be found at **www.tucel.com/cgi-bin/store/agora.cgi** in the Floor and Wall Clean section. Some of these items include brooms, mops, and dust pans. Contact them at 800-558-8235, fax 802-247-6826, or via e-mail at **info@tucel.com**.

Ventilation

Effective ventilation is critical to remove grease, heat, smoke, and steam from the food preparation area. It also improves the quality of the air and can reduce the risk of fire from accumulations of grease. It eliminates condensation and airborne contaminants. It also reduces dirt, gas, fumes and odors, humidity, and potential mold growth. Here are ways to ensure good ventilation in the facility:

- **Use exhaust fans** to remove smoke and odors.

- **Use hoods with exhaust fans** in cooking areas and over dishwashers.

- **Properly maintain exhaust fans and hoods.**

- **Clean vent filter** using manufacturer's instructions.

Restrooms

Public restrooms should be convenient, and employee restrooms should be centrally located in the work area. They must all be sanitary and stocked with toilet paper, antiseptic liquid soap, disposable paper towels or air blowers, and a covered trash can with a foot pedal to lift the lid.

A staff member or two should be scheduled to check the public restrooms throughout the shifts. Employee restrooms need nail brushes and sanitizing solution. Use the checklist at the end of this chapter to monitor restroom sanitation.

Sanitation Practices

At the end of this chapter you will find a checklist that is comprehensive and covers each area of your non-commercial food service facility.

Dishware

Employees need to use care when handling dishware. Share these tips with your employees on how to handle dishware without contaminating areas that touch food or mouths.

1. Use tongs, scoops, or food grade rubber gloves to handle food items.

2. Glasses should be picked up from the outside.

3. Hold cups and mugs by the handle.

4. Use handles to pick up silverware.

5. Plates should be carried by the bottoms or the edges. Dishes, cups, and saucers should not be stacked.

6. Employees' hands must be washed after they handle dirty dishes and pans.

7. One more time. Always wash your hands before putting gloves on. After you use the gloves, discard them and wash your hands again. Then put on fresh gloves.

8. Never use a utensil to taste more than one item.

Gloves Information

Multi-use gloves may save money, but they can be breeding grounds for bacteria. You must wash, sanitize, and rinse them after each use. If the gloves are dirty or the inside becomes contaminated, throw them out. Never use slash-resistant gloves with ready-to-eat food because they can't be sanitized easily.

Natural Latex Rubber Gloves can cause allergic reactions for some people even if they only eat food that was prepared with them.

Either type you choose will help you protect patrons of your non-commercial food service facility from bacteria and contamination. If you would like additional information, the federal government and the local health department will help. There is more work involved in their suggestions, but they will help protect your facility and patrons.

DayMark Safety Systems is an excellent resource for all types of gloves from cut gloves to disposable options. For more information call 800-847-0101 or visit **www.daymarksafety.com**.

Sanitary Self-Service

No matter how much you train your employees, it is also possible that customers could contaminate the food. They haven't received training in sanitation practices. It is advisable to watch for customers or employees who do these things:

- **Touch food or silverware** with their hands.

- **Touch the edges** of utensils or equipment.

- **Sneeze or cough** on food or self serve displays.

- **Touch the tops of salt and pepper shakers**, sugar bowls and condiment containers.

- **Return uneaten food** to the hot holding or self service trays. If you or any staff members see anything questionable, you are responsible to remove food that could be contaminated. Whenever you are in doubt, throw it out. Here are two ways to protect your patrons: purchase breadsticks, crackers, and condiments in sealed containers and wrap, label, and date any sandwiches that you will sell.

Rosseto dispensers are a safe and sanitary way for customers to serve themselves and to help you control contamination. Toppings, cereal and other items are beautifully displayed and customers get measured portions. These items are ideal for salads, snacks, cereal, and ice cream. The design keeps your toppings fresh longer. The equipment is easy to use and easy to clean. Visit **www.rosseto.com** or call for more details 847-491-9166.

If your facility offers a salad bar, use the checklist at the end of this chapter to monitor the sanitary condition of the area.

Cross-Contamination Concerns

Cross-contamination is a common cause of food-borne illness. It is the transfer of bacteria and viruses from food to food, hand to food, or equipment to food.

> **Food to Food** — Raw, contaminated ingredients can be added to foods. Fluids from raw foods may drip into uncooked foods. This is why it was mentioned several times that meat should not be stored on upper refrigerator shelves where the juices can drip

onto prepared foods.

Hand to Food — Bacteria is everywhere: in hair, clothing, mouth, nose, throat, intestinal tract, and on skin, scabs, or scars from wounds. It ends up on hands and can easily be spread to food. It is possible to transfer bacteria by touching raw food and then touching cooked or ready-to-eat food.

Equipment to Food — Bacteria can pass to food when equipment touches contaminated food and is used to prepare other food without being cleaned and sanitized.

Plastic wrap can hold bacteria and transfer it to other containers and food. A can opener, boxes of wrap, or a food slicer creates cross-contamination when not sanitized properly.

Contributing to Food-borne Illness

A Centers for Disease Control (CDC) study shows that the most common reason for food-borne illnesses is mishandling food. The CDC's Surveillance for Food-borne Disease Outbreaks (1988-1992) cite these major factors:

Using leftovers	4 percent
Improper Cleaning	7 percent
Cross-Contamination	7 percent
Contaminated raw food	7 percent
Insufficient reheating	12 percent
Improper hot storage	16 percent
Insufficient cooking	16 percent
Infected people touching food	20 percent
Time between preparing and serving	21 percent
Improper cooling of foods	40 percent

Control

Here are a few ways to control bacteria. Maintain good personal hygiene, control cross contamination, monitor time and temperature, and implement an effective sanitation program.

One way to control contamination is by limiting access to the food receiving, storage, and preparation areas. This is another reason that your receiving person needs to verify that all items and boxes are clean and pest free when they arrive at your facility.

Your staff members can avoid contamination by controlling time and temperatures. Bacterial disease begins to develop between 41°F and 140°F. So when food is cooked, reheated, and stored between the correct temperatures, potential problems are reduced. It is hard to believe, but bacteria can double every 15 minutes to produce more than a million bacterial cells in only five hours. This means that enough bacteria can develop in four hours to cause food-borne illnesses.

Foods will be at risky temperatures at times. You must minimize these times by being watchful. When staff members take breaks, food should be placed back in the refrigerator until the break is over.

Bacteria

Bacteria are everywhere: air, your facility, and the bodies of your staff members. Some bacteria are good, but keep in mind that a small amount of bad bacteria can cause food to spoil and will cause food poisoning when it is eaten. There are types of bacteria that can live in less than ideal situations, including during cooking, in high-salt environments and while frozen, but given "ideal" conditions they multiply and cause illness.

Bacteria need these things to reproduce: food, acid, temperature, time, oxygen, and moisture.

Food — High protein or carbohydrate foods like meats, poultry, seafood, cooked potatoes, and diary products.

Acid — Most bacteria flourish in a neutral environment, but they can grow in foods that have pH levels between 4.5 and 9.0. (The "pH" indicates how acidic or alkaline a food is.) pH ranges from 0.0 to 14.0, with 7.0 being neutral. High acid foods discourage the growth of bacteria. You can limit the hazard of lower pH foods by adding acidic ingredients to increase the pH level.

Temperature — Most disease-causing bacteria grow at between 41°F to 140°F. Listeria monocytogenes causes food-borne illnesses to arise from processed luncheon meats and can grow below 41°F.

Time — Bacteria needs about four hours to reproduce enough cells to cause a food-borne illness.

Oxygen — Aerobic and anaerobic bacteria contain different oxygen requirements. Aerobic bacteria need oxygen, but anaerobic bacteria do not and grow well in vacuum packed or canned items.

Moisture — The amount of water in a food to support bacterial growth is called water activity. It's measured on a scale of 0.0 and 1.0. The water activity must be greater than 0.85 to support bacterial growth.

Bacteria growth depends on how favorable these conditions are. Bacteria prefer moisture-saturated foods, and they won't grow in dry conditions.

Dangerous Bacteria

There are an estimated 76 million cases of food-borne disease in the United States each year. Most of these are mild and don't last long. The CDC estimates 325,000 hospitalizations and 5,000 deaths are caused by food-borne diseases each year. The elderly and the young are the most at risk. These are precautions that those at high risk should take:

- Pregnant women, the elderly, and those with weakened immune systems need to be careful not to eat undercooked animal products. They should avoid alfalfa sprouts and un-pasteurized juices.

- A bottle-fed infant is at high risk for bacteria that can grow in a bottle of warm formula if it is left at room temperature for many hours. Baby bottles need to be thoroughly cleaned after they are used.

- Anyone with liver disease is susceptible to infections with a rare microbe found in oysters. They should avoid eating raw oysters.

- The most commonly recognized food-borne infections are those caused by the bacteria campylobacter, salmonella, and E. coli O157:H7, and by a group of viruses known as the Norwalk and Norwalk-like viruses.

- Campylobacter causes fever, diarrhea, and abdominal cramps. Eating undercooked chicken or food contaminated with juices dripping from raw chicken is the most frequent source of this infection.

- Salmonella causes fever, diarrhea, and abdominal cramps. When these bacteria attack a person with poor health, they can cause serious infections.

- E. coli O157:H7 is usually caused by consuming water that's contaminated with microscopic amounts of cow feces. It causes severe and bloody diarrhea and painful abdominal cramps without much fever. If the condition becomes more severe, it includes temporary anemia, profuse bleeding, and kidney failure.

- Calicivirus, or Norwalk-like virus, causes an acute gastrointestinal illness, characterized with more vomiting than diarrhea. It only lasts about two days. It's usually spread from one infected person to another. Infected kitchen staff can contaminate cold foods during preparation. Visit **www.cfsan.fda.gov/~mow/intro.html** for more information.

Employee Hygiene Concerns

Maintaining personal hygiene is the most effective and easiest way to stop the growth of bacteria. The hands of your staff members are a big source of contamination, and all staff members should wash their hands throughout the day. Sneezing and scratching your head will expose all hands to bacteria. When employees' hands are contaminated, bacteria is passed on to other things they touch. Staff members can prevent the spread of bacteria by using anti-bacterial soaps, disposable gloves, and nail brushes. Employees need to follow these hygiene basics:

- Short hair and/or use of a hair net.

- Clean-shaven face.

- Clean clothes/uniforms.

- Clean hands and short nails.

- No unnecessary or large jewelry.

- A daily shower or bath.

- No smoking in or near the kitchen.

- Hand washing, prior to work, periodically, and after handling foreign objects such as any body parts, money, food, boxes, or trash.

There are times when employees should not be around food: when they are getting a cold or the flu and when they have a cut. Small cuts can be covered with a bandage, but larger cuts cannot be fully covered and some bandages are a breeding ground for bacteria.

There are some businesses that require prospective employees to take a complete medical exam, including blood and urine test. Of course, not all employers can afford this.

Hand washing is the most critical part of our personal hygiene. The only time employees should touch raw food is when they wash fruits and vegetables. They can use gloves, spatulas, spoons, tongs, or deli paper.

Employees must always wash their hands after any of these activities:

- Smoking
- Using the restroom
- Touching raw food
- Coughing or sneezing
- Taking a break

- Eating
- Handling money
- Touching or combing their hair
- Blowing their nose
- Handling anything dirty

You should make sure all employees know and practice proper hand washing procedures. Posters are an excellent on-going reminder. Atlantic Publishing offers three different handwashing posters: "Wash Your Hands" (Item #FSP1-PS), "Step-By-Step Handwashing" (Item #FSP2-PS) and "Wash Your Hands After" (Item #FSP3-PS), Each brightly colored poster is in both Spanish and English and laminated with sealed edges. They are $8.95 each and available at **www.atlantic-pub.com** or by calling 800-814-1132.

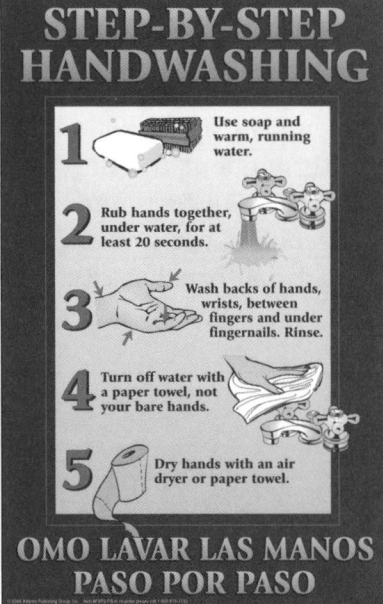
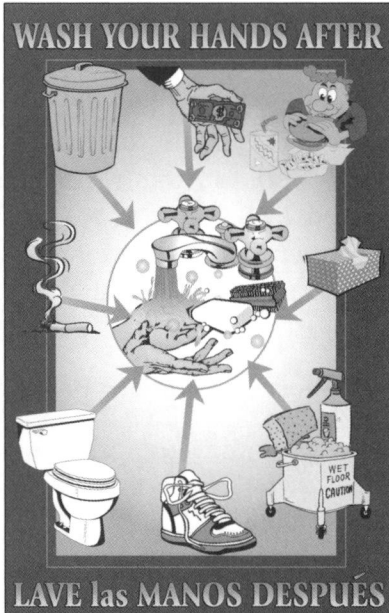

The information and forms at the end of this chapter will help you track the facility policy and procedure for personal hygiene. This is only a suggestion and you can tweak this to make it effective for your facility.

Clothing

It is common to touch our clothes while we're working, and clothes hold bacteria when they are dirty. Touching clothing and then touching food transfers bacteria to the food. Customers get concerned when they see employees in dirty clothes. There will be days when employees go through many aprons because of flour, sauce, and other ingredients. These are signs of working hard, but have them change into a clean uniform or apron when needed.

"Aprons, Etc" offers many apron styles that are washable and disposable choices. The name of the facility can be printed on the aprons. To see the full line of aprons available, visit **www.apronsetc.com/aprons.htm#1.**

Dickie's Chef Aprons and Hats offer high quality products that are durable and functional. Their aprons have oversized pockets and are comfortable for your staff. They are available with a soil resistant finish. To see Dickie's selection of aprons, chef hats, shirts, pants, and vests, visit **www.dickieschef.com**, call 866-262-6288, or fax 877-353-9044.

Royal Industries also offers aprons, chef's coats, and chef's hats. They are innovative leaders in the food service industry. Visit **www.royalindustriesinc.com**, call 800-782-1200, or fax 800-321-3295.

Some uniform options available from Aprons, Ect.

Eating, Drinking, or Using Tobacco

As a manager, you need to prohibit eating, smoking, and drinking in the food preparation areas.

Anyone who has worked in a kitchen knows how hot it can be. Employees can have closed drink containers in these areas, but always insist they be placed near the back of any work surface and away from the food.

Eyes, Nose, and Mouth

Employees with a cold or allergies are going to sneeze and cough, contaminating anything close: food, utensils, equipment, dishes, and linens. While they are sick, employees should be assigned duties away from food preparation and sanitizing areas.

Hair Restraints

Customers worry about hair contaminating their food. Because of this concern, employees need to use caps and hair nets. This is the easiest way to keep hair out of the food. Staff members can also contaminate their food by touching their hair while they are working.

Hand Contamination

Hands are another common way that food is contaminated through burns, cuts, and infections. These potential problem areas need to be bandaged before starting to work each day. When staff members wash their hands, they need to follow these instructions:

1. Remove jewelry.

2. Use water as hot as you can stand it.

3. Moisten hands and forearms to the elbows.

4. Lather thoroughly with soap.

5. Rub hands together, wash between fingers and up to the elbows for at least 20 seconds.

6. Scrub under nails with a brush.

7. Rinse hands and forearms with hot water.

8. Dry hands and forearms with a paper towel or a hand dryer.

This is a simple and effective way to eliminate cross-contamination. When you train new employees to wash their hands, use this exercise to test their technique. Start with a fluorescent substance and a black light. (One source for this is Atlantic Publishing's Glo Germ Training Kit. See **www.atlantic-pub.com/HACCP_Main.htm** or call 800-814-1132.)

Use this procedure to show trainees the dirt they are missing on their hands:

1. Dip hands in the fluorescent substance.

2. Have employees wash their hands.

3. Hold their hands under the black light to see how much "dirt" is still there.

4. Explain the steps of the proper hand-washing technique.

5. Employees should wash their hands again, with the proper hand-washing technique.

6. Have employees once again hold their hands under the black light.

Food Safety Inspections

There are many ways to prepare for an inspection and I will include some tips, suggestions, and checklists for you to study and use as you see fit. We talked earlier about doing self-inspections in your facility. This is another area where those inspections would be beneficial.

For an online mock inspection, visit **www.metrokc.gov/health/foodsfty/mockinspection.htm**. This Web site walks you through the steps of an inspection, although the specific details may vary in your area. However, this will give you an idea of the things take place.

The City of Pasedena's Web site offers all sorts of valuable information at **http://www.ci.pasadena.ca.us/publichealth/environmental_health/food_safety_%20services/inspection_violation_codes.asp**. On this page you will find specific information about the following topics:

Type I Violations

1. Food Service

2. Personnel

3. Temperature Control

4. Sanitization Rinse

5. Water/Sewage/Plumbing Systems

6. Hand Washing and Toilet Facilities

7. Pest Control

8. Toxic Items

Type 2 Violations

9. Food Labeling and Protection

10. Improper Equipment Design and Construction

11. Testing Devices

12. Improper Cleaning of Equipment and Utensils

13. Utensils – Single Service Articles

14. Physical Facilities

15. Other Operations

This site offers more information on each of these headings and various subheadings. But you can also learn why each element of this list is significant to public health. I would highly recommend that you take a look at this information to gain additional insights into many of the things we discussed in this chapter.

Food Safety and Inspection Service (FSIS) is the public health agency in the U.S. Department of Agriculture which ensures the nation's commercial supply of meat, poultry, and egg products is safe, wholesome, and correctly labeled and packaged. Visit them at **www.fsis.usda.gov**. There is a wealth of safety information at **www.fsis.usda.gov/Food_Safety_Education/index.asp.**

You can also subscribe to their Food Safety Newsletter for up-to-date information. This newsletter reports on new food safety educational programs and materials and emerging science concerning food safety risks. The newsletter is distributed up to four times a year. This publication is free for print subscribers. Electronic copies may be downloaded from the Web site. E-mail questions to **fsis.outreach@usda.gov**.

How to Prepare for an Inspection

Inspections can be traumatic for food service managers if you do not maintain the proper environment and procedures each day. This section will include some tips to help you prepare for these inspections and to alleviate some of the stress associated with inspections. They are a necessary part of the business, so it's better to be prepared for them. At the end of this chapter are a couple of checklists that you can use in your self inspection. This Web site offers a Sanitation Survey Report you can use: **www.metrokc.gov/health/foodsfty/inspectionform.pdf.**

At the end of this chapter there is a form that will help you set up and maintain a daily sanitation schedule, a wonderful way to establish sanitary practices for your facility.

There is an online step-by-step inspection which can help you see what will be checked and to be better prepared. Your inspection can be different, but this is an example of some of the things you should expect. **www.metrokc.gov/health/foodsfty/mockinspection.htm.**

Preparing for an Inspection

Preparation

Here are some things you need to do to prepare for an inspection.

- Use a form similar to the local health department's for your self inspections.

- View the facility from the inspectors view-point, not your own.

- Begin your self-inspection from the outside and work your way through the entire facility.

- Immediately after your inspection, hold a brief meeting with your staff members to review the problems you found. This will illustrate how important this is to you.

- Several priorities in your inspection should include: food temperatures in storage, preparation, serving, reheating, food type awareness, and proper hand washing techniques.

- You cannot emphasize the importance of hand washing too much. Hang posters and reminders for staff members in the kitchen and restrooms.

- Any managers should be trained to keep up-to-date about the latest food safety information and techniques.

- Stay current about the local health code and requirements.

The Visit

- **Most important—don't panic.** Be prepared and eliminate the possibility of panic.

- **When inspectors arrive, ask to see their credentials.**

- **If you are unsure about their credentials**, call the health department to verify their identity.

- **Never refuse to allow inspectors to do an inspection.** They can get an inspection warrant if needed, but the resulting inspection will be more thorough if these measures are needed. Refusing to allow an inspection will cause unneeded animosity with the inspector who is there to help you make the facility better and safer.

- **Follow the inspector and make notes about any problems.** Make the effort to fix any problems while the inspector is there. Show you are willing to make the needed changes.

- **Never offer food or other items to the inspector.** They could be viewed as a bribe to influence the inspector.

- **Sign the report after the inspection is complete.** Your signature does not indicate your agreement with the details but merely that you received a copy of the report.

- **Ask inspectors to explain any findings to you and your staff members.** They can also offer suggestions on how to make necessary improvements. Remember that even the cleanest food service facilities can have health department citations.

The Violations

- **Fix any small problems before inspectors leave your facility** to show your willingness to make improvements.

- **Ask for additional explanation** if you have questions or need clarification.

- **You have the right to appeal any findings**, but keep your thoughts to yourself until after the inspector leaves.

Visit **http://www.ci.pasadena.ca.us/publichealth/environmental_health/food_safety_ %20services/inspection_violation_codes.asp** to get more information about each violation and additional information which may explain the public health significance for each violation. Categories include:

1. Food Source

2. Personnel

3. Temperature Control

4. Sanitization Rinse

5. Water/Sewage/Plumbing Systems

6. Hand Washing and Toilet Facilities

7. Pest Control

8. Toxic Items

9. Food Labeling and Protection

10. Improper Equipment Design and Construction

11. Testing Devices

12. Improper Cleaning of Equipment and Utensils

13. Utensils – Single Service Articles

14. Physical Facilities

15. Other Operations

For additional information about HACCP and safe food handling practices, you should see *HACCP & Sanitation in Restaurants and Food Service Operations: A Practical Guide Based on the USDA Food Code* by Atlantic Publishing (**www.atlantic-pub.com**).

Circle either "True" or "False"

1. The five major risk factors related to employee behaviors and preparation practices in retail and food service establishments that contribute to foodborne illness are improper holding temperatures, inadequate cooking; contaminated equipment, food from unsafe sources, and poor personal hygiene.
    True
    False

2. The average cost to a food service operation for an outbreak of food poisoning (to cover medical and legal fees, etc.) is $50,000.
    True
    False

3. HACCP is the abbreviation for Hazard Analysis of Critical Control Points. This is a system to reduce food-borne illnesses by using specific procedures in food preparation.
    True
    False

4. The annual cost of foodborne illness in terms of pain and suffering, reduced productivity, and medical costs are estimated to be $10 - $83 billion.
    True
    False

5. An outbreak of food poisoning can cause loss of customers, loss of reputation, low employee morale and the need to retrain employees.
    True
    False

6. Leftover foods should be covered, labeled with the name, labeled with the date and properly stored.
    True
    False

7. Plastic wrap can hold bacteria and transfer it to other containers and food.
    True
    False

8. A can opener, boxes of wrap, or a food slicer creates cross-contamination when not sanitized properly.
    True
    False

9. It is generally safe to combine leftovers and fresh food.
    True
    False

10. Leftovers should be heated to at least 110°F.
    True
    False

11. Leftover batter, breading and marinade can be properly stored and reused once before discarding.
    True
    False

12. Meats should be thawed at room temperature because it is the safest method.
    True
    False

13. Soups, stews, and sauces should be cooled in shallow pans and stirred to help release the heat.
    True
    False

14. Wiping cloths should be stored in a sanitizing solution because they can cause cross-contamination.
    True
    False

15. When you are stocking foods, put the new stock in front of the old stock.
    True
    False

16. Raw foods (such as raw meats) should only be stored on shelves above cooked foods.
    True
    False

17 When in doubt, throw it out.
    True
    False

18. Check the temperature of foods by feel, then use a thermometer if you are unsure.
    True
    False

19. Keep foods out of the Danger Zone (45°F-140°F).
    True
    False

20. For deliveries, inspect foods thoroughly and store immediately using the first in, first out method.
    True
    False

21. Clean and sanitize all equipment, tools, tables, etc., after each use.
    True
    False

22. Food mass is not a factor when chilling. Smaller amounts of food chill at the same rate as large amounts.
    True
    False

23. For preschool age children, older adults in health care facilities, and those with impaired immune systems, foodborne illness is serious and may be life threatening.
    True
    False

24. Slash-resistant gloves should be used with ready-to-eat food because they can be sanitized easily.
    True
    False

25. When sanitizing equipment, towel drying can contaminate the equipment and remove the solution before it is finished working..
    True
    False

Circle either "True" or "False"

1. The five major risk factors related to employee behaviors and preparation practices in retail and food service establishments that contribute to foodborne illness are improper holding temperatures, inadequate cooking; contaminated equipment, food from unsafe sources, and poor personal hygiene.
    ☆ **True**
    False

2. The average cost to a food service operation for an outbreak of food poisoning (to cover medical and legal fees, etc.) is $50,000.
    True
    ☆ **False. It is $75,000.**

3. HACCP is the abbreviation for Hazard Analysis of Critical Control Points. This is a system to reduce food-borne illnesses by using specific procedures in food preparation.
    ☆ **True**
    False

4. The annual cost of foodborne illness in terms of pain and suffering, reduced productivity, and medical costs are estimated to be $10 - $83 billion.
    ☆ **True**
    False

5. An outbreak of food poisoning can cause loss of customers, loss of reputation, low employee morale and the need to retrain employees.
    ☆ **True**
    False

6. Leftover foods should be covered, labeled with the name, labeled with the date and properly stored.
    ☆ **True**
    False

7. Plastic wrap can hold bacteria and transfer it to other containers and food.
    ☆ **True**
    False

8. A can opener or a food slicer can create cross-contamination when not sanitized properly.
    ☆ **True**
    False

9. It is generally safe to combine leftovers and fresh food.
    True
    ☆ **False. These should never be combined.**

10. Leftovers should be heated to at least 110°F.
    True
    ☆ **False. Leftovers should be heated to 165°F.**

11. Leftover batter, breading and marinade can be properly stored and reused once before discarding.
    True
    ☆ **False. It cannot be reused.**

12. Meats should be thawed at room temperature because it is the safest method.
    True
    ☆ **False. This is not a safe method of thawing.**

13. Soups, stews, and sauces should be cooled in shallow pans and stirred to help release the heat.
    ☆ **True**
    False

14. Wiping cloths should be stored in a sanitizing solution because they can cause cross-contamination.
    ☆ **True**
    False

15. When you are stocking foods, put the new stock in front of the old stock.
    True
    ☆ **False. Use the first in, first out method and move older items to the front.**

16. Raw foods (such as raw meats) should only be stored on shelves above cooked foods.
    True
    ☆ **False. They should only be stored under cooked foods.**

17. When in doubt, throw it out.
    ☆ **True**
    False

18. Check the temperature of foods by feel, then use a thermometer if you are unsure.
    True
    ☆ **False. Always use a thermometer.**

19. Keep foods out of the Danger Zone (45°F-140°F).
    ☆ **True**
    False

20. For deliveries, inspect foods thoroughly and store immediately using the first in, first out method.
    ☆ **True**
    False

21. Clean and sanitize all equipment, tools, tables, etc., after each use.
    ☆ **True**
    False

22. Food mass is not a factor when chilling. Smaller amounts of food chill at the same rate as large amounts.
    True
    ☆ **False. Smaller amounts chill faster.**

23. For preschool age children, older adults in health care facilities, and those with impaired immune systems, foodborne illness is serious and may be life threatening.
    ☆ **True**
    False

24. Slash-resistant gloves should be used with ready-to-eat food because they can be sanitized easily.
    True
    ☆ **False. Slash-resistant gloves are more difficult to sanitize.**

25. When sanitizing equipment, towel drying can contaminate the equipment and remove the solution before it is finished working..
    ☆ **True**
    False

FOOD PREPARATION EQUIPMENT TRAINING CHECKLIST

All employees must be trained on equipment before use to avoid injury. The following chart can be used as a training record for each employee. After training has been completed, both the trainer and employee should initial in the appropriate area.

EMPLOYEE NAME _____

SUPERVISOR NAME _____

Equipment	Dates	Trained By	Trainers Initials	Employee Initials
Slicer				
Fryer				
Electronic Mixers				
Steamers				
Vegetable Cutter				
Deep Fat Fryer				
Garbage Disposal				
Knives				
Dish machine				
Convection Ovens				
Gas Range				
Blender				
List others:				

EMPLOYEE PERSONAL HYGIENE CHECKLIST

Date	
Employee Name	
Supervisor Name	
Purpose	To protect employees, patients, and customers by minimizing the possibility of contamination.

Procedure:

The Supervisor should observe the employee to observe the following items

1. The employee has no visible, open cuts, abrasions or skin lesions.
   ❏ yes ❏ no

2. Any cuts, abrasions or skin lesions are properly bandaged.
   ❏ yes ❏ no

3. The employee does not display any symptoms of cold, infectious diseases or illness.
   ❏ yes ❏ no

4. The employee wears protective gloves as needed.
   ❏ yes ❏ no

5. The employee knows and follows proper handwashing procedures.
   ❏ yes ❏ no

6. The employee wears proper hair restraints.
   ❏ yes ❏ no

7. The employee wears a clean uniform and has a well-groomed appearance..
   ❏ yes ❏ no

8. The employee wears only approved jewelry.
   ❏ yes ❏ no

9. The employee's fingernails are clean, unpolished and cut short.
   ❏ yes ❏ no

10. The employee uses proper safety precautions to prevent cuts, burns or other injuries.
    ❏ yes ❏ no

List any comments or areas that need improvement:

_____
_____
_____
_____
_____
_____
_____

Use the following worksheet as a handout to help educate employees on the dangers of Salmonella.

WHAT ARE SALMONELLA?

Salmonella are bacteria. The Salmonella consist of a range of very closely related bacteria, many of which cause disease in humans and animals.

Salmonellae does not survive with proper cooking. The cooked internal temperatures of meat should be:

Cook all meat and poultry thoroughly. Check the internal temperature with a properly calibrated thermomter. This applies to microwaving as well as using traditional ovens.

ADDITIONAL COOKING TIPS:

- If meat is too thin for a thermometer, cook until the juices run clear. Be sure to follow the recipe.

- Cook continually without interruption.

- After thawing foods in the microwave, cook them immediately.

- If rehearsing leftovers, cover and reheat thoroughly to 165°F. Bacteria can survive during refrigeration or freezing.

- Never store cooked meat or poultry in an off or warm oven. Hold the food above 140°F. Within 2 hours after cooking, refrigerate the food.

COOLING TIPS:

Be aware that refrigeration and freezing do not kill all salmonella or other bacteria. However, proper cooling can prevent salmonellae from multiplying. Follow these cooling guidelines:

- Keep all raw meat and poultry refrigerated until cooking.

- Any cooked food containing meat or poultry should be refrigerated within 2 hours of cooking.

- Refrigerate or freeze cooked meat or poultry casseroles in covered shallow pans. Make sure there is space around the containers to let cold air circulate.

- Use only proper thawing methods: in the refrigerator, under cold running water or with the microwave.

- Remember that refrigeration can't correct a mistake such as leaving cooked poultry at room temperature for more than two hours. If in doubt, throw the food out.

DATE:	9:00 a.m. EMPLOYEE:
	3:00 p.m. EMPLOYEE:
	10:00 p.m. EMPLOYEE:

Receiving & Storage — Cold Storage	9:00 a.m.	3:00 p.m.	10:00 p.m.
Walk-in refrigerator temperature	_____ °F	_____ °F	_____ °F
Walk-in freezer temperature	_____ °F	_____ °F	_____ °F
Other storage temperature (list area) _____	_____ °F	_____ °F	_____ °F
Raw meats stored in separate location or below any fruits, vegetables or cooked/prepared foods	❑ Y ❑ N	❑ Y ❑ N	❑ Y ❑ N

Back-of-House Preparation Area	9:00 a.m.	3:00 p.m.	10:00 p.m.
Temperature of concentrate(s), list:			
_____	_____ °F	_____ °F	_____ °F
_____	_____ °F	_____ °F	_____ °F
_____	_____ °F	_____ °F	_____ °F
Temperature of soup(s), list:			
_____	_____ °F	_____ °F	_____ °F
_____	_____ °F	_____ °F	_____ °F
_____	_____ °F	_____ °F	_____ °F
_____	_____ °F	_____ °F	_____ °F
Temperature of water in steam table	_____ °F	_____ °F	_____ °F
Effective sanitizing solution available	❑ Y ❑ N	❑ Y ❑ N	❑ Y ❑ N
Handwashing sink stocked with soap and disposable, single-use towels	❑ Y ❑ N	❑ Y ❑ N	❑ Y ❑ N

Grill Area	9:00 a.m.	3:00 p.m.	10:00 p.m.
Temperature inside service refrigerator	_____ °F	_____ °F	_____ °F
Sandwich boards and cutting boards cleaned and sanitized	❑ Y ❑ N	❑ Y ❑ N	❑ Y ❑ N
Forks and spatulas on hot grill	❑ Y ❑ N	❑ Y ❑ N	❑ Y ❑ N

Sandwich Preparation Area	9:00 a.m.	3:00 p.m.	10:00 p.m.
Temperature inside service refrigerator	_____ °F	_____ °F	_____ °F
Temperature of mayonnaise or dressings	_____ °F	_____ °F	_____ °F
Temperature inside reach-in freezer	_____ °F	_____ °F	_____ °F
Cold table above refrigerator covered	❏ Y ❏ N	❏ Y ❏ N	❏ Y ❏ N
Cutting boards clean and sanitized	❏ Y ❏ N	❏ Y ❏ N	❏ Y ❏ N
Microwaved products cooking times are clearly marked	❏ Y ❏ N	❏ Y ❏ N	❏ Y ❏ N

Cold Food Preparation Area	9:00 a.m.	3:00 p.m.	10:00 p.m.
Temperature inside pie/salad refrigerator	_____ °F	_____ °F	_____ °F
Temperature inside service refrigerator	_____ °F	_____ °F	_____ °F
Temperature of mayonnaise or dressings	_____ °F	_____ °F	_____ °F
Temperature of side items (list):	_____ °F	_____ °F	_____ °F
_____	_____ °F	_____ °F	_____ °F
_____	_____ °F	_____ °F	_____ °F
_____	_____ °F	_____ °F	_____ °F
Microwaved products cooking times clearly marked	❏ Y ❏ N	❏ Y ❏ N	❏ Y ❏ N
Sanitizing solutions available and accessible	❏ Y ❏ N	❏ Y ❏ N	❏ Y ❏ N

NOTES:

_____

_____

_____

_____

_____

_____

_____

_____

_____

_____

_____

PRODUCT:	DATE:

Process Step	
Hazard Description	
CCP Description	
Monitoring Procedures/ Frequency/ Person Responsible	Who: What: When: How:
Corrective Actions	
HACCP Records	
Verification Procedures/ Person Responsible	

Equipment Inspected: _____

Inspected By: _____ **Inspection Date:** _____

Condition:_____

Improvements Needed:_____

Equipment Inspected: _____

Inspected By: _____ **Inspection Date:** _____

Condition:_____

Improvements Needed:_____

Equipment Inspected: _____

Inspected By: _____ **Inspection Date:** _____

Condition:_____

Improvements Needed:_____

Equipment Inspected: _____

Inspected By: _____ **Inspection Date:** _____

Condition:_____

Improvements Needed:_____

Equipment Inspected: _____

Inspected By: _____ **Inspection Date:** _____

Condition:_____

Improvements Needed:_____

Equipment Inspected: _____

Inspected By: _____ **Inspection Date:** _____

Condition:_____

Improvements Needed:_____

FOOD ITEM: **DATE:**

RECEIVING/STORING

CONTROL CRITERIA
☐ Approved source
☐ Item(s) inspected
☐ Shellfish tags
☐ Raw/cooked/separated in storage
☐ Refrigerated at 45°F or less
☐ Product condition (dents, open products, torn bags)

MONITORING
☐ Shellfish tags available and complete
☐ Food temperature checked
☐ Raw foods stored below cooked or ready-to-eat foods

ACTION
☐ Discard food
☐ Return food
☐ Separate raw and cooked food
☐ Discard cooked food contaminated by raw food
☐ Discard if food temperature is more than 45°F for 2 hours, or more than 70°F

THAWING

CONTROL CRITERIA
☐ Refrigeration
☐ Under running water less than 70°F
☐ Microwave
☐ Cooked in frozen state (less than 3 lbs. only)

MONITORING
☐ Select thawing method, check food temperature

ACTION
☐ Discard if food temperature is more than 45°F for 2 hours, or more than 70°F

PRE-COOKING

CONTROL CRITERIA
☐ Food temperature no more than 45°F

MONITORING
☐ Observe quantity of food at room temperature
☐ Observe time food held at room temperature

ACTION
☐ Discard if food temperature is more than 45°F for 2 hours, or more than 70°F

REHEATING

CONTROL CRITERIA
☐ Food temperature at thickest part more than or equal to 165°F

MONITORING
☐ Measure food temperature at thickest part during reheating

ACTION
☐ Food temperature at thickest part less than 165°F, continue reheating

HOT HOLDING

CONTROL CRITERIA
☐ Food temperature at thickest part at least _____°F

MONITORING
☐ Measure food temperature at thickest part during hot holding every _____ minutes

ACTION
☐ Food Temperature: 140°F–120°F More than or equal to 2 hours, discard; less than 2 hours, reheat to 165°F and hold at 140°F

  120°F–45°F More than or equal to 2 hours, discard; less than 2 hours, reheat to 165°F and hold at 140°F

COOKING

CONTROL CRITERIA
☐ Temperature to kill pathogens: Food temperature at thickest part at least _____°F

MONITORING
☐ Measure food temperature at thickest part

ACTION
☐ Continue cooking until food temperature at thickest part is at least _____°F

FOOD ITEM: **DATE:**

PROCESSING

CONTROL CRITERIA

Prevent contamination by:

- ☐ Employees' hands not touching ready-to-eat food
- ☐ Employees wash hands correctly and frequently
- ☐ No ill employees
- ☐ All utensils clean and sanitized
- ☐ Cold, potentially hazardous food at a temperature less than or equal to 45°F
- ☐ Hot, potentially hazardous food at a temperature more than or equal to 140°F

MONITORING

- ☐ Use of gloves and utensils
- ☐ Handwashing techniques and frequency
- ☐ Observe employees' health
- ☐ Use pre-chilled ingredients for cold foods
- ☐ Minimize quantity of food at room temperature

ACTION

Discard food if any of the following is observed:

- ☐ Cold, potentially hazardous food: More than 45°F more than or equal to 2 hours, discard; more than 70°F, discard
- ☐ Hot, potentially hazardous food: 140°F–120°F More than or equal to 2 hours, discard; less than 2 hours, reheat to 154°F and hold at 140°F 120°F–45°F More than or equal to 2 hours, discard; less than 2 hours, reheat to 154°F and hold at 140°F
- ☐ If raw food has contaminated other food or equipment/utensils, discard food in question or reheat to 165°F
- ☐ Ill worker handling food

COOLING

CONTROL CRITERIA

- ☐ Food 120°F to 70°F in 2 hours; 70°F to 45°F in 4 additional hours by the following methods:
- ☐ Product depth 4 inches or less
- ☐ Ice water bath, stirring
- ☐ Rapid-chill refrigeration
- ☐ Do not cover until cold

MONITORING

- ☐ Measure food temperature every ____ minutes
- ☐ Food depth
- ☐ Food iced
- ☐ Food stirred
- ☐ Food size
- ☐ Food placed in rapid-chill refrigeration unit
- ☐ Food uncovered

ACTION

- ☐ Food Temperature: 120°F–70°F More than 2 hours, discard food

  70°F–45°F More than 4 hours, discard food

  45°F or less But cooled too slowly, discard food

TRANSPORTING

CONTROL CRITERIA

- ☐ Hot Food: Temperature at thickest part at least 140°F
- ☐ Cold Food: Temperature at thickest part at least 45°F

MONITORING

- ☐ Measure food temperature at thickest part during hot holding every ____ minutes

ACTION

- ☐ Cold holding, potentially hazardous food: More than 45°F more than or equal to 2 hours, discard; more than 70°F, discard
- ☐ Hot holding, potentially hazardous food: 140°F–120°F More or equal to 2 hours, discard; less than 2 hours, reheat to 154°F and hold at 140°F

  120°F–45°F More or equal to 2 hours, discard; less than 2 hours, reheat to 165°F and hold at 140°F

NOTES

GUIDELINES

1. **Time & Temperature** – Always record the time when the temperature is taken.

2. **Final Cooking** – The foods' internal temperature must reach a minimum of 170°F.

3. **Initial Cooling** – Initial cooling begins at 140°F. Meet all cooling requirements:
   - Cool foods from 140°F to 70°F within 2 hours; and from 70°F to below 41°F within 4 hours, for a total of 6 hours. If food item goes directly into hot holding after cooking, cooling is not required.

4. **2-Hour Requirement** – Internal temperature must reach 70°F within 2 hours of initial temperature.

5. **4-Hour Requirement** – Internal temperature must reach below 41°F within 4 hours from the time the food is 70°F.

6. **Total Cooling Time 6 hours** – The final column should be initialed by the employee to certify the food has been cooled properly and checked at each increment.

7. **Reheating** – Reheat to proper internal temperature within 2 hours and serve. Reheat only once to 170°F and repeat chill process or discard food item.

8. **Corrective Action** – Continue to cook to required HACCP temperature for each food. Corrective actions should be listed below:

_____

_____

_____

EMPLOYEE:					DATE:

PRODUCT	FINAL COOKING		INITIAL TEMP		2 HOURS		4 MORE HOURS		INITIALS
	TIME	TEMP	TIME	TEMP	TIME	TEMP	TIME	TEMP	

Vending Locations

Date: **Employee:**

❏ YES   ❏ NO   1.   Is the vending area cleaned and uncluttered, with no trash or other debris?

❏ YES   ❏ NO   2.   Is the vending machine area clean, in good condition and protected from overhead water, waste or sewer piping leakage and condensation?

❏ YES   ❏ NO   3.   Does the vending area have adequate lighting and proper ventilation?

❏ YES   ❏ NO   4.   Is the vending area free of insects and rodents?

❏ YES   ❏ NO   5.   Are cold, potentially hazardous foods held at the proper temperatures (41°F or less) at all times?

❏ YES   ❏ NO   6.   Are hot, potentially hazardous foods held at the proper temperatures (140°F or higher) at all times?

❏ YES   ❏ NO   7.   Do the vending machines have thermometers that are checked daily to ensure machines are maintaining safe, accurate temperatures?

❏ YES   ❏ NO   8.   Is food sold in the vending machines properly packaged and protected from contamination?

❏ YES   ❏ NO   9.   Are all vending machines cleaned on a regular basis?

❏ YES   ❏ NO   10.   Is a trash receptacle located near vending machines to properly dispose of food cartons and other debris?

Action Plan: **Completed By:**   **Comments:**

Supervisor:

Vending/Catering Food Transport Vehicles

Date: **Employee:**

❑ YES   ❑ NO   1.   During transport, are cold, potentially hazardous foods held at the proper temperatures (41°F or less) at all times?

❑ YES   ❑ NO   2.   During transport, are hot, potentially hazardous foods held at the proper temperatures (140°F or higher) at all times?

❑ YES   ❑ NO   3.   Are insulated containers used for food transport?

❑ YES   ❑ NO   4.   If warming cabinets are used, is the temperature 140°F or higher when handling or transporting hot foods?

❑ YES   ❑ NO   5.   Are foods and beverages protected from contaminations such as dirt, dust and insects?

❑ YES   ❑ NO   6.   Are vehicles cleaned and sanitized after each use?

Action Plan: **Completed By:**   **Comments:**

Supervisor:

PRODUCT: **DATE:**

Process Step/CCP	Critical Limits	Monitoring Procedures (Who/What/When/How)	Corrective Actions
		Who: What: When: How:	1. 2. 3. 4.
		Who: What: When: How:	1. 2. 3. 4.
		Who: What: When: How:	1. 2. 3. 4.

SUPPLIER: **TIME OF DELIVERY:**   a.m./p.m.

❑ Y ❑ N   Frozen products arrive frozen solid   ❑ Y ❑ N   Refrigerated products put away within 30 minutes of delivery

❑ Y ❑ N   Refrigerated products arrive at a temperature below 41°F   ❑ Y ❑ N   Refrigerated and frozen products dated and stored for FIFO usage

❑ Y ❑ N   Frozen products put away within 15 minutes of delivery   ❑ Y ❑ N   Damaged products rejected

EMPLOYEE CHECKING IN PRODUCTS: **DATE:**

SUPPLIER: **TIME OF DELIVERY:**   a.m./p.m.

❑ Y ❑ N   Frozen products arrive frozen solid   ❑ Y ❑ N   Refrigerated products put away within 30 minutes of delivery

❑ Y ❑ N   Refrigerated products arrive at a temperature below 41°F   ❑ Y ❑ N   Refrigerated and frozen products dated and stored for FIFO usage

❑ Y ❑ N   Frozen products put away within 15 minutes of delivery   ❑ Y ❑ N   Damaged products rejected

EMPLOYEE CHECKING IN PRODUCTS: **DATE:**

SUPPLIER: **TIME OF DELIVERY:**   a.m./p.m.

❑ Y ❑ N   Frozen products arrive frozen solid   ❑ Y ❑ N   Refrigerated products put away within 30 minutes of delivery

❑ Y ❑ N   Refrigerated products arrive at a temperature below 41°F   ❑ Y ❑ N   Refrigerated and frozen products dated and stored for FIFO usage

❑ Y ❑ N   Frozen products put away within 15 minutes of delivery   ❑ Y ❑ N   Damaged products rejected

EMPLOYEE CHECKING IN PRODUCTS: **DATE:**

NOTES/CONCERNS:

TEMPERATURE LOG

Month: _____ Freezer: _____ Refrigerator: _____

DATE	TIME	TEMP	INITIALS	DATE	TIME	TEMP	INITIALS

SANITATION TEMPERATURES FOR UTENSILS & SILVERWARE

165°F - 180°F   74°C - 82°C
Dishmachine final rinse*

170°F   77°C
Manual sanitizing rinse water

150°F - 165°F   66°C - 74°C
Dishmachine wash water*

120°F - 140°F   49°C - 60°C
Chemical dishmachine wash water*

75°F - 120°F   24°C - 49°C
Chemical dishmachine final rinse water*

75°F   24°C
Manual chemical sanitizing rinse water

* *Temperature range may vary depending on type of dish machine.*

FOOD HANDLING, COOKING AND STORAGE TEMPERATURES

212°F   100°C
Water boils

165°F   74°C
Minimum cooking temperature for poultry and reheating potentially hazardous foods

160°F   71°C
Minimum cooking temperature for pork and beef

140°F   60°C
Holding temperature of cooked foods (at or above 140°F)

65°F - 85°F   18°C - 29°C
Room temperature

32°F   0°C
Water freezes

0°F   -18°C
Storage of frozen foods

Dry Storage

Date: **Employee:**

❑ YES   ❑ NO   1.   Are all food goods stacked neatly, labeled and in proper containers?

❑ YES   ❑ NO   2.   Are all storage shelves or racks at least 6 inches off the floor?

❑ YES   ❑ NO   3.   Are shelves and storage area clean, free of dust, empty cartons and other debris?

❑ YES   ❑ NO   4.   Is storage area swept daily?

❑ YES   ❑ NO   5.   Are food items rotated properly using the "first in, first out" system?

❑ YES   ❑ NO   6.   Is temperature of the the dry storage area regulated (between 60°F and 70°F) and ventilated to avoid dampness?

❑ YES   ❑ NO   7.   Is the storage area large enough for ease of use?

❑ YES   ❑ NO   8.   Is the storage area inspected for evidence of rodents and insects on a regular basis?

❑ YES   ❑ NO   9.   Are food supplies stored separately from chemicals, cleaners and pesticides?

❑ YES   ❑ NO   10.   Are water or sewer lines located in a separate area away from food storage?

❑ YES   ❑ NO   11.   Is contaminated or spoiled food promptly discarded?

❑ YES   ❑ NO   12.   Is the storage area well-lit?

Action Plan: **Completed By:**   **Comments:**

Supervisor:

Refrigerator & Freezer Storage

Date: **Employee:**

❏ YES ❏ NO 1. Is the interior temperature of the refrigerators 41°F or lower?

❏ YES ❏ NO 2. Are all refrigerators and freezers equipped with interior and exterior thermometers?

❏ YES ❏ NO 3. Are the interior and exterior thermometers of the refrigerators and freezers calibrated regularly?

❏ YES ❏ NO 4. Are refrigerators cleaned on a regular basis (including coils, grills and compressor area) and free of mold and odors?

❏ YES ❏ NO 5. Isshelving at least 6 inches from the floor and free from dust or other debris?

❏ YES ❏ NO 6. Arefoods and products covered, dated and properly spaced to provide adequate air circulation?

❏ YES ❏ NO 7. Arefoods stored to allow "first in, first out" usage?

❏ YES ❏ NO 8. Are raw meats stored on the bottom shelves, away from cooked or prepared food?

❏ YES ❏ NO 9. Are all spills cleaned up immediately?

❏ YES ❏ NO 10. Are cooked foods labeled and stored in clean, sanitized, covered containers?

❏ YES ❏ NO 11. Is the temperature of freezer units 0°F or lower?

❏ YES ❏ NO 12. Are products in the freezer stored above floor level?

❏ YES ❏ NO 13. Are all frozen foods wrapped and covered to avoid freezer burn?

❏ YES ❏ NO 14. Are freezers clean, in good working condition and defrosted on a regular basis?

Action Plan:	Completed By:	Comments:
	Supervisor:	

COOL FOOD PROPERLY
To Prevent Contamination & Bacterial Growth

1. **Pour food into shallow pan (large pots should not be used to cool food).**

2. **Food in pan should not be more than 2 inches in depth.**

3. **Surround with another large container filled with ice.**

4. **Stir frequently.**

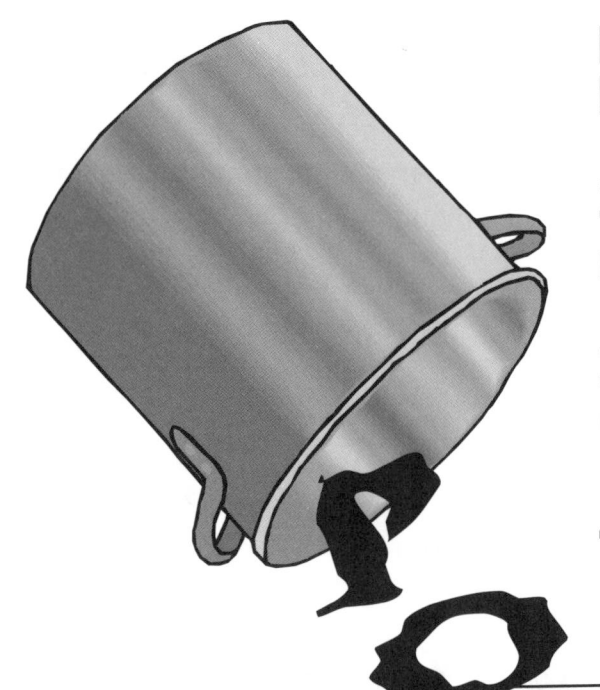

ITEM	CLEANING TASK	WHEN
Beverage dispensers	Wipe spills and splashes Take apart, clean and sanitize dispenser spouts Clean drain tray	Upon each occurrence Daily Once per shift
Breath guards	Wipe spills and splashes Clean and sanitize all surfaces	Upon each occurrence Once per shift
Can openers	Clean and sanitize	After every use, and once per shift
Carts, food transport equipment	Wipe spills and splashes Clean and sanitize shelves and racks	Upon each occurrence Daily, after use
Coffee and tea machines	Wipe spills and splashes Rinse baskets, urns and pots Take apart, clean and sanitize spray heads and spouts	Upon each occurrence After each use Daily
Deep fryer	Clean outside surfaces Clean and filter grease	Once per shift Once per shift
Dishwashing machines	Take apart and clean Clean doors, gaskets and surfaces	On a regular basis to remove build-up and ensure clean water Daily
Floors	Wipe spills Sweep Damp mop Sanitize and scrub	Upon each occurrence As needed After each shift Daily
Frozen dessert machines	Wipe spills and splashes Clean drain tray Take apart, clean and sanitize parts, interior surfaces and dispenser spouts	Upon each occurrence Once per shift Daily
Grill, griddle, broiler	Clean and brush grill surfaces Clean surrounding surfaces and grease tray Clean cooking surfaces and backsplash	As needed, or once per shift Once per shift Daily
Hot holding	Wipe spills Clean interior surfaces and racks Clean exterior surfaces	Upon each occurrence Daily Daily

ITEM	CLEANING TASK	WHEN
Ice machine	Clean doors, gaskets and exterior surfaces	Daily
Microwave	Wipe spills Clean and sanitize interior surfaces Clean and sanitize fan shield and tray Clean outside surfaces	Upon each occurrence Once per shift Daily Daily
Mixers, slicers, and food processors	Take apart, clean and sanitize parts, surfaces and work tables	After each use, or between each food item change
Ovens	Wipe spills	Upon each occurrence
Range	Wipe spills Clean and sanitize work surfaces	Upon each occurrence Once per shift
Reach-in refrigerators and freezers	Wipe spills Clean outside, doors and gaskets	Upon each occurrence Daily
Scales	Clean and sanitize weighing tray Clean and sanitize exposed surfaces	After each use Daily
Sinks	Clean and sanitize sink interior Clean exterior surfaces and backsplash	After each use Daily, at closing
Steam tables	Drain water and clean wells Clean outside and surrounding surfaces	Once per shift Once per shift
Steamer	Wipe spills Clean and sanitize interior surfaces and racks Clean exterior surfaces	Upon each occurrence Daily Daily
Walk-in refrigerators and freezers	Wipe spills Sweep and damp mop (freezer, sweep only) Clean door surfaces and gaskets Scrub floors	Upon each occurrence Once per shift Daily Daily (except freezer)
Walls	Splashes Wash walls in prep and cooking areas	Upon each occurrence Daily, at closing
Work tables	Clean and sanitize tops and shelves each shift	After each use and after

Weekly Cleaning

ITEM	CLEANING TASK
Carts and transport equipment	Thoroughly clean and sanitize supports and exterior
Coffee and tea machines	Clean and brush urn, pots and baskets using cleaner specified by manufacturer
Deep fryer	Boil out fryers
Ovens	Clean interior surfaces and racks
Range	Take apart burners, and empty and sanitize catch trays
Reach-in refrigerators	Empty, clean and sanitize
Sinks	Clean legs and supports
Steam tables	De-lime
Walk-in refrigeration and freezer units	Wipe clean and sanitize walls
Work tables	Clean legs and supports; empty, clean and sanitize drawers

Monthly Cleaning

ITEM	CLEANING TASK
Dishwashing machines	De-lime machine
Ice machine	Drain ice, clean and sanitize interior surfaces Flush ice-making unit Defrost and clean
Reach-in freezers	Empty, clean and sanitize
Reach-in refrigeration and freezer units	Defrost
Steamer	De-lime
Walk-in refrigeration and freezer units	Clean fans Empty, clean racks, walls, floors and corners Defrost freezer

ITEM	CLEANING TASK	WHEN
Carpets	Vacuum	Daily
Chairs	Clean and sanitize seat	After each use
Dining tables	Clean and sanitize	After each use
Display cabinets	Clean and sanitize surfaces	Once per shift
Drains	Scrub covers	Daily
Dry storage areas	Sweep and mop floors	Daily
Employee areas	Clean and sanitize tables used for eating Sweep and mop, if applicable	After each use Once per shift
Floors	Wipe spills Sweep Damp mop Scrub	Upon each occurrence As needed, or between meals Once per shift Daily
Garbage cans	Scrub clean and sanitize cans with hot water or steam and detergent	After emptying, or at closing
Hoods	Clean walls and exposed surfaces of hoods Clean removable filters	Daily Daily
Office areas	Sweep and mop, if applicable Clean work surfaces	Daily Daily
Self-service beverage areas	Wipe spills and splashes Clean and sanitize surfaces	Upon each occurrence Once per shift
Self-service condiment areas	Wipe spills and splashes Clean and sanitize surfaces Take apart, clean and sanitize dispensers	Upon each occurrence Once per shift Daily
Upholstery	Vacuum or brush clean	Daily
Walls	Splashes Wash	As soon as possible Daily (in kitchen and cooking areas)

Weekly Cleaning

ITEM	CLEANING TASK
Chairs	Clean chair backs, rails and legs
Dining tables	Clean table bases
Display cabinets	Clean cabinet interior
Drains	Flush drains with disinfectant
Dry storage areas	Clean shelves, scrub floors, baseboards and corners
Employee areas	Clean employee lockers and storage areas
Fans	Clean fan guards
Floors	Scrub baseboards and corners
HVAC system	Clean air intake and output ducts
Walls	Wash all walls

Monthly Cleaning

ITEM	CLEANING TASK
Carpets	Steam clean and shampoo, bi-monthly
Ceilings	Wash
Floors	Strip and reseal twice per year
Grease traps	Remove grease and clean
Hoods	Clean and degrease hood system, bi-monthly
HVAC system	Check filters
Light fixtures	Clean shields and fixtures
Upholstery	Steam clean or shampoo, bi-monthly
Walls	Wash all walls

EMPLOYEES

❑ Yes   ❑ No   Employees are wearing clean uniforms or clothing.

❑ Yes   ❑ No   Employees use hair restraints and remove all jewelry.

❑ Yes   ❑ No   Employees are presentable and practice good personal hygiene.

❑ Yes   ❑ No   Eating or drinking is not allowed in food preparation area.

❑ Yes   ❑ No   Ill or infectious employees are not allowed to work.

FOOD HANDLING PRACTICES

❑ Yes   ❑ No   Fresh foods are in good condition, and properly labeled and stored.

❑ Yes   ❑ No   Canned goods are sealed and have no dents, bulges, swelling or leaks and rust.

❑ Yes   ❑ No   Cereals, sugar, dried fruits, flour and other dry bulk items are labeled and stored in proper containers and free from insect infestation.

❑ Yes   ❑ No   Refrigeration and freezer units are clean and free of excess ice buildup.

❑ Yes   ❑ No   Refrigerator temperature _____ °F.

❑ Yes   ❑ No   Freezer temperature _____ °F.

❑ Yes   ❑ No   Refrigeration (or other approved method) is used for thawing.

❑ Yes   ❑ No   Milk and milk products are inspected upon delivery, stored in unopened individual containers, and have a temperature of 41°F or lower.

❑ Yes   ❑ No   Cold foods are maintained at 41°F or lower and temperature checked every 2 hours.

❑ Yes   ❑ No   Hot foods are maintained at 140°F or higher and temperature checked every 2 hours.

❑ Yes   ❑ No   Leftovers are properly labeled with time, date and use-by date.

❑ Yes   ❑ No   All foods are properly cooked and/or reheated (165°F).

❑ Yes   ❑ No   All foods are properly cooled (140°F to 70°F within 2 hours; 70°F to 41°F in 4 hours).

FOOD EQUIPMENT AND UTENSILS

❑ Yes   ❑ No   Food contact and work surfaces are constructed of proper materials, installed correctly and in good, workable condition.

❑ Yes   ❑ No   Proper dishwashing facilities are available (a three-compartment sink or dish machine) and used correctly.

❑ Yes   ❑ No   Signs with correct dishwashing procedures (pre-flush, scrape, wash, rinse, sanitize and air-dry) are posted and visible in area.

❑ Yes   ❑ No   Dishwashing machine clean, free of food particles or residue, uses proper levels of sanitizer and maintains correct water temperature.

❑ Yes   ❑ No   All food service equipment and utensils are cleaned, sanitized and stored correctly to prevent contamination.

❑ Yes   ❑ No   Clean in-place equipment is adequately cleaned and sanitized, with no leftover food residue.

FACILITY/STRUCTURE

❑ Yes   ❑ No   Floors, walls, ceilings and fixtures are clean and properly constructed.

❑ Yes   ❑ No   Lighting is adequate and well-shielded.

❑ Yes   ❑ No   Water sources are safe, with adequate supplies of pressurized hot and cold water.

❑ Yes   ❑ No   All handwashing sinks have hot and cold water and are stocked with soap, single-use paper towels and covered waste receptacles.

❑ Yes   ❑ No   Sewage and wastewater is correctly piped for proper disposal.

❑ Yes   ❑ No   Plumbing is installed professionally and maintained with back-flow and back-siphonage devices.

❑ Yes   ❑ No   Ventilation systems are in place and working properly.

GARBAGE/INSECT CONTROL

❑ Yes ❑ No All garbage containers have tight-fitting covers to prevent insect and rodent infestation.

❑ Yes ❑ No There are adequate garbage containers available and they are not overfilled.

❑ Yes ❑ No Garbage containers are cleaned often and no offensive odors exist.

❑ Yes ❑ No Outside refuse storage area is clean and enclosed.

❑ Yes ❑ No Outer openings are protected from insects and rodents, with functional, self-closing doors.

NOTE VIOLATIONS AND CORRECTIVE ACTIONS BELOW:

Hot Food Production

Date: **Employee:**

❏ YES   ❏ NO   1. Before and after food preparation, are all equipment and utensils cleaned and sanitized (including work surfaces)?

❏ YES   ❏ NO   2. Are frozen foods thawed correctly, either in the refrigerator, under cold, running water or thawed during the cooking process?

❏ YES   ❏ NO   3. Are potentially hazardous foods cooked thoroughly with proper internal temperatures: poultry, 165°F; beef, 155°F; pork, 155°F; and eggs, 145°F?

❏ YES   ❏ NO   4. Are hot, potentially hazardous foods cooled quickly by one of the following methods: with a rapid, cool stirring device, stirring while in an ice bath, in a blast chiller, by adding ice to the food, in shallow, iced pans or by separating food into smaller portions?

❏ YES   ❏ NO   5. Are leftovers heated to 165°F?

❏ YES   ❏ NO   6. Are sinks used for food preparation cleaned and sanitized between each use?

❏ YES   ❏ NO   7. Are handwashing sinks accessible and properly stocked with single-use towels and soap dispensers so employees can wash hands before food preparation?

❏ YES   ❏ NO   8. Are spills wiped up immediately?

❏ YES   ❏ NO   9. Are floors kept clean with regular sweeping and mopping?

❏ YES   ❏ NO   10. Does every workstation have easy access to sanitizing solution?

Action Plan: **Completed By:**   **Comments:**

Supervisor:

Line Serving Areas

Date: **Employee:**

❑ YES   ❑ NO   1.   Do all refrigerators have properly calibrated thermometers and maintain a temperature of 41°F or below?

❑ YES   ❑ NO   2.   Are all deli or line items items refrigerated until placement on the deli bar?

❑ YES   ❑ NO   3.   Are all items held at 45°F while on the deli bar?

❑ YES   ❑ NO   4.   Are properly calibrated thermometers used regularly to check product temperatures?

❑ YES   ❑ NO   5.   Are floors kept clean with regular sweeping and mopping?

❑ YES   ❑ NO   6.   At the end of each day, is all the deli bar equipment cleaned and sanitized?

❑ YES   ❑ NO   7.   Does every workstation have easy access to sanitizing solution?

Action Plan:	Completed By:	Comments:
	Supervisor:	

Line Service/Hot Foods

Date: **Employee:**

❑ YES   ❑ NO   1.   Do all refrigerators have properly calibrated thermometers and maintain a temperature of 41°F or below?

❑ YES   ❑ NO   2.   Are refrigerated items stored properly, with cooked or ready-to-eat items above raw products?

❑ YES   ❑ NO   3.   Are all refrigerated products stored in properly covered containers and labeled?

❑ YES   ❑ NO   4.   Is raw meat refrigerated prior to cooking?

❑ YES   ❑ NO   5.   Is the grill clean, in good working order and properly maintained?

❑ YES   ❑ NO   6.   Is the steam table clean and in good working condition?

❑ YES   ❑ NO   7.   Are all hot, cooked foods held at 140°F or higher?

❑ YES   ❑ NO   8.   Do soup kettles have a temperature of 140°F or higher?

❑ YES   ❑ NO   9.   Are properly calibrated thermometers used to take frequent temperature checks?

❑ YES   ❑ NO   10.   Are spills wiped up immediately?

❑ YES   ❑ NO   11.   Are floors mopped and swept on a regular basis?

Action Plan: **Completed By:**   **Comments:**

Supervisor:

Restrooms

Date: **Employee:**

❑ YES   ❑ NO   1.   Are restrooms clean and odor-free?

❑ YES   ❑ NO   2.   Are restrooms well-ventilated?

❑ YES   ❑ NO   3.   Do toilet stalls have self-closing, locking doors?

❑ YES   ❑ NO   4.   Are soap and towel dispensers well-stocked and working properly?

❑ YES   ❑ NO   5.   Does the sink(s) and have faucets with pressurized hot and cold water?

❑ YES   ❑ NO   6.   Are the trash containers cleaned and emptied on a regular basis?

❑ YES   ❑ NO   7.   Is the restroom used for storage of food, utensils, equipment or supplies?

Action Plan: **Completed By:**   **Comments:**

Supervisor:

DATE: _____ TIME: _____ EMPLOYEE(S): _____

			Notes or Concerns:

JANITORIAL ROOM

Is it clean and neat?	Yes No	
Are buckets empty and stored upside down?	Yes No	
Are there rodent or insect droppings visible?	Yes No	
Are all toxic materials (including pesticides) in their original containers and clearly labeled?	Yes No	

DISHWASHING AREA

	MAIN KITCHEN	AUX KITCHEN
Wash cycle temperature	_____ °F	_____ °F
Rinse cycle temperature	_____ °F	_____ °F
Are there any obstructions or contaminants in the jets and nozzles (such as food particles)?	Yes No	Yes No
Is the dishwashing equipment cleaned daily to remove food particles, chemicals and debris?	Yes No	Yes No
Is the proper amount or level of detergent and/or sanitizer being used consistently in the wash cycle?	Yes No	Yes No
Do separate employees remove and store clean tableware?	Yes No	Yes No
Do dishwashing employees practice proper hand-washing between handling soiled tableware and sanitized ware?	Yes No	Yes No
Do employees pre-scrape and flush dishes and utensils prior to washing?	Yes No	Yes No
Once dishes and utensils are cleaned and sanitized, are they stored in a clean, dry location (off the floor)?	Yes No	Yes No
Are utensils and tableware toweled properly?	Yes No	Yes No

DATE: _____ TIME: _____ EMPLOYEE(S): _____

SERVICES AREA	MAIN KITCHEN	AUX KITCHEN	Notes or Concerns:
Are floors, tables and chairs clean and dry in the dining area?	Yes No	Yes No	
Is the floor being swept or cleaned while food is being served or when customers are eating?	Yes No	Yes No	
Is the temperature correct in the dining area for customer comfort?	Yes No	Yes No	
Does the dining area have any unpleasant odors?	Yes No	Yes No	
Are the dishes and silverware clean, sanitized and stored correctly to prevent contamination?	Yes No	Yes No	
Are condiment containers clean and in good repair?	Yes No	Yes No	
Are menus clean and in good repair, without food marks or stains?	Yes No	Yes No	
Are food warmers or steam tables used to re-heat prepared foods?	Yes No	Yes No	
Is food being held in the hot-holding equipment at or above 140°F?	Yes No	Yes No	
Is cold food being held at 41°F or lower?	Yes No	Yes No	
Are cold- and hot-holding cabinets equipped with thermometers?	Yes No	Yes No	
Are tongs or other serving utensils available and used to pick up rolls, bread, butter pats, ice or other food to be served?	Yes No	Yes No	
Are tableware towels clean, dry and only used for wiping food spills?	Yes No	Yes No	
Are servers wearing proper uniforms that are clean and in good condition?	Yes No	Yes No	
Do servers show any signs of illness, such as coughing or wiping their noses?	Yes No	Yes No	
Do servers handle drinking glasses and silverware properly, without touching glass tops or silverware blades?	Yes No	Yes No	

DATE: _____ TIME: _____ EMPLOYEE(S): _____

	MAIN KITCHEN	AUX KITCHEN	Notes or Concerns:
PERSONAL SANITATION			
Are all employees involved with food handling properly dressed in clean uniforms or attire?	Yes No	Yes No	
Are employees wearing jewelry other than a wedding band?	Yes No	Yes No	
Are employees wearing hair restraints?	Yes No	Yes No	
Do employees have a noticeable odor (such as strong perfume or body odor)?	Yes No	Yes No	
Do employees have properly groomed hands, without fingernail polish and with short, clean fingernails?	Yes No	Yes No	
If employees have any wounds, are they properly covered and free of infection?	Yes No	Yes No	
Do employees show any signs of illness, such as sneezing or coughing?	Yes No	Yes No	
Do employees scratch their head, face or body?	Yes No	Yes No	
Are employees seen eating in food preparation or serving areas?	Yes No	Yes No	
GENERAL SANITATION			
Are cleaning supplies and chemicals stored separately from the food preparation and service areas?	Yes No	Yes No	
Is prepared food held correctly (at the correct temperature and in the proper containers?	Yes No	Yes No	
Are clean, sanitary towels available?	Yes No	Yes No	
Are frozen foods thawed correctly, either in the refrigerator, under cold, running water or thawed during the cooking process?	Yes No	Yes No	
Is a separate sink available for food preparation that is not used for handwashing or cleaning?	Yes No	Yes No	

DATE: _____ TIME: _____ EMPLOYEE(S): _____

GENERAL SANITATION (continued)	MAIN KITCHEN	AUX KITCHEN	Notes or Concerns:
Is preparation equipment cleaned and sanitized between and after each use, or at the end of the day?	Yes No	Yes No	
Are equipment and utensils not in use clean?	Yes No	Yes No	
Are all dishes, pots, pans and other utensils stored correctly to prevent contamination?	Yes No	Yes No	
Is food stored in coolers and freezers covered and spaced correctly to allow air circulation?	Yes No	Yes No	
Are cutting boards in good condition and used only for specific types of food preparation to avoid cross-contamination?	Yes No	Yes No	
Are cutting boards cleaned and sanitized after each use?	Yes No	Yes No	

DRY STORAGE	MAIN KITCHEN	AUX KITCHEN	
Is the food storage area enclosed, dry and free from dampness?	Yes No	Yes No	
Are food supplies labeled, dated and stored to ensure "first in, first out" use?	Yes No	Yes No	
Is food stored separately from non-food supplies?	Yes No	Yes No	
Is there any evidence of insects or rodent droppings in the storage areas?	Yes No	Yes No	
Is the food storage area clean and free of dust, empty food cartons and other debris (including shelves and floor)?	Yes No	Yes No	
Are shelves at least 4 inches away from walls and floors?	Yes No	Yes No	
Is the area underneath the shelves easily accessible for cleaning?	Yes No	Yes No	

DATE: _____ TIME: _____ EMPLOYEE(S): _____

WALK-IN FREEZERS	MAIN KITCHEN	AUX KITCHEN	Notes or Concerns:
Temperature	_____ °F	_____ °F	_____
Are shelves and floor clean and free of empty cartons or debris?	Yes No	Yes No	_____
Are all foods properly stored and covered?	Yes No	Yes No	_____
Are food supplies labeled, dated and stored to ensure "first in, first out" use?	Yes No	Yes No	_____
Can air circulate freely around stored food?	Yes No	Yes No	_____
Does freezer need defrosting?	Yes No	Yes No	_____

WALK-IN REFRIGERATORS	MEAT	DAIRY	VEGE	AUX KITCHEN
Temperature	_____ °F	_____ °F	_____ °F	_____ °F
Are refrigerators clean, with no mold or offensive odors?	Yes No	Yes No	Yes No	Yes No
Can air circulate freely around stored food?	Yes No	Yes No	Yes No	Yes No
Is food stored on the the floor of the refrigerators?	Yes No	Yes No	Yes No	Yes No
Are foods labeled, dated and stored to ensure "first in, first out" use?	Yes No	Yes No	Yes No	Yes No
Are large-quantity containers used for storing cooked foods (ground meat, dressing or gravy)?	Yes No	Yes No	Yes No	Yes No
Are all containers clearly labeled with date and food item?	Yes No	Yes No	Yes No	Yes No
Is spoiled or outdated food promptly discarded?	Yes No	Yes No	Yes No	Yes No
Are proper storage techniques used, with cooked food on the top and raw meats or poultry on the bottom shelves?	Yes No	Yes No	Yes No	Yes No
Are shelves at least 6 inches from the floor to allow cleaning underneath?	Yes No	Yes No	Yes No	Yes No
Are cooked foods stored in clean, sanitized, covered containers (not their original cartons)?	Yes No	Yes No	Yes No	Yes No

Salad Bar

Date: **Employee:**

❑ YES   ❑ NO   1.   Are salad bar utensils and dishes properly cleaned, sanitized and stored?

❑ YES   ❑ NO   2.   Is the area underneath the counter clean?

❑ YES   ❑ NO   3.   Are all salad bar crockery or containers in good condition, without chips or cracks?

❑ YES   ❑ NO   4.   Is the salad bar area cleaned and sanitized daily?

❑ YES   ❑ NO   5.   Are all spills cleaned up immediately?

❑ YES   ❑ NO   6.   Are all salad bar items kept at a temperature of 41°F?

❑ YES   ❑ NO   7.   Is the floor around the salad bar regularly swept and mopped?

❑ YES   ❑ NO   8.   Are ingredients on the salad bar refrigerated for at least 24 hours before use?

❑ YES   ❑ NO   9.   If ingredients need to be refilled, are the refill items from refrigerated materials?

❑ YES   ❑ NO   10.   Are all vegetables and fruits properly washed before placement on the salad bar?

❑ YES   ❑ NO   11.   Is the temperature of salad bar items maintained and checked on a regular basis?

❑ YES   ❑ NO   12.   Do all food-handling employees wear gloves during salad preparation?

Action Plan: **Completed By:**   **Comments:**

Supervisor:

Employee Personal Hygiene

Date: **Employee:**

❑ YES   ❑ NO   1. Are employees wearing clean uniforms or approved garments?

❑ YES   ❑ NO   2. Is all jewelry removed (except plain wedding band) during working hours?

❑ YES   ❑ NO   3. Are employees' fingernails clean and short, with no false fingernails or nail polish?

❑ YES   ❑ NO   4. Do employees refrain from touching hair or scratching head and face while on duty?

❑ YES   ❑ NO   5. Do employees practice proper handwashing techniques using soap or sanitizer?

❑ YES   ❑ NO   6. Do employees wash hands after any activity that may cause contamination including when working between raw food and ready-to-eat foods, after coughing or sneezing, after touching soiled equipment or utensils and after using restrooms?

❑ YES   ❑ NO   7. Do employees wear hats or hair coverings in the food preparation and serving areas?

❑ YES   ❑ NO   8. Do employees refrain from eating, smoking, chewing gum and using toothpicks while on duty?

❑ YES   ❑ NO   9. Do employees use tobacco products only in designated areas, away from food preparation, storage and service areas?

❑ YES   ❑ NO   10. Do employees show any sign of illness such as coughing or sneezing?

❑ YES   ❑ NO   11. Have employees been trained in safe food handling procedures and food safety?

Action Plan: **Completed By:**   **Comments:**

Supervisor:

Hazard Analysis Critical Control Points

DATE _____ **OBSERVER**_____

PERSONAL DRESS AND HYGIENE

Employees wear proper uniform including proper shoes.
❏ YES ❏ NO Corrective Action _____

Hair restraint is worn.
❏ YES ❏ NO Corrective Action _____

Fingernails are short, unpolished and clean.
❏ YES ❏ NO Corrective Action _____

Jewelry is limited to watch, simple earrings and plain ring.
❏ YES ❏ NO Corrective Action _____

Hands are washed or gloves are changed at critical points.
❏ YES ❏ NO Corrective Action _____

Open sores, cuts, splints or bandages on hands are completely covered while handling food.
❏ YES ❏ NO Corrective Action _____

Hands are washed thoroughly using proper hand-washing techniques at critical points.
❏ YES ❏ NO Corrective Action _____

Smoking is observed only in designated areas away from preparation, service, storage and warewashing areas.
❏ YES ❏ NO Corrective Action _____

Eating, drinking and chewing gum are observed only in designated areas away from work areas.
❏ YES ❏ NO Corrective Action _____

Employees take appropriate action when coughing or sneezing.
❏ YES ❏ NO Corrective Action _____

Disposable tissues are used and disposed of when coughing/blowing nose.
❏ YES ❏ NO Corrective Action _____

LARGE EQUIPMENT

Food slicer is clean to sight and touch.
❏ YES ❏ NO Corrective Action _____

Food slicer is sanitized between uses when used with potentially hazardous foods.
❏ YES ❏ NO Corrective Action _____

All other pieces of equipment are clean to sight and touch — equipment on serving lines, storage shelves, cabinets, ovens, ranges, fryers and steam equipment.
❏ YES ❏ NO Corrective Action _____

Exhaust hood and filters are clean.
❏ YES ❏ NO Corrective Action _____

REFRIGERATOR, FREEZER AND MILK COOLER

Thermometer is conspicuous and accurate.
❏ YES ❏ NO Corrective Action _____

Temperature is accurate for piece of equipment.
❏ YES ❏ NO Corrective Action _____

Food is stored 6 inches off floor in walk-ins.
❏ YES ❏ NO Corrective Action _____

Unit is clean.
❏ YES ❏ NO Corrective Action _____

Proper chilling procedures have been practiced.
❏ YES ❏ NO Corrective Action _____

All food is properly wrapped, labeled and dated.
❏ YES ❏ NO Corrective Action _____

FIFO (First In, First Out) inventory is being practiced.
❏ YES ❏ NO Corrective Action _____

FOOD STORAGE AND DRY STORAGE

Temperature is between 50° F and 70° F.
❏ YES ❏ NO Corrective Action _____

All food and paper supplies are 6 to 8 inches off the floor.
❏ YES ❏ NO Corrective Action _____

All food is labeled with name and delivery date.
❏ YES ❏ NO Corrective Action _____

FIFO (First In, First Out) inventory is being practiced.
❏ YES ❏ NO Corrective Action _____

There are no bulging or leaking canned goods in storage.
❏ YES ❏ NO Corrective Action _____

Food is protected from contamination.
❏ YES ❏ NO Corrective Action _____

All surfaces and floors are clean.
❏ YES ❏ NO Corrective Action _____

Chemicals are stored away from food and other food-related supplies.
❏ YES ❏ NO Corrective Action _____

HOT HOLDING

Unit is clean.
❏ YES ❏ NO Corrective Action _____

Food is heated to 165° F before placing in hot holding.
❏ YES ❏ NO Corrective Action _____

Temperature of food being held is above 140° F.

HOT HOLDING *continued*

❏ YES   ❏ NO   Corrective Action _____

Food is protected from contamination.
❏ YES   ❏ NO   Corrective Action _____

FOOD HANDLING

Frozen food is thawed under refrigeration or in cold running water.
❏ YES   ❏ NO   Corrective Action _____

Food is not allowed to be in the "temperature danger zone" for more than 4 hours.
❏ YES   ❏ NO   Corrective Action _____

Food is tasted using proper method.
❏ YES   ❏ NO   Corrective Action _____

Food is not allowed to become cross-contaminated.
❏ YES   ❏ NO   Corrective Action _____

Food is handled with utensils, clean-gloved hands or clean hands.
❏ YES   ❏ NO   Corrective Action _____

Utensils are handled to avoid touching parts that will be in direct contact with food.
❏ YES   ❏ NO   Corrective Action _____

Reusable towels are used only for sanitizing equipment surfaces and not for drying hands, utensils, floor, etc.
❏ YES   ❏ NO   Corrective Action _____

UTENSILS AND EQUIPMENT

All small equipment and utensils, including cutting boards, are sanitized between uses.
❏ YES   ❏ NO   Corrective Action _____

Small equipment and utensils are air dried.
❏ YES   ❏ NO   Corrective Action _____

Work surfaces are clean to sight and touch.
❏ YES   ❏ NO   Corrective Action _____

Work surfaces are sanitized between uses.
❏ YES   ❏ NO   Corrective Action _____

Thermometers are washed and sanitized between each use.
❏ YES   ❏ NO   Corrective Action _____

Can opener is clean to sight and touch.
❏ YES   ❏ NO   Corrective Action _____

Drawers and racks are clean.
❏ YES   ❏ NO   Corrective Action _____

Small equipment is inverted, covered or otherwise protected from dust and contamination when stored.
❏ YES   ❏ NO   Corrective Action _____

CLEANING AND SANITIZING

Three-compartment sink is used.
❏ YES   ❏ NO   Corrective Action _____

Three-compartment sink is properly set up for ware-washing (wash, rinse, sanitize).
❏ YES   ❏ NO   Corrective Action _____

Chlorine test kit or thermometer is used to check sanitizing process.
❏ YES   ❏ NO   Corrective Action _____

The water temperatures are accurate.
❏ YES   ❏ NO   Corrective Action _____

If heat-sanitizing, the utensils are allowed to remain immersed in 170° F water for 30 seconds.
❏ YES   ❏ NO   Corrective Action _____

If using chemical sanitizer, it is the proper dilution.
❏ YES   ❏ NO   Corrective Action _____

The water is clean and free of grease and food particles.
❏ YES   ❏ NO   Corrective Action _____

The utensils are allowed to air dry.
❏ YES   ❏ NO   Corrective Action _____

Wiping clothes are stored in sanitizing solution while in use.
❏ YES   ❏ NO   Corrective Action _____

GARBAGE STORAGE AND DISPOSAL

Kitchen garbage cans are clean.
❏ YES   ❏ NO   Corrective Action _____

Garbage cans are emptied as necessary.
❏ YES   ❏ NO   Corrective Action _____

Boxes and containers are removed from site.
❏ YES   ❏ NO   Corrective Action _____

Loading dock and are around dumpster are clean.
❏ YES   ❏ NO   Corrective Action _____

Dumpster is closed.
❏ YES   ❏ NO   Corrective Action _____

PEST CONTROL

Screen on open windows and doors are in good repair.
❏ YES   ❏ NO   Corrective Action _____

No evidence of pests is present
❏ YES   ❏ NO   Corrective Action _____

DATE: _____

BATHROOM MIRRORS

WHEN: Once per shift   **HOW:** As needed
CLEANSER: Glass cleaner

PERSON RESPONSIBLE: _____
INITIAL UPON COMPLETION: _____

BATHROOM SUPPLIES

WHEN: Once per shift
HOW: Hand soap, paper towels, toilet paper

PERSON RESPONSIBLE: _____
INITIAL UPON COMPLETION: _____

BATHROOM FIXTURES AND SURFACES (other than floor, tiles and mirror)

WHEN: Daily
HOW: Spray, rinse and wipe
CLEANSER: Bathroom cleaner with disposable towel

PERSON RESPONSIBLE: _____
INITIAL UPON COMPLETION: _____

CONDIMENT CONTAINERS

WHEN: Daily   **HOW:** Wash, rinse, sanitize
CLEANSER: Dish machine

PERSON RESPONSIBLE: _____
INITIAL UPON COMPLETION: _____

COOLING RACKS

WHEN: Daily
HOW: Wipe clean of food debris   **CLEANSER:**
Water and sanitizer 200ppm with in-use wiping cloth

PERSON RESPONSIBLE: _____
INITIAL UPON COMPLETION: _____

COUNTERS/SHELVES (FRONT)

WHEN: End of shift   **HOW:** Wash, rinse, sanitize
CLEANSER: Cleanser, fresh water and sanitizer 200ppm

PERSON RESPONSIBLE: _____
INITIAL UPON COMPLETION: _____

COUNTERS/SHELVES (COOLER)

WHEN: End of shift   **HOW:** Wash, rinse, sanitize
CLEANSER: Cleanser, fresh water and sanitizer 200ppm

PERSON RESPONSIBLE: _____
INITIAL UPON COMPLETION: _____

COUNTERS (DELIVERY)

WHEN: End of shift   **HOW:** Wash, rinse, sanitize
CLEANSER: Cleanser, fresh water and sanitizer 200ppm

PERSON RESPONSIBLE: _____
INITIAL UPON COMPLETION: _____

COUNTERS (PREP)

WHEN: Between uses   **HOW:** Wash, rinse, sanitize
CLEANSER: Cleanser, fresh water and sanitizer 200ppm

PERSON RESPONSIBLE: _____
INITIAL UPON COMPLETION: _____

DISH RACKS

WHEN: Daily   **HOW:** Wash, rinse, sanitize
CLEANSER: Cleanser, fresh water and sanitizer 200ppm

PERSON RESPONSIBLE: _____
INITIAL UPON COMPLETION: _____

DOORS (FRONT ENTRY)

WHEN: As needed   **HOW:** Spot clean glass;
CLEANSER: Glass cleaner wipe clean other surfaces
PERSON RESPONSIBLE: _____
INITIAL UPON COMPLETION: _____

DRAIN COVERS

WHEN: Daily
HOW: Clear debris; wash, rinse, sanitize
CLEANSER: Dish machine

PERSON RESPONSIBLE: _____
INITIAL UPON COMPLETION: _____

DRY STORAGE AREAS

WHEN: Daily   **HOW:** Sweep/mop
CLEANSER: Approved sanitizer

PERSON RESPONSIBLE: _____
INITIAL UPON COMPLETION: _____

FLOORS

WHEN: Daily/as needed   **HOW:** Sweep/mop
CLEANSER: Approved sanitizer

PERSON RESPONSIBLE: _____
INITIAL UPON COMPLETION: _____

FREEZERS

WHEN: Daily
HOW: Sweep/mop if walk-in;   wipe exterior
CLEANSER: Approved sanitizer

PERSON RESPONSIBLE: _____
INITIAL UPON COMPLETION: _____

HANDWASHING SINK

WHEN: Every 4 hours
HOW: Wash, rinse, sanitize
CLEANSER: Cleanser, fresh water and sanitizer 200ppm

PERSON RESPONSIBLE: _____
INITIAL UPON COMPLETION: _____

HOOD FILTERS

WHEN: Every other p.m., end of shift
HOW: Soak in degreaser, spray
CLEANSER: Non-caustic degreaser clean with fresh water,
air dry

PERSON RESPONSIBLE: _____
NITIAL UPON COMPLETION: _____

HOOD GREASE PANS

WHEN: Bi-weekly
HOW: Empty into grease bin; run through dishwasher
CLEANSER: Dish machine:
PERSON RESPONSIBLE: _____
INITIAL UPON COMPLETION: _____

ICE CARRIERS

WHEN: Every 4 hours
HOW: Wash, rinse, sanitize run through dishwasher
CLEANSER: Dish machine
PERSON RESPONSIBLE: _____
INITIAL UPON COMPLETION: _____

ICE CREAM DIPPER WELL

WHEN: Daily
HOW: Wash, rinse, sanitize
CLEANSER: Cleanser, fresh water and sanitizer 200ppm

PERSON RESPONSIBLE: _____
INITIAL UPON COMPLETION: _____

KNIFE HOLDERS

WHEN: Every 4 hours
HOW: Wash, rinse, sanitize
CLEANSER: Cleanser, fresh water and sanitizer 200ppm

PERSON RESPONSIBLE: _____
INITIAL UPON COMPLETION: _____

MIXER BASE/EXTERIOR

WHEN: Daily
HOW: Wash, rinse, sanitize
CLEANSER: Cleanser, fresh water and sanitizer 200ppm

PERSON RESPONSIBLE: _____
INITIAL UPON COMPLETION: _____

MOPS/BRUSHES

WHEN: Daily
HOW: Wash, rinse and sanitize in mop sink; hang
upside down to drip dry over sink
CLEANSER: Cleanser, fresh water and sanitizer 200ppm

PERSON RESPONSIBLE: _____
INITIAL UPON COMPLETION: _____

PIZZA OVEN

WHEN: Throughout shift
HOW: Wipe interior with clean, moist towel
CLEANSER: Water only

PERSON RESPONSIBLE: _____
INITIAL UPON COMPLETION: _____

PREMISES EXTERIOR

WHEN: Daily
HOW: Sweep entire areas of debris/trash
CLEANSER: Water spray if needed

PERSON RESPONSIBLE: _____
INITIAL UPON COMPLETION: _____

PREPARATION AREAS

WHEN: Each use
HOW: Wash, rinse, sanitize
CLEANSER: Cleanser, fresh water and sanitizer 200ppm

PERSON RESPONSIBLE: _____
INITIAL UPON COMPLETION: _____

REACH-IN HANDLES

WHEN: Daily
HOW: Wipe exterior with moist cloth
CLEANSER: Sanitizer bucket at 200ppm

PERSON RESPONSIBLE: _____
INITIAL UPON COMPLETION: _____

REACH-INS AND WELLS

WHEN: Daily   **HOW:** Wash, rinse, sanitize
CLEANSER: Cleanser, fresh water and sanitizer 200ppm

PERSON RESPONSIBLE: _____
INITIAL UPON COMPLETION: _____

ROTISSERIE:
HOLDING DRAWERS, EXTERIOR

WHEN: Daily
HOW: Wash, rinse, sanitize, buff exterior
CLEANSER: Cleanser, fresh water and sanitizer 200ppm
PERSON RESPONSIBLE: _____
INITIAL UPON COMPLETION: _____

SCALES

WHEN: Between each use, and every 4 hours
HOW: Wash, rinse, sanitize
CLEANSER: Cleanser, fresh water and sanitizer 200ppm
PERSON RESPONSIBLE: _____
INITIAL UPON COMPLETION: _____

SLICERS AND STAND

WHEN: Between each use (Stand: Daily)
HOW: Wash, rinse, sanitize
CLEANSER: Cleanser, fresh water and sanitizer 200ppm
PERSON RESPONSIBLE: _____
INITIAL UPON COMPLETION: _____

STORAGE BINS

WHEN: Daily
HOW: Wipe exterior with moist cloth
CLEANSER: Sanitizer at 200ppm

PERSON RESPONSIBLE: _____
INITIAL UPON COMPLETION: _____

THREE-COMPARTMENT SINK

WHEN: Daily or between use
HOW: Wash, rinse, sanitize
CLEANSER: Cleanser, fresh water and sanitizer 200ppm

PERSON RESPONSIBLE: _____
INITIAL UPON COMPLETION: _____

TRASH RECEPTACLES

WHEN: Daily
HOW: Wipe exterior with disposable cloth
CLEANSER: Water and sanitizer 200ppm

PERSON RESPONSIBLE: _____
INITIAL UPON COMPLETION: _____

UTENSILS (IN-USE)

WHEN: Every 4 hours or between products
HOW: Wash, rinse, sanitize
CLEANSER: Dish machine

PERSON RESPONSIBLE: _____
INITIAL UPON COMPLETION: _____

WALK-IN

WHEN: Daily
HOW: Sweep and clean floor
CLEANSER: Tile cleaner

PERSON RESPONSIBLE: _____
INITIAL UPON COMPLETION: _____

WIPING CLOTHS (IN-USE)

WHEN: Every 4 hours
HOW: Put in designated container to launder

PERSON RESPONSIBLE: _____
INITIAL UPON COMPLETION: _____

CHAPTER TWELVE

Safety and Risk Management

All business owners and managers need to be concerned about safety in their facility for the benefit of their employees and customers. This chapter discusses many of the common safety concerns and ways to manage risk in the facility.

Many facilities choose one or two employees to be the safety or risk manager. Some businesses offer special training for their safety and risk coordinator. If you feel this would be beneficial for your facility, discuss the possibility with your supervisor. Otherwise, you need to be up to date on the safety and risk concerns in your facility. A safety and risk coordinator should also give periodic reports at your staff or team meetings. From time to time, the coordinator could give short presentations or handouts to teach other employees about safety and risk concerns. Here are some areas which your safety coordinator needs to check.

- The area around fire extinguishers, pull alarms, and electrical panels must be kept clear.

- You need an 18" vertical clearance from the fire sprinkler heads.

- Cabinets, equipment, and furniture higher than four feet need to be braced or anchored.

- Food and drink must be stored and consumed away from toxic and infectious materials.

- Label all refrigerators and freezers with "Food and Drink Only" or "No Food and Drink." Then maintain this criterion.

- Extension cords and power strips should not be piggybacked.

- Extension cords should not be used on a permanent basis.

- Any exposed wires and damaged electrical cords must be replaced.

- Keep floors, aisles, and hallways clear of clutter and debris.

- Keep floors dry and free of any hazards that could cause falls.

The checklists at the end of this chapter could also help you or your safety coordinator track the safety in the facility.

Local, State, and Federal Agencies

The agencies listed below will come to your non-commercial food service facility and offer safety training for your employees.

Red Cross

Red Cross training includes first aid, abdominal thrust, and CPR. Each of these is helpful in any business environment. The abdominal thrust is especially useful in a food service setting, and first aid and CPR can be needed at any time. You can contact them at **www.redcross.org.**

Local Fire Department

The local fire department offers training to teach employees how to use fire extinguishers. Fires are most common in food service settings. This makes it necessary that all employees know how to operate fire extinguishers. There are different types of extinguishers and employees need to understand the differences and when to use each type.

Have fire extinguishers available throughout the facility. You need to be sure that they are available and operational in case of a fire. Another key thing is to train your employees to avoid fires and how to handle a fire if it does happen. This training must include an evacuation plan for your team members and customers, but it is critical to call the fire department before you use a fire extinguisher.

Knowing what to do in the event of a fire is critical for everyone's safety. When there is a fire, time is of the essence. If you have a fire, well trained and prepared staff members must help to get everyone to safety. There is a recommended order for responding to a fire. See below for the correct first responses.

1. **Human Lives** — The first priority is to get all employees and patrons from the facility.

2. **Contain the Fire** — The second priority is to close all doors to keep the fire from spreading.

3. **Fire Alarms** — Activate the fire alarms. All staff members need to be informed of the location of the alarms. Make it understood that they are only to be used in case of an actual fire.

4. **Call the Facility Switchboard** — In a non-commercial food service facility you are often located inside a larger facility. Call the central switchboard to report the location of the fire.

5. **Fire Extinguishers** — Use the proper fire extinguishers to contain the fire. This step necessarily follows those above.

OSHA

OSHA stands for Occupational Safety and Health Agency. It is a government agency that oversees safety in the workplace, and it can provide safety training information for your staff members. Further, your facility must be in compliance with their regulations. Fines and penalties for violations are stiff. Food service facility requirements and training materials are available at their Web site, **www.osha.gov**.

Develop Safety Requirements

Your facility needs to have established safety policies and requirements. It is a good idea to include these details in your employee manual which we will discuss in Chapter 13. The following areas include some of the information and headings that should be included in your manual.

First Aid

All non-commercial food service facilities need well-trained employees who know safe working practices. When your staff members are not trained to work safely, they can create hazardous conditions. It is necessary to hold first aid and safety meetings to train your employees to work safely and to handle first aid emergencies. You need to have a safety plan in place for the facility and to train the staff members to use the plan. It is critical that they respond in a calm, quick, and efficient manner when there are emergencies. A great resource for safety training materials is located on the Training Network's Web site, **www.safetytrainingnetwork.com**.

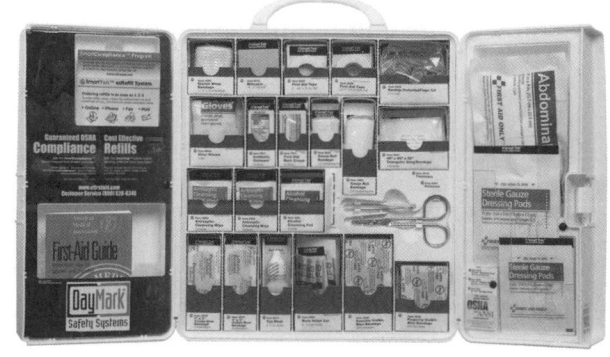

You should be sure to have a comprehensive first aid kit in a prominent location in your facility. DayMark's patented first aid cabinet is stocked with OSHA compliant first aid products for those accidents that typically occur in the food service industry such as burns, cuts, sticks, and common workplace injuries. With the high risk of accidents in the food service industry, it's always challenging to maintain a first aid program that's both cost effective and up-to-date on current safety regulations. This process is easy and cost effective with the only first aid program with guaranteed OSHA compliance. For more information call 800-847-0101 or visit **www.daymarksafety.com**.

Fire

The local fire department can give you more information about their regulations and suggestions for your facility. These suggestions can include: fire extinguishers, fire alarms, carbon monoxide alarms, and smoke detectors. It is good to make a note on your office calendar to replace all equipment batteries every six months. There are various types of fire extinguishers: dry chemical, halon, and water and carbon dioxide.

The type of fire extinguisher that should be used depends on the type of fire. This is why all fire extinguishers are labeled as follows.

- **Class A** — Ordinary Combustibles

- **Class B** — Flammable Liquids

- **Class C** — Electrical Equipment

The labels may carry a graphic to illustrate the type of fire. Remember that all fire extinguishers need to be serviced once a year. Here are some duties of your safety coordinator. Have a list of all emergency phone numbers placed prominently throughout the restaurant and especially the kitchen area. Create a simple facility map noting your evacuation plan near the doors in the entry way, dining area, kitchen, and any other areas that you think would be beneficial. Depending on the layout of the facility, you may need several evacuation plans.

Accidents

No matter how careful you are, anyone can have an accident. Here are some tips to reduce your chances of an accident.

- Ground your electrical outlets.

- Clean walkways and clear any debris and clutter.

- Shovel and salt all walks and steps when you have bad weather.

- Provide adequate outdoor lighting.

- Provide adequate lighting in any hallways that lead to the facility.

- Place handrails along all steps.

- Provide adequate interior lighting.

- Install solid doors at all entrances and exits.

- Use good locks on windows and doors.

- Have a quality security system installed.

Ask staff members to suggest additional ways to create a safe environment to get them involved and make them more conscientious about being safe and avoiding accidents.

This chart will offer some examples of potential safety hazards. My hope is that this will help staff members identify problems before someone is hurt.

Potential Safety Hazards

Potential Hazards	What is Needed	Some Examples
Bending	Proper Training	Moving heavy boxes
Breaking Boxes	Proper Training	Staples, box edges
Carpet	Appropriate Shoes	
Carts Above Eye Level	Storage Training	Supply Cart and Shelves
Chemicals	Chemical Training	Cleaning Products
Dry Ice	Gloves and Training	Ice chest or storage
Electrical Equipment	Prep Training	Slicer, grinder
Frozen Foods	Storage Training	Dry Ice
Glass	Dishwashing Training	Broken glass, china
Hot Liquids	Serving and Prep Training	Coffee, soup, water
Hot Metal Items	Prep and Serving Training	Oven, oven racks, pans
Other People	Proper Training	
Pouring Hot Beverages	Prep and Serving Training	Hot coffee, water, tea
Plugs	Equipment Training	Any electrical equipment
Pushing	Proper Training	
Reaching	Proper Training	Step Ladder, High Shelf
Refrigerator/Freezer	Equipment Training	Pinching Fingers, cold exposure
Steam	Prep and Serving Training	Dishwasher, stove, oven, serving areas
Walking	Proper Training	Crowded kitchen and serving areas
Wet Areas	Proper Boots and Shoes	Dishwasher and spills

There are forms at the end of this chapter which are useful for reporting injury on the job or follow up on the safety of the facility. Each of these reports will help you understand safety issues in the facility.

Effective Staff Training

All staff members need to learn proper work systems and procedures to create a safe work environment. Schedule a department or facility orientation for all new employees to cover basic safety training discussed in this chapter and in chapter 11. Additional safety training depends on the job each staff member performs. The training should be appropriate and customized for the person's job requirements; for example, a hostess or cashier needs less intense training than a receiving person or a cook.

Staff member orientation can include basic safety on the job, proper lifting procedures, fire hazards, proper cleaning, and sanitizing products, and identifying the safety coordinator.

The facility can emphasize additional safety training in periodic meetings. If your facility has a newsletter or a bulletin board, use them to disseminate additional safety tips and suggestions.

Atlantic Publishing offers a series of work place safety posters with tips for many facets of workplace safety. These can be found at **www.atlantic-pub.com/poster.htm**. The posters are available in English and Spanish. The set of 10 posters can be purchased for $79.95 or for $8.98 each. They are pictured on the next page.

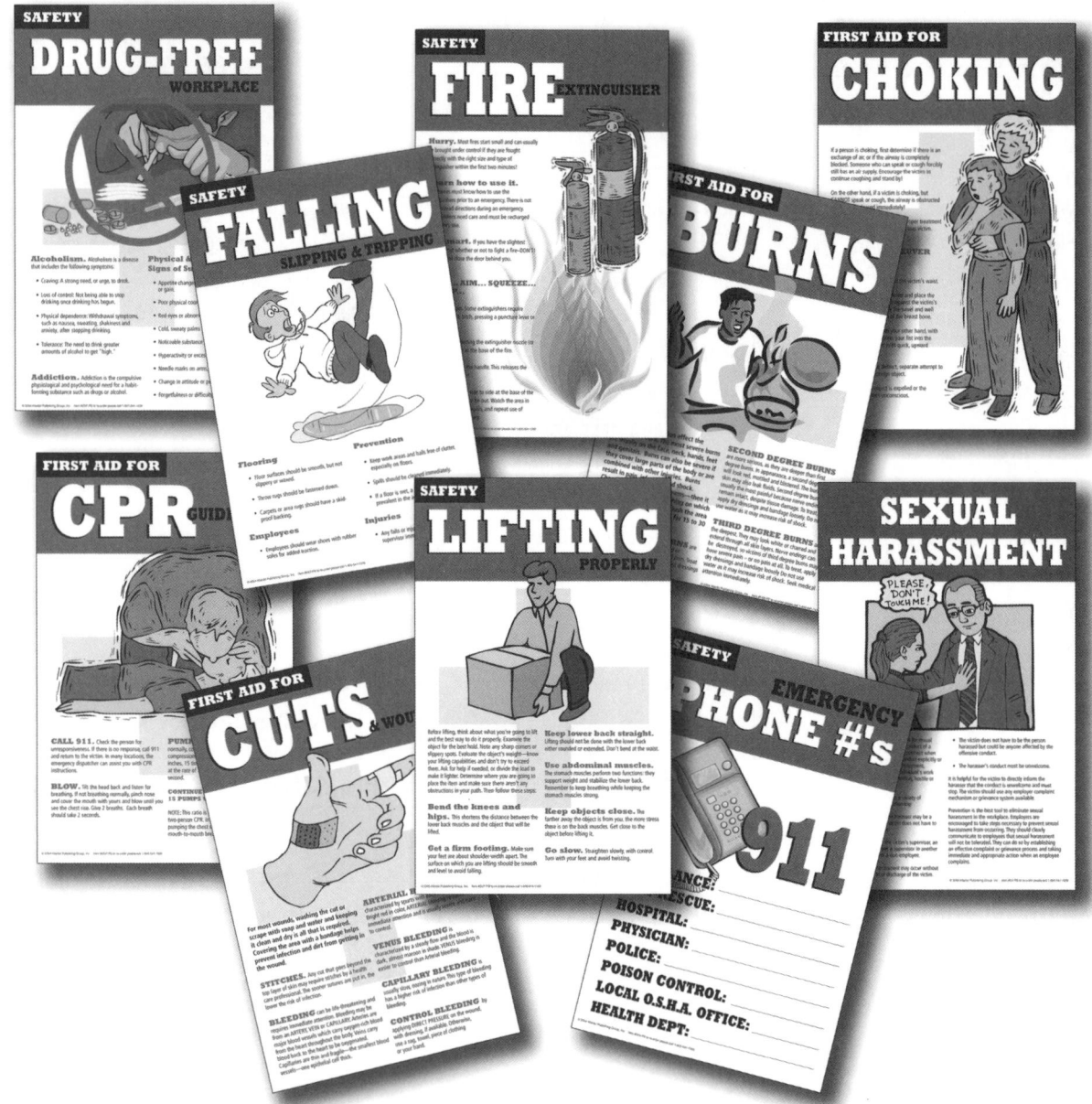

Common Safety Concerns

Any food service facility has many possible hazards, particularly because of equipment, tools, heat, and liquids.

Safety in the Kitchen

The kitchen is usually the focus of safety concerns. Here are areas where accidents can be prevented with the proper training.

Heat and Burns

There are many opportunities every day for staff members to be burned. The good news is that many of them can be avoided if employees learn to be careful when working with grills, hot food, drinks, ovens, splatters, splashes, spills, and stoves.

To Prevent Burns

- **Use thick, dry pot holders** when touching or moving hot pans and dishes.

- **Use long-handled spoons** to stir hot foods.

- **Think ahead when using hot water** or dealing with steam.

- **Use insulated rubber gloves** when rinsing with hot water.

- **Read and follow all instructions** when using steam equipment.

- **Expel all steam** before opening steam equipment doors.

- **Always lift lids on hot foods away from you.**

- **Don't overfill kettles** so as to eliminate splatters and splashes.

- **Keep an eye on hot foods** to avoid a boil-over.

- **Remember that oil and water don't mix**; all food should be dry before being placed in hot oil to avoid unnecessary spatter.

- **Avoid having too many hot pans on the stove.** Remove any emptied pans from the cooking surface.

- **Always let oil cool** before beginning to clean fryers.

- **Have plenty of insulated gloves** when taking hot pans from the oven.

- **Look to be sure no one is close** when you take hot pans from the oven.

- **Never wear clothes that drape or hang** and could catch fire.

Kitchen Grips offer a great way to grab hot items safely up to 500°F. They are heat resistant, water repellent, and stain resistant. Visit their Web site for more information **www.kitchengrips.com**, call 800-785-4449, or fax 661-257-8123.

DayMark Safety Systems also offers a complete line of oven mitts and burn protection gloves which offer protection in temperatures up to 900°F. For more information call 800-847-0101 or visit **www.daymarksafety.com**.

Cuts

It is easy for staff members to be cut while they are working. Knives, blades, broken glass, dishes, and sharp equipment are all potential hazards. Your receiving person must understand the safe way to open cardboard boxes to avoid and remove nails and staples. Taking items out of boxes safely eliminates future hazards and makes a neater and better organized storage area. Here are some precautions your staff members need to understand.

1. Use tools to dispose of broken glass. These shards should be placed in a different trash container to prevent future hazards.

2. Use a cutter to cut rolls of kitchen wrap.

3. Be careful with the edges of open cans. Never use a knife to open cans or to pry the lid up. It is also good to place cut lids inside the empty cans before disposal. An employee compacting garbage by hand will be at risk otherwise. Always use a pusher and not your hands when feeding food into a grinder.

4. Grinders and slicers must be unplugged before removing food and cleaning.

5. Train your staff members to use guards on grinders and slicers.

6. Clean blades and replace them promptly. They should never be left out of machines.

7. Left handed staff members need additional training on how to use slicers and other equipment safely as most safety features are designed for right handed people.

A Few Additional Suggestions:

1. Keep knives sharp because dull blades are a greater hazard than sharp knives.

2. Do not place knives and blades in the bottom of any sink.

3. Hold knives by the handle and turn the tip away from you.

4. Never try to catch a falling knife.

5. Cut away from yourself when using cutting boards.

6. Slice smoothly and do not hack at items.

7. Choose the right knife for the project you are working on at the time.

8. Store and clean knives and equipment in a safe manner.

9. Knives and other sharp tools should be stored in a separate area.

10. Wash glasses separately to prevent possible breakage and injury.

11. Glasses and cups should not be stacked inside each other.

12. Look for nails, staples, and sharp edges while opening and unpacking cardboard boxes.

A good way to prevent cuts is to make sure all employees have proper equipment. DayMark Safety Systems offers a variety of gloves that prevent punctures, cuts and abrasions and are made specifically for food service. Here are some of their options:

- **DayMark's FingerArmor™ Cut Gloves** are made with highly cut resistant fabric, and protect food service workers from accidental cuts and pokes by shielding the most vulnerable parts of the hand—the middle finger, index finger, and thumb. Dual sided for superior protection, FingerArmor™ Cut Gloves can be worn under latex, vinyl, nitrile or poly gloves, making them ideal for food preparation. With their flexible fit, FingerArmor™ Cut Gloves give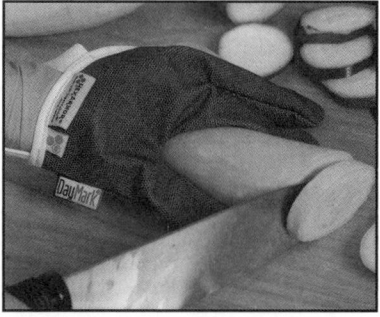

operators full range of motion, significantly reducing slippage. The gloves are machine washable and can be easily sanitized.

- **DayMark's 5 Finger HexArmor/Spectra Combination Cut Gloves** help employees feel safer and work faster. The traditional spectra cut glove with the DayMark Personal Safety touch. HexArmor fabric is added to the most often cut areas, the thumb and first finger.

- **DayMark's HexArmor® Oyster Gloves** protect operators' palms from cuts caused by sharp mussel shells and oyster shucking knives. Made with high cut, puncture and abrasion resistant fabric, the HexArmor Oyster Gloves provide superior protection on the palm and thumb crotch without limiting finger movement. The HexArmor Oyster Gloves are machine washable and can be easily sanitized.

- **DayMarks' Restaurant General Purpose Work Gloves** offer protection like none other in its class. It fits and feels like a mechanic's style glove, grips like a gel palm glove and protects like a cut and puncture resistant glove. Provides the highest level of cut protection based on the ISEA hand protection guidelines. Great for us in receiving, inventory rotation, pull thaw/slacking products, freezer/walk-in work, or kitchen organization and heavy restaurant maintenance.

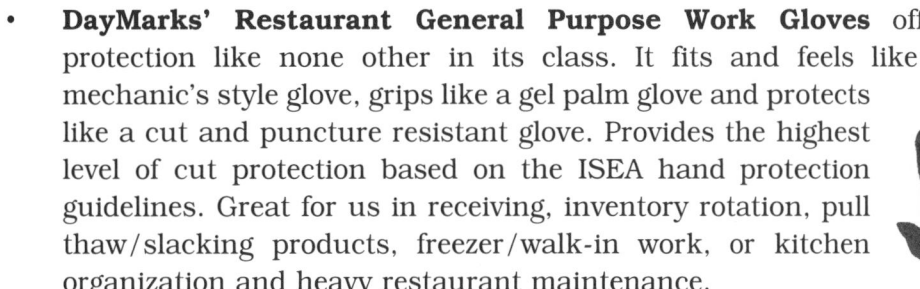

For the complete glove product line or more information call 800-847-0101 or visit **www.daymarksafety.com**.

Knife Safety

This is the procedure to safely hold a knife – hold the handle with all four fingers and place your thumb against the side of the blade. Grip the item to be cut with your other hand. Your knuckles should be used to guide the knife blade. Hold the knife at a 45 degree angle to the cutting surface and move the blade forward and down. The tip of the knife should remain on the cutting surface.

Tips for Knife Safety

- Use the proper knife for the job.

- Sharpen knives on a regular basis.

- Cut away from your body.

- Don't use knives to open cans or bottles.

- Always use a cutting board.

- Place a damp cloth under the cutting board to keep it from slipping.

- Carry knives at your side with the point down and the edge turned away from you.

- Let a knife fall when it slips.

- Don't place dirty knives in a sink of soapy water because they cannot be seen. Lay all dirty knives to the side of the sink.

- Don't leave knives on the edge of any table or other surface.

- Store knives in a rack or case to protect the blades.

Electric Shock

Food service facilities contain many types of electrical equipment creating electric shock a real concern for all food service workers. These suggestions will help prevent electrical shock.

- Ground all electrical equipment.

- Check wires for worn or frayed electrical cords and replace immediately.

- Be sure that employees can reach all switches without touching or leaning against metal tables or counters.

- Unplug equipment before beginning to clean.

- Dry hands before using electrical equipment.

- Know and label locations for electrical switches and breakers for quick shutdown in an emergency.

Strains

Staff members can strain their arms, backs, and legs when carrying heavy food items and equipment. To prevent strains:

- Place heavy food items and equipment on low shelves for easy access.

- Use dollies or carts to move heavy objects.

- Use carts with rollers to move objects around the restaurant.

- Use a cart to carry excessive or heavy objects.

- Ask for help when lifting large or heavy objects.

- Bend from your knees, not with your back, when lifting heavy items.

Slipping and Falling

Slips and falls can cause bad injuries. Tips to prevent slips and falls:

- Clean spills immediately.

- Use signs or cones on wet floors. Staff members should wear shoes with non-slip soles.

- Don't stack boxes high; they can fall and hit people or cause them to trip.

- Keep boxes, ladders, step stools, and carts away from walkways.

Matrix Engineering offers Grip Rock and Super G floor mats. These are ideal for preventing slip-and-fall accidents, a leading cause of injury in workplaces. They are durable, lightweight, and long-lasting to make wet, greasy, hazardous areas safe for your staff. To contact Matrix call 800-926-0528, fax 772-461-7185, or e-mail **griprock@gate.net**. You can find more information at their Web site **www.griprock.com**. These are some of the mat characteristics:

Grip Rock slip-resistant safety mat is:

- Slip-resistant in water, grease, and oil

- Extremely tough and durable

- Flexible even in freezing temperatures

- Lightweight and thin ($\frac{1}{8}$" thick; a 3' x 10' is only 25 lbs.)

- No installation needed

- Easy to handle, clean, and maintain

Dur-A-Flex flooring offers a variety of flooring options. Attractive, functional flooring systems are ideal for your facility. They are formed from heat resistant epoxy to withstand temperatures to 250°F and can be used to resurface floors in dining areas and restrooms. These floors resist penetration of grease or stains. Visit **www.dur-a-flex.com/ByIndustry/industries/restaurant.html** for the full line of food service facility flooring options or contact Dur-A-Flex at 800-253-3539 or by fax at 860-528-2802.

Exposure to Hazardous Chemicals

Hazardous chemicals include pesticides and sanitizers. Special precautions are necessary when working with them because they can injure or poison people. The law states clearly that precautions must be taken. OSHA is the agency that requires each facility have a current inventory of all hazardous materials.

Manufacturers are required to label all hazardous materials properly and supply a Material Safety Data Sheet for each chemical to be kept on file in each food service facility. The MSDS includes: chemical name, physical and health hazards, and emergency procedures. It is the responsibility of each manager to keep this book up-to-date and available in case of an emergency. All employees need to be trained about how to use the MSDS. Prevent Improper Exposure to Hazardous Materials in these ways:

- Only trained workers may handle hazardous chemicals.

- Safety equipment must be used when working with them.

- Nonporous gloves and goggles must be worn when using sanitizing and cleaning agents.

People can be hurt through accidental mishandling of food items or chemicals, only one of the reasons that it's critical for all employees to be trained to use chemicals and to understand how to use MSDS in case of emergencies. Successful food service facilities must build and maintain a reputation for offering quality food in a safe and sanitary environment. When your customers have doubts about the quality of your product, that hard-earned reputation is lost. The safety and sanitary policies discussed in this chapter and in Chapter 11 are easy to implement and can be valuable for the facility.

Good Ergonomics

The official definition of ergonomics is "the study and engineering of human physical interaction with space and objects during activities." Benefits of good ergonomic design can include employee well being, safety, productivity, and comfort. One example of bad ergonomics is any work area that requires staff members to stretch to reach needed supplies. Doing so is awkward and can cause accidents. Use these suggestions to reorganize your facility to work well with people.

- Design mini work areas which have the food, utensils, tools, and preparation space close at hand.

- Arrange your storage areas to limit the amount of bending, lifting, and reaching needed for staff members to do their jobs.

- Provide stools and chairs that offer support for employees' backs and feet when they are not standing.

- Evaluate your tools and equipment for accessibility of employees of various heights.

- Obtain important tools for left-handed staff members.

- Provide stable, heavy-duty ladders for employees to reach shelves or other storage areas.

- Does the current facility layout make things easier or more difficult for customers, employees, and vendors to do their jobs or to enjoy their food?

- When you shop for equipment and fixtures, find items that can be moved and rearranged easily.

Safety in Dining and Serving Areas

The following is a list of safety concerns in the dining and serving areas.

Choking

Children aren't the only ones who eat fast or talk while they are eating. Adults can choke just as easily as children. All staff members need to be aware of what is happening throughout the facility so such an incident doesn't go unnoticed.

When a person grips his throat and is unable to talk or cough, they are choking. Do not pat a person's back if he can talk, cough, or breathe. Use the Heimlich maneuver and call for help right away if the person cannot talk, cough, or breathe.

All staff members should be trained in the proper way to execute the Heimlich maneuver and are able to perform it in an emergency situation. Posters with these instructions can be posted in the employee areas.

Environmental Issues

Employees and patrons want and need healthy air inside and outside your facility. "Poor air" quality can add to employee absence and unhappy patrons. Following are some ways to offer better air quality.

Fresh Indoor Air

There are rigid air and work environment regulations in many areas regarding grease, smoke, and wood burning. Unpleasant odors contribute to "poor" air quality. Char broilers, fryers, or wood burning stoves can create unhealthy or unpleasant air conditions in and around the facility. Routing enough outside air into the facility can give you an improved indoor air quality. It is accomplished by filtering air properly, circulating, and redirecting the facility's airflow. Use these tips to improve facility air quality:

- **Smoking and non-smoking areas** — Airflow should be directed away from non-smoking tables. Employees must not smoke in the kitchen and dining room.

- **Install an air cleaner/filtration system** to reduce airborne particles and dust.

- **Radon, mold, and biological dangers** are possible during remodeling and renovation of old or vacant buildings.

- **EPA reports** about air quality can be located at **www.epa.gov/iaq/pubs/insidest.html**.

- **Unhealthy emissions from carpet, paint, and cleaning products.** Sick Building Syndrome is explained in detail at the National Safety Council site at **http://www.nsc.org/ehc/indoor/sbs.htm**.

- **Hire an HVAC contractor or engineer with restaurant experience.** Hire contractors to install new systems or to maintain existing systems.

Outdoor Air Quality

Ovens, fryers, and other cooking equipment emit particulates, gases, grease, and odors, regulated by local, state, and federal environmental standards. Local and state standards vary so it's best to talk with the local health department to verify the regulations in your area. Federal Air Quality Standards may supersede the local requirements. It's critical to pay close attention to the regulations, because penalties can be severe. Follow these suggestions to meet emission regulations:

- **Hire a professional, industrial air-cleaning firm** to install emission-control systems, handle grease, smoke, CO_2, and odors.

- **Inspect and repair exterior vents, hoods, and intake ducts.** Proper maintenance improves air quality and saves energy costs. Dirty and inadequate systems waste electricity.

- **Install a catalytic oxidizer that converts gases and smoke to water.** Read the article at **www.pfonline.com/articles/010203.html** for more details.

- **Contact your gas and electric companies** along with the county or state environmental and health departments for air quality information, resources, and financial incentives.

- **Hire an air quality consultant** to help you comply with more complex emission issues and stringent regulations.

- The Environmental Protection Agency's Web site **www.epa.gov** provides information on restaurant-specific regulations.

- **Implementing these steps will result in less stress** due to operating a safe non-commercial food service facility.

Theft

A 2002 National Retail Security Survey indicates employee theft accounts for 48.5 percent of business losses.

- 31.3 percent is shoplifting

- 15.1 percent is administrative errors

- 5.1 percent is vendor fraud.

Managers should be the only people to handle money and especially cash. Some facilities have problems with staff members stealing other items because they can, but a conscientious manager can halt attempts at theft. If you are suspicious, it might be good to have cameras on your exterior doors, doors out of view, and the delivery door. A friend who was a security expert once told me that the majority of things are stolen through the dumpster and trash chute. Employees throw items out and then dig them out of the dumpster. It sounds disgusting with food items, but they can be packaged or sealed before they are thrown out.

When you enter all transactions into your computer system, it is easier to detect that items are missing. Frequent inventory counts will also allow you to discover missing items quickly. If you have to issue a refund or give any items away for promotion, be sure to enter the items into the computer at a zero amount. This keeps your financial records straight and ensures the food usage is calculated correctly. These concepts make the system work effectively:

- Document all tasks, activities, and transactions completely.

- Enforce the use of the established standards with all employees.

- Several different people should be involved in tracking. This was mentioned in Chapters 6 and 7 when we discussed having different people receiving and doing inventory.

- Do these things in a timely manner to catch and eliminate problems early.

- It is also important to determine whether you are spending more money to track these expenses than you are saving.

FOOD SERVICE SAFETY POLICY

Policy Number: STV424

Date Issued: August 29, 2007

Issued By: Colton Hall, Director of Food Service/Dietary

It is the goal of the dietary department to provide a safe work environment for all employees in accordance with the hospital policies. Maintaining a safe work environment is the responsibility of each member of the Food Service/Dietary department.

The following work practices are required to avoid accidents:

1. **New Employee Orientation.** All employees hired for food service positions will be required to attend orientation and training pertaining to his or her job. All training must be documented and the documentation signed by the employee, trainer and supervisor. Records will be kept in the departmental training manual and employee records kept in the department.

2. **On-Going Education.** All employees must attend hospital and departmental in-service programs related to safety. Records will be kept in the departmental training manual and employee records kept in the department.

3. **Respect.** Employees must treat each other with respect. Horseplay, rough housing or boisterous language is not permitted as it is distracting and unsafe.

4. **Uniforms.** All employees are required to wear the St. Vincent food service uniform which consists of clean white pants and shoes. Aprons, hats and other protective equipment are issued with every shift. Appropriate duty shoes are also required. Employees must be clean, well-groomed and follow personal hygiene stands (see departmental infection control manual) at all times.

5. **Employee Responsibilities.** Employees must maintain adequate physical fitness to handle job responsibilities, practice efficient work habits, receive adequate rest and nourishment. Employees must lift correctly, walk with care, and report hazardous conditions and/or injuries to their supervisor immediately.

6. **Work Area Cleanliness.** It is every employee's responsibility to keep dietary work areas clean and orderly with equipment, materials, and tools properly maintained. Spills must be wiped up immediately.

7. **Sanitary Practices.** Employees may not eat or drink food items in production, storage, trayline, or dishroom areas. Food may only be consumed in designated breakrooms at designated break times.

8. **Safety Manual.** A safety manual is maintained in the director's office and contains all dietary department and hospital policies related to safety, fire, disasters, respiratory protection, waste management, managing spills, "Right-To-Know" policies, smoking, and injuries on duty. All employees have the right to review this manual upon request.

9. **MSDS Sheets/ Chemical Records.** MSDS sheets contain health and safety information about each hazardous chemical in the workplace. An MSDS is required for each hazardous chemical in the workplace. All MSDS sheets are readily accessible by employees and can be found in the Food Service management office, as well as in the chemical storage area.

FOOD SERVICE SAFETY POLICY (CONTINUED)

ST. VINCENT'S
MEDICAL
CENTER

11. **Food Service/Dietary Safety Plan.** A departmental safety plan is in place and revised annually. The departmental safety committee is composed of representatives from each department and meets at least twice per year to review accidents, develop plans for improved safety, and complete inspections. The departmental safety plan is based on committee findings and the accidents that occurred the prior year. Our goal is to reduce accidents and involve all employees in developing safety awareness. A copy of the most recent safety plan can be found in the Food Service management office and is available for all employees to review upon request.

12. **Accidents.** All accidents are monitored and must be reported immediately to immediate supervisors. An accident incident report must be filled out and signed by all parties involved. Supervisors are responsible for counseling employees who have recurrent accidents about the importance of safe work practices and the implications of a poor safety record. A safety chart is also maintained in the department. Each year, the area with the greatest improvement in reducing accidents receives an award and hospital wide recognition.

13. **Equipment Safety.** Operating and cleaning instructions must be posted adjacent to all equipment and safety devices for equipment must be used correctly. Preventive maintenance of equipment will be monitored by the maintenance and engineering department.

14. **Safety Conditions and Inspections.** Overall safe conditions are monitored by all supervisors. Food service department safety checks will be conducted monthly by managers and members of the department safety committee. The following safety issues will be monitored:

- Floors must be maintained, dry, and in good repair.

- Walkways must be kept clear.

- Ladders and/or step stools must be used, when necessary.

- Light bulbs must be guarded.

- All materials must be stored at least 20 inches away from light fixtures.

- Nonfood items such as chemicals have a separate storage area way from food items and food storage.

- All food items are stored properly on shelves at least 6 inches from the floor and walls.

FOOD SERVICE SECURITY POLICY

Policy Number: STV425

Date Issued: September 14, 2007

Issued By: Colton Hall, Director of Food Service/Dietary

ST. VINCENT'S
MEDICAL
CENTER

It is the goal of the dietary department to provide a secure work environment for all employees in accordance with the hospital policies. This policy ensures
- Employees and supplies are in a safe environment
- Unauthorized persons are not allowed.
- Supplies are to be protected by a security system..

The following practices are required for the security of employees and supplies:

1. **Security Personnel and Monitoring.** St. Vincent's Medical Center employees 24-hour security guards to watch the premises. An electronic video surveillance system is operational in the cafeteria, food service/dietary department and at all entrance. The Security office and control room is located off the northwest corner of the main lobby.

2. **Entrances.** The main hospital entrance is opens at 5 a.m. and is locked at 10 p.m. The Emergency entrance is open 24-hours. All other doors are locked after 9:00 p.m. until 6:00 a.m. Doors are watched by monitors in the Control Room.

3. **Food Service Equipment and Supplies.** All food service equipment and supplies are kept locked before issue and when not in use. All freezers and walk-in coolers in the dietary department are kept at all times.

4. **Authorized Personnel Only.** No unauthorized person is allowed in any food storage area. These areas must be locked when not in use.

5. **General Dry Storage Area** The general dry food and storage area is well lighted and ventilated. It houses dry food items on shelves at least 6 inches from the floor and walls, and 20 inches from the light fixtures.. The dry storage area is protected from fire by a sprinkler system. A dry chemical extinguisher is also available. The area is also protected from insects and rodents through the pest control program.

6. **Storeroom locks.** Storeroom locks are changed annually.

7. **Food Security.** Employees receiving food and supplies must follow the food check-out and rotation procedures (see departmental issuing manual). Responsible employees must check to be sure they have received the exact quantity and weight requested and sign the proper receipt. The items shall be checked again for quantity, weight, and condition upon delivery to the department. Frequent checks, comparing the amounts of food prepared against the number of savings consumed, are conduct to insure proper use of food in the preparation and pre-preparation areas.

8. **Theft.** Inspection of garbage areas shall be made by security personnel to assure that only authorized items are being removed from the premises. Employees are not allowed to bring personal packages into the area.

FOOD SERVICE SECURITY POLICY (CONTINUED)

9. **Food Consumption.** Employees may not eat food other than those authorized to be eaten. This will be considered theft.

10. **Supplies.** All non-food supply levels are monitored by food service management staff. Extensive use of hospital supplies such as paper goods, soaps, and cleaning supplies shall be investigated and action taken to prohibit abuses. The removal of any kind of food, equipment, or property without proper request, constitutes a theft.

11. **Cash Handling.** Cash is handled only by designated employees. Money is secured in locked safes with restricted combination under the control of the supervisor. Cash handling procedures are reviewed by the Internal Auditor.

ST. VINCENT'S
MEDICAL
CENTER

FOOD SERVICE ACCIDENT AND ILLNESS REPORTING POLICY

Policy Number: STV426

Date Issued: October 3, 2007

Issued By: Colton Hall, Director of Food Service/Dietary

ST. VINCENT'S
MEDICAL
CENTER

It is the goal of the dietary department to provide a safe work environment for all employees. If an accident or illness occurs in the workplace, we require the parties involved to record all details to ensure fair and adequate treatment. Timely recording of accidents and illnesses will also ensure that employees receive benefits to which they are entitled.

The following practices are required in the event of an accident or illness:

1. **Minor Illness/Sick Days.** When ill and unable to work, employees must phone their immediate supervisor as soon as possible prior to the start of his or her scheduled shift. See St. Vincent's Employee Handbook for details on benefits and sick days.

2. **Long-Term Illness.** In the event of a long-term illness, coordination of return to work occurs between the attending physician, the employee, and the Director of Food Service/Dietary. It will be handled on a case-by-case basis.

3. **On-the-Job Illness.** An employees who becomes ill at work must report to his or her supervisor to be excused from work.

4. **Accidents.** All accidents, no matter how minor, must be reported to the supervisor on duty. An Employee Incident Report must be completed and signed. Questions regarding compensation are handled by the Personnel Department.

DINING ROOM SAFETY INSPECTION FORM

Completed By: _____ Date _____

EMERGENCY PROCEDURES

Is there a functional emergency lighting system?   ❑ Yes   ❑ No

Are all employees instructed in emergency procedures?   ❑ Yes   ❑ No

Are the emergency numbers clearly posted for fire, police, hospital and ambulance?   ❑ Yes   ❑ No

Are any employees trained in first aid procedures such as CPR or Heimlich Maneuver?   ❑ Yes   ❑ No

Comments or Corrective Actions Needed: _____

_____

_____

ELECTRICAL

Are all electrical switches and outlets covered?   ❑ Yes   ❑ No

Are there any extension cords in use?   ❑ Yes   ❑ No

Are all exposed electrical cords untangled, properly insulated and in good condition?   ❑ Yes   ❑ No

Comments or Corrective Actions Needed: _____

_____

_____

EQUIPMENT

Is all equipment clean, well-maintained and in good working order?   ❑ Yes   ❑ No

Do hot beverage machines, such as coffee urns, have scald warnings posted?   ❑ Yes   ❑ No

Before using any piece of equipment, are all employees properly trained?   ❑ Yes   ❑ No

Comments or Corrective Actions Needed: _____

_____

_____

FLOORING, STAIRWAYS & EXITS

Are floor mats in use, especially near wet or greasy areas?   ❑ Yes   ❑ No

For high-traffic areas, are rugs and runners utilized?   ❑ Yes   ❑ No

Is there adequate lighting in areas with steps or staircases?   ❑ Yes   ❑ No

Are steps equipped with handrails and slip guards?   ❑ Yes   ❑ No

Do all exits have properly lit exit signs?   ❑ Yes   ❑ No

Are all exits free from obstructions?   ❑ Yes   ❑ No

Do all exit doors have panic bars?   ❑ Yes   ❑ No

Do all exit doors open easily?   ❑ Yes   ❑ No

Comments or Corrective Actions Needed: _____

_____

EMPLOYEE INVOLVED

Name:_____

Address: _____

Phone: _____

Date of birth: _____

SS#: _____

Emergency contact:_____

ACCIDENT DETAILS

Date of accident occurred:_____

Time of accident occurred:_____

Location accident occurred:_____

Manager on duty: _____

Date reported:_____

Time reported: _____

EMPLOYMENT STATEMENT

To whom was the accident reported? _____

_____

Specify work area where accident occurred:

_____

_____

Part of body injured: _____

_____

Specify machine, appliance, substance or object connected with accident: _____

_____

Describe what you were doing when accident occurred:

_____

_____

_____   _____

Employee's Signature   Date

SUPERVISOR'S DESCRIPTION OF ACCIDENT

_____

_____

_____

_____

_____

_____

_____

_____

INJURY DETAILS

Disabling injury ❏ Yes ❏ No

Sent to hospital ❏ Yes ❏ No

Return to regular job ❏ Yes ❏ No

Return to light duty ❏ Yes ❏ No

Estimated days of disability: _____

Date to return to work: _____

Initial medical diagnosis:_____

_____   _____

Manager's Signature   Date

This form should be used in conjunction with an Accident Report, within 24 hours of the incident. It will help determine the cause of the accident.

Employee(s) invloved: _____ Date of Accident:_____

Summarize the Accident _____

_____

_____

CAUSE OF THE ACCIDENT

Check one and fill out appropriate section below ❑ Employee ❑ Procedure ❑ Equipment

EMPLOYEE

Did the employee make an error? ❑ Yes ❑ No If yes, explain the error and possible reason. _____

_____

_____

Did employee receive medical care? ❑ Yes ❑ No If yes, detail treatment._____

_____

_____

Would safety equipment have prevented this accident? ❑ Yes ❑ No If yes, list equipment_____

_____

_____

PROCEDURE

Is there a procedure for the specific task? ❑ Yes ❑ No If yes, explain the procedure.

_____

_____

If yes, was employee following it? ❑ Yes ❑ No If not, was employee counselled? ❑ Yes ❑ No

Is further training needed for all employees on this procedure? ❑ Yes ❑ No

If yes, list dates training will be offered.

_____

Does the procedure need to be modified? ❑ Yes ❑ No If yes, explain how and expected completion.

_____

_____

_____

_____

EQUIPMENT

What equipment was involved? _____

_____

Does the equipment need repair? ❑ Yes ❑ No If yes, explain how and expected completion.

_____

_____

Was other equipment of that type checked? ❑ Yes ❑ No

Was safety equipment available to prevent accident? ❑ Yes ❑ No Was it being used? ❑ Yes ❑ No

Signature of Supervisor_____Date

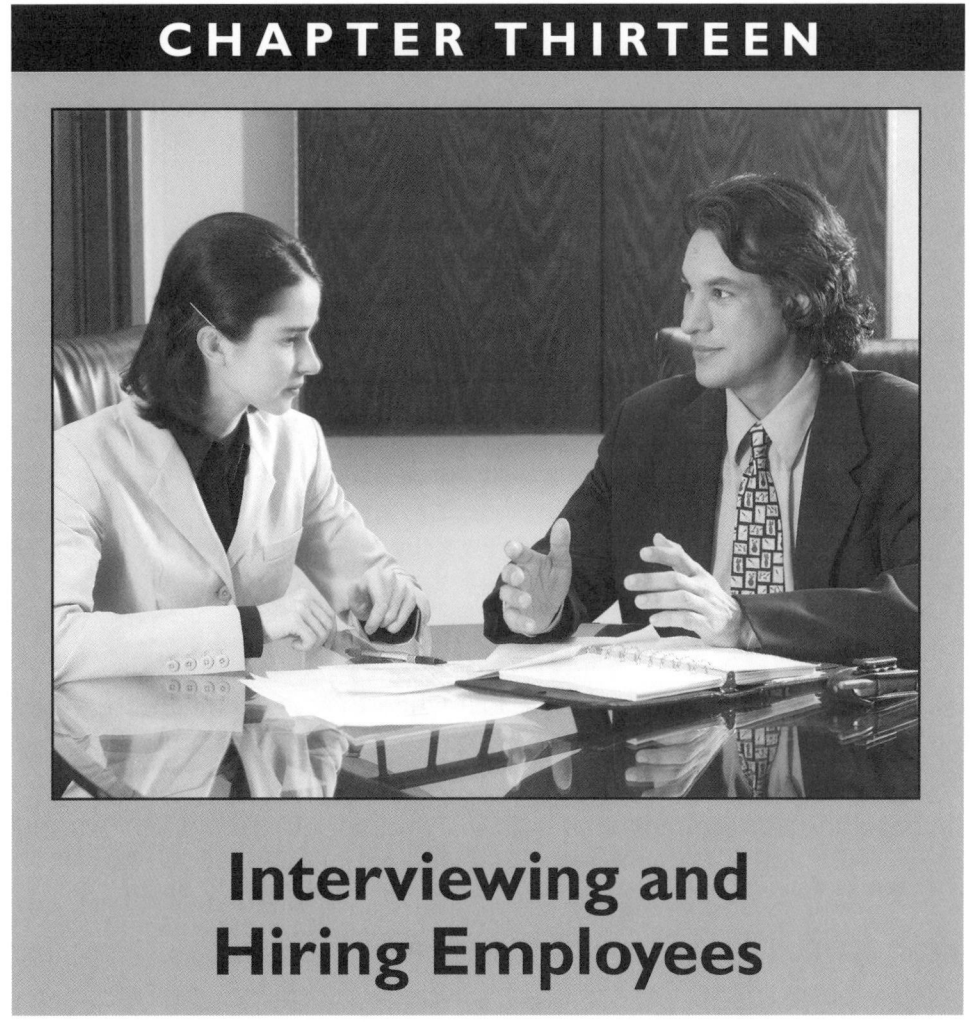

CHAPTER THIRTEEN

Interviewing and Hiring Employees

As a non-commercial food service manager, you will invest time and money in nothing that is as critical as your selection of staff members. A business must have employees to make it work, and great people make your food service facility great. To have great employees, you must be a great manager.

The Value (and Cost) of Employees

Your employees have the biggest effect on the quality of your food and its presentation to your patrons. Train your employees and keep them motivated and satisfied to help maintain the quality standards that you set for the facility. You can motivate them by making them feel like part of a team and by making their job rewarding. Some simple provisions to make their working conditions better are employee lockers, separate restrooms, break room, air conditioning, sufficient lighting, and the right tools and equipment for the job. These things aren't complicated, but they make a big difference in the employees' attitude and performance.

In a perfect world, here are the things you would provide to staff members: higher salaries; thorough and effective training; health, dental, vision, and life insurance programs, flexibility in the scheduling; shorter work weeks while paying a full wage; tools needed to increase productivity and reduce stress in a safety situation; a safe and clean work environment; effective employee evaluations while listening to employee feedback; benefit packages; an opportunity for advancement in the company; and a pleasant and structured work environment.

Remember that many of the items listed above are not provided by other food service businesses so it may be unrealistic for staff members to expect these things from your facility.

Do not offer things to prospective employees that you cannot do.

When you review the wish lists of valuable staff members, consider the cost of replacing employees. You need to figure the cost of unmotivated and unhappy employees who are preparing food for the facility. People rarely give their best when they are unhappy, meaning that your patrons won't get a quality product or outstanding customer service. Most business managers know that positive word-of-mouth advertising can be great, but you can get negative word-of-mouth, even if the food was wonderful, but the server or cashier was rude.

Another concern is that unhappy employees are not worried about your business. They may break things, lose things, be rude to others, or absent without notice. It's hard for staff members to care about the business's profits when they feel they are underpaid. These are some of the costs included in replacing that employee:

- **Advertisements for applications** to fill the position.

- **The interviewer's salary** and their time lost when they are pulled from other duties.

- **Administrative costs** for paperwork and payroll for a new hire.

- **Time to train the new employee** and added work for others until they are trained.

- **Loss of sales and the cost of supplies** because of training mistakes.

- **Labor expenses** until the new staff member is fully trained.

- **Expense and time needed to terminate an employee**, such as paperwork, exit interview, and possibly unemployment compensation.

The American Management Association reports the cost to replace an employee is about 30 percent of his annual salary. The cost for a skilled employee can be one-and-a-half times his annual salary. So retaining good, quality workers affects profitability and effectiveness.

Everyone wants to work for employers who appreciate their skills and give them adequate compensation. It is good to check the Department of Labor in Washington, D.C., and your state employment commission for detailed breakdowns of current pay rates for various jobs to keep your pay scale within local parameters. It also helps you know when you are offering employees more than other businesses in your area.

Atlantic Publishing **www.atlantic-pub.com** offers a book entitled *365 Ways to Motivate and Reward Employees Every Day—With Little or No Money*. Managers know that rewarding employees will help motivate them. It is best to find ways to keep quality employees in your facility. You may hear that the only way to keep employees is to give them more money, but this is not necessarily true.

Computing your turnover rate can be enlightening. The form at the end of this chapter gives you the information to determine your turnover rate and the cost to your facility.

Design Employee Applications

Does your facility have a form application? Do you feel that it asks questions that help you screen applicants? If you feel the applications aren't effective in getting the preliminary information you need, ask your supervisor if you can make changes. The person who screens the applications needs to gather specific information to choose which applicants to interview.

It might be helpful to look at applications that other facilities use. These could give you unique ideas of the questions you would like to ask. I am not suggesting that you steal an application, but you can use pieces of these to form you own. At the end of this chapter you will find some applications that you can use and a questionnaire to learn a little more about the applicant.

Here are some suggested questions targeted for food service applicants.

- Name three food service places where you have worked.

- What type of food service facility was each of these businesses?

- What was your position and what were your responsibilities?

- Which one of these businesses would you be proud to own? Why?

- Which one would you be ashamed to own? Why?

- What do you like most about working in food service?

- What is your least favorite thing about food service employment?

- Why do you feel qualified to work in this food service department?

- What do you have to contribute to this department?

If you plan to interview people from inside the company or even the food service facility, you can use the application at the end of this chapter for a current employee.

Screen Applicants

It is normal to have a large pile of applications when you advertise a job opening. So how do you tackle this mound of applications? Many business managers review every application to decide which people to interview. One process is detailed below.

Sort the Applications

Consider your best employees. You could talk to the human resource department and pull their applications to check their backgrounds. Check for past employment that would qualify them for the open position.

I managed one business where everyone who applied was invited to the office for an interview. The job involved one-on-one contact with customers and employees, and we wanted to see how applicants interacted with people. I scheduled every person with useful skills, normally 15 to 20 people for each group interview. Their expressions betrayed their reactions when they were told that all of these people would be in the interview.

We reviewed the applications and marked our favorites; however, our choices sometimes changed after we met the person. We handed out paper and a pen to each person and asked a series of questions. Most were job-related but some were personal preferences. One specific question was regarding our work hours which were unusual and they didn't suit many people.

During the interviews, I made notes about the applicants' behavior and their interaction with the others. We considered the results overnight and discussed our thoughts the next morning. At that point we called three or four people in simultaneously for face-to-face interviews. Because we had formed opinions about the applicants, we personalized the interviews. It was an unusual technique, but it allowed us to watch the applicants interact with people, something that you don't see when you talk with them individually. You might find this technique useful in your facility.

When you need to hire a new employee, make a list of the qualities for the "perfect" applicant. What experience and background do you want? Create a clear picture in your mind of what you are looking for in an employee. When you know what you want, review the applications. Your criteria should include:

1. **Definite Interview** — People with the background and experience needed. An interview will determine if they have the personality and attitude you need.

2. **Possible Interview** — People with some background and experience that you need. You need more information about them to make a decision. Personality and attitude could be a factor with these applicants.

3. **Do Not Interview** — Many people apply who are simply not qualified. Reviewing their work history will reveal they don't have the background you need.

Once you have three piles, focus on the first two and determine who has the background and experience you need. There may be other specific things that you are looking for in applicants. This is a time when a customized application is beneficial.

In one job, I interviewed perspective kitchen employees in our little workroom when it was fairly busy. The atmosphere was intimidating, but I needed to see if they could handle working close to others. If applicants wanted a solitary workspace, they would never survive in the department. Some obviously were uneasy, but others seemed comfortable around the activity. A big part of the job involved pulling supplies and restocking carts. Accuracy and speed were critical. During our "interview," I asked applicants to help me with an inventory sheet. I watched to see if they chatted or if they pulled the supplies accurately. Most of the people I wanted to hire were well suited for the job. Those interviews helped me see if they could focus on the things that I felt were important.

First, hire quality people to work in your non-commercial food service facility. You need to develop effective interviewing skills to find the best people. It may seem funny, but the quality of your help-wanted ad can affect the type of people you attract. When you design the ad, be honest: "Seeking hardworking and skilled applicants with previous experience and with the drive to do a superior job." What sort of people would this ad attract? "Busy cafeteria desperately needs anyone who can complete an application." A qualified individual wouldn't be attracted to a desperate business.

The applications are coming in. Now what should you do? Atlantic Publishing **www.atlantic-pub.com** offers a book titled *501+ Great Interview Questions for Employers and the Best Answers for Prospective Employees*. It contains 501 well written questions to help interviewers draw out the answers they need. There are specific techniques when you ask questions that help you get the answers needed to screen applicants.

Screening Potential Employees

Pre-screening gives you a chance to eliminate candidates who are not qualified for the position before spending time on a lengthy interview. This saves time for everyone involved. Pre-screening should be done by a staff member who knows the qualities and experience needed for the job. Interviews with job candidates may be scheduled with the manager. In some facilities, the supervisor does the initial interview, and then the department manager does a separate interview. Check with your supervisor or human resources department to make sure you understand the procedures that affect your area. Be sure that all applicants are treated fairly and have an equal opportunity to get the job. This is an important part of public relations for the facility. These are the criteria for preliminary screening:

1. **Experience** — Is the applicant qualified to handle the job you have available? Examine past job experience. Check all references.

2. **Appearance** — Is the applicant clean and neatly dressed? If the applicant will deal with the public, what kind of impression will they make? In a food service facility, cleanliness is of prime importance. Some staff members will have more contact than others with the public, and that could affect your decision.

3. **Personality** — Does the applicant's personality complement other employees, and will it impress patrons? Is he outgoing, but not overbearing? Is this the sort of person who can be managed?

4. **Legality** — Does the applicant meet the legal requirements to work in the facility?

5. **Availability** — Can the person work the hours you need to fill? Does he have reliable transportation to work?

6. **Health and physical ability** — Can your applicant do the physical work required? Some businesses require potential employees to have a complete physical before starting to work. Be careful not to discriminate against people with disabilities, but if you have any doubts, check with human resources or legal counsel for the facility.

7. Is the application signed and dated?

CASE STUDY: POLICIES AND PROCEDURES

Here is a good place to advise you to have written Policies and Procedures, Job Descriptions (the key phrase being 'performs other duties as required'), Work Schedules, and that all supervisor/employee interactions are documented. They will prove of inestimable value at your next Labor Relations Board hearing where you will occupy the seat labeled "BAD GUY."

Ed Hulse

Effective Interviewing

All effective managers need good team members. Count your blessings if you are able to handpick the members of your team. However, most managers must work with a team another person assembled. Either of these approaches works, but I prefer to pick my own employees.

Remember that your team members will need to help you accomplish tasks and they can make you and the facility look good. Think about these questions:

- **What type of people** do you prefer to work around?

- **What qualities** are the most important?

- **What types of people** work well with you and your team?

- **Do you put interviewees at ease** when you talk with them?

- **Do you avoid questions which prompt short answers?** More detailed answers will give you more insights into the potential employee. However, don't use loaded or leading questions.

- **Do you ask one or more questions at a time?** Ask one and give the applicant the chance to answer completely. Their answer could affect the next question.

- **Do you use language and grammar to show you have a reasonable level of education?**

- **Always listen to the applicants** to learn about them.

- **Do you tell the applicant that you will be in touch?** How will you follow up after the interview?

Consider these things carefully when you interview people and make the final decisions about who to hire. Ask key and valued employees to make a list of what experience, background, and qualities they feel are needed to work in the facility. They work there every day and have the best ideas about the experience and knowledge needed to do their jobs. Add your thoughts to their ideas and file them in a safe place. They can help you screen applicants and can affect the questions you ask in the interviews. Prepare the list before you start the interviews and be familiar with the list before you talk to an applicant.

Before you schedule any interviews, determine how you will conduct the interviews. Have a complete and concise description of the job you need to fill. I liked to have a one-page overview of the job requirements and duties. This helped the applicant see and hear what was involved in the job. There have been times when a complete explanation of job requirements was enough to help an applicant know the job wasn't right for them. If you notice concern or hesitation in the interviewees, make it easy for them to leave without feeling obligated. You do not want someone to pursue a job for the wrong reasons. If they do not feel competent to handle the job, they shouldn't be considered.

It is important to be honest about negative aspects of the job. Giving the applicant a rosy picture of what is needed won't help anyone. These unrealistic expectations will create an unhappy employee, and it is likely that you will have to replace another person. The goal of an effective manager is to find the best possible person to fill the position in the facility. To do this, you must be honest with the interviewees. Can they work unusual or night hours? Will they work outside? Are the conditions uncomfortable?

One job where I was a manager didn't have any windows and only two solid doors. We spent the majority of our day in the basement where claustrophobic people would have freaked out. Another job involved working near 400°F ovens. There were people who couldn't work in the intense heat. These are the sort of things you need to explain to applicants.

When I managed a pizza shop, almost all my team members were college students. They were required to work Friday and Saturday nights, and everyone had to work during the Super Bowl. I spent a great deal of time trying to make the schedule fair, but I made these conditions clear in their interviews. It was critical that the store be staffed during these peak times.

At the pizza shop, one employee was "on call" every Friday and Saturday night. This required that they not drink. I gave them a simple bonus for being on call. If I called, they had to be sober. This was made clear in the beginning and I never had a problem.

Once you have explained the positives and negatives, determine if the applicant is still interested. Mention the starting pay, benefits, holiday and vacation policies, and any other benefits the job offers. Do not make promises about pay raises, time off, and other things you cannot control. Even if you say, "I will try to...." the applicant may hear "I will make it happen." You didn't say those words, but they will believe you did.

Your interviews should not feel like an inquisition. Ask open ended questions that begin with: who, what, when, where, why, and how, and cannot be answered by "yes" or "no." Some goals of your questions include information about their education, work experience, attendance record, and the reasons they left their last jobs.

It can be helpful to have form such as the ones at the end of this chapter to keep your interview on track and to make notes.

Here are some questions to get inside the applicant's mind:

- What type of job do you picture yourself in at this time?

- Why would you pick that job?

- Why are you qualified for that position?

- Who was your best supervisor?

- What made that person a great boss?

- Do you have any of these qualities?

- How could a manager improve on the things your ideal boss did?

- Who was your worst supervisor?

- What made him the worst?

- Do you have similar qualities?

- How would you overcome these qualities?

These questions make people look inside themselves and give you insights into the sort of boss and situation the applicant prefers. Are you that type of boss? These insights will indicate if you can work together.

It never hurts to analyze our interviewing skills to see if there are ways to improve. Take a closer look at your interviewing skills. Are there ways to improve the way you interview?

Unlawful Pre-Employment Questions

This section includes details about equal and fair employment practices. These suggestions should not be used as a substitute to talking to your attorney or state and federal labor offices. This chapter gives you a basic understanding, but the people and agencies mentioned above can give you complete information applicable for your location. Have your attorney review any specific information or forms before using them for the non-commercial food service facility.

The Federal Civil Rights Act of 1964 and other state and federal laws ensure that a job applicant must be treated on a fair and equal basis. Because of these regulations, there are questions you cannot ask about:

- Race and/or National Origin
- Religion
- Sex
- Age
- Marital Status
- Disabilities
- Criminal Record
- Physical Abilities

You cannot legally inquire into these personal matters, but many answers are obvious. Many disabilities are evident during interviews. The only time a disability makes a difference is when it would make it impossible for the person to do the job. Tread carefully around these situations and speak to legal counsel if you have any doubts or concerns.

The form at the end of this chapter will provide some tips to help you avoid questions that can leave the facility open to lawsuits.

Age/date of birth is important for food service facilities that serve alcohol. It is also an issue if the person is below the legal age to work. Age is a sensitive question, because the Age Discrimination in Employment Act **www.eeoc.gov/policy/adea.html** protects employees 40 years and older. You can ask applicants whether they are under 18.

Drugs and Smoking

You can ask whether the applicant smokes or uses drugs. The application gives you a chance to have the applicant agree to be bound by the employer's drug and smoking policies and to submit to drug testing. Use the form at the end of this chapter to acquire the applicant's consent for drug and alcohol screening.

Other problem areas to consider

- **Questions about credit rating** or credit references are believed to be discriminatory against minorities and women.

- **Asking whether an applicant owns a home** is discriminatory against minority members, since a greater number of minority members do not own their own homes.

- **You can ask if the person was in the military** but not about his or her discharge.

- **You cannot ask about disabilities,** health problems, and medical conditions.

Focus on the positive things in interviews. These include experiences that fit into the job requirements. Ask if they have done similar work? What personality characteristics do they have suited for the job? Some of these traits include:

- Achievements
- Energy and enthusiasm
- Physical condition
- Attitude
- Job attendance
- Ability to pay attention to the interviewer

Make Interviews More Successful

It is natural for people to be nervous during an interview so make an effort to help the interviewee feel relaxed. Don't make notes during the interview because this can distract the person. Instead, make mental notes during the interview and write them down after the interview is over.

Do not initiate comments about the applicant's personal life out of the process. If an applicant mentions children or a spouse, then you can pursue it. Did you notice any inconsistencies in the applicant's story? The person could only be nervous, but follow up on these things and ask for specifics. It may take practice to keep your expression and tone even during interviews. Try not to show your shock if the applicant says something that surprises you. I've been amazed at some of the things people say in interviews.

You may feel tempted to rush interviews especially when many people are scheduled. There is plenty of work to do, but don't make the person feel rushed. Glancing at your watch can make the interviewee shut down, and the interview won't be productive. Give the person your undivided attention and take your time.

Key Points for Conducting Employment Interviews

There are many things you need to discuss during job interviews. Some of them are listed here.

- **Be genuinely interested in all applicants,** even if you probably won't hire them. Each applicant is a potential customer.

- **Be on time and be ready to talk at the appointed time.** Being late or changing the time gives the impression you are disorganized. Applicants may be discouraged by your poor impression and not reschedule.

- **Know all details about the job you are offering.** You need to understand what the job involves to find the right person to do it.

- **Conduct all interviews in private.** A private office is the best place for interviews. Let your staff members know they need to keep interruptions to a minimum.

- **Help the applicant feel at ease.** Give them a comfortable place to sit. Be conversational and interested in what the applicants say.

- **Give the person a chance to ask questions.** The questions will be revealing so listen carefully; you will hear about past jobs, past supervisors, and school experiences. Watch for contradictions, excuses, and defensive or negative reactions. Any questions they avoid could indicate possible problems.

- **Don't indicate your disapproval** of things any applicant does or says; appear open-minded. But be careful not to condone obvious mistakes.

- **Have some unexpected questions prepared.** What do they do to relax? What are their hobbies? What is the last book they read? These reveal things about their attitudes, personalities, and energy levels.

I ask what they didn't like about their last job and supervisor. Sometimes their answers will tell you immediately whether they would be happy. Many food service applicants "like dealing with people" or "like dealing with food." Which applicants seem to be qualified for the job? Include one or more behavior-based questions to give an indication of how the applicant responds in real-life work situations and whether the person can handle them. For example: "How would you help a patron who complained his 'soup just doesn't taste right'?" Customer complaints must be handled carefully and to their satisfaction.

Things to Look for in Potential Employees

Each manager has key qualities that they want in a potential employee. Here are some of the more common qualities:

- **Stability** — It is better for you and the facility if new hires stay around. Check their past employment records. Stability also includes their emotional makeup which can be evident in the interview.

- **Leadership qualities** — It is productive to have team members who want to achieve things in their professional lives. This doesn't mean someone who is after your job at all costs, but team members can be successful in any position in a company. Review their past employment records for growth.

- **Motivation** — Why is the person applying to your non-commercial food service facility? Is it an interest in the non-commercial industry in general? Does he want a career or a temporary job? Is he domineering or being motivated by someone else?

- **Independence** — Is the applicant on his own? Is he financially secure? When did he leave his parents' home and why?

- **Maturity** — Are the applicants mentally and emotionally mature enough to handle a stressful environment? Can they communicate with team members and customers who are older or younger?

- **Determination** — Does the applicant finish projects that he starts? Does he seek out or hide from challenges?

- **Work habits** — Does the applicant understand the physical work involved in a non-commercial food service facility? Has he or she done similar work? Is he or she neat and organized? Is the application filled out properly? Look at the applicant's job history for pay increases and promotions.

After you learn what the person is looking for, these are some things to focus on and discuss in more detail. At this point you already know they are interested in the position you need to fill.

- Money, benefits, and steady employment.

- Interesting and challenging work.

- Opportunities for advancement in a safe and pleasant environment.

- Any social, recreational, or sports events the facility offers.

- Any support the facility offers for advanced education and training.

- The opportunity to be cross-trained in different skills.

Americans with Disabilities Act (ADA)

People who sponsored the ADA found that disabled people were discriminated against in many areas including: employment, housing, public accommodations, transportation, communication, recreation, institutionalization, health services, voting, and access to public services. Something had to be done to help people with disabilities to have some recourse. These are some of the accomplishments of the ADA.

- **Clear and comprehensive mandate to eliminate discrimination** against people with disabilities on a national level.

- **The standards would be clear, consistent, enforceable**, and would strongly address discrimination against people with disabilities.

- **There would be power to enforce the 14th amendment** and to deal with discrimination that disabled people face each day.

- **The federal government would play a central role in enforcing the standards** established by the ADA to help disabled people.

The first section of the Act deals with discrimination in employment situations. This includes discrimination against employees and applicants in:

1. Hiring
2. Treatment
3. Accommodating disabilities
4. Training
5. Applying for a job
6. Promotion and advancement
7. Compensation for job done
8. Benefits
9. Layoff
10. Termination
11. Job Assignments
12. Leave

People who are protected under this act include:

- Those with mental or physical impairments that severely limit at least one major activity in life.

- Those with a history of impairments.

- Those who are regarded as having such impairments and can perform the job with or without reasonable accommodation.

There are various solutions available to disabled people which include: compensatory and punitive damages, back pay, restored benefits, attorney's fees, reasonable accommodation by the employer, reinstatement, and job offers.

Who is Qualified?

The Act defines "qualified" as "an individual with a disability who satisfies the requisite skill, experience, and educational requirements of the employment position such individual holds or desires, and who, with or without reasonable accommodation, can perform the essential functions of each position."

Most people agree that "essential function" is the important key in making the decision about who is or is not "qualified." This will depend on what the person is hired to do. If they are hired to prepare food, they must be able to perform the preparation duties needed.

Does the Business Have Any Defense?

There are some conditions under which the business has some defense about whom to hire. These include:

1. **Business Necessity** — Accommodations would pose an unreasonable hardship on the business operations.

2. **Contagious/Infectious Disease** — The applicant has a contagious or infectious disease that poses a significant risk to people in the workplace.

3. **Religious Entity Defense** — The ADA allows people to limit their hiring to others of their own faith, but they cannot refuse to hire someone of their faith because of a disability.

4. **Drug/Alcohol Use** — Employers may prohibit the use of alcohol and illegal drugs in the work place. Most also refuse to allow employees to work while under the influence of drugs or alcohol. Employees must follow these rules to keep their jobs.

What Are Reasonable Accommodations?

The EEOC defines an accommodation as "any change in the work environment or in the way things are customarily done that enables an individual with a disability to enjoy equal employment opportunities." There are three reasons for making accommodations:

1. **To help the person apply for the job.**

2. **To enable the person to perform necessary functions of the job.**

3. **To allow disabled people to enjoy the same "benefits and privileges"** that employees without disabilities enjoy.

Reasonable accommodations can include:

- Acquiring or modifying the needed equipment or tools.

- Restructuring job descriptions and procedures.

- Varying hours and work schedules.

- Reassigning a vacant position.

- Adjusting or modifying examinations, training materials, and facility policies.

- Providing readers and interpreters.

- Offering an accessible and usable work place.

When Does "Reasonable Accommodation" become an "Undue Hardship"? This is an important factor that business managers need to understand. Undue hardship would alter the nature of the business or be unduly costly, extensive, disruptive, or substantial.

Consider the costs involved, size of the business, financial resources, and the nature and structure of the business. When one accommodation is ruled out, you must search for another option. Is there financing available from another source? This would make a difference in whether it is an undue hardship for your facility. Vocational rehabilitation agencies or other agencies may be able to fund the necessary accommodations.

Compliance is mandatory and enforceable by law. For more details visit their Web site at **www.usdoj.gov/crt/ada**. This page will give you access to all ADA information and updates about new and proposed regulations. One of the first things you can do is to analyze the job to get additional information to make an educated decision. The form at the end of this chapter will help you verify the facts.

Hiring

The form shown on the next page could be helpful when you are comparing one applicant to another. Use your notes to make an educated and effective decision. This gives you a chance to evaluate each applicant side by side. If there is anything else you would like to add, feel free to make any changes to make it more helpful.

Applicant's Name
To what degree do they meet the requirements?
Degree of General Knowledge
Degree of Technical Skills
Total Score
Comments

You need a thorough and accurate job description because it helps you and the applicant know what is expected. Existing and dependable employees can give you details about their duties. The form at the end of this chapter can be helpful in explaining what a job involves.

CASE STUDY: PRISON STAFFING

Supervisors interview inmates for job positions. All inmates work 30 hours a week. There are two shifts. The pay scale starts at 20 cents per hour and can reach 45 cents per hour at the six-month evaluation.

There is very little training for the job. When a person is hired he is told where to work. With practice, he picks up the way things are done. In some cases an inmate will have training in food service or has been to cook/baker school. These individuals will have knowledge of the way things are done in a food service facility.

Lawrence Shearer, Chef

Reduce Potential Turnover

Effective hiring will reduce potential turnover. Carefully consider what you need in an employee and conduct a great interview. Unhappy people have a higher chance of tardiness and low-quality work. We all know how hard it is to be enthusiastic about a job that we dislike. When you aren't happy, it's difficult to give your best.

Do you know how much it costs the facility when you hire the wrong person? The U.S. Department of Labor reports, "A bad hire will cost a company the equivalent of that employee's salary for a six month period." This not only includes that person's payroll amount. There is much more to consider. The following amounts listed are averages, but the amounts will surprise you.

Adding an Unskilled Worker	$5,000
Keeping an Unqualified Person	$20,000
Training a New Employee	$2,000

Most people don't realize a bad hire can cost a business that much money. Consider what it actually costs the facility when you have employee turnover. Include these expenses in your calculations.

- **Overtime needed** to get the work done.

- **Management time to review applications** and conduct interviews.

- **Expenses to pay employees to train new employees** who work at a lower productivity rate while they are training.

High employee turnover can easily cause budget problems, but it has a negative impact in the facility. All team members are required to do additional work while the facility is understaffed. High turnover rates are discouraging to the people who train the new hires. Training is difficult, and their work falls further behind.

When reviewing applications, look for experience and personalities that fit into the facility, and then sort out the people who fit the job. However, qualifications and experience are only two things to consider.

Southwest Airlines takes this idea to an unusual level. The company's hiring policies are unorthodox. They hire people based on their attitude. A person with less experience and a better attitude is usually hired instead of a person who has experience but a less attractive attitude. We know that employees can be trained to do their jobs, but a bad attitude is hard to change. Southwest Airlines looks for: "team spirit, cheerfulness, optimism, decision-making ability, communication, self-confidence, and self starter skills."

Some companies give tests to potential employees. There is a wide variety of tests that can be used. If you decide to use one, find one that produces results pertaining to the qualities you need. Find tests that are easy to understand, realizing that there are many people who simply cannot take tests, in which case you may miss out on a wonderful team member. So test scores should not be the only determining factor when you decide who to hire. When the tests don't get the results you want, try new tests or stop using them all together.

When you review your notes after an interview, listen to your gut feelings. There are times when we get a good or bad feeling about a person. If you have been right about people in the past, pay attention to your feelings.

Earlier we talked about making a list of qualities and qualifications for potential employees. Keep this handy when you make the final decisions. Which qualities are the most important to you? Some are more critical than others. Have these points clearly in mind when you review the final applicants.

Every application I've ever seen has a section for references. It is common to ask for references and ironic since personal references are basically useless. In 20 years of conducting interviews, only one person listed an acquaintance who told me how awful he was.

However, business references are critical. Be sure the applicant includes business references and check them. References can't legally tell you very much, but they can give you a sense about the person. Some of the things you can learn about applicants through their business references include their:

- Previous job
- Pay and any raises or bonuses
- Attendance record

- Responsibilities
- Length of employment
- Reason for leaving the job

When you check references, it is a good time to verify information the applicant gave you and the impressions you have about them. I've called many references and usually got a good sense about potential employees. This is possible even when they couldn't directly answer my questions. Many people say that hiring anyone without checking references is crazy. It's an easy way to learn more about the applicant.

The forms at the end of this chapter offer various ways to track the information you receive from an applicants' references. One or more may be perfect for your needs. You can also make changes so the form will work better for you. One of the forms is especially for taking notes from a phone reference check.

It is difficult to decide whom to hire. Sometimes there are too many qualified applicants and other times you can't find any. When you make the final decision, consider the applicant as a "total package." It could help to make a list of the pros and cons for each applicant. Do you have someone who knows the job well and whose opinion you trust? Why not ask this person to say hello to the applicants? This should be subtle and can even be a simple "Hello, how are you today?" but it gives them a chance to talk with the person. Ask about their impressions. Review all of the points below with your most qualified applicant, making sure the person understands the details.

- **Salary** — Starting pay, pay range, realistic pay increases, time sheet procedures, payday, company benefits, vacations, and insurance.

- **Job description** — Job duties, hours, your expectations, accepting added responsibility, ways to increase their chance of getting pay raises.

- **Start time, date, and where he should report** on the first day of work.

Then ask the applicant if he is interested and would like to accept the job. Some people say no, but by this time in the process, they usually say yes. It is common for some applicants to take the evening to think about it just to be sure.

You may want to review the following information about job descriptions before meeting with potential employees. This will help you have the job responsibilities firmly in mind. Atlantic Publishing offers a computer program which includes job descriptions of many food service positions. To order visit **www.atlantic-pub.com** – Item FSJ-CS.

Rejecting Applicants

All experienced managers know how hard it is to reject job applicants, but the majority will be rejected. Some people may ask why they were rejected. In these cases, be honest and tactful. This shouldn't be a confrontation, and it can help them to find jobs they are more qualified to do. Sometimes it is enough to say there was a more experienced or better qualified applicant.

Employee Handbooks

Employee handbooks can ensure employee consistency in their training and understanding of the job. They provide a written record of the facility policies and what is expected from employees. A written manual can help you overcome communication problems. Employees need to be required to read the manual and then sign a statement for their personnel file. This is useful when problems arise.

Writing an effective and comprehensive manual is time-consuming. Atlantic Publishing **www.atlantic-pub.com** has a standard handbook for the food service industry. The title is *Design Your Own Effective Employee Handbook*. You simply edit the information so it matches your policies. It is written in Microsoft Word, facilitating customization.

Atlantic Publishing also offers a computer program to help you create an employee handbook. There are 100 policies included, and you can make simple changes to suit your facility. The information about your facility can be entered where prompted and you can insert forms for your employees to sign. Contact **www.atlantic-pub.com** – Item EHB-CS.

EMPLOYEE HANDBOOK TOPICS		
Absenteeism	Acts of Misconduct	Affidavit of Receipt
Availability to Work	Benefit Eligibility	Benefit Program
Bereavement Leave	Bonus Plan	Break Policy
Communication	Company Property	Company Vehicle
Confidentiality	Conflict of Interest	Criminal Convictions
Discipline	Educational Assistance	Employing Relatives
Employee Conduct	Employee Discount	Employment References
Equal Opportunity Employer	Family Leave of Absence	Harassment
Holidays	Hours for Work	Insurance
Insurance Continuation	Job Abandonment	Job Classification
Jury Duty	Mandatory Meetings	Medical Leave
Military Leave	Neatness in Work Area	Office Equipment
Orientation	Overtime	Outside Employment
Payroll	Performance Release	Performance Reviews
Personal Mail	Personal Phone Calls	Personal Appearance
Personnel Files	Pre Tax Deductions	Problem Resolution
Recording Time	Rehiring Employees	Reimbursable Expense
Safety	Salary and Wage Increases	Searches
Separation Forms	Severe Weather Policy	Shift Substitutions
Social Security	Solicitation and Contributions	Standards of Conduct
Substance Abuse	Suggestions	Termination Procedures
Tools and Equipment	Travel Expenses	Unemployment
Vacation	Violence and Weapons	Voluntary Resignation
Work Performance	Worker's Compensation	Workplace Monitoring

These are examples of some of the many topics that you should discuss in your employee handbook. Each facility will have different needs, but these are a great start.

Personnel Files

A personnel file needs to be created when the applicant is hired. This file will contain the following information:

- Completed application

- W-4 Form and social security number

- Name, address, and phone number (update as needed)

- Emergency contact phone numbers

- Employee hire date

- Job title and beginning pay rate

- Performance evaluations, signed by manager and employee

- Signed form to confirm he read and understood the Employee Handbook/Personnel Policy Manual

- Notes regarding any problems or positive events during his employment

- Termination date, if applicable, and a detailed account of the reasons for termination.

Obviously, you won't have all the information in the beginning, but all of these items and details need to be added at the appropriate time.

Now that you have hired your new employee, it's time to move on to training and managing staff members. We'll discuss that in Chapter 14.

PREPARED BY: _____

DATE: _____

EMPLOYEE TURNOVER RATE

Number of Completed W-2s _____

(-)

Current Number of Employees _____

(=)

Number of Past Employees _____

Number of Past Employees _____

(÷)

Average Number of Employees Employed _____

(x 100)

Employee Turnover Rate Percentage _____ %

COST OF EMPLOYEE TURNOVER

Number of Past Employees _____

(x)

Cost to Hire Each Employee $_____

(=)

Cost of Employee Turnover $_____

Notice to Applicant: We are an Equal Opportunity Employer and do not discriminate on the basis of applicant's race, color, religion, sex, national origin, citizenship, age, physical or mental disability, or any other characteristic.

PERSONAL INFORMATION (please print)

Name: _____ Social Security Number: _____

Address: _____

_____

_____

City: _____ State: _____ Zip: _____

Phone Number: _____

POSITION INFORMATION

Position applied for (check all that apply):

❑ Executive Chef	❑ Expediter	❑ Assistant Manager
❑ Host/Hostess	❑ Baker	❑ Kitchen Manager
❑ Banquet Manager	❑ Prep Cook	❑ Bartender
❑ Pantry Cook	❑ Beverage Manager	❑ Server
❑ Bus Person	❑ Cashier	❑ Cocktail Server
❑ Cook	❑ Counter Person	❑ Dining Room Manager

❑ Other _____

Have you ever worked for this organization: ❑ Yes ❑ No

If yes, date(s): _____

Prior position: _____

Reason(s) for leaving: _____

_____

_____

EDUCATION *(List from present to past)*

School/Institution	Major or Area of Study	Degree or Number of Years

OTHER INFORMATION

Name of friends and/or relatives employed by this organization:_____

_____

Position(s) held: _____

_____

If you are eligible, are you interested in health insurance? ❏ Yes ❏ No

AWARDS/ACHIEVEMENTS

_____

_____

_____

_____

REFERENCES *(Please list at least three people who are not related to you)*

Name	Occupation	Phone Number

EMERGENCY CONTACT *In the event of an emergency, who should we contact?*

Name: _____ Relationship to applicant: _____

Address: _____

City:_____ State: _____ Zip: _____

Phone Number:_____

ACKNOWLEDGMENT *(please read carefully)*

I hereby certify that the information contained in this application form and in any attachments (hereafter made a part of this application) is true and correct to the best of my knowledge and agree to have any of the statements checked by the organization unless I have indicated to the contrary. I authorize the references listed above to provide the company any and all information concerning my previous employment and any pertinent information that they may have. Further, I release all parties and persons from any and all liability for any damages that may result from furnishing such information to the company as well as from the use or disclosure of such information by the organization or any of its agents, employees or representatives. I understand that any misrepresentation, falsification or material omission of information on this application may result in my failure to receive an offer or, if I am hired, in my dismissal from employment.

Applicant's Signature _____ **Date** _____

PERSONAL

Last Name _____ First Name _____ Middle _____ Date _____

Street Address _____

City, State, Zip _____

Home Phone _____ Business Phone _____

Social Security Number _____ E-mail _____

Position Desired _____ Pay Expected _____

Are you available for full-time work? ❑ Yes ❑ No   If no, what hours can you work? _____

Will you work overtime if asked? ❑ Yes ❑ No   Are you legally eligible for employment in the United States? ❑ Yes ❑ No

When are you available to begin work? _____

Please list any additional training or skills (languages, certifications, specialty training, etc.): _____

_____

_____

EDUCATION

School	Name and Location of School	Course of Study	Years Completed	Did You Graduate?	Degree or Diploma
GRADUATE				❑ Yes ❑ No	
COLLEGE				❑ Yes ❑ No	
TRADE/TECHNICAL				❑ Yes ❑ No	
HIGH SCHOOL				❑ Yes ❑ No	
ELEMENTARY				❑ Yes ❑ No	

MEMBERSHIPS

Please list professional or civic organizations to which you belong. You may exclude those which may disclose your race, color, religion or ethnic origin.

_____

_____

_____

_____

EMPLOYMENT HISTORY

Starting with your present or most recent employer, give an accurate, complete employment record (include both full-time and part-time). We reserve the right to contact any employer listed below unless you indicate not to do so.

Company Name _____ Telephone_____

Address _____

Employed From (month/year) _____ To _____ Name of Supervisor _____

Weekly Pay Starting _____ Weekly Pay Leaving _____ Job Title _____

Description of Job Duties _____

_____

Reason for Leaving _____ May we contact this employer? ❏ Yes ❏ No

Company Name _____ Telephone_____

Address _____

Employed From (month/year) _____ To _____ Name of Supervisor _____

Weekly Pay Starting _____ Weekly Pay Leaving _____ Job Title _____

Description of Job Duties _____

_____

Reason for Leaving _____ May we contact this employer? ❏ Yes ❏ No

Company Name _____ Telephone_____

Address _____

Employed From (month/year) _____ To _____ Name of Supervisor _____

Weekly Pay Starting _____ Weekly Pay Leaving _____ Job Title _____

Description of Job Duties _____

_____

Reason for Leaving _____ May we contact this employer? ❏ Yes ❏ No

Company Name _____ Telephone_____

Address _____

Employed From (month/year) _____ To _____ Name of Supervisor _____

Weekly Pay Starting _____ Weekly Pay Leaving _____ Job Title _____

Description of Job Duties _____

_____

Reason for Leaving _____ May we contact this employer? ❏ Yes ❏ No

MILITARY

Did you serve in the Armed Forces? ❏ Yes ❏ No   If yes, what branch? _____

Describe any training received relevant to the position for which you are applying.

_____

_____

ADDITIONAL INFORMATION

DO NOT ANSWER ANY QUESTION IN THIS SECTION UNLESS THE BOX IS CHECKED.

If the employer has checked the box next to the question, the information requested is needed for legally permissible reason, including, without limitation, national security considerations, a legitimate occupational qualification or business necessity. The Civil Rights Act of 1964 prohibits discrimination in employment because of color, religion, sex or national origin. Federal law also prohibits discrimination based on age, citizenship and disability. The laws of most states also prohibit some or all of the above types of discrimination as well as some additional types such as discrimination based upon ancestry, marital status or sexual preference.

❏ Provide dates you attended school: Elementary From _____ To _____   High School From _____ To _____

College From _____ To _____   Other (give names and dates) _____

❏ Sex ❏ Male ❏ Female   Number of dependents, including yourself: _____   Are you a Vietnam veteran? ❏ Yes ❏ No

❏ Marital Status ❏ Single ❏ Engaged ❏ Married ❏ Separated ❏ Divorced ❏ Widowed   Date of Marriage: _____

❏ What was your previous address? _____

How long at present address? _____   How long at previous address? _____

❏ Have you ever been bonded? ❏ Yes ❏ No   If yes, with what employer(s)? _____

❏ Are you over 18 years of age? ❏ Yes ❏ No   If no, employment is subject to verification of age.

❏ Have you been convicted of a crime in the past ten years, excluding misdemeanors and summary offenses, which has not been annulled, expunged or sealed by a court? ❏ Yes ❏ No   If yes, please describe: _____

SIGNATURE

The information provided in this Application for Employment is true, correct and complete. Any misstatement or omission of fact on this application may result in my dismissal. I understand that acceptance of an offer of employment creates no obligation upon you, the employer, to continue to employ me in the future.

_____   _____
                    Signature   Date

PERSONAL INFORMATION

Name (last name first): _____ Social Security Number: _____

Present Address: _____ Apt No.: _____ City: _____ State: _____ Zip: _____

Permanent Address: _____ Apt No.: _____ City: _____ State: _____ Zip: _____

Phone: _____ Are you 18 years or older? ❏ Yes ❏ No

DESIRED EMPLOYMENT

Position: _____ Date you can start: _____ Desired salary: _____

Are you currently employed? ❏ Yes ❏ No   If yes, may we contact your present employer? ❏ Yes ❏ No

Have you applied to this company before? ❏ Yes ❏ No   Where? _____ When? _____

Have you worked for this company before? ❏ Yes ❏ No   Where? _____ When? _____

Reason for leaving: _____

_____

Name of last supervisor at this company: _____

Who referred you to this company? ❏ Employment Agency ❏ Newspaper Ad ❏ Friend ❏ State Employment Office
                                  ❏ College Placement Service ❏ Walk In ❏ Other

EDUCATION

School	Name and Location of School	Course of Study	Years Completed	Did You Graduate?
ELEMENTARY				❏ Yes ❏ No
HIGH SCHOOL				❏ Yes ❏ No
COLLEGE				❏ Yes ❏ No
TRADE/TECHNICAL				❏ Yes ❏ No

GENERAL

Subject of special study or research work	Special training	Special skills
_____	_____	_____
_____	_____	_____
_____	_____	_____
_____	_____	_____

Last

First

Middle

REFERENCES Please list the names of three persons (not relatives) whom you have known at least one year.

Name	Address	Business	Years Acquainted
_____	_____	_____	_____
_____	_____	_____	_____
_____	_____	_____	_____
_____	_____	_____	_____

FORMER EMPLOYERS Please start with the most recent employer.

Name of Previous Employer: _____ Telephone: _____

Address: _____ City: _____ State: _____ Zip: _____

Employed From (month/year): _____ To: _____ Name of Supervisor: _____

Weekly Starting Salary: _____ Weekly Leaving Salary: _____ May we contact this employer? ❑ Yes ❑ No

Job Title: _____ Description of Job Duties: _____

Reason for Leaving: _____

Name of Previous Employer: _____ Telephone: _____

Address: _____ City: _____ State: _____ Zip: _____

Employed From (month/year): _____ To: _____ Name of Supervisor: _____

Weekly Starting Salary: _____ Weekly Leaving Salary: _____ May we contact this employer? ❑ Yes ❑ No

Job Title: _____ Description of Job Duties: _____

Reason for Leaving: _____

Name of Previous Employer: _____ Telephone: _____

Address: _____ City: _____ State: _____ Zip: _____

Employed From (month/year): _____ To: _____ Name of Supervisor: _____

Weekly Starting Salary: _____ Weekly Leaving Salary: _____ May we contact this employer? ❑ Yes ❑ No

Job Title: _____ Description of Job Duties: _____

Reason for Leaving: _____

MILITARY SERVICE

Branch of Service	Rank	Discharge Date

ADDITIONAL INFORMATION

Have you ever been convicted of a felony? ❏ Yes ❏ No If yes, please explain (this will not necessarily exclude you from consideration for the position).

_____

_____

_____

_____

_____

AUTHORIZATION

I certify that the information contained in this application is factual, true and complete to the best of my knowledge. I understand that, if employed, falsified statements on this application shall be grounds for immediate dismissal.

I authorize investigation of all statements contained herein and the references and employees listed herein to give you any and all information concerning my previous employment and any pertinent information they may have, personal or otherwise, and release the company from all liability for any damage that may result from the utilization of such information.

I also understand and agree that no representative of the company has the authority to enter into any agreement for employment for any specified period of time, or to make any agreement contrary to the foregoing, unless it is in writing and signed by an authorized company representative.

_____   _____

Signature   Date

FOR INTERVIEWER'S USE ONLY

Interviewed By: _____ Date: _____

Comments: _____

_____

_____

_____

_____

_____

_____

_____

Interviewed By: _____ Date: _____

Comments: _____

_____

_____

_____

_____

_____

_____

_____

Interviewed By: _____ Date: _____

Comments: _____

_____

_____

_____

_____

_____

_____

_____

Candidate was ❏ Hired   ❏ Rejected For Position: _____

Salary: _____ Starting Date: _____

Supervisor: _____

Manager: _____

Comments: _____

_____

_____

Name		Phone Number		Date

Address		City	State	Zip Code

Position Applying For	Social Security No.	Date of Birth	Marital Status

---

Present or Previous Employer		Dates of Employment

Address	City	State	Zip Code	Phone Number

Job Title and Duties

Reason for Leaving	Starting Salary	Ending Salary

Present or Previous Employer		Dates of Employment

Address	City	State	Zip Code	Phone Number

Job Title and Duties

Reason for Leaving	Starting Salary	Ending Salary

	Degree/Course of Study	Dates Attended	Did You Graduate?
Grammar School	Degree/Course of Study	Dates Attended	❏ Yes ❏ No
High School	Degree/Course of Study	Dates Attended	❏ Yes ❏ No
College	Degree/Course of Study	Dates Attended	❏ Yes ❏ No
Other	Degree/Course of Study	Dates Attended	❏ Yes ❏ No

Reference Name	Address	Occupation	Phone Number
Reference Name	Address	Occupation	Phone Number
Reference Name	Address	Occupation	Phone Number

Applicant's Signature

Notice to Applicant: We are an Equal Opportunity Employer and do not discriminate on the basis of applicant's race, color, religion, sex, national origin, citizenship, age, physical or mental disability or any other characteristic.

Personal Information (please print)

Name:_____ Social Security Number: _____

Address: _____

City: _____ State: _____ Zip: _____

Phone Number:_____

Position Information

Position applied for: _____

Department/Group: _____

Have you ever worked for this organization: ❏ Yes ❏ No   If yes, date(s): _____

Prior position: _____

Reason(s) for leaving: _____

_____

Education (List from present to past)

School/Institution	Major or Area of Study	Degree or Number of Years

Other Information

Name of friends and/or relatives employed by this organization: _____

_____

Position(s) held: _____

_____

If you are eligible, are you interested in health insurance? ❏ Yes ❏ No

Awards/Achievements

_____

_____

_____

References (Please list at least three people who are not related to you)

Name	Occupation	Phone Number

_____

_____

_____

_____

Emergency Contact In the event of an emergency, who should we contact?

Name:_____

Relationship to applicant:._____

Address: _____

City: _____ State: _____ Zip: _____

Phone Number: _____

Name:_____

Relationship to applicant:._____

Address: _____

City: _____ State: _____ Zip: _____

Phone Number: _____

Acknowledgment (please read carefully)

I hereby certify that the information contained in this application form and in any attachments (hereafter made a part of this application) is true and correct to the best of my knowledge and agree to have any of the statements checked by the organization unless I have indicated to the contrary. I authorize the references listed above to provide the company any and all information concerning my previous employment and any pertinent information that they may have. Further, I release all parties and persons from any and all liability for any damages that may result from furnishing such information to the company as well as from the use or disclosure of such information by the organization or any of its agents, employees or representatives. I understand that any misrepresentation, falsification or material omission of information on this application may result in my failure to receive an offer or, if I am hired, in my dismissal from employment.

_____

Applicant's Signature   Date

FOOD SERVICE APPLICANT QUESTIONNAIRE SAMPLE

Following are some questions that you may wish to ask that are pertinent specifically to food service.

Why are you interested in working in food service?

_____

_____

_____

If you have worked in food service before, please list the names of the establishments:

_____

_____

_____

What is the most challenging aspect of working in food service?

_____

_____

_____

_____

What qualities do you possess that make you a good candidate to work in food service?

_____

_____

_____

Please give one specific example that demonstrates your food service capabilities (for example, what did you excel at in your previous positions)?

_____

_____

_____

_____

Do you feel food service offers you an opportunity for advancement or a long-term career? Why or why not?

_____

_____

_____

APPLICATION FOR AN IN-HOUSE CANDIDATE

Personal Information (please print)

Name:_____ Date: _____

Address: _____

City: _____ State: _____ Zip: _____

Phone Number: _____

Current Position Information

Current Position: _____

❑ Full-Time   ❑ Part-Time

Length of Employment: _____

Current Supervisor: _____

Position Information

Position applied for: _____

Department/Group: _____

❑ Full-Time   ❑ Part-Time

Reason(s) for applying for new position (check all that apply): ❑ Opportunity for advancement

❑ Preferred shift   ❑ Variety of job duties   ❑ Other (please list)

_____

_____

_____

_____

_____

IN HOUSE RESULTS TO BE FILLED OUT BY SUPERVISOR

Application Results

❑ Accepted   ❑ Denied

If accepted, list start date _____

If denied, check reason:

❑ Did not meet job requirements   ❑ Another employee with more seniority was selected

❑ Attendance record is not acceptable ❑ Other _____

_____

_____

Signature of Supervisor

Applicant: _____

Job Title: _____ ❏ General Interview ❏ Promotion Interview

Interviewer: _____ Title: _____

❏ 1st Interview   ❏ 2nd Interview   ❏ 3rd Interview

PERSONALITY TRAITS

Briefly list the personality traits the ideal candidate for this position would possess:

_____

_____

_____

- ❏ Great for this position.
- ❏ Good for this position.
- ❏ Acceptable for this position.
- ❏ Not very good for this position.
- ❏ Not acceptable for this position.

Comments: _____

_____

_____

_____

EXPERIENCE

Briefly list the ideal type of experience and training the best candidate for this position would possess:

_____

_____

_____

- ❏ Exceptional experience and background.
- ❏ Above-average experience and background.
- ❏ Average experience and background.
- ❏ Below-average experience and background.
- ❏ No experience and background not applicable.

Comments: _____

_____

_____

JOB FAMILIARITY

- ❏ Exceptional familiarity; no training needed.
- ❏ Above-average familiarity.
- ❏ Rudimentary familiarity, but able to meet job performance standards.
- ❏ Below-average familiarity; training needed.
- ❏ Applicant has no familiarity in this field.

Comments: _____

_____

_____

WORK FIELD UNDERSTANDING

- ❏ Exceptional understanding of the field.
- ❏ Above-average knowledge and understanding.
- ❏ Average knowledge of this field.
- ❏ Below-average knowledge of this field.
- ❏ Poor knowledge and understanding in this field.

Comments: _____

_____

_____

MOTIVATION

- ❏ Very strong desire to work; excellent level of motivation
- ❏ High level of interest in job.
- ❏ Basic desire to work.
- ❏ Interest in the position is minimal.
- ❏ Little or no interest in the position.

Comments: _____

_____

_____

AMBITION & ENTHUSIASM

- ❑ Extremely high; very resourceful.
- ❑ Positive drive to succeed.
- ❑ Average goals.
- ❑ Lacks goals and enthusiasm
- ❑ Relies on others; no goals or ambition.

Comments: _____

_____

_____

_____

ORIGINALITY & APTITUDE

- ❑ Exceptional creativity; seems original and proposes new ideas.
- ❑ Above-average creativity.
- ❑ Average level of creativity.
- ❑ Few ideas or suggestions.
- ❑ Poor creativity—little or no suggestions.

Comments: _____

_____

_____

_____

POISE & COMPOSURE

- ❑ Very self-assured and capable.
- ❑ Able to handle problems well.
- ❑ Fair composure and control.
- ❑ Below-average composure.
- ❑ Seemly unstable.

Comments: _____

_____

_____

_____

APPEARANCE

- ❑ Neat and very well-groomed.
- ❑ Above-average personal appearance.
- ❑ Average personal appearance.
- ❑ Disheveled, disregard for personal appearance.

Comments: _____

_____

_____

OVERALL

- ❑ Excellent for this position.
- ❑ Highly possible for other position.
- ❑ A possible candidate.
- ❑ An unlikely candidate.
- ❑ Unsatisfactory.

Comments: _____

_____

_____

_____

RATE THE APPLICANT:

Carefully consider all factors in this evaluation. Then rate the candidate on a scale from 1 to 10, with 10 being the highest possible score.

1 2 3 4 5 6 7 8 9 10

Other position this applicant seems to have

experience for: _____

Comments: _____

_____

_____

_____

_____

Interviewer's Signature   Date

Applicant: _____ **Job Desired:** _____

REFERENCE CHECK

Company Name _____ Telephone_____

Person Contacted _____

Results _____

_____

_____

Company Name _____ Telephone_____

Person Contacted _____

Results _____

_____

_____

Company Name _____ Telephone_____

Person Contacted _____

Results _____

_____

_____

TEST RESULTS

Tested Administered	Raw Score	Rating	Analysis and Comments

INTERVIEW QUESTIONS

Interviewer: _____ Title: _____

❑ 1st Interview   ❑ 2nd Interview   ❑ 3rd Interview

1.   What are your strengths? _____

2.   What are your weaknesses? _____

3.   How would your current (or last) boss describe you? _____

4   What were your boss's responsibilities? _____

5.   What's your opinion of him or her? _____

6.   How would your co-workers or subordinates describe you professionally? _____

_____

7.   Why do you want to leave your present employer? _____

8.   Why should we hire you over the other finalists? _____

_____

9.   What qualities or talents would you bring to the job? _____

10. Tell me about your accomplishments. _____

11. What is your most important contribution to your last (or current) employer? _____

12. How do you perform under deadline pressure? Give me an example. _____

13. How do you react to criticism? _____

14. Describe a conflict or disagreement at work in which you were involved. How was it resolved? ____

_____

15. What are two of the biggest problems you've encountered at your last (or current) job and how did you overcome them? _____

_____

16. Think of a major crisis you've faced at work and explain how you handled it. _____

17. Give me an example of a risk that you took at your last (or current) job and how it turned out. _____

_____

18. What's your managerial style like? _____

19. Have you ever hired employees, and, if so, have they lived up to your expectations? _____

20. What type of performance problems have you encountered in people who report to you, and how did you motivate them to improve? _____

_____

21. Describe a typical day at your current (or last) job. _____

22. What do you see yourself doing five years from now? _____

Other _____

_____

_____

INTERVIEW ANALYSIS

APPEARANCE

- ❏ Neat, well-groomed, very presentable.
- ❏ Pays extra attention to personal appearance.
- ❏ Standard personal appearance.
- ❏ Neglects details in personal appearance.
- ❏ Not groomed and untidy.
  Notes:_____
  _____
  _____

PERSONALITY TRAITS (His/her personality suitable for position)

- ❏ Exceptional for this position.
- ❏ Good for this position.
- ❏ Workable for this position.
- ❏ Personality may not fit this position.
- ❏ Unsuitable for this position.
  Notes:_____
  _____
  _____

COMPOSURE

- ❏ Good control; very calm; thrives under pressure.
- ❏ Appears to handle problems well.
- ❏ Typical composure.
- ❏ Seems bothered or stressed
- ❏ Uneasy; shows concern.
  Notes:_____
  _____
  _____

MOTIVATION

- ❏ Very motivated; strong desire to work.
- ❏ Quite interested in job.
- ❏ Desires to work.
- ❏ Low level of interest in position.
- ❏ Impassive and not interested in position.
  Notes:_____
  _____
  _____

INITIATIVE

- ❏ Driven to succeed and sets very high goals.
- ❏ Possesses confidence and makes an effort.
- ❏ Takes some initiative; has goals.
- ❏ Rather irresponsible; few goals.
- ❏ Little direction; minimal goals, relies on others too often.
  Notes:_____
  _____
  _____

JOB EXPERIENCE

- ❏ Excellent experience, education and background.
- ❏ Good experience and background.
- ❏ Standard experience and background.
- ❏ Has some background experience.
- ❏ Background not relevant to position.   Notes:_____
  _____
  _____
  _____

JOB KNOWLEDGE

- ❏ Highly knowledgeable; little training needed.
- ❏ Very efficient; may need some training.
- ❏ Basic, training required.
- ❏ Extensive training needed.
- ❏ Not related to this position.
  Notes:_____
  _____
  _____

GENERAL WORK FIELD INFORMATION

- ❏ Very knowledgeable and high level of understanding in this field.
- ❏ Above-average knowledge and understanding.
- ❏ Average work field knowledge.
- ❏ Slight understanding of field.
- ❏ Very poor knowledge and understanding.
  Notes:_____
  _____
  _____

OVERALL

- ❏ Exceptional—highly recommended.
- ❏ Above average.
- ❏ Average.
- ❏ Below average.
- ❏ Unsatisfactory.
  Notes:_____
  _____
  _____

ANALYSIS

- ❏ Applicant is recommended for position.
- ❏ A possible candidate for the position.
- ❏ A very unlikely candidate.
  Notes:_____
  _____
  _____
  _____

Interviewer's Signature: _____ **Date:** _____

The following checklist can be used to make sure your interviewing process is consistent with every candidate. Being organized will help you focus on hiring the most qualified candidate for the position.

APPLICANT INFORMATION

Name: _____ Date applied: _____

Address: _____

City:_____ State: _____Zip: _____

Phone Number:_____

Before interviewing, check each item when complete:

❑ The applicant has submitted an application and it has been reviewed to make sure all information was completed properly.

❑ Information pertinent to the position has been verified (such as age verification as required by law or citizenship status).

❑ The applicant has been pre-screened based on qualifications specific to the position

❑ The applicant has notified as to testing needed and has agreed to testing (list date of testing) _____

❑ Previous employment has been verified (list dates) _____

_____

_____

_____

_____

❑ References have been checked (list) _____

_____

_____

_____

❑ Interview questions pertinent to the position have been developed and assessed for legality.

❑ The information given to each applicant has been a standardized—benefits, schedules, work performance expectations, etc.?

❑ An interview time has been set. (list date and time) _____

❑ A private interview location is arranged (list) _____

❑ A tour of the prospective workplace is arranged.

Employee Name: _____

Test Date: _____

Social Security Number: _____

Department: _____

Employee Start Date: _____

Supervisor: _____

I, _____, freely give my consent for this drug and/or alcohol test. I have been fully informed of the reason for this urine test and I understand that the results will be forwarded to my supervisor.

If the test results are positive, I will be given the opportunity to explain the results before any action is taken.

Signature: _____

Date: _____

Interviews are designed to determine the best candidate for your position. However, asking illegal or improper questions (even inadvertently) can result in compliance actions or lawsuits. Unfortunately, there is no way to guarantee that you will never be sued. However, the risk can be minimized by following some basic guidelines:

Review laws carefully.
Do some research on federal, state and local laws on proper interview questions. Use the Internet, bookstores or the local library for references.

Know what questions to ask.
Develop a list of pre-planned questions. Ask the same question of every applicant, and document responses. Even informal "chatting" can be a problem if questions are asked about marital status or children.

Document each step.
The interview should be documented in two ways: with notes taken during the interview and recap documentation. Inform the applicant that you will be taking notes. Once the interview is complete, your recap documentation is an overall analysis and recommendation. All records should be carefully maintained and preserved, and ready-made forms used when possible.

Treat each applicant respectfully. This applies not only to the interview, but specifically to your rejection methods. Be as professional, respectful and kind as possible.

Be aware of bias.
A biased individual has a tendency to find traits and attitudes that fulfill preconceived beliefs. If you know a manager is biased, do not allow him or her to conduct interviews, as their personal opinions and beliefs may be inadvertently communicated to the applicant in the interview.

Consider rejected applicants' challenges.
Take the time to review all rejected applicants' challenges and provide a method for rejected applicants to voice their dissatisfaction. If there is error on the part of the company, rectify the error.

Be aware of staffing. It's much better to do an internal review of hiring practices than have a third party review your records after a complaint. Don't just review the process annually for the affirmative action plan. Know what your selection rates are. If there appears to be an adverse impact, fully investigate the matter, advise management of risks and enlist managers in finding solutions.

REFERENCE CHECK

TO:

Company Name: _____ Telephone: _____

Address: _____ City: _____ State: _____ Zip: _____

Attention: _____ Title: _____

FROM:

Company Name: _____ Telephone: _____

Address: _____ City: _____ State: _____ Zip: _____

Name: _____ Title: _____

TO BE FILLED OUT BY APPLICANT

Previous employer: I have made application for employment with the company above. I authorize you to furnish the this company with any information requested concerning my employment records, character, habits and ability. I do hereby release (fill in previous employer's company name) _____ from any claims, suits and liabilities for any damage resulting from their actions and conduct in responding to this request and supplying the information.

Name While in Your Employ: _____

Social Security Number: _____

Dates of Employment: _____ Department : _____

Start Position: _____ Salary: _____ Per ❑ hour ❑ week ❑ month ❑ annual

End Position: _____ Salary: _____ Per ❑ hour ❑ week ❑ month ❑ annual

Immediate Supervisor: _____

_____
Signature

TO BE FILLED OUT BY EMPLOYER

Was the applicant employed by your company? ❑ Yes ❑ No

Is all the information stated above correct? ❑ Yes ❑ No

If no, what is incorrect? _____

_____

What were the applicant's responsibilities? _____

_____

_____

TO BE FILLED OUT BY EMPLOYER

Please rate the applicant's performance in the following areas:

Attendance	❏ Above Average	❏ Average	❏ Below Average
Reliability	❏ Above Average	❏ Average	❏ Below Average
Quality of Work	❏ Above Average	❏ Average	❏ Below Average
Teamwork & Cooperation	❏ Above Average	❏ Average	❏ Below Average
Skill Level	❏ Above Average	❏ Average	❏ Below Average
Enthusiasm & Initiative	❏ Above Average	❏ Average	❏ Below Average
Productivity	❏ Above Average	❏ Average	❏ Below Average

While working for your company, what were this person's strong points? _____

_____

_____

What were his or her weak points? _____

_____

_____

Would you consider rehiring this person? ❏ Yes ❏ No   Why or why not?_____

What was his or her reason for leaving?_____

_____

_____

Additional Comments: _____

_____

_____

_____

Completed By:_____ Date: _____

Company:_____

APPLICANT: ....

POSITION: ....

Reference: ....

Company: ....

Address: ....

....

Phone: ....

Dates of Employment: ....

Job Title: ....

Duties: ....

....

....

Why did the applicant leave your employment?

....

....

....

What were the applicant's best job skills? ....

....

....

....

In what areas could the applicant improve? ....

....

....

....

Did the applicant get along with supervisors?

❑ Yes   ❑ No   With peers? ❑ Yes   ❑ No

In comparison to others with the same position, please rate the applicant:

❑ Above average   ❑ Average   ❑ Below average

Following is a list of personal characteristics. Using a scale from 1 to 10 (with 10 being the highest), please rate the applicant, based on your experience working together.

Punctual	1	2	3	4	5	6	7	8	9	10
Pleasant	1	2	3	4	5	6	7	8	9	10
Honest	1	2	3	4	5	6	7	8	9	10
Flexible	1	2	3	4	5	6	7	8	9	10
Organized	1	2	3	4	5	6	7	8	9	10
Composed	1	2	3	4	5	6	7	8	9	10
Reliable	1	2	3	4	5	6	7	8	9	10
Competent	1	2	3	4	5	6	7	8	9	10
Professional	1	2	3	4	5	6	7	8	9	10
Safety-Conscious	1	2	3	4	5	6	7	8	9	10
Team Player	1	2	3	4	5	6	7	8	9	10
Lazy	1	2	3	4	5	6	7	8	9	10
Inconsistent	1	2	3	4	5	6	7	8	9	10
Inattentive	1	2	3	4	5	6	7	8	9	10
Temperamental	1	2	3	4	5	6	7	8	9	10
Antagonistic	1	2	3	4	5	6	7	8	9	10

Would you rehire this person? ❑ Yes   ❑ No

Why or why not? ....

....

....

Do you have any additional comments on this individual's character or work habits? ....

....

....

....

....

CHECKED BY:..

DATE: ....

GOOD CANDIDATE ❑ YES   ❑ NO

APPLICANT: ....

POSITION: ....

Reference: ....

Company: ....

Address: ....

....

Phone: ....

How long did you work with the applicant? ....

What was your job? ....

What was the applicant's job? ....

....

What were the applicant's principal duties? ....

....

....

What did you like about working with the applicant?

....

....

....

What did you dislike about working with the applicant?

....

....

....

Was this person easy to get along with? ....

....

....

....

Following is a list of personal characteristics. Using a scale from 1 to 10 (with 10 being the highest), please rate the applicant, based on your experience working together.

Punctual	1	2	3	4	5	6	7	8	9	10
Pleasant	1	2	3	4	5	6	7	8	9	10
Honest	1	2	3	4	5	6	7	8	9	10
Flexible	1	2	3	4	5	6	7	8	9	10
Organized	1	2	3	4	5	6	7	8	9	10
Composed	1	2	3	4	5	6	7	8	9	10
Reliable	1	2	3	4	5	6	7	8	9	10
Competent	1	2	3	4	5	6	7	8	9	10
Professional	1	2	3	4	5	6	7	8	9	10
Safety-Conscious	1	2	3	4	5	6	7	8	9	10
Team Player	1	2	3	4	5	6	7	8	9	10
Lazy	1	2	3	4	5	6	7	8	9	10
Inconsistent	1	2	3	4	5	6	7	8	9	10
Inattentive	1	2	3	4	5	6	7	8	9	10
Temperamental	1	2	3	4	5	6	7	8	9	10
Antagonistic	1	2	3	4	5	6	7	8	9	10

Would you like to work with this person again?

❏ Yes   ❏ No   Why or why not? ....

....

....

Do you have any additional comments on this individual's character or work habits? ....

....

....

....

....

CHECKED BY: ....

DATE: ....

GOOD CANDIDATE ❏ **YES**   ❏ **NO**

TELEPHONE REFERENCE CHECK FORM

APPLICANT INFORMATION

Name:_____Date applied: _____

Address: _____

City:_____ State: _____Zip: _____

REFERENCE INFORMATION

Name:_____

Address: _____

City:_____ State: _____Zip: _____

Phone Number:_____

Date Called: _____ Time Called: _____

Job Title: _____

List Type of Reference (ie. previous employer, character): _____

FILL OUT THE INFORMATION BELOW IF PREVIOUS EMPLOYER

Verification of Dates of Employment: From_____ To_____

Eligible for Rehire? _____

What were the employee's main responsibilities and duties? _____

_____

_____

On a scale of 1 to 5, with 5 being the best, please rate how well did the employee performed his or her duties. (circle response)   1   2   3   4   5

On a scale of 1 to 5, with 5 being the best, please rate how the employee related to his/her supervisor and other employees?   1   2   3   4   5

FILL OUT THE INFORMATION BELOW IF OTHER REFERENCE

_____ is being considered for _____, which

involves _____. What in your opinion are the applicant's abilities in these areas?

Additional Comments:

Interviewer:_____ Date _____

Position: _____

Prepared By: _____ **Date Prepared:** _____

Salary Range: _____ Department/Supervisor: _____

Primary Tasks

1. _____
2. _____
3. _____
4. _____
5. _____
6. _____
7. _____
8. _____
9. _____
10. _____
11. _____
12. _____

Personality Traits or Characteristics Required

1. _____
2. _____
3. _____
4. _____
5. _____

Notes

_____

_____

_____

JOB DESCRIPTION TEMPLATE

Job Title: _____ Company Job Code: _____

FLSA Status: _____ Division/Department:_____

EEO Code: _____ Reports To: _____

Salary Grade/Band: _____ Last Revision Date: _____

SUMMARY

This section provides an overview or summary of the job.

PRIMARY RESPONSIBILITIES

This section lists the primary job functions. Responsibilities should be listed in order of importance and/or time spent. Duties listed here should be considered "essential" to help define "essential functions" for the purposes of the Americans with Disabilities Act. If an applicant cannot perform most, if not all, of the essential functions, the applicant will not be considered.

ADDITIONAL RESPONSIBILITIES

This section provides additional functions of the job that are desirable but not required. Since these duties are not "essential functions," an applicant who cannot perform these duties will still be considered for the position.

KNOWLEDGE AND SKILL REQUIREMENTS

Specific knowledge and skill requirements are listed here. Examples would include sales techniques, generally accepted accounting principles and physical requirements. Also listed here are the years of experience needed and/or education requirements.

WORKING CONDITIONS

This section contains information on non-standard working conditions such as extensive travel, high noise levels and frequent lifting of over "_____" pounds.

ACKNOWLEDGMENT

The dated signature lines for the manager/supervisor and employee provides a record that the employee was shown and understands the job responsibilities.

Manager's Name (print)_____ Signature_____ Date:_____

Employee's Name (print)_____ Signature_____ Date:_____

CHAPTER FOURTEEN

Train and Manage Employees

After new employees are trained, you need to manage them in the best way possible. Each of the following duties will be discussed in this chapter.

Orientation and Instruction

Here is a checklist of ideas for a successful orientation.

1. Explain some basic information about the company.

2. Introduce other employees.

3. Introduce trainer and supervisor.

4. Explain company policies and present the Employee Manual.

5. Outline objectives and goals of the training schedule and plan:

   a. Describe where and how training will take place.

b. Describe information to be learned.

c. Describe skills and attitudes to develop.

6. Establish a schedule which includes:

a. Date, day, and time to begin training.

b. Introduce the person who will handle the training.

c. Explain what should be learned and accomplished each day.

d. Expected date to complete training.

The form at the end of this chapter is a sample orientation checklist. You can use this as a template to create your own checklist. When you have the information written the way you want it, let several long-term staff members offer suggestions. Then rework the form. It is a good way to remember everything when you and a trainer handle new employee orientation.

Training and Motivation

The final decision has been made about whom to hire. There may be times when your first choice for the job will turn it down. It may take several calls to find a person who accepts the job. This is unusual, but you should be prepared in case it happens to you.

After the person is hired, training is in order. What should you do to help the person get started in the best way? The training the person receives will make a big difference in his or her performance. Employees need a good start.

Your first priority is to put a new employee at ease. I always informed team members when we had a new employee starting, and I counted on them to make the new person feel welcome. Do not overwhelm a new team member on the first day. Help them feel welcome and be available to give the help they need.

How did you feel on your first day? Did you want to run out the door? Your new employee will probably feel all of these things. What would have made your first day better? What do you need to do for new employees?

Give a quick tour on the first day to help new employees get settled. Introduce them to their new coworkers. At one job, we wore name tags the first week to help new people learn names. People won't remember everything from their first day, so don't overload them with information. Set a reasonable pace and check to make sure the person is learning new things each day. Also be sure they remember the things. I had a couple of employees who seemed to understand, but the next day they had forgotten everything. The need for reinforcing information can be a big problem and something to identify as soon as possible.

The new employee needs to understand how your lunch schedule works. He or she needs instruction about the work week, how to submit time cards, and how to collect paychecks. This leads into how scheduling, sick days, and vacation work. You may find it useful to have employees submit written requests for vacation. At the end of this chapter is an example of a form you could use.

After the facility tour and meeting coworkers, review the job duties. Be sure to tell the new person that you are available when he or she has questions. New employees need to know you won't abandon them.

Choose their trainer carefully. Arrange the training person and schedule before the new person begins to work. Good trainers generally are

- Patient

- Detail oriented

- Well trained, competent, and familiar with all aspects of the job

- Positive about the facility and company

- Willing to train a new employee

- Aware of the time involved in training

After you turn the new employee over to his or her trainer, follow up often. Schedule a brief meeting with the new employee each day for the first couple of weeks. This gives you a chance to discuss concerns or questions. You can use these times to evaluate their progress.

New employees should start with simple projects and add more challenges. This is a good way to gauge new employees' progress without overwhelming them in the beginning. It's good to keep challenging them and to avoid letting them get bored. These things help new hires become strong members of the team.

A manager cannot expect employees to do the job without proper training. This training needs to explain what to do, how to do it properly, and why procedures are in place.

Training involves more than just providing information. It's good to involve trainees in what is being done. They won't learn if they just watch. This will help you to be sure the person can do the job. Provide a list with the job description and physically check off each item on the list. When you train someone, learn about his or her interests, goals, and desires. These help you learn what motivates him or her to do a good job.

When new employees are trained, help them understand how the job fits with other duties in the non-commercial facility. This enables the employee to understand the overall picture and his or her importance to the company.

Not everyone can teach. The trainer must be a model employee with the ability and willingness to train and even then a great employee may not be qualified to teach. An effective trainer needs to communicate well and be patient and understanding. The trainer should give details about how fast the new employee is learning. These updates need to be in writing and can be filed in the employee's personnel file. New material needs to be added as the new employee learns. It's also good to explain how the various tasks build on each other.

The trainer should submit a report when training is complete to include details about how the trainee did. What are the trainee's strengths and weaknesses, quality of work, and understanding of all aspects of the job? The form included at the end of this chapter shows some ways to pinpoint things missed in new employee training.

You need to congratulate the trainee on successfully completing training. Ask the employee about his or her training: What was helpful? Was there anything that would be helpful for future trainers? After a couple of weeks, follow up with questions about whether the training prepared him or her for the actual job.

Outside Training

Some outside businesses offer training that could be beneficial for your employees. It's best to find people who are experts in their fields. Many times you only need to ask and be sure to reward them for their help with a complimentary gift certificate or some other gift for their time and effort.

Here are some examples of great resources for outside training information to assist you in training programs: videos, posters, books, and software. One source for all these products is Atlantic Publishing. Visit their Web site at **www.atlantic-pub.com**.

Speakers and Subjects

- **State Liquor Agent** — Liquor laws and compliance (if applicable)

- **Health Department** — Health and sanitation practices/requirements.

- **Red Cross Instructor** — First Aid, Heimlich Maneuver, and CPR procedures.

- **Some Equipment Distributors** — Assistance in learning to use the items they sell.

Effective Staff Meetings

When you learn new things and need to relay them to your team members, what is the best way to accomplish this goal? You need a great, truly effective staff meeting. Most staff meetings are boring. They usually create lower employee energy and the staff could feel that management is upset with them. When you have information to impart, you have a good reason for a staff meeting. Do not wait to call them when there are problems. Effective staff meetings are not just a chance to gather employees together while one person gives out information; it is a meeting that generates positive feeling and productivity in the entire group. Effective staff meetings have these three main goals:

1. To generate positive group feeling.

2. To start a dialogue.

3. To train.

Positive Group Feeling

A positive group feeling helps your team members discover what they have in common and to think about working together, instead of working as individuals. Share good news to build good feeling. At times you will have to search for good news, but there is always something positive to share. Staff meetings should not be used to address individual or group shortcomings. They are opportunities to generate a supportive feeling and get people talking.

Dialogue

Good dialogue is a comfortable way to share ideas and help your staff feel they are a part of the facility. It helps you to learn from the staff, and they learn from you. It encourages the flow of ideas and reduces or eliminates the "Us versus Them" mentality in your staff and puts everybody on the same team. If everybody is on the same team, service improves, and productivity and profits go up.

Training

Effective staff meetings allow the chance to share ideas for better performance. If you do not do this, you share the belief that things are as good as they could possibly be, or that anyone can prepare food and serve the patrons. Almost anyone can, but are your staff members doing it to the best of their ability and in the best way to serve your patrons? No matter how good people are, there is always room for improvement. It is also a chance to pass along tips to your staff and to let them learn from each other. Your staff members are intelligent people. They know what works and what does not. Encourage them to share thoughts about work, and it can turn staff meetings into a forum for discussing ideas. This atmosphere increases their learning curve dramatically.

It is good to hold staff meetings before each shift. Be careful about canceling or rescheduling staff members as doing so will send the message that you don't think meetings are important. They will also develop the feeling that you don't think their thoughts and opinions are important. Both of these things can be detrimental to the facility and employee morale.

An effective pre-shift meeting shouldn't exceed 15 minutes. Longer meeting will cause you to lose people's attention—shorter, you won't say enough. Pick a length, then start and finish on time. Include all employees in the meetings. What sort of information do you need to convey to your staff on a daily basis? These things should be included in your meetings.

Format for Brief Pre-shift Meeting

Before you start, remember that your own state of mind determines how your meeting will go. Are you looking at your staff as a group of dedicated people committed to doing a great job or as a bunch of layabouts looking to milk the system? Are you a coach on the playing field seeking to facilitate and encourage people's best performances, or a judge looking to identify and punish people's mistakes? Rest assured that whichever it is, your staff feels it, and it will affect the work they do. Get committed to building on people's strengths and holding energizing staff meetings.

- **Good news (1–2 minutes)** — Acknowledge what works and create a good mood. Feature something about the business that shows people doing a good job and making guests happy. Acknowledge the doer or bearer of the news with sincerity.

- **Daily news (2–3 minutes)** — Outline today's specials and upcoming events.

- **Ask your staff (5 minutes)** — This is the most important part of the meeting. This is your opportunity to find out what's really going on in your facility and what people are thinking about. Listen. Do not interrupt with your own thoughts, and do not judge people's comments. Let them share and know you are being given a gift. Create a safe space for people to share what is on their minds and to learn from each other. How well you listen directly affects how much they are willing to say. Since they are the restaurant, as well as your access to the nitty-gritty, get them talking. If they are shy, ask them questions: What is working for you guys? What is making things tough? Where have things broken down? What questions from customers have you been unable to answer? Once you get the ball rolling you may find it hard to stop! Good. That means people have things to say, and you will benefit. Asking the rest of the staff if they feel the same way as the speaker is a great way to see if there is a group sentiment and to gauge the size of the issue being presented.

- **Training: The latest news (3–5 minutes)** — If staff comments run over, let it cut into this time. It is important that your staff learns from you, but it is more important for you to learn from them. Plus they will be open to learning from you if they know you are listening to them. Use this time to talk about a single point you want your staff to focus on during this shift, to give out specific knowledge about a product or to train in another targeted way. Focus is important. If you tell people how long the meeting will last and hold to that, they will give you their attention. If you go over, you will lose their attention and their trust. Get to the point and trust that they got it.

It takes time to become good at running staff meetings But it is worth the effort. Doing so will translate into helping the staff feel like a team which should be one of your main goals. It will help them care about the facility and find ways to improve services and products you offer. You can be more effective because your staff takes some weight off your shoulders by helping the facility run better and making your job easier.

Staffing & Scheduling

We will discuss effective cost cutting with proper scheduling in Chapter 17. Many managers rush through schedule writing, but effective scheduling involves the most efficient use of employees in the job or on a shift to give you maximum productivity for the minimal cost.

It can take an hour or more to create an effective schedule. The time will be determined by the number of employees you have, the number of patrons you have, and the number of shifts your facility is open. That time frame will decrease as you become more familiar with schedule writing and your team members' abilities and scheduling needs. Try to achieve these goals as you write a schedule:

1. **Sufficient staffing for peak periods** without having too many staff members (specific hours or days of the week).

2. **Determine when you need the maximum production.**

3. **Plan ahead for special events;** use staff or require staff to work outside the facility. (We will discuss that in Chapter 19 – Catering and Special Events.)

4. **Consider the skills and productivity level of each employee.**

5. **Each employee's desired schedule.**

It could take time to assess how many staff members are needed to handle the facility's business. In the beginning, it's better to overstaff the facility to maintain customer service. Schedule employees throughout the work day and have your best people scheduled at the most critical times. When is your busiest time—when you open, the lunch or dinner rush, or late night? Whatever time is most critical for you, be sure to have sufficient staff to handle the work load.

I always promote cross-training your team members to perform more than one job to give you a better chance of filling your schedule during vacations, illness, and special events. This makes weekly schedules and emergency situations easier to staff. The variety can keep employees from getting bored with your duties. The team members who become involved, interested, and concerned about the non-commercial facility will perform better than people who remain uninvolved.

When I interviewed and hired new team members, they were told from the beginning that they were being hired for a specific job but were expected to help anywhere in the facility that they were needed. If that would be a problem, they could be passed over for the job. Flexibility is a key issue in business and especially in the beginning. The more flexible staff members can be, the better service you can give to your patrons. Be clear about what you expect in the initial interview so that new team members know what is expected.

When you have too many people scheduled, it is good to send someone home or find other work the person can do. This can be any sort of preparation work or other jobs needed. If you decide to send someone home, the fairest thing is to ask who would like to go home. Usually, there is someone who wants to leave. This is much more positive for your staff members than indiscriminately sending people home.

The work that you need will depend on the time of day. Staff members can start closing work or prepare for the next shift or the next day. They could post flyers on bulletin boards or distribute menus or coupons to the different departments or break rooms. The type of business you work in will make a difference in how you use additional staff members. Get creative when you have idle people on the clock.

Various software programs can assist you in scheduling employees. They can track labor costs as the shift progresses to give suggestions about the best times to cut staff. Even with these programs, use your experience, knowledge, and common sense.

If you prefer to work on a hard copy of your schedule, forms on this topic at the end of this chapter. There are slight differences in these schedules and you can check to see which one works best for your needs.

You may want to keep a record of particular employee attendance records, especially helpful if an employee is tardy, leaving early, or missing shifts. Forms at the end of this chapter will help you track these problems.

Periodic Employee Evaluations

Managers need an effective way to evaluate their employees' performance. Therefore, they need to know:

- How to create an evaluation form.

- How to review it with their team members.

- What to do when their employees disagree with them.

Effective evaluations enable your team members to grow. They are a great way to help employees understand how they are doing and what needs to be improved. At evaluation time you need the notes about employees' specific information. We discussed this earlier when I mentioned it is good to make positive and negative notes about staff members.

You can start separate files for special positive and negative notes, if needed, about performance and attitude. Keep these files locked in your office. Share them only with your boss and the human resource department.

The more employees you have, the more difficult it is to keep notes compiled; therefore, write your notes immediately after an incident to substantiate your claims in case of problems. As a non-commercial food service manager you have enough things to remember.

Performance evaluations are not the answer to all your problems, but they are a useful tool in identifying problems that need to be addressed. Evaluations help you review the positives and negatives of the previous year and focus on team members individually in more depth than usual. What should you do if you tried solutions to issues during the year, but the employee did not respond? The evaluation is the best time to revisit those problems again, but that does not mean they will suddenly improve.

You may wish to give instructions and assistance to employees to resolve ongoing problems along with deadlines for resolving the situations to coincide with their annual evaluations. In extreme cases, review their employment status during the evaluation, only as a last resort, to provide a deadline for difficult employees to improve their attitude, behavior, or performance.

Most businesses provide instructions for completing the forms. Your boss could work with you on the first one. Your supervisor or a human resources person can give you a list of evaluation schedules. Some companies do all evaluations at one time, while others are done on employee hire date anniversaries.

Most evaluations include a list of statements and questions you need to present to employees with a score from one to five, one being the lowest and five the highest. Determine the individual rating for each section in the evaluation and total these ratings. The result is used to determine the employee's raise.

When your staff members receive a positive evaluation, they will get a raise. The Payroll Adjustment form at the end of this chapter will help you track their raise and should be submitted to the human resource department or the bookkeeper who works in the facility. This form can also be used when you need to lower an employee's pay.

Many forms use these standards for rating employee performance:

1. **Unacceptable** — Failure to perform the job. Immediate improvement is needed to maintain employment.

2. **Needs Improvement** — Occasionally fails to perform the job. Performance must improve to meet job expectations.

3. **Meets Expectations** — Performs all job duties in a satisfactory manner. Some supervision and guidance is needed.

4. **Exceeds Expectations** — Frequently exceeds job requirements. Objectives were accomplished above established standards.

5. **Superior** — Consistently works at above average level. Exceeds employer expectations.

This is also the time to acknowledge the positive things about each employee. Evaluations can be quarterly, annually, or on a different schedule. These sessions offer the opportunity to discuss thoughts, ideas, and problems with the employee.

See an example of two Employee Evaluation Forms at the end of this chapter. A third form at the end of this chapter can help guide you through employee evaluations and the needed follow up.

Here are key points to consider when you complete evaluation forms:

- **Be familiar with the employee's job description.** It's important to understand their duties to evaluate how they perform the job.

- **Conduct the evaluation in private.** Meet in your office or another private setting. If performing an evaluation for an employee of the opposite sex, you might want to leave the door cracked open. Use your judgment based on your knowledge of the person being evaluated. Schedule enough time to evaluate everything in one session.

- **Don't over-emphasize one incident.** Consider the complete picture of the employee's work since their last evaluation. A totally negative evaluation doesn't motivate a poor employee. Focus on his positive contributions and describe the changes required. No matter how bad an employee performs, there are one or two things that you can applaud. Any employee that deserves a totally negative evaluation should be terminated.

- **Review past evaluations, but don't dwell on them.** They are a good resource to find areas of improvement or decline of performance has taken place.

- **Give examples to support your appraisals.** It is important to allow enough time for the employee's comments because there is a chance that your conclusions are wrong.

- **Don't cover too much material at one time or expect a drastic change overnight.** The evaluation is the first step in directing the employee.

- **It's best to begin with the employee's positive attributes** and then move to areas where they need improvement.

- **Some traits and deficiencies may not change.** Don't focus on them too much, but explain how these things affect their performance and the performance of others in the facility.

- **Wrap up the evaluation on a positive note** leaving a good feeling with the employee about his positive contributions to the facility and firm ideas on how to improve.

- **After the evaluation, follow up with the employee on the thoughts, recommendations, and ideas that you discussed in the evaluation.** If you do not have a follow-up, the evaluation is of little value.

- **Always remember that evaluations are confidential.** File them in the employee's personnel file and ensure that no one else has access to them there.

You may want to create customized employee evaluations. Atlantic Publishing offers the book *199 Pre-Written Employee Performance Appraisals: The Complete Guide to Successful Employee Evaluations and Documents—With Companion CD-ROM* which is a valuable resource to create these forms. It helps you understand what to include, how to ask questions, and how to respond to employee concerns. The accompanying CD will help you create customized employee evaluations. Contact **www.atlantic-pub.com**.

Create Effective Evaluations

Whether you create your own evaluation or use the company's form, determine what you want to accomplish before starting the evaluation process.

- Can you find a way to praise the employee?

- Are there problems that you need to address?

- Do you have notes about any things that were done well?

- How should you tell them what is wrong and why it is wrong?

- Explain what they need to change in detail.

- Explain how the employee can make the needed changes.

Do you work for a company that does not have evaluation forms? Ask your supervisor to ask if you can develop an evaluation for your team members. Here is a good list of standard items on a personalized evaluation form.

• Adaptability	• Administration (if applicable)
• Attendance	• Attitude
• Behavior	• Communication
• Complete Work	• Cooperation

- Delegation (if applicable)
- Enthusiasm
- Interpersonal Skills
- Knowledge, Skills, and Abilities
- Maintaining Expenses
- Meeting Quotas
- Meeting Deadlines
- Promptness
- Quality of Work
- Sticking to a Schedule
- Training Attendance

- Dependability
- Initiative
- Judgment
- Leadership
- Maintaining Inventory
- Meeting Attendance
- Planning and Organization
- Punctuality
- Scheduling Ability
- Technical Skills
- Work Habits

If you get a chance to personalize the evaluation form, include skills and tasks important in your facility. Think about the tasks the team members do and what abilities are needed. You can add these items to the list if your supervisor agrees. The information in the next section will help you make your evaluations more effective. You can find some sample evaluations at the end of this chapter.

You can go over an evaluation with employees quarterly, as needed, or once a year. Some employees have home and personal problems that cause temporary problems at work. The form at the end of this chapter will help you identify short periods of problems and give you an overview of their performance to create a thorough and accurate evaluation. The scheduling decision is up to you based on the needs of individual employees.

It might be good to share a self-evaluation form with employees to help them prepare for the evaluation to give you some interesting insights into how they view their job duties.

Conducting Evaluations

Remind employees a week or so before their evaluations. There needs to be a set time to meet in a private place. When the day arrives do not put them off. Any employee evaluation needs to be a priority. When the day arrives, you have filled out an evaluation for each employee and are ready to conduct the evaluation.

New managers may want to look over old evaluations to get an idea of employees' past performance, but never complete your evaluation based on the old scores unless your boss instructs you to do so. In that case, note that fact beside your signature and write how many months you worked with the employee. When you conduct the evaluation and tally their score, employees should fall into one of these three categories:

1. **Above Average** — Above average evaluation usually means a good raise and is recognition for outstanding work.

2. **Average** — Most employees will fall into this category. Each point on the evaluation still needs a rating, but there won't be really good or bad points. Some employees may feel they are above average, but your individual ratings will show the areas where they need to improve. This is another reason to fill out the complete evaluation form.

3. **Below Average** — Any employees will complain if they fall into this category. Below average employees need to put more effort and make the needed changes. We will discuss on the following pages what to do when they refuse to improve.

Even when employees know they deserve a low rating, many will argue with you. No one wants a low score in his or her file, and evaluation forms are included in the official personnel file. Again, your individual ratings will support the score that they received. Feel free to add additional comments to substantiate specific problems. Details are always good when there are future problems or issues.

If the ratings total seems wrong, review the evaluations. Make sure you are satisfied with the results before meeting with the employee. Be confident about them before meeting with any team members because you need to stand behind them. Sometimes evaluations need specific goals for the following year, based on changes in the facility or areas where the employee is lacking. Your suggestions and recommendations need to be logical, and you must be able to explain them.

During the evaluation, explain any high or low scores. High scores include praise for a job that was done well. In turn, the low scores focus on the problem areas.

What should you do if the same problem was already discussed with the employee? It must be included in the evaluation and discussed with the employee. Part of your job is to determine why the employee is not rectifying these problems. They may have reasons for failing to make the needed changes. Give them a chance to explain, but this should not be a rant session. If you are not satisfied with the exchange, review the section below about reprimanding employees.

When the evaluation is complete, let employees look over the form and give them a chance to add their comments and then sign the form.

Some managers aren't comfortable giving evaluations, even though they are an important part of the management process. Periodic reviews help you gauge problems and trends in your facility. The evaluation form puts details in front of you and is a great way to monitor how the team is doing, helping you detail a plan of action to improve the team and to find individual weaknesses. Keep these key points in mind when you review evaluations with specific employees:

- How is the employee doing?

- Are there duties they should perform differently?

- List the employee's strengths.

- List the employee's weaknesses.

- Are there ways they can improve?

- What help can you offer to help them excel?

- How can you help them to improve?

You need to help team members understand how their responsibilities fit into the facility to create a team atmosphere. During the evaluation, show each employee his part to explain why performance is important.

An evaluation is not just a once-a-year meeting with your employees. Some parts of this work can and should be done during the year. Keep track of the good and bad things that employees do. Deal with issues as they arise and don't wait until the evaluation to mention the problems.

When you discuss your evaluation, be clear about what the employee did and did not do well. Be specific and give examples. Once you have explained the details, initiate a discussion with the employee. This lets you see how the employee feels about your comments. It also gives the employee a chance to explain why they agree or disagree with your thoughts.

Even experienced managers know It can be difficult to help employees understand what will happen if their performance doesn't improve. When you try to work with an employee repeatedly without improvement, it's time to discuss further action. This may mean putting the employee on probation. With any ongoing performance issues, take a firm stand. This is especially important after discussing the necessary changes when the employee didn't make the needed changes.

Start by telling the employee what they did well. Can you use any past successes to improve their current performance? The employee may not know how to use the necessary skills on a different task. This is a great opportunity to help an employee improve. After you discuss the situation, develop a plan to help the employee reach these goals. When you expect an employee to improve, you must provide the "tools" to make it happen. These tools don't need to be detailed; simply list some specific things that were discussed in the evaluation to help the employee.

When you put an employee on probation, it is critical that you follow up with the person. It is a waste of your time and the employee's time if you leave the person dangling. When you do a progress check, it's good to offer suggestions and praise.

When Workers Disagree With Your Evaluations

Workers usually feel you should give them higher marks. Everyone has opinions about how much they are worth and how good they are. If you are new to the facility, some employees might say they deserve higher ratings, but you don't know enough to give them a correct evaluation. This is a situation that you should discuss with your supervisor.

If you anticipate that an employee will complain about their evaluation, review it with your supervisor before meeting with the employee. Do not take more than a few minutes of your supervisors' time but provide a copy of the evaluation and review the problem areas. When the employee is dissatisfied, he or she will complain to your supervisor. By handling the situation this way, the supervisor is prepared for the complaint. You may inform the employee that you already reviewed it with your boss. I had my supervisor initial that they agreed with my conclusions. This approach will defuse the situation before it gets out of hand.

Before taking it to your boss, make certain your evaluation is fair and not clouded by your personal opinions because the employee may have no rational recourse. Remember, you will be evaluated on your employee evaluation skills. When they are handled well, they benefit the facility. They also become easier for you with practice. The first few may be difficult, but supervisor boss can help you with those.

Reprimand and Discipline Employees

There are times when constructive criticism is all a team member needs to get back on track. Here are some tips in making the most of constructive criticism.

- **Wait until the employee calms down** before you reprimand them. It is better to wait until you calm down too.

- **Do not reprimand an employee in front of other staff members.** This does much more harm than good.

- **Ask the employee how they feel about the problem.** This will help you understand what they think.

- **Never compare one employee to another.** Use the facility policies and standards as a gauge to measure the employee's behavior.

- **The most important thing is to show the employee how to improve.**

When an employee is not performing well, further action is needed. Talk to the employee and then give the person a chance to correct problems. If they cannot or will not make the needed changes, the employee needs to be terminated. Doing so can be difficult, but it is a necessary part of being a manager. It is much worse to keep unsatisfactory employees. Their behavior attitude and problems can affect the morale of your entire staff.

Weigh the positive and negative impact of whether to retrain the employee or to terminate him. It is a good idea to ask for input from any managers or shift runners to get a complete picture of their performance. Review their past evaluations, training, and performance. Once you decide to terminate the employee, schedule a meeting with the employee as soon as possible.

There are some reasons for immediate employee termination. Here is a list of the most common ones.

1. Misuse or destruction of facility property or equipment.

2. Any theft of money, equipment, personal, or facility items.

3. Changing a patron's bill.

4. Any use of alcohol or drugs during work or being under the influence at work.

5. Being absent for a shift without prior approval.

6. Falsifying any documentation—application, paperwork, time cards.

7. Threatening or trying to harm another employee.

8. Intentionally giving away any chargeable facility items.

9. Being rude or unkind to a patron.

10. Serving alcohol to a minor.

11. Any safety violation in preparation or service of food or beverages.

12. Any unauthorized disclosure or other use of confidential information.

13. Sleeping or being lazy on the job.

14. Any sort of dishonesty.

15. Gambling on the job.

The form at the end of this chapter will provide a checklist for corrective action to be taken against an employee. Use it to make note of your answers and place it in their personnel file for future reference. If things do not improve, you then complete the Disciplinary Suspension Form and put a copy in the personnel file.

Exit Interviews

An exit interview is valuable for the employer and the employee. You may learn new things about the facility, and you can correct these things with future employees. The employee can also gain information that can help them in the future. Here are important elements of an exit interview:

- **Use a private room.**

- **Allow no interruptions.**

- **If you anticipate problems**, have some other supervisor or human resource person in the room.

- **When the employee disagrees with you**, give him or her the opportunity to discuss his or her objections. Before the discussion, make sure you have documentation to support you.

- **Remain seated and calm during the proceedings;** don't get up quickly or move suddenly. This can make the employee defensive.

- **Never touch the employee, except when shaking hands.** These actions may be mis-interpreted and lead to a confrontation.

- **Fill out a report about the exit interview and place it in the employee's personnel file.** This report is important if the employee tries to challenge the action.

- **Place an ad for a new employee as soon as possible.** You know from experience that it takes several months before a new employee is fully productive.

Be honest about the employee's performance and the reason for the termination. Document the chances you gave the employee to improve before your decision to terminate him. All of these records need to be placed in the personnel file in case the employee challenges the termination. The notes don't have to be detailed but should include the details, the date, and your recommendations for the employee.

At times, other employees perceive an employee termination as a threat to them. On the other hand, some employees will be relieved because the problem was resolved. This is a great chance to explain that you will not tolerate substandard work. If needed, give your staff members a simple explanation. Remember, always document everything.

DEPARTMENT ORIENTATION CHECKLIST SAMPLE

New Employee _____ Position _____

After completing this form, please return it to the secretary of your department for filing. Both employee and supervisor should sign at the bottom.

❏	1.	Introduce yourself to the employee and explain your role as a supervisor.
❏	2.	Double check that the employee attended a general orientation.
❏	3.	Verify the employee's telephone number and address.
❏	4.	Go over dress code, personal hygiene, and ID badge wearing policy with employee.
❏	5.	Explain telephone policy regarding use of phones for personal calls.
❏	6.	Explain system for scheduling. Give employee his or her schedule and a locker (if applicable).
❏	7.	Explain policy regarding payment for sick time.
❏	8.	Show employee where, when, and how to use the time clock. Explain the importance of following the proper procedure.
❏	9.	Review job duties and explain the job again.
❏	10.	Explain lunch and break times, cafeteria use, and the meal policy.
❏	11.	Explain the departmental disaster plan.
❏	12.	Review fire procedures and exits from department.
❏	13.	Discuss the hazardous materials list with employee (if applicable).
❏	14.	Show employee any areas of the building he or she will be using.
❏	15.	Review the paging system codes.
❏	16.	Introduce employee to co-workers and show where he or she will be working. Assign employee to a work station with one of the experienced employees for on the job training.

Supervisor's Signature_____ Date _____

I certify that all of the above items have been explained and reviewed to my satisfaction and that I am aware of where to look or whom to contact should any questions arise concerning the above list.

Employee's Signature_____ Date _____

EMPLOYEE INFORMATION

Name: _____ Date: _____

Employee Number: _____ Department: _____

Vacation Days Available: _____ **As Of (Date):** _____

VACATION REQUEST

Dates/Times Requested Off: _____ ❏ Approved ❏ Denied

_____ ❏ Approved ❏ Denied

_____ ❏ Approved ❏ Denied

_____ ❏ Approved ❏ Denied

_____ ❏ Approved ❏ Denied

Alternative Days Requested, If Denied:

_____ ❏ Approved ❏ Denied

_____ ❏ Approved ❏ Denied

_____ ❏ Approved ❏ Denied

Employee's Signature: _____ **Date:** _____

Manager's Signature: _____ **Date:** _____

Comments: _____

_____

_____

_____

_____

_____

_____

_____

_____

Shift: _____ **Date:** _____

Labor Category: _____ **Labor Budget:** _____

EMPLOYEE	SCHEDULE	HOURS SCHEDULED	RATE	TOTAL COST
TOTAL				

Week Of: _____ **Department:** _____

Date Prepared: _____ **Prepared By:** _____

POSITION	NAME	SUN	MON	TUE	WED	THUR	FRI	SAT
	scheduled lunch break here ➜							
	scheduled lunch break here ➜							
	scheduled lunch break here ➜							
	scheduled lunch break here ➜							
	scheduled lunch break here ➜							
	scheduled lunch break here ➜							
	scheduled lunch break here ➜							
	scheduled lunch break here ➜							
	scheduled lunch break here ➜							
	scheduled lunch break here ➜							
	scheduled lunch break here ➜							

WORK SCHEDULE II

Prepared By: _____   Week Of: _____

Approved By: _____

EMPLOYEE	SUN	MON	TUE	WED	THUR	FRI	SAT	TOTAL

WEEK OF:

Employee	Sunday	Monday	Tuesday	Wednesday	Thursday	Friday	Saturday

Week Of: _____

Employee	PH #	SUN	MON	TUE	WED	THUR	FRI	SAT

DATE																
EMPLOYEE	L	D	L	D	L	D	L	D	L	D	L	D	L	D

EMPLOYEE ATTENDANCE RECORD

Name: _____ Date of Employment: _____ Year: 20_____

Employee Number: _____ Department: _____

Mark each instance of missing work below with the reason for the absence.

| **S** = Sick **V** = Vacation **H** = Holiday **I** = Injury **D** = Death in the Family **J** = Jury Duty |
| **L** = Leave without Pay **U** = Unexcused **P** = Personal Time **F** = Maternity Leave/Family Leave Act |

	Jan	Feb	March	April	May	June	July	Aug	Sept	Oct	Nov	Dec
1												
2												
3												
4												
5												
6												
7												
8												
9												
10												
11												
12												
13												
14												
15												
16												
17												
18												
19												
20												
21												
22												
23												
24												
25												
26												
27												
28												
29												
30												
31												

Absence Summary

S _____   V _____   H _____   I _____   D _____

J _____   L _____   U _____   P _____   F _____

Name: _____ Date Of Employment: _____

Employee Number: _____ Department: _____

First Date Absent: _____ Expected Return Date: _____

REASON FOR ABSENCE

❏ Sick   ❏ Vacation   ❏ Holiday   ❏ Injury

❏ Death in the Family   ❏ Jury Duty   ❏ Leave without Pay   ❏ Unexcused

❏ Personal Time   ❏ Maternity Leave/Family Leave Act   ❏ Suspension

❏ Other _____

Explanation _____

_____

_____

_____

ABSENCE DETAIL

This absence was:

Expected in Advance   ❏   Yes   ❏ No

Reported in Advance of Shift   ❏ Yes   ❏ No

Considered by Supervisor as   ❏ Unexcused   ❏ Excused

_____
Signature of Supervisor or Manager   Date

EMPLOYEE INFORMATION

Name: _____ Date: _____

Position: _____

TYPE OF ABSENCE (check one and fill in the appropriate section)

❑ **Anticipated Sick**

❑ **Unanticipated Sick**

❑ **Unanticipated Sick with Insufficient Notification of Sick Leave**

❑ **Tardiness**

❑ **Unexcused Absence**

Sick Day(s) ❑ **Anticipated**   ❑ **Unanticipated** failed to notify supervisor 1½ hours before scheduled shift.

Day(s) _____ Date _____

Notification was made at: _____

Person Notified: _____

Shift Employee was Scheduled for: _____

Reason for Absence: _____

_____

_____

Time off taken as (circle one): sick leave, deduct, vacation, holiday

Number of absences _____ within 6 months for the period _____ to _____.

❑ Excused   ❑ Unexcused

Comments: _____

_____

_____

_____

_____

Employee's Signature _____ Date _____

Supervisor's Signature _____ Date _____

Tardiness

Day(s) _____ Date _____

Shift Employee was Scheduled for: _____

Time Arrived/Amount Tardy: _____

Notification was/was not made:_____

Person Notified: _____

Reason for Tardiness: _____

_____

_____

Number of tardiness _____within 6 months for the period _____ to _____.

❑ Excused   ❑ Unexcused

Comments: _____

_____

_____

Employee's Signature _____ Date _____

Supervisor's Signature _____ Date _____

Unexcused Absence

Day(s) _____ Date _____

Notification was made at: _____

Person Notified: _____

Shift Employee was Scheduled for: _____

Reason for Absence: _____

_____

_____

Number of absences _____within 6 months for the period _____ to _____.

Comments: _____

_____

_____

Employee's Signature _____ Date _____

Supervisor's Signature _____ Date _____

Name: _____ Date of Employment: _____

Employee Number: _____ Payroll Number: _____

Date Payroll Adjustment Effective: _____

Authorized By: _____

NEW ADDRESS

Street Address: _____

City, State, Zip: _____

Home Phone: _____

FOR NEW EMPLOYEES ONLY Social Security Number: _____ Date of Birth: _____

CHANGE (existing employees only)

JOB From: _____ To: _____

SHIFT From: _____ To: _____

DEPARTMENT From: _____ To: _____

PAY From: _____ To: _____

REASON FOR CHANGE

❏ Hired ❏ Rehired ❏ Promotion ❏ Demotion

❏ Transfer ❏ Merit Increase ❏ Resignation ❏ Layoff

❏ Termination ❏ Probation Completed ❏ Retirement ❏ Union Contract

❏ Other _____

LEAVE OF ABSENCE

From: _____ To: _____

Charged to Vacation ❏ Yes ❏ No Family Leave Act ❏ Yes ❏ No

_____
Signature of Supervisor or Manager   Date

Name: _____ Position: _____

Interviewer: _____ Date: _____

Last Evaluation Date: _____ Current Salary: _____

For each of the following categories, grade the employee's performance on a sliding scale of 1 to 10 (see scale below). The overall grade is the average of all scores plus the interviewer's comments.

1-2 poor   3-4 below average   5 average   6-7 above average   8-9 very good   10 exceptional

1. **KNOWLEDGE OF JOB** procedures, paperwork, skill, function   1 2 3 4 5 6 7 8 9 10
   Comments: _____
   _____

2. **QUALITY** up to specification, accuracy, consistency   1 2 3 4 5 6 7 8 9 10
   Comments: _____
   _____

3. **ATTITUDE** towards work, management, other employees, customers   1 2 3 4 5 6 7 8 9 10
   Comments: _____
   _____

4. **LEADERSHIP** ability to give direction   1 2 3 4 5 6 7 8 9 10
   Comments: _____
   _____

5. **RELIABILITY** dependable, on time, follows through on assignments   1 2 3 4 5 6 7 8 9 10
   Comments: _____
   _____

6. **PRODUCTIVITY** volume, utilization of time   1 2 3 4 5 6 7 8 9 10
   Comments: _____
   _____

7. **APPEARANCE** uniform, neat   1 2 3 4 5 6 7 8 9 10
   Comments: _____
   _____

8. **SERVICE** alert, fast   1 2 3 4 5 6 7 8 9 10
   Comments: _____
   _____

OVERALL RATING: _____ / 80

SALARY ADJUSTED: ❏ YES ❏ NO   **NEW SALARY:** _____

Signature of reviewer: _____

The Employee Development & Performance Plan is a detailed, step-by-step program designed to improve communication between employees and supervisors, enhance customer service, increase overall productivity and boost company morale. It is divided into three sections: preview, preparation and feedback. Each section can be specifically tailored for any establishment by adding company-specific details.

STEP 1: PREVIEW SESSION

The first step of the Employee Development & Performance Plan (EDPP) is the Preview Session, where the supervisor schedules a time to discuss with the employee the program details. It is appropriate to schedule the Preview Session one week prior to the Feedback Session to allow the employee appropriate preparation for the EDPP.

The employee's immediate supervisor is designated the evaluator, unless the employee is a member of a self-managed work team and has no supervisor. In that case, a evaluator must be decided prior to the EDPP.

Follow the steps below for the Preview Session:

1. Review all EDPP instructions carefully. Discuss each step of the process and answer any questions the employee may have. Next, incorporate any specific company evaluation policies into the EDPP.

2. Establish a timeline for the EDPP.

3. Review the employee's job description to make sure duties and responsibilities are accurate and up to date.

4. Review the employee's Personal Performance Standards. The Performance Standards should include particular behaviors, special assignments, specific goals or results, special training, etc., that relate directly to the employee.

5. Review the Performance Elements listed on the following page. Determine which are relevant to the employee's job and what may need to be added. Unlike Performance Standards (which are more personal), the Performance Elements should be used universally for all employees in that work unit to which they are applicable.

STEP 2: EDPP PREPARATION

The employee and the supervisor should each draft their own individual responses to Parts I through III of the EDPP. The responses should be based on performance of the employee's duties and responsibilities, Personal Performance Standards and the relevant Performance Elements.

Both the employee and supervisor should demonstrate how the employee's job and performance standards relate to the organization's goals, values, objectives and quality improvement efforts.

Finally, Part IV of the EDPP is completed by the employee only. This is the employee's opportunity to give the supervisor feedback on the supervisor's effectiveness, communication and leadership.

STEP 3: FEEDBACK SESSION

After completing Parts I through III of the EDPP, the employee and supervisor meet to discuss their individual responses. An open and constructive discussion is the main objective. This conversation should result in a clear understanding of the employee's past performance, future expectations and development objectives. Finally, the employee should present his or her review of the supervisor from Part IV. If the employee is uncomfortable doing this personally, it can be presented to the supervisor in writing after the Feedback Session.

If any problems or conflicts occur during the feedback session, another manager should function as a mediator at the request of either the supervisor or the employee.

Once the Feedback Session is complete, the supervisor compiles a final review form for the employee to review and sign. This form should contain all comments from Parts I through IV of the EDDP. The supervisor also signs the EDPP, and then gives the form to the reviewer whose signature indicates that the EDDP has been completed properly. The reviewer does not make changes or comments relative to the employee's performance. The supervisor gives the employee a copy and places the original in the employee's personnel file.

The following "performance elements" should be considered, where applicable, in assessing employee performance (Part I) and determining future performance expectations and development needs (Parts II and III). Other performance elements may be added as needed.

PERFORMANCE ELEMENTS

PERSONAL MANAGEMENT TRAITS

- Using work time effectively.
- Punctuality.
- Possessing integrity and honesty.
- Following company rules and procedures.
- Absences and attendance record.
- Being open to constructive feedback for self and others.
- Proper use of equipment and resources.
- Proper maintenance of equipment.
- Proper safety procedures.
- Seeking and fulfilling additional responsibilities as suitable.
- Treating others with respect and dignity.
- Focusing on the situation, problem or behavior rather than on the person.
- Other: _____
  _____
  _____
  _____

TEAMWORK

- Communicating with others openly and honestly.
- Working with others towards the team and organization's goals.
- Realizing the benefits of teamwork.
- Offering assistance to others and recognizing the contributions of others.
- Viewing the organization's success more important than individual achievement.
- Working towards team cohesion and productivity.
- Sharing information internally and externally.
- Other: _____
  _____
  _____

WORK PROCESSES & RESULTS

- Achieving results.
- Establishing and adhering to priorities.
- Using sound judgment.
- Meeting productivity standards and deadlines.
- Working accurately with minimal supervision.
- Providing products and services above or beyond the customers' needs and expectations.
- Beingaware of customer satisfaction.
- Utilizing problem-solving to improve processes.
- Evaluating information to make informed decisions.
- Striving for efficiency in the use of resources.
- Informing supervisor of problems and offering solutions.
- Other: _____
  _____
  _____
  _____

INNOVATION AND CHANGE

- Looking for creative and innovative ways to contribute to organizational and individual goals.
- Adapting willingly to new situations.
- Striving to be open to new ideas and explore different options.
- Avoiding being overly defensive.
- Seeking ways to improve work processes.
- Helping others adapt to changes.
- Other: _____
  _____
  _____
  _____

PERFORMANCE ELEMENTS (CONTINUED)

GROWTH & PROGRESSION

- Actively striving for ways to increase knowledge.
- Participating in opportunities that are offered by the organization to enhance skills.
- Developing or upgrading knowledge and skills independent of job position through self-initiative.
- Actively applying new skills acquired from developmental opportunities.
- Teaching others new processes or systems.
- Using technology effectively, when appropriate.
- Other: _____
  _____
  _____
  _____

COMMUNICATION

- Actively participating in meetings.
- Interacting with others in a cooperative and courteous manner.
- Giving oral presentations before groups in clear and effective manner.
- Competently communicating verbally in small groups and one-on-one.
- Writing clearly and concisely.
- Responding quickly and properly to other's verbal requests or e-mail, phone messages and mail.
- Other: _____
  _____
  _____
  _____

CUSTOMER SERVICE

- Being responsive to customers' needs.
- Striving to be accessible, timely and responsive to customers.
- Handling customer inquiries promptly and politely.
- Dealing with customer complaints courteously and in a non-judgmental manner.
- Expending extra effort to satisfy customer needs and expectations.
- Other: _____
  _____
  _____
  _____

SUPERVISORY PERFORMANCE

- Offering clear directions to staff.
- Giving regular, ongoing feedback to staff.
- Clearly communicating organization's goals and mission to employees.
- Supporting staff's efforts to succeed.
- Facilitating and coaching employees.
- Recognizing individual's efforts and performance.
- Recognizing team efforts and performance.
- Supporting workplace diversity.
- Following through on instructions.
- Making appropriate decisions regarding employee selection and promotions.
- Other: _____
  _____
  _____
  _____

Name: _____   Date of Employment: _____

Job Position: _____   Date of Preview Session: _____

Evaluated By: _____   Evaluation Period: _____

Purpose of Evaluation: ❏ Annual Review ❏ Trial Service Review ❏ Probationary Review ❏ Other

PART I: PERFORMANCE FEEDBACK

1. Assess the employee's overall performance in relation to carrying out job responsibilities and performance standards.

2. Evaluate the employee's contribution to helping the organization achieve its goals and be successful.

3. Review all Performance Elements and describe how well the employee has done in relation to each relevant area.

PART II: PERFORMANCE EXPECTATIONS

1. Review the employee's Personal Performance Standards in relation to job duties, special assignments and skills the employee need to focus on in order to further his/her success and contribution to the organization.

2. Note any areas in which the employee could improve.

PART III: FUTURE TRAINING & DEVELOPMENT

1. Identify training and development opportunities that could improve and enhance the employee's existing skills and performance.

PART IV: ORGANIZATIONAL SUPPORT
(TO BE COMPLETED BY THE EMPLOYEE)

1. Please list at least five ways your supervisor, co-workers and company can support you in the present job and with future career goals.

2. What do you perceive as your supervisor's greatest strength?

3. Are there any areas in which your supervisor could improve?

PART V: COMMENTS AND SIGNATURES

By signing below, the evaluator agrees that this report is based on his or her judgment. By signing below, the employee agrees that he or she has had an opportunity to review and discuss this report.

_____
Evaluator's Signature

_____
Title   Date

_____
Employee's Signature

_____
Title   Date

I have reviewed this report and, in my judgment, the process has been properly followed.

_____
Reviewer's Signature

_____
Title   Date

Upon completion of this report and signatures of evaluator, employee and reviewers, a final copy should be provided to the employee and the original report placed in the employee's personnel file.

Date: _____

Type of Review: ❑ Mid-Term Probationary   ❑ Final Probation   ❑ Annual

Employee Name: _____

Date of Employment: _____   Job Position: _____

Evaluated By: _____

DIRECTIONS

- Schedule review with employee at least one week in advance. At this time, give employee a copy of his or her current Job Description for review.

- Hold the performance appraisal in a quiet, private place where you will not be interrupted. Have the employee discuss his or her view of job performance.

- Discuss the employee's performance regarding: Job Responsibilities, Performance Standards, and Performance Criteria.

- Ask for the employee's feedback on your review.

- List specific objectives for both the employee and supervisor to maintain and/or improve the employee's job performance.

- Give the employee a written copy of his or her performance review. Let the employee review it and write any of his or her additional comments. Once it has been reviewed by all parties, the performance appraisal should be signed by the reviewer, employee and employee's supervisor. Once copy should be given to the employee and another placed in the employee's permanent file.

- After the performance review, determine if the employee's Job Description needs to be revised. If so, make revisions and give a revised copy to employee.

RATING PERFORMANCE

Use the following numerical system for rating the employee.

1	2	3	4	5
Does not meet basic job duties and responsibilities. Needs improvement.	Meets some but not all job duties and responsibilities. Needs improvement.	Meets most job duties and responsibilities at a minimal level. Could be improved.	Meets job duties and responsibilities on a consistent basis but does not exceed them.	Performs at a level which significantly exceeds job duties and responsibilities on a consistent basis.

PERFORMANCE REVIEW

Rate each criteria below.

Work Record, Scheduling and Personal Appearance

Starts work on time	1 2 3 4 5
Ends work on time	1 2 3 4 5
Takes breaks only at scheduled break times	1 2 3 4 5
Appearance is clean and well groomed	1 2 3 4 5
Follows dress code/wear appropriate uniform	1 2 3 4 5
Attends inservice and employee meetings as scheduled	1 2 3 4 5
Follows infection control and safety policies	1 2 3 4 5

Comments: _____

_____

_____

_____

Attitude, Communication, Cooperation, and Personal Relations

Is polite and courteous to supervisors, co-workers and other staff	1 2 3 4 5
Is a team player and works in a combined effort with others	1 2 3 4 5
Is sensitive and non judgmental towards patients, families and visitors	1 2 3 4 5
Maintains strict confidentiality of privileged information	1 2 3 4 5

Comments: _____

_____

_____

_____

GOALS

List any job-related development goals and employee career goals, along with action and date to be completed.

_____

_____

_____

_____

_____

_____

APPROVALS

Employee's Signature_____ Date _____

Supervisor's Signature_____ Date _____

Reviewer's Signature_____ Date _____

PERFORMANCE REVIEW AND WORK PLANNING SUMMARY SHEET SAMPLE

Date: _____

Employee Name: _____

Date of Employment: _____ **Job Position:** _____

Meeting Date: _____

List People in Attendance _____

_____

_____

_____

_____

_____

_____

Goal(s) of Meeting: _____

_____

_____

_____

List Specific Topics to be Discussed at this Meeting: _

_____

_____

_____

_____

_____

_____

_____

List Additional Performance Expectations:_____

_____

_____

_____

_____

_____

List Employee's Concerns Regarding Topics and Performance Expectations: _____

_____

_____

_____

_____

_____

_____

_____

_____

List Relevant Problems and Solutions Discussed _____

_____

_____

_____

_____

_____

_____

_____

_____

_____

_____

List Employee's Accomplishments Since Last Meeting:

_____

_____

_____

_____

_____

_____

_____

_____

_____

Set Specific Objectives to be Accomplished in the

Next Time Period:_____

_____

_____

_____

_____

_____

_____

_____

_____

_____

_____

_____

_____

_____

List Additional Goals: _____

_____

_____

_____

_____

_____

_____

_____

_____

_____

_____

_____

_____

_____

_____

_____

_____

_____

Projected Date of Next Review:_____

APPROVALS

Employee's Signature_____   Date _____

Supervisor's Signature_____   Date _____

Reviewer's Signature_____   Date _____

Employee Name: _____

Date of Employment: _____ Job Position: _____

RATING PERFORMANCE

Use the following numerical system for rating your job performance.

1	2	3	4	5
Does not meet basic job duties and responsibilities. Needs improvement.	Meets some but not all job duties and responsibilities. Needs improvement.	Meets most job duties and responsibilities at a minimal level. Could be improved.	Meets job duties and responsibilities on a consistent basis but does not exceed them.	Performs at a level which significantly exceeds job duties and responsibilities on a consistent basis.

Performance	1st Quarter Date_____	2nd Quarter Date_____	3rd Quarter Date_____	4th Quarter Date_____
Attendance (rate missed days of work)				
Tardiness (rate times late for work)				
Work Quality				
Work Effort				
Appearance				
Attitude				
Cooperation with Co-Workers				
Works Safely				
Motivation				
TOTAL SCORE				

Employee Comments

Quarter 1	Signature of Employee	Date Signed
Quarter 2	Signature of Employee	Date Signed
Quarter 3	Signature of Employee	Date Signed
Quarter 4	Signature of Employee	Date Signed

MANAGER'S EVALUATION FORM

Employee Name: _____

Date of Employment: _____ Job Position: _____

RATING PERFORMANCE

Use the following numerical system for rating the employee.

1	2	3	4	5
Does not meet basic job duties and responsibilities. Needs improvement.	Meets some but not all job duties and responsibilities. Needs improvement.	Meets most job duties and responsibilities at a minimal level. Could be improved.	Meets job duties and responsibilities on a consistent basis but does not exceed them.	Performs at a level which significantly exceeds job duties and responsibilities on a consistent basis.

Performance	1st Quarter Date_____	2nd Quarter Date_____	3rd Quarter Date_____	4th Quarter Date_____
Attendance (rate missed days of work)				
Tardiness (rate times late for work)				
Work Quality				
Work Effort				
Appearance				
Attitude				
Cooperation with Co-Workers				
Works Safely				
Motivation				
TOTAL SCORE				

Manager Comments

Quarter 1	Signature of Manager	Date Signed
Quarter 2	Signature of Manager	Date Signed
Quarter 3	Signature of Manager	Date Signed
Quarter 4	Signature of Manager	Date Signed

EMPLOYEE'S SELF EVALUATION QUESTIONNAIRE

Date: _____

Employee Name: _____

Date of Employment: _____ **Job Position:** _____

Please complete the following questions regarding your job and job performance. Be prepared to share the answers with your supervisor and to discuss your performance so that you know how well you are meeting expectations.

Outline the course of a typical work day, listing your

duties as they are performed. Be specific as possible.

_____

_____

_____

_____

_____

_____

Please list any possible solutions to the problems you

have described.

_____

_____

_____

_____

_____

_____

_____

_____

Please list any problem areas that affect job job per-

formance

_____

_____

_____

_____

_____

_____

_____

_____

Please list any ways you feel your job performance could be improved. _____

_____

_____

_____

_____

_____

_____

_____

_____

Please list any work related goal you would like to accomplish in the next year._____

_____

_____

_____

_____

_____

_____

_____

_____

Please list any ways you feel your supervisor could help improve your job performance. _____

_____

_____

_____

_____

_____

_____

_____

_____

_____

_____

_____

Additional Comments. _____

_____

_____

_____

_____

_____

_____

_____

_____

_____

_____

_____

Employee's Signature_____   Date _____

Supervisor's Signature_____   Date _____

Reviewer's Signature_____   Date _____

Date: _____

Employee Name: _____

Date of Employment: _____ **Job Position:** _____

Your Name: _____

Review the following form and fill in answers where appropriate. This will help you summarize the problem and determine the corrective action to be taken.

Briefly describe the current problem

_____

_____

_____

_____

_____

What is the past record of the employee? *Consider if the employee was disciplined previously for the same type of offense and when that occurred. Be specific in listing dates or include copies of documented warnings.* _____

_____

_____

_____

_____

Has the employee had a chance or made an effort to improve? *Consider if the employee has been given full instruction or explanations and if the rules and standards at the time of the infraction are clearly outlined. Give examples.* _____

_____

_____

_____

What is the best course of action to take? *Review any procedural manuals for written guidelines. Review how similar problems were handled with other employees. Note answers or attach samples.* _____

_____

_____

_____

What are the impending effects of your actions? *Consider other employees and schedules in your disciplinary actions and note any anticipated effects.* _____

_____

_____

_____

_____

_____

_____

Are you responsible for administering the corrective action? *Review any procedural manuals for written guidelines and talk to your supervisor to confirm procedures if needed.* _____

_____

_____

_____

What possible actions are there? *Will your action improve the work output in your department and help the employee to improve? Should he or she be warned or suspended? List consequences and alternatives.*

_____

_____

_____

_____

EMPLOYEE DISCIPLINARY ACTION WRITTEN NOTICE

Date: _____

Employee Name: _____

Date of Employment: _____ Job Position: _____

Supervisor Name: _____

You are hereby given written warning for infractions of company policy. Please review the statements below, add your comments if needed, sign and return to your supervisor. The purpose of notice is to make you aware of your mistakes and to help improve your work habits. Repeated violations or failure to improve your work habits can lead to dismissal.

INFRACTION
(To be filled out by supervisor. Check all that apply).

❏ Unexcused Absence ❏ Late for Work ❏ Behavior ❏ Work Performance ❏ Other (specify below)

Date(s) Incident Occurred:_____

Briefly describe the incident if needed:_____

_____

_____

_____

_____

_____

_____

This is the ❏ 1st Offense ❏ 2nd Offense ❏ 3rd Offense ❏ Other _____

If the employee has been warned about this problem before, please list details below including date of late offense, type of warning given (written or verbal), and the name of the supervisor :_____

_____

_____

_____

_____

Comments: _____

_____

_____

_____

_____

Employee's Signature_____ Date _____

Supervisor's Signature_____ Date _____

EMPLOYEE DISCIPLINARY SUSPENSION NOTICE

Date: _____

Employee Name: _____

Date of Employment: _____ Job Position: _____

Supervisor Name: _____

YOU ARE HEREBY GIVEN WRITTEN NOTICE OF SUSPENSION FOR DISCIPLINARY PURPOSES.

SUSPENSION DETAILS

Reason for Suspension: _____

_____

_____

_____

_____

_____

_____

_____

You will be suspended for the following time period: **FROM** _____ **TO** _____

Suspension is ❏ Unpaid   ❏ Paid

SUSPENSION CONSEQUENCES

Is is the recommendation of your supervisor that:

❏ Your next salary increase be denied.

❏ You be placed on probation for a period of _____

Comments: _____

_____

_____

_____

_____

EMPLOYEE ACKNOWLEDGEMENT

I have been made aware of the reason(s) for this disciplinary suspension. I understand that my signature does not imply agreement or disagreement with this action.

Employee's Signature_____ Date _____

Supervisor's Signature_____ Date _____

CHAPTER FIFTEEN

Operational Management

There are various ways to produce, serve, and deliver food and beverage items. This chapter deals with these options. Much of the information in this chapter is based on health care food service facilities, but the information is valuable for any non-commercial food service facility.

Food Production

In Chapter 4 we discussed menu planning in detail. That work must be done before any food production decisions are made. This is because the way food is produced is affected by the items to be prepared. Food production decisions should be based on several criteria that include:

1. Menu requirements
2. Food purchasing
3. Available equipment
4. Distribution and service procedures
5. Available personnel
6. Finances available

Two menu factors have an impact on the type of production to be used. They include:

1. **Menu Style or Format** — Earlier we discussed nonselective and selective menus. You can prepare meal plates beforehand, but the selection may not suit the employees or patients. When you do not offer the option to use substituted items, there is lower satisfaction and food acceptance.

2. **Menu Variety** — Take a close look at your menu items. Can they be prepared in different ways? The production choices you make must be compatible with the menu items. If the production choice will only accommodate some of the menu items, there are usually added expenses for the facility.

Let's discuss some of the options to see which would be the right choice for your facility. Remember, if you are hired to work in an established facility, you might want to offer suggestions or changes to save money and effort. There are four common food production categories. They include:

FOOD PRODUCTION CATEGORIES			
Cook - serve	Assembly - serve	Cook - freeze - serve	Cook - chill - serve

CASE STUDY: ORGANIZATIONAL STRUCTURE

The chain of command in a non-commercial environment is just as vital to the operation as it is in a commercial setting. The entire process of food service is continuously under the microscope with respect to several issues such as: Food Cost, Licensing, Sanitation, Productivity, and Menu design and implementation

It is still an important issue to have a chain of command in the event of any uncomfortable situation arising that requires a major decision.

To give an example, a small community here in our province recently held a fundraiser that involved the preparation of food for a local church takeout dinner. A large number of people became very ill and had to be hospitalized. It became a media frenzy, and nobody was accepting responsibility for the problem or attempting to handle it in a professional manner. If there had been a chain of command in place, one person could have come forward and handled the situation quickly and effectively as opposed to a large group of people getting involved resulting in a massive amount of misinformation getting out to the media.

Non-commercial institutions still have to be accountable for their actions, and it is vital to their success to have a chain of command in the event of an emergency.

Chef Eric King • College of the North Atlantic (Culinary Arts Program) • **www.cna.nl.ca**

"Cook–Serve" Production

This is a common method which uses raw foods on the premises prepared daily for each meal. The food is prepared and served with minimal holding time. A factor to consider is the limited number of skilled staff members you have. Therefore, not all of the items are prepared from scratch and some convenience foods are used. For example, a butcher shop might cube, grind, and portion meats.

A wide variety of items could be frozen and prepared on site to include: cakes, cookies, frozen pies, or pie shells. Bread and rolls can be purchased from commercial bakers. Once the food is prepared, there is a plan to distribute meals to the patients. The food is portioned, placed on plates or trays, and presented without further heating.

All food is prepared at the same time in most facilities, but in some, one meal is prepared and served. The kitchen is cleaned and preparation begins for the next meal. This is an example of how employees can be scheduled.

6 – 9 a.m.	9-11 a.m.	11–2 p.m.	2-4 p.m.	4-6 p.m.	6-7 p.m.
Morning	Morning	Morning	Morning		
		Afternoon	Afternoon	Afternoon	Afternoon

Morning Shift – Prepares Breakfast and Lunch   Afternoon Shift – Prepares Lunch and Dinner

One primary concern with the overlapping work hours is that productivity will suffer and labor costs will soar if the manager doesn't keep a close eye on the staff. However, it is nice to have additional staff members for lunch, normally the busiest meal in most businesses.

ADVANTAGES OF COOK–SERVE	DISADVANTAGES OF COOK–SERVE
• Menu flexibility. • Fresh appearance. • Diner satisfaction. • Variety of menu items.	• Added employee stress during rush periods • Skilled employees must be scheduled every day meals are served • Overlap of shifts causes lower productivity and increased labor costs

"Assemble-Serve" Production

With the "assemble–serve" method, food is purchased after being prepared by another source. Food items are prepared and frozen in bulk until the facility is ready to use them. Here are the common steps at the point when the facility is ready to prepare the food: 1) thaw the items, 2) plate the food, 3) assemble each item, and 4) distribute to diners.

Employee meals are heated in disposable containers, saving washing expenses, and served on a standard counter or serving area. Some other items that can be purchased already prepared include:

1. Precut and prepared salad mix

2. Frozen dessert items and rolls

3. Prepared vegetable plates and combinations

4. Prepared entrees

The word for using prepared entrees but preparing other items is "semi-convenient." It can be a great way to save on equipment and labor expenses. It is critical for the non-commercial food service manager to remember that cost is not the top priority. The critical factors are:

• Acceptability by diners

• Quality and nutritional value

• Variety offered by the distributor

It does not do you any good to save money if the patrons and patients won't eat the food.

If you go with this food production method, there could be a need for more freezer space and more reheating equipment.

Some facilities like to use nice china and fine serviceware along with garnishes to "dress up" the prepared items they use. Of course, nice presentation of any food items is encouraged.

ADVANTAGES OF ASSEMBLE–SERVE	DISADVANTAGES OF ASSEMBLE–SERVE
• Labor costs are reduced – skilled cooks are not necessary. • Food waste is reduced. • Equipment purchase and maintenance costs are reduced. • Food portions are consistent. • Purchasing, accounting, and inventory are simplified.	• Increased food costs. • Limited food modification to suit diner preferences. • Unavailability of particular products. • Limited control over production of food items. • High equipment costs – heating and freezer equipment. • Negative reactions to "prepared" foods, especially when served in disposable containers.

**CASE STUDY:
ASSISTED LIVING FOOD PRODUCTION**

We use the cook-serve and assemble-serve production technique. This method still works well for our operation. Cook-freeze and cook-chill require extensive production, labor, and very expensive equipment purchases.

Kathy L. Hilbert, Director of Dining Services
Bridgewater Retirement Community

"Cook–Freeze–Serve" Production

There is a wide variety of "cook–freeze" options. The procedure to serve diners includes

1. Preparing items.

2. Packaging individual portions.

3. Blast freezing.

4. Storing in freezer.

5. Thawing items when needed.

6. Assembling products as needed.

7. Distributing.

8. Reheating at the point of service.

9. Serving to diners.

One such procedure was developed by the researchers at Cornell's School of Hotel Administration.

- **Prepare food in large quantities.** Skilled cooks work five days a week and prepare multiple foods each day.

- **Prepare single portions** that can be re-thermalized as needed.

- **Blast-freeze items** and store in a freezer unit.

- **Use a simple reheating process** such as "boil in bag" or microwave heating.

- **Control food quality** by using on-premise preparation.

- **Cater to local tastes** and satisfy preferences.

Prepare other items in-house. In-house items could be appetizers, vegetables, soup, bread, and desserts. Your decision about which to prepare in-house depends on the facility, the resources, and the number of skilled and unskilled staff members.

In medical food service facilities, some adjustments are needed to meet dietary and nutritional needs for the patients and employees. Cafeterias that use these pre-prepared items for their patrons would thaw the needed food items a day early. These items are thawed in a refrigerator or in a thaw refrigerator which thaws food faster.

A variation is the "Leeds Cook–Freeze" system which was created by the United Leeds Hospitals in England. They use the following steps to prepare these foods: casseroles, desserts, egg dishes, entrees, soups, starches, and vegetables.

1. **Leave food slightly undercooked and finish cooking just before serving.**

2. **Place six to eight servings in a polyethylene mold** while hot and then blast freeze.

3. **Remove food from blast packs.**

4. **Heat-seal packs in polyethylene bags** and pack in boxes to freeze.

5. **Place frozen slabs in reusable metal pans** to be heated in conventional oven on the wards.

6. **Assemble food and serve to patients on the wards.**

This method of freezing multiple portions is different from the other "cook-freeze-serve" methods. Keep in mind that decentralized heating and plating cause the manager to lose control of the product's finished quality.

The "cook-freeze-serve" method is only useful for patient meals and is not used with employee meals. Many facilities find it easier to have one method that can be used for all their patrons. This means that the "cook-freeze-serve" method is not useful for the majority of the specialties discussed in this book.

ADVANTAGES OF COOK-FREEZE-SERVE	DISADVANTAGES OF COOK-FREEZE-SERVE
• Simplified employee scheduling. Skilled employees work eight-hour shifts Monday-Friday. • Individual items can be prepared in bulk, limiting the number of times the items need to be prepared. • Bulk preparation can reduce labor costs. • There are no more peak production workloads, ensuring that employees can be used consistently during their shift without the added stress of peak production.	• Added equipment costs in the beginning including additional freezer space, packaging supplies, reheating equipment. It may also require some facility renovation. • Employees who are required to work weekends may be resentful of employees who don't work weekends.

Genpak oven-ready baking trays are ready to fill, freeze, and bake food items in the same package. The design and clear lids make it possible to promote items at the counter. You can use these items with clear lids, or they can be film-sealed as well. See the full line of products at **www.genpak.com** or contact them at **www.genpak.com/cfm/inforequest.cfm.**

This is an example of someone else's cooking and freezing, but your serving the food. You may want to offer an appetizer of wings or chicken tenders, one example of a "cook-freeze-serve" option. La Nova provides various wing flavors to satisfy any customer's taste: barbecue, oven-roasted, Italian-style, and hot 'n' spicy. Customers love the taste, and you'll love the easy preparation. According to Restaurants and Institutions magazine, the best-selling appetizers are chicken strips and wings. These items are popular with food service managers because they are easy to store, prepare, and serve. For full information, visit their Web site **www.lanova.com** or call 800-6LA-NOVA.

"Cook-Chill-Serve" Production

Basic principles of this method are conventional cooking, quick chilling, packaging, and chilled storage. It originated in the 1960s at Nagka Hospital in Stockholm, Sweden. Here are the procedures used:

1. **Food can be cooked by any conventional means** including boiling, frying, roasting, stewing, or any method that brings the temperature to 176°F.

2. **Five portions of the hot food are transferred to plastic bags.**

3. **Excess air is extracted from the plastic bags before sealing with a Cryovac machine.**

4. **Each bag is boiled for three minutes.** (They recommend a rectangular kettle for rapid heating.)

5. **Sealed bags are then passed through a tunnel** for one hour with running water at a beginning temperature of 50°F that is lowered to 37°F.

6. **Packages are quick-dried** and stored at a maximum 37°F.

7. **When the food is needed, it is placed in boiling water for 30 minutes.**

8. **Food is opened and served.**

There are many possible variations of this procedure. These prepared items can be stored for as little as one day or as long as three weeks, depending on the chilling method used. For a hospital, remember this system can also require special equipment and a preparation area on the wards.

There are some exceptions to this method. They include:

1. **Raw or partially cooked food is placed in the pouches.** The cooking process can be completed in water baths with controlled temperatures.

2. **Once the processing is complete, the items can be chilled in ice tanks**, then stored between 28°F and 32°F.

3. **The prepared pouches can be delivered to other units or facilities** in covered plastic containers surrounded with ice.

4. **Sealed pouches can be placed in a hot water bath for 30-40 minutes.** The items should be heated to 160°F.

5. **Plate the hot food and microwave for 10 to 20 seconds** just before the meals are taken to patients.

Whichever process you choose, it must be organized to maintain control of the food and labor costs. One way to create this organization is through the use of the worksheet shown at the end of this chapter.

Determine how many sheets are needed based on the number of items you serve and the volume of business your facility does. There can be one sheet for baking, one for cooking, one for salad, and one for appetizer preparation. Here are details on how to use the sheet most effectively. Each item on the sheet is listed along with instructions on how to complete it.

1. **Food Item** — List the item just as it is on the menu. Only the manager should make any changes.

2. **Amount Needed** — The amount you need will be determined by the number of servings you plan to prepare. Make adjustments for the day of the week, the number of patients in the facility, and any other variable that can affect the portions you need. The form was made with spaces to note the number of regular and modified diets. The column on the left is for regular diets and the other columns are for special diet requirements.

3. **Prepared By** — The chef or kitchen manager can use the sheet to assign individual preparation duties to staff members; there is a written record of who prepared each item in case there are problems.

4. **Time of Preparation** — It is critical that foods are prepared at the right time, not too early or too late. This potential problem can be eliminated by including the time items are to be prepared.

5. **Instruction** — This can be handled by writing which recipe number to use. Each facility has the master recipe book and each recipe is numbered. to prevent confusion about which item is needed. Also include instructions about any unusual details such as larger-than-usual portions being used.

6. **Amount Used** — This part will not be completed until the end of the shift. Gather information about the total servings and enter that number on the worksheet.

7. **Amount Left** — Subtract the amount used from the amount that was prepared. This can be used in future projections and to determine waste or over usage of food.

8. **Disposition** — All remaining food needs to be accounted for in some way. Mark whether leftovers were frozen, refrigerated, or thrown away.

At the bottom of the form, include information about unusual factors that had an impact on the amount of food that was used. This could include weather, patient census, a holiday, special event in the facility, unusually high traffic, or anything that affected your sales numbers for that day or shift. When it is used properly, the sheet helps the manager predict irregularities.

CASE STUDY: PRISON FOOD PRODUCTION

All meals are prepared the day before for a smooth schedule. Usually inmates and staff work half a month and are then off for half a month. They work two shifts, working three and a half days and then are off three and a half days. Only two meals are served on weekend days and holidays. There is a great deal of waste in the prison facility. Enough food is prepared, but not all the inmates show up for meals which is one reason for leftovers.

Each meal there can be 4- to 6-inch pans to be thrown out. There are no seconds except for kitchen inmates and staff.

Employee theft is a big thing in the prison environment. The penalty when someone is caught stealing is being fired or removed from the job for 90 days with no income. There are inconsistent policies and a lack of communication from the top to the bottom, and there are no mandatory meetings where supervisors could communicate with the staff.

Lawrence Shearer, Chef

Produce Food for Modified Diets

This is especially important in hospitals, nursing homes, and school cafeterias. Increasingly, people have health concerns such as food allergies and intolerances that should be addressed by modified diets. It can be a critical or life threatening situation for some people. This section will help you understand how to handle modified diet requirements.

Modified items can be prepared with the meals for regular diet, staff, and guest meals. Usually these do not have additional seasonings or added fat. The simplest way is to make plain, unseasoned items. Individuals who can have salt, for example, would simply add it for themselves.

It is a common belief that food service personnel do not usually take the time to make tasty and attractive meals for people on modified diets, that more emphasis is put on making meals appetizing for doctors, administrators, staff, and guests who eat in cafeterias. Remember that each patron is paying for a nutritious and appetizing meal.

Some health care food service facilities have a separate section to prepare modified diets. This is a great way to cater to patients with modified diets, but the facility would have to justify the added expense.

Here are some of the benefits of this system:

1. The staff members have time to make individual meal preparations.

2. Cooks can add some seasonings approved for the modified diet to offer the patron a more appetizing meal.

3. The facility can offer more specialty items that would meet the modified diet requirements.

4. There is time to prepare complicated or diets with multiple restrictions.

5. The staff could also have the time to prepare combination meals for the patrons while still meeting the modified requirements.

Vending Services

Vending services are another option that is nice option for staff members and visitors when the facility cafeteria is not open. It could be serviced in-house or by an outside company. This is especially true in facilities that have employees and patients 24 hours a day. Some facilities opt to have the cafeteria open around the clock, but others have vending services. It is a decision that has to be made by each facility.

The advantages of vending machines are

- **Cold items like fruit and salads can be served.** The facility can provide a microwave.

- **Food quality must be maintained** by removing uneaten items daily and replacing them with fresh items.

- **Machines must be cleaned daily to ensure safe and sanitary conditions.** Temperatures in the machines must be checked daily, and freshness dates should be stamped on all items.

- **Outside vending companies only offer foods with an extended shelf life.**

- **It is good to have a staff person who is able to repair the equipment** when there are problems.

As with everything in life, there are also disadvantages to using vending services.

- **Additional staff can be needed to prepare foods in an attractive manner.**

- **Staff members need to be trained on how to load, rotate, clean, and operate the machines.**

- **The facility needs to make additional menu plans.**

- **Safety and sanitary concerns require additional supervision.** This includes: dating the food, cleaning, and sanitizing the machines and controlling the machine temperatures.

- **The machines and additional equipment will cost money to get started.** There is the possibility to rent or purchase the necessary machines. Also consider the needed repairs, maintenance, and all paper supplies. There will also be an additional area to clean on a regular basis.

Additional Food Production Issues

We have discussed many food production methods, but is that the only thing to consider? There are other considerations when evaluating and implementing a food production technique. Some concerns are food, labor, supply costs, energy use, equipment needs, food quality, food safety, ingredient availability and control, scheduling, and skilled labor availability. Let's take a closer look at these concerns.

Food and Labor Costs

Take a look at all elements of a proposed method. Some will involve more food costs, while others are labor intensive, and others involve added equipment costs. The individual facility and the economics of the area can be determining factors in which method to use. Every decision we make is a trade off. Which elements are better suited for the facility where you work? If you come into an established facility, this would be a chance to suggest possible changes which would be more appropriate for the facility, the area, and the staff members.

Food Costs

Some methods may be more attractive because they lessen the potential food loss, therefore reducing food costs. However, take a closer look to be sure your assumptions are correct. One method actually averages 10 to 20 percent food losses even though the food is stored in bags. This is especially true when the food is steamed in kettles, pumped into bags, re-thermalized, and placed into steam tables. The potential loss with some food items can be as much as 25 percent. Studies show that the lowest potential food loss is with the "cook–freeze" system.

Labor Costs

On paper the motivating reason to use ready food and convenience production is to reduce labor costs. Production costs may be less, but often the service costs are higher for ready-to-use foods. These costs need to be figured into any decision to make changes. It is strange that facility case studies show a decrease in labor costs, but studies do not support this claim. With methods that include some food re-thermalization on the wards, it could appear that labor costs have been decreased, while the cost is being spread around. Another thing that could skew the results is having a facility that is already over-staffed. When this is the case, you can change methods and not need any additional people or may need fewer because you are watching more closely. This will not give accurate results or a complete evaluation of the new technique.

A study in 1973 by Rappole, examined the results from hospitals, colleges, and universities that began using convenience products. The results showed that the facilities did not realize any significant or obvious savings after changing to the convenience product methods. Here are some of the particular elements of the method which seem to influence the labor costs involved:

1. The type of production system used.

2. The use of hot and cold tray lines.

3. The use of re-thermalization.

4. The work involved in tray finishing on patient floors.

Each of these elements must be evaluated to make an accurate decision.

School Food Production

With school food service, there are many regulations which govern how food is prepared and served. It is critical that the person in charge of planning and serving is familiar with the breakfast and lunch meal patterns and the laws and regulations that pertain to school meals.

There are various ways to produce the food needed for your school facility meals. Menu planning is also a part of the food production process. Details about school menu planning were discussed in Chapter 4.

Producing Food On-Site

This is the most common production system used. The cost of on-site production is high unless there is a large volume of meals being served and unless labor costs are contained. Unfortunately, many school systems do not have another choice. Below are some alternatives.

Satellite Food Production

This is a feasible option when there are multiple schools in one school district. The kitchen in one school is used to prepare part of the food and another school will finish the preparation and serve the meals. In some districts, one kitchen prepares the food for several schools. These are a few ways to use satelliting:

1. Food is transported in bulk to each facility to be served.

2. Food is transported already placed on plates and ready to serve.

3. Food is transported and needs to be finished and served.

The amount of final preparation needed will depend on the personnel and facilities in each school facility. If any of these methods are used, there is some specialized equipment the facility must have, including carriers that hold temperatures.

Keep in mind that even though in-house production costs are lower, you still need a limited number of people to serve the meals. Food already placed on plates can require only one or two servers. However, any considerations and decisions need to be based on a variety of information and not just the number of employees needed. The local school district may not allow any of these options, but it is something to consider.

Convenience Foods

There was a time when convenience foods were a low-quality option. In recent years quality has improved, increasing its use and decreasing labor costs. If costs do not change, there is a problem in the facility operation that needs to be evaluated. The labor cost is figured into the price, which makes this option generally more expensive than preparing the items from scratch. As this industry grows, the price of convenience foods could drop. It might be advantageous to keep an eye on them.

It is good to keep production records for the facility. This can be a valuable tool for a school food service manager to track the menu pattern used and to satisfy state and local school districts. The proper use of a production record can help you control food costs and waste. A sample form is included at the end of this chapter.

Distribution and Service

In a health care situation, after food is prepared, it must be delivered to the patients. The food served to patients is based on their menu selections or based on their physician's orders. This is an example of the procedures that lead up to the patient's menu choices.

1. **Gather** physician's orders.

2. **Discuss** options and doctor's orders with the patient.

3. **Record** pertinent information in the patient's chart.

4. **Plan** menu based on established menu patterns, using patient preferences.

5. **List** menu choices for the food service department and include any special instructions.

6. **Serve** meals to patients.

Each department should have policies to handle the following exceptions:

1. Lack of time to place orders.

2. Changes in diet orders.

3. Special food requests.

4. New admissions.

5. Delay of trays.

6. Orders for unusual diets.

7. Providing diet instructions for patients to follow after leaving the hospital. This is slightly different in nursing homes where the patient stays are longer. There are fewer changes in the diets because the same patients are being served. Census sheets in a hospital can be rewritten each day, but in a nursing home they may only be needed once a week. Below is an example of a census sheet.

CENSUS SHEET	
Ward _____ Date _____	
Room No.	
Patient's Name	
Type of Diet – Include diabetic insulin and restriction level	

Before each meal, nurses prepare a diet change order that is sent to the food service department before each meal. It is best to discourage any changes by phone and to require wards to submit changes in writing. These changes should also be submitted at least 30 minutes before tray assembly.

A sample of a diet change sheet can be found at the end of this chapter.

Menu Item Selection

All patients on regular and modified diets can order when selective menus are used. We discussed selective menus in Chapter 4. They give patients and residents the option to look at a restaurant-type menu and make their personal choices. They are encouraged to make nutritional choices with their selections. In most cases their choices will be monitored by a dietician.

Meal Assembly and Deli

The method used to assemble trays will be dictated by the production methods used in the facility. Some methods will require a delay between preparation time and assembly, while others do not.

In centralized tray service, all patient trays are assembled in one location near the food production area. The food service staff members assemble the trays using the patient menu selection sheets to ensure the patient gets the items they ordered. These are the steps in the tray assembly process:

1. Review patient order and assemble tray.

2. Check tray for accuracy.

3. Load assembled trays on food carts or other distribution equipment.

It is convenient to have some smaller equipment like coffee makers or toasters near a conveyor belt in the production area. The food items are plated, placed on trays, and carried down the line. As we discussed above, in some food production techniques the food is assembled immediately.

Decentralized tray service involves taking food in bulk to the food preparation area on each ward. This area is equipped with hot and cold holding equipment and dishwashing facilities. The decentralized system is not used frequently because technology has advanced and there are too many other options. There are some major problems associated with decentralization. They include:

1. **High Labor Costs** — Some employees must be assigned to work in each tray area for assembly, distribution, and cleanup.

2. **Limited Supervision** — With employees spread in many locations, it is impossible for a supervisor to oversee and control food portioning.

3. **Costly Equipment** — Excessive amounts of equipment are needed to prepare and distribute the food.

4. **Questionable Environments** — There is limited control over the work area used to assemble food.

To maximize effectiveness of a centralized system, these steps should be followed:

1. **You need standardized assembly instructions to maintain consistency and to speed the assembly process.** It can be helpful to provide a diagram of where each item should be placed on the tray.

2. **Trays that contain modified diets** need to be prepared at the same time and placed on racks so all meals can be delivered together.

3. **Trays can be assembled in two phases if needed.** Cold food should be placed on the tray first and then the hot food can be added.

Again, each tray needs to be checked for accuracy before it is delivered to the patient.

FOOD PRODUCTION SAMPLE

DATE _____ **PREPARED BY:**_____

DAY SU M T W TH F SA   **MONTH** Jan Feb Mar April May June July Aug Sept Oct Nov Dec

MENU ITEM :

Portion Size	No. of Portions Forecast	No. of Portions Prepared	Quantity of Food Used
Portions Leftover	Portions Served	Cost/Serving	Total Cost

MENU ITEM :

Portion Size	No. of Portions Forecast	No. of Portions Prepared	Quantity of Food Used
Portions Leftover	Portions Served	Cost/Serving	Total Cost

MENU ITEM :

Portion Size	No. of Portions Forecast	No. of Portions Prepared	Quantity of Food Used
Portions Leftover	Portions Served	Cost/Serving	Total Cost

Comments and Special Instructions:_____

_____

_____

DATE _____ PREPARED BY:_____

PROJECTED NUMBER OF MEALS_____

ACTUAL MEALS SERVED_____

FOOD ITEM :

Total Amount Needed: *(breakdown into dietary restrictions below)*

Regular Meals _____	Restricted Calorie _____	Restricted Sodium _____
Restricted Fat _____	Restricted Fiber _____	Liquid _____
Other (list) _____		

Prepared by:		Time of Preparation:
Amount Used:	Amount Left:	Disposition:

Instructions:

FOOD ITEM :

Total Amount Needed: *(breakdown into dietary restrictions below)*

Regular Meals _____	Restricted Calorie _____	Restricted Sodium _____
Restricted Fat _____	Restricted Fiber _____	Liquid _____
Other (list) _____		

Prepared by:		Time of Preparation:
Amount Used:	Amount Left:	Disposition:

Instructions:

FOOD ITEM :

Total Amount Needed: *(breakdown into dietary restrictions below)*

Regular Meals _____	Restricted Calorie _____	Restricted Sodium _____
Restricted Fat _____	Restricted Fiber _____	Liquid _____
Other (list) _____		

Prepared by:		Time of Preparation:
Amount Used:	Amount Left:	Disposition:

Instructions:

Day _____

Month _____

Ward _____

Room and Bed	Patient's Name	N.P.O.	Change in Diet	Omit Next Meal Only	Delay Next Meal Only	Special Meal (Test)	Isolation—Protection	Discharge	Admission	Transfer to:	Type of Diet: If diabetic, include insulin order. If restricted, indicate level.

Signature of Charge Nurse Must Appear Below:

6:00 a.m. _____   11:00 a.m. _____

2:00 p.m. _____   6:00 p.m. _____

CHAPTER SIXTEEN

Operate an Effective Dining Area

Dining room management and work varies in non-commercial food service. The wait staff does not take orders, bring all food, remove all dirty dishes, and bring the check. However, the amount of work done in the dining areas for non-commercial food service facilities will vary from one location to another. The hospital cafeteria works differently from the prison or school cafeteria.

Keep in mind that not all information discussed below will apply in each facility, but there is a wealth of information to use in making decisions about how your patrons will be served in your dining area. Each of these decisions is up to the manager or the supervisors who oversee the food service operations, but the information here provides suggestions for changing your facility, or it may convince you that operations are being handled correctly.

A mess hall works similar to cafeterias you would find in other situations. However, there are some distinct differences. The rank and marital status of military personnel determines how much they are charged to eat in the mess hall.

- Enlisted troops living in the barracks pay nothing.

- Married personnel are given a monthly subsistence allowance which is used to pay for meals.

- Duty Officers eat for free during their shifts.

There is a buffet style setup and plenty of food to choose from for each meal.

In boot camp there are assigned areas for people to sit. In regular mess halls there are areas set aside for junior enlisted troops, staff NCOs and officers.

Personnel working in the mess halls are responsible for maintaining a safe and clean environment. They take immediate action to rectify any abnormal situation.

Non-appropriated clubs on the bases are another option for military personnel. There are various clubs which are for troops of different ranks. For example:

- Enlisted - includes junior enlisted troops

- Staff NCO - includes senior enlisted and Non-Commissioned Officers

- Officer's Club - All Officer ranks are included, and they pay dues

At times civilians or government employees will eat in the mess hall. Some personnel on (TAD), Temporary Active Duty, will eat in the mess hall and they will have orders which state whether they are to pay for meals.

The amount charged to eat in the mess hall is far less than the cost for military personnel to eat at other establishments,; however, more are choosing to eat at McDonalds, Wendy's, Starbucks, and other businesses which are operating on the bases.

Mel Trimble, Retired Marine

Take Orders

In non-commercial cafeterias, orders are taken differently. In schools, there are usually limited menu options. A prison offers limited choices. In some facilities your patrons will have the opportunity to look at a printed menu or a menu board to make their decisions.

Even if there is no choice, your service line staff members should have a thorough knowledge of the dishes served because your patrons may have questions about them. Should a customer have a hard time making a decision, a staff member may recommend that they step back to let others go in front of them. This situation should be handled tactfully, but you don't want the line to be delayed. Most patrons will be on a short lunch break and need to be served as quickly as possible.

If your facility offers to prepare special orders or even cooked to order meals, you might want to write "checks" for their orders. This will allow you to have a record of what they want and will let them check out while the item is being prepared. Preprinted forms usually have consecutive numbers to help you track any misuse of checks. These consecutive numbers tell you when a check was written but not charged. For facilities that use written checks for any orders, train employees to keep checks even if they made mistakes.

Many facilities have patrons get the food items they want and then charge them before they are seated, simplifying checkout, and making it easier for individuals to return to work after their meal.

Facilities using written checks for any of their orders need a process to get these to the kitchen so the food will be prepared. Some use a turnstile that holds the check. Others have a spindle to hold the check until the cook gets it. There many possibilities, but it's important to decide which system to use and train all employees to use this system. One important thing is to have the staff member who prepares the check initial it in case the cook has any questions.

Also train the staff members not to tell the cook they are "in a hurry" for their orders. There is an order to how and when orders are prepared and the cooks know these procedures. At times, fast service will be necessary. So don't push the cooks when it isn't an emergency. Along these lines, the staff member should know how long a special order will take to get it to the patron as soon as possible.

Opening Responsibilities

Every food service facility has a list of opening duties. If certain staff members handle specific areas of the dining area, they can be responsible to prepare those areas for the shift. The opening responsibilities will vary depending on how the facility operates. Some possibilities include:

- Are there beverage service areas in the dining area?

- Are there condiments on each table or in a common area?

- If the facility uses cloth napkins and tablecloths, they need to be restocked before opening each day.

- All counters, walls, shelves, furniture, and equipment should be cleaned and polished each day before opening and cleaned as needed throughout the day. Also sweep, mop and/or vacuum as needed.

No matter how well an area is prepared for a shift, its better to have additional items close. A beverage area should have clean glasses, ice, and pitchers for beverages that are refilled for free. It is good to have some clean dishes in the dining area and certainly a supply of silverware. If you use linen table cloths and napkins, or even paper napkins, keep some near the dining area. Additional condiment containers, sugar, salt, and pepper should be conveniently located.

A staff member who is responsible to keep the dining area looking attractive and clean should wipe and straighten tables and chairs. Busers need to clean tables as soon as possible. Never hold up patrons because vacant tables are dirty. Will the bus person keep track of the dining area or should other staff members notify him when tables need to be bused?

Side-Work Responsibilities

Additional duties that food service staff members perform before or after rushes are called "side work." They can be time-consuming and should be shared among several employees. Some of this "side work" includes:

- **Sugar bowls** — Empty, clean, dry, and refill sugar bowls as needed. If you use sugar packets, be sure there are sufficient packets of sugar and artificial sweeteners on each table.

- **Salt and pepper shakers** — Wash salt and pepper shakers with a bottle brush. A toothpick can be used to unclog any holes in the lids. Clean salt and pepper shakers and allow to dry before refilling.

- **Miscellaneous containers** — Any containers refilled need to be cleaned and dried on a regular basis. Clean thoroughly on the inside and outside and then refill them as needed.

- **Condiment Bottles** — Clean condiment bottles and wipe the outside with a damp cloth. All caps need to be cleaned regularly. Schedule regular times to empty and clean all condiment containers to ensure they are clean and the contents are fit to consume.

- **Creamer Containers** — Does the facility use creamer containers? If so, they must be washed on a regular basis. Always cool these containers before refilling, using a container with a spout.

- **Ashtrays** — If smoking is permitted in your facility, clean all ashtrays on a regular basis, especially important during serving hours. During peak periods, ashtrays can be emptied and wiped clean with a damp rag as the table is bused.

- **Keep all foreign items out of ice used for drinks and food preparation.** Handle ice cubes with tongs or a large scoop and use specific containers to move ice. Handle ice the same way you would handle any other food item.

- **Crumbs and other debris should be removed from chairs.** Seats should be dusted each time the table is bused. The remaining parts of the chair should be dusted at least once a day.

- **Silver or stainless utensils need to be cleaned according to the manufacturer's directions.** If your facility has actual silverware, it needs to be cleaned following these directions when using a cream polish. The items should be rubbed with a soft cloth or a small brush over the surface and well into the embossed pattern of the silverware. Then the silver should be thoroughly washed, rinsed, and polished with a dry cloth to remove all traces of the silver cream.

Seasons Harvest knew people would enjoy their family recipes, so they wanted to share them. They were a small company that needed to expand to meet customer orders. They started with the barbecue sauce from grandfather's recipe. Heartland Barbecue Sauce was the first product. From those simple and uncomplicated beginning, the company has reproduced some of the really good flavors from those days. There were no shortcuts, additives, artificial colorings, or nifty processors, just fabulous know-how, fresh, and natural ingredients in recipes learned and handed down from one generation to another. Visit **www.seasonsharvest.com** or call 800-621-5075.

All soy sauces are not dark or black. White soy sauce is a golden condiment which was used for its characteristic flavor and functions. White soy sauce plays a surprising, unique role. It can be found at **www.Whitesoysauce.com** or call 559-740-8543. For all sorts of product details, visit **www.whitesoysauce.com/Products.html**.

Service Responsibilities

These are some of the responsibilities of the dining room staff members:

- Circulate and refill drinks.

- Clean an assigned area.

- Replenish food, dishes, trays, and silverware for each area.

- Restock food and equipment on steam tables.

- Carry food to tables for patrons as needed.

- Clean up any spills, broken dishes, glasses, and empty bottles.

- Refill beverage and ice dispensers before they are empty.

- Staff members working on a cafeteria line can use care in placing food on plate to look appetizing and even garnish with simple items.

- Is there a salad bar in the dining area? If so, there are various duties to set up and maintain it.

- Are dirty dishes removed for patrons or do they remove their trays? Either option requires people to remove dishes or to keep the disposal area clean during and after the shift. If staff members clean tables, they need to do so promptly.

- Scrape and stack dirty dishes. Take all tableware to the kitchen promptly to be cleaned.

- Even if patrons remove their trays, a staff member needs to wipe the table before the next patron sits down.

- Staff members might circulate with rolls and butter for patrons, depending on the policy for the facility.

- Clear and wipe tables and seats with a damp rag–not wet.

- Find all items requested by customers.

Closing Responsibilities

In some facilities "closing duties" may be difficult to perform. If your facility is open 24 hours a day, "end of the day duties" can be performed at a specific time each day. They include:

- **Stripping the tables** if you use table cloths.

- **Restocking all items** on the tables for the next day.

- **Clean and fill sugar bowls, salt and pepper shakers**, and condiment containers.

- **If the facility uses cloth napkins and tablecloths**, they need to be taken to the laundry facility to be cleaned.

Hosting

When new staff members are trained, they need to understand that every employee is a host in your facility, and they need to treat all patrons as guests, even when the dining area is busy. Each staff member needs to feel comfortable helping patrons.

Is there a delay in getting a special order for a customer? Is something causing a wait in the cafeteria line? Is there a disturbance in the dining area? Each of these problems needs to be addressed right away. Assure inconvenienced patrons that a staff member is working to fix the problem right away. It is better if the problem is fixed quickly so patrons do not have time to notice, but that is not always possible.

This is another time when staff members need to be able to answer questions about your menu items. In a cafeteria situation all staff members who are in the dining area and behind the serving area need to be able to answer questions about the items the facility serve. A way to make this easier is by placing promotional signs on the tables.

Nature of Hosting

Your staff members are the most visible representatives to your customers. Do they present the appearance and level of service that you want for the facility? If not, their image needs to change.

Staff members are a valuable resource to communicate the image of your facility. They can relay suggestions and complaints. These staff members need to show tact and sound judgment with customers.

The number of employees who work in the dining area will be determined by the size of the facility and the number of customers served on a daily basis.

Information a Host Needs

If the facility has one primary person as host, that person needs to understand policies and regulations that affect the business. This could include normal sanitation, handling, and safety regulations. The host will be more effective when they understand these details. They need to understand specifics which involve:

- Dealing with customers.

- Overseeing service in the dining area.

- Helping management execute business policies.

- Knowing the servers' duties.

- Distinguishing bus persons' duties.

Receiving Customers

Even in a non-commercial food service facility, a host can help expedite many responsibilities. Any host should be gracious to customers and make patrons feel welcome. Here are some tips to help the host do a thorough job and to be sure your patrons are served.

1. **Acknowledge patrons when they arrive.** The host can change locations depending on

the time of day. As your breakfast, lunch, or dinner rush begins, it may be best to be near the entrance. When these rushes begin to slow, it could be better to be near the exit. In between, the host should be in the dining area to ensure customer concerns are addressed.

2. **It is always good to say, "Good Morning," "Good Afternoon," or "Good Evening."** If possible, the patrons should be greeted by name.

3. **During especially busy times, it would be good to help people to the right size table**, meaning seating two at a table for two, not a table for four or six. In slow times doing so is not as critical.

4. **Try to have people sit in different areas so that each service person has a reasonable number of people to serve.** This is better than having all patrons in one area, since this makes it more difficult for a server to handle everyone in a timely manner. There will be times when all tables are full, but at other times patrons can be spaced more reasonably.

5. **It is important to clean tables quickly but especially during rush periods.** Customers should not have to wait to be seated or to push dirty dishes out of their way to eat. Bus staff and servers need to be conscientious about clearing tables.

6. **It never hurts to pull a chair out for patrons or to take their tray away after they are seated.** There are many "nice" things that make a great impression of patrons and only take a moment of the staff members' time.

Handle Customer Complaints

Every facility will have occasional complaints. An unusually high number of complaints is a reason to be concerned. Take each complaint seriously, but also keep a list of people who complain on a regular basis. Many hosts find that handling customer complaints can be the most difficult parts of their job. Your host needs to learn how to handle customers' concerns and complaints. Customers leave your facility with positive feelings when their concerns and complaints are handled properly, and they leave with negative feelings if no one addresses their complaints.

It is important to have a policy in place to help the host handle complaints properly. There should also be a policy that lists the conditions under which the host needs to summon the manager to handle customer complaints. It is good to establish complaint resolution procedures to make sure concerns are handled without the need to involve management each time there is a problem. Here are some tips for a host to handle complaints in a positive manner.

1. **Be positive and friendly when approaching the customer.** This should prevent most customers from becoming defensive.

2. **Get the full story from the customer.** Listen to what they have to say.

3. **Repeat the basic points to the customer** to be sure you understand the complaint.

4. **Apologize for the problem** and be sincere.

5. **Can the host offer a substitution for items** which were not satisfactory?

6. **If the facility has specific policies that apply to the patron's complaint**, the host might need to mention these to the patron.

7. **There are times when a complaint or request must be denied.** When this happens, the host needs to explain why it is denied.

8. **A sincere apology must be given** when the restaurant is to blame for the problem.

9. Many customers are actually helping you when they bring problems to your attention. **Thank them** for bringing issues to you.

10. When these customers return, make sure their visit is flawless.

11. Difficult and unreasonable complaints should be referred to the manager.

Dealing with Difficult Customers

Some customers are more difficult to deal with than others. It might be their attitude or because they have special needs. Your host must handle them in a tactful way and must use good judgment. Here are some of the difficult situations that your host needs to be prepared to handle.

1. **Early Customer** — Some patrons may be on their lunch hour early for some reason. If so, they will want to be served early. This can cause a problem if they arrive too early, and food is not prepared. They also may arrive before the food has been moved to the steam table or before the menu items are set up for the meal.

2. **Late Customer** — Some patrons may be running late and want to be served anyway. This is not a problem if food is left over. However, the food is not at its freshest after certain wait times. Help the patron understand that you will do everything possible to get the food they want, but they must be prepared if it is difficult or impossible because of their timing.

3. **Hurried Customer** — This can be difficult since everyone may be rushed and you need to be careful not to offend your other patrons who are in line and waiting for service.

4. **Friendly Customer** — Over time your staff members may become familiar with your regular customers. They still need to treat them courteously. Some staff members may fall into long conversations with familiar customers. They should never be rude but they need to avoid being overly familiar.

5. **Grouchy Customer** — Be cheerful even when customer is being grumpy. Avoid an argument and be pleasant. Try to stay calm and don't overreact to his complaints.

6. **Angry Customer** — Listen and apologize for the problem. Do every reasonable thing to resolve the problem. Express appreciation for the fact that the customer brought the problem to your attention.

7. **Trouble-making Customer** — The host still needs to be courteous, even to the troublemaker. It is critical not to be drawn into an argument. This is what the troublemaker wants. The host must be careful not to say anything that can be misconstrued. Troublemakers are good at twisting the words they hear. If a known troublemaker comes into the facility, it is good to warn staff members to avoid antagonizing the person.

8. **Tired Customer** — This can also apply to an overstressed or upset patron. Try to give the person a quiet or peaceful table. Do everything you can to make their visit stress free and as pleasant as possible.

The next couple of sections will focus on the three basic meals of the day.

Clerical Work

Many hosts handle a variety of clerical responsibilities in the facility. The size of the facility and the number of employees determine how many duties the host will be given. These clerical duties include:

- Checking menu boards and flyers for any errors. Make the needed changes.

- Helping with scheduling special groups. We will discuss this in more detail in Chapter 19 about catering opportunities.

- Assisting with recording employee work hours.

- Helping track items sold or consumed if sales analysis is handled manually.

- Giving any suggestions to the manager in writing concerning complaints from staff members and customers.

Breakfast Specific

Your patrons will be in a hurry to eat and get to work. Morning is a fascinating time of day. Some people are not "morning people," others must have their coffee before they face the day, and others just need a little something to keep them from getting hungry before lunch. We all want to start our day out right, and a positive and helpful attitude at breakfast can really help.

Most breakfast items taste best when prepared fresh and served at the right temperatures. Many breakfast items can be prepared in a short period of time and to the customer's preferences. It is also critical to serve these items quickly for the best taste possible.

Specific staff members should circulate through the dining room to be sure that the patrons have sufficient water and coffee with their meals. Butter and other condiments are important. These staff members can also have a successful system to get special orders to customers in an efficient manner.

Many items can be sold as an impulse buy as the customer pays the bill or are they are walking through the serving line. This creates a need for display cases. For a variety of display cases, you can visit **www.calmil.com/products.asp?ID=9** or call 800-321-9069, fax 760-630-5010, or e-mail **info@calmil.com**.

Lunch Specific

One of the real benefits I found when I worked in a local hospital was that I could eat in the cafeteria without being rushed. If I left the building, I also had to find another parking spot, usually a problem. Eating on the premises and getting a good quality meal at a reasonable price was more convenient.

There is a myriad of menu item possibilities for lunch. Some are easier, but it is good to have interesting options for your customers. Train your serving staff to keep the serving line moving without making the customers feel rushed. You may have some special orders during any meal, so train staff members to handle these promptly and correctly.

Dinner Specific

Dinner can be less rushed in many facilities. Many prisons only serve breakfast and dinner, but in facilities where the same people may eat lunch and dinner, plan to have sufficient variety between the two meals.

The amount of time that patrons have depends on the type of facility. Nursing homes will offer more time for residents, while employees will generally have shorter meal times. Each of these variables influences the way your staff needs to serve your patrons.

Some tips to offer better service at any meal of the day.

- Use warm plates for hot foods and chilled plates for cold foods.

- For special orders, find out how foods are to be cooked.

    1. Fried, scrambled, or boiled eggs and length of cooking time.

    2. Steaks or burgers–rare, medium, medium well, or well done.

    3. Toast–buttered or dry

- Refill water and tea glasses as needed. It is good to ask before refilling some beverages such as coffee in case it took some time to sweeten it to the customers' taste.

- Offer crackers, bread, Melba toast with salads and soup according to the facility policies.

Clear the Table

Staff members need to clear the table in a different manner in a non-commercial atmosphere. This can be decided for each facility, but below are some suggestions to incorporate into your policies.

1. **Remove dirty dishes as patrons finish.** Be careful not to rush patrons, but it is helpful to remove dirty dishes and speed up cleaning tables for the next patrons.

2. **Ask before removing any glasses or cups.** If the patron is finished, the items can be removed.

3. **A wonderful little effort is to be sure to leave the silverware on the table when plates and bowls are removed.** This is a simple thing and saves inconvenience for the patron and the serving staff.

4. **Water glasses need to stay on the table throughout the meal** and should be refilled as needed.

5. **If your facility allows smoking, keep an eye on ashtrays throughout the meal** and empty or replace as needed.

6. **If you offer tablecloths, there may be times when these need to be replaced**

during a meal. This can be necessary for extensive spills. When a tablecloth needs to be replaced, turn the soiled cloth halfway back, lay the clean cloth half open in front of the guest, and transfer the tableware to the clean cloth. The soiled cloth may then be drawn from the table and the clean one pulled smoothly into place. If this exchange of linen is accomplished skillfully, the guest need not be disturbed unduly during the procedure. Soiled linen should be properly disposed of immediately after it is removed from the table.

Courtesy to Departing Customers

Don't forget to be courteous when your patrons leave the facility. Some simple things that can make a difference include:

- "Have a nice day."

- "Hope we see you soon."

- "Take care."

- "Let us know if there is anything we can do to help you."

These are simple efforts, but when you take a minute to speak to and look the patron in the eye, it can mean much to them. It's a simple personal touch that shows you know they are there and took a minute to acknowledge that fact.

Supervise Service Employees

The main responsibility of the host or hostess is to provide hospitality. It is the host's job to make patrons feel welcome. Make sure they get good service. So that they feel that they are valued customers. This is different in a school or prison atmosphere where there is little choice, but it's still nice to show you care about them. All service employees need to be trained to be:

- Courteous.

- Cheerful.

- Interested in patrons.

The hosts also need to:

- Interpret facility policies and standards.

- Be a conduit between management and patrons.

Your host's effectiveness is important in helping patrons have a satisfying meal.

Inspect Dining Room

The facility host needs to oversee the appearance, cleanliness, and order in the dining area. The host needs to check on these specifics before the meals are served.

1. Verify order and cleanliness and fix any problems before mealtimes.

2. Adjust curtains, blinds, and shades to provide sufficient light and block direct sunlight.

3. Set the temperature and ventilation for the correct temperature.

4. Double check that tables are ready for the next meal.

5. See that service areas are stocked with appropriate and adequate supplies.

6. Be sure tent cards are on each table if your facility uses them.

7. If you have any special parties, arrange tables and areas before the patrons arrive.

8. Inspect all flowers and plants. Prune and water as needed.

Provide Adequate Service for Special Parties

These are the responsibilities of the host to provide adequate service for special events.

- **Schedule** enough wait staff, cooks, and bus people.

- **Prepare order** for additional linens and dishes as needed.

- **Give instructions** for how room and tables are to be set up.

- **Check** to be sure the room and tables are ready.

- **Verify** the correct number of seats and tables are prepared.

- **Instruct** each server on their responsibilities.

- **Kitchen staff needs to know what is required** and when to be prepared.

- **Notify** all staff members when items should be served.

- **Be sure the serving begins on time** and that used dishes are removed on time.

- **Have special items ready** for the event.

- **Provide additional supplies,** like water pitchers in certain areas. If there is to be a speaker, make sure all items to be supplied are available.

Large Party Policies

Here are some specific policies you may implement for special events.

- Which rooms and areas can be used for events?

- How many people can be accommodated?

- How few people can use special rooms and parties?

- Is there any flexibility with these numbers?

- At what times and on which days can special events be held?

- Is there a minimum price for a special event? Is there an average price?

- Can the facility provide flowers and other decorations?

- **Does the facility have a stage** and table for events?

- **Are electrical outlets available around the rooms?** Can you provide extension cords, slide projector, or overhead projector?

- **How are tips handled for large groups?**

- **Do the usual staff members work special parties,** or will different people work these events? How many people can be brought in for large events?

- **Can guests use office telephones?**

- **Are special menus or flyers provided as souvenirs?** Is there a charge?

- **Are items made to order** or are standard recipes the only option?

Special events are a wonderful way to increase the facility's revenue. Remember that all staff members need to be trained to handle all patrons with respect and courtesy. Without patrons, you have no facility. Handling a dining room effectively is key to making your patrons feel welcome and to encourage their continued and increased patronage.

Decorate Your Dining Room

The atmosphere of the facility will make a difference in the look and décor used in the facility. Below are some possibilities for your facility.

Art Marble Furniture brings a unique elegance to your non-commercial facility. Their granite top tables are affordable, durable, and lightweight. They offer a beautiful choice for your dining room. Check the selection of chairs and stools that were designed to complement granite top tables at **www.artmarblefurniture.com** or by calling 866-400-1688.

Art Marble Furniture dining options

Gasser Chair Company offers a variety of chair options. They were the first to design a unique style of aluminum framed seating specifically for the hospitality industry. The second generation of the Gasser family is still guided by the founders' principles and proudly continues the tradition of introducing new ideas and innovations. Visit their Web site at **www.gasserchair.com** or call 330-759-2234, fax 330-759-9844, or e-mail **sales@gasserchair.com**.

There is a solution for wobbly tables, and you can find it at **www.tableshox.com.** Wobbly tables are the number one customer complaint. Call 800-457-6454.

Hilden America offers fine table linens for food service facilities. Standard linens range from 100 percent Egyptian cotton products, 50/50 cotton and polyester, and 100 percent spun polyester. The full catalog is available on their Web site at **www.hildenamerica.com** or you can contact them by phone at 800-431-2514 or fax 434-572-4781. Some of these items would be ideal for upscale special events and catering events.

Booth from Gasser Chair Company

Royal Industries offers a wide variety of table and chair options. They also offer highchairs, children's chairs, and booster seats. For the full line of products, please visit **www.royalindustriesinc.com/source/furniture.php** or contact Royal Industries at 800-782-1200 or fax 800-321-3295.

Candle Lamp Company offers quality lighting options. These lamps enhance your atmosphere and the dining experience.

Hilden America Table Linens

The design team and staff will help you make the right purchase for your facility. Visit **www.candlelamp.com** or call 877- 526-7748 or fax 951-784-5801.

Royal Industries offers a wide variety of table and chair options

Another alternative is Dining by Candlelight which offers candles, holders, and lamps to fit any décor. Below are a few examples and more can be seen at their Web site **www.diningbycandlelight.com**. Food service customers like the ambiance created by candlelight. These candles and lamps offer various designs and options. Call 800-375-8023 or fax 905-273-6905.

Dining by Candlelight which offers candles, holders, and lamps.

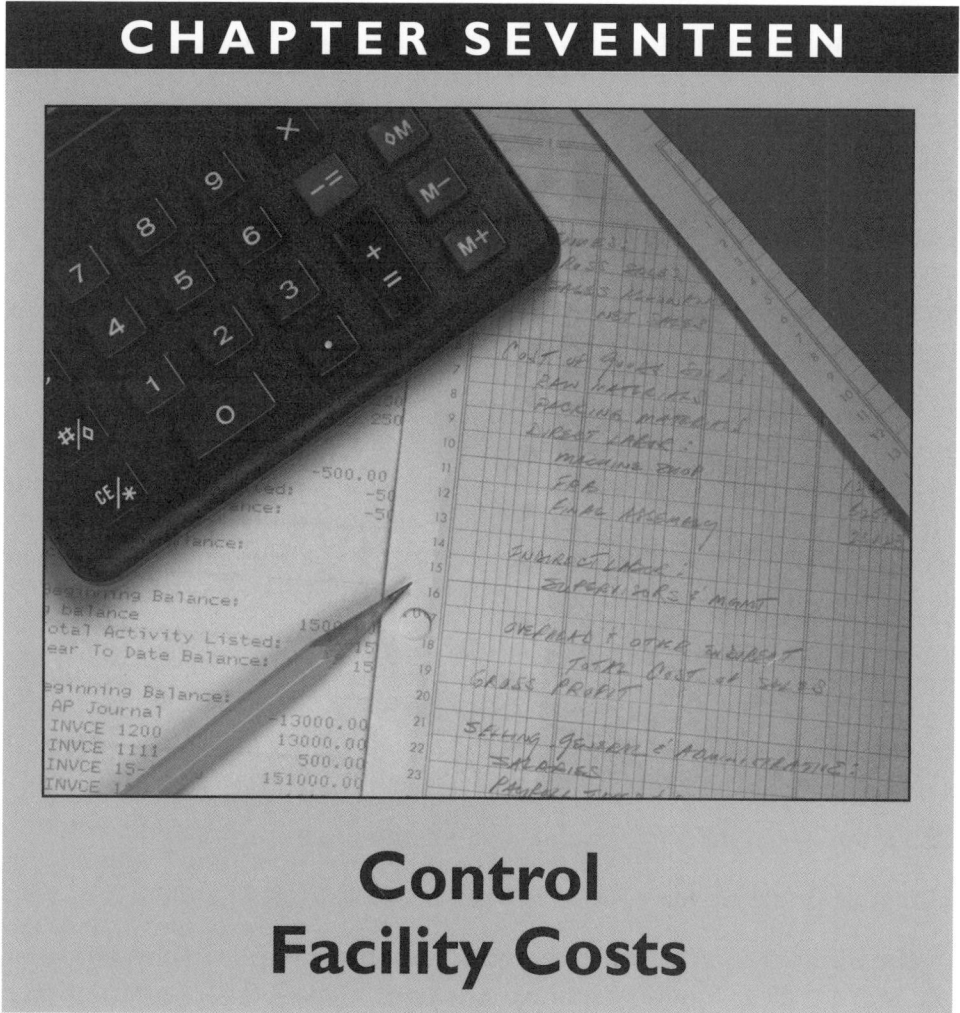

CHAPTER SEVENTEEN

Control
Facility Costs

In most businesses, expenses are up and profits are down. Even in a non-commercial environment, you need to break even and strive to make a profit. Keeping an eye on the bottom line and controlling costs are great ways to improve your profit margin. When you take the time to study your costs, they are easier to control. Keep an eye on these specific costs:

- New items
- Food
- Inventory

- Labor
- Marketing

You need to control these items from the beginning and train every employee to do so as well. Many people have to take a loss before they learn this lesson, but you can learn from other people's mistakes. There are also many managers who race around "putting out fires." A much more effective way to manage is to prevent these fires because they waste time and money.

Profits Do Not Guarantee Success

Don't assume that profits mean you are doing things the right way. There are instances when a business is making a profit, but you could increase that profit by controlling your costs. If you don't control costs, it will become obvious when your sales drop.

Budgeting

Budgeting will give you an idea of where the facility income needs to be spent. Sometimes it helps to have these numbers in front of us. These are a few forms to help a non-commercial food service manager project costs and then record actual expenses. It's good to track these numbers in one place to make it easier to spot problem area.

Controlling Costs Does Work

Controlling costs is something that you need to do all the time, not just when it's convenient. Doing so will give you the chance to serve the best quality product and make the most money possible for the facility.

The first step in controlling costs is to evaluate how and where you are spending your money. It can be difficult to spot the areas where you are wasting money. This is why the daily, weekly, and monthly reports are valuable. When you learn to use these, they will help you spot problem areas and to find solutions. It's important for you to know that controlling costs does not have anything to do with bookkeeping. These are the things you need to accomplish:

- Determine the efficiency of each area of the facility.

- Determine if your expenses are in your budget.

- Prevent fraud and theft by employees and customers.

- Establish short-term and long-terms goals for the business.

- Maximize your profit, do not minimize your losses.

In many cases the facility employees may see cost control measures as an indication that they are not trusted. Make it clear that a lack of trust is not the reason you are implementing these policies, but you should know that theft prevention and detection are the means of monitoring and controlling costs.

Atlantic Publishing, **www.atlantic-pub.com**, offers a couple of books to help you cut costs and to save money in the business. *2,001 Innovative Ways to Save Your Company Thousands by Reducing Cost: A Complete Guide to Creative Cost Cutting and Boosting Profits* is helpful for any manager who understands that every dollar counts. There is a wealth of practical advice on how to save money without sacrificing service and quality. Tips in the book are from business people who tried these techniques and proved that they work.

Another resource from Atlantic Publishing, **www.atlantic-pub.com**, is *The Food Service Manager's Guide to Creative Cost Cutting and Cost Control: Over 2,001 Innovative and Simple Ways to Save Your Food Service Operation Thousands by Reducing Expenses*. This book offers experiences from successful business operators who found practical ways to cut costs and save money. You will find these tips and suggestions are useful in the day-to-day operation of your facility to cut costs and increase the bottom line.

What Do the Numbers Mean?

There is a difference between controlling costs and reducing costs.

CONTROL COSTS	REDUCE COSTS
Compiling and interpreting the numbers about the facility income and the facility expenses.	Bringing costs within budgetary constraints.

Purchasing

An effective inventory system is necessary. Place and review all orders thoroughly. The facility will be charged for each item ordered, so be sure you need everything on the order since the bill will tie up your working capital. Over time you learn how much food is needed for unexpected rushes and sales.

- **Give yourself a cushion** between deliveries but keep it to a minimum.

- **Analyze non-perishable costs and usage** to determine if buying in larger volume is wise.

- **Establish an order system** and make adjustments based on your sales projections.

- **Have a complete list of all suppliers, order units, product detail, and prices.**

- **Renegotiate prices with vendors every six months.** Use your records to find the quantities you order and ask about volume discounts. This also lets the vendor know that you are watching the service, products, and prices on a regular basis.

Receiving

Double-check your orders when they arrive.

- Verify brand, grade, types, weight, amount, and prices.

- Note any problems with your order and get credit or return items.

Storage

Foods must be stored at correct temperatures with adequate ventilation to limit possible contamination.

- Expensive items should be in a safe place to prevent theft.

- Organize storage to make it easier to manage inventory.

Usage

Remove items from inventory when they are used. Keep an accurate record of your beginning inventory, how much was sold and the ending inventory.

Portioning

Set standards for the ingredient amounts to be used. This is especially critical with expensive ingredients, but it's important to track all items.

Order Taking

Enter each item in the computer or cash register when it is sold or given away. This keeps food usage records accurate. Everything needs to be entered, even drinks and snacks. Start this on the first day and enforce it. You aren't accusing staff of theft but rather are tracking your usage and profits. You can provide employee meals, snacks, and beverages, but track them.

Cash Receipts

Monitor sales-to-cost controls. Discrepancies must be investigated daily while staff memories are still fresh and reliable. The sales information is used to compile your financial record and to make future projections.

Bank Deposits/Accounts Payable

Verify deposit amounts. Every staff member needs to control costs. When creating your cost control plans, keep them simple and easy to explain. Be prepared for the questions from employees about why they have to control costs. Keep an open mind because the plan will need periodic changes and revisions. Keep these five key thoughts in mind for an effective cost-control strategy:

1. Always plan ahead.

2. The techniques need to be clearly written and explained.

3. Evaluate the program on a regular basis to determine what changes are needed and then be willing to make those changes.

4. The strategy must be enforced with your staff members.

5. Everyone needs to use the program, including managers.

Consider these questions:

1. Do you have the information needed?

2. Is the information brought to you in a timely manner?

3. Is the bookkeeping system easy to use and teach to employees?

4. Is the system saving more money than it costs to implement?

The last question is especially important. If the cost-controlling measures cost you more than you are saving, changes need to be made. Re-evaluate and make the needed changes.

What is Cost Control?

Cost control is a necessary part of any business. Without controlling costs, a workable budget and profit are almost impossible. Each non-commercial facility needs a budget for all operating expenses. Learning to control costs will enable you to get as much work and food as possible for each dollar that you spend. This will inevitably increase your profit and the quality of service which you offer to your customers.

Food Cost Controls

Let's start with controlling food costs. This was an area where my crew had problems and failing to control food costs can eat into your profit quickly. This is especially true depending on what items are being over used.

Food Purchasing

As a new manager, you may feel that you are ordering food all the time, but keep in mind that food service facilities must have a steady flow of food to serve their patrons. However, as we discussed in Chapters 6 and 7, you need to try not to over order and buy items needed for your menu plans. When you buy too much, the money is tied up while the items sit on the shelf. Here are some purchasing tips to help you:

- **Buy in Bulk** — You can usually save money if you buy items in bulk (larger quantities), but do not over order food that will spoil before it's used.

- **Name Brands versus Generic** — Buying "name brands" does not guarantee that you get a better quality of food. Your patrons won't usually notice a difference between name brands and other brands as long as the quality is the same.

- **Purchase Locally** — Fresh produce suppliers in your area may be able to supply fresher, cheaper, and better quality produce directly. This may not always work, but it can be a nice option that you should check into.

- **Menu Items with Similar Ingredients** — One way to make ordering easy and to enable you to buy bulk purchases is to plan menu choices that use similar items. A wide variety of items use pasta sauce. You can order a large quantity of pasta sauce and then prepare lasagna, pizza, spaghetti, or chicken cacciatore. Doing so will also make receipt and inventory easier.

- **Samples** — You may have the option of getting test samples of new products that you are considering for the facility so that you can make educated decisions about them. The availability may depend on your relationship with the sales representative at your distributor.

- **Effective Receiving** — In Chapter 7 we discussed having a person responsible for verifying your order items and amounts so that you are not cheated. It is possible that you are charged for more than you received or that prices are being adjusted without your knowledge.

- **Food List** — The inventory person in your facility should create a list of the items you need and items that are running low. Inventory and purchasing should be handled by a person who is most familiar with usage and spoilage.

- **Inventory Tracking** — In Chapter 3 we discussed computer programs for your facility. Some programs enable you to track your inventory and food usage. The inventory is calculated based on the items prepared and the amount consumed. This software can also make it simpler to place accurate food orders based on the inventory you have on hand. ChefTec software for inventory control, recipe, menu costing, and nutritional analysis is available at **www.atlantic-pub.com**, 800-814-1132.

- **www.foodprofile.com** — This site can be used to collect product information. It is part of the Efficient Foodservice Response (EFR) initiative. Distributors list their products on this site. There are more than 65,000 items listed with up-to-date information available, serving suggestions, nutritional information, cooking instructions, and lists of ingredients. EFR strives to improve the purchasing efficiency in the food service industry. You can learn more about the Efficient Foodservice Response at **www.efr-central.com.**

- **Running Out of Food** — You can waste money when you run out of the necessary supplies. When you order too little food, you have to run to the local grocery store to get the items you need. There is normally a big price difference when you buy items from the grocery store instead of your established suppliers. Effective menu planning and ordering can eliminate this problem.

In Chapter 8 we discussed ways to save money on food items without sacrificing quality. As a reminder, this can be done by using an item that was prepared in a different way. Tomatoes for salad or for sauce and peaches to be served as peach halves or for cobbler are two good examples. For one menu item you need whole tomatoes or peaches, for the other pieces would be acceptable and will save you money without sacrificing quality. Some simple and accepted ingredient substitutions are shown on the chart at the end of this chapter.

Buying Strategy to Reduce Food Costs

Have you developed a buying strategy? If not, you need to develop one–now! An effective buying plan is a quick and easy way to reduce food costs. Food cost cutting should start with your purchasing practices. Don't worry about making it overly complicated; just think it through and be straightforward. This simple five-point strategy will help you buy the right product, of the right quality, at the right price, at the right time, from the right source.

- **Purchasing must be done on a recurring basis, not just once or twice.** There is more to ordering than just calling in a random order. Two key things to remember are that you do not want to run out of food and you do not want to waste money and space by buying too much.

- **The items you buy, how you buy them, and when you buy must be based on the facility.** They should be based on the items you have on hand, the menus you have planned, and the preferences of your patrons.

- **When you develop the purchasing strategy, write it down on paper or save it to your computer's hard drive.** This will keep the details handy for you and will make it easier to train others to help you.

- **Look at the overall situation.** Keep in mind that your buying will be based on long-term fixed prices and on current prices.

Tighten Your Purchasing Belt

Here are some basic ways to "tighten" your food purchasing to help you cut costs.

- **Your purchasing strategy should be a step-by-step guide.** It takes time to create but will also save time and money over the long term. There are many things that a non-commercial food service manager must keep in mind at all times. A guide can help you keep track of the little things and eliminate the need to backtrack and duplicate your work.

- **How is your timing?** Timing is critical. A good way to ensure your timing is to subscribe to market reports. They will give you a chance to make buying and menu adjustments before prices go up. If you are planning something and the price of ingredients is about to increase dramatically, make the decision to buy the items early or change your menu plans.

- **Track Vendors** — Keep an eye on your vendors for the quality of their products, their reliability, consistency of products, delivery timing, flexibility, cleanliness, and pricing. Never be afraid to talk with your vendors about your concerns and questions. They should be available to address your issues and always keep an eye on the prices they are charging. Are price increases accurate? If the price is lowered, are you getting the same quality product?

Purchasing Ideas

These are some tips to cut costs:

1. **Barter Clubs** — These clubs let you trade some items for other items. Verify they freshness of any items when you use this system. Some sites include: **www.barterwww.com** and **www.netlabs.net/biz/index.htm.**

2. **Bread Baskets** — This may not be an issue with your non-commercial facility, but if you do offer free bread, these tips may help. Ask before offering free bread and then offer less to cut back on waste.

3. **Condiments** — Use refillable dispensers instead of individual packets.

4. **Cost-Watch Web site** — This Web site has regional reports to compare your expenses and food costs **www.cost-watch.com.**

5. **Inexpensive Fish** — There are some lower-priced fish that your customers may like including Alaskan halibut, farm-raised salmon, fresh-water perch, mahi-mahi, shark, skate, and tilapia. Make sure fish is fresh.

6. **Prepared Items** — In Chapter 15 we discussed prepared food options. Although the food costs more, you can decrease your labor costs. You can figure how many labor hours are spent preparing the items and determine if the prepared food would be cost-effective for your facility.

7. **Shelled Eggs** — If you use more than three cases a week, they can be an alternative. They reduce the cardboard to be thrown away, and you can reuse the buckets they are shipped in.

Buy Quality

The quality of your food sets the tone for the entire facility. Never sacrifice quality to save money because doing so can be an expensive mistake. Here are some tips to help you maintain quality in the non-commercial facility.

- **Insist on Quality** — Purchase quality products from the beginning.

- **Buy Appropriate Products** — Buy the right product for the items you will prepare. Suitable ingredients create better quality products.

- **Quality throughout the Facility** — All aspects of the facility need to offer quality to your patrons.

- **Do Not Compromise** — Don't be taken in by poor quality offers and products just to save some money. This is a common trap that managers can fall into if they aren't careful.

- **Most Expensive is not always the Best** — Don't assume that the expensive item is the best. It's better to investigate the products available.

- **Double Check Vendors** — It is acceptable to ask for samples from vendors whom you are considering working with in the future. They can also supply quality specifications for the items they offer to help you to avoid misunderstandings.

Reduce Purchasing Costs

Your purchasing person or department is the key to cutting costs because conscientious buying practices give you the best chance of getting quality products at the best cost. These tips will help you make the most of your purchasing dollars.

- **Market Trends** — Stay current with the current market trends. There is a wealth of resources to help you know the current and projected costs for many food items. Use this information to negotiate with your vendors. It will show them that you are serious about your costs and that you keep up with the current prices.

- **New Ideas** — Keep an open mind about new ideas, new products, and alternative possibilities. Play potential vendors against one another for the best prices and ask for promotional offers and discounts.

- **"Opportunity Buys"** — At times your vendor will offer special buys and overstock merchandise for a special price. These specials can save you money. Just verify the freshness and expiration dates on the items.

- **Cooperative Buying** — This is a situation where several businesses pool their buying power to get better terms and prices. I would suggest that you have a solid agreement in writing, signed by everyone involved before entering into this sort of arrangement.

- **Purchase Different Size Units** — Some items can be purchased in larger quantities without being concerned about waste and spoilage.

- **Place Multiple Orders** — When you purchase multiple items from one vendor, more discounts will be available to you and you will save some delivery expenses. Ask your vendor what advantages they can offer if you order more from them.

The "Want Sheet" can be a great asset when the food order is compiled. Train all employees to list items that they want or need and then use the list when the food order is put together. The manager or purchasing person can opt not to purchase any items, but this is an organized way for employees to notify you of items that were used.

Inventory Levels Affect Cash Flow

Maintaining an inventory can be a balancing act. You need enough to prepare your menu items without running out of ingredients, but you don't want to buy too much and waste money. When you plan your menus, remember that the more inventory items there are to manage, the harder it is to control. Here are some tips to help you maintain your inventory:

- **Know Your Customers** — The better you learn the customer habits in your facility, the easier it is to manage your inventory and to plan successfully.

- **Keep Inventory at Minimal Levels** — Do not keep it so low that you run out of items. Your accuracy will improve over time. The frequency of your food deliveries and projected facility sales will determine how much you need to order each time.

- **Special Promotions** — When you discover that you over ordered or under ordered, you can make adjustments in your menus and planned menu items. This is easier when you do frequent inventory checks.

- **Weekly Deliveries** — As mentioned above, learn to work food orders around the scheduled deliveries.

Reduce Pilferage

Pilferage can make a big dent in facility profits. The amount of security needed will depend on the size of the facility. Below are some suggestions to increase security and limit opportunities for theft.

- **Storeroom Keys** — Locks and combinations should be changed on a regular basis. All keys need to stay in the facility, with limited access.

- **Screens and Locked Cabinets** — Roll down screens can be a great way to make an area inaccessible. Locked cabinets can be used to protect certain hazardous, expensive items.

- **Limited Access** — Limit the number of staff members who have access to storage areas and money vaults. You can also set specific times for food to be issued to limit access to the storage areas.

- **Locked Cooler Storage** — Refrigerators and walk-in coolers should have working locks. A lockable shelf or unit in the refrigerator is good for expensive items.

There are several forms to help you track food usage (shown at the end of this chapter). These can help you pinpoint problems or potential problems.

- **Sign Out Sheet** — This form will track what is used, how much was used, and which employee issued the items.

- **Daily Preparation Form** — This form tracks food items, how much of the items were used, and how much you had at the beginning of the shift.

- **Minimum Amount Needed Form** — This form is a great asset when you work on a food order. It tracks individual food items and the amount needed for each day.

- **Daily Yield Form** — The form tracks each food item and how many portions you will get from the items used.

Control Labor Costs

I have talked to many people who think the only way to cut labor costs is to cut hours and terminate people. This is an immediate solution, but is not a long-term answer as it will reduce productivity, decrease quality and service, and produce high turnover. High quality employees will not stick around if they see you indiscriminately let people go when costs are out of control. Being involved in the daily management of the facility will help you control labor costs.

Scheduling

A key way to control labor costs is through effective scheduling. A badly written or unused schedule can cost money. Qualified managers can overcome a bad schedule, but it will cause hard feelings with the staff members. The person who creates the schedule needs to give consideration to the staff members and to review past sales to create an accurate sales projection before creating a schedule. How do you determine the number of staff members needed if you don't have any idea how business will be done?

There are all sorts of variables you can use in the creation of a schedule. One tactic I used that bridged the rough areas was having a couple of people in "short shifts" who came in just before rush and who could stay longer if needed. I always had people who wanted to work a few short shifts.

Remember that it will take some time to get familiar with a new facility and with the trends with the patrons and the staff members. Each of these things affects your scheduling and you will become familiar with all of these elements.

The form shown at the end of this chapter will help you compute the payroll costs for each day. If you enter the employees, hours, and payroll amounts and find you are spending too much, you need to make scheduling adjustments. This form can be especially useful when beginning to write schedules or if you are implementing changes. The form summarizes the employees, their position, pay, and the labor hours you plan to use.

Computer Software to Improve Scheduling

Computer software can give you a huge advantage in scheduling and tracking labor costs. There are programs that track time, attendance, and payroll to save you money and improve employee satisfaction and retention. The software ranges from a few hundred to several thousand dollars. Here are some scheduling programs available.

1. Visit Asgard Systems at **www.asgardsystems.com**.

2. Staff Trak at **www.staftrak.com**.

3. Madrigal Soft Tools at **www.madrigalsoft.com**.

4. **www.restaurantresults.com** for a listing of other software.

It is better to learn how to schedule properly instead of cutting wages. During your busiest times, you need your best people. Knowing the strengths and weaknesses of your staff members will help you to create the most effective schedules. People can start at different times, end at different hours, and the shifts can overlap if needed.

- **Determine labor cost per shift** — After you write the schedule, multiply employee hours by their hourly wage to get the labor cost for each shift. Use your projected sales figures and divide that amount into your labor dollars to find the labor percentage. If the resulting percentage is too high, you need to lower labor costs or raise sales.

- **Others can write schedules** — The assistant manager and/or shift runners should help write schedules. It will be a learning experience and can help them understand about maintaining costs. You have to be able to count on team leaders to maintain costs, or they should be replaced.

- **Tips** — The people who write schedules need to remember to: give each employee one or two days off per week, avoid employee burnout from over-scheduling, schedule alternate employees in case of emergencies, schedule one manager or leader for each shift and assign each employee enough hours to make it worth their while to come in.

On-Call Schedule

I implemented this for Friday and Saturday nights. It was difficult with all college students for employees, but it worked. One or two employees would be "on call," and I would only call if I was slammed. (Slammed means being too busy to handle the rush without additional personnel.) We had special college events and local events that packed the hotels, and it was impossible to plan for some of those things. Having someone on call gave me more peace of mind and allowed me to send a driver home when it slowed down without being concerned that we would be busy later. I had to call people in only a few times.

Productivity

Making and keeping an efficient staff productive is a huge help in maintaining costs and being able to give superior customer service. Here are some ideas for increasing efficiency.

- **Simple** — Buy additional trash cans and place throughout the facility.
- **Complex** — Commission work-motion studies to evaluate the facility.
- **Free** — Overcome poor work habits and retrain staff members.
- **Costly** — Remodel the entire kitchen and improve layout.
- **Physical** — Build a facility with no steps.
- **Psychological** — Create an "ownership" attitude among your employees.

At times you have to invest in the staff and their training. Well-trained, happy employees are more productive and less prone to leave, and they have less stress. It can be as easy as making layout changes to the facility or purchasing equipment that makes the work easier.

Productive People

One of the best ways to make your employees more "cost-effective" is to get them to work harder. When they do more work in the same or fewer hours, the facility saves money. Another way is to get the same amount of work with fewer employees. The last way is to get the same amount of work from fewer employees in less time. Following are some suggestions to make this work.

- **Make It Important** — Making the facility a success needs to be important to everyone. Help employees see how their performance affects customer satisfaction and the overall success of the facility.
- **Don't Waste Time** — Employees should clock in and get to work as soon as they arrive. If you have a manual time card system, a manager needs to initial time cards right away. At the end of the shift, have employees clock out on time. These bits of time will add up.
- **Ask for Input** — Your employees can be a valuable source of suggestions on how to make the job better and easier.
- **Follow-Up** — Acknowledge your employees' contributions and let them know their input is important to you.
- **Be Clear and Concise** — Give thorough details to staff members. Detailed and written job descriptions can eliminate most problems and questions. The description is valuable

when employees are trained or retrained.

- **Clear Standards** — Explain facility standards to employees. It is good to encourage employees to look for more efficient ways to do a job, but be clear that they must maintain the same quality standards.

- **Suggestions for Improvement** — Offer suggestions to individual employees on ways to do their job better. When they do, reward them.

- **Right Person for the Job** — You will get more out of each employee when you match the right person with the right job. Each task should be assigned to the lowest paid employee who is able to do it well.

- **Don't Keep It to Yourself** — Share information. Be helpful to your staff. Orientation for new employees and periodic staff meetings are a great time to share information.

- **Drive It Home** — When you explain things to staff members, use handouts, diagrams, bulletin boards, and Web pages to explain details.

- **Encourage** — Do not discourage self-motivated employees. You may need to offer some specific guidance or harness their enthusiasm.

- **Reward Employees** — Additional pay is not the only way to reward employees. Ask local businesses to offer gifts that you can use for staff member rewards.

- **Be Involved** — Many managers feel that they can sit in their office and shuffle papers. Effective managers are involved in the daily operations and work with their employees. I learned long ago that your employees work better when they respect their manager. Work alongside them, earn their respect, and they will work harder for you.

- **Reduce Stress** — Keep in mind that 60 percent of employee burnout is emotional and 40 percent is physical. Lower their stress and they can remain productive.

- **Cross-Train** — Staff members who can work in more than one area are more valuable to you. You can help them avoid burnout by offering some diversity in their job duties.

- **Follow-Up** — Be sure that employees continue to improve. When they receive additional training, be sure they use the new training.

Help Employees Recharge

Employees should have a rest area or break room. It doesn't need to be elaborate, but it should be a separate room. Here are some additional ideas to help employees recharge.

- **Music in Work Areas** — Appropriate music played at a reasonable volume will increase productivity and reduce stress.

- **Employee Restrooms** — If possible, give employees a restroom separate from the public.

- **Covered Outdoor Area** — Employees can be recharged when they step outside for their break. Give them a covered area to block the sun or bad weather.

Streamline Tasks

Is there a way for your employees to do their job better? The following are some areas to keep in mind when looking to improve efficiency.

- **Be flexible** — There is more than one right way to do things.

- **Replace bad habits** — easier than breaking bad habits.

- **One thing at a time** — Do not try to fix everything at once. Focus on one or two things at once and do them right.

- **First things first** — Find a couple of positive things to begin and to encourage the staff members to work as a team.

- **Review your menu** — Take a look at individual menu items to determine whether there are enough sales to justify orders, inventories, preparations, and labor costs. Can the recipe be altered to make it easier? Could you purchase some items already prepared to save some work?

- **Less service** — Many non-commercial facilities require less personal service. Evaluate your facility to see if you need more or fewer service personnel. But do not sacrifice quality to save money.

Productive Layout and Design

The layout that you use in the facility can make a big difference in labor costs. Take a serious look at your food preparation area. Does the layout make it easy to work? Is there an easy flow between food storage, preparation, and serving areas? Do your staff members have to backtrack to get their work done?

The facility layout can make work easier or more difficult for staff members. I've been in kitchens where people were literally falling over one another, a safety and productivity nightmare. Employees should be able to get the supplies they need and do their jobs without difficulties. If you have specialty items that require special equipment, are the necessary items stored close to the preparation area to save time?

Remember that wasted movement cost time and labor dollars. Here are some tips to help you create a more productive work area.

- **Rearrange the Area** — Employees can work faster when fewer steps are required.

- **Evaluate Walkways and Hallways** — Allow room to walk without bumping into one another. Too little room can be a safety issue.

- **Watch Where They Walk** — Is there an easier way to move or arrange the area to make their work easier?

- **Eliminate Unnecessary Movements** — These unnecessary movements can include bending, stooping, and reaching for common items they need each day. Sometimes the solution is as simple as a new shelf or table.

You can improve productivity by creating three different types of storage spaces: active, backup and long-term. This is how they work:

- **Active Storage is accessed throughout each day** and needs to be located near the main work area.

- **Backup Storage is where you store bulk items** that will be used throughout the week. It can be farther away from the main work area.

- Long-Term Storage is for items used on rare occasions. It should be in the least accessible area of the work space.

If busy non-commercial food service facilities have many people in small spaces where too much work has to be done, some rearranging can make the flow of work easier and increase productivity.

- **Aisles** — Aisles need to be at least 30" wide or wide enough for any carts that you use. If your facility is busy, you might need 48" aisles.

- **In and Out** — When you install a door for kitchen access, they should be two feet apart. They should swing one way with a clear and unbreakable window in each door. Mark them with "In" and "Out" signs easy to see and read. Each door should be at least 42" wide. Another less attractive option is two swinging doors at least 44" wide total.

Kitchen Design

If possible, hire consultants to organize the kitchen. They will evaluate the budget, food preparation needs, safety issue, and space limitations. These limitations are addressed without sacrificing quality, productivity, or the sanity of your staff. To make these assessments, you need a clear understanding of the menu items served. This will include the storage space, preparation space, and supplies that each item requires.

You can make the kitchen more productive by dividing it into self-contained workstations. In each of these areas, you should have the tools, ingredients, equipment, and supplies close for the items to be prepared.

A simple way to increase productivity and decrease unnecessary steps is to buy additional trash containers and place them throughout the facility. You can also use different containers if you recycle your refuse.

While you are planning the work space and traffic areas, be sure to leave ample open space. Staff members will need to walk past each other, carts will be rolled around, shelves may be moved, buckets will be rolled around, and trays will be lifted and moved. There must be safe spaces for all of these activities.

Labor-Saving Equipment

Some menu items require limited preparation, but others are more involved. In most phases of the preparation process, there are tools and pieces of equipment to make the job easier and faster. These are some useful resources and ideas to help you.

- **Cost** — Consider the amount of labor hours to be saved over the long term when you consider the cost of specific equipment.

- **Will it last?** — Evaluate the costs to maintain a piece of equipment and the expected lifespan of the equipment.

- **Test it first** — Always test equipment before making the purchase. Many vendors have test kitchens where you can test the items. If you are talking with a distributor who will not let you test the equipment, reconsider dealing with them.

- **Do you need the features?** — Be sure to buy what you need without overbuying. If you don't need extra features, then buy the basic model.

- **Train employees** — Offer complete training for your staff members on any new equipment. Remember that your sales representative should be there to help you.

- **Is it easy to clean?** — You want to know how much time is needed to clean and maintain the equipment before making a final decision.

Kitchen Equipment

There are many ways to save money inside the kitchen. Computerized ovens can be programmed to bake and hold your items. A conveyor belt dishwashing unit will carry dishes from the serving area to the dish room. These are only two examples of equipment to save labor hours each day. Here are some more equipment suggestions that make work easier for the facility.

- Equipment that is easy to move, clean, and operate.

- Buy quality tools, equipment, and materials.

- Select easy-to-use equipment.

Cooking Equipment

Some of the options to cook faster include microwave, conveyor, convection, and impingement (pressured hot air) ovens. Get the best equipment for your needs. Not all items should be cooked quicker, so you may consider a combination oven. These ovens provide the speed of microwaves without the taste and appearance negatives associated with microwave cooking. See Chapter 9 for more details on equipment.

More Cooking-Equipment Tips

Here are some additional cooking tips to save the facility money.

- **Use timers and buzzers** to leave employees free to work rather than timing ovens.

- **Accurate thermometers** can increase staff productivity and food safety.

- **Portion control dispensers and scales** are valuable in maintaining costs.

- **Use a grease collector.** Clean oil is piped to your fryers and used grease is piped out for recycling. Or you can use an "oil-free" fryer that uses infrared technology or flash heat to activate oil in frozen and pre-browned foods.

Other Cooking Innovations

Don't wrap and rewrap pans. Use see-through lids for steam-table pans from Cambro, **www.cambro.com**. This saves time and money for the facility. You can also save a lot of time using pan liners to reduce dish soaking and scrubbing. DayMark Safety Systems offers wide variety of sizes. Plus, leftovers can store, chill and reheat in the same liner. a For more information call 800-847-0101 or visit **www.daymarksafety.com**.

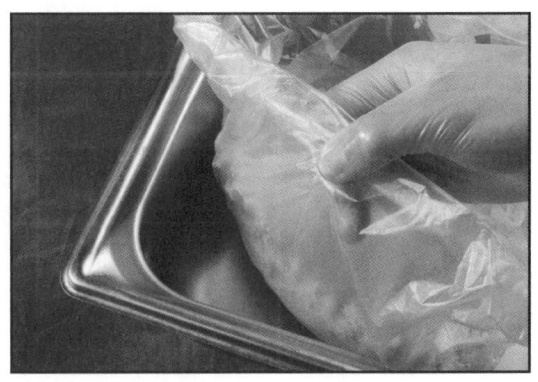

Tired of waiting for the pot to fill with water? Wall-mounted flow fillers are available from Fisher at **www.fisher-mfg.com** or call 800-421-6162.

Need a sharp edge fast? Chef's Choice knife sharpener can hone a razor-sharp edge in 60 seconds and re-sharpen knives in less than 15 seconds. Visit the Edgecraft Web site at **www.edgecraft.com.**

Never scrape off a steam-table pan label again. Buy wash-off labels from DayMark Food Safety Systems 800-847-010, **www.dissolveaway.com**.

Use an air door to separate hot and cold areas, preserving energy and improving traffic flow. Visit Air Door World at **www.airdoorworld.com** for more information.

Labor-Saving Equipment Resources

Food service equipment manufacturers are learning that their clients want to cut costs. They are constantly adding new models to save labor costs, floor space, energy, and service costs. This is a list of some commercial cooking equipment manufacturers to help you save you money. Check with your local distributor about which brands are used in your community.

Check the items available that suit your budget. Below is a list of manufacturers which offers articles, reviews, and other resources to help you in your search for the right equipment.

- Food Service Central — **www.foodservicecentral.com.**

- Gas Foodservice Equipment Network — **www.gfen.org/content/foodservice/ equipment.html.**

- Supply and Equipment Food Service Alliance — **www.sefa.com.**

- Food Service Equipment Reports — **www.fermag.com.**

- FoodService.com — **www.foodservice.com.**

- Food Service Equipment Magazine — **www.fesmag.com.**

- ESelNet Food Service (used equipment) — **www.eselnet.com.**

- Kitchen-Today (small equipment, tools) — **www.kitchens-today.com.**

Item	Budgeted	%	Actual	%
SALES				
Food				
Liquor				
TOTAL SALES				
MATERIALS				
Food Costs				
Liquor Costs				
Wine Costs				
TOTAL COSTS				
GROSS PROFIT				
LABOR				
Manager Salary				
Employee				
Overtime				
TOTAL LABOR COSTS				
Controller Oper. Costs				
China & Utensils				
Glassware				
Kitchen Supplies				
Dining Room Supplies				
Uniforms				
Laundry/Linen				
Services				
Trash Pick-Up				
Laundry Cleaning				
Protection				
Freight				
Accounting				
Maintenance				
Payroll				

PERIOD: _____ **DATE:** _____

PREPARED BY: _____

Item Description	Budget	Actual	% of Budget
Meals Served			
Income			
Food Expense			
Labor Expense			
Other Expenses (List below)			
Total Expenses			
PROFIT			

Ingredient

Recipe Substitutions

Ingredient	Recipe Substitutions
1 tsp allspice	$1/2$ tsp cinnamon + $1/2$ tsp ground cloves
1 tsp baking powder	$1/4$ tsp baking soda + $1/2$ tsp cream of tartar + $1/4$ tsp cornstarch, or $1/3$ tsp baking soda + $1/2$ tsp cream of tartar
1 cup bread crumbs	$2/3$ cup all-purpose flour
1 cup butter	1 cup margarine, or 1 cup shortening + $1/2$ tsp salt, or $7/8$ cup cooking oil + $1/2$ tsp salt
1 cup buttermilk	1 Tbsp vinegar or lemon juice + enough milk (or plain yogurt) to make 1 cup; let stand 5 minutes
1 cup catsup	1 cup tomato sauce + $1/2$ cup sugar + 2 Tbsp vinegar
1 oz chocolate, unsweetened	3 Tbsp unsweetened cocoa + 1 Tbsp oil
$1/4$ cup cocoa	1 ounce (square) chocolate (decrease fat called for in recipe by $1/2$ Tbsp)
1 cup cornmeal (self-rising)	$7/8$ cup plain cornmeal + $1 1/2$ Tbsp baking powder + $1/2$ tsp salt
1 Tbsp cornstarch	2 Tbsp all-purpose flour, or 2 Tbsp granulated tapioca
1 cup corn syrup	$3/4$ cup sugar + $1/4$ cup water or 1 cup honey
1 cup cream, half and half	$7/8$ cup milk + $1 1/2$ Tbsp melted butter
1 cup cream, heavy	$3/4$ cup milk + $2 1/2$ Tbsp fat
$1/2$ tsp cream of tartar	$1 1/2$ tsp lemon juice or vinegar
1 large egg, whole	4 Tbsp beaten egg, or 2 yolks + 1 Tbsp water
1 egg yolk	2 Tbsp sifted, dry egg yolk powder + 2 tsp water, or $1 1/3$ Tbsp thawed frozen egg yolk
1 cup flour, all-purpose	1 cup + 2 Tbsp cake flour, or $1/2$ cup all-purpose flour + $1/2$ cup whole-wheat flour, or 1 cup rolled oats, $1/2$ cup all-purpose flour + $1/2$ cup bran, or $5/8$ cup potato flour, or $7/8$ cup cornmeal, or $1 1/4$ cups rye flour
1 Tbsp flour, all-purpose (as thickener)	$1/2$ Tbsp cornstarch, potato starch or arrowroot, or 2 tsp quick-cooking tapioca
1 cup flour, self-rising	1 cup all-purpose flour + $1 1/4$ tsp baking powder + $1/4$ tsp salt
Flour, whole wheat (any amount)	Substitute whole wheat flour for $1/4$ to $1/2$ of the white flour called for

Ingredient

Recipe Substitutions

1 medium clove garlic	$^1/_8$ tsp garlic powder or instant minced garlic, or $^1/_2$ to 1 tsp garlic salt (reduce amount of salt called for in recipe)
3-ounce package gelatin, flavored	1 Tbsp plain gelatin and 2 cups fruit juice
1 Tbsp ginger, fresh, minced	$^1/_4$ tsp ground ginger
1 Tbsp herbs, fresh	1 tsp whole dried, or $^1/_4$ tsp ground
1 cup honey	$1^1/_4$ cups granulated sugar + $^1/_4$ cup liquid
1 Tbsp horseradish, fresh, grated	2 Tbsp prepared horseradish
1 tsp lemon juice	$^1/_2$ tsp vinegar
2 cups maple syrup	2 cups sugar and 1 cup water, bring to clear boil; take off heat; add $^1/_2$ tsp maple flavoring
1 cup milk, skim	$^1/_3$ cup instant nonfat dry milk + water to make 1 cup, or $^1/_2$ cup evaporated skim milk + $^1/_2$ cup water
1 cup milk, whole	2 tsp melted butter + enough skim milk to make 1 cup, or $^1/_2$ cup evaporated milk + $^1/_2$ cup water, or 1 cup soy milk, or $^1/_3$ cup nonfat dry milk + water to make 1 cup + 1 Tbsp fat
1 can milk, sweetened condensed	Heat the following ingredients until sugar and butter are dissolved: $^1/_3$ cup and 2 Tbsp evaporated milk + 1 cup sugar + 3 Tbsp butter or margarine
1 small onion	1 tsp onion powder, or 1 Tbsp instant minced onion
1 tsp pumpkin pie spice	$^1/_2$ tsp cinnamon, $^1/_4$ tsp ginger, $^1/_8$ tsp allspice, and $^1/_8$ tsp nutmeg
1 cup sour cream	1 cup yogurt or $^1/_3$ cup butter + $^3/_4$ cup buttermilk
4 Tbsp soy sauce	3 Tbsp Worcestershire sauce + 1 Tbsp water
1 cup sugar, granulated	1 cup packed brown sugar, or $1^3/_4$ cups powdered sugar (do not substitute in baking), or $1^1/_2$ cups corn syrup (reduce liquid in recipe by $^1/_2$ cup), or 1 cup honey (reduce liquid in recipe by $^1/_4$ to $^1/_3$ cup)
1 cup tomato juice	$^1/_2$ cup tomato sauce + $^1/_2$ cup water + 1 dash salt
1 cup tomato puree	$^1/_2$ cup tomato paste + $^1/_2$ cup water
1 Tbsp yeast, dry active	1 package ($^1/_4$ oz) active dry yeast, or 1 cake compressed yeast
1 cup yogurt, plain	1 cup buttermilk, or 1 cup sour milk

ITEM	EMPLOYEE	APPROVED	ORDERED ON	RECEIVED

ITEM	DATE	AMOUNT/WT.	EMPLOYEE

ITEM	MINIMUM AMOUNT	AMOUNT DEF./ORD.	BEGINNING AMOUNT	AMOUNT PREPPED	STARTING TOTAL

ITEM	MON	TUES	WED	THURS	FRI	SAT	SUN

ITEM	STARTING WEIGHT (OZ.)	# OF PORTIONS	TOTAL PORTION WEIGHT (OZ.)	YIELD %	PREP/ COOK

DATE PREPARED: _____ WEEK OF: _____

PREPARED BY: _____

HOURLY EMPLOYEES

EMPLOYEE NAME	POSITION	PAY RATE	HOURS	OVERTIME	TOTAL EARNED
				TOTAL	

Allowance for Social Security, Medicare, Federal & State Unemployment Taxes:

Total Hourly Wages _____ x Rate _____ = _____

EMPLOYEE MEALS & TOTALS

Estimated Number of Meals _____ Cost _____ **Total Cost of Meals** _____

TOTAL (Wages & Meals) _____

Estimated Sales for Week _____

Estimated Payroll Cost Percentage for Week _____

Payroll Cost Percentage Goal _____

CHAPTER EIGHTEEN

Marketing and Promotion

We discussed a number of ways to promote your facility in Chapter 10. Those ideas combined with the information in this chapter will help you find ways to promote the facility to potential and existing customers.

Advertising and marketing are not the same. Marketing is more involved than advertising and may be needed in many non-commercial food service facilities. Cafeterias located in businesses, hospitals, military installations, and nursing homes can bring in more revenue by marketing to increase business and revenue. When managers decide to market the business, they need to know who their customers are and what their customers want.

Finding the answers to these questions will enable them to meet the needs of more potential customers. This is marketing. Traditional marketing is made up of four parts: product or service, promotion, price, and place.

- **Product** — or service being sold includes all features of the good or service, packaging of the product, brand name of the product, and the total package.

- **Promotion** — This includes communicating the necessary information to potential customers and being able to convince them to make a purchase.

- **Price** — Will customers think the price is fair, too high, or too low? The price will be determined by the people you are targeting. Is the company trying to survive or to lead the market? Many companies that want to lead the market need to drop their prices to gain enough business to lead the market. On the other hand, many people believe that a high price is a sign of high quality. In this case, price is part of the image. The facility operations will dictate the minimum price charged, but the market will determine the maximum charged.

- **Place** — How is the product or service brought to the customer? A great product or service can easily fail with a bad location. In turn, a mediocre product can succeed with the right location.

Almost any food service facility can serve a hot, nutritious, well portioned meal. However, it is more challenging to present the items with the proper garnish, color contrast, varied shapes, and textures on the plate. The difference requires attention to detail and the added effort to make the meal picture perfect. This difference is the essence of marketing.

Determine Your Market

As a manager, you must identify your target market and find an effective way to reach it to be successful. Without information about your target market, you cannot satisfy their needs. An example of this would be offering gourmet food to a meat-and-potatoes crowd. The more you know about your potential customers, the better you can satisfy their needs. You also need to determine the right portions, prices, and types of food to offer. The secret is to find the right product, at the right location, for the right price, and promote it in the right way–not as easy as it might seem. But these elements are necessary to help you offer the right product to the right customers.

Mystery Shoppers

"Mystery Shoppers" are a way to get comments about your facility. The most effective way is to bring in a new customer and have the person evaluate your facility. There are many mystery shopper programs on the Internet. People who would like to eat at various establishments join the program and are scheduled to eat at your facility. These people are reimbursed for their meal, and sometimes they are paid an additional amount for their time. However, not all programs pay an additional amount of money.

Mystery shoppers have a "training" session to learn how your facility is supposed to operate. It can include how the employees should dress, how the facility should look, how the food items are to be presented to patrons, and how employees and managers should act.

The questionnaires they complete after their visit are detailed. An example of a questionnaire can be found at the end of this chapter.

The patron is asked to evaluate all phases of the operation. You would probably like to make adjustments to this form, but it will give you an idea of the sort of questions that can be asked.

The patron is given a time to visit the facility. During their visit, they make mental or written notes about the points on the questionnaire. After the visit they complete the form and return it along with their receipt. Once the forms are checked to be sure they are complete, the forms are approved for payment. It is a good way to get unbiased, outsider opinions about the operation of your facility.

You could organize something like this yourself, or work with an established mystery shopping company. Here is a partial list of mystery shopping companies.

- **www.mystery-shoppers.com**
- **www.volition.com/mystery/html**
- **www.mystiqueshopper.com**
- **www.secretshoppercompany.com**
- **www.shopperscritique.com**

These sites offer reviews of some of the programs available: **www.topsitereviews.info/ shopping.html?gclid=COHC1Zr8wIUCFQYLHgod1zqevA** and **www.betterbusinessratings. org/shopping/**.

Do-It-Yourself Marketing

Start by asking yourself these questions: Do you really want to learn about marketing? Should you use your time to promote? Can you be objective? Are you a creative person?

When you decide to coordinate your own promotional efforts, the checklist at the end of this chapter will help you track your efforts and evaluate the results.

CASE STUDY: MILITARY MARKETING AND PROMOTION

The non-appropriated clubs on the bases have a monthly calendar of events. These calendars alert all members of the entertainment or special events which will be held at the facility. The calendars are posted around the base and can be distributed to all applicable personnel. One of these special events is the Marine Corps Ball which is a formal event that is held at the Officers Club.

Mel Trimble, Retired Marine

Guerrilla Marketing

Guerrilla marketing guru Jay Conrad Levinson offers these techniques to give managers the ability to be effective marketers without exceeding their budget. His books, business tools, and his Web site, **www.gmarketing.com**, are filled with hands-on advice. His Web site contains dozens of free marketing articles. He also has free newsletters, radio programs, seminars, and individual coaching. Here are some guerrilla marketing books, CDs and DVDs you will find helpful:

Patience is Crucial

Most of your customers will need you on an ongoing basis. This is a positive for you. But first you have to convince them to eat with you. Then you have to impress them with your product and service. It is good to have your operations and employee training in place before starting to do any major promotion. Ask yourself whether the facility is ready to offer a quality product each time and to give the best possible service? If the answer is yes, you are ready to promote the facility. Also keep in mind that it can take time to bring people in the door. Marketing requires patience. You will get some results overnight, but most results will take time and effort. Work hard, be patient, and they will come.

Repetition for Emphasis

Running an ad or displaying flyers just once won't get decent results. You need to repeat these efforts to be effective. Many marketing experts state that it takes three to seven exposures to your offer before people make the decision to buy. You can make some small changes to your promotional wording, but be sure your words are consistent. Your customers are busy, so you must keep your name before them. Promotion can also reactivate customers who haven't dealt with you for some time.

CASE STUDY: CHURCH MEAL PROMOTION

Churches do not market their meals. Sunday noon and Wednesday evening seem to be popular times for church meals. They can be promoted in the church newsletter, on a bulletin board, reminder screen in the foyer, and other ways in-house. Some of the church meals are prepared in-house, and others are pot luck dinners where the parishioners bring some of the dishes.

Gary Douylliez • St Francis Inn
Casa de Solana Inn • **www.stfrancisinn.com**

What Benefits Do You Offer?

To draw customers in, you need to let them know "what you can do for them."

- **Are you open late?** Market to students and 2nd and 3rd shift workers.

- **Do you offer discounts for large orders?**

- **Do you cater special events?** We'll discuss this in the next chapter.

Should You Have a Web Presence?

Every day there are millions of people using the Internet for work, play, shopping, and research.

Does the business where your facility is located have a Web site? If so, it should be simple to have a page or series of pages added to promote the food service options.

A Web page is a wonderful way to tell people about your facility, who you are, what you offer, who you serve, where you are located, how to find you, when you are open, why to buy from you, and how to place special orders. Your Web pages can:

1. **Be changed quickly.** (You do not have to throw out printed items to make changes. Share mouth-watering pictures of menu items.)

2. **Contain copies of your upcoming menus.**

3. **Allow people to place orders.**

4. **Be any amount of exposure you want and need.**

5. **Be interactive** — let potential diners offer their thoughts.

6. **Build community spirit** — promote the business and local community and charity events.

Some businesses have password-protected sections to share information with their employees, explain benefits, and post work schedules.

There are some advantages to having a Web presence. They include:

- Gathering marketing information.

- Evaluating marketing information.

- Generating additional sales.

- Establishing communication with customers and employees.

- Supplementing employee training with updates and bulletins.

- Broadcasting press releases.

- Identifying prospective employees.

- Providing immediate access to your menu.

- Permitting customers to place orders online.

According to Nielsen/tings, 67.8 percent of the U.S. population uses the Internet.

After you have a Web page, include your link on any promotional items and flyers. If possible, have the Web master give you a simple URL (Web address). There also needs to be an easy-to-find link on the company or business Web site. Include an obvious link to your menu online. Coupons and other specials can be offered on your Web site.

What to Put on Your Web Site

Web pages should reflect the personality and atmosphere of your facility. Use fonts, color, and graphics consistent with your store. Here are some suggestions for things to include on your site:

- **Show What You Have to Offer**. How do your food items look? What do customers see when they walk in your doors? Show the atmosphere in your facility. Include a picture of your friendly, cheerful staff.

- **Share the News** — You can develop a Web-site based newsletter to share information about your facility, employee news, and specials. Use it to include your customers in the operation of the facility. You could gather information about customer promotions, birth dates, and anniversaries with their permission. You could include the information in your newsletter or in a section of your Web pages.

- **Menus** — Your Web pages give you a chance to include full color pictures with your online menu.

- **Directions** — Offer a location and building map to help people in the business and in the community to find your facility.

- **History** — Is there interesting local history, neighborhood history, or business background that Web page visitors would find interesting? Share the story. You can also have local individuals share some interesting stories that you.

- **Educational Info** — Give potential patrons information about the items you offer, and you could even include the nutritional information. Throughout the book we discussed programs that provide information that could be listed on your Web pages. More and more food service businesses are providing in-depth information about the nutritional value of their items.

The focus and content of your Web pages are only limited by your imagination. It is useful to incorporate information that educates visitors, giving your site wider appeal and your visitors a reason to tell others about your site.

You Need an Effective Web Site

These are important points to discuss with the company's Web site designer.

1. **Create a Professional Look** — An unprofessional or amateurish look reflects badly on your facility.

2. **User Friendly** — Be sure visitors can navigate your pages. Do all your links work? Are there links to all your pages? It never hurts to double check the function ability of your pages when it is posted.

3. **Search Engine Friendly** — 75 percent of all online activity comes from search engines. The Web master needs to optimize your pages for search engines.

4. **Content that Promotes Sales** — Does the company have a person to write Web page content? If you have someone qualified to write the content for your facility, mention that to the Web designer. The content needs to give the feel of your facility, information for potential visitors, and to be written in a way that works with search engines.

Marketing Tools

You need to develop marketing tools to expand your business. Press releases, mail campaigns, and telephone solicitation are just some of the ways you can reach your target markets. A Web site is also a must for any catering business today. The catering options can be included on the facility Web site. Here are some common types of promotion and the goals for each type.

COUPONS	SPECIAL EVENTS	NEWSLETTERS
Identify a product and set a value for the product	Call attention to facility and products you offer	Call attention to facility and products you offer
Make customers aware of a specific product	Create excitement about the products and facility	Provide information about products and facility
Promote product by offering a discount	Can increase average ticket price for facility	Establish benefits of products and facility

Low Cost Marketing Ideas

Most facilities have limited money to promote their business. This is one of the reasons I mentioned guerrilla marketing earlier in this chapter. The limited budget makes it necessary to find creative and inexpensive marketing approaches. Many marketing ideas can be implemented for a reasonable cost. The following list includes some low cost but effective marketing tools.

- **Develop a portfolio** — Use a high-quality camera and take pictures at unique and special events that you host. Make sure the person taking pictures is qualified since you will use these pictures in your promotion and they should be a nice addition to your Web pages. These pictures should show staff members in uniform, food displays, and happy guests.

- **Market your Reputation** — This is especially important in the beginning. Don't cut corners. Being part of a large and respected company in the community will help your reputation. Spend marketing dollars effectively and productively. Your compensation may not be monetary – the facility reputation is valuable.

- **Develop a brochure** — An effective brochure will include color photos and text that moves people to make a purchase. Include information about the background and experience of your staff. Include information about any notable clients or awards received. Details about your food and services need to be included, along with a guarantee for your services. Brochures should be easy to read, and it is best to be concise and to the point.

- **Print business cards** — Business cards and stationery should reflect your facility. Staff members should have business cards with the facility address, contact information, and Web page address. If the facility offers catering and special event coordination, include information about these services.

Word of Mouth

The most reasonable and powerful marketing tool is word of mouth. One of the keys to positive word of mouth is to provide excellent service and to offer an excellent product. This can apply to your daily menu offerings and any special event work that you do. Make a great impression and people will tell others. Our local hospital has a cafeteria so good that people go out of their way to have lunch or dinner there.

Another way to encourage word of mouth is to ask satisfied customers for a written testimonial. These can be included on a Web page or in promotional items. The more noteworthy the person is, the more effective the testimonial will be.

You want potential customers to think about you in a positive way. This can be accomplished by educating your patrons. Show your patrons why you are different, and they will tell their friends.

An effective word-of-mouth program will:

- Inform and educate your patrons.

- Make your guests into informal salespeople for your business.

- Give guests reasons to return.

- Provide unique and personal service.

- Distinguish your business from the competition.

You should exude "quality service." Satisfied patrons will tell others about you. This is important in your daily business and with special event planning. When you cater an event, do a little something extra. You can prepare snack items for the customer and they will remember your facility. It doesn't take long or cost much, but the customer will appreciate the fact that you thought to do something special for them.

Networking

It can be beneficial to become an active member of groups such as the Chamber of Commerce, Rotary, Lions, Elks, churches and synagogues, and special interest groups. The first key is to be active. Second, you are not asking them to contract catering work, but they will get to know you and will contact your facility when they need catering services.

Write Effective Press Releases

Write at least six press releases per year. These press releases need to contain something of relevance to the community, or they won't be printed. Read local newspapers and listen to local radio stations to get a feel for what they cover. Keep it short and to the point. This is a link to an article that I wrote about writing an effective press release. The link is **www.affcommunity.com/write-an-effective-press-release.2020.html**. I've gotten great feedback on the information contained in the article. Keep in mind that smaller papers are usually more willing to print press releases which pertain to local businesses and people.

Community Service

Working with community service organizations will give you a better public image. Starbucks is a master at promoting their good deeds work. Their employees wear T-shirts advertising the company's involvement with causes such as fighting breast cancer. Any local organization that raises money to help others is a good potential partner for your facility. Donate your space and staff for a charity fundraiser. These are things that you can mention through your contacts in the community—the Chamber of Commerce, local clergy, alumni organizations, or civic groups.

Yellow Pages

Not all businesses need yellow-page ads. You are locking yourself into a year contract or possibly more when you run a yellow page ad. I will also say that not all yellow page sales representatives are concerned with your well being. Keep in mind that they make money when they sell you an ad. I work with a number of yellow page representatives and after years in marketing, I finally have a helpful and conscientious representative for one phone book company. Helpful representatives have been few and far between for me.

Marketing Literature

Each of the items mentioned above is worth the time and money to produce them. However, think about how you will use these and only get the items you will use. Many facilities use brochures and promotional folders to promote your services to potential clients. These folders contain a business card, sample menus, letters of recommendation, lists of services, and possibly photographs. These folders must look professional. Make sure your literature is eye-catching and inviting because your information needs to stand out from the crowd.

Whether you use a designer only as a consultant or for the whole project, there are many sources to find qualified individuals. A local college might have an art program. Contact the school to see if anyone is interested in increasing their portfolio. Many of these students can produce professional designs even without on-the-job experience.

There are many freelance designers. Contact professional design organizations such as the American Institute of Graphic Arts (AIGA) to see if they can provide you with a directory of freelancers. The AIGA can be contacted at: AIGA, 164 Fifth Avenue New York, NY 10010, telephone 212-807-1990, or fax 212-807-1799. Their Web site is **www.aiga.org**. Also check **www.sologig.com**, **www.guru.com**, and **www.elance.com** for freelancers.

Business Cards

There is less space on business cards, but they are an effective way to promote any business. On business cards, you need to get to the point quickly. The layout and text need to be eye catching or people will toss your cards aside. This is a case of "less is more" so simplicity is best. Use an image as the focal point of your card and include pertinent information, including business name, address, phone number, fax, and Web site address. This will leave little room for anything else. A couple of alternatives are two-sided cards and a folding card with information inside. Poynteronline, **www.poynter.org**, has several helpful design pages you might want to investigate. There is one on color typography and one that discusses using a grid for design. Search Poynteronline for articles such as:

- *Understanding Color*

- *Elements of Typography*

- *The Structure of Design*

Remember, there are many things you can do with business cards, and they are an inexpensive way to advertise. I recently purchased 1,000 heavy card stock, color cards for three cents each from **www.vistaprint.com**. It's hard to get your business name and contact information into someone's hand for three cents. Give your cards away freely. Many businesses let you leave a stack of your cards in their offices/buildings or on their message boards. When you go to networking events, be sure to take a pile of your cards and hand them out freely.

Promotional Items

There are many promotional items that you can offer as gifts or prizes in your facility.

You can grab people's attention by giving them useful items. One of these items is a durable and attractive plastic cup or a set of cups. Berry Plastics has a great selection of cups in various sizes. They can customize these with your logo, slogan, address, phone number, or a special offer for people who have a cup. (Discounted refill when they bring the cup back to the facility is one example.) Check their selection at **www.berryplastics.com/souvenir.html** and **www.berryplastics.com/specialty.html**, call them at 812-424-2904, or e-mail **www. berryplastics.com/contact.html#phone**.

These are wonderful items to give to customers. Send your dine-in customers home with a drink refill, or you can stuff these cups with coupons, magnets, menus, or anything else and then put a lid on them. Students, families, and most anyone will appreciate these at special events. Use the stuffed cups to promote your facility to potential customers for possible catering and special event clients.

T-shirts are a wonderful way to promote your business whether you give them to customers or have your staff members wear them. You could hold a drawing each week and award a T-shirt to one customer. This can be a great way to get business cards from customers or e-mail addresses for other promotional pieces. One business that offers custom T-shirts which include your logo or other information is **www.campus-collection.net/custom.php3** or call **800-BUY-T-SHIRTS** at 800-289-8744. These pictures show some of the possibilities.

Use Marketing Literature

After these items are designed and printed, you need to distribute them. Get creative about distributing your cards and brochures. Anyone who is a potential customer or who can refer you to others should get some of your business cards and brochures. This may sound broad, but keep in mind that business cards are inexpensive and people collect them. An attractive brochure is a great way to get the word out to people. When you join networking groups and organizations, be sure to take plenty of promotional materials with you to meetings and gatherings. Brochures can be displayed in the non-commercial food service facility or other areas of the business where your facility is located, and if you cater events, be sure to have cards and brochures handy. You should not display them on tables without permission from your current customer, but have them close at hand. It's hard to determine how much business is lost by the simple fact that a caterer did not have a card to give a guest who loved the food at the last party you catered.

Coupons

You should never underestimate the value of coupons in the food business. Many consumers love coupons. There are many types of coupons you can use. These include:

- A specific dollar amount discount.

- A percentage off the total price.

- A free item with a qualifying order.

- A special price for large orders.

These are just a few ideas. Be creative and figure your food costs to be sure it's cost effective for you. To create effective coupons to attract your customers, you need to know what those customers like. Computer programs will track which items sell the most and which sell the least to help you decide what sort of coupons to offer.

How will you circulate your coupons? They can be posted on company bulletin boards, included in a newsletter, or you can send a stack through inter office mail. But you might want to coordinate that with the department that distributes company mail. It would be better not to send coupons to all departments on the same day as it might overwhelm the mailroom and because you want to reach different departments on different days.

A company that prints custom coupons is National Tickets. Visit their Web site at **www.nationalticket.com/Ticket_Printing/coupon_books.asp**. They offer coupons, coupon books, and gift certificates for your facility. Call 800-829-0829 or fax 800-829-0888 or e-mail **ticket@ nationalticket.com**.

If you decide that you would like to do a direct mail campaign, these companies have something to offer for your facility.

As a non-commercial food service manager, you may want to target people who are new to your area. You should be the first one to contact them. Moving Targets is a company that specializes in attracting new neighbors. Their Web site is **http://www.movingtargets.com/ ourprograms.asp** or call 800-926-2451. See their sample at the right.

Another promotional idea is to send postcards to specific geographic groups of people: neighborhoods or business districts, for example. They can be given to existing customers and to re-activate inactive customers. Postcard Press also offers business cards for businesses. The Web site is: **www.postcardpress.com** and they offer a variety of sizes, shapes, and patterns for you. Call 800-957-5787 from 7:15 a.m. to 6 p.m. (PST) for more information.

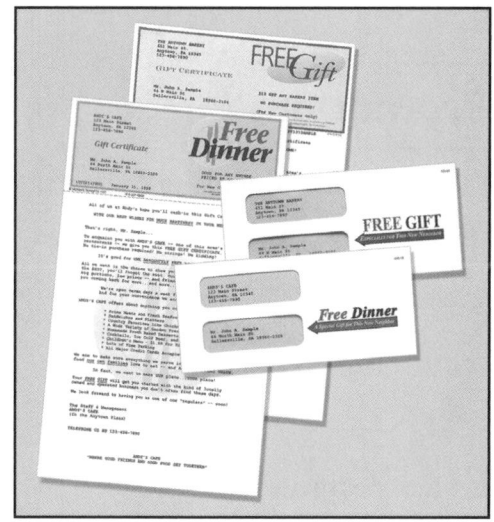

Moving Targets Materials

Incentives

Incentives are great because they reward people for what they do. You are giving them a reward for coming back to your facility. You can do this in three ways:

1. Discounts.

2. Promotions.

3. Customer loyalty programs.

Discounts

The most effective deals give your guests a discount and generate a profit for the facility. This is especially effective when you make a sale that you might not have made otherwise. For this to work well, you can offer items with high profit margins. The customer gets a great deal and the facility makes money.

Internal Coupons

This is a way to increase repeat business. Three widely used offers are:

- **Courtesy coupons** — Use wallet-sized coupons that staff members carry. Give them to guests and they can be used on return visits. (They are great for patrons who had a complaint or are upset with the product or service they received.) Or use them to reward customers for repeated patronage.

- **Cross-marketing coupons** — Offer a special discount for your slower hours to encourage patrons to eat during periods when you are not busy and they will get a discount and more attention. They can offer a free or discounted appetizer, drink, or dessert on specific days or during certain hours.

- **Companion coupons** — Encourage your regulars to bring a friend. A business cafeteria is a great chance for employees to spend their lunch break with a friend or family member without having to fight traffic, travel to a commercial restaurant, and still try to get back to work. There can be special dishes or offers for two or four people.

Promotions

Five great promotional opportunities are:

1. Birthdays

2. Anniversaries

3. Holidays

4. Special Events

5. Festivals

There is no reason that a company food service facility cannot offer specials for these employee events. On-the-job promotions to a new position are also a good excuse for a promotional event.

- **Birthdays and Anniversaries** — Make an irresistible offer for patrons who celebrate their birthdays or anniversaries with you. It may be a special day for them, but they probably still have to work. Give them a treat in the middle of their work day. Patron surveys are a great place to ask for this information. (*Hint:* When they sign up, let them know you're asking about these dates to offer them specials on their birthdays and anniversaries; otherwise they could feel their privacy is being invaded.) Make your offer valid for more than just the actual date being celebrated—in the month is effective—because people need some flexibility.

- **Holidays** — All businesses can use holidays to offer specials. Retail businesses do this for every holiday. There is no need to tell your patrons that a holiday is coming, but post flyers to let them know what a great deal they'll get if they visit you. I know how irritating it is for health care workers to work on holidays. Offering a special deal for these workers can be popular.

- **Special Events** — Special events can help you promote business. We will discuss special events and catering in more detail in Chapter 19.

When your facility has a special event, a custom banner can be valuable. Banners Across America offers banner kits to create custom banners. The sizes and prices can be seen at **www.bannersacrossameri-ca.com**. These kits include reversible letters, built-in grommets, heavy-duty vinyl, durable plastic pockets to hold letters and numbers, and nylon rope to secure signage. Call 214-352-7015.

Lunch and Earn a unique program that could be beneficial for your facility. Would you like to build your lunch business? Most businesses do a decent business at lunch but would like to do more. **LunchandEarn.com** brings the pharmaceutical industries' huge online lunch orders to you! They have the inside track to the pharmaceutical industry. In addition, they market your facility online at no cost to you. There are no set-up fees, no monthly dues, and no fees of any kind to join **LunchandEarn.com**. All you need is a fax line. Sign up completely risk free at **www.LunchandEarn.com** or call 888-70-LUNCH.

Customer Loyalty Programs — Frequent Diner Programs

These can be a huge benefit to your facility. Rewarding your customers for continued loyalty gives them an added incentive to choose you over their other options and will bring them back. These are the most common variations:

- **Punch cards** — Inexpensive cards can be used for punch cards. They are punched each time a patron purchases a specific item. It is best to find an unusual hole-punch to eliminate the chance of people punching the cards themselves. After a patron purchases a certain number of items they receive something for free. These cards are easy and cheap to produce. You can also keep the patron's cards at the cash register and then locked up at the end of the day.

- **Point systems** — These are usually dollar-for-point systems, where patrons accumulate points towards free food or merchandise. This can be a great way for guests to "eat their way" to free merchandise. This is more involved than punch cards and you can get outside businesses to donate prizes in exchange for free promotion in the company.

Punch cards and point systems are ways to monitor your patrons, reward them for coming back, and increase your opportunities to delight them. Take time to figure out which promotion is right for you.

Delight Your Guests

You must exceed the expectations of your patrons every time they deal with you. Many businesses have horrible customer service, giving you a chance to surpass your customers' expectations. Remind your staff they are in the hospitality business. Guests want a quality product served by a friendly staff at a reasonable price. It is a tall order, but it is possible to attain.

Remember that your items and service will be evaluated by all patrons. In schools this includes the students, faculty, and sometimes their parents. In prisons this includes the inmates and the staff members. Health care facilities serve employees, visitors, and patients. The military food service facilities cater to many different people on any given day. Church food service also serves a variety of patrons. You just never know who will be eating in your facility. So every day you and your staff need to prepare excellent food and offer outstanding customer service.

CASE STUDY: SCHOOL FOOD SERVICE

When I first started here, I was amazed that the only apples served were Red Delicious. At the middle schools, we did an apple promo where we had 2 varieties Gala versus Granny Smith or Fuji versus Granny Smith, and the students ate a slice of each. Then they voted on their preference. Granny Smith won with the students; faculty and adult volunteers' preference was always the other kind of apple. That was a simple lesson to me about how students' and adults' food preferences differ. Children love sour!

Along with this promo, we had table tent displays that touted the nutritional value of apples, staff dressed up in apple costumes (lent from AMC), and various apple dishes were on the menu.

Sandy Neff • Augusta County School Board
School Nutrition Program

Maintain Employee Relations

Happy employees treat patrons better and are more productive. They will also say positive things outside your facility. Customers want to be treated right, and they remember this when they judge the food and the service. You need to have happy employees to keep patrons happy and eager to return.

Another way to keep your employees happy is by training them well. They need to understand how to do their job and that you expect a high level of service. Give them every opportunity to give the best possible service. These employees generate repeat business and help your business grow. Here are some ways to communicate with your staff and keep them involved.

- Communicate information about training and job openings.

- Discuss staff weddings, birthdays, accomplishments, or life events.

- Don't say they are important, show them.

These things help employees feel you care and create a team atmosphere. Show that you understand the contributions they make to the facility by effective communication with them. They can provide valuable information and suggestions on how to improve business. Have meetings with your staff, create a newsletter, and offer orientations and training for employees to show you care and encourages them to make a difference.

All of these things help you generate positive PR and a great environment for your employees and customers. Give back to the community and boost the image of the non-commercial food service facility.

Market Research

Good information about your prospective market will enable you to make a good decision. The easiest way to get a thorough idea of what is needed is through a market survey. These are creative ways to get the information you need from existing and potential customers.

Market surveys are a great way for a food service manager to determine if special programs are needed and how much demand there is for special items. There are government funds available for food service facilities who address special nutritional needs, such as programs for elderly patients and nursing home residents.

Title XII of the Older Americans Act of 1965 provides that the federal government will give funding for nutritional services for elderly Americans. The government realizes that many elderly Americans are at risk nutritionally and getting proper nutrition will reduce medical problems. These provisions contain many regulations, but some of these include:

1. Health care and other related facilities are the natural location to produce these meals.

2. Health care facilities can sponsor these programs in conjunction with state and/or local governments. The actual meal production can be sub-contracted to the health care facility.

3. Funds can be used (with limits) to reimburse the facility for some costs incurred for management, production, and service. Specific supplies used for these meals can also be reimbursed.

4. Nutritional training programs can be funded through this program.

A simple written or phone survey can be done to determine the need in the community. Flyers or information can be posted at local grocery stores, community centers, and libraries.

RESERVATION PROCESS

The telephone call to make the reservation was answered within three rings. ❑ Yes ❑ No

The employee answering the phone was pleasant, identified himself/herself and the restaurant. ❑ Yes ❑ No

The employee taking the reservation was courteous, repeated your reservation information and thanked you. ❑ Yes ❑ No

The employee taking the reservation was knowledgeable, helpful and able to answer any questions (e.g., directions to restaurant). ❑ Yes ❑ No

Additional Notes: _____

_____

_____

_____

_____

RESTAURANT EXTERIOR

The restaurant's sign was easily seen from a distance, easy to read, and in good condition. ❑ Yes ❑ No

The restaurant's parking lot and grounds were free of debris and well-maintained. ❑ Yes ❑ No

The area around the dining room was landscaped and well-lit. ❑ Yes ❑ No

The restaurant had adequate parking. ❑ Yes ❑ No

Additional Notes: _____

_____

_____

_____

_____

ARRIVAL & SEATING

You were greeted quickly upon entering. ❑ Yes ❑ No

The host/hostess was appropriately dressed, smiling and pleasant. ❑ Yes ❑ No

The host/hostess asked your smoking preference. ❑ Yes ❑ No

You were seated within a reasonable time. ❑ Yes ❑ No

The lounge was offered as an alternative if you had to wait for your table.	❏ Yes	❏ No
The booths and tables were not crowded and easily accessible.	❏ Yes	❏ No
The table or booth was comfortable and appropriate for your party.	❏ Yes	❏ No
The host/hostess distributed menus for each guest and they were easily within reach.	❏ Yes	❏ No
The host/hostess informed you of specials.	❏ Yes	❏ No
The host/hostess told you the server's name.	❏ Yes	❏ No
The host/hostess had a pleasant demeanor and treated you graciously.	❏ Yes	❏ No

Additional Notes: _____

_____

_____

_____

_____

MENU

The menu was in good, clean condition.	❏ Yes	❏ No
The menu matched the restaurant's theme.	❏ Yes	❏ No
The menu size was physically easy to handle.	❏ Yes	❏ No
Available specials were listed prominently or separately.	❏ Yes	❏ No
The menu was well-organized, with selections grouped in an easy-to-read and easy-to-find manner.	❏ Yes	❏ No
The type on the menu was easy to read.	❏ Yes	❏ No
The number of selections was appropriate.	❏ Yes	❏ No
Appetizing descriptions were provided for menu items.	❏ Yes	❏ No
The menu had complete descriptions of side orders included or offered for each item.	❏ Yes	❏ No
The menu offered additional information as a marketing tool.	❏ Yes	❏ No
Vegetarian portions were offered.	❏ Yes	❏ No
Children's portions were offered.	❏ Yes	❏ No

Senior citizens' portions were offered.   ❏ Yes   ❏ No

Additional Notes: _____

_____

_____

_____

_____

WAITSTAFF

The waiter's or waitress's uniform was clean and attractive.	❏ Yes	❏ No
The waiter's or waitress's hands and fingernails were clean.	❏ Yes	❏ No
The waiter or waitress approached your table within three minutes after being seated.	❏ Yes	❏ No
The waiter or waitress greeted you pleasantly and introduced himself or herself.	❏ Yes	❏ No
The waiter or waitress smiled, was cordial, and created a genial atmosphere.	❏ Yes	❏ No
The waiter or waitress was familiar with the menu and able to answer questions.	❏ Yes	❏ No
The waiter or waitress used suggestive selling techniques, such as offering appetizers, in a friendly and non-offensive manner.	❏ Yes	❏ No
The waiter or waitress served beverage items promptly and from the left.	❏ Yes	❏ No
The waiter or waitress served food items in a timely manner and from the left.	❏ Yes	❏ No
The timing between courses was well-spaced.	❏ Yes	❏ No
The waiter or waitress knew each guest's selections and served them correctly.	❏ Yes	❏ No
The waiter or waitress returned to the table to check on satisfaction and provide additional service after the main course arrived.	❏ Yes	❏ No
It was not necessary to summon the waiter or waitress during the meal.	❏ Yes	❏ No
The waiter or waitress was attentive to guests' needs during the meal.	❏ Yes	❏ No
The waiter or waitress seemed to enjoy their job.	❏ Yes	❏ No
Overall, the waiter or waitress did a good job.	❏ Yes	❏ No

Additional Notes: _____

_____

_____

BUS STAFF

The busperson provided water quickly after being seated.	❑ Yes	❑ No
The busperson made sure water glasses were refilled promptly.	❑ Yes	❑ No
The busperson was responsive to any service requests.	❑ Yes	❑ No
The busperson removed dirty dishes quickly, so they were not left sitting on the table after being emptied.	❑ Yes	❑ No
The busperson removed dirty dishes from the right.	❑ Yes	❑ No
The busperson removed dirty ashtrays properly and replaced them quickly.	❑ Yes	❑ No
The busperson was polite and courteous.	❑ Yes	❑ No
The busperson was presentable, clean and well-groomed.	❑ Yes	❑ No
The busperson's uniform was clean and attractive.	❑ Yes	❑ No
The busperson did a good job, and service was not disruptive.	❑ Yes	❑ No

Additional Notes: _____

_____

_____

_____

_____

FOOD

Food matched its menu description.	❑ Yes	❑ No
All items ordered were available.	❑ Yes	❑ No

Appetizer
Please list appetizer(s) ordered: _____

_____

_____

Please rate overall appetizer quality:	❑ Excellent	❑ Good	❑ Fair	❑ Poor
Appetizing appearance		❑ Yes	❑ No	
Proper temperature (hot items hot, cold items cold)		❑ Yes	❑ No	
Tasted good		❑ Yes	❑ No	

Soup

Please list soup(s) ordered: _____

_____

Please rate overall soup quality: ❑ Excellent   ❑ Good   ❑ Fair   ❑ Poor

Appetizing appearance   ❑ Yes   ❑ No

Proper temperature (hot items hot, cold items cold)   ❑ Yes   ❑ No

Tasted good   ❑ Yes   ❑ No

Bread

Please list type of bread(s) ordered: _____

_____

Please rate overall bread quality: ❑ Excellent   ❑ Good   ❑ Fair   ❑ Poor

Appetizing appearance   ❑ Yes   ❑ No

Proper temperature (hot items hot, cold items cold)   ❑ Yes   ❑ No

Tasted good   ❑ Yes   ❑ No

Salad

Please list type of salad(s) ordered: _____

_____

Please rate overall salad quality: ❑ Excellent   ❑ Good   ❑ Fair   ❑ Poor

Appetizing appearance   ❑ Yes   ❑ No

Proper temperature (hot items hot, cold items cold)   ❑ Yes   ❑ No

Tasted good   ❑ Yes   ❑ No

Dressing choices adequate   ❑ Yes   ❑ No

Dressing amount correct   ❑ Yes   ❑ No

Entrée

Please list entrée(s) ordered: _____

_____

_____

_____

Please rate overall entrée quality: ❑ Excellent   ❑ Good   ❑ Fair   ❑ Poor

Appetizing appearance   ❑ Yes   ❑ No

Proper temperature (hot items hot, cold items cold)   ❑ Yes   ❑ No

Tasted good   ❑ Yes   ❑ No

Portions appropriate   ❑ Yes   ❑ No

Side Orders

Please list side order(s) ordered: _____

_____

_____

Please rate overall side orders quality: ❑ Excellent	❑ Good	❑ Fair	❑ Poor
Appetizing appearance		❑ Yes	❑ No
Proper temperature (hot items hot, cold items cold)		❑ Yes	❑ No
Tasted good		❑ Yes	❑ No
Portions appropriate		❑ Yes	❑ No

Dessert

Please list dessert(s) ordered: _____

_____

_____

Please rate overall dessert quality: ❑ Excellent	❑ Good	❑ Fair	❑ Poor
Appetizing appearance		❑ Yes	❑ No
Proper temperature (hot items hot, cold items cold)		❑ Yes	❑ No
Tasted good		❑ Yes	❑ No
Portions appropriate		❑ Yes	❑ No

Additional Notes: _____

_____

_____

_____

DINING AMBIANCE

Noise level in dining room is not too loud.	❑ Yes	❑ No
Music pleasant, not too loud and not distracting.	❑ Yes	❑ No
Lighting in dining room is not too bright or dim.	❑ Yes	❑ No
Table decorations are clean and attractive.	❑ Yes	❑ No
Table decorations are unobtrusive and do not block diners' view of each other.	❑ Yes	❑ No
The restaurant presented a unified theme in décor, music, employee uniforms and overall atmosphere.	❑ Yes	❑ No
Décor, furnishings and plants are in good physical condition and tastefully exhibited.	❑ Yes	❑ No

Additional Notes: _____

_____

FACILITY CLEANLINESS

The entrance, lounge, bar and dining room were clean. ❑ Yes ❑ No

The dining table is clean, in good condition, and has no food residue, crumbs or stains. ❑ Yes ❑ No

Chairs and booths are clean, stain-free and stable. ❑ Yes ❑ No

Glasses are clean and do not have water spots. ❑ Yes ❑ No

Flatware is clean and does not have water spots. ❑ Yes ❑ No

Dishes are clean and do not have water spots. ❑ Yes ❑ No

Napkins are clean, not stained, and folded nicely. ❑ Yes ❑ No

The ceiling is clean and in good condition. ❑ Yes ❑ No

Lighting fixtures are working and clean. ❑ Yes ❑ No

The walls and floors are clean and well-maintained. ❑ Yes ❑ No

Additional Notes: _____

_____

_____

_____

_____

RESTROOMS

Men's and women's restrooms clearly marked and in an easy-to-find location. ❑ Yes ❑ No

The restroom door is clean and well-maintained. ❑ Yes ❑ No

Overall, the restroom is clean and doesn't have any objectionable odors. ❑ Yes ❑ No

The restroom lighting is in good working order and sufficiently bright. ❑ Yes ❑ No

The restroom is adequately stocked with toiletries, soap and disposable paper towels (or a hot-air hand dryer). ❑ Yes ❑ No

The restroom sink areas and fixtures are clean. ❑ Yes ❑ No

The restroom mirrors are clean. ❑ Yes ❑ No

The restroom walls, floors and windows are clean and well-maintained. ❑ Yes ❑ No

An infant changing area is available, clean and in good condition. ❑ Yes ❑ No

Additional Notes: _____

_____

_____

_____

_____

DEPARTURE

The check was presented in an appropriate and timely manner. ❑ Yes ❑ No

The check was placed in a discreet location. ❑ Yes ❑ No

The check is itemized, readable and easy to understand. ❑ Yes ❑ No

The check is totalled correctly and reflects the items ordered. ❑ Yes ❑ No

The waiter or waitress informs you that he or she will return for payment at your convenience. ❑ Yes ❑ No

The waiter or waitress properly tabulated and processed credit card payment. ❑ Yes ❑ No

The waiter or waitress brought your correct change directly from the cashier. ❑ Yes ❑ No

The waiter or waitress thanked you upon receiving payment. ❑ Yes ❑ No

The waiter or waitress thanked you for coming and said "It was a pleasure to server you" and "Please come again." ❑ Yes ❑ No

Exits were well-lit and departure from dining room was free of obstacles. ❑ Yes ❑ No

Additional Notes: _____

_____

_____

_____

_____

OVERALL RATINGS

Overall service quality was:

❑ Excellent   ❑ Good   ❑ Fair   ❑ Poor

Overall food quality was:
❑ Excellent   ❑ Good   ❑ Fair   ❑ Poor

Overall dining experience was:
❑ Excellent   ❑ Good   ❑ Fair   ❑ Poor

Please note any areas of service that could be improved:

_____

_____

_____

_____

_____

_____

_____

_____

_____

_____

_____

Please note any areas of service that were exceptional or above ordinary:

_____

_____

_____

_____

_____

_____

_____

_____

_____

_____

_____

Additional Notes:

_____

_____

_____

_____

_____

PROMOTION INFORMATION

Promotion Name:	Date(s) of Promotion:
Person in Charge of Promotion:	Meal Period(s):

Briefly Describe Promotion:

Financial Objectives:	Non-Financial Objectives:
Projected Sales Impact:	Projected Customer Count Impact:

Promotion Pricing Strategy. List incentives and Appeals.

POINT OF PURCHASE MATERIALS

Check all that are needed:
❏ Menu Cards   ❏ Price Cards   ❏ Signs   ❏ Banners   ❏ Other (list)

MENU CARDS (describe briefly and fill in specs below)

Size:	Quantity Needed:	Date to Order:	Budget:
Color: b/w 2-color full (4-color)	Paperstock:	Date Needed by:	Placement::
Vendor I (list contact info and price quote):		Vendor I (list contact info and price quote):	

POINT OF PURCHASE MATERIALS (CONTINUED)

PRICE CARDS (describe briefly and fill in specs below)

Size:	Quantity Needed:	Date to Order:	Budget:
Color: b/w 2-color full (4-color)	Paperstock:	Date Needed by:	Placement::
Vendor 1 (list contact info and price quote):		Vendor 1 (list contact info and price quote):	

SIGNS (describe briefly and fill in specs below)

Size:	Quantity Needed:	Date to Order:	Budget:
Color: b/w 2-color full (4-color)	Paperstock:	Date Needed by:	Placement::
Vendor 1 (list contact info and price quote):		Vendor 1 (list contact info and price quote):	

BANNERS (describe briefly and fill in specs below)

Size:	Quantity Needed:	Date to Order:	Budget:
Color: b/w 2-color full (4-color)	Paperstock:	Date Needed by:	Placement::
Vendor 1 (list contact info and price quote):		Vendor 1 (list contact info and price quote):	

PRINTED MATERIALS NEEDED

Check all that are needed:
❑ Posters   ❑ Flyers   ❑ Table Tents   ❑ Coupons   ❑ Other (list)

POSTERS (describe briefly and fill in specs below)

Size:	Quantity Needed:	Date to Order:	Budget:
Color: b/w 2-color full (4-color)	Paperstock:	Date Needed by:	Placement::
Vendor 1 (list contact info and price quote):		Vendor 1 (list contact info and price quote):	

FLYERS (describe briefly and fill in specs below)

Size:	Quantity Needed:	Date to Order:	Budget:
Color: b/w 2-color full (4-color)	Paperstock:	Date Needed by:	Placement::
Vendor 1 (list contact info and price quote):		Vendor 1 (list contact info and price quote):	

TABLE TENTS (describe briefly and fill in specs below)

Size:	Quantity Needed:	Date to Order:	Budget:
Color: b/w 2-color full (4-color)	Paperstock:	Date Needed by:	Placement::
Vendor 1 (list contact info and price quote):		Vendor 1 (list contact info and price quote):	

PRINTED MATERIALS NEEDED (CONTINUED)

COUPONS (describe briefly and fill in specs below)

Size:	Quantity Needed:	Date to Order:	Budget:
Color: b/w 2-color full (4-color)	Paperstock:	Date Needed by:	Placement::
Vendor 1 (list contact info and price quote):		Vendor 1 (list contact info and price quote):	

OTHER (describe briefly and fill in specs below)

Size:	Quantity Needed:	Date to Order:	Budget:
Color: b/w 2-color full (4-color)	Paperstock:	Date Needed by:	Placement::
Vendor 1 (list contact info and price quote):		Vendor 1 (list contact info and price quote):	

OTHER (describe briefly and fill in specs below)

Size:	Quantity Needed:	Date to Order:	Budget:
Color: b/w 2-color full (4-color)	Paperstock:	Date Needed by:	Placement::
Vendor 1 (list contact info and price quote):		Vendor 1 (list contact info and price quote):	

PREMIUMS

Check all that are needed:

❏ T-shirts ❏ Hats ❏ Buttons ❏ Balloons ❏ Aprons ❏ Mugs ❏ Toys ❏ Pens ❏ Key chains

❏ Other (List) _____

T-SHIRTS (describe briefly and fill in specs below)

Size(s):	Quantity Needed of each: :	Date to Order:	Budget:
		Date Needed by:	Placement::

Vendor I (list contact info and price quote):	Vendor I (list contact info and price quote):

HATS (describe briefly and fill in specs below)

Size(s):	Quantity Needed of each: :	Date to Order:	Budget:
		Date Needed by:	Placement::

Vendor I (list contact info and price quote):	Vendor I (list contact info and price quote):

BALLOONS (describe briefly and fill in specs below)

Size:	Quantity Needed:	Date to Order:	Budget:
Color:	Imprint (if any):	Date Needed by:	Placement::

Vendor I (list contact info and price quote):	Vendor I (list contact info and price quote):

PREMIUMS			

APRONS (describe briefly and fill in specs below)

Size:	Quantity Needed:	Date to Order:	Budget:
Color:	Imprint (if any):	Date Needed by:	Placement::

Vendor 1 (list contact info and price quote):	Vendor 1 (list contact info and price quote):

MUGS (describe briefly and fill in specs below)

Size:	Quantity Needed:	Date to Order:	Budget:
Color:	Imprint (if any):	Date Needed by:	Placement::

Vendor 1 (list contact info and price quote):	Vendor 1 (list contact info and price quote):

TOYS (describe briefly and fill in specs below)

Size:	Quantity Needed:	Date to Order:	Budget:
Color:	Imprint (if any):	Date Needed by:	Placement::

Vendor 1 (list contact info and price quote):	Vendor 1 (list contact info and price quote):

PREMIUMS			

PENS (describe briefly and fill in specs below)

Size:	Quantity Needed:	Date to Order:	Budget:
Color:	Imprint (if any):	Date Needed by:	Placement::

Vendor 1 (list contact info and price quote):	Vendor 1 (list contact info and price quote):

KEY CHAINS (describe briefly and fill in specs below)

Size:	Quantity Needed:	Date to Order:	Budget:
Color:	Imprint (if any):	Date Needed by:	Placement::

Vendor 1 (list contact info and price quote):	Vendor 1 (list contact info and price quote):

OTHER (describe briefly and fill in specs below)

Size:	Quantity Needed:	Date to Order:	Budget:
Color:	Imprint (if any):	Date Needed by:	Placement::

Vendor 1 (list contact info and price quote):	Vendor 1 (list contact info and price quote):

ADVERTISING

TYPES OF ADVERTISING (Briefly list type of advertising planned)

PRINT ADS

Publication Name:	Size::	Run Date:	Cost:
Color:	Ad Layout due:	Publication Rep & Contact info:	
Publication Name:	Size::	Run Date:	Cost:
Color:	Ad Layout due:	Publication Rep & Contact info:	

OTHER ADVERTISING SUPPORT MATERIAL NEEDED (LIST):

EVALUATE PROMOTION

SUMMARY OF PROMOTION (Once the promotion is complete, write a summary of what was successful and what was not)

Projected Financial Objectives:	Projected Non-Financial Objectives:	Financial Objectives Achieved:	Non-Financial Objectives Achieved::
Projected Sales Impact:	Projected Customer Count Impact:	Actual Sales Impact:	Actual Customer Count Impact:

EMPLOYEE(S) REACTION:

CHAPTER NINETEEN

Catering and Special Events

Add Catering to a Food Service Facility

As the manager of a non-commercial food service facility, should you consider adding catering to your services? Consider these points before you make a decision.

- Customer profile
- Facility style/concept
- Staffing possibilities
- Menu options
- Layout of the building and available space

The proximity of your restaurant to other businesses is a determining factor when you consider catering. If you are close to heavily populated areas with offices or universities you may be a candidate to incorporate business catering into your existing facility. Most non-commercial facilities serve two or three meals a day, so seriously consider the difficulty that catering could cause with your existing kitchen and staff. Can you realistically handle the added business? Can catering be done without sacrificing the quality for your established patrons?

Social catering is another option. Again, consider how you will work catering into your existing schedule. For a small increase in food and labor cost you can significantly increase weekly or monthly sales. It is possible that some of your existing patrons will need some catering services. Start with them, and the word can begin to spread. Place signs, table tents, and text in your menu. Here are some questions you should consider:

- Is your facility big enough to handle the added production work?

- Is there enough space for on-site catering?

- Does your facility serve complete dinners or simple lunches?

- How much storage space do you have for the food preparation and supplies needed for the catering services?

The space you have available and your menu items may determine the feasibility of catering. Consider dinners to go or another type of take out service. Dinners to go can be a great attraction for workers in the facility. There are nights when busy people simply won't have time to prepare dinner. Carry out dinners could be a great option for busy facility staff members.

Many facilities can cater on-premise events and off-premise opportunities. This is a great way to take advantageous of the money that was invested in professional production equipment, lowering your overall operational costs and increasing your sales numbers. The increase will happen without having to spend money on expanding the dining room or kitchen area. These are some goals to pursue:

Flexibility — Blending both types of catering in a restaurant-catering operation will allow you to prepare foods in the facility and employ outside labor or using your existing staff, if possible.

Expertise — Because of the flexibility offered by dual catering operations, you can draw on a greater pool of specialist expertise. This means that you will be in greater demand for a wider range of significant events.

Exclusivity — Determine your exclusive target market. Serving exclusive clients gives you an advantage over other caterers in the area, bringing you recognition and market dominance.

Seasonal niche — Be aware of special annual and seasonal events and consider the pros and cons of preparing food on your own premises to be served on or off-premises. The off-site catering usually allows you to serve a greater number of people. Here are some suggestions to develop your catering business:

- **Decide whether your catering operation will be in-house or off premises.** In-house allows you to use your kitchen and equipment but may limit the size of events. Off-premises work allows for more exposure, multiple daily events, and more revenue, but you must abide by the rules of each venue.

- **Choose your staff smartly.** A temp agency might be a good option to staff your large catering events while your existing staff may be sufficient for small events. Your employees will appreciate making the extra money, but be sure to avoid overtime expenses because they will reduce any profits.

- **Use your menu.** There is no need to create a new menu for catered events. Which items on your menu are cater-friendly? For off premises catering, choose items that hold their temperature during transport and can be partially cooked ahead of time.

- **Food transportation can be difficult.** Safety and successful transportation are two major concerns. Each staff member should be trained to handle transported food properly to prevent outbreaks of food-borne illness.

- **Some items you need for off-site catering can be rented if you do limited off-site work.** These items could include things like stoves and hot boxes.

- **Create complete lists of food items, job duties, and equipment.**

- **Never let your regular facility business suffer for your catering business.** Quality will suffer in both businesses if you stretch too far. Know your limits and live by them.

Staffing

Be sure that the additional business merits hiring extra personnel. At first, your existing workers will be required to handle multiple job duties. Here is a partial list of the positions available in a large catering facility.

- **Director of Catering** — Oversees catering functions and marketing efforts, interacts with clients, coordinates sales, creates menus with the chef.

- **Assistant Catering Director** — Works with clients and helps with marketing.

- **Catering Manager** — Works with clients and maintains client contacts.

- **Catering Sales Manager** — Oversees sales office and sales staff.

- **Catering Sales Representative** — Performs outside and inside sales.

- **Banquet Setup Manager** — Supervises banquet set-up; orders tables, chairs, and other equipment; supervises tear-down of the event.

- **Scheduler** — Maintains master log of events, coordinates functions. Schedules meeting rooms and other rooms, keeps thorough records to avoid overbooking or double booking, and communicates information to appropriate departments.

- **Server** — Food servers and cocktail servers work the event. They handle and serve food and beverage items to guests.

- **Bartender** — Serves drinks during events and restocks bar inventory. May keep track of drinks for pricing of the event.

- **Clerical staff** — Handles correspondence: typing Banquet Event Order forms (BEOs), contracts, and handles phone messages.

- **Cashier** — Collects money for cash bars, sells drink tickets and meal tickets, if needed.

- **Cook/Food Handler** — Prepares food product according to the Banquet Event Order form (BEO).

To staff your catered events, ask your staff members who would like some additional work. If you need to hire temporary help, most areas have a large pool of people who want to work temporary catering jobs. The event staff will be paid a set amount for each event they work. Temporary workers and your staff members need to be paid the same way. An average amount for catering personnel can be $15 to $20 per hour. This amount does not include a tip that the host or hostess may offer. It is good to talk with local caterers to find what the average is in your area.

Skills for a Successful Caterer

There is money to be made in catering, but you need to remember that catering is hard work, and the easiest part of the job could be cooking. Coordination is important to arrange events. Even small events require work and organization. Imagine organizing an off-premise event for 250 people. Someone will need to load, unload, reload, and unload crates of china, silverware, and glasses. Usually that person is you!

Catering requires long hours and will usually take place on holidays when others are socializing, and the work is not limited to the day of the event. Organization, planning, and execution can be overwhelming. If any of these plans fail, there can be a domino effect with other problems to be handled.

You must be a person who can multi-task, organize your time to the minute and be ready for the unexpected. No matter how good you are, there will probably be unexpected things that happen. Do you have the skills necessary to handle catering and special event planning?

You are an excellent cook, able to present food artistically, have basic business knowledge and love working with people—that means you have the basic skills, but there are many skills and competencies needed to be an effective and successful caterer.

Cook and Food Presentation Skills

Catered events are usually devoted to a special event like a wedding, a product launch, or a special business meeting so customers expect more at a catered function: the food and presentation need to be outstanding. Any staff members need to be familiar and qualified with food preparation and presentation.

Display Equipment

The display equipment that you use in catering can make a big difference in the presentation. A non-commercial food service facility will have many pieces of equipment needed, but there are some pieces you may need. Don't feel obligated to buy additional equipment, but be on the lookout for items that would improve the presentation and safety of the food.

Cal Mil Plastics has a wide assortment of display items. These products include beverage serving items, pastry, and cookie displays, covered food containers and more. Visit **www.calmil.com/products.asp** for more information or call 800-321-9069 or 760-630-5100.

Dover Metals offers tiered serving displays and many other unique items for food serving needs. Visit **www.dovermetals.com** or call 269-849-1411.

Gourmet Display also offers a wide selection of serving trays and tiered display units. Two of their serving options are pictured below. Visit **www.gourmetdisplay.com**, or call 800-767-4711 for more information.

Other Catering Equipment

Portable cooking equipment could be a nice attraction for off site or outdoor events. These items could fill that need for you..

For more than 43 years, Big John Grills and Rotisseries has designed, manufactured, packaged, and distributed the best outdoor cooking equipment available. This family-run business has become the standard of the outdoor cooking Industry. An issue to consider with either of these options is whether you have anyone qualified to use these items safely.

Euipment shown at the right is available from Big John's Grills. They offer a wide selection of gas grills, charcoal grills, and portable and built in grills. To see all the possibilities, visit **www.bigjohngrills.com** or call 800-326-9575. They would be happy to send you a catalog.

Cookshack, Inc., offers a variety of smokers for every need. Cookshack was started in the early 1960s by Gene and Judy Ellis, Ponca City, Oklahoma. Mr. Ellis was an inventor and entrepreneur who loved barbecue and wanted to find "a better way" to produce great barbecue. The two collaborated on the recipes that became the formulas for their spicy sauce and dry spice blends. Cookshack sells a selection of recipes and wood along with their smokers to give you and your customers a great barbecue experience. They have an informative site at **www.cookshack.com** or call 800-423-0698.

Holstein Manufacturing offers smokers, roasters, grills, stoves, kettle corn cookers, deep fat fryer, and even trailers for transporting the equipment to off site locations. You can see the full line of products at **www.holsteinmfg.com** or call 800-368-4342.

One great way to keep drinks and some other items cold is with a chill and fill table. Chillin' Products offers these tables, snow cone machines, table shirts, granite mixers, cotton candy, and popcorn machines for your events. Visit **www.chillinproducts.com** or call 866-932-4455.

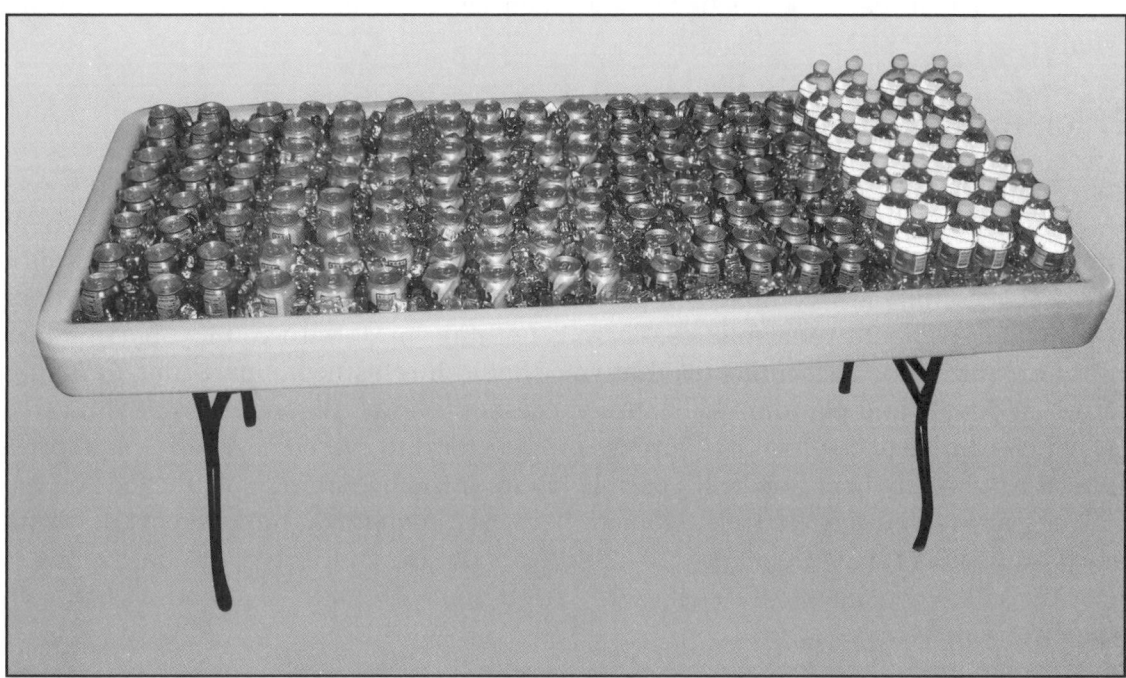

Each food service manager has the problem of keeping buffet items hot and other items cold while still presenting an appealing appearance. Satellite Cool has products to help you maintain safe temperatures and avoid wasted food. Since the units are portable, they are ideal for catering and special events. Visit **www.satellitecool.com** or call 888-365-2665 or 888-365-COOL.

Belson is your outdoor superstore. Any item you need for an outdoor event is available. They offer barbecue grills, trash receptacles, bleachers, bike racks, picnic tables, park benches, food service equipment, tables and chairs, camp stoves, concession equipment, pool furniture, drinking fountains, smokers, cigarette receptacles,

Satellite Cool portable cooling units

sports equipment, planters, parking lot equipment, and sanitation equipment. They are your one-stop for outdoor event supplies. Visit **www.belson.com** or call 800-323-5664.

Planning and Organizational Skills

If you don't plan smart, you will have a hectic, unsuccessful event with unhappy clients. Planning is more critical with off-premises catering because you can't run into the kitchen to grab what you need. You need a plan to keep hot food hot and cold food cold. You need to know what item gets served on which platter so that you have all necessary serving dishes or serving ware on hand. Silverware items need to be counted and recounted.

In a typical food service facility, 70 percent of your work is food-oriented with 30 percent involving service and organization. These percentages are swapped with the catering business. With catering, 70 percent of the work is organization and planning and 30 percent involves the food. You also need to include delivery, transporting food, lining up rental equipment, and juggling personnel. In catering, each day and each event is different making organizational skills vital!

Be Efficient and Stay Calm

Efficiency is important. Do you work well under pressure? Do you struggle to keep your head above water? Or do you manage to get the task done after a long time and with errors? The other option would be if you are a person who thrives on a complicated task. There is a big difference between handling complicated projects and managing to get the minimum done. Be honest with yourself about your abilities. There is nothing wrong with you if you cannot handle the project organization. That indicates that you should hire someone part time to handle the more involved details and planning to ensure successful events. Remember that you rarely get more than one chance to create a first impression. It is hard to overcome a bad first impression, so you need to be ready to do the best possible job from the beginning. In catering you have to deal with the stress and make sure customers never see the stress. Remain cool and smile no matter what chaos is racing through your mind or body. No matter what is happening, when you meet the customer, have your chef jacket on, a smile on your face, and a cool, calm air that reassures your client.

Crisis Management

A caterer spends time "putting out fires," literally and figuratively. Expect problems and be prepared to solve them quickly and creatively. Crisis management and problem solving skills are necessary in catering. This is especially true with off-premise catering because of all the unknown variables. You will handle site problems, serving food at unfamiliar locations, finding delivery entrances and parking spots. No matter what happens, you have to be creative and the event must go on.

Assess Your Skills Profile

To be a successful caterer you need to prepare delicious food and present it in an appetizing, mouth-watering way, while maintaining a profit. You might want to work a few catering events to get an idea of how they work. There are many chances to work during late spring, early summer, and the holidays, when catering businesses are especially busy with special events and holiday events. This is a great way to see how the events work and to understand what is involved. Depending on where you work, you may get to ask lots of questions.

Spend some time seriously considering what you are about to do and ask yourself some questions to determine if this is the decision you want to make. These answers will help you determine whether you are ready to open a catering business and whether you have the resources to do it.

- What are your goals for the catering operation?

- What type of personality do you have? Do you like to interact with other people? Do you thrive on activity and crisis?

- Does your family support this decision and are they prepared to sacrifice time with you?

The Non-Commercial Food Service Manager's Handbook

• What management experience do you have?

Be realistic. If you are a night owl, you should not consider catering brunches or other morning events. In turn, if you are a morning person, you should not cater late night events. Food service work is tough when you love it; do not make the work harder by mismatching the work and your personality.

Catering and Profits

The potential profit margin in catering is extremely high. Some caterers manage to walk away with 66 percent pre-tax profits. This figure may seem hard to believe, but there are many ways for caterers to keep their overhead costs low. About 70 percent of caterers report they are profitable each of their last five years in business.

If you are working out of your own kitchen, your initial investment can be as low as $1,000. This is one of the benefits of expanding an existing food service facility to offer catering because many of the fixed costs are being met by the non-commercial food service facility. However, it is important to choose the types of catering that fit your skills and expectations.

Types of Catering

Catering is categorized by the type of event being hosted. Caterers usually work at business and social events. Social events are normally scheduled at night and on weekends, while business events are scheduled during normal business hours. The types of events you handle are dictated by your interests and your schedule. The information below will give you some additional details about the types of catering.

Off-Premise Catering – Off-premise catering is for a business that has a kitchen but no dining facilities. All food and other items are transported to different locations. These services could be provided in people's homes, at facilities that have no kitchens, at parks for outdoor weddings, at office business meetings. Off-premise catering is more challenging because each situation and location are new while with on-site catering you are in a familiar location. With off-premise catering each event is unique and so are the potential problems. But off-premise catering has some advantages over on-premise catering. The events can be more exciting and rewarding if you enjoy the challenge of working in unusual and unique locations and dealing with new people. One interesting specialized type of off-premise catering is mobile catering, where a caterer feeds a basic menu to a large group of people like forest firefighters, disaster relief workers, construction-site workers, people taking camping trips, or excursions. The caterer develops a seasonal menu and a picnic table concept on the back of a properly equipped truck. The fare is usually hot or cold sandwiches, beverages, soup, coffee, bagels, or burritos. This is not as glamorous as some catering, but it is profitable and less stressful. There are two important considerations for any type of catering.

- **Teamwork** — Strong leaders can build a strong team. A team that does off-premise catering will become strong, and all members will learn to handle just about everything that can go wrong.

- **Subcontractors** — Off-premise catering costs are generally lower than for on-premises catering, so you may be able to hire subcontractors for particular aspects of the event such as floral design, music, and entertainment. Check the yellow pages under "entertainment" for such agencies or you can ask other caterers which companies they use for flowers or music. Networking with business people in your community will help you find resources of talent and expertise.

Four Keys to Success in Off-Premise Catering

1. **Be Prepared** — You need to be organized, plan ahead, and visualize in advance all of the aspects of a catered event. It's important to make lists and check these lists repeatedly before an event. Let a trusted person, who may catch something you missed, check the lists.

2. **Visit the Event Site** — When you cater an event off-premises visit the site. This should be done early and again as the event gets closer.

3. **Be Involved** — You must be in the center of the action and especially when you are working off-site. Ask clients and guests for feedback. Keep an eye on your staff to ensure they are performing to your established standards. You need to jump in and help when things need to be done.

4. **Stay Calm** — Five things are going wrong at once. You still need to appear calm and in control. You also need to be in control. Learn how to deal with stress. One good way to start is to manage your time effectively.

On-Premise Catering

On-premise catering is held on your facility's premises. There are estimates that on-premise catering accounts for two thirds of all catering sales in the United States. Some food service businesses have banquet facilities and offer on-premise catering. Other facilities close their operations to the public for a night and rent the space for a private function. This option would depend on the number of meals that your facility is required to serve each day.

On-premise catering offers an advantage to clients because they do not have the added stress of finding and securing a site for their function, decorate, and set up the area for their event.

Tips for Success

Specialize

Find a niche for your catering business. Weddings can yield high profits, largely because of the additional purchases included in a single event. However, you should include a bridal consultant on your staff. This person is valuable to handle expectations of brides. They also understand cultural differences and customs that you must work around. There are many Web sites devoted to planning weddings. Visit these to see the concerns couples will have. One Web site is at **www.usabride.com**.

Streamline

The layout of your premises needs to work with you, rather than against you. Convenience is critical since you will be working under pressure. The biggest advantage of catering on-premises is that everything is in reach.

Comfort

Determine how many people can be comfortably seated in your facility. Can you provide entertainment? Are you able to prepare various menu items at the last minute?

Catering For Businesses

Corporate sales make up approximately 75 percent of the total catering sales in the United States. This is a partial list of business events that require catering: meetings/conventions, incentive events, new product introductions, building openings, recognition events, training sessions, anniversaries, annual meetings, team meetings, and employee appreciation events. The kinds of business events are varied, and the corporate catering market is divided into three segments: shallow, mid-level, and deep.

Shallow Market

These include low-budget events like employee appreciation lunches. They have limited budgets and resources and do not include lead-time. They usually are for non-profit businesses, schools, and the military. These events may be less profitable, but they fill a niche for caterers. This type of event can fill in time between larger events. Some money is better than no money.

Mid-level Market

These are clients such as local associations that host regular training meetings. Price is important in this sector, but the resources are not as limited as in the shallow market. Clients are willing to spend more for an impressive event. This work often leads to repeat business and word of mouth advertising.

Deep Market

These are elegant, upscale events like university presidential inaugurations or board of director dinners. Cost is not a factor in this market. The client needs to provide an excellent and memorable event and will pay what is required.

Social Event Catering

Individuals usually book these events. They are scheduled around occasions in a person's life such as anniversaries, bar mitzvahs, birthdays, births, fund raising events, graduations, holiday parties, reunions, and weddings. Social catering is considered to be the catering business. While it is actually the smaller sector of the business, but caterers are drawn to these events because they are fun and lively, and people can relate to a birthday or anniversary as opposed to the launch of new product or a new building opening.

There are many facets to business catering and you need to decide what combination of services appeals to you and fits your skills and objectives.

Menus

Catering menus are developed by several people. They are often reviewed in customers' own homes or offices prior to meeting with food service personnel. The customer may review several different operations at the same time. When creating your catering menus consider:

- What items on your menu are popular?

- What products do you have on hand?

- Which items on your menu can be stored and transported if needed?

- Which items can be mass produced easily?

- How much storage space do you have available.

It isn't necessary to start from scratch. If certain items sell well, can be stored to maintain quality, and can be mass produced, use them on your catering menu. Your menu sales analysis sheets and sales history can be used to determine the popular, cost effective recipes that you already use. At the end of this chapter is a sample catering menu to give you an idea of the way to present the information for your clients.

When you plan an event you need to consider the food and portions needed. The form shown at the end of this chapter will help you plan this specific information and help you compile a realistic budget for the event.

Marketing

Your catering services need to be promoted. Your existing customer base is a great place to start with some internal marketing. These techniques are used with customers in your facility. Here are some internal marketing tips:

- **Set up table tents or signs** that let your customers know you cater.

- **Have carryout catering menus at the cashier or hostess station** along with brochures and business cards.

- **You can serve a tray of appetizers from your catering menu in the facility** during a reasonably busy time.

- **A popular idea is to have people drop business cards in a fishbowl and draw one, once a week.** The winner receives a free lunch catered for six.

- **These business cards can be used to create an e-mail list.** A well-thought-out e-mail can be sent to promote your catering business.

- **Create T-shirts with your logo and catering information and sell these at the hostess stand.** You can hold a drawing to give one away each week.

- **Give each server a button that says "Ask me!"** Servers can tell customers about your new catering services and give them a brochure.

We have discussed creating an e-mail list which is is a fast and easy way to contact your customers through their e-mail accounts. Using e-mail is fast and inexpensive. If this is a promotional avenue that appeals to you, call 800-309-7228 or check the Web site at **www.loyalrewards.com/merchant.asp** for information about this program to promote your business. They offer interesting ways to build your mailing list.

Know exactly what you want to promote before beginning external promotions. Advertising is costly and there is no guarantee that it will succeed. These are some ideas for external ways to promote your catering services.

Booking an Event

To book an event you need detailed information: number of guests, budget, decorations, menu choices, dietary restrictions, entertaining, floral preferences, and the style of service. It is necessary to meet with potential clients face to face without interruption to discuss their preferences. It may be necessary to create an enclosed office space to meet with potential clients or you can meet in the dining room during off hours.

You should create an event order form to have specific details in one place. The example at the end of this chapter of a Catering and Event Checklist will help you get the initial details to prepare for the event. Make sure these records are in a safe place like a folder to hold all records for the individual events you cater.

After you book an event and complete the event order sheet, it is necessary to complete a contract with the person who is authorized to arrange the event. Be sure that the person in charge of the event signs the contract. An example of a catering contract can be found at the end of this chapter. You need to fill in the specifics for each individual event.

The letters at the end of this chapter are examples of a confirmation letter that should be sent to each catering client, a letter to thank them for contacting you, a sample agreement and a letter to confirm last-minute details. You can also include a second copy and ask them to sign and return it to you. This is just an idea to provide suggestions to create a series of letters of your own.

Is catering a feasible option for your facility? This chapter has given you some basic information to help you begin to make an educated decision. For much more in-depth information about catering, you should read *The Professional Caterer's Handbook How to Open and Operate a Financially Successful Catering Business* from Atlantic Publishing **www.atlantic-pub.com**. This book offers detailed information about how to establish and run a successful catering business, and it comes with a CD that provides many helpful forms and a sample business plan for your review.

Another great resource from Atlantic Publishing Company that discusses how to plan special events is *The Complete Guide to Successful Event Planning With Companion CD-ROM* by Shannon Kilkenny (Item # SEP-01, $39.95). This book goes into great detail about exactly what all you need to know to plan a large or small event as well as excellent information on "greening" an event. Atlantic Publishing Company can be reached via their Web site at **www.atlantic-pub. com** or by phone at 800-814-1132,

Planning an event can be tedious and you don't want to over look any details. This software could be beneficial for you. Caterease software offers something for everybody. There are three versions of this software, Express, Standard, and Professional. All three offer comprehensive event and client management. The Standard version offers more advanced tools and reports to simplify your workday. The Professional version offers all the bells and whistles, providing cutting-edge features with a focus on saving your company time.

EVENT FOOD PRODUCTION AND PORTION CONTROL FORM

Name of Event: _____ Date of Event: _____

Prepared By: _____ Day of Week of Event: _____

Guaranteed Guest Count: _____ Amount to Prepare Count: _____ Confirmed Count: _____

○ Full-Service   ○ Buffet   ○ Other _____   Food Service Time: _____

Menu Item	Quantity Prepared	Portion Size	Possible Number	Weight of Amount Left	Portions of Amount Left	Amount Used

EVENT ORDER	
Customer:	Judith Jones
Contact:	Judith Jones
Phone:	555-555-5555
Event date:	12/14/06
Location:	J. Jones' house: 1516 Periwinkle Way
No. of guests:	60
Setup time:	5 p.m.
Event type:	Coworker Christmas dinner party

Schedule:

5 p.m.	Caterer arrives
6 p.m.	Guests arrive/serve appetizers/open bar
6:30 p.m.	Serve dinner
7:45 p.m.	Serve dessert
9 p.m.	Guests depart

Menu:

- Smoked salmon mousse on endive
- Fruit and cheese display with crackers
- New potatoes filled with sour cream and caviar
- Beef tenderloin glazed with reduced balsamic vinegar
- Wild mushroom cobbler
- Roasted green beans
- Bread and butter
- Individual chocolate soufflé cakes

Rentals:

- Six 60" round linens
- Six 10-foot rounds
- Two 5-ft banquet tables for buffet

Appetizers

- Curried chicken salad in phyllo cups
- Cheese, fruit and cracker display with strawberries, grapes, brie, sharp cheddar, dill and Havarti, and assorted crackers
- Hummus and vegetables
- Smoked salmon and cream cheese roll ups

DINNER

- Mixed green salad with champagne vinaigrette
- Smoked pork tenderloin with apple chutney
- Grilled chicken breast stuffed with leeks and mushrooms
- Roasted fingerling potatoes
- Haricot verts

DESSERT

- Client will provide anniversary cake. Servers to cut and serve with truffles and coffee.

SEATING

- There will be a head table with anniversary couple plus 8 other family members. Table to be round like other dining tables; place in front by stage.

ENTERTAINMENT

- Taped music for dinner (client will provide tape). A swing band will play after dinner.

CATERING AND EVENT CHECKLIST

Date of Event:	Time: : a.m./p.m. to : a.m./p.m.
Private or Open Event?	Name of Party

DESCRIPTION OF EVENT

Approx. Covers Last Event*: * Approx. "Cover" formula: # of Seats x # of Hours	**Sales Last Similar Event:** $
Number of Guests:	

MENU

	PORTION PP	ORDER UNIT/ PORTION #	ESTIMATED SERVINGS	AMOUNT TO ORDER
Entrée				
1.				
2.				
3.				
Side Dishes				
Side 1				
Side 2				
Side 3				
Side 4				
Bread or Other				
1.				
Dessert				
1.				
2.				
3.				
Beverages				
1.				
2.				
3.				

CATERING AND EVENT CHECKLIST				
Other Ingredients/ Items to Order Increase				
1.				
2.				
3.				
4.				
5.				
6.				
7.				
8.				
9.				
10.				
11.				
12.				
13.				
14.				
15.				
16.				
17.				

CATERING AND EVENT CHECKLIST				
KITCHEN SETUP	**TIME TO DO**	**PERSON RESPONSIBLE**	**RETRIEVE ITEM FROM**	**PLACE ITEM WHERE?**
Product Prepping				
Prep Sheet Filled Out				
Prep Items Labeled				
Clean event area				
Equipment Setup				
Cooking Setup				
Tongs/#				
Spatulas/#				
Cold Side Dish Containers/ # plus backups				
Spoons for Cold Sides/ #				
Hot Dish Containers/ # plus backups				
Serving Spoons #				

CATERING AND EVENT CHECKLIST

Basting Brush				
Condiment Containers/ #				
Cold Holding Setup (40°)				
Aprons/#				
Food Handlers' Gloves				
Trash Cans Strategically Placed and Lined				
KITCHEN/ STAFFING PERSON	**POSITION**	**HOURS SCHEDULED**	**RATE**	**PRIVATE PARTY CHARGE?**

CATERING AND EVENT CHECKLIST					
SERVICE SET-UP	**TIME TO DO**	**PERSON RESPONSIBLE**	**RETRIEVE ITEM FROM**	**PLACE ITEM WHERE?**	
Table/Chairs Placement					
Tablecloths on Tables					
SERVICE SET-UP	**TIME TO DO**	**PERSON RESPONSIBLE**	**RETRIEVE ITEM FROM**	**PLACE ITEM WHERE?**	
Condiments					
Beverages					
Cups					
Forks, Knives and Spoons					
Straws, Sugar, Cut Lemons					
GUEST BRINGING CAKE?					
Plates					
Cake Cutter					
Candles					
FULL BAR OR WINE?	**Cash 'n Carry**	**Host Bar**	**Cork Fee?**	**Cost PP**	**$NA**
Set Up Bar					
Register					

CATERING AND EVENT CHECKLIST				
SERVICE STAFFING FOR EVENT/ PERSON	POSITION	HOURS SCHEDULED	RATE	CHARGE TO PARTY?
				NA
				NA
				NA
				NA
				NA
				NA
				NA
				NA
				NA
				NA
				NA
				NA
				NA
				NA
				NA
				NA
				NA
				NA
				NA
				NA

DAPHNE'S CATERING

In consideration of the services to be performed by [insert Caterer's name here] ("Caterer") for the benefit of [insert Client's name here] ("Client") at the event scheduled for [insert event's date here], 200_, ("Event") as set forth in the attached invoice, Client agrees to the following terms and conditions:

1. In arranging for private functions, the attendance must be specified and communicated to Caterer by 12:00 p.m. (noon), at least seven (7) days in advance. If the actual number in attendance is greater than the amount confirmed, Caterer cannot guarantee that adequate food will be available for all persons attending. If the actual number is more than 20 percent less than the number confirmed, Caterer reserves the right to increase the price per person.

2. In order to reserve the date of the Event, Client must deliver a copy of this Agreement to Caterer along with a Deposit ("Deposit") of 50 percent of the invoice amount. The balance is due and payable no later than the day on which the Event is scheduled to be held.

3. If Client fails to make any payments when due, this Agreement may be cancelled or rejected by Caterer, and Client agrees that Caterer shall not thereafter be obligated to provide any services hereunder. Client agrees that Caterer may retain 50 percent of the Deposit, as liquidated damages and not as a penalty, which represents a reasonable estimation of fair compensation to Caterer for damages incurred by Caterer resulting from such failure to pay or cancellation by Client.

4. Menu requirements are to be followed as discussed and agreed upon with Client. All food and beverage is subject to __ percent sales tax and __ percent service charge. No beverages of any kind will be permitted to be brought into the premise by Client or any of the guests or invitees from the outside without the special permission of Caterer, and Caterer reserves the right to make a charge for the service of such beverages.

5. Performance of this Agreement is contingent upon the ability of Caterer to complete the same and is subject to labor troubles, disputes or strikes; accidents; government requisitions; restrictions upon travel; transportation; food; beverages; or supplies; and other causes beyond Caterer's control that may prevent or interfere with performance. In no event shall Caterer be liable for the loss of profit, or for other similar or dissimilar collateral or consequential damages, whether on breach of contract, warranty, or otherwise.

6. Client agrees to indemnify and hold harmless Caterer for any damage, theft, or loss of Caterer's property (including without limitation, equipment, plates, utensils, and motor vehicles) occurring at the Event that is caused by persons attending the Event.

January 22, 2007

Ms. Eleanor Smith
The XYZ Marketing Company
Tallahassee, FL 32301
850-844-8444

Ms. Smith,

Thank you for your interest in Elite Catering, Co. It is the perfect way to bring professionally prepared, exciting menu creations to your guests. Elite Catering, Co. is a fully licensed and insured corporation that represents 20 years of serving the Tallahassee business community. We are prepared to meet every challenge while delivering exceptional services.

I've enclosed a flyer, sample menus, and business references for your review. Please note that prices do not include additional services such as rental equipment, decorations, and alcoholic beverages. I look forward discussing this information with you. I will call next Wednesday to answer any questions you may have.

Sincerely,

Peter Wilson, Elite Catering, Co.
President/Chef

May 28, 2007

Ms. Eleanor Smith
The XYZ Marketing Company
Tallahassee, FL 32301
850-844-8444

Eleanor,

I am looking forward to your employee picnic on Saturday, June 17, 2006, at the Elite Catering, Co.. We are in receipt of a final guarantee of 350 guests.

Your deposit of $_____ will be deducted from the final invoice presented at the end of the event.

We ask that any alcoholic beverages be delivered to the park site by 11:30 a.m. that day to ensure proper cooling and handling. Your rental and softball equipment are scheduled to arrive by noon. Our chefs are skilled in preparation and service, and their first duty is to prepare the finest meal possible and serve the food to each table, hot or cold, in a timely manner.

We look forward to adding your name of our list of satisfied clients. We will arrive on Saturday at 11:00 a.m. to begin preparations for your event.

See you on the 17th of June.

Peter Wilson, Elite Catering, Co.
President/Chef

February 10, 2006

Ms. Eleanor Smith
The XYZ Marketing Company
Tallahassee, FL 32301
850-844-8444

Re: June 17, 2006, afternoon employee picnic with 350 adults
Ducks Community Park
300 South 11th Street, Tallahassee, FL 32301

Ms. Smith,

Thank you for selecting Elite Catering, Co. to prepare and serve your employee picnic on Saturday, June 17, 2006, at 1:30 p.m. The menu will begin with the food and beverage service prior to the softball game. After the game, we will present the dessert about 3 p.m.

MENU
Regular Hot Dogs and Hamburgers
Cold Cuts, Sliced Cheese, and Sub Rolls,
Potato Chips, Macaroni Salad, and Cold Slaw

6 oz. Cartons of Orange Juice
Assorted 20 oz. Soft Drink & Juice Bottles
Thermos of Hot Water
Decaf & Regular Coffee
Nondairy Creamer, Sugar, and Sugar Substitutions

Paper plates, plastic utensils, napkins, straws, stir sticks, tablecloths
Plastic coffee cups with handles
Plastic cups for soft drinks
Condiments Packets

DESSERT
Cantelope Squares, ½ Chocolate/ ½ Yellow Sheet Cake with Flower Frosting, Cookies

RENTAL
2 – 20-cup coffee urns, 2 x-large grills, charcoal and lighter
24 – 8' tables for seating
8 – 6' tables for food service

The cost of your menu is $5.95 per person plus tax. The dessert is $1.75 per person plus tax. Charges for your chefs will be $50 per chef for a 3-hour minimum period. Rentals are $952 plus tax.

Please remit a deposit of $1,500.00 made payable to Elite Catering, Co. The balance of your charges are due at the end of the event. Please review and sign the enclosed working agreement. I will plan to meet with you at the Park in mid-May.

Sincerely,

Peter Wilson, Elite Catering, Co.
President/Chef

March 8, 2006

Ms. Eleanor Smith
The XYZ Marketing Company
Tallahassee, FL 32301
850-844-8444

Eleanor,

The following is an agreement between Ms. Eleanor Smith, representative of the The XYZ Marketing Company and Elite Catering, Co. Please review, sign, and retain a copy for your records.

Regarding the XYZ Marketing Company employee picnic on Saturday, June 17, 2006, afternoon employee picnic for 350 adults to be held at Ducks Community Park, 300 South 11th Street, Tallahassee, FL 32301.

1. XYZ Marketing Company, as buyer, mains the services of Elite Catering, Co. to provide, food (as outline in attached menu) and service for the XYZ Marketing Company employee picnic on the day at the location stated above for 350 guests. The cost is $5.95 per person plus tax. The dessert is $1.75 per person plus tax. Charges for your chefs will be $50 per chef for a 3-hour minimum period. Rentals are $952 plus tax.

2. XYZ Marketing Company agrees to provide all alcoholic beverages and convey them to the site. Elite Catering, Co. will provide bartenders for the service of the alcoholic beverages. Elite Catering, Co. is insured for Dram Shop insurance by Liberty Insurance Group for $1,500,000.00). Attached is a copy of our certificate of insurance for our Dram Shop coverage.

3. XYZ Marketing Company agrees to a deposit of $1,500.00 made payable to Elite Catering, Co. 15 days prior to the event date. Elite Catering, Co. agrees to perform all catering services as services listed in the attached party confirmation letter.

4. A final invoice will be submitted to XYZ Marketing Company no more than seven business days after the function and is payable at that time. Any charges other than food or service (e.g., equipment, rental, decorations, use fees) are the responsibility of XYZ Marketing Company and are payable directly to the vendors providing them.

I have read and understand the information outlined above.

_____

Ms. Eleanor Smith, The XYZ Marketing Company

_____

Peter Wilson, President/Chef, Elite Catering, Co.

Conclusion

Job opportunities are available, and now you have information on each of them to help you pursue these options. Would you like to work in a hospital cafeteria or a nursing home? Does a high school or college cafeteria seem like a better fit? Either of these is possible.

All effective managers need to understand the basics of account management and how to cut costs in a facility. Cutting costs is about more than saving money: you also need to maintain customer and employee relations. We discussed the various ways that non-commercial menus are developed and how to calculate profitable prices.

Some of the most critical things in any food service facility are: purchasing, receiving, storage, and inventory. Once the food is safely brought into the facility, all staff members need to learn to handle food safely and to maintain sanitary conditions. These topics were presented along with a wealth of forms, worksheets, and additional resources to help you learn all elements of your job.

Employees can be valuable or a nightmare. The difference begins with effective interviewing, hiring, and training practices.

These are just a sample of the information we discussed in these pages. The CD included with this book will be valuable to you in creating useful forms for your facility. The case studies sprinkled throughout the book are also meant to give you information from people who have worked in the food service industry.

Each of these combines to help you make an educated decision about whether to look into the non-commercial industry as a career choice. After you make the decision, this book will help you develop and fine tune your skills as a non-commercial food service manager.

Biographies

Douglas R. Brown is a best-selling author in the area of food service management, having worked for both national chains and independent restaurants, as well as providing consulting services. He is the author of several new books and numerous articles on food service management. In 1982 he established Atlantic Publishing Group, Inc., and today the company is the leader in providing training materials including books, videos, posters, tools and software to the food service industry. Visit **www.atlantic-pub.com** to view a complete selection of products.

Shri Henkel is from the Shenandoah Valley of Virginia. She had a strong desire to create and write since she was young. She owns a Management and Marketing Consulting business and is a freelance writer and marketing professional.

This is her third non-fiction book being released during 2006-2007. Each one focuses on business management. One is a guide for first time managers. The second book is specifically targeted to pizza and sub shop managers or owners. Each will be available from Atlantic Publishing. She also wrote a book on *Successful Meetings* which was released February 2007.

Shri has 21 years of business management and 15 years of marketing experience. The knowledge she gained in this work was used to create helpful handbooks for business managers. These experiences include suggestions about things that work and warnings about things that don't.

In addition to her non fiction work, she has 2 novels in print under her pen name, Nikki Leigh. She is working on her third and fourth novels and two novellas. Her love of the coast, history and lighthouses is apparent in her stories. On a trip to Cape Ann with her brother, Chris, she discovered the area which is setting for a series of books. The rugged land, hardworking people and rich history were too compelling to ignore. Cape Ann, Eastern Point and Gloucester, Massachusetts are the setting for her books which focus on the "Stormy View" lighthouse.

For more information about her work, visit her fiction Web site at **www.nikkileigh.com** or her business Web site **www.sandcconsulting.com**. She also invites you to visit her and other friends at the Readers Station. This is a site to help readers understand more about the settings and characters that make up your favorite stories. You also have a chance to meet and talk with authors. The Web site is: **www.readersstation.com**

Glossary

A

A LA CARTE Items are prepared to order and each one is priced separately.

AP WEIGHT As-purchased weight.

ACCOUNTANT A person skilled in keeping and adjusting financial records.

ACCOUNTS PAYABLE Money owed for purchases.

ACCOUNTS RECEIVABLE Money owed by the customers.

ACTUAL-PRICING METHOD All costs plus the desired profits are included to determine a menu selling price.

ADVERSE IMPACT Impact of employer practices that result in higher percentages of employees from minorities and other protected groups.

ADVERTISING Purchase of space, time, or printed matter for the purpose of increasing sales.

AFFIRMATIVE ACTION Steps to eliminate the present effects of past discrimination.

AGE DISCRIMINATION IN EMPLOYMENT ACT OF 1967 Protects individuals over 40 years old.

AMBIANCE Sounds, sights, smells and attitude of an operation.

AMERICANS WITH DISABILITIES ACT (ADA) Prohibits discrimination against disabled persons.

ANNUAL Happening once in 12 months.

ANNUAL BONUS Monetary incentive tied to company profitability and designed to encourage continuous improvement in employee performance.

ANNUITY Promise of a definite payment for a specific period.

APPLICATION FORM A form that, when filled out by a potential employee, gives information on education, prior work record and skills.

ARBITRATION Third-party intervention, in which the arbitrator has the power to determine and dictate the terms.

AS PURCHASED (AP) Item as purchased or received from the supplier.

AS SERVED (AS) Weight, size or condition of a product as served or sold after processing or cooking.

ASSESSOR Someone who estimates the value of property for the purpose of taxation.

ASSETS Anything of value; all property of a person, company or estate that can be used to pay debts.

AUTOMATION Automatic control of production by electronic devices.

B

BALANCE The amount that represents the difference between debit and credit sides of an account.

BALANCE SHEET Written statement that shows the financial condition of a person or business. Exhibits assets, liabilities or debts, profit and loss, and net worth.

BANK NOTE A note issued by a bank that must be paid back upon demand. Used as money.

BASELINE BUDGET Based on a past budget and adjusted for current conditions.

BASIC MARKETING MOVES Basic moves that an operation should use to increase its sales volume.

BATCH PREP RECIPE Lists prices per ingredient for a detailed recipe for the purpose of obtaining a total cost for one batch of a meal.

BATCHING Adjusting recipes for equipment or recipe size constraints.

BEGINNING INVENTORY The quantity and value of beverage and food products or operational supplies in stock at the beginning of an accounting period.

BEHAVIOR MODELING A training technique. Trainees are shown good management techniques by role-play or viewing a film. Trainees are then asked to play roles in a simulated situation, and supervisors give feedback.

BEHAVIORISTIC APPROACH TO CONTROL Control through workers' desire to perform for the best interests of the organization.

BENCHMARK JOB The job that is used to secure the employer's pay scale and around which other jobs are systematized in order of relative worth.

BENCHMARKING Analyzing operation features in comparison to the best of its competitors in the industry.

BENEFITS Indirect payments given to employees. These may include paid vacation time, pension, health and life insurance, education plans and/or rebates on company products.

BID SHEET A sheet that is used in comparing item prices from different vendors.

BLIND RECEIVING When there are no quantities or weights printed on packages. The receiver must count or weigh items.

BLOCK SCHEDULING Workers begin and end work at the same time on a specified shift.

BONA FIDE OCCUPATIONAL QUALIFICATION (BFOQ) Requirement that an employee be of a certain religion, sex or national origin where this is reasonably necessary to the organization's normal operation. Specified by the 1964 Civil Rights Act.

BOTTLE MARK A label or ink stamp with information that identifies bottled products as company property.

BOTTOM UP BUDGET Secondary employees prepare a budget and then send it to upper management for approval and combining.

BOUNCEBACK CERTIFICATE OR COUPON A coupon good for a product upon a return visit. The customer is "bounced back" to the business.

BREADING The process of placing an item in flour, egg wash (egg and milk), then bread crumbs before frying or baking.

BREAKEVEN ANALYSIS A computative method used to find the sales amount needed for a food-service operation to break even.

BREAKEVEN CHART A chart that shows the relationship between the volume of business and the sales income, expenditures and profits or losses.

BREAKEVEN POINT Association between the amount of business and the resulting sales income, expenditures and profits or losses. When income and costs are equal.

BUDGET A plan for a specific period that estimates activity and income and determines expenses and other adjustments of funds. Planning the company's expenditures of money, time, etc.

BUDGET CALENDAR The dates/time that a budget should be finished.

BURGLARY Unlawful entry.

BURNOUT Depletion of physical and mental capabilities usually caused by setting and attempting unrealistic goals.

BUSINESS INTERRUPTION INSURANCE Insurance that covers specific costs when a business cannot operate as normal.

BUSINESS PLAN Defines the business image, clarifies goals, calculates markets and competition and determines costs and capital needs.

BUTCHER AND YIELD TESTS Testing of products to determine usable amounts after preparation.

BY-PRODUCT Item or items that are made in the course of producing or preparing other items.

C

CALCULATE Compute or estimate an amount.

CALENDAR YEAR Consisting of 365 days. The period that begins on January 1 and ends on December 31.

CAPACITY The volume limit.

CAPACITY MANAGEMENT The use of an operation's resources to serve the greatest number of guests.

CAPITAL Financial assets.

CAPITAL ACCUMULATION PROGRAMS Long-term incentives. Plans include stock options, stock appreciation rights, performance achievement plans, restricted stock plans, phantom stock plans and book value plans.

CAPITAL BUDGET Equipment, building and other fixed assets.

CARRYOVER Amount left over.

CASE STUDY METHOD Method in which the manager is given a written description of an organizational problem to diagnose and solve.

CASH BUDGET The amount of money received, the amount of money disbursed, and the resulting cash position.

CASH FLOW Profit plus depreciation allowances.

CASH ON DELIVERY (COD) Merchandise must be paid for on delivery or prior to delivery.

CASH OR CASH OUTLAY FOR PROJECT Annual net income (or savings) from project before depreciation but after taxes.

CASHBOOK A book containing records of all income and expenses of a business operation.

CELSIUS A unit used to measure temperature in the metric system, divided into 100 equal parts called degrees; previously called centigrade.

CENTIGRADE See Celsius.

CENTIMETER One hundredth part of a meter.

CENTRAL TENDENCY The disposition to rate all employees the same way, such as rating them all average.

CERTIFICATE Authorizing document issued by a bank indicating that a specific amount of money is set aside and not subject to withdrawal except on surrender of the certificate.

CHAIN OF COMMAND A top authority and a clear line of authority from that top to each person in the organization. Also called the scalar principle.

CIPHER Zero.

CITATIONS SUMMONS Informs employers and employees of regulations and standards that have been violated.

CIVIL RIGHTS ACT Law that makes it illegal to discriminate in employment on the basis of race, color, religion, sex or national origin.

CIVIL RIGHTS ACT OF 1991 (CRA 1991) Places the burden of proof back on employers and permits compensatory and punitive damages.

CLASSES Groupings of jobs based on a set of rules for each grouping. Classes usually contain similar jobs.

CLASSICAL PRINCIPLES (OR THEORY) OF ORGANIZATION Focuses on enterprise structure and work allocation.

CLASSIFICATION (OR GRADING) METHOD Categorizing jobs into groups.

CLASSIFICATION RANKING SYSTEM Constitutes grades and categories to rank various jobs.

COLLECTIVE BARGAINING Representa-tives of management and the union meet to negotiate the labor agreement.

COMMISSION An individual's pay based on the amount of sales personally derived.

COMMITTED ITEM A product that is scheduled for production between the time it is ordered and the time it is received.

COMMON SIZE ANALYSIS Analysis of financial statements by dividing each item on two or more statements by the total revenue for the period.

COMPARATIVE ANALYSIS Analysis of displaying the difference of line items on financial statements for two or more financial periods or two or more financial dates along with the percentage changes.

COMPENSABLE FACTOR A fundamental, compensable element of a job, such as skills, effort, responsibility and working conditions.

COMPENSATION Something given in return for a service or a value.

COMPETITIVE ADVANTAGE The elements that allow an organization to distinguish its product or service from those of its competitors.

COMPOUND Composed of more than one part.

COMPUTERIZED By means of a computer or computers.

CONFIGURATION An arrangement.

CONFRONTATION MEETINGS The method of explaining and bringing up intergroup misconceptions and problems so that they can be resolved.

CONSIGNMENT PRODUCTS Items provided to a company by a vendor who charges for them after they are used.

CONSUMER ORIENTATION The needs of consumers determine management decisions.

CONTRIBUTION RATE The contribution margin, in dollars, divided by sales.

CONTROL To have charge of.

COOK/CHILL SYSTEM Cooking food item to "almost done" state, packaging it (above pasteurization temperature) and chilling it rapidly.

CO-OP BUYING A group of similar operations working together to secure pricing through mass purchasing at quantity discount prices.

CORPORATION A group of people who obtain a charter giving them (as a group) certain legal rights and privileges distinct from those of the individual members of the group.

COST The amount paid to acquire or produce an item.

COST ALLOCATION The process of distributing costs among departments.

COST CONTROLLER The person or persons whose responsibilities include analyzing expenses, revenues and staffing levels.

COST FACTOR Cost calculated by dividing the cost per servable pound by the purchase price per pound.

COST LEADERSHIP Being the low-cost leader in an industry.

COST OF SALES Food and beverage cost for menu items in relation to the sales attained by these items during a specific period.

COST PER PORTION The cost of one serving calculated by total recipe cost divided by the number of portions.

COST PER SERVABLE POUND The cost calculated by multiplying the purchase price by the cost factor.

COST-BENEFIT ANALYSIS Determining the cost, in monetary terms, of producing a unit within a program.

COST-EFFECTIVENESS ANALYSIS Identifying the cost, in nonmonetary terms, of producing a unit.

COST-PLUS Paying vendors cost plus a percentage.

COUNT The number of units or items.

CPA (CERTIFIED PUBLIC ACCOUNTANT) An accountant who has fulfilled certain requirements and abides to rules and regulations prescribed by the American Institute of Certified Public Accountants.

CPP (COST PER POINT) BUDGETING Method used to obtain an advertising level at a predetermined cost.

CRITERION VALIDITY Validity is based on showing that scores on a test are related to job performance.

CULTURAL CHANGE Changes in a company's shared values and aims.

CURRENT LIABILITY A debt or obligation that will become due within a year.

CURRENT RATIO Current assets divided by current liabilities.

CUTTING LOSS Weight lost from a product during fabrication.

CVP The relationship between cost, volume and profit.

D

DAILY PRODUCTION REPORT A list of items and quantities produced during a specific shift or day.

DEAD STOCK ITEM Item no longer offered.

DEBIT Showing something owed or due.

DECIMAL A system of counting by tens and powers of ten.

DECIMETER Equal to one tenth of a meter.

DEDUCTION A value that may be subtracted from taxable income.

DEFAULT Failure to pay when due.

DEFERRED PROFIT-SHARING PLAN A plan in which a certain amount of profits are credited to an employee's account. May be payable at retirement, termination or death.

DEFINED BENEFIT PENSION PLAN A formula for determining retirement benefits.

DEFINED-CONTRIBUTION PLAN The employer makes specific contributions to an employee's pension but does not guarantee the amount.

DEGREE DAY The difference between outside temperature and 65° F.

DECAMETER Equal to 10 meters.

DELEGATION Distribution of authority and responsibility downward in the chain of command.

DEMOGRAPHIC SEGMENTATION Segmentation based on human population variables such as age, gender and family size.

DENOMINATOR Common trait or standard.

DEPOSIT To put in a place, especially a bank, for safekeeping.

DEPRECIATION Lessening or lowering in value.

DESIGNATE Point out; indicate definitely.

DIFFERENTIAL (BEVERAGE) Difference of the sales value of a drink from the standard sales value of beverages used.

DIFFERENTIATE To distinguish a product or service from similar products or services.

DIFFERENTIATION Trying to be unique within an industry with dimensions that are valued by buyers.

DIRECT COSTS (FOOD) The costs associated with direct purchases.

DIRECT ISSUE Items that are directly delivered and charged to a food-and-beverage outlet—not stored in a central storeroom.

DIRECT LABOR Labor used directly in the preparation of a food item.

DIRECT PURCHASES Food delivered directly into the kitchen and charged as a food cost on that day.

DIRECTING Showing and explaining to others what needs to be done and helping them do it.

DISCIPLINE A correction or action towards a subordinate when a rule or procedure has been violated.

DISMISSAL Involuntary termination of employment.

DIVIDEND An owner's share of the surplus when a company shows a profit at the end of a period.

DIVISOR A number by which another (the dividend) is divided.

DOWNSIZING The process of reducing the size of an operation.

E

EARNINGS PER SHARE Earnings of a company divided by the number of its stock shares outstanding.

EARNINGS RATIO The net profit before taxes divided by net sales.

ECONOMIC ORDER QUANTITY (EOQ) Determines a purchase quantity that does the best of minimizing purchases and inventory costs.

ECONOMIC STRIKE A strike resulting from a failure to agree about terms of a contract that involve wages, benefits and other employment conditions.

EDIBLE PORTIONS (EP) The actual yield available for processing a food item.

ELASTICITY OF DEMAND How demand for a product can fluctuate in response to other factors.

ELASTICITY OF SUPPLY The response of output to changes in price. Quantity supplied divided by the percentage change in the price.

ELECTRONIC DATA INTERCHANGE (EDI) Allows a food-service operator to receive prices electronically and generate an order form to send back.

ELECTRONIC SPREADSHEET Computerized worksheet with vertical and horizontal columns that are easily manipulated.

EMBEZZLEMENT Taking of property by someone to whose care it has been entrusted.

EMPLOYEE ADVOCACY Human Resources takes responsibility for defining how management should treat employees and represent the interests of employees within the framework of its obligation to senior management.

EMPLOYEE ASSISTANCE PROGRAM (EAP) Program employers promote to help employees overcome employee assistance program, usually in regard to alcoholism, drug abuse,

EMPLOYEE COMPENSATION Any form of pay or reward an employee gets from his or her employment.

EMPLOYEE ORIENTATION Introduction of basic company background information to new employees.

EMPLOYEE RETIREMENT INCOME SECURITY ACT (ERISA) The law that provides government protection of pensions for all employees with pension plans.

EMPLOYEE STOCK OWNERSHIP PLAN (ESOP) A company contributes shares of its own stock to a trust to which additional contributions are made annually. Upon retirement or separation from service the trust distributes the stock to employees.

EMPOWERMENT Giving lower-level employees the opportunity, responsibility and authority to solve problems.

ENDING INVENTORY The quantity and value of items in strock at the end of a period.

ENTREE The main dish of a meal.

ENTROPY Lack of useful input causing a system to solidify or run down.

EP WEIGHT Edible portion weight. The usable portion after processing.

EQUAL EMPLOYMENT OPPORTUNITY COMMISSION (EEOC) The commission empowered to investigate job discrimination complaints and sue on behalf of complainants.

EQUAL PAY ACT OF 1963 An amendment to the Fair Labor Standards Act designed to require equal pay for women doing the same work as men.

EQUIPMENT Machines or major tools necessary to complete a given task.

EQUITY FINANCING Financing by owners of the organization or company.

EQUIVALENT Equal in value or power.

ESTIMATE Judgment or guess determining the size, value, etc., of an item.

EVALUATE To find the value or amount of.

EXCEPTION PRINCIPLE Recurring decisions are handled in the normal manner and specific ones are referred upward for appropriate action.

EXPECTANCY CHART Shows the relationship between test scores and job performance.

EXPENDITURE Amount spent.

EXPIRATION The date on which a food or beverage product ceases to be usable.

EXPLODED RECIPE Changing recipe quantities to create the number of portions required.

EXTENSION To equate out, lengthen or widen.

EXTRA INDUSTRY Comparison of your practices with other industries.

F

FABRICATED Made or made up.

FABRICATED PRODUCT The item after trimming, boning, portioning, etc.

FABRICATED YIELD PERCENTAGE The yield, or edible portion, of an item shown as a percentage of the item as purchased.

FACTOR One of two or more quantities, multiplied.

FACTOR SYSTEM Raw food cost is multiplied by a factor to determine a menu selling price.

FAIR LABOR STANDARDS ACT Passed in 1936 to provide for minimum wages, maximum hours, overtime pay and child labor protection.

FINANCES Funds, money or revenue; financial condition.

FINANCIAL POSITION The status of a company's assets, liabilities and equity.

FINANCIAL STATEMENTS Used in a business operation to inform management of its exact financial position.

FINISHED GOODS Menu items that are prepared and ready to serve.

FIRM PRICE The price agreed to by the purchaser and vendor.

FISCAL YEAR The time between one yearly settlement of financial accounts and another.

FIXED BUDGET Budget figures based on a definite level of activity.

FIXED EMPLOYEES Employees who are necessary no matter the volume of business.

FLEX PLAN A plan giving employees choices regarding benefits.

FLEXIBLE BUDGET Projected revenue and expenditures based on production.

FLEXIBLE CAPACITY STRATEGY Handling varying volumes of business without having high overhead costs.

FLEXTIME A system that allows employees build their workdays around a core of midday hours.

FLIGHT The period of an advertiser's campaign.

FLUCTUATE Change continually.

FOOD COST The cost of food items purchased for resale.

FOOD INGREDIENT DATABASE Contains basic information about each food item. Name, cost, purchase units, inventory units, issue units, vendors and conversion factors are included.

FOOD ITEM DATA FILE (FIDF) NUMBER The number assigned to a food item in a database.

FOOD COST PERCENTAGE Cost of food divided by sales from that food.

FORECAST A prediction.

FORECASTING Estimating future revenue and expense.

FORMAT Refers to size, shape and general arrangement of a book, magazine, etc.

FORMULA A recipe or equation.

FOUR Cs OF CREDIT Character, capital, collateral and the capacity to repay.

FOUR-DAY WORKWEEK An arrangement that allows employees to work four ten-hour days instead of the more usual five eight-hour days.

FRACTION One or more of the equal parts of a whole.

FRANCHISE A franchise grants the right to use a name, methods and product in return for franchise fees.

FRANCHISEE The person or organization acquiring the franchise.

FRANCHISOR The person or company selling the franchise.

FREEZER BURN Fat under the surface of food having become rancid and possibly having caused a brown deterioration.

FTE, OR FULL-TIME EQUIVALENT A method of measuring labor costs with use of overtime pay.

FUNDAMENTAL EQUATION ASSETS
Liabilities plus equity.

G

GARNISH To decorate.

GELATIN A tasteless, odorless substance that dissolves easily in hot water and is used in making jellied desserts and salads.

GENERAL LEDGER (GL) A ledger containing all financial statement accounts.

GOURMET A lover of fine foods.

GRADUATED Arranged in regular steps, stages or degrees.

GRAM Twenty-eight grams are equal to one ounce.

GRATUITY/TIP A gift or money given in return for a service.

GRAZING When employees consume food, unauthorized.

GRIEVANCE A complaint against the employer that may include factors involving wages, hours or conditions of employment.

GROSS The overall total.

GROSS COST The total cost of food consumed.

GROSS MARGIN Sales minus the cost of food.

GROSS PAY Money earned before deductions are subtracted.

H

HARD WATER Water containing excessive calcium and magnesium.

HEALTH MAINTENANCE ORGANIZATION (HMO) Health-care providers that use their own physicians and facilities.

HECTOMETER Equal to 100 meters.

HEDGING A contract on a future price entered into to secure a fixed price.

HOMOGENEOUS ASSIGNMENT A form of specialization that assigns an employee to one job or limits the employee to a related specific task.

HORIZONTALLY On the same level.

HOST/HOSTESS The person who receives guests.

HOUSE BRAND The brand of liquor normally served by a given bar.

HVAC Heating, ventilation and air-conditioning.

HYPOTHETICAL Assumed or supposed.

I

IMPERIAL SYSTEM A measurement system using pounds and ounces for weights and pints for volume.

INDICATOR That which points out.

INGREDIENT One part of a mixture.

INGREDIENT ROOM Where non-cooking personnel prepare food before it is sent to cooking personnel.

INSTALLMENT Part of a sum of money or debt to be paid at regular times.

INSUBORDINATION Willful disobedience or disregard of a boss's authority.

INSURANCE Trading the possibility of a loss for the certainty of reimbursement. Paid by small premiums.

INTEGRATED BEVERAGE CONTROL SYSTEM An automatic beverage dispensing system integrated with a computer or point-of-sale register.

INTEREST Money paid for the use of borrowed money.

INTERNAL CONTROL Methods and measures within a business to safeguard assets, check the accuracy and reliability of accounting data, and promote operational efficiency.

INVENTORY A list of items with their estimated value and the quantity of each.

INVENTORY CONTROL System used for maintaining inventories.

INVENTORY CONTROL METHOD (BEVERAGE) Method in which the beverage amount used is determined from guest checks and then reconciled with replacement requisitions.

INVENTORY TURNOVER The amount of times inventory turns over during a specific period.

INVENTORY VARIANCE ACCOUNTING The amount of sales of an item is compared with the number used from inventory records, and the variance is noted.

INVERT Turn upside down.

INVOICE Shows prices and amounts of goods sent to a purchaser.

ITEMIZE To state by item.

J

JIGGER Used to serve a volume predetermined of a beverage.

JOB ANALYSIS Job description and specifications.

JOB DESCRIPTION A description of tasks and duties required on a job.

JOB SHARING Allowing two or more people to share a single full-time job.

JOB SPECIFICATIONS The qualifications needed to hold a job. Includes educational, physical, mental and age requirements.

K

KILOGRAM Equal to 1,000 grams.

KILOMETER Equal to 1,000 meters.

KLEPTOMANIA The persistent impulse to steal.

L

LAPPING A type of embezzlement when funds are taken from an account then covered with later receipts.

LEAST SQUARES ANALYSIS In-depth method of calculating an average of variable or fixed costs.

LEGUMES Vegetables, especially beans and peas; technically, plants in the pea family, or the fruits and seeds of such plants.

LEVERAGING Using borrowed money to acquire assets to make money.

LIABILITY Being under obligation or debt.

LINE MANAGER The manager who is authorized to direct work and is responsible for accomplishing the company's goals.

LINE OF IMPLEMENTATION Division of planning and organizing activities from "doing" activities.

LIQUIDITY RATIOS Ratios that show the ability to meet short-term obligations.

LIQUOR COST Amount paid for liquor after discounts.

LIQUOR COST PERCENT The portion cost divided by the selling price.

LITER Metric system measure of volume.

LOCKOUT When an employer refuses to provide opportunities to work.

LOGO Trademark.

LONG-TERM DEBT Fixed liabilities.

LOSS CONTROL Attempting to prevent losses.

M

MAITRE D' Person in charge of dining room service.

MANAGEMENT BY OBJECTIVES (MBO) Setting measurable goals with employees and periodically reviewing their progress.

MANAGEMENT PROCESS Five basic functions of planning, organizing, staffing, leading and controlling.

MANAGEMENT PROFICIENCY RATIO Net profit after taxes divided by total assets.

MANUAL Done by hand.

MARGIN The difference between the cost and the selling price.

MARGINAL COST The amount of output by which aggregate costs are changed if the volume of output is increased or decreased by one unit.

MARKET Groups with similar characteristics, wants, needs, buying power and willingness to spend for dining or drinking out.

MARKET PRICE INDEX Used to show the change in the cost of raw foods.

MARKET SHARE The share of a market that a business has for its products or services.

MARKETING Means by which an outlet is exposed to the public.

MARKETING OBJECTIVES Measurable and achievable goals that marketing efforts are intended to accomplish.

MARKETING PERSPECTIVE Consumer satisfaction is placed first in all planning, objectives, policies and operations.

MARKETING POLICY A course of action to be followed as long as conditions exist.

MARKETING SEGMENTATION Dividing the market into smaller submarkets or segments.

MARKETING STRATEGY Overall plan of action that enables the outlet to reach an objective.

MARKUP Amount by which a higher price is set.

MBWA Management by walking around.

MEASURE A lineal measure equal to a thousandth of a meter.

MEAT TAG Used for identification and verification.

MEDIA Various types of advertising, such as television, radio and newspapers.

MEDIATION Intervention using a neutral third party to help reach an agreement.

MEDICARE A federal health insurance program for people 65 or older and certain disabled people.

MENU A list of dishes served at a meal.

MENU ENGINEERING Technique that is used for analyzing menu profitability and popularity.

MENU MIX Menu popularity calculation.

MENU PREFERENCE FORECASTING Predicts how various items will sell when in competition with other items.

MENU PRICE The amount that will be charged for an item.

METRIC Pertains to the meter or to the system of weights and measures based on the meter and the kilogram.

MILL When dealing with monetary

numbers, the third place to the right of the decimal.

MILLIGRAM One thousandth part of a gram.

MILLILITER One thousandth part of a liter.

MILLIMETER One thousandth part of a meter.

MISSION STATEMENT A statement giving the reason why the organization exists and what makes it different from other organizations.

MODEM ORGANIZATION THEORY A behavioral approach to organization.

MODULE A discrete and identifiable program.

MONETARY To do with money or coinage.

MOVING AVERAGE The total of demand in previous periods divided by the number of periods.

MUNICIPAL SOLID WASTE (MSW) Waste products that are deposited in landfills.

N

NATIONAL EMERGENCY STRIKES Strikes that might "imperil the national health and safety."

NET The remaining amount after deducting all expenses.

NET PRESENT VALUE (NPV) The present value of future returns discounted at the appropriate cost of capital minus the cost of the investment.

NET PROFIT Profit after all product costs, operating expenses and promotional expenses have been deducted from net sales.

NET PURCHASE PRICE The price paid by the company for one unit.

NET WORTH Excess value of resources over liabilities.

NORRIS-LAGUARDIA ACT This law marked the era of strong encouragement of unions and guaranteed each employee the right to bargain collectively "free from interference, restraint or coercion."

NUMERAL Symbol for a number.

O

OCCUPATIONAL MARKET CONDITIONS Published projections of labor supply and demand for various occupations by the Bureau of Labor Statistics of the U.S. Department of Labor.

OCCUPATIONAL SAFETY AND HEALTH ACT Law passed by Congress in 1970 assuring every working man and woman in the nation safe and healthful working conditions to preserve our human resources.

OCCUPATIONAL SAFETY AND HEALTH ADMINISTRATION (OSHA) The agency created within the Department of Labor to set safety and health standards for all workers in the United States.

ON-THE-JOB TRAINING (OJT) Training to learn a job while working it.

OPEN BAR Practice at banquet functions whereby customers are not charged individually for the drinks they consume. The host pays for banquet-goers' consumption.

OPEN DEPARTMENT REGISTER KEYS Keys that break down sales by categories.

OPEN MARKET BUYING Food purchasing method where competitive bids are secured for various items.

OPERATING BUDGET Detailed revenue and expense plan for a determined period.

OPERATING RATIO Net profit divided by net sales.

ORGANIZATIONAL CHART Shows the relationships of jobs to each other with lines of authority, responsibility and communication.

ORGANIZATIONAL DEVELOPMENT INTERVENTIONS Techniques aimed at changing employees' attitudes, values and behavior.

OUTPUT The end product.

OUTSOURCING Calling upon other companies help supply your products.

OVERHEAD-CONTRIBUTION METHOD All non-food cost percentages are subtracted from 100. The resulting figure is divided into 100 and that figure times the raw food cost equals the menu selling price.

OVERTIME Time exceeding regular hours.

P

P AND L SHEET Profit and loss statement.

PAR STOCK Stock levels established by management for individual inventory items in varying locations.

PARKINSON'S LAW Workers adjust pace to the work available.

PAYBACK PERIOD Period of time required to recover an expenditure.

PAYROLL A list of employees and amounts to pay them, as well as records pertaining to these payments.

PENSION BENEFITS GUARANTEE CORPORATION (PBGC) Established under ERISA to ensure that pensions meet vesting obligations and to insure pensions should a plan terminate without sufficient funds to meet its vested obligation.

PENSION PLANS Plans that provide a fixed sum when employees reach a predetermined retirement age or when they no longer work due to disability.

PERCENTAGE CONTROL SYSTEM Wherein the cost of food or beverage is divided by sales to provide a percentage.

PERCEPTION OF VALUE A consumer's perception of what a product is worth.

PERPETUAL Continuous, endless.

PERPETUAL INVENTORY Accounting for inventory changes. Beginning and ending inventory figures are changed along with any sales or purchases.

PHYSICAL INVENTORY A count of all items on hand.

PIECEWORK The system of pay based on the number of items produced by each individual worker.

POINT-OF-SALE (POS) SYSTEM A sales transaction register and processor.

POPULARITY INDEX Total sales of an item divided by total number of that item sold.

PORTION One serving.

PORTION CONTROL Ensures that the correct amount is being served each time.

PORTION COST The cost of one serving.

PORTION SERVED The amount served to a customer.

PORTION SIZE A specific portion amount.

POSITION REPLACEMENT CARD A card prepared for each position in a company. Shows possible replacement candidates and their qualifications.

POTENTIAL COST Calculating what the expected cost of an item should be.

PPBSE Planning, programming, budgeting, staffing and evaluating.

PRE-CHECKING SYSTEM
Independent record of what is ordered from a kitchen.

PRE-COST/PRE-CONTROL
Accounting system that determines what the food cost should be, compares it with the actual food cost, and includes sales analysis.

PREFERRED PROVIDER ORGANIZATIONS (PPOS) Groups of health-care providers that contract with employers, insurance companies or third-party payers to provide medical care services at a reduced fee.

PREP YIELD PERCENTAGE Ratio of product yield after preparation to the quantity of product as purchased.

PRICE ELASTICITY The change in the rate of sales due to the change in price.

PRICE INDEXING Measures the effect of product price changes.

PRICE LOOK-UP (PLU) Assigned menu item numbers in POS systems.

PRIMAL CUT Primary division for cutting meat into smaller cuts.

PRIME COST The cost of a product after calculating and adding in labor.

PRINCIPAL Sum of money on which interest is paid.

PRIVILEGE CONTROL SYSTEM A system that permits or denies access to restricted areas.

PRO FORMA Statement prepared on the basis of anticipated results.

PROCEDURE The method of doing a task.

PRODUCT SPECIFICATION A listing of quality and service requirements necessary for each product to be purchased from a vendor.

PRODUCTION SCHEDULE The items and quantities that must be produced for a specific meal, day, etc.

PROFILE Data creating an outline of significant features.

PROFIT Gain.

PROPORTION The relationship between one thing and another with regard to size, number or amount.

PROPRIETORSHIP Ownership.

PSYCHOGRAPHIC SEGMENTATION Segmentation based on lifestyles.

PURCHASE SPECIFICATIONS Standard requirements established for procuring items from suppliers.

PURVEYOR One who supplies provisions or food.

Q

QUALITY CONTROL Assuring the execution of tasks and responsibilities according to established standards.

QUANTITATIVE FORECASTING Forecasting based on past and present numerical data.

QUANTITATIVE METHODS Using numbers to help make decisions.

QUANTITY The amount; how much.

QUICK RATIO Current assets less inventory value divided by current liabilities.

R

RANDOM WALK Assuming a present period of sales will be the same as a past period.

RANKING METHOD Ranks each job relative to all other jobs.

RATIO The ratio between two quantities is the number of times one contains the other.

RATIO ANALYSIS A technique for determining staff needs by using ratios between sales volume and the number of employees needed.

REACH Percentage of people in a target audience who will see or hear a specific advertising message.

RECEIPT A written statement that something has been received.

RECEIVING REPORT A report that indicates the value and quantity of items received.

RECIPE Directions used for preparing a menu item.

RECIPE COST The total cost of all ingredients in a recipe.

RECIPE YIELD The weight, count or volume of food that a recipe will produce.

RECONSTITUTE Put back into original form, especially by re-hydration.

RED-LINING Placing a red mark on a guest check so it cannot be used again.

RE-ENGINEERING To change an enterprise to be more customer oriented or more efficient.

REPORT An account of facts used to give or get information.

REQUISITION To apply for something needed.

RESIDUAL INCOME ANALYSIS (RIA) Comparing the return on an investment to the cost of invested capital.

RETURN ON INVESTMENT A ratio found by dividing profit by investment.

REVENUE Income.

REVENUE CENTER Outlet or department that produces revenue.

RFP Request for proposal.

ROI (RETURN ON INVESTMENT) Incremental sales dollars divided by total costs.

ROP (RUN OF PAPER/RUN OF PRESS) Placement of advertisement anywhere within a publication that the publisher elects.

ROTATING MENU A menu that alternates in a series. Usually set up on a yearly basis.

S

SALARY A regular payment for services rendered.

SALES MIX The number of sales of individual menu items.

SALES REVENUE Money from the sale of certain items.

SCATTER PLOT Helps identify the relationship between two variables.

SEAT TURNOVER The number of times a seat is occupied during a meal period. Calculate by dividing the number of guests seated by the number of available seats.

SENSIBLE HEAT Heat measured by a thermometer.

SERVER BANKING When the server or bartender also does the cashier duties.

SHRINKAGE The amount of food lost due to cooking, dehydration or theft.

SHRINKAGE (INVENTORY) The difference between what is on hand and what should be on hand.

SIMPLE RANKING SYSTEM Ranking jobs in order of difficulty or importance.

SIMPLIFY To make easier to understand or carry out.

SMART CARD A credit card with a computer chip that holds data.

SOCIAL APPROACH TO MANAGEMENT Considers management's responsibilities to employees, customers and community as well as to its stockholders.

SOLO INSERT Usually printed on different stock than that used by the publication, this page is printed by the advertiser and inserted into a magazine or newspaper by the publisher.

SOLVENCY RATIOS Ratios that show an organization can meet its long-term debt obligations.

SPECIFICATION A detailed statement of the particulars of an item.

SPILLAGE The alcohol lost during the drink making process.

SPOILAGE Loss due to poor food handling.

STAFF MANAGER The manager who assists and advises line managers.

STAGGERED SCHEDULING Scheduling employees to start and stop at different times according to the work pattern.

STAGGERED STAFFING Employees are staffed according to business volume.

STANDARD HOUR PLAN An employee is paid a basic hourly rate and an extra percentage of his or her base rate for production exceeding the standard.

STANDARD RECIPE Producing a particular food or drink item by a definite formula.

STANDARD-COST METHOD (BEVERAGE) Determines the cost of beverages from the number of each beverage sold then compares it to the cost of beverage requisitions.

STANDARDIZE To make the same in size, shape, weight, quality, quantity, etc.

STANDARDIZED RECIPE Directions describing the way an establishment prepares a particular dish.

STANDARD-SALES METHOD (BEVERAGE) Comparing actual beverage sales with the sales value of the beverage.

STANDING ORDER An order for delivery that is automatic.

STATEMENT OF INCOME Shows whether an operation has made or lost money.

STATIC MENU A menu that rarely changes.

STEPPED COSTS Costs which increase in elongated steps but at regular intervals.

STOCK OPTION The right to purchase a stated number of shares in a company at today's price at a future time.

STOCKHOLDER The owner of stocks or shares in a company.

STOREROOM PURCHASES Items are placed into storage rather than sent to the kitchen.

STORES (FOOD COST) The value of food that is in storage.

STRAIGHT LINE METHOD Used when figuring depreciation on an item.

STRATEGIC CHANGE A change in a company's strategy, mission or vision.

SUMMARIZE Briefly express, stating the main points.

SUNK COSTS Costs already incurred that cannot be recouped.

SYSTEM Components working together in the most efficient way.

T

TABLE D'HOTE A complete meal at a set price.

TARGET FOOD COST The amount a company hopes to spend for a particular menu item.

TENDER KEYS Cash register keys that break down sales by payment method.

THERM 100,000 Btu.

TIE-INS Joint venture promotions involving your company and another.

TIME AND MOTION STUDY A study done to establish a standard time for each job.

TIPPING FEE The cost of disposing of waste at a landfill.

TITLE VII OF THE 1964 CIVIL RIGHTS ACT States that an employer cannot discriminate on the basis of race, color, religion, sex or national origin.

TOP DOWN BUDGET A budget prepared by upper management and "passed on" to operating units.

TOTAL QUALITY MANAGEMENT (TQM) A program aimed at maximizing customer satisfaction through continuous improvements.

TRAINING Teaching new employees the basic skills needed to perform their jobs.

TREND ANALYSIS Study of a company's past employment needs over a time period of years to predict future needs.

TRIM The part or quantity of a product removed during preparation.

TRIPLICATE Three identical copies.

TUMBLE CHILL SYSTEM Pumpable foods prepared with steam kettles and then rapidly chilled.

U

U.S. SYSTEM The system of measurement used in the United States, whereby weight is measured in pounds and ounces, and volume is measured in cups and gallons.

UNIFORM PRODUCT CODE (UPC) A computer readable code on a package.

UNIT Refers to the number or amount in a package.

UNIT COST The purchase price divided by the applicable unit.

USABLE PORTION The part of a fabricated product that has value.

USAGE METHOD (OF FOOD PURCHASING) Purchasing food based on past consumption.

V

VARIABLE COST The production cost that changes in direct proportion to sales volume.

VARIABLE EMPLOYEES Employees whose time requirements change with changes in business volume.

VARIABLE RATE Variable costs divided by sales.

VARIATION The extent to which a thing changes, or the change itself.

VENDOR The person or company who sells.

VERBALLY Expressed in words.

VERSATILE Easily changing or turning from one action to another.

VERTICAL Straight up and down.

VOLUME Calculated as length times width times height.

VOUCHER Evidence of payment in written form such as a receipt.

W

WAGES Amount paid or received for work.

WEIGHT The measurement of mass or heaviness of an item.

WELL DRINK A drink not made with name-brand liquor.

WITHHOLDING TAX The deduction from a person's paycheck for the purpose of paying income taxes.

WORK SAMPLES Job tasks used in testing an applicant's performance.

WORK SIMPLIFICATION Finding the easiest and most productive way to perform a job or task.

WORKING CAPITAL The difference between current assets and current liabilities.

X

X MODE Allows reports to be produced on the POS register without resetting totals.

Y

YIELD The total created or the amount remaining after fabrication. The usable portion of a product.

YIELD CONVERSION FACTORS A factor that when multiplied by the gross weight amount of an item purchased shows how much will be available.

YIELD PERCENTAGE/YIELD FACTOR The ratio of the usable amount to the amount purchased.

Z

Z MODE Produces final reports and clears information from a POS register.

ZERO-BASED BUDGET A budget prepared without previous budget figures.

Manufacturers Reference

The following manufacturers submitted photos and information to be used as references in *The Non-Commercial Food Service Manager's Handbook.*

Accardis Systems, Inc.
20061 Doolittle Street
Montgomery Village, MD 20886
1-800-852-1992
www.accardis.com

Accubar
9457 S University Blvd
#261
Highlands Ranch, CO 80126
1-800-806-3922
www.accubar.com

Amana Commercial Products
2800 220th Trail
Amana, IA 52204
1-888-262-6271
www.amanacommercial.com

America Corporation
PO Box 91
13686 Red Arrow Highway
Harbert, MI 49115
1-800-621-5075
www.america-americabirchtrays.com

Aprons, Etc.
PO Box 1132
9 Ellwood Court
Mauldin, SC 29662
1-800-460-7836
www.apronsetc.com

Belson Outdoors, Inc
111 North River Rd
North Aurora, IL 60542
1-630-897-8489
www.belson.com

Big John Grills & Rotisseries
770 W College Ave
Pleasant Gap, PA 16823
1-800-326-9575
www.bigjohngrills.com

Biocorp
15301 140th Ave
Becker, MN 55308
1-866-348-8348
www.biocorpaavc.com

Blodgett
44 Lakeside Avenue
Burlington, VT 05401
1-800-331-5842
www.blodgett.com

Browne-Halco, Inc.
2840 Morris Ave
Union, NJ 07083
1-888-289-1005
www.halco.com

Buffet Enhancements International
PO Box 1000
Point Clear, AL 36564
1-800-990-0990
www.buffetenhancements.com

Caterease Software
1020 Goodlette Road N
Naples, FL 34102
1-800-863-1616
www.caterease.com

Chillin' Products, Inc.
1039 Railroad Street
Rockdale, IL 60436
1-866-932-4455
www.chillinproducts.com

CommLog
2509 E Darrel Rd
Phoenix, AZ 85042
1-800-962-6564
www.commlog.com

Cookshack, Inc.
2304 N Ash St
Ponca City, OK 74601
1-800-423-0698
www.cookshack.com

DayMark Food Safety Systems
12830 South Dixie Highway
Bowling Green, OH 43402
1-800-847-0101
www.daymarksafety.com

Duncan Industries
PO Box 802822
Santa Clarita, CA 91380
1-800-785-4449
www.kitchengrips.com

EasyBar Beverage Management Systems
19799 SW 95th Ave, Suite A
Tualatin, OR 97062
1-503-624-6744
www.easybar.com

Franklin Machine Products
101 Mt. Holly Bypass
Lumberton, NJ 08048
1-800-257-7737
www.fmponline.com

General Espresso Equipment Corporation
7912 Industrial Village Road
Greensboro, NC 27409
1-336-393-0224
www.geec.com

Genpak
PO Box 727
Glen Falls, NY 12801
1-518-798-9511
www.genpak.com

Gourmet Display
6040 South 194th, Ste #102
Kent, WA 98032
1-206-767-4711
www.gourmetdisplay.com

Henny Penny Corporation
1219 U.S. 35 West
Eaton, OH 45320
1-800-417-8417
www.hennypenny.com

Holstein Manufacturing
5368 110th St
Holstein, IA 51025
1-800-368-4342
www.holsteinmfg.com

iSi North America, Inc.
175 Rt 46 West
Fairfield, NJ 07004
1-800-447-2426
www.isinorthamerica.com

Motoman Inc.
805 Liberty Lane
West Carrollton, OH 45449
1-937-847-6200
www.motoman.com

OZEM Corp.
832 Harvard Dr
Holland, MI 49423

1-866-617-3345
www.ozwinebars.com

Polar Ware Company
2806 North 15th St
Sheboygan, WI 53083
1-800-237-3655
www.polarware.com

Precision Pours, Inc.
12837 Industrial Park Blvd
Plymouth, MN 55441
1-800-549-4491
www.precisionpours.com

Regal Ware, Inc.
1675 Reigle Dr
Kewaskum, WI 53040
1-262-626-2121
www.regalwarefoodservice.com

Sabert
879-899 Main St
Sayreville, NJ 08872
1-800-722-3781
www.sabert.com

Satellite Cooling
308 Washington Blvd, Ste
A-105
Mundelein, IL 60060
1-888-356-2665
www.satellitecool.com

Scannabar
101 Federal Street, Suite 1900
Boston, MA 02110
1-888-666-0736
www.scannabar.com

Sitram USA
4081 Calle Tesoro, Ste G
Camarillo, CA 93012
1-800-515-8585
www.sitramcookware.com

Slecta Corp dba Dickies Chef
13780 Benchmark Dr.
Farmers Branch, TX 75234
1-866-262-6288
www.dickiechef.com

Sunkist Foodservice Eq.
720 E Sunkist St
Ontario, CA 91761
1-800-383-7141
www.sunkistfs.com/equipment

Tucel Industries
2014 Forestdale Road
Forestdale, VT 05745
1-800-558-8235
www.tucel.com

Vinotemp International
17621 S Susanna Rd
Rancho Dominguez, CA 90221
1-310-886-3332
www.vinotemp.com

Wes-Pak, Inc.
9100 Frazier Pike
Little Rock, AR 72206
1-800-493-7725
www.wespakinc.com

Winekeeper
625 E Haley St
Santa Barbabra, CA 93103
1-805-963-3451
www.winekeeper.com

WNA Comet
6 Stuart Road
Chelmsford, MA 01824
1-888-962-2877
www.wna-inc.com

Zing Zang Inc
950 Milwaukee Ave
Glenview, IL 60025
1-888-891-7489
www.zingzang.com

Zojirushi America Corp
6259 Bandini Blvd
Commerce, CA 90040
1-800-733-6270
www.zojirushi.com

Index

D

Nutritional value 73

O

P

Q

R

S

DID YOU BORROW THIS COPY?

Have you been borrowing a copy of *The Non-Commercial Food Service Manager's Handbook: A Complete Guide For Hospitals, Nursing Homes, Military, Prisons, Schools And Churches: With Companion CD-ROM* from a friend, colleague, or library? Wouldn't you like your own copy for quick and easy reference? To order, photocopy the form below and send to:

Atlantic Publishing Company • 1405 SW 6th Ave. Ocala, FL 34474-7014

YES!

Send me___copy(ies) of *The Non-Commercial Food Service Manager's Handbook* (Item # NCF-02) for $79.95 + $6.00 for USPS shipping and handling.

(Please Print) *Name* _____

Organization Name _____

Address _____

City, State, Zip _____

Phone, Fax _____

❑ Please charge my: ❑ MasterCard ❑ VISA ❑ American Express ❑ Discover

Credit Card # _____

Expiration Date: _____ *Signature:* _____

❑ My check or money order is enclosed. *Please make checks payable to Atlantic Publishing Company.*

❑ My purchase order is attached. *PO #* _____

www.atlantic-pub.com
Order toll-free 800-814-1132 • FAX 352-622-1875

HACCP & Sanitation in Restaurants and Food Service Operations:
A Practical Guide Based on the FDA Food Code

According to the FDA, it is estimated that up to 76 million people get a food-borne illness each year. Since people don't go to the doctor for mild symptoms, the actual number of illnesses can't be known, but 5,000 people a year die from food-borne illness in the United States, and many others suffer long-term effects.

Most all of this sickness and death could have been prevented with the proper procedures that are taught in this comprehensive book. If these numbers don't upset you, realize that a food-borne outbreak in your establishment can put you out of business, and if the business survives, it will certainly be severely damaged; this, of course, after the lawsuits are resolved. If you do not have proper sanitation methods and a HACCP program in place, you need them today.

This book is based on the FDA Food Code and will teach the food service manager and employees every aspect of food safety, HACCP and sanitation, from purchasing and receiving food to properly washing dishes. They will learn:

- Time and temperature abuses
- Cross-contamination
- Personal hygiene practices
- Biological, chemical and physical hazards
- Proper cleaning and sanitizing
- Waste and pest management
- Basic principles of HACCP
- Bacteria, viruses, fungi and parasites
- Various food-borne illnesses
- Safe food-handling techniques
- Purchasing, receiving and food storage
- Food preparation and serving
- Sanitary equipment and facilities
- Explain what safe food is and how to provide it facilities
- Accident prevention and crisis management
- Food safety and sanitation laws

Item # HSR-02 $79.95
600 Pages Hardbound
ISBN 0910627-35-5

To order call toll-free
800-814-1132 or visit
www.atlantic-pub.com

The companion CD-ROM contains all the forms and posters needed to establish your HACCP and food-safety program.

Simply the BEST QUICK Reference Guides

The Food Service Professional GUIDE TO SERIES

This series from the editors of *The Food Service Professional Magazine* are the best and most comprehensive books for serious food service operators available. Step-by-step guides on specific management subjects that are easy to read and understand. The information is "boiled down" to the essence. They are filled to the brim with up-to-date and pertinent information. These books cover all the bases, providing clear explanations and helpful, specific information. All titles in the series include the phone numbers and Web sites of all companies discussed. Each book is 144 pages and **$19.95 each**.

1-800-814-1132 Call toll-free 24 hours a day, 7 days a week. Or fax completed form to: **1-352-622-1875**. Order Online!   Just go to **www.atlantic-pub.com** for fast, easy, secure ordering.

Qty	Order Code	Book Title	Qty	Order Code	Book Title
	Item # FS1-01	Restaurant Site Location		Item # FS9-01	Building Restaurant Profits
	Item # FS2-01	Buying & Selling a Restaurant		Item # FS10-01	Waiter & Waitress Training
	Item # FS3-01	Restaurant Marketing & Advertising		Item # FS11-01	Bar & Beverage Operation
	Item # FS4-01	Restaurant Promotion & Publicity		Item # FS12-01	Successful Catering
	Item # FS5-01	Controlling Operating Costs		Item # FS13-01	Food Service Menus
	Item # FS6-01	Controlling Food Costs		Item # FS14-01	Restaurant Design
	Item # FS7-01	Controlling Labor Costs		Item # FS15-01	Increasing Restaurant Sales
	Item # FS8-01	Controlling Liquor & Beverage Costs		**Item # FSALL-01**	**Entire 15-Book Series for $199.95**
Subtotal		Shipping	Sales Tax		**TOTAL DUE**

SHIP TO:

Name_____Phone(_____) _____

Company Name_____

Mailing Address _____ City _____State _____Zip

FAX _____E-mail _____

❏ My check or money order is enclosed   ❏ Please send my order COD   ❏ My authorized purchase order is attached

❏ Please charge my: ❏ Mastercard ❏ VISA ❏ American Express ❏ Discover

Card # ☐☐☐☐ – ☐☐☐☐ – ☐☐☐☐ – ☐☐☐☐   Expires ☐☐☐☐

Please make checks payable to: **Atlantic Publishing Company** • 1405 SW 6th Ave. • Ocala, FL 34474-7014   USPS Shipping/Handling: add $5.00 first item and $2.50 each additional or $15.00 for the whole set. Florida residents PLEASE add the appropriate sales tax for your county.